TOM THE DANCING BUG
AWAKENS

BOOK DESIGN BY ROBBIE ROBBINS

This is the 6th volume in
The Complete Tom the Dancing Bug.

TOM THE DANCING BUG AWAKENS

ISBN: 978-1-951038-08-3

FIRST PRINTING OCTOBER 2021

4 3 2 1 21 22 24 25

PRINTED IN KOREA

CLOVER PRESS:
MATT RUZICKA, PRESIDENT
ROBBIE ROBBINS, VICE PRESIDENT/ART DIRECTOR
HANK KANALZ, PUBLISHER
TED ADAMS, FACTOTUM
TIM BELL, SHIPPING
CHRISTIAN RUZICKA, SHIPPING ASSISTANT

Clover Founders:
Ted Adams, Elaine LaRosa, Nathan Murray, Robbie Robbins

CLOVER PRESS

SAN DIEGO, CA

WWW.CLOVER**PRESS**.US

TOM THE DANCING BUG
AWAKENS

Comics
by
**Ruben
Bolling**

About Tom the Dancing Bug

Tom the Dancing Bug is the weekly comic strip by Ruben Bolling that appears in newspapers across North America and on the internet. It takes a sketch-comedy approach to comic strip cartooning, with varying new or recurring characters, formats and even art styles each week.

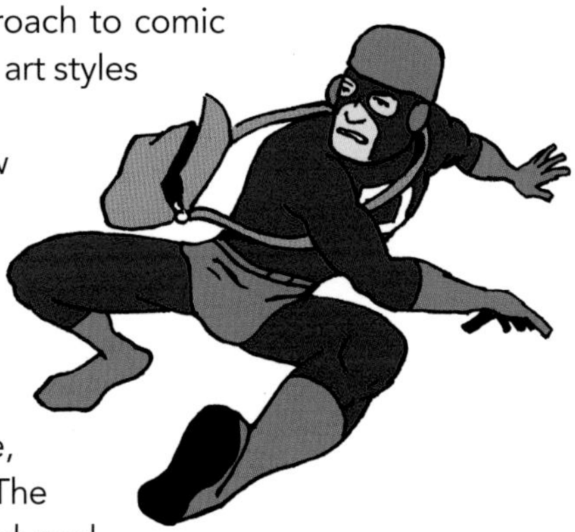

It started its professional incarnation in 1990 in a small newspaper in New York City, *New York Perspectives* (now defunct), and Bolling self-syndicated it to many other newspapers until 1997, when the company now known as Andrews McMeel Syndication took on syndication, which it continues to this day.

In its early years, its subject matter was only occasionally political, and it featured such characters as Max & Doug, Charley the Australopithecine, Louis Maltby, Harvey Richards: Lawyer for Children, God-Man, Sam Roland: The Detective Who Dies, and Billy Dare: Boy Adventurer. In 1997, Bolling introduced the popular Super-Fun-Pak Comix format, which simulates a surreal daily comics page.

In the 1990s, the comic strip's readership grew, with a newspaper client list exceeding 100, including leading daily newspapers (such as *The Washington Post*), and leading alternative newsweeklies (such as *The Village Voice*). Alternative newspapers were a particularly important part of the comic's distribution and growth, and in the space of eight years, it won five Association of Alternative Newsweekly Best Comic awards.

Tom the Dancing Bug shifted after September, 2001, when Bolling, a New Yorker, felt the urgent need to inject more politics and topical matters into the comic strip's content. New characters of a political bent, like Lucky Ducky and Nate the Neoconservative were introduced, and the comic's political satire became more frequent and increasingly pointed and specific.

As more print newspaper clients (especially alternative newspapers) disappeared or downsized in the late 2000s and early 2010s, the internet became a more important part of the comic's distribution. In that time, *Tom the Dancing Bug* gained important web clients BoingBoing.net, DailyKos.com and GoComics.com, which dramatically increased the size and enthusiasm of its readership. In 2012, Bolling launched the "Inner Hive," an email subscription club that emails members each week's comic before it's published on the web, plus other exclusive content, commentary, comics and benefits.

Bolling conceived the social satire feature "Chagrin Falls" in 2013, in which the Smythe family grapples with their increasingly marginalized middle class American lives. One of these installments, dated November 18, 2013 in this volume, was the 2014 Gold Medal Winner for the Society of Illustrators Comic Strip Awards.

In 2016, *Tom the Dancing Bug* took an even sharper political turn when Bolling recognized that Donald Trump represented the political phenomenon of his lifetime, and devoted much of the comic strip to the campaign, which carried over (to Bolling's chagrin) to Trump's election and administration.

This led to greater recognition of *Tom the Dancing Bug*, including a 2017 National Cartoonists Society Award, a 2017 Herblock Prize, and a 2018 Robert F. Kennedy Journalism Award. Ruben Bolling was a Finalist for the Pulitzer Prize in 2019 and 2021.

TO JOIN TOM THE DANCING BUG'S "INNER HIVE," GO TO
tomthedancingbug.com

TOM the DANCING BUG'S
SUPER-FUN-PAK COMIX
EDITED BY RUBEN BOLLING

IN THE BASEMENT

YES! DIRECT HIT!

OH, NO! I HIT A VILLAGE!

PASS THE DORITOS!

WHOA--IT'S 3AM! WE'D BETTER CALL IT A NIGHT, DUDES!

WHAT'S ON FOR TOMORROW?

PAKISTAN, YEMEN, AND LAS CRUCES, N.M.

DRONE OPERATIONS U.S AIR FORCE

AT HOME WITH DR. PROFESSOR

THIS PLACE IS A MESS! HOW CAN YOU EVER FIND ANYTHING?

AW, DAD!

AND THIS CLOSET... HEY!

SO THAT'S WHERE DARK MATTER IS! I HAVE TO CALL THE OBSERVATORY!

CLASSIX COMIX
Not a substitute for reading the text or for classroom discussion of the text.

The Sun Also Rises

The sun has set, my friends. It is all over. Goodbye.

The world, in a permanent, apocalyptic darkness!

Well, what do you know!

End

NEXT~ The sun has set, my friends...

SUPERHERO FANTASIES FOR THE MIDDLE-AGED

WOW! YOUR STRENGTH REPRESENTS AN ADOLESCENT WISH FOR POWER AND FAIRNESS?

AARR NO!

RIP

UNDIRECTED ADOLESCENT RAGE?

NO!

I'M GOING TO REARRANGE PARKED CARS TO MAKE A SPOT!

FUN SCIENCE FACTS FOR THE DEPRESSED

MODERN SCIENCE AND IRREFUTABLE MATHEMATICS HAVE PROVEN DEFINITIVELY...

IT IS **ALL YOUR FAULT.**

INCOMPREHENSIBLE SUFFERING FUNNIES

HEY, VINCENT. WHY IS THERE A BANDAGE ON YOUR EAR?

WHAT?

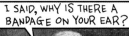

I SAID, WHY IS THERE A BANDAGE ON YOUR EAR?

WHAT?

WHY IS THERE A BANDAGE ON YOUR EAR?

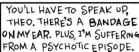

YOU'LL HAVE TO SPEAK UP, THEO. THERE'S A BANDAGE ON MY EAR. PLUS, I'M SUFFERING FROM A PSYCHOTIC EPISODE.

DIST. BY THE UNIVERSAL UCLICK SYNDICATE - ©2012 R. Bolling - 1069 - tomthedancingbug.com twitter.com/rubenbolling

1/2/12

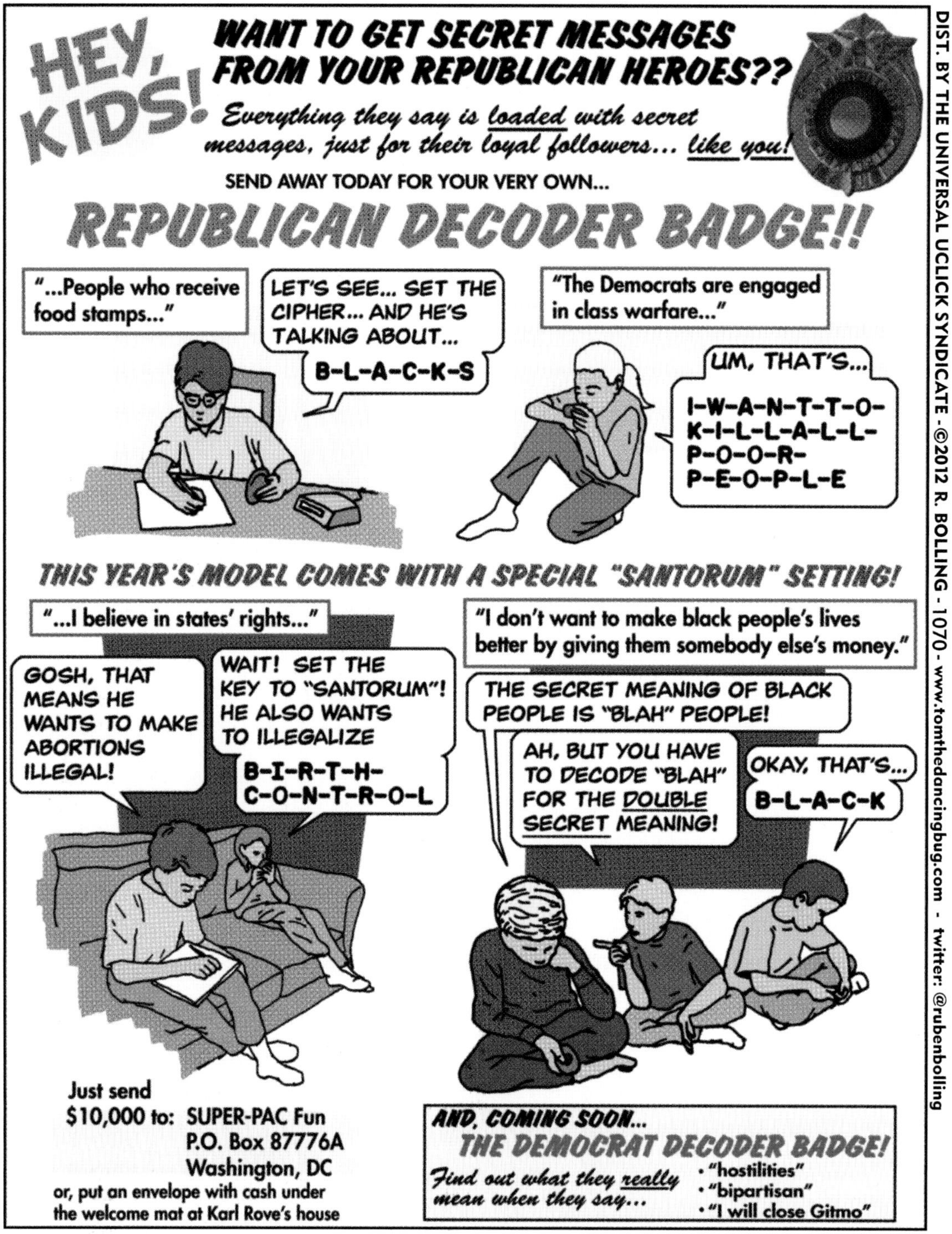
HEY, KIDS!
WANT TO GET SECRET MESSAGES FROM YOUR REPUBLICAN HEROES??
Everything they say is loaded with secret messages, just for their loyal followers... like you!
SEND AWAY TODAY FOR YOUR VERY OWN...
REPUBLICAN DECODER BADGE!!
"...People who receive food stamps..."
LET'S SEE... SET THE CIPHER... AND HE'S TALKING ABOUT... B-L-A-C-K-S
"The Democrats are engaged in class warfare..."
UM, THAT'S... I-W-A-N-T-T-O-K-I-L-L-A-L-L-P-O-O-R-P-E-O-P-L-E
THIS YEAR'S MODEL COMES WITH A SPECIAL "SANTORUM" SETTING!
"...I believe in states' rights..."
GOSH, THAT MEANS HE WANTS TO MAKE ABORTIONS ILLEGAL!
WAIT! SET THE KEY TO "SANTORUM"! HE ALSO WANTS TO ILLEGALIZE B-I-R-T-H-C-O-N-T-R-O-L
"I don't want to make black people's lives better by giving them somebody else's money."
THE SECRET MEANING OF BLACK PEOPLE IS "BLAH" PEOPLE!
AH, BUT YOU HAVE TO DECODE "BLAH" FOR THE DOUBLE SECRET MEANING!
OKAY, THAT'S... B-L-A-C-K
Just send $10,000 to: SUPER-PAC Fun P.O. Box 87776A Washington, DC
or, put an envelope with cash under the welcome mat at Karl Rove's house
AND, COMING SOON... THE DEMOCRAT DECODER BADGE!
Find out what they really mean when they say...
• "hostilities"
• "bipartisan"
• "I will close Gitmo"
DIST. BY THE UNIVERSAL UCLICK SYNDICATE - ©2012 R. BOLLING - 1070 - www.tomthedancingbug.com - twitter: @rubenbolling

1/9/12

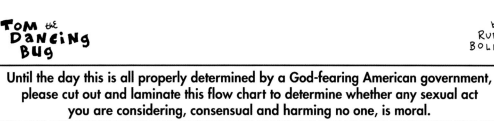

TOM the DANCING BUG
by RUBEN BOLLING
Until the day this is all properly determined by a God-fearing American government, please cut out and laminate this flow chart to determine whether any sexual act you are considering, consensual and harming no one, is moral.
SEX-ACT MORALITY FLOW CHART
Would the act satisfy an urge placed within you by God?
Yes
No
Does the act exist in the 1950s TV world of "Leave It to Beaver"?
Would the act satisfy an urge that should have been placed in you by God, but He forgot to?
Yes, and that conversion therapy weekend at the Ramada TOTALLY worked!
Yes
No
No
It is NATURAL, so God wants you to do it.
It is NATURAL, and thus animalistic, so God wants you to resist it.
It is UNNATURAL; God placed the urge in you due to some foul-up.
But...
But...
Are you married to your partner?
No
Are you married to your partner?
Yes
Are you in a loving, committed relationship with your partner?
Yes
Are you doing it solely for procreative purposes?
No
Just kidding! It is or should be ILLEGAL to marry your partner.
No
What partner?
Yes, I will close my eyes and think of babies.
MORAL
Feel free to remove your sweater-vest.
IMMORAL
If you engage in this repulsive act, what's to stop multiple genders, species, appliances and mythical creatures from writhing naked on the floors of our places of worship, demanding to be married?
DIST. BY THE UNIVERSAL UCLICK SYNDICATE - ©2012 R. BOLLING - 1071 - www.tomthedancingbug.com - twitter: @rubenbolling

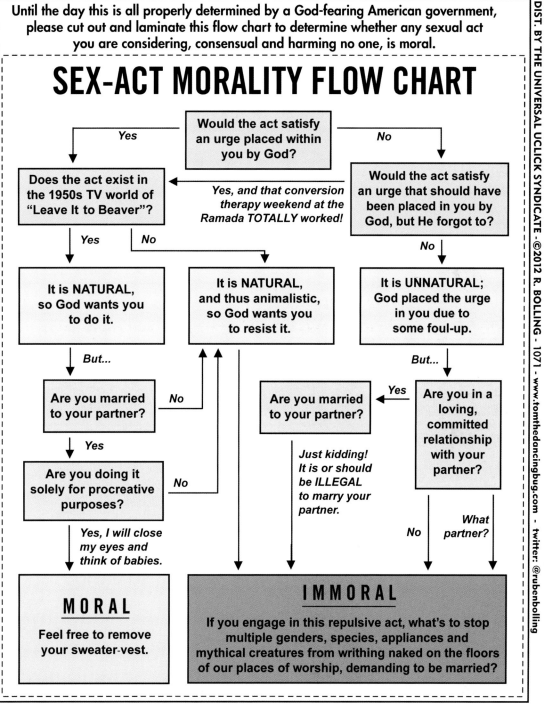

1/16/12

TOM the DANCING BUG

by RUBEN BOLLING

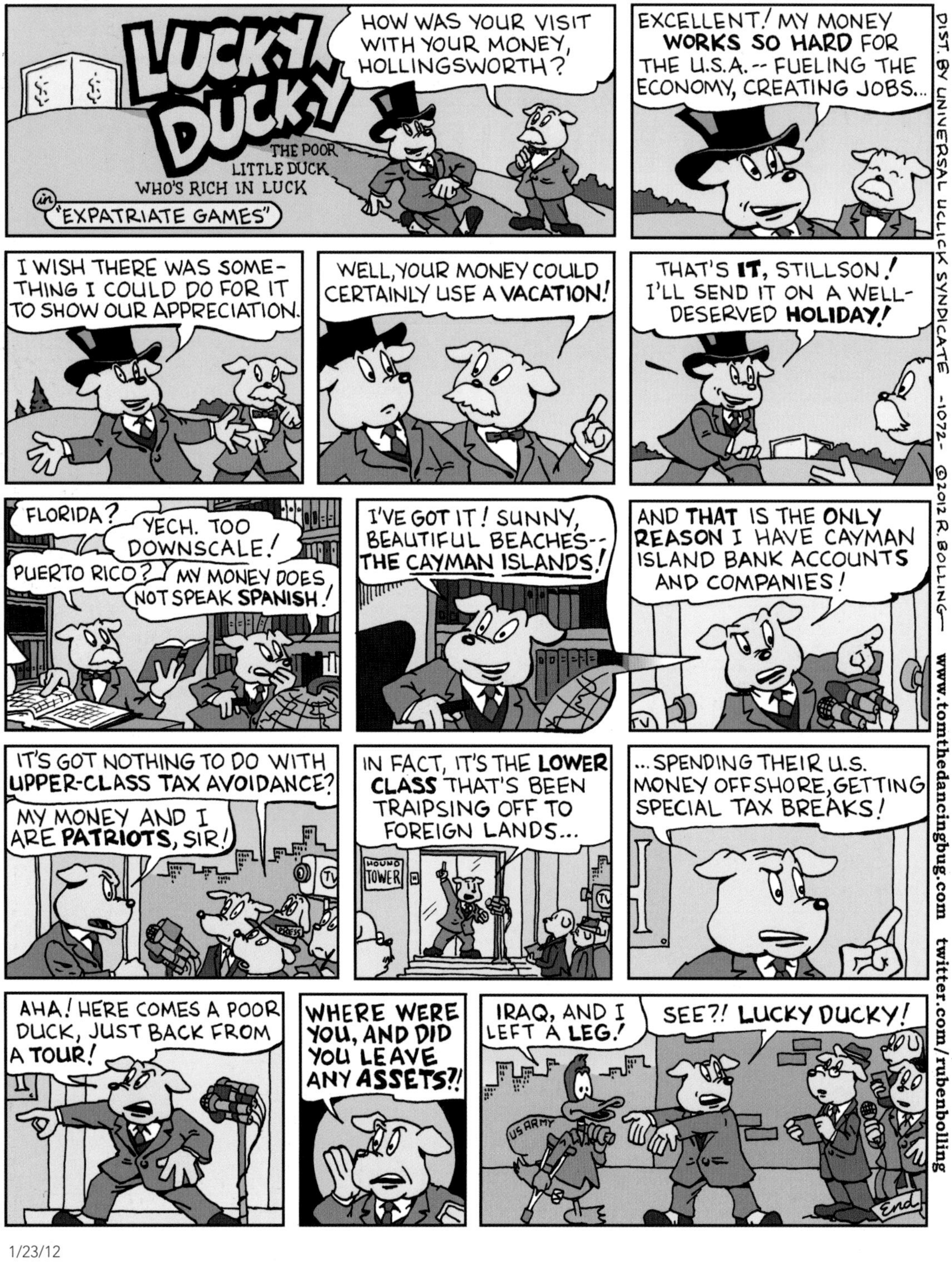
LUCKY DUCKY
THE POOR LITTLE DUCK WHO'S RICH IN LUCK
in "EXPATRIATE GAMES"
HOW WAS YOUR VISIT WITH YOUR MONEY, HOLLINGSWORTH?
EXCELLENT! MY MONEY WORKS SO HARD FOR THE U.S.A.-- FUELING THE ECONOMY, CREATING JOBS...
I WISH THERE WAS SOMETHING I COULD DO FOR IT TO SHOW OUR APPRECIATION.
WELL, YOUR MONEY COULD CERTAINLY USE A VACATION!
THAT'S IT, STILLSON! I'LL SEND IT ON A WELL-DESERVED HOLIDAY!
FLORIDA?
YECH. TOO DOWNSCALE!
PUERTO RICO?
MY MONEY DOES NOT SPEAK SPANISH!
I'VE GOT IT! SUNNY, BEAUTIFUL BEACHES-- THE CAYMAN ISLANDS!
AND THAT IS THE ONLY REASON I HAVE CAYMAN ISLAND BANK ACCOUNTS AND COMPANIES!
TV
IT'S GOT NOTHING TO DO WITH UPPER-CLASS TAX AVOIDANCE?
MY MONEY AND I ARE PATRIOTS, SIR!
TV
PRESS
IN FACT, IT'S THE LOWER CLASS THAT'S BEEN TRAIPSING OFF TO FOREIGN LANDS...
HOUND TOWER
TV
...SPENDING THEIR U.S. MONEY OFFSHORE, GETTING SPECIAL TAX BREAKS!
AHA! HERE COMES A POOR DUCK, JUST BACK FROM A TOUR!
WHERE WERE YOU, AND DID YOU LEAVE ANY ASSETS?!
IRAQ, AND I LEFT A LEG!
US ARMY
SEE?! LUCKY DUCKY!
End
DIST. BY UNIVERSAL UCLICK SYNDICATE -1072- ©2012 R. BOLLING
www.tomthedancingbug.com twitter.com/rubenbolling

1/23/12

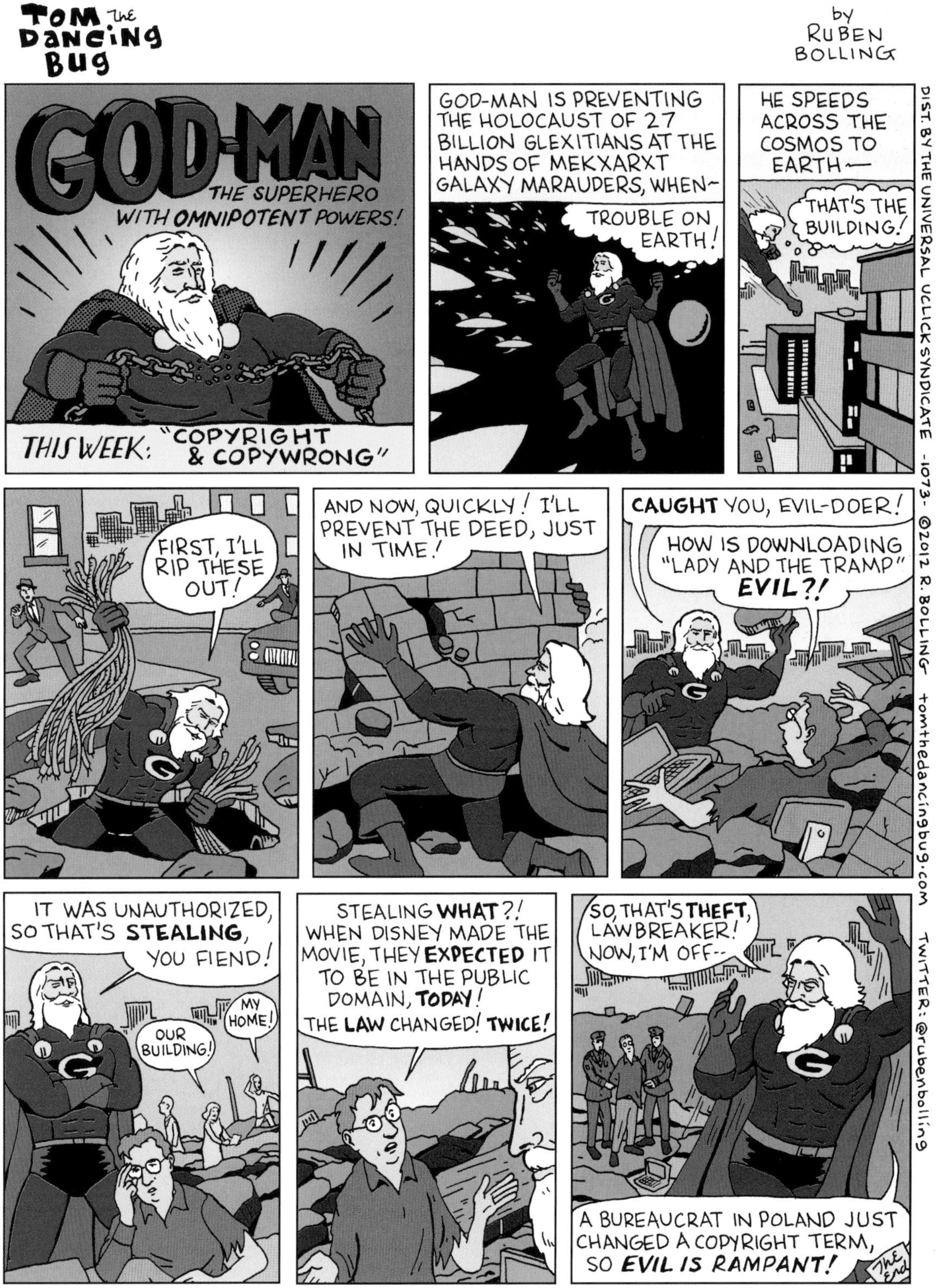
TOM the DANCING BUG
by RUBEN BOLLING
GOD-MAN
THE SUPERHERO WITH OMNIPOTENT POWERS!
THIS WEEK: "COPYRIGHT & COPYWRONG"
GOD-MAN IS PREVENTING THE HOLOCAUST OF 27 BILLION GLEXITIANS AT THE HANDS OF MEKXARXT GALAXY MARAUDERS, WHEN~
TROUBLE ON EARTH!
HE SPEEDS ACROSS THE COSMOS TO EARTH—
THAT'S THE BUILDING!
FIRST, I'LL RIP THESE OUT!
AND NOW, QUICKLY! I'LL PREVENT THE DEED, JUST IN TIME!
CAUGHT YOU, EVIL-DOER!
HOW IS DOWNLOADING "LADY AND THE TRAMP" EVIL?!
IT WAS UNAUTHORIZED, SO THAT'S STEALING, YOU FIEND!
OUR BUILDING!
MY HOME!
STEALING WHAT?! WHEN DISNEY MADE THE MOVIE, THEY EXPECTED IT TO BE IN THE PUBLIC DOMAIN, TODAY! THE LAW CHANGED! TWICE!
SO, THAT'S THEFT, LAWBREAKER! NOW, I'M OFF--
A BUREAUCRAT IN POLAND JUST CHANGED A COPYRIGHT TERM, SO EVIL IS RAMPANT!
THE END
DIST. BY THE UNIVERSAL UCLICKSYNDICATE -1073- ©2012 R. BOLLING tomthedancingbug.com TWITTER: @rubenbolling

1/30/12

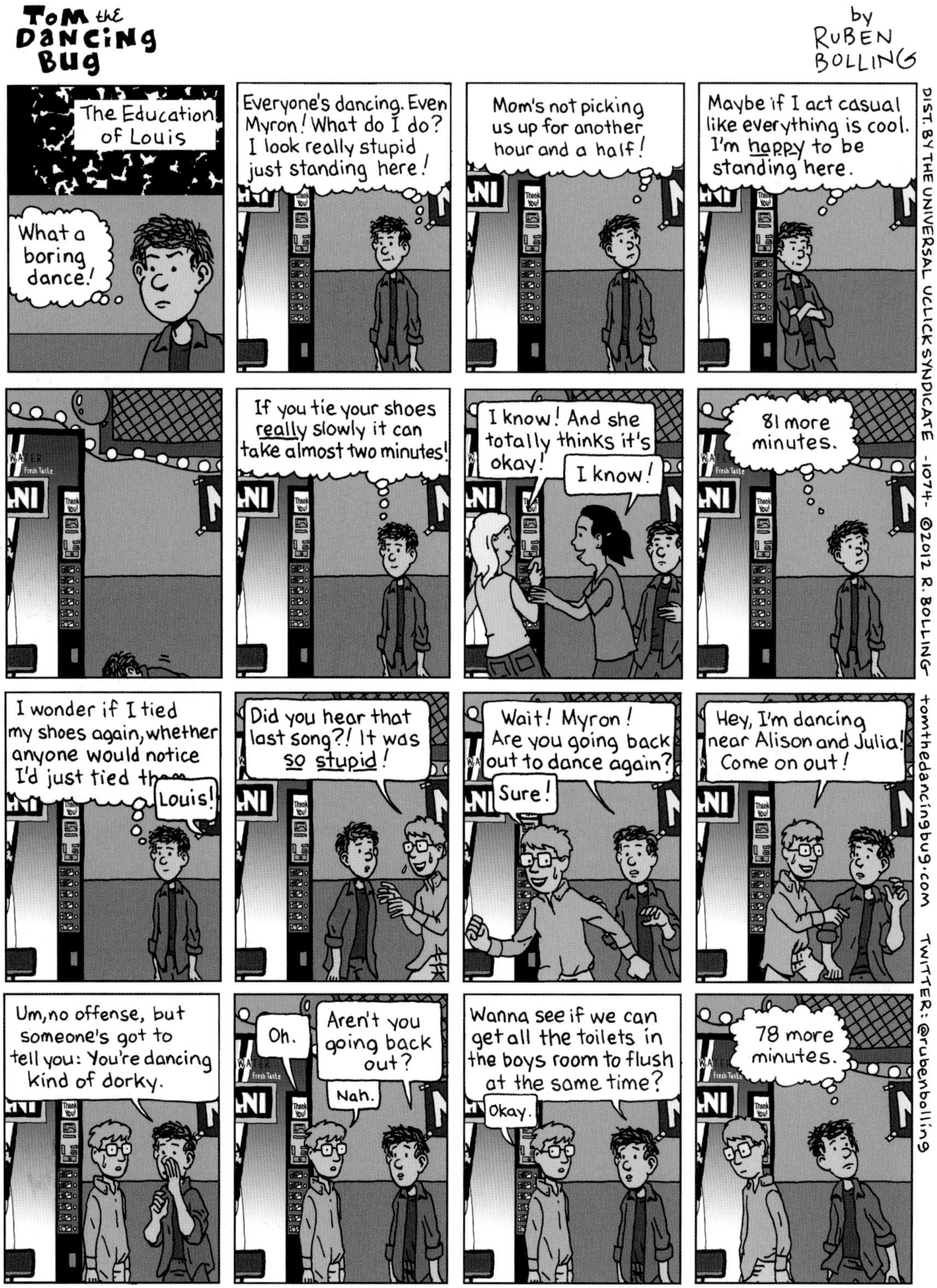
Tom the Dancing Bug
by Ruben Bolling
The Education of Louis
What a boring dance!
Everyone's dancing. Even Myron! What do I do? I look really stupid just standing here!
Mom's not picking us up for another hour and a half!
Maybe if I act casual like everything is cool. I'm happy to be standing here.
If you tie your shoes really slowly it can take almost two minutes!
I know! And she totally thinks it's okay!
I know!
81 more minutes.
I wonder if I tied my shoes again, whether anyone would notice I'd just tied them
Louis!
Did you hear that last song?! It was so stupid!
Wait! Myron! Are you going back out to dance again?
Sure!
Hey, I'm dancing near Alison and Julia! Come on out!
Um, no offense, but someone's got to tell you: You're dancing kind of dorky.
Oh.
Aren't you going back out?
Nah.
Wanna see if we can get all the toilets in the boys room to flush at the same time?
Okay.
78 more minutes.
DIST. BY THE UNIVERSAL UCLICK SYNDICATE -1074- ©2012 R. BOLLING
tomthedancingbug.com TWITTER: @rubenbolling

2/6/12

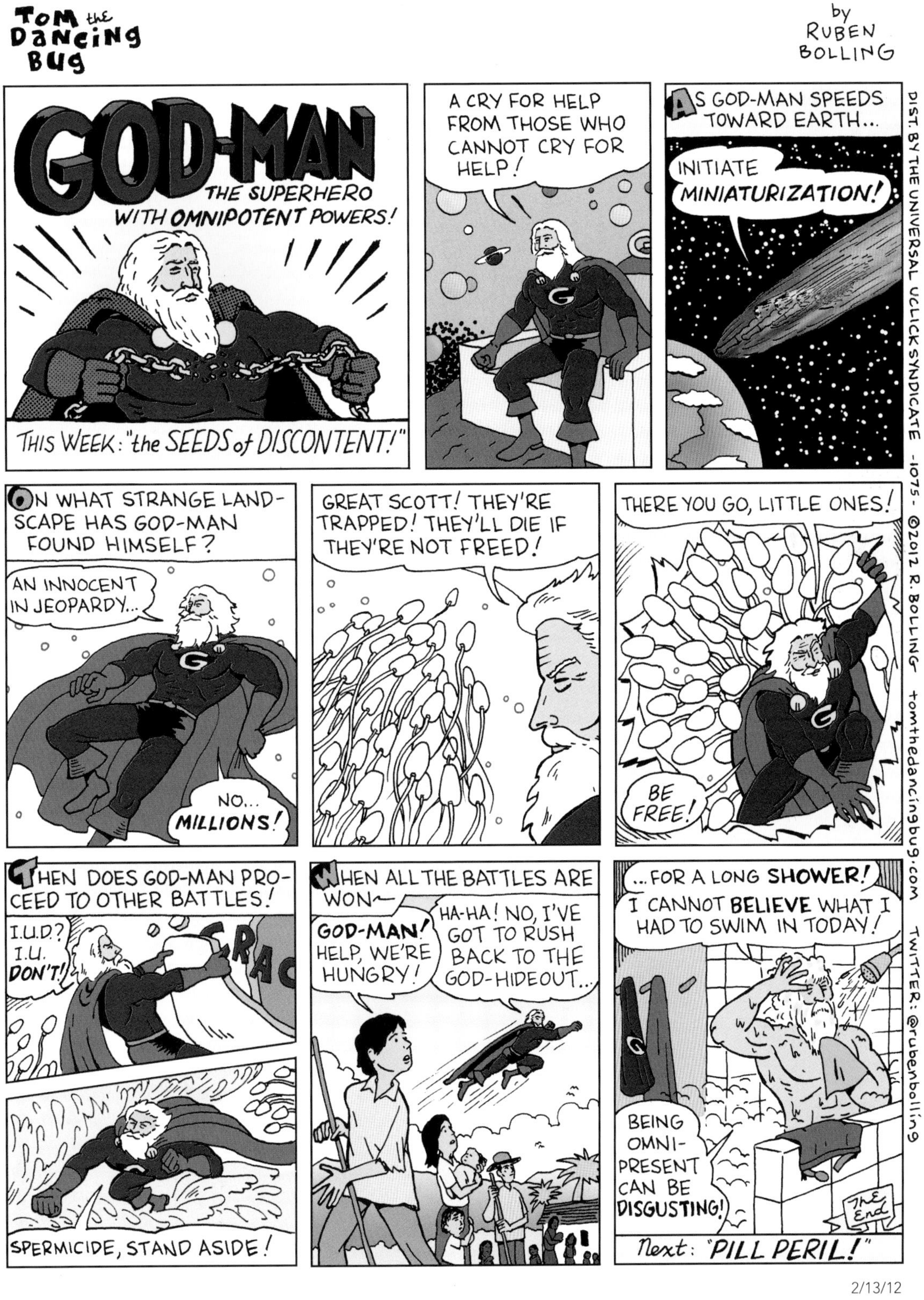

TOM the DANCING BUG
by RUBEN BOLLING
GOD-MAN
THE SUPERHERO WITH OMNIPOTENT POWERS!
THIS WEEK: "the SEEDS of DISCONTENT!"
A CRY FOR HELP FROM THOSE WHO CANNOT CRY FOR HELP!
AS GOD-MAN SPEEDS TOWARD EARTH...
INITIATE MINIATURIZATION!
ON WHAT STRANGE LANDSCAPE HAS GOD-MAN FOUND HIMSELF?
AN INNOCENT IN JEOPARDY...
NO... MILLIONS!
GREAT SCOTT! THEY'RE TRAPPED! THEY'LL DIE IF THEY'RE NOT FREED!
THERE YOU GO, LITTLE ONES!
BE FREE!
THEN DOES GOD-MAN PROCEED TO OTHER BATTLES!
I.U.D.? I.U. DON'T!
CRAC
SPERMICIDE, STAND ASIDE!
WHEN ALL THE BATTLES ARE WON—
GOD-MAN! HELP, WE'RE HUNGRY!
HA-HA! NO, I'VE GOT TO RUSH BACK TO THE GOD-HIDEOUT...
...FOR A LONG SHOWER!
I CANNOT BELIEVE WHAT I HAD TO SWIM IN TODAY!
BEING OMNIPRESENT CAN BE DISGUSTING!
THE End
Next: "PILL PERIL!"
DIST. BY THE UNIVERSAL UCLICK SYNDICATE -1075- ©2012 R. BOLLING tomthedancingbug.com TWITTER: @rubenbolling

2/13/12

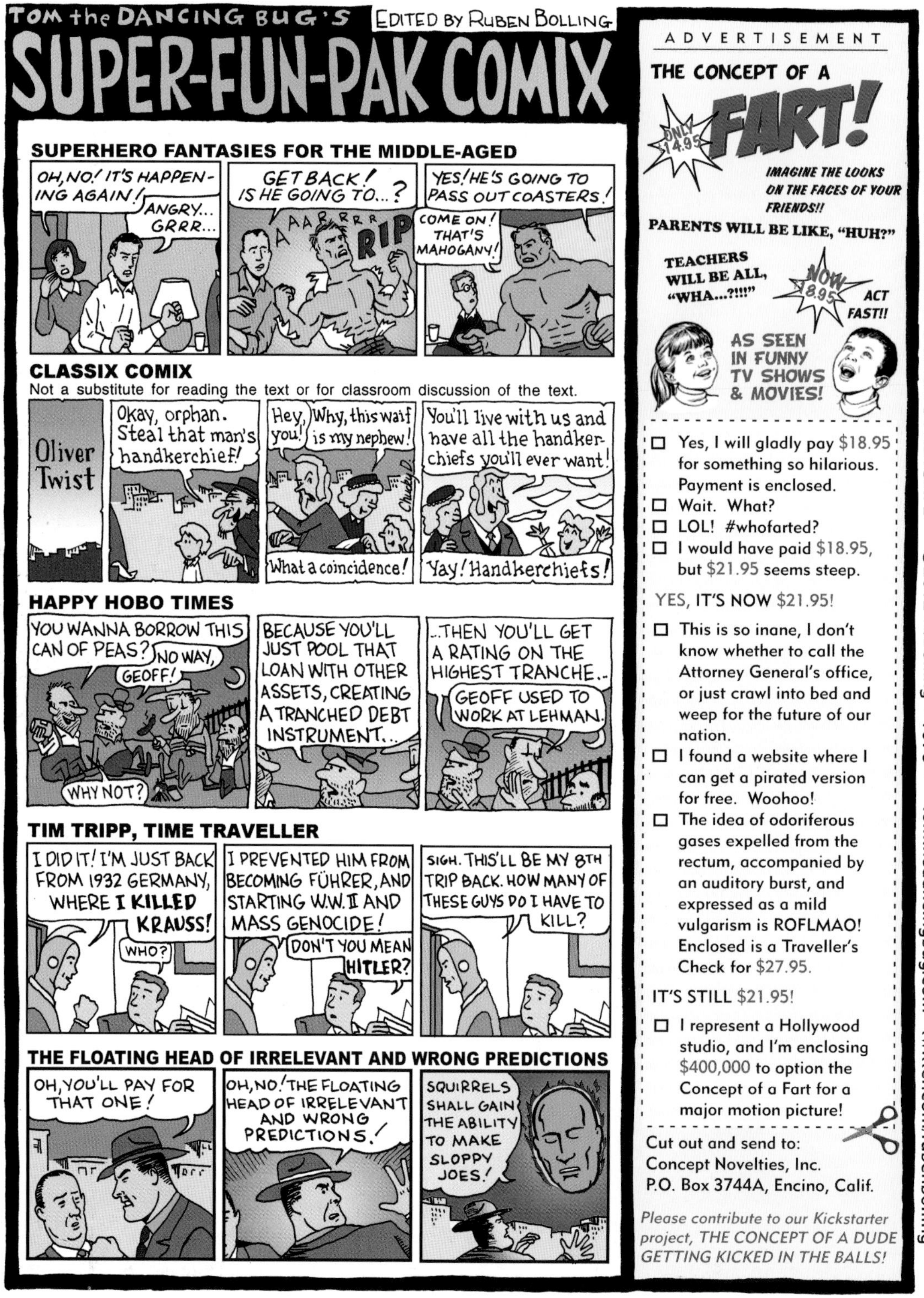

TOM the DANCING BUG'S
EDITED BY RUBEN BOLLING
SUPER-FUN-PAK COMIX
SUPERHERO FANTASIES FOR THE MIDDLE-AGED
OH, NO! IT'S HAPPENING AGAIN!
ANGRY... GRRR...
GET BACK! IS HE GOING TO...?
AAARRRR
RIP
YES! HE'S GOING TO PASS OUT COASTERS!
COME ON! THAT'S MAHOGANY!
CLASSIX COMIX
Not a substitute for reading the text or for classroom discussion of the text.
Oliver Twist
Okay, orphan. Steal that man's handkerchief!
Hey, you!
Why, this waif is my nephew!
What a coincidence!
You'll live with us and have all the handkerchiefs you'll ever want!
Yay! Handkerchiefs!
HAPPY HOBO TIMES
YOU WANNA BORROW THIS CAN OF PEAS?
NO WAY, GEOFF!
WHY NOT?
BECAUSE YOU'LL JUST POOL THAT LOAN WITH OTHER ASSETS, CREATING A TRANCHED DEBT INSTRUMENT...
...THEN YOU'LL GET A RATING ON THE HIGHEST TRANCHE...
GEOFF USED TO WORK AT LEHMAN.
TIM TRIPP, TIME TRAVELLER
I DID IT! I'M JUST BACK FROM 1932 GERMANY, WHERE I KILLED KRAUSS!
WHO?
I PREVENTED HIM FROM BECOMING FÜHRER, AND STARTING W.W.II AND MASS GENOCIDE!
DON'T YOU MEAN HITLER?
SIGH. THIS'LL BE MY 8TH TRIP BACK. HOW MANY OF THESE GUYS DO I HAVE TO KILL?
THE FLOATING HEAD OF IRRELEVANT AND WRONG PREDICTIONS
OH, YOU'LL PAY FOR THAT ONE!
OH, NO! THE FLOATING HEAD OF IRRELEVANT AND WRONG PREDICTIONS!
SQUIRRELS SHALL GAIN THE ABILITY TO MAKE SLOPPY JOES!
ADVERTISEMENT
THE CONCEPT OF A
FART!
ONLY $14.95
IMAGINE THE LOOKS ON THE FACES OF YOUR FRIENDS!!
PARENTS WILL BE LIKE, "HUH?"
TEACHERS WILL BE ALL, "WHA...?!!!"
NOW $18.95
ACT FAST!!
AS SEEN IN FUNNY TV SHOWS & MOVIES!
☐ Yes, I will gladly pay $18.95 for something so hilarious. Payment is enclosed.
☐ Wait. What?
☐ LOL! #whofarted?
☐ I would have paid $18.95, but $21.95 seems steep.
YES, IT'S NOW $21.95!
☐ This is so inane, I don't know whether to call the Attorney General's office, or just crawl into bed and weep for the future of our nation.
☐ I found a website where I can get a pirated version for free. Woohoo!
☐ The idea of odoriferous gases expelled from the rectum, accompanied by an auditory burst, and expressed as a mild vulgarism is ROFLMAO! Enclosed is a Traveller's Check for $27.95.
IT'S STILL $21.95!
☐ I represent a Hollywood studio, and I'm enclosing $400,000 to option the Concept of a Fart for a major motion picture!
Cut out and send to:
Concept Novelties, Inc.
P.O. Box 3744A, Encino, Calif.
Please contribute to our Kickstarter project, THE CONCEPT OF A DUDE GETTING KICKED IN THE BALLS!

2/20/12

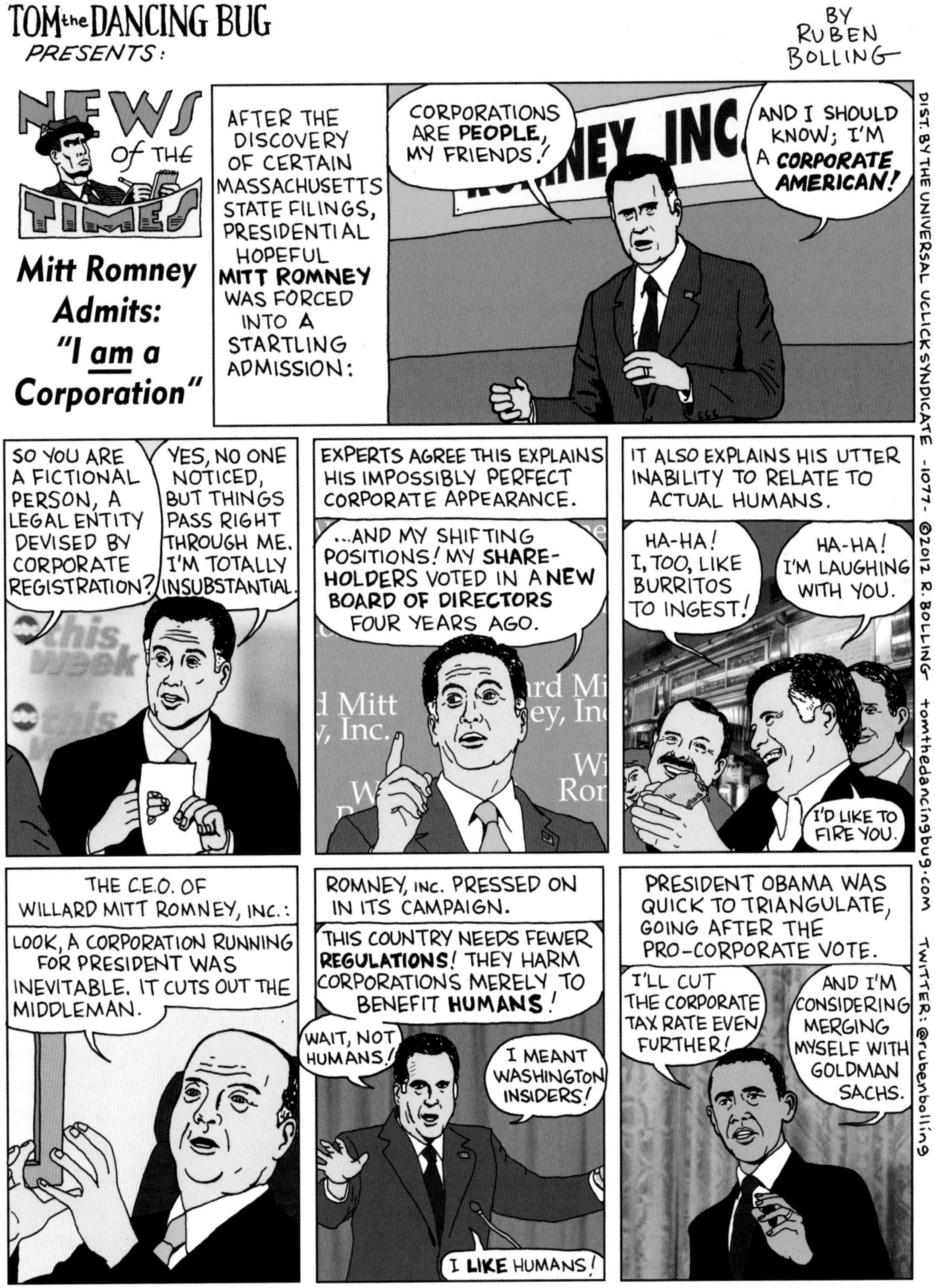
TOM the DANCING BUG PRESENTS:
BY RUBEN BOLLING
NEWS of the TIMES
Mitt Romney Admits: "I am a Corporation"
AFTER THE DISCOVERY OF CERTAIN MASSACHUSETTS STATE FILINGS, PRESIDENTIAL HOPEFUL MITT ROMNEY WAS FORCED INTO A STARTLING ADMISSION:
CORPORATIONS ARE PEOPLE, MY FRIENDS!
AND I SHOULD KNOW; I'M A CORPORATE AMERICAN!
SO YOU ARE A FICTIONAL PERSON, A LEGAL ENTITY DEVISED BY CORPORATE REGISTRATION?
YES, NO ONE NOTICED, BUT THINGS PASS RIGHT THROUGH ME. I'M TOTALLY INSUBSTANTIAL.
EXPERTS AGREE THIS EXPLAINS HIS IMPOSSIBLY PERFECT CORPORATE APPEARANCE.
...AND MY SHIFTING POSITIONS! MY SHAREHOLDERS VOTED IN A NEW BOARD OF DIRECTORS FOUR YEARS AGO.
IT ALSO EXPLAINS HIS UTTER INABILITY TO RELATE TO ACTUAL HUMANS.
HA-HA! I, TOO, LIKE BURRITOS TO INGEST!
HA-HA! I'M LAUGHING WITH YOU.
I'D LIKE TO FIRE YOU.
THE C.E.O. OF WILLARD MITT ROMNEY, INC.:
LOOK, A CORPORATION RUNNING FOR PRESIDENT WAS INEVITABLE. IT CUTS OUT THE MIDDLEMAN.
ROMNEY, INC. PRESSED ON IN ITS CAMPAIGN.
THIS COUNTRY NEEDS FEWER REGULATIONS! THEY HARM CORPORATIONS MERELY TO BENEFIT HUMANS!
WAIT, NOT HUMANS!
I MEANT WASHINGTON INSIDERS!
I LIKE HUMANS!
PRESIDENT OBAMA WAS QUICK TO TRIANGULATE, GOING AFTER THE PRO-CORPORATE VOTE.
I'LL CUT THE CORPORATE TAX RATE EVEN FURTHER!
AND I'M CONSIDERING MERGING MYSELF WITH GOLDMAN SACHS.
DIST. BY THE UNIVERSAL UCLICK SYNDICATE -1077- ©2012 R. BOLLING tomthedancingbug.com TWITTER: @rubenbolling

2/27/12

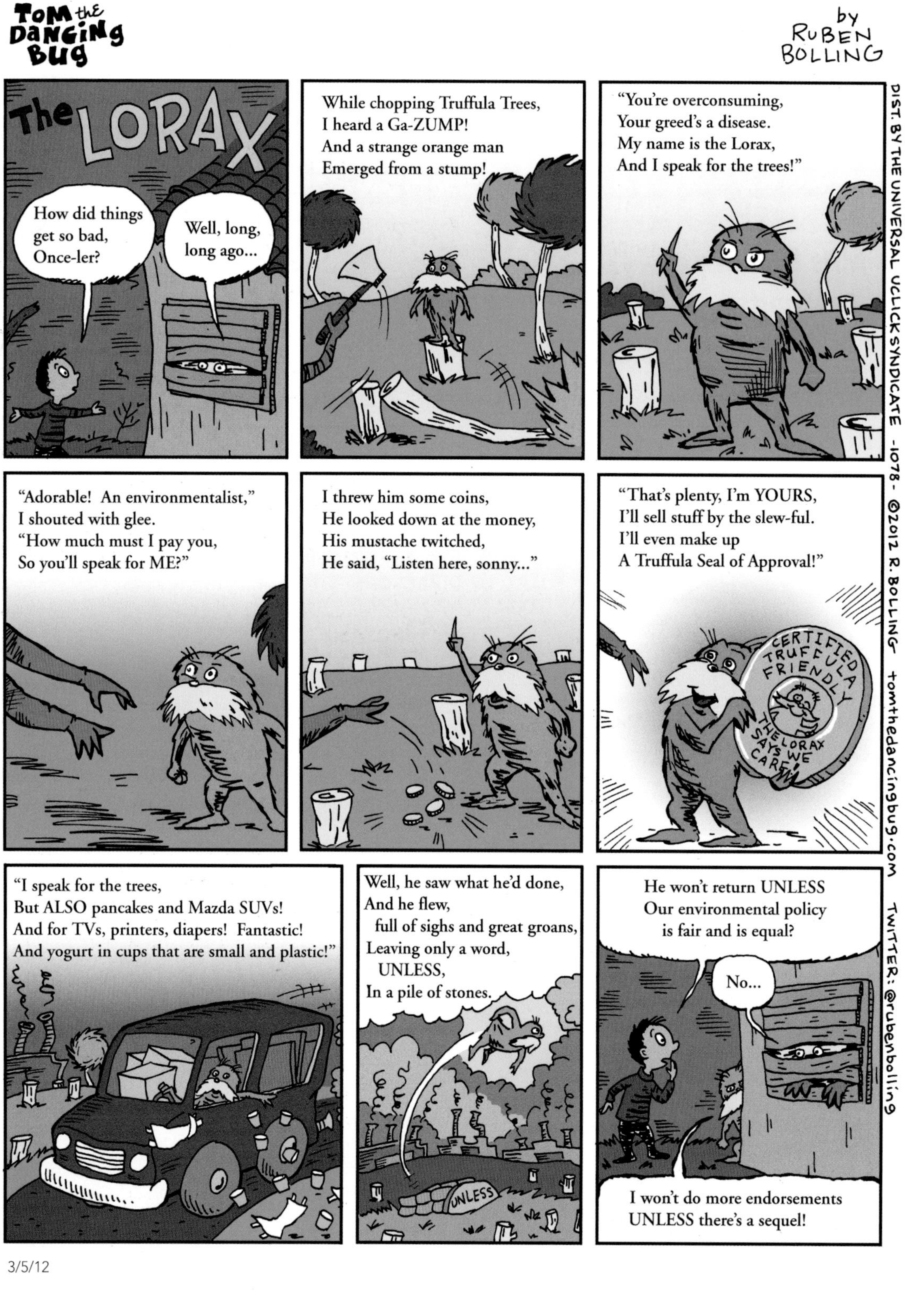
TOM the DANCING BUG
by RUBEN BOLLING
The LORAX
How did things get so bad, Once-ler?
Well, long, long ago...
While chopping Truffula Trees, I heard a Ga-ZUMP! And a strange orange man Emerged from a stump!
"You're overconsuming, Your greed's a disease. My name is the Lorax, And I speak for the trees!"
"Adorable! An environmentalist," I shouted with glee. "How much must I pay you, So you'll speak for ME?"
I threw him some coins, He looked down at the money, His mustache twitched, He said, "Listen here, sonny..."
"That's plenty, I'm YOURS, I'll sell stuff by the slew-ful. I'll even make up A Truffula Seal of Approval!"
CERTIFIED TRUFFULA FRIENDLY
THE LORAX SAYS WE CARE!
"I speak for the trees, But ALSO pancakes and Mazda SUVs! And for TVs, printers, diapers! Fantastic! And yogurt in cups that are small and plastic!"
Well, he saw what he'd done, And he flew, full of sighs and great groans, Leaving only a word, UNLESS, In a pile of stones.
UNLESS
He won't return UNLESS Our environmental policy is fair and is equal?
No...
I won't do more endorsements UNLESS there's a sequel!
DIST. BY THE UNIVERSAL UCLICK SYNDICATE -1078- ©2012 R. BOLLING tomthedancingbug.com TWITTER: @rubenbolling

3/5/12

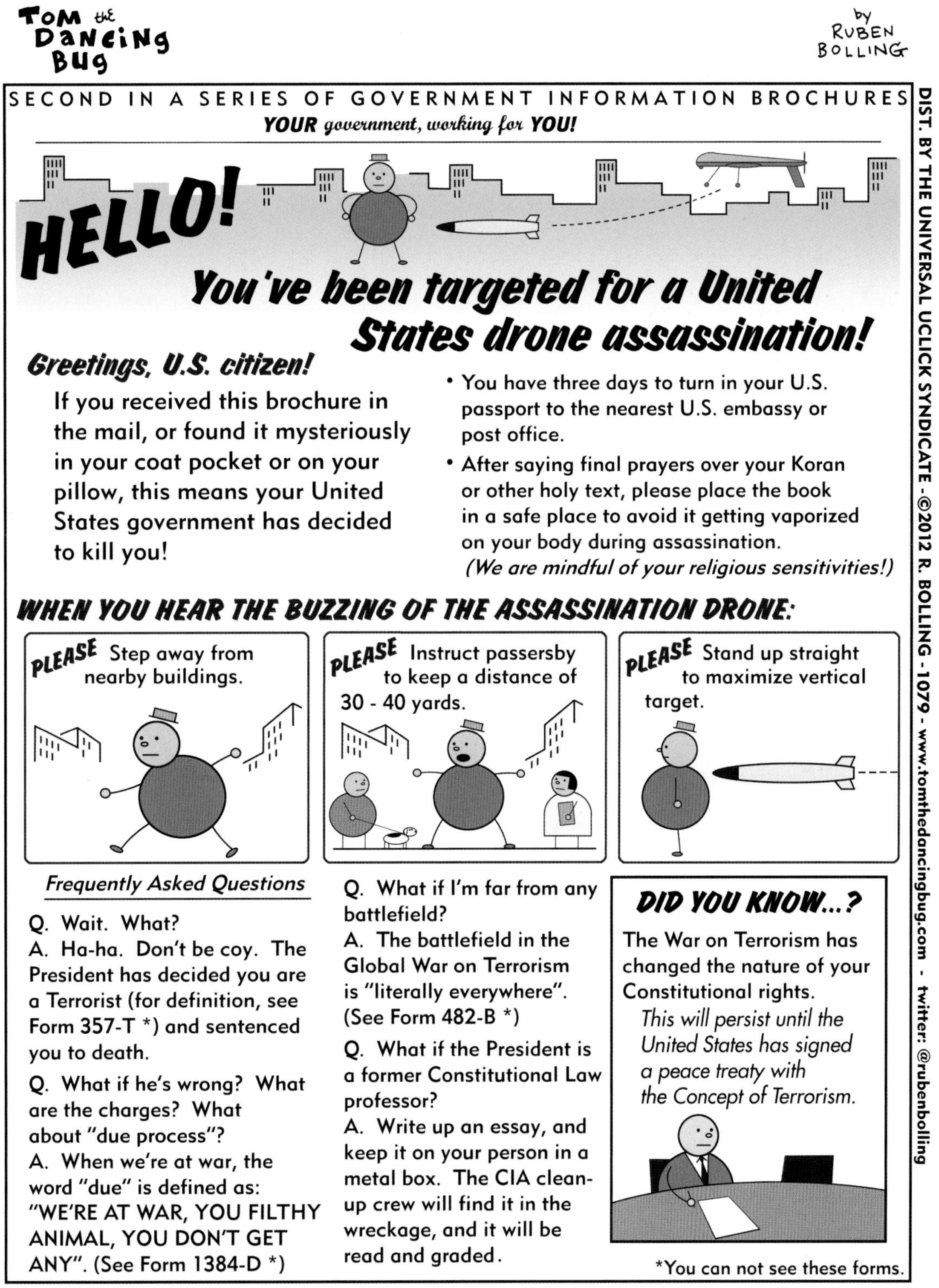

TOM the DANCING BUG

by RUBEN BOLLING

DIST. BY THE UNIVERSAL UCLICK SYNDICATE - ©2012 R. BOLLING - 1079 - www.tomthedancingbug.com - twitter: @rubenbolling

SECOND IN A SERIES OF GOVERNMENT INFORMATION BROCHURES

YOUR *government, working for* **YOU!**

HELLO!

You've been targeted for a United States drone assassination!

Greetings, U.S. citizen!

If you received this brochure in the mail, or found it mysteriously in your coat pocket or on your pillow, this means your United States government has decided to kill you!

- You have three days to turn in your U.S. passport to the nearest U.S. embassy or post office.
- After saying final prayers over your Koran or other holy text, please place the book in a safe place to avoid it getting vaporized on your body during assassination.
  (We are mindful of your religious sensitivities!)

WHEN YOU HEAR THE BUZZING OF THE ASSASSINATION DRONE:

PLEASE Step away from nearby buildings.

PLEASE Instruct passersby to keep a distance of 30 - 40 yards.

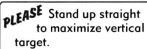

PLEASE Stand up straight to maximize vertical target.

Frequently Asked Questions

Q. Wait. What?
A. Ha-ha. Don't be coy. The President has decided you are a Terrorist (for definition, see Form 357-T *) and sentenced you to death.

Q. What if he's wrong? What are the charges? What about "due process"?
A. When we're at war, the word "due" is defined as: "WE'RE AT WAR, YOU FILTHY ANIMAL, YOU DON'T GET ANY". (See Form 1384-D *)

Q. What if I'm far from any battlefield?
A. The battlefield in the Global War on Terrorism is "literally everywhere". (See Form 482-B *)

Q. What if the President is a former Constitutional Law professor?
A. Write up an essay, and keep it on your person in a metal box. The CIA clean-up crew will find it in the wreckage, and it will be read and graded.

DID YOU KNOW...?

The War on Terrorism has changed the nature of your Constitutional rights.
This will persist until the United States has signed a peace treaty with the Concept of Terrorism.

*You can not see these forms.

3/12/12

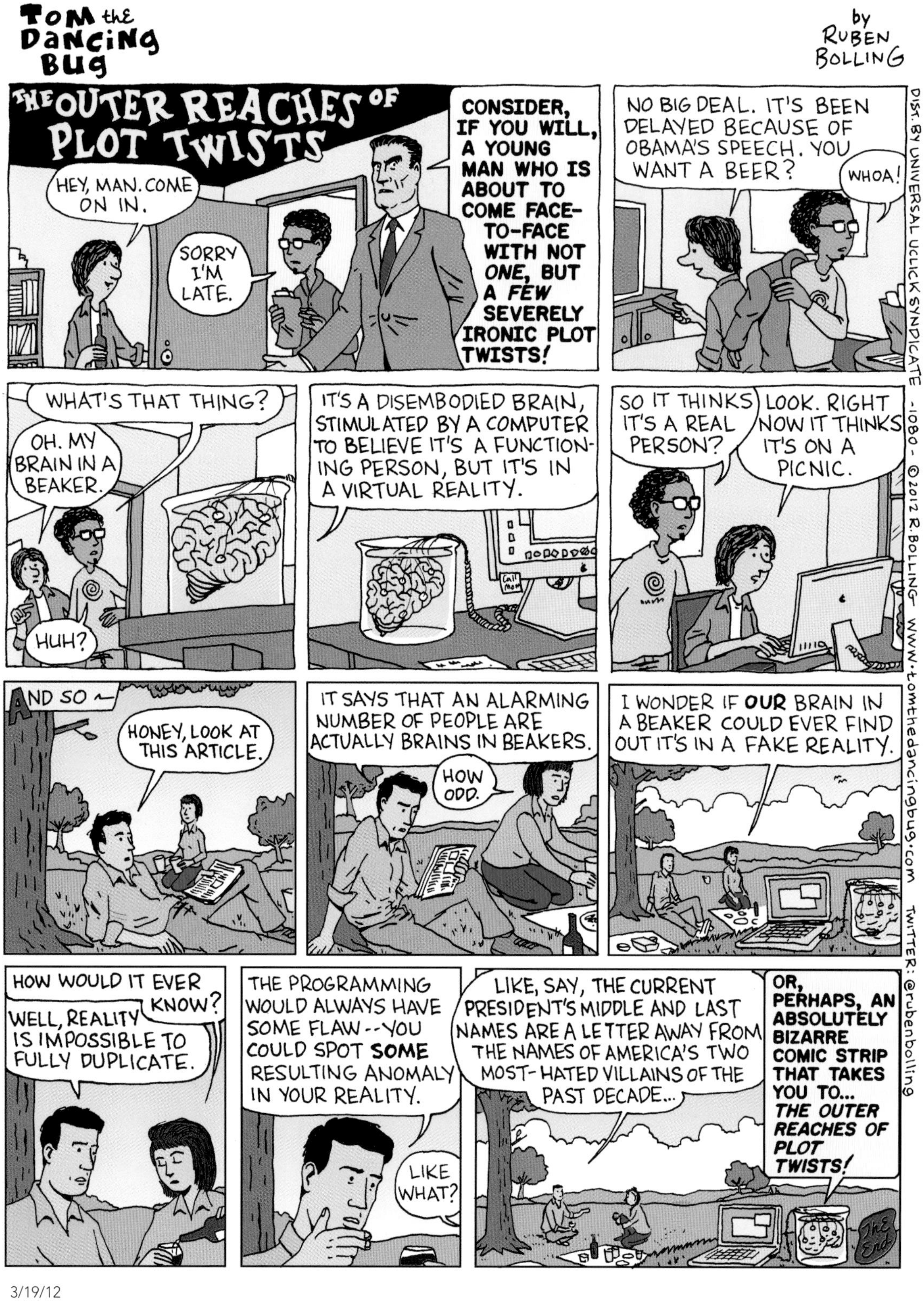
TOM the DANCING BUG
by RUBEN BOLLING
THE OUTER REACHES OF PLOT TWISTS
HEY, MAN. COME ON IN.
SORRY I'M LATE.
CONSIDER, IF YOU WILL, A YOUNG MAN WHO IS ABOUT TO COME FACE-TO-FACE WITH NOT ONE, BUT A FEW SEVERELY IRONIC PLOT TWISTS!
NO BIG DEAL. IT'S BEEN DELAYED BECAUSE OF OBAMA'S SPEECH. YOU WANT A BEER?
WHOA!
WHAT'S THAT THING?
OH. MY BRAIN IN A BEAKER.
HUH?
IT'S A DISEMBODIED BRAIN, STIMULATED BY A COMPUTER TO BELIEVE IT'S A FUNCTIONING PERSON, BUT IT'S IN A VIRTUAL REALITY.
Call Mom
SO IT THINKS IT'S A REAL PERSON?
LOOK. RIGHT NOW IT THINKS IT'S ON A PICNIC.
AND SO ~
HONEY, LOOK AT THIS ARTICLE.
IT SAYS THAT AN ALARMING NUMBER OF PEOPLE ARE ACTUALLY BRAINS IN BEAKERS.
HOW ODD.
I WONDER IF OUR BRAIN IN A BEAKER COULD EVER FIND OUT IT'S IN A FAKE REALITY.
HOW WOULD IT EVER KNOW?
WELL, REALITY IS IMPOSSIBLE TO FULLY DUPLICATE.
THE PROGRAMMING WOULD ALWAYS HAVE SOME FLAW--YOU COULD SPOT SOME RESULTING ANOMALY IN YOUR REALITY.
LIKE WHAT?
LIKE, SAY, THE CURRENT PRESIDENT'S MIDDLE AND LAST NAMES ARE A LETTER AWAY FROM THE NAMES OF AMERICA'S TWO MOST-HATED VILLAINS OF THE PAST DECADE...
OR, PERHAPS, AN ABSOLUTELY BIZARRE COMIC STRIP THAT TAKES YOU TO... THE OUTER REACHES OF PLOT TWISTS!
THE END
DIST. BY UNIVERSAL UCLICK SYNDICATE -1080- ©2012 R. BOLLING- www.tomthedancingbug.com TWITTER: @rubenbolling

3/19/12

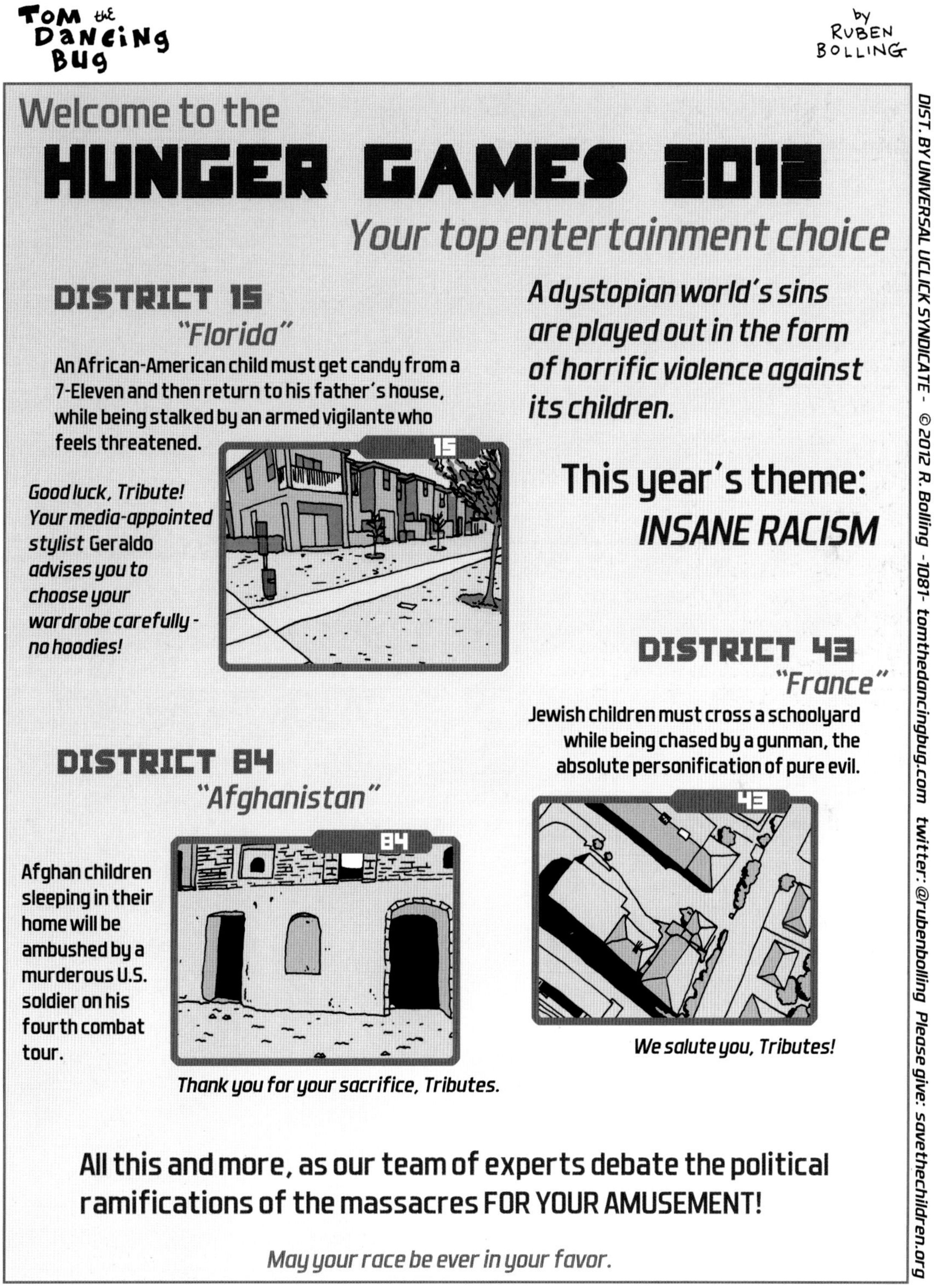
Tom the Dancing Bug
by Ruben Bolling
Welcome to the
HUNGER GAMES 2012
Your top entertainment choice
DISTRICT 15
"Florida"
An African-American child must get candy from a 7-Eleven and then return to his father's house, while being stalked by an armed vigilante who feels threatened.
15
Good luck, Tribute! Your media-appointed stylist Geraldo advises you to choose your wardrobe carefully - no hoodies!
A dystopian world's sins are played out in the form of horrific violence against its children.
This year's theme: INSANE RACISM
DISTRICT 43
"France"
Jewish children must cross a schoolyard while being chased by a gunman, the absolute personification of pure evil.
43
We salute you, Tributes!
DISTRICT 84
"Afghanistan"
84
Afghan children sleeping in their home will be ambushed by a murderous U.S. soldier on his fourth combat tour.
Thank you for your sacrifice, Tributes.
All this and more, as our team of experts debate the political ramifications of the massacres FOR YOUR AMUSEMENT!
May your race be ever in your favor.
DIST. BY UNIVERSAL UCLICK SYNDICATE - © 2012 R. Bolling -1081- tomthedancingbug.com twitter: @rubenbolling Please give: savethechildren.org

3/26/12

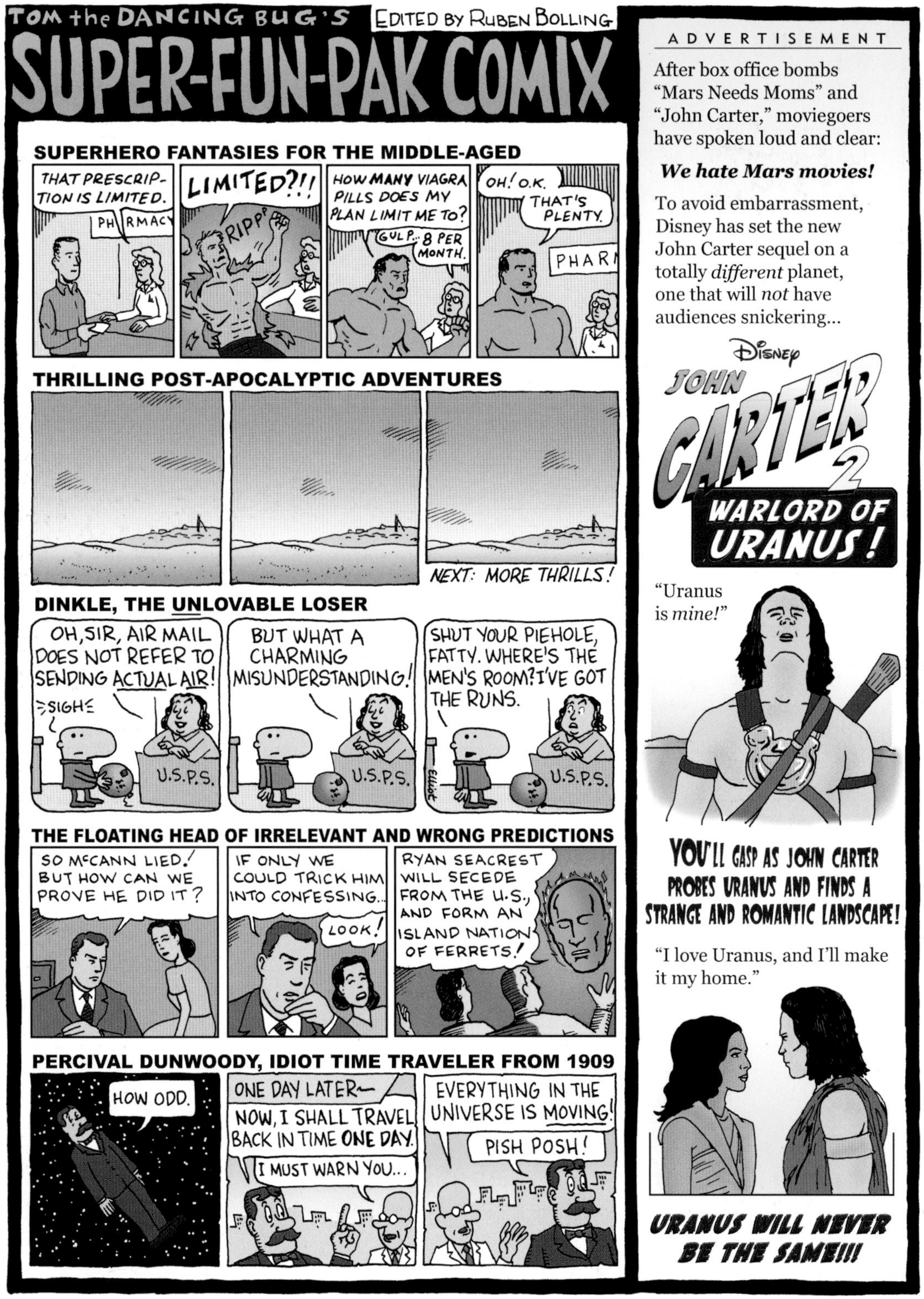
TOM the DANCING BUG'S
EDITED BY RUBEN BOLLING
SUPER-FUN-PAK COMIX
SUPERHERO FANTASIES FOR THE MIDDLE-AGED
THAT PRESCRIP-TION IS LIMITED.
PH RMACY
LIMITED?!!
RIPP
HOW MANY VIAGRA PILLS DOES MY PLAN LIMIT ME TO?
GULP... 8 PER MONTH.
OH! O.K.
THAT'S PLENTY.
PHAR
THRILLING POST-APOCALYPTIC ADVENTURES
NEXT: MORE THRILLS!
DINKLE, THE UNLOVABLE LOSER
OH, SIR, AIR MAIL DOES NOT REFER TO SENDING ACTUAL AIR!
SIGH
U.S.P.S.
BUT WHAT A CHARMING MISUNDERSTANDING!
U.S.P.S.
SHUT YOUR PIEHOLE, FATTY. WHERE'S THE MEN'S ROOM? I'VE GOT THE RUNS.
U.S.P.S.
THE FLOATING HEAD OF IRRELEVANT AND WRONG PREDICTIONS
SO McCANN LIED! BUT HOW CAN WE PROVE HE DID IT?
IF ONLY WE COULD TRICK HIM INTO CONFESSING...
LOOK!
RYAN SEACREST WILL SECEDE FROM THE U.S., AND FORM AN ISLAND NATION OF FERRETS!
PERCIVAL DUNWOODY, IDIOT TIME TRAVELER FROM 1909
HOW ODD.
ONE DAY LATER
NOW, I SHALL TRAVEL BACK IN TIME ONE DAY.
I MUST WARN YOU...
EVERYTHING IN THE UNIVERSE IS MOVING!
PISH POSH!
ADVERTISEMENT
After box office bombs "Mars Needs Moms" and "John Carter," moviegoers have spoken loud and clear:
We hate Mars movies!
To avoid embarrassment, Disney has set the new John Carter sequel on a totally different planet, one that will not have audiences snickering...
Disney
JOHN CARTER 2
WARLORD OF URANUS!
"Uranus is mine!"
YOU'LL GASP AS JOHN CARTER PROBES URANUS AND FINDS A STRANGE AND ROMANTIC LANDSCAPE!
"I love Uranus, and I'll make it my home."
URANUS WILL NEVER BE THE SAME!!!

4/2/12

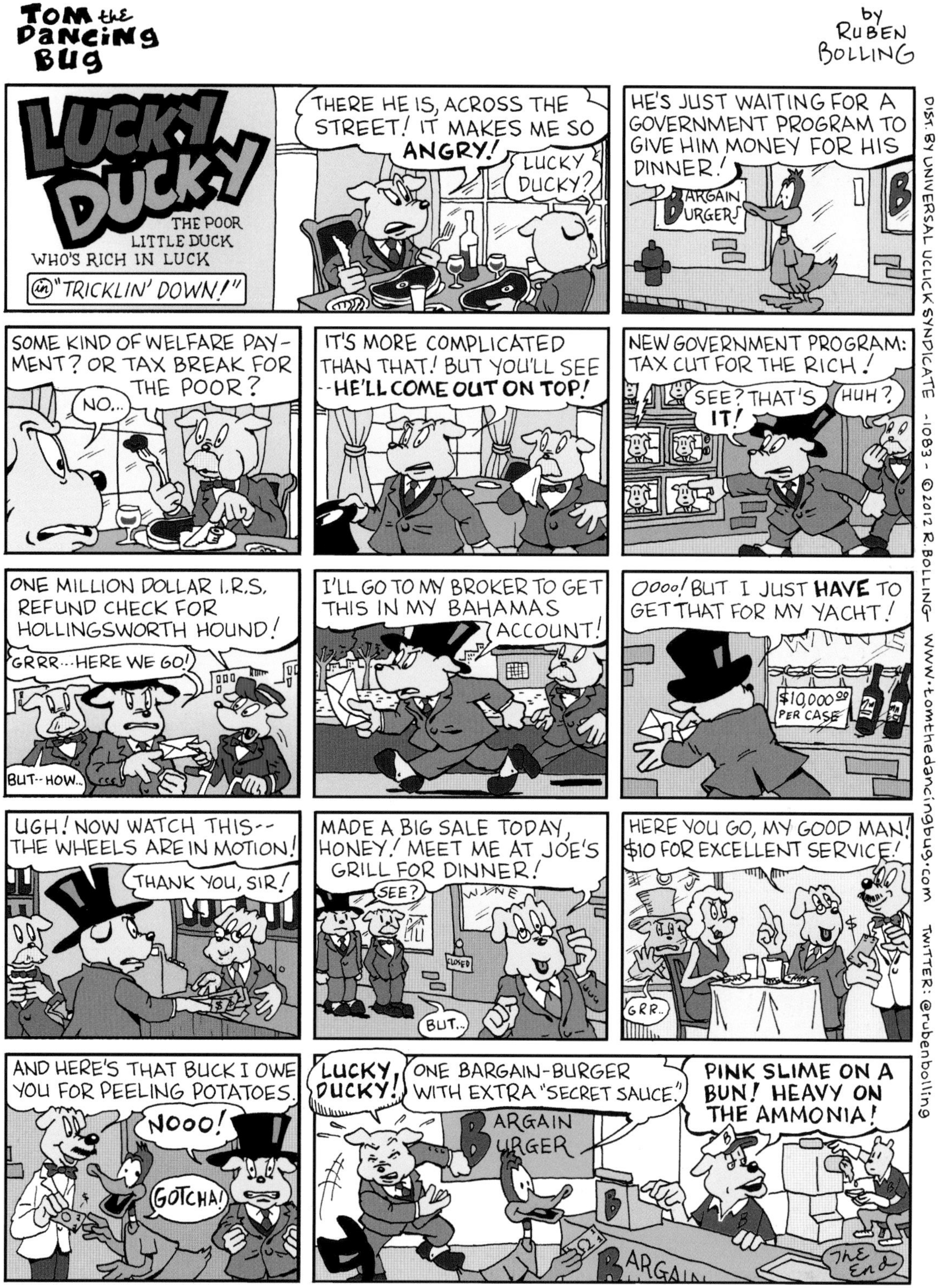
TOM the DANCING BUG
by RUBEN BOLLING
LUCKY DUCKY
THE POOR LITTLE DUCK WHO'S RICH IN LUCK
in "TRICKLIN' DOWN!"
THERE HE IS, ACROSS THE STREET! IT MAKES ME SO ANGRY!
LUCKY DUCKY?
HE'S JUST WAITING FOR A GOVERNMENT PROGRAM TO GIVE HIM MONEY FOR HIS DINNER!
BARGAIN BURGER
SOME KIND OF WELFARE PAYMENT? OR TAX BREAK FOR THE POOR?
NO...
IT'S MORE COMPLICATED THAN THAT! BUT YOU'LL SEE --HE'LL COME OUT ON TOP!
NEW GOVERNMENT PROGRAM: TAX CUT FOR THE RICH!
SEE? THAT'S IT!
HUH?
ONE MILLION DOLLAR I.R.S. REFUND CHECK FOR HOLLINGSWORTH HOUND!
GRRR... HERE WE GO!
BUT-- HOW..
I'LL GO TO MY BROKER TO GET THIS IN MY BAHAMAS ACCOUNT!
OOOO! BUT I JUST HAVE TO GET THAT FOR MY YACHT!
$10,000.00 PER CASE
UGH! NOW WATCH THIS-- THE WHEELS ARE IN MOTION!
THANK YOU, SIR!
MADE A BIG SALE TODAY, HONEY! MEET ME AT JOE'S GRILL FOR DINNER!
SEE?
BUT..
CLOSED
HERE YOU GO, MY GOOD MAN! $10 FOR EXCELLENT SERVICE!
GRR..
AND HERE'S THAT BUCK I OWE YOU FOR PEELING POTATOES.
NOOO!
GOTCHA!
LUCKY DUCKY!
ONE BARGAIN-BURGER WITH EXTRA "SECRET SAUCE."
PINK SLIME ON A BUN! HEAVY ON THE AMMONIA!
BARGAIN BURGER
THE End
DIST. BY UNIVERSAL UCLICK SYNDICATE -1083- © 2012 R. BOLLING— www.tomthedancingbug.com TWITTER: @rubenbolling
4/9/12

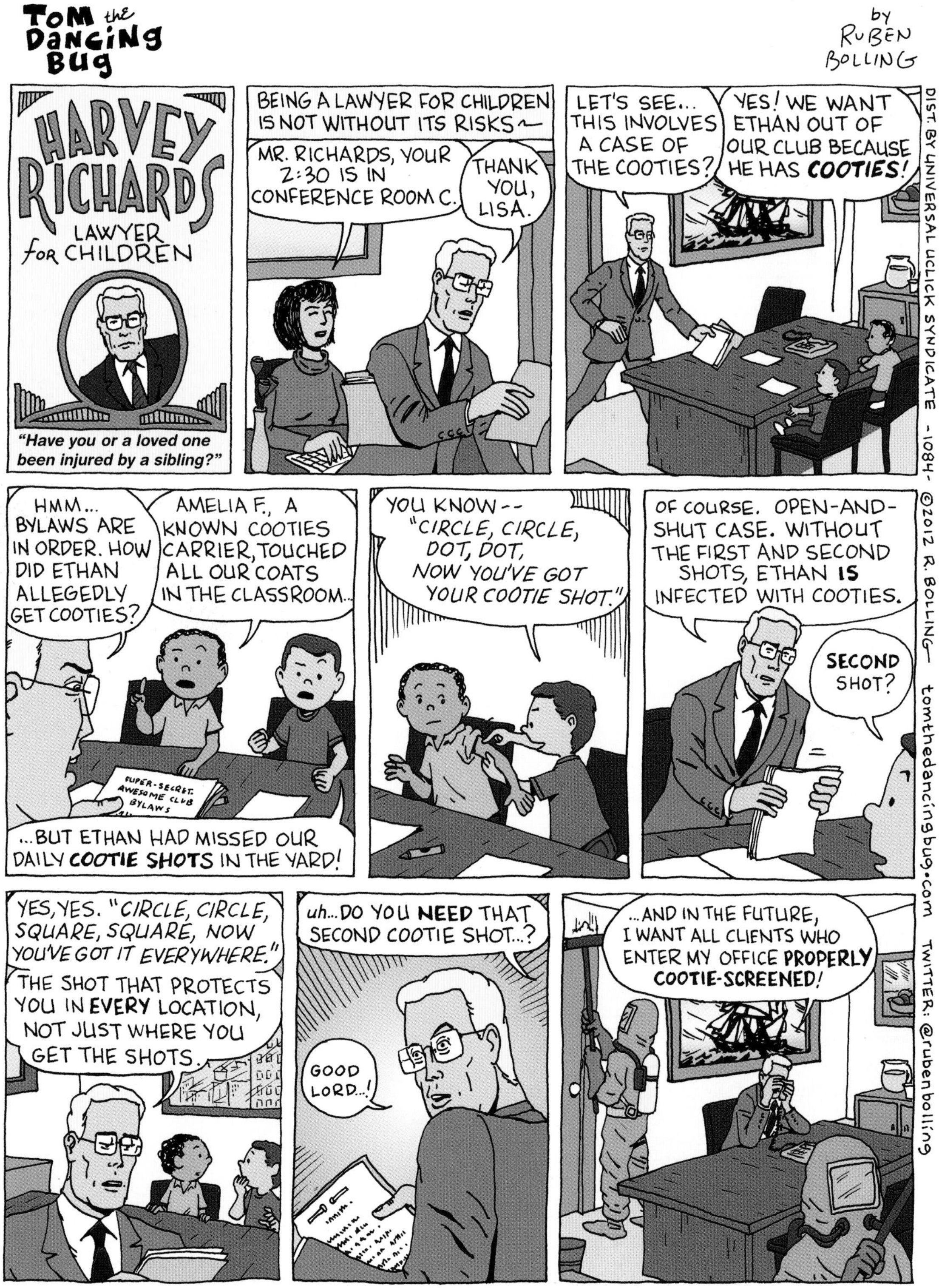
TOM the DANCING BUG
by RUBEN BOLLING
HARVEY RICHARDS
LAWYER for CHILDREN
"Have you or a loved one been injured by a sibling?"
BEING A LAWYER FOR CHILDREN IS NOT WITHOUT ITS RISKS~
MR. RICHARDS, YOUR 2:30 IS IN CONFERENCE ROOM C.
THANK YOU, LISA.
LET'S SEE... THIS INVOLVES A CASE OF THE COOTIES?
YES! WE WANT ETHAN OUT OF OUR CLUB BECAUSE HE HAS COOTIES!
HMM... BYLAWS ARE IN ORDER. HOW DID ETHAN ALLEGEDLY GET COOTIES?
AMELIA F., A KNOWN COOTIES CARRIER, TOUCHED ALL OUR COATS IN THE CLASSROOM...
SUPER-SECRET AWESOME CLUB BYLAWS
...BUT ETHAN HAD MISSED OUR DAILY COOTIE SHOTS IN THE YARD!
YOU KNOW-- "CIRCLE, CIRCLE, DOT, DOT, NOW YOU'VE GOT YOUR COOTIE SHOT."
OF COURSE. OPEN-AND-SHUT CASE. WITHOUT THE FIRST AND SECOND SHOTS, ETHAN IS INFECTED WITH COOTIES.
SECOND SHOT?
YES, YES. "CIRCLE, CIRCLE, SQUARE, SQUARE, NOW YOU'VE GOT IT EVERYWHERE."
THE SHOT THAT PROTECTS YOU IN EVERY LOCATION, NOT JUST WHERE YOU GET THE SHOTS.
uh...DO YOU NEED THAT SECOND COOTIE SHOT...?
GOOD LORD...!
...AND IN THE FUTURE, I WANT ALL CLIENTS WHO ENTER MY OFFICE PROPERLY COOTIE-SCREENED!
DIST. BY UNIVERSAL UCLICK SYNDICATE -1084- ©2012 R. BOLLING— tomthedancingbug.com TWITTER: @rubenbolling

4/16/12

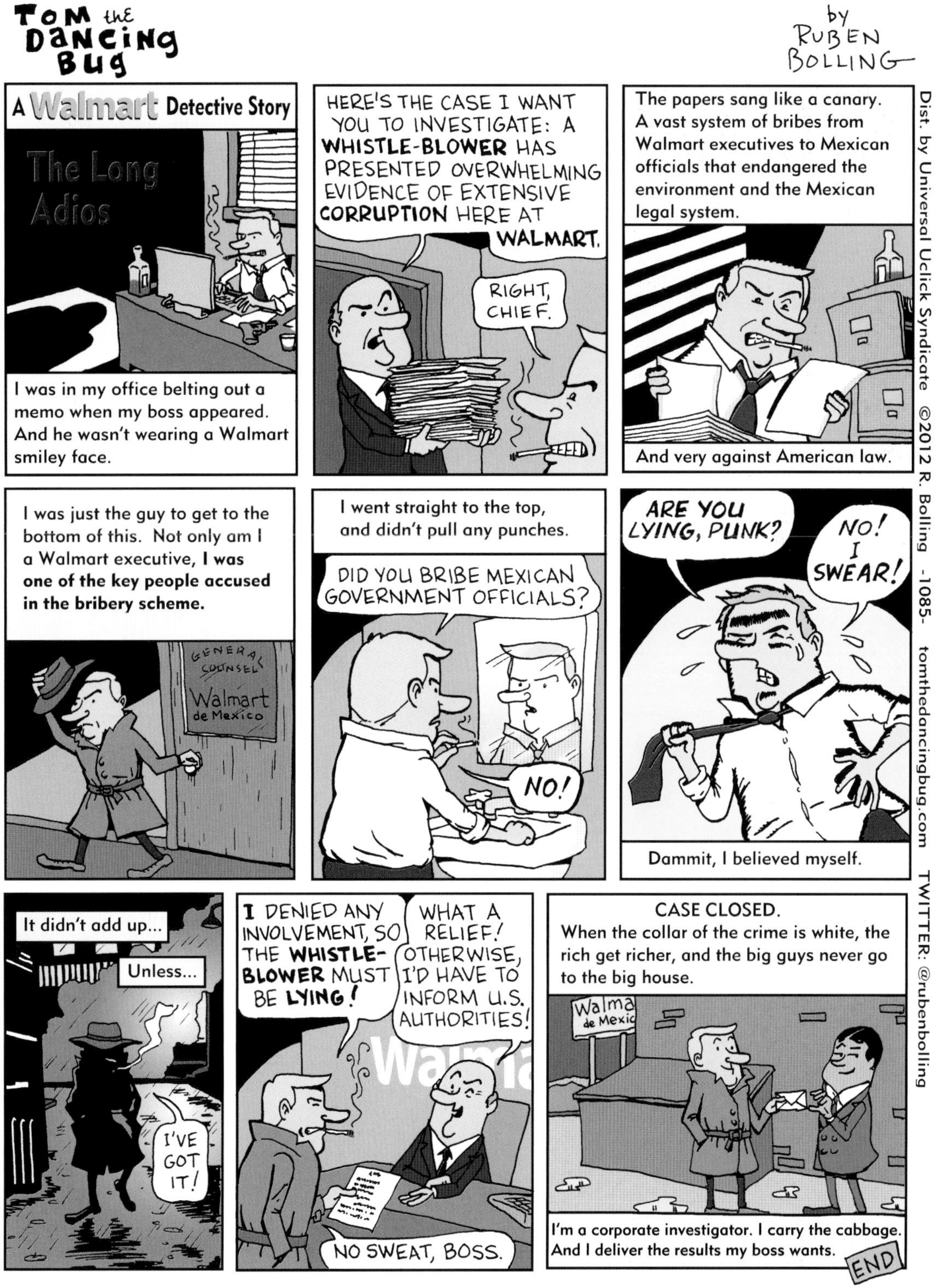

TOM the DANCING BUG
by RUBEN BOLLING
A Walmart Detective Story
The Long Adios
I was in my office belting out a memo when my boss appeared. And he wasn't wearing a Walmart smiley face.
HERE'S THE CASE I WANT YOU TO INVESTIGATE: A WHISTLE-BLOWER HAS PRESENTED OVERWHELMING EVIDENCE OF EXTENSIVE CORRUPTION HERE AT WALMART.
RIGHT, CHIEF.
The papers sang like a canary. A vast system of bribes from Walmart executives to Mexican officials that endangered the environment and the Mexican legal system.
And very against American law.
I was just the guy to get to the bottom of this. Not only am I a Walmart executive, I was one of the key people accused in the bribery scheme.
GENERAL COUNSEL
Walmart de Mexico
I went straight to the top, and didn't pull any punches.
DID YOU BRIBE MEXICAN GOVERNMENT OFFICIALS?
NO!
ARE YOU LYING, PUNK?
NO! I SWEAR!
Dammit, I believed myself.
It didn't add up...
Unless...
I'VE GOT IT!
I DENIED ANY INVOLVEMENT, SO THE WHISTLE-BLOWER MUST BE LYING!
WHAT A RELIEF! OTHERWISE, I'D HAVE TO INFORM U.S. AUTHORITIES!
NO SWEAT, BOSS.
CASE CLOSED.
When the collar of the crime is white, the rich get richer, and the big guys never go to the big house.
Walma de Mexic
I'm a corporate investigator. I carry the cabbage. And I deliver the results my boss wants.
END
Dist. by Universal Uclick Syndicate ©2012 R. Bolling -1085- tomthedancingbug.com TWITTER: @rubenbolling

4/23/12

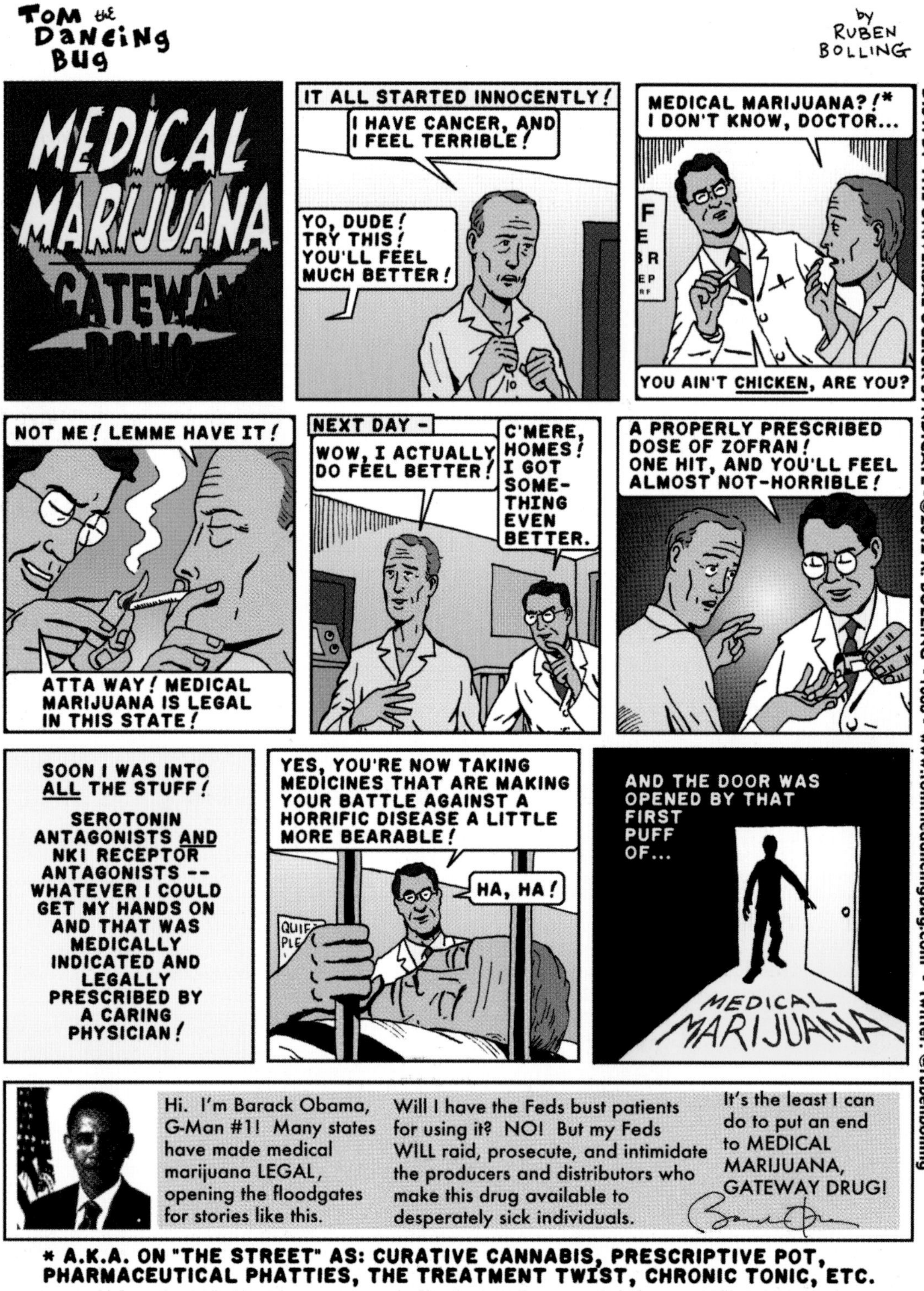
TOM the DANCING BUG
by RUBEN BOLLING
MEDICAL MARIJUANA
GATEWAY DRUG
IT ALL STARTED INNOCENTLY!
I HAVE CANCER, AND I FEEL TERRIBLE!
YO, DUDE! TRY THIS! YOU'LL FEEL MUCH BETTER!
MEDICAL MARIJUANA?!* I DON'T KNOW, DOCTOR...
YOU AIN'T CHICKEN, ARE YOU?
NOT ME! LEMME HAVE IT!
ATTA WAY! MEDICAL MARIJUANA IS LEGAL IN THIS STATE!
NEXT DAY –
WOW, I ACTUALLY DO FEEL BETTER!
C'MERE, HOMES! I GOT SOMETHING EVEN BETTER.
A PROPERLY PRESCRIBED DOSE OF ZOFRAN! ONE HIT, AND YOU'LL FEEL ALMOST NOT-HORRIBLE!
SOON I WAS INTO ALL THE STUFF!
SEROTONIN ANTAGONISTS AND NK1 RECEPTOR ANTAGONISTS -- WHATEVER I COULD GET MY HANDS ON AND THAT WAS MEDICALLY INDICATED AND LEGALLY PRESCRIBED BY A CARING PHYSICIAN!
YES, YOU'RE NOW TAKING MEDICINES THAT ARE MAKING YOUR BATTLE AGAINST A HORRIFIC DISEASE A LITTLE MORE BEARABLE!
HA, HA!
AND THE DOOR WAS OPENED BY THAT FIRST PUFF OF...
MEDICAL MARIJUANA
Hi. I'm Barack Obama, G-Man #1! Many states have made medical marijuana LEGAL, opening the floodgates for stories like this.
Will I have the Feds bust patients for using it? NO! But my Feds WILL raid, prosecute, and intimidate the producers and distributors who make this drug available to desperately sick individuals.
It's the least I can do to put an end to MEDICAL MARIJUANA, GATEWAY DRUG!
* A.K.A. ON "THE STREET" AS: CURATIVE CANNABIS, PRESCRIPTIVE POT, PHARMACEUTICAL PHATTIES, THE TREATMENT TWIST, CHRONIC TONIC, ETC.
DIST. BY THE UNIVERSAL UCLICK SYNDICATE - ©2012 R. BOLLING - 1086 - www.tomthedancingbug.com - twitter: @rubenbolling

4/30/12

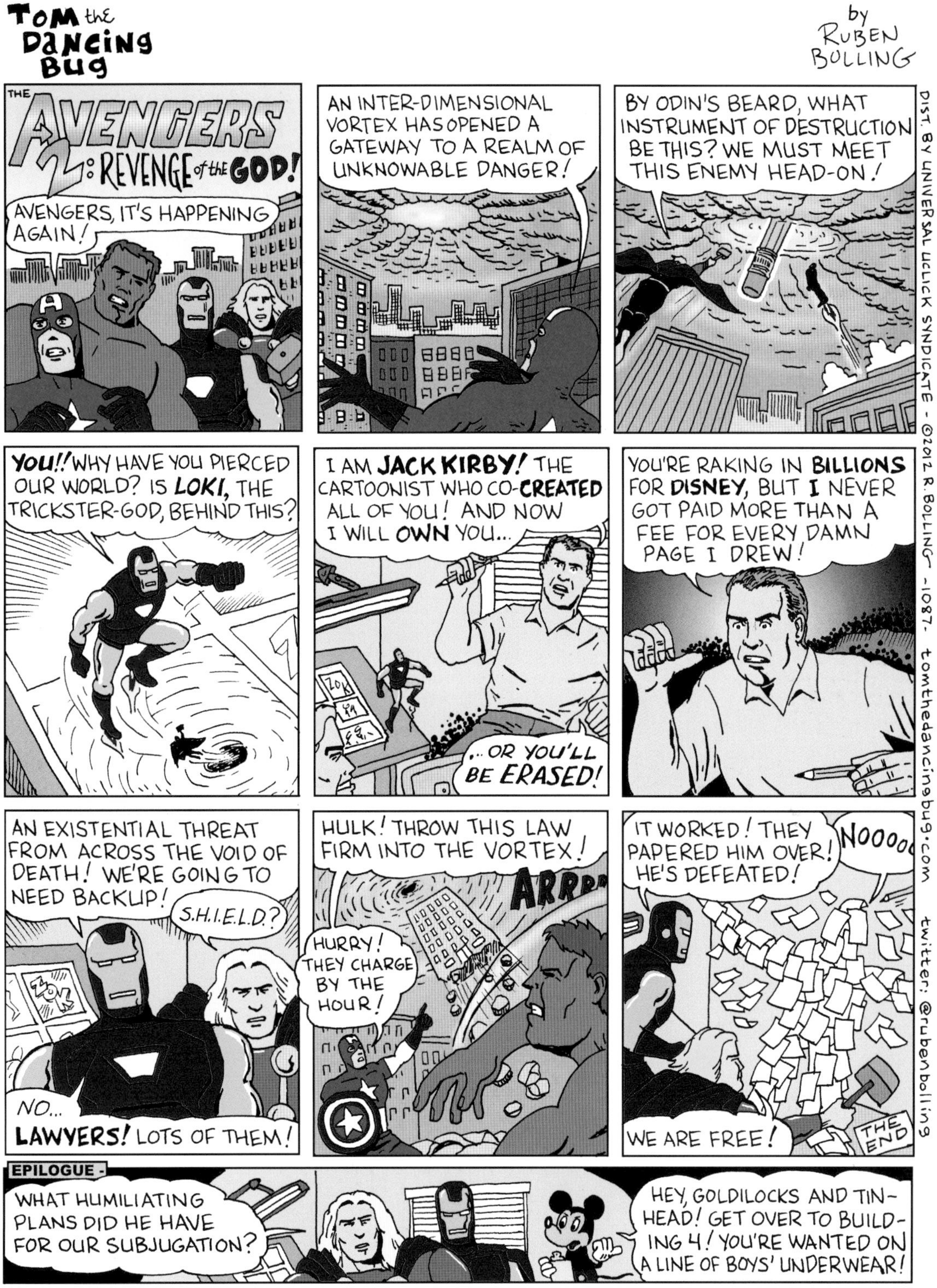
Tom the Dancing Bug
by Ruben Bolling
THE AVENGERS 2: REVENGE of the GOD!
AVENGERS, IT'S HAPPENING AGAIN!
AN INTER-DIMENSIONAL VORTEX HAS OPENED A GATEWAY TO A REALM OF UNKNOWABLE DANGER!
BY ODIN'S BEARD, WHAT INSTRUMENT OF DESTRUCTION BE THIS? WE MUST MEET THIS ENEMY HEAD-ON!
DIST. BY UNIVERSAL UCLICK SYNDICATE - ©2012 R. BOLLING -1087- tomthedancingbug.com twitter: @rubenbolling
YOU!! WHY HAVE YOU PIERCED OUR WORLD? IS LOKI, THE TRICKSTER-GOD, BEHIND THIS?
I AM JACK KIRBY! THE CARTOONIST WHO CO-CREATED ALL OF YOU! AND NOW I WILL OWN YOU...
...OR YOU'LL BE ERASED!
YOU'RE RAKING IN BILLIONS FOR DISNEY, BUT I NEVER GOT PAID MORE THAN A FEE FOR EVERY DAMN PAGE I DREW!
AN EXISTENTIAL THREAT FROM ACROSS THE VOID OF DEATH! WE'RE GOING TO NEED BACKUP!
S.H.I.E.L.D.?
NO... LAWYERS! LOTS OF THEM!
HULK! THROW THIS LAW FIRM INTO THE VORTEX!
ARRRR
HURRY! THEY CHARGE BY THE HOUR!
IT WORKED! THEY PAPERED HIM OVER! HE'S DEFEATED!
NOOOOO
WE ARE FREE!
THE END
EPILOGUE -
WHAT HUMILIATING PLANS DID HE HAVE FOR OUR SUBJUGATION?
HEY, GOLDILOCKS AND TIN-HEAD! GET OVER TO BUILDING 4! YOU'RE WANTED ON A LINE OF BOYS' UNDERWEAR!

5/7/12

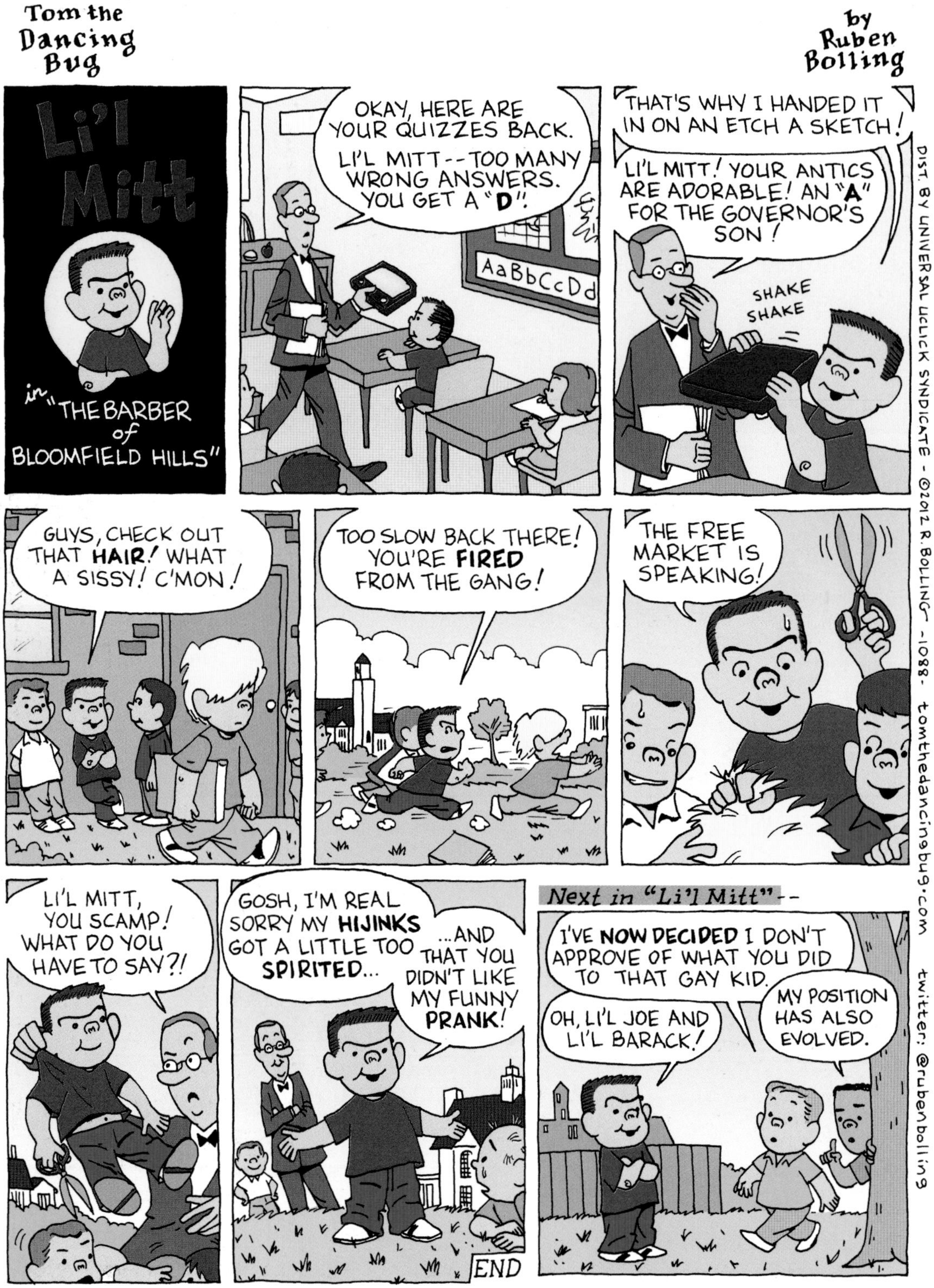

Tom the Dancing Bug
by Ruben Bolling
Li'l Mitt
in "THE BARBER of BLOOMFIELD HILLS"
OKAY, HERE ARE YOUR QUIZZES BACK.
LI'L MITT--TOO MANY WRONG ANSWERS. YOU GET A "D".
AaBbCcDd
THAT'S WHY I HANDED IT IN ON AN ETCH A SKETCH!
LI'L MITT! YOUR ANTICS ARE ADORABLE! AN "A" FOR THE GOVERNOR'S SON!
SHAKE SHAKE
GUYS, CHECK OUT THAT HAIR! WHAT A SISSY! C'MON!
TOO SLOW BACK THERE! YOU'RE FIRED FROM THE GANG!
THE FREE MARKET IS SPEAKING!
LI'L MITT, YOU SCAMP! WHAT DO YOU HAVE TO SAY?!
GOSH, I'M REAL SORRY MY HIJINKS GOT A LITTLE TOO SPIRITED...
...AND THAT YOU DIDN'T LIKE MY FUNNY PRANK!
END
Next in "Li'l Mitt"--
I'VE NOW DECIDED I DON'T APPROVE OF WHAT YOU DID TO THAT GAY KID.
OH, LI'L JOE AND LI'L BARACK!
MY POSITION HAS ALSO EVOLVED.
DIST. BY UNIVERSAL UCLICK SYNDICATE - ©2012 R. BOLLING -1088- tomthedancingbug.com twitter: @rubenbolling

5/14/12

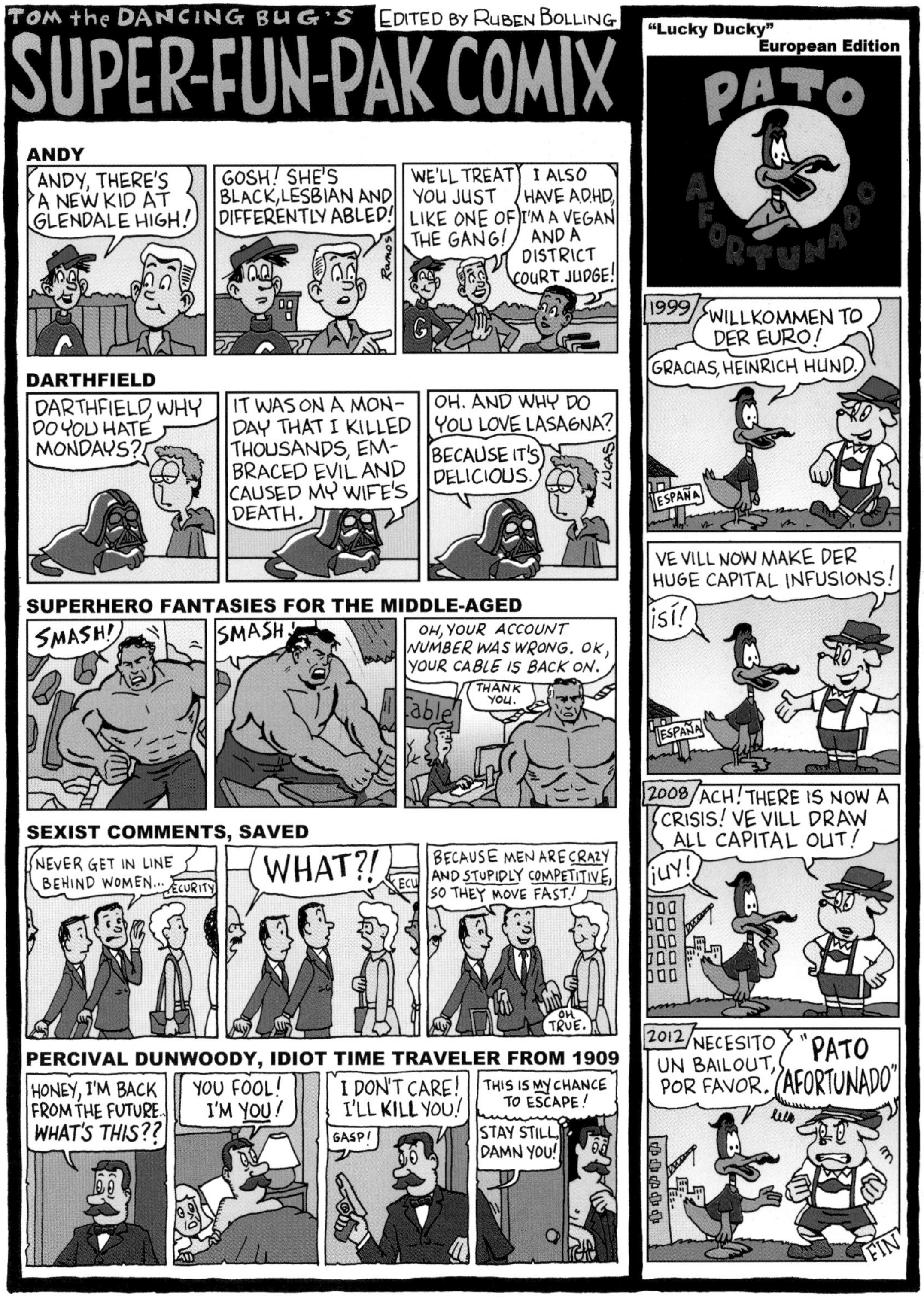
TOM the DANCING BUG'S
EDITED BY RUBEN BOLLING
SUPER-FUN-PAK COMIX
ANDY
ANDY, THERE'S A NEW KID AT GLENDALE HIGH!
GOSH! SHE'S BLACK, LESBIAN AND DIFFERENTLY ABLED!
RAMOS
WE'LL TREAT YOU JUST LIKE ONE OF THE GANG!
I ALSO HAVE A.D.H.D., I'M A VEGAN AND A DISTRICT COURT JUDGE!
DARTHFIELD
DARTHFIELD, WHY DO YOU HATE MONDAYS?
IT WAS ON A MON-DAY THAT I KILLED THOUSANDS, EM-BRACED EVIL AND CAUSED MY WIFE'S DEATH.
OH. AND WHY DO YOU LOVE LASAGNA?
BECAUSE IT'S DELICIOUS.
LUCAS
SUPERHERO FANTASIES FOR THE MIDDLE-AGED
SMASH!
SMASH!
OH, YOUR ACCOUNT NUMBER WAS WRONG. OK, YOUR CABLE IS BACK ON.
THANK YOU.
Cable
SEXIST COMMENTS, SAVED
NEVER GET IN LINE BEHIND WOMEN...
ECURITY
WHAT?!
BECAUSE MEN ARE CRAZY AND STUPIDLY COMPETITIVE, SO THEY MOVE FAST!
OH TRUE.
PERCIVAL DUNWOODY, IDIOT TIME TRAVELER FROM 1909
HONEY, I'M BACK FROM THE FUTURE... WHAT'S THIS??
YOU FOOL! I'M YOU!
I DON'T CARE! I'LL KILL YOU!
GASP!
THIS IS MY CHANCE TO ESCAPE!
STAY STILL, DAMN YOU!
"Lucky Ducky"
European Edition
PATO AFORTUNADO
1999
WILLKOMMEN TO DER EURO!
GRACIAS, HEINRICH HUND.
ESPAÑA
VE VILL NOW MAKE DER HUGE CAPITAL INFUSIONS!
¡SÍ!
ESPAÑA
2008
ACH! THERE IS NOW A CRISIS! VE VILL DRAW ALL CAPITAL OUT!
¡UY!
2012
NECESITO UN BAILOUT, POR FAVOR.
"PATO AFORTUNADO"
FIN

5/21/12

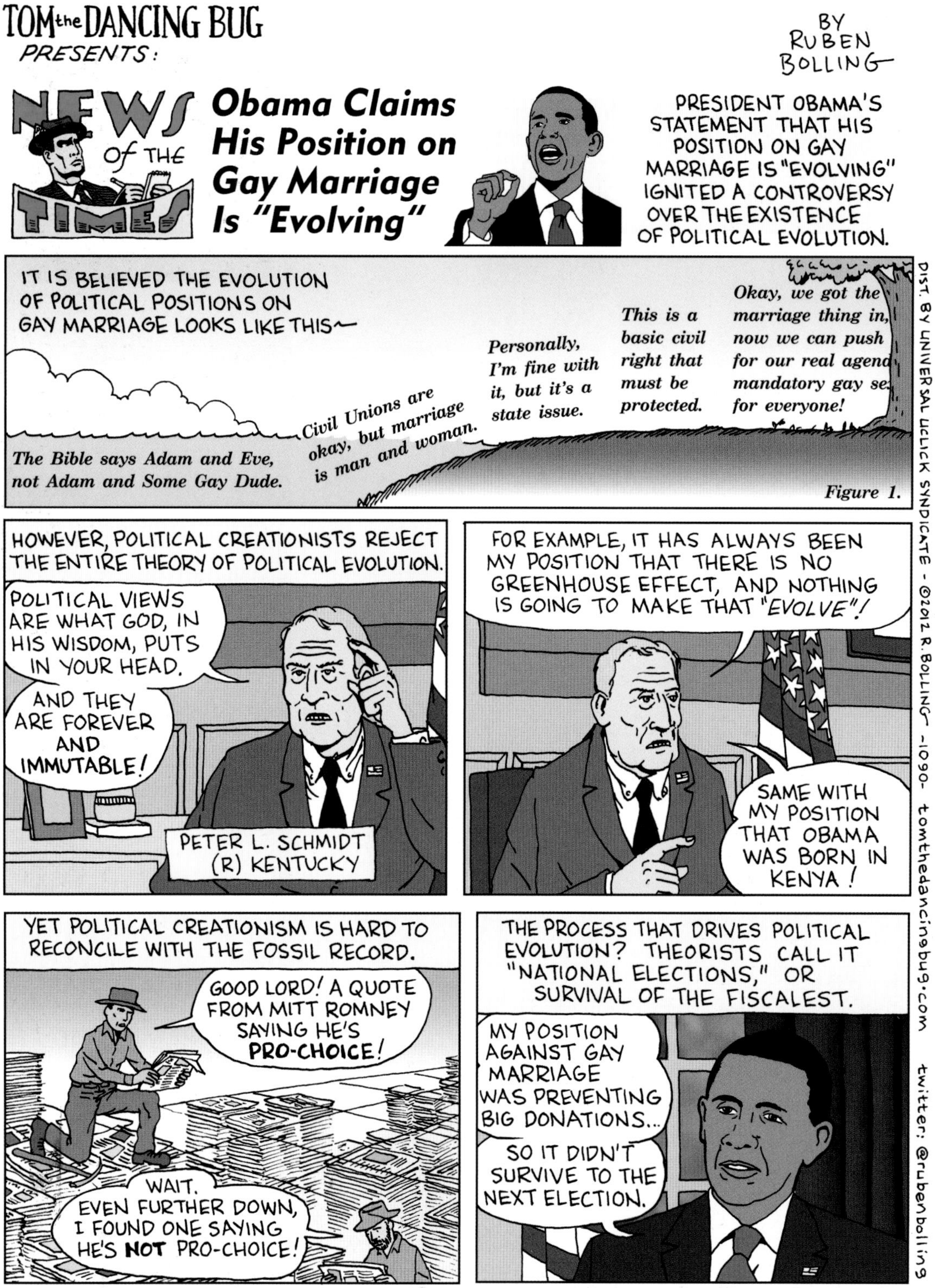
TOM the DANCING BUG
PRESENTS:
BY RUBEN BOLLING
NEWS of THE TIMES
Obama Claims His Position on Gay Marriage Is "Evolving"
PRESIDENT OBAMA'S STATEMENT THAT HIS POSITION ON GAY MARRIAGE IS "EVOLVING" IGNITED A CONTROVERSY OVER THE EXISTENCE OF POLITICAL EVOLUTION.
IT IS BELIEVED THE EVOLUTION OF POLITICAL POSITIONS ON GAY MARRIAGE LOOKS LIKE THIS~
The Bible says Adam and Eve, not Adam and Some Gay Dude.
Civil Unions are okay, but marriage is man and woman.
Personally, I'm fine with it, but it's a state issue.
This is a basic civil right that must be protected.
Okay, we got the marriage thing in, now we can push for our real agend mandatory gay se for everyone!
Figure 1.
HOWEVER, POLITICAL CREATIONISTS REJECT THE ENTIRE THEORY OF POLITICAL EVOLUTION.
POLITICAL VIEWS ARE WHAT GOD, IN HIS WISDOM, PUTS IN YOUR HEAD.
AND THEY ARE FOREVER AND IMMUTABLE!
PETER L. SCHMIDT (R) KENTUCKY
FOR EXAMPLE, IT HAS ALWAYS BEEN MY POSITION THAT THERE IS NO GREENHOUSE EFFECT, AND NOTHING IS GOING TO MAKE THAT "EVOLVE"!
SAME WITH MY POSITION THAT OBAMA WAS BORN IN KENYA!
YET POLITICAL CREATIONISM IS HARD TO RECONCILE WITH THE FOSSIL RECORD.
GOOD LORD! A QUOTE FROM MITT ROMNEY SAYING HE'S PRO-CHOICE!
WAIT. EVEN FURTHER DOWN, I FOUND ONE SAYING HE'S NOT PRO-CHOICE!
THE PROCESS THAT DRIVES POLITICAL EVOLUTION? THEORISTS CALL IT "NATIONAL ELECTIONS," OR SURVIVAL OF THE FISCALEST.
MY POSITION AGAINST GAY MARRIAGE WAS PREVENTING BIG DONATIONS...
SO IT DIDN'T SURVIVE TO THE NEXT ELECTION.
DIST. BY UNIVERSAL UCLICK SYNDICATE - ©2012 R. BOLLING -1090- tomthedancingbug.com twitter: @rubenbolling

5/28/12

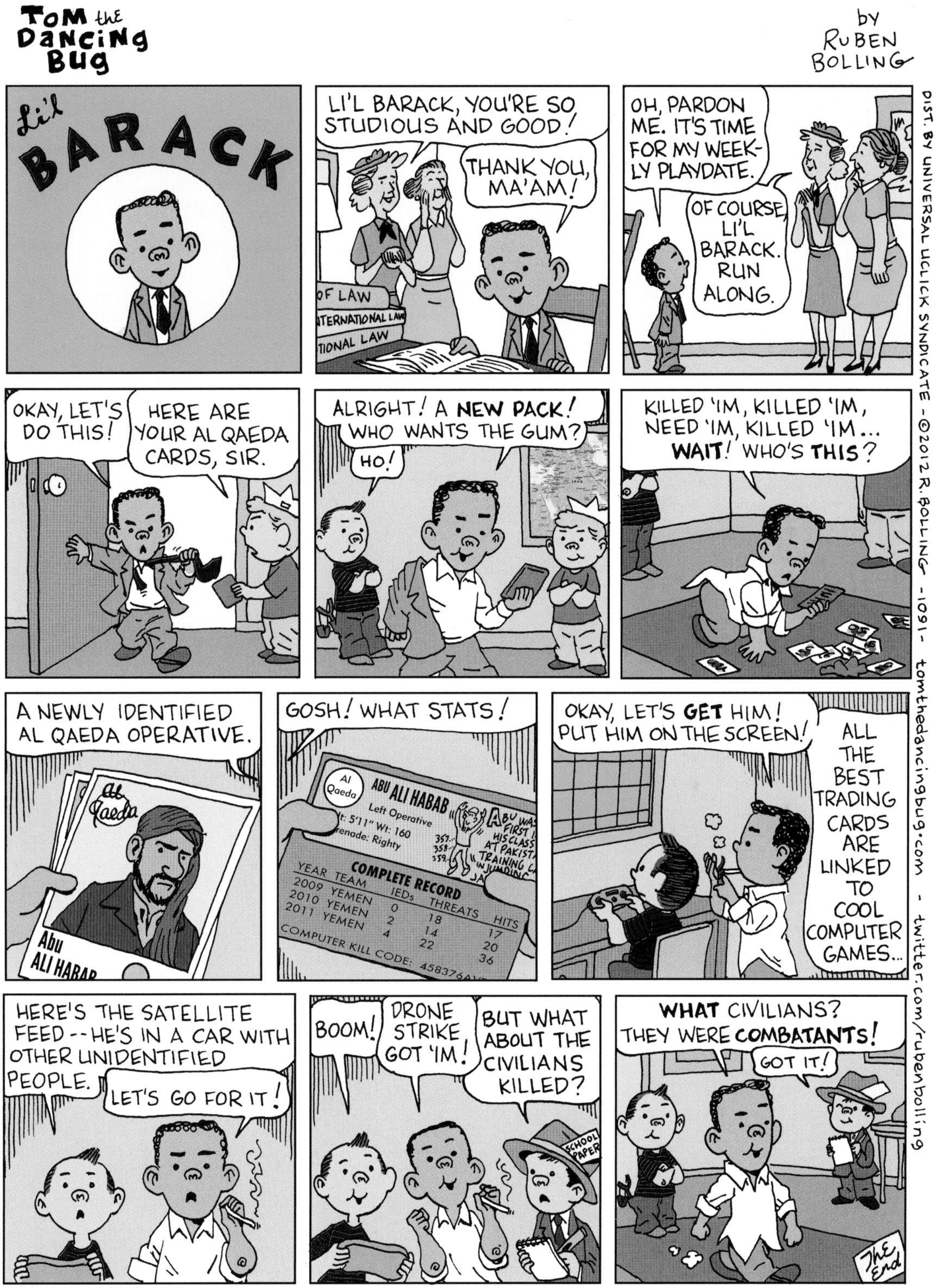
TOM the DANCING BUG
by RUBEN BOLLING
Li'l BARACK
LI'L BARACK, YOU'RE SO STUDIOUS AND GOOD!
THANK YOU, MA'AM!
OF LAW
INTERNATIONAL LAW
TIONAL LAW
OH, PARDON ME. IT'S TIME FOR MY WEEKLY PLAYDATE.
OF COURSE, LI'L BARACK. RUN ALONG.
OKAY, LET'S DO THIS!
HERE ARE YOUR AL QAEDA CARDS, SIR.
ALRIGHT! A NEW PACK! WHO WANTS THE GUM?
HO!
KILLED 'IM, KILLED 'IM, NEED 'IM, KILLED 'IM... WAIT! WHO'S THIS?
A NEWLY IDENTIFIED AL QAEDA OPERATIVE.
Al Qaeda
Abu ALI HABAB
GOSH! WHAT STATS!
Al Qaeda
ABU ALI HABAB
Left Operative
Wt: 160
Righty
COMPLETE RECORD
YEAR TEAM IEDs THREATS HITS
2009 YEMEN 0 18 17
2010 YEMEN 2 14 20
2011 YEMEN 4 22 36
COMPUTER KILL CODE:
OKAY, LET'S GET HIM! PUT HIM ON THE SCREEN!
ALL THE BEST TRADING CARDS ARE LINKED TO COOL COMPUTER GAMES...
HERE'S THE SATELLITE FEED--HE'S IN A CAR WITH OTHER UNIDENTIFIED PEOPLE.
LET'S GO FOR IT!
BOOM!
DRONE STRIKE GOT 'IM!
BUT WHAT ABOUT THE CIVILIANS KILLED?
SCHOOL PAPER
WHAT CIVILIANS? THEY WERE COMBATANTS!
GOT IT!
THE End
DIST. BY UNIVERSAL UCLICK SYNDICATE - ©2012 R. BOLLING -1091- tomthedancingbug.com - twitter.com/rubenbolling

6/4/12

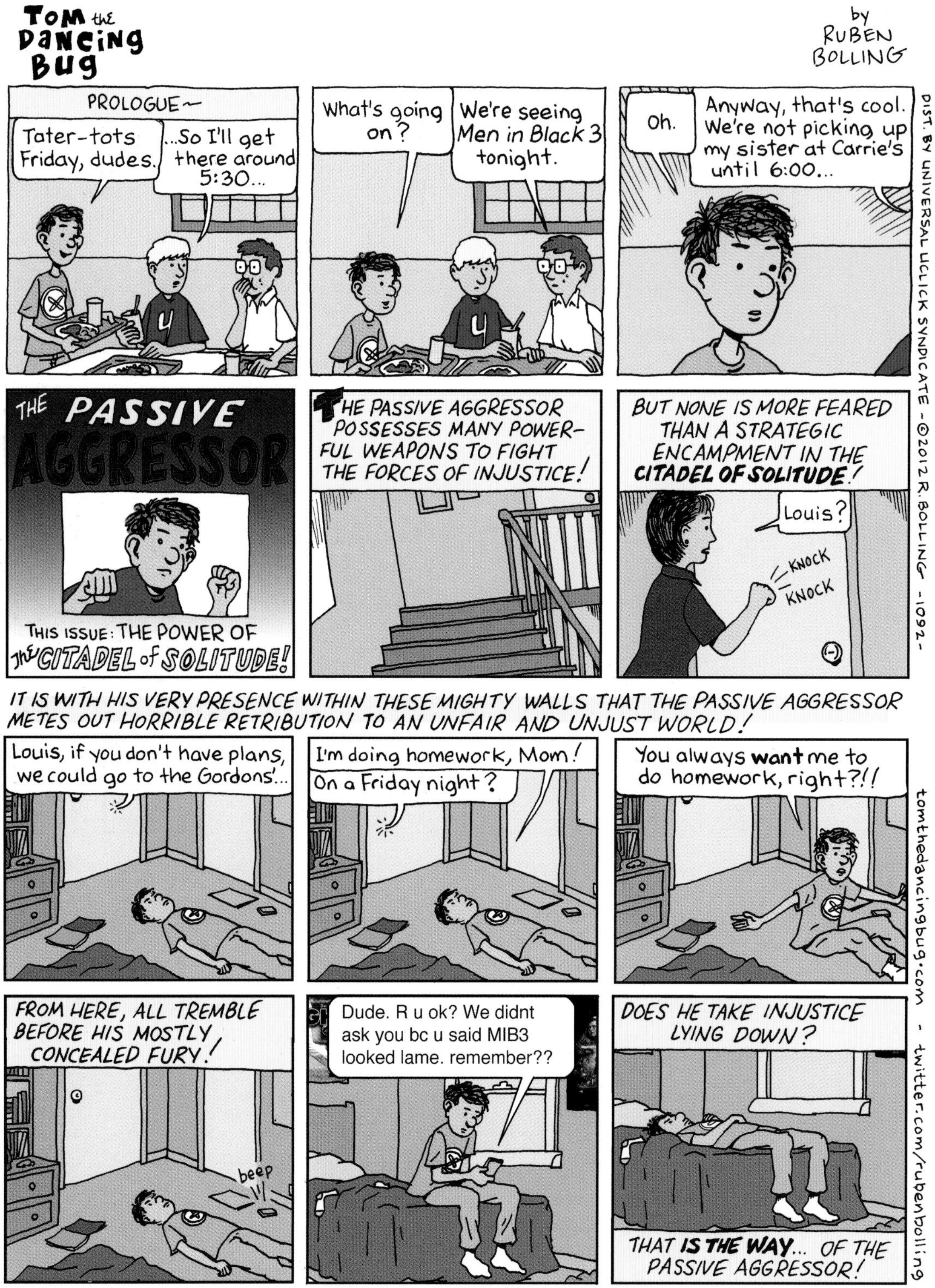
TOM the DANCING BUG
by RUBEN BOLLING
PROLOGUE~
Tater-tots Friday, dudes.
...So I'll get there around 5:30...
What's going on?
We're seeing Men in Black 3 tonight.
Oh.
Anyway, that's cool. We're not picking up my sister at Carrie's until 6:00...
DIST. BY UNIVERSAL UCLICK SYNDICATE - ©2012 R. BOLLING -1092-
THE PASSIVE AGGRESSOR
THIS ISSUE: THE POWER OF THE CITADEL of SOLITUDE!
THE PASSIVE AGGRESSOR POSSESSES MANY POWERFUL WEAPONS TO FIGHT THE FORCES OF INJUSTICE!
BUT NONE IS MORE FEARED THAN A STRATEGIC ENCAMPMENT IN THE CITADEL OF SOLITUDE!
Louis?
KNOCK
KNOCK
IT IS WITH HIS VERY PRESENCE WITHIN THESE MIGHTY WALLS THAT THE PASSIVE AGGRESSOR METES OUT HORRIBLE RETRIBUTION TO AN UNFAIR AND UNJUST WORLD!
Louis, if you don't have plans, we could go to the Gordons'...
I'm doing homework, Mom!
On a Friday night?
You always want me to do homework, right?!!
FROM HERE, ALL TREMBLE BEFORE HIS MOSTLY CONCEALED FURY!
beep
Dude. R u ok? We didnt ask you bc u said MIB3 looked lame. remember??
DOES HE TAKE INJUSTICE LYING DOWN?
THAT IS THE WAY... OF THE PASSIVE AGGRESSOR!
tomthedancingbug.com - twitter.com/rubenbolling

6/11/12

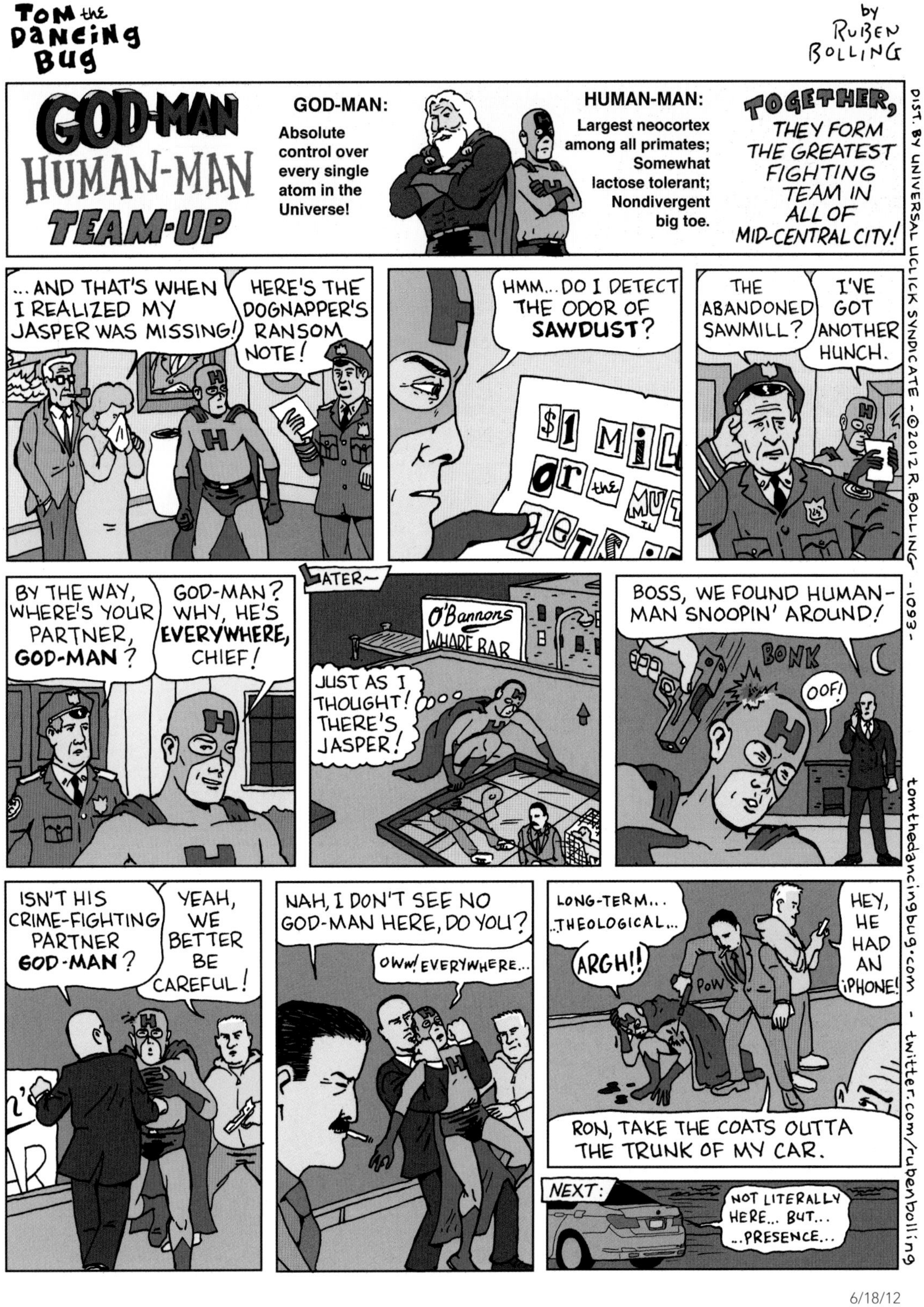

TOM the DANCING BUG
by RUBEN BOLLING
GOD-MAN HUMAN-MAN TEAM-UP
GOD-MAN:
Absolute control over every single atom in the Universe!
HUMAN-MAN:
Largest neocortex among all primates; Somewhat lactose tolerant; Nondivergent big toe.
TOGETHER, THEY FORM THE GREATEST FIGHTING TEAM IN ALL OF MID-CENTRAL CITY!
...AND THAT'S WHEN I REALIZED MY JASPER WAS MISSING!
HERE'S THE DOGNAPPER'S RANSOM NOTE!
HMM... DO I DETECT THE ODOR OF SAWDUST?
$1 MIL OR THE MUT GET
THE ABANDONED SAWMILL?
I'VE GOT ANOTHER HUNCH.
BY THE WAY, WHERE'S YOUR PARTNER, GOD-MAN?
GOD-MAN? WHY, HE'S EVERYWHERE, CHIEF!
LATER~
O'Bannons WHARF BAR
JUST AS I THOUGHT! THERE'S JASPER!
BOSS, WE FOUND HUMAN-MAN SNOOPIN' AROUND!
BONK
OOF!
ISN'T HIS CRIME-FIGHTING PARTNER GOD-MAN?
YEAH, WE BETTER BE CAREFUL!
NAH, I DON'T SEE NO GOD-MAN HERE, DO YOU?
OWW! EVERYWHERE...
LONG-TERM...
...THEOLOGICAL...
ARGH!!
POW
HEY, HE HAD AN iPHONE!
RON, TAKE THE COATS OUTTA THE TRUNK OF MY CAR.
NEXT:
NOT LITERALLY HERE... BUT... ...PRESENCE...
DIST. BY UNIVERSAL UCLICK SYNDICATE - ©2012 R. BOLLING - 1093 -
tomthedancingbug.com - twitter.com/rubenbolling

6/18/12

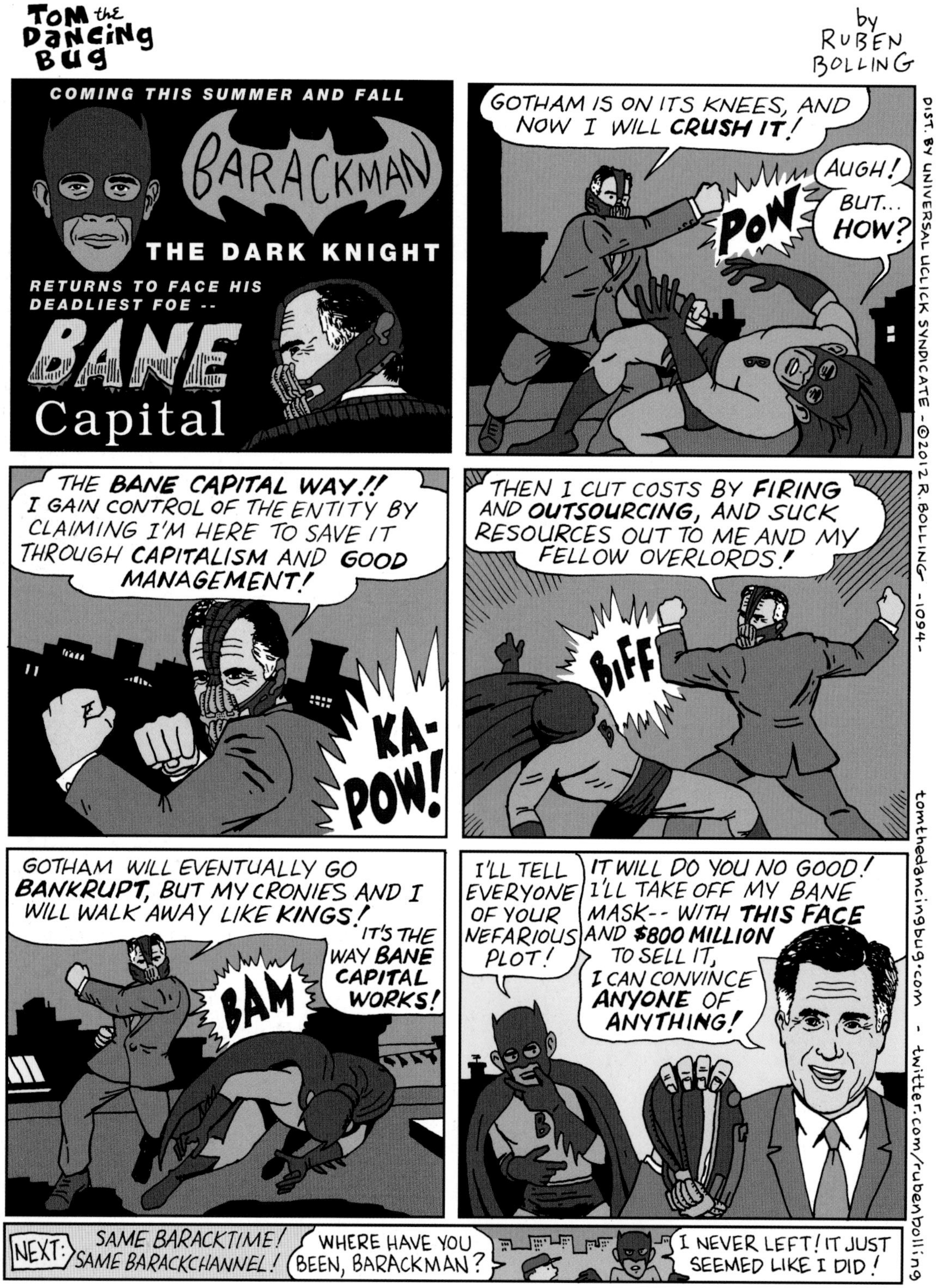
TOM the DANCING BUG
by RUBEN BOLLING
COMING THIS SUMMER AND FALL
BARACKMAN
THE DARK KNIGHT
RETURNS TO FACE HIS DEADLIEST FOE --
BANE Capital
GOTHAM IS ON ITS KNEES, AND NOW I WILL CRUSH IT!
POW
AUGH!
BUT... HOW?
THE BANE CAPITAL WAY!! I GAIN CONTROL OF THE ENTITY BY CLAIMING I'M HERE TO SAVE IT THROUGH CAPITALISM AND GOOD MANAGEMENT!
KA-POW!
THEN I CUT COSTS BY FIRING AND OUTSOURCING, AND SUCK RESOURCES OUT TO ME AND MY FELLOW OVERLORDS!
BIFF
GOTHAM WILL EVENTUALLY GO BANKRUPT, BUT MY CRONIES AND I WILL WALK AWAY LIKE KINGS!
IT'S THE WAY BANE CAPITAL WORKS!
BAM
I'LL TELL EVERYONE OF YOUR NEFARIOUS PLOT!
IT WILL DO YOU NO GOOD! I'LL TAKE OFF MY BANE MASK-- WITH THIS FACE AND $800 MILLION TO SELL IT, I CAN CONVINCE ANYONE OF ANYTHING!
NEXT: SAME BARACKTIME! SAME BARACKCHANNEL!
WHERE HAVE YOU BEEN, BARACKMAN?
I NEVER LEFT! IT JUST SEEMED LIKE I DID!
DIST. BY UNIVERSAL UCLICK SYNDICATE - ©2012 R. BOLLING - 1094 -
tomthedancingbug.com - twitter.com/rubenbolling

6/25/12

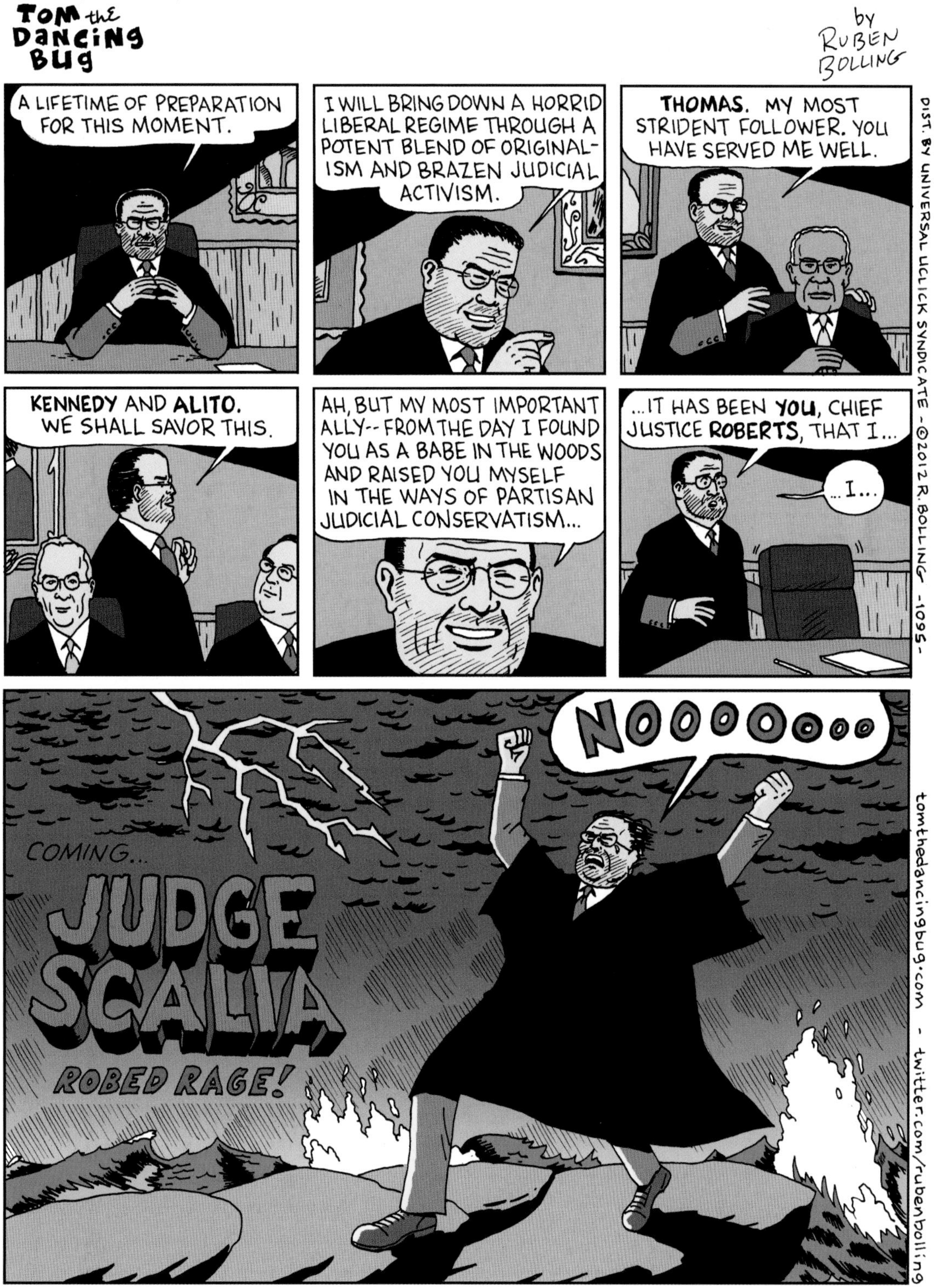
TOM the DANCING BUG
by RUBEN BOLLING
A LIFETIME OF PREPARATION FOR THIS MOMENT.
I WILL BRING DOWN A HORRID LIBERAL REGIME THROUGH A POTENT BLEND OF ORIGINAL-ISM AND BRAZEN JUDICIAL ACTIVISM.
THOMAS. MY MOST STRIDENT FOLLOWER. YOU HAVE SERVED ME WELL.
DIST. BY UNIVERSAL UCLICK SYNDICATE - ©2012 R. BOLLING -1095-
KENNEDY AND ALITO. WE SHALL SAVOR THIS.
AH, BUT MY MOST IMPORTANT ALLY-- FROM THE DAY I FOUND YOU AS A BABE IN THE WOODS AND RAISED YOU MYSELF IN THE WAYS OF PARTISAN JUDICIAL CONSERVATISM...
...IT HAS BEEN YOU, CHIEF JUSTICE ROBERTS, THAT I...
...I...
NOOOOOoo
COMING...
JUDGE SCALIA
ROBED RAGE!
tomthedancingbug.com - twitter.com/rubenbolling

7/2/12

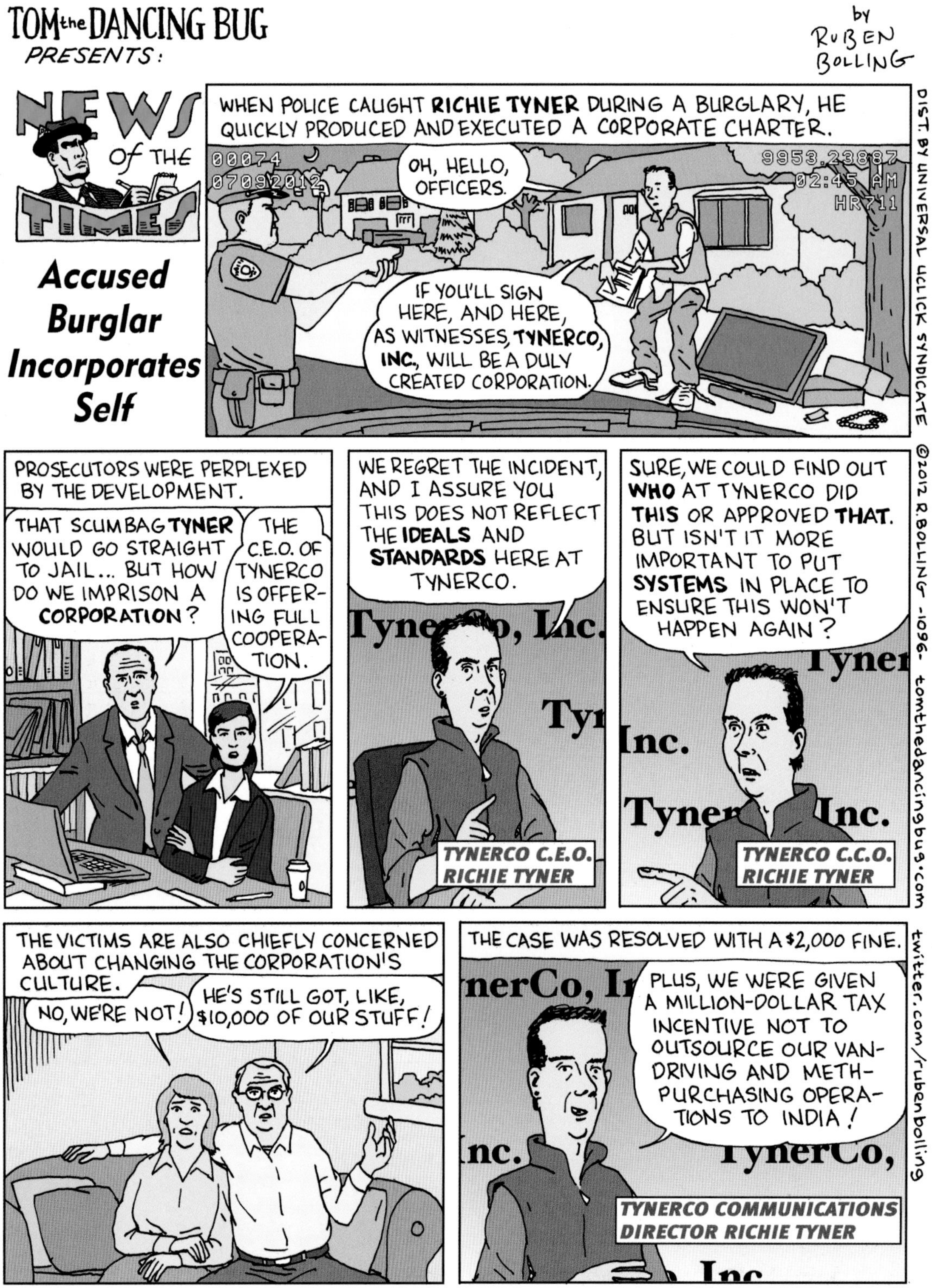
TOM the DANCING BUG
PRESENTS:
by RUBEN BOLLING
NEWS of THE TIMES
Accused Burglar Incorporates Self
WHEN POLICE CAUGHT **RICHIE TYNER** DURING A BURGLARY, HE QUICKLY PRODUCED AND EXECUTED A CORPORATE CHARTER.
00074
07092012
9953.23887
02:45 AM
HR711
OH, HELLO, OFFICERS.
IF YOU'LL SIGN HERE, AND HERE, AS WITNESSES, **TYNERCO, INC.**, WILL BE A DULY CREATED CORPORATION.
PROSECUTORS WERE PERPLEXED BY THE DEVELOPMENT.
THAT SCUMBAG **TYNER** WOULD GO STRAIGHT TO JAIL... BUT HOW DO WE IMPRISON A **CORPORATION**?
THE C.E.O. OF TYNERCO IS OFFERING FULL COOPERATION.
WE REGRET THE INCIDENT, AND I ASSURE YOU THIS DOES NOT REFLECT THE **IDEALS** AND **STANDARDS** HERE AT TYNERCO.
TYNERCO C.E.O. RICHIE TYNER
SURE, WE COULD FIND OUT **WHO** AT TYNERCO DID **THIS** OR APPROVED **THAT**. BUT ISN'T IT MORE IMPORTANT TO PUT **SYSTEMS** IN PLACE TO ENSURE THIS WON'T HAPPEN AGAIN?
TYNERCO C.C.O. RICHIE TYNER
THE VICTIMS ARE ALSO CHIEFLY CONCERNED ABOUT CHANGING THE CORPORATION'S CULTURE.
NO, WE'RE NOT!
HE'S STILL GOT, LIKE, $10,000 OF OUR STUFF!
THE CASE WAS RESOLVED WITH A $2,000 FINE.
PLUS, WE WERE GIVEN A MILLION-DOLLAR TAX INCENTIVE NOT TO OUTSOURCE OUR VAN-DRIVING AND METH-PURCHASING OPERATIONS TO INDIA!
TYNERCO COMMUNICATIONS DIRECTOR RICHIE TYNER
DIST. BY UNIVERSAL UCLICK SYNDICATE ©2012 R. BOLLING -1096- tomthedancingbug.com twitter.com/rubenbolling

7/9/12

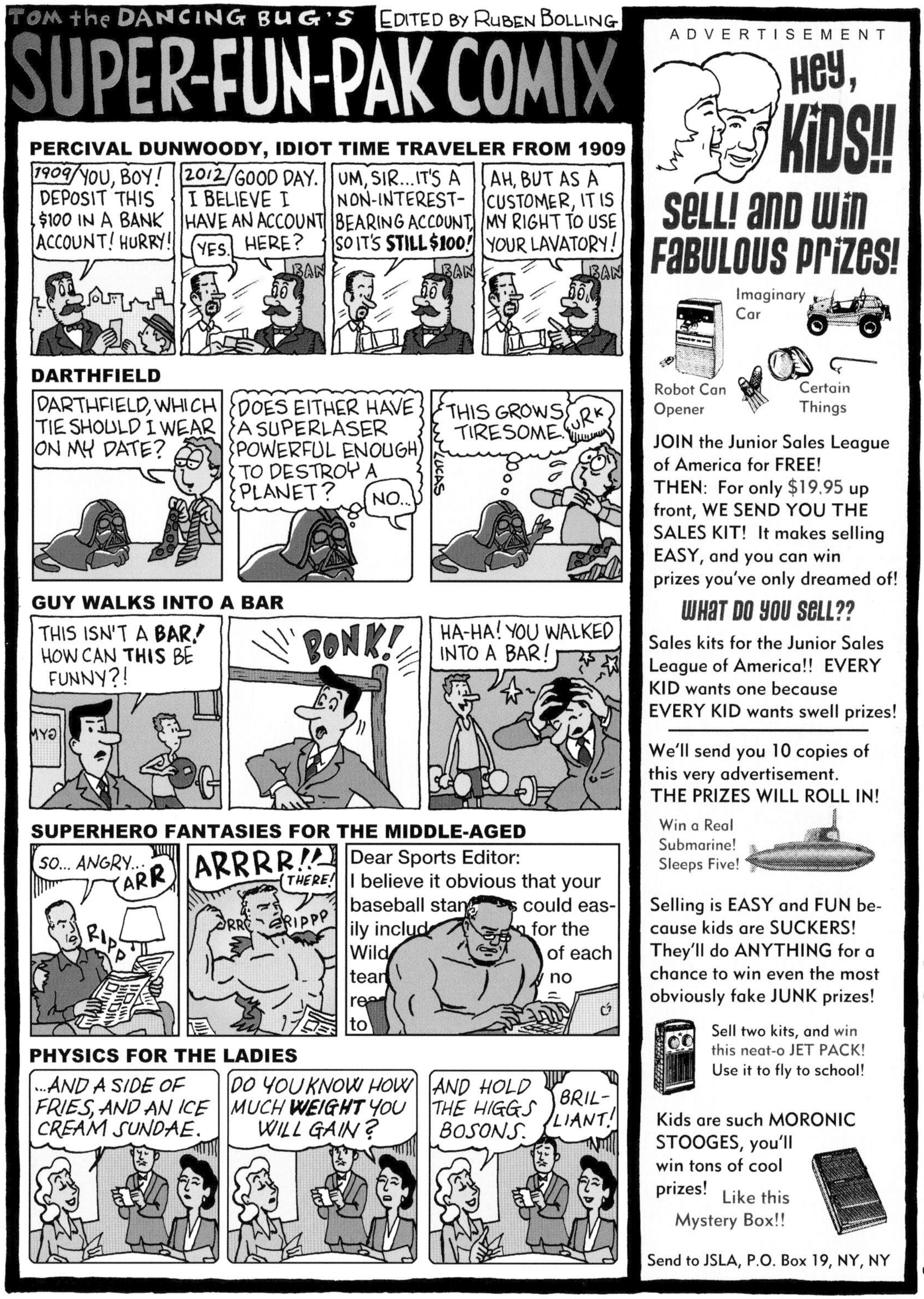
TOM the DANCING BUG'S
EDITED BY RUBEN BOLLING
SUPER-FUN-PAK COMIX
PERCIVAL DUNWOODY, IDIOT TIME TRAVELER FROM 1909
1909
YOU, BOY! DEPOSIT THIS $100 IN A BANK ACCOUNT! HURRY!
2012
GOOD DAY. I BELIEVE I HAVE AN ACCOUNT HERE?
YES.
UM, SIR... IT'S A NON-INTEREST-BEARING ACCOUNT, SO IT'S STILL $100!
AH, BUT AS A CUSTOMER, IT IS MY RIGHT TO USE YOUR LAVATORY!
DARTHFIELD
DARTHFIELD, WHICH TIE SHOULD I WEAR ON MY DATE?
DOES EITHER HAVE A SUPERLASER POWERFUL ENOUGH TO DESTROY A PLANET?
NO...
THIS GROWS TIRESOME.
URK
LUCAS
GUY WALKS INTO A BAR
THIS ISN'T A BAR! HOW CAN THIS BE FUNNY?!
BONK!
HA-HA! YOU WALKED INTO A BAR!
SUPERHERO FANTASIES FOR THE MIDDLE-AGED
SO... ANGRY...
ARR
RIPP
ARRRR!!
THERE!
RIPPP
Dear Sports Editor:
I believe it obvious that your baseball stan could eas-ily includ for the Wild of each tean no re to
PHYSICS FOR THE LADIES
...AND A SIDE OF FRIES, AND AN ICE CREAM SUNDAE.
DO YOU KNOW HOW MUCH WEIGHT YOU WILL GAIN?
AND HOLD THE HIGGS BOSONS.
BRIL-LIANT!
ADVERTISEMENT
Hey, KIDS!!
SELL! AND WIN FABULOUS PRIZES!
Imaginary Car
Robot Can Opener
Certain Things
JOIN the Junior Sales League of America for FREE!
THEN: For only $19.95 up front, WE SEND YOU THE SALES KIT! It makes selling EASY, and you can win prizes you've only dreamed of!
WHAT DO YOU SELL??
Sales kits for the Junior Sales League of America!! EVERY KID wants one because EVERY KID wants swell prizes!
We'll send you 10 copies of this very advertisement.
THE PRIZES WILL ROLL IN!
Win a Real Submarine! Sleeps Five!
Selling is EASY and FUN be-cause kids are SUCKERS! They'll do ANYTHING for a chance to win even the most obviously fake JUNK prizes!
Sell two kits, and win this neat-o JET PACK! Use it to fly to school!
Kids are such MORONIC STOOGES, you'll win tons of cool prizes!
Like this Mystery Box!!
Send to JSLA, P.O. Box 19, NY, NY

7/16/12

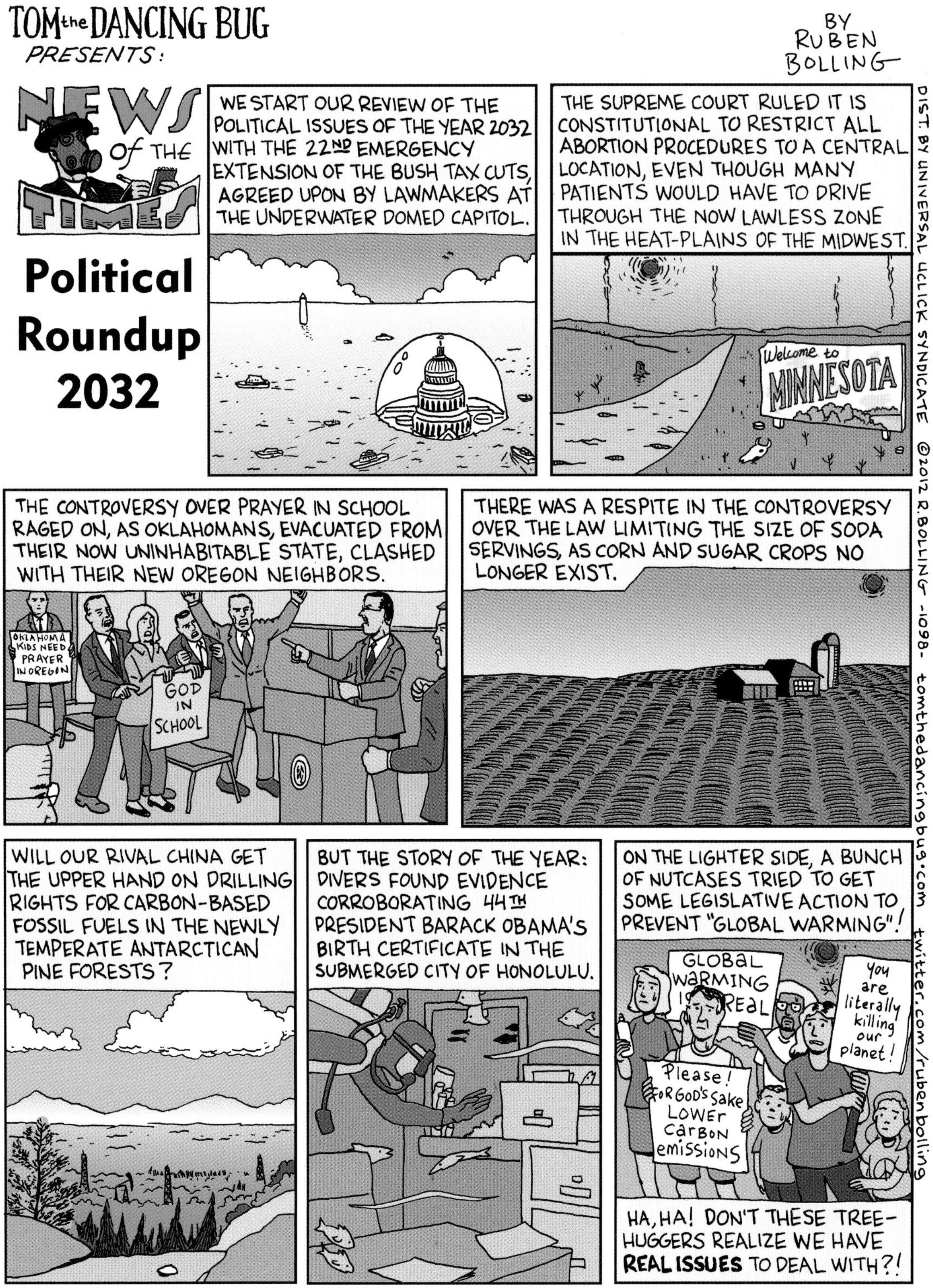
TOM the DANCING BUG PRESENTS:
BY RUBEN BOLLING
NEWS of THE TIMES
Political Roundup 2032
WE START OUR REVIEW OF THE POLITICAL ISSUES OF THE YEAR 2032 WITH THE 22ND EMERGENCY EXTENSION OF THE BUSH TAX CUTS, AGREED UPON BY LAWMAKERS AT THE UNDERWATER DOMED CAPITOL.
THE SUPREME COURT RULED IT IS CONSTITUTIONAL TO RESTRICT ALL ABORTION PROCEDURES TO A CENTRAL LOCATION, EVEN THOUGH MANY PATIENTS WOULD HAVE TO DRIVE THROUGH THE NOW LAWLESS ZONE IN THE HEAT-PLAINS OF THE MIDWEST.
Welcome to MINNESOTA
DIST. BY UNIVERSAL UCLICK SYNDICATE ©2012 R. BOLLING -1098- tomthedancingbug.com twitter.com/rubenbolling
THE CONTROVERSY OVER PRAYER IN SCHOOL RAGED ON, AS OKLAHOMANS, EVACUATED FROM THEIR NOW UNINHABITABLE STATE, CLASHED WITH THEIR NEW OREGON NEIGHBORS.
OKLAHOMA KIDS NEED PRAYER IN OREGON
GOD IN SCHOOL
THERE WAS A RESPITE IN THE CONTROVERSY OVER THE LAW LIMITING THE SIZE OF SODA SERVINGS, AS CORN AND SUGAR CROPS NO LONGER EXIST.
WILL OUR RIVAL CHINA GET THE UPPER HAND ON DRILLING RIGHTS FOR CARBON-BASED FOSSIL FUELS IN THE NEWLY TEMPERATE ANTARCTICAN PINE FORESTS?
BUT THE STORY OF THE YEAR: DIVERS FOUND EVIDENCE CORROBORATING 44TH PRESIDENT BARACK OBAMA'S BIRTH CERTIFICATE IN THE SUBMERGED CITY OF HONOLULU.
ON THE LIGHTER SIDE, A BUNCH OF NUTCASES TRIED TO GET SOME LEGISLATIVE ACTION TO PREVENT "GLOBAL WARMING"!
GLOBAL WARMING IS REAL
You are literally killing our planet!
Please! FOR GOD'S Sake LOWER CarBON emissions
HA, HA! DON'T THESE TREE-HUGGERS REALIZE WE HAVE REAL ISSUES TO DEAL WITH?!

7/23/12

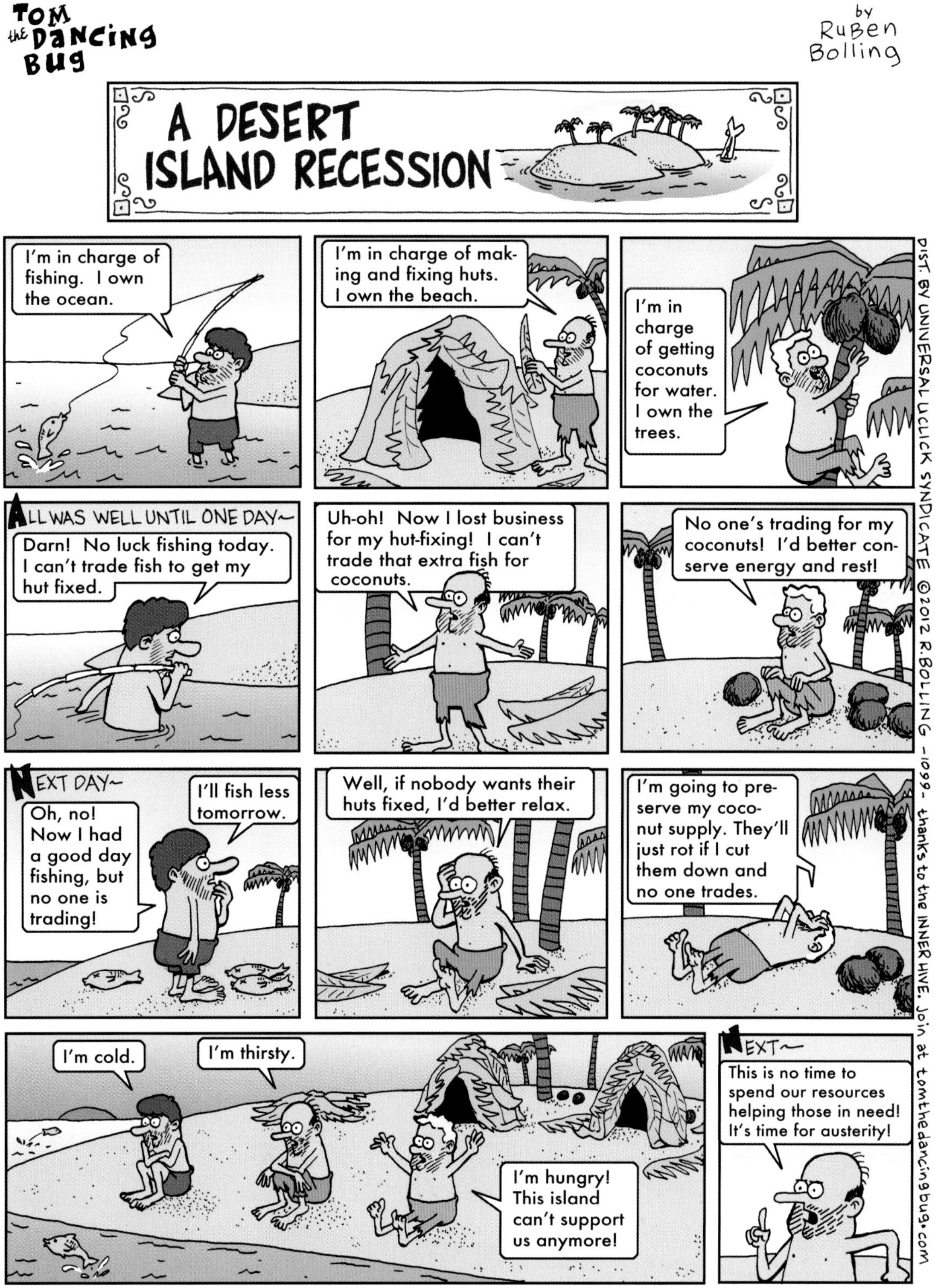
TOM the DANCING BUG
by Ruben Bolling
A DESERT ISLAND RECESSION
I'm in charge of fishing. I own the ocean.
I'm in charge of making and fixing huts. I own the beach.
I'm in charge of getting coconuts for water. I own the trees.
ALL WAS WELL UNTIL ONE DAY~
Darn! No luck fishing today. I can't trade fish to get my hut fixed.
Uh-oh! Now I lost business for my hut-fixing! I can't trade that extra fish for coconuts.
No one's trading for my coconuts! I'd better conserve energy and rest!
NEXT DAY~
Oh, no! Now I had a good day fishing, but no one is trading!
I'll fish less tomorrow.
Well, if nobody wants their huts fixed, I'd better relax.
I'm going to preserve my coconut supply. They'll just rot if I cut them down and no one trades.
I'm cold.
I'm thirsty.
I'm hungry! This island can't support us anymore!
NEXT~
This is no time to spend our resources helping those in need! It's time for austerity!
DIST. BY UNIVERSAL UCLICK SYNDICATE ©2012 R. BOLLING -1099- thanks to the INNER HIVE. Join at tomthedancingbug.com

7/30/12

TOM the DANCING BUG

by Ruben Bolling

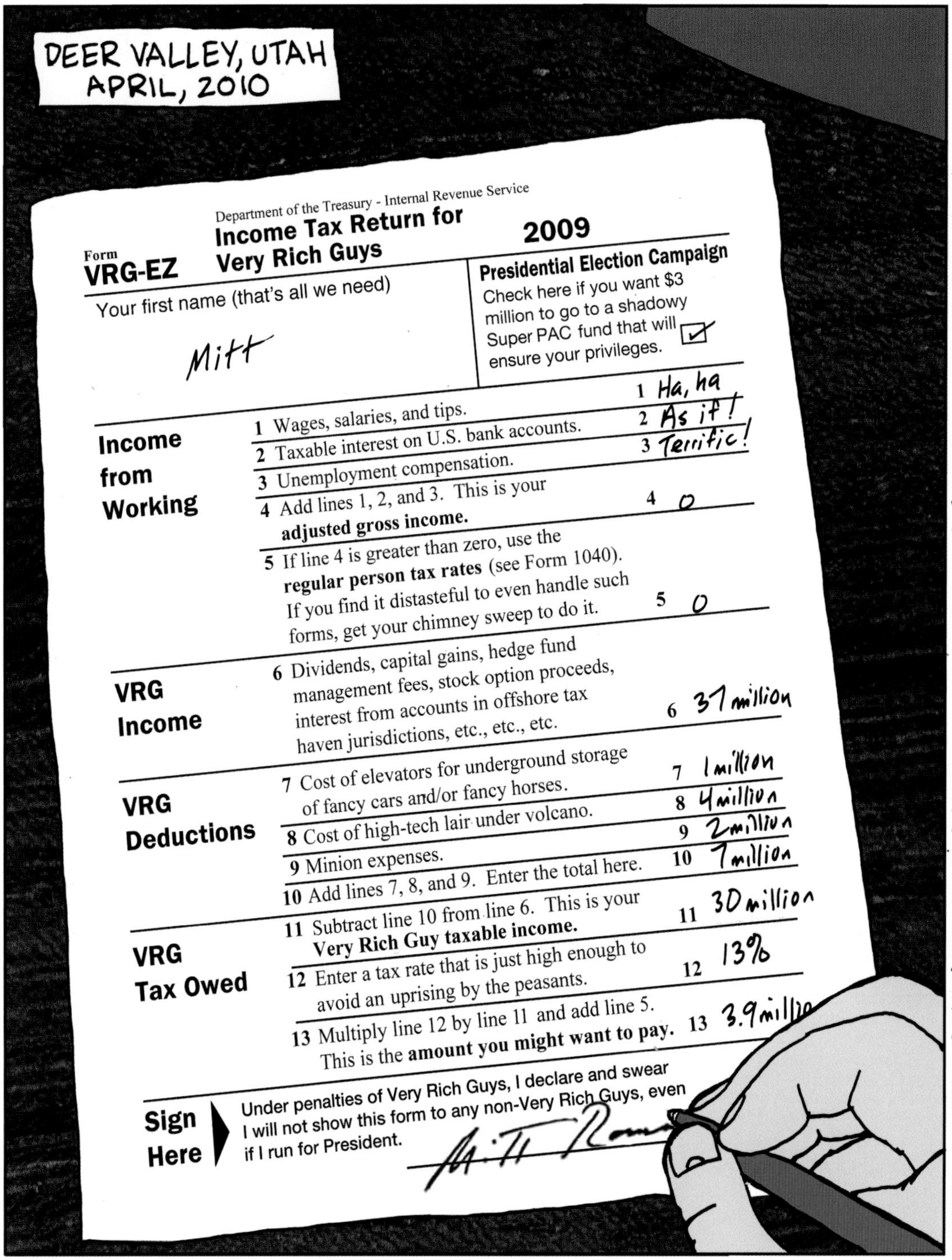

8/6/12

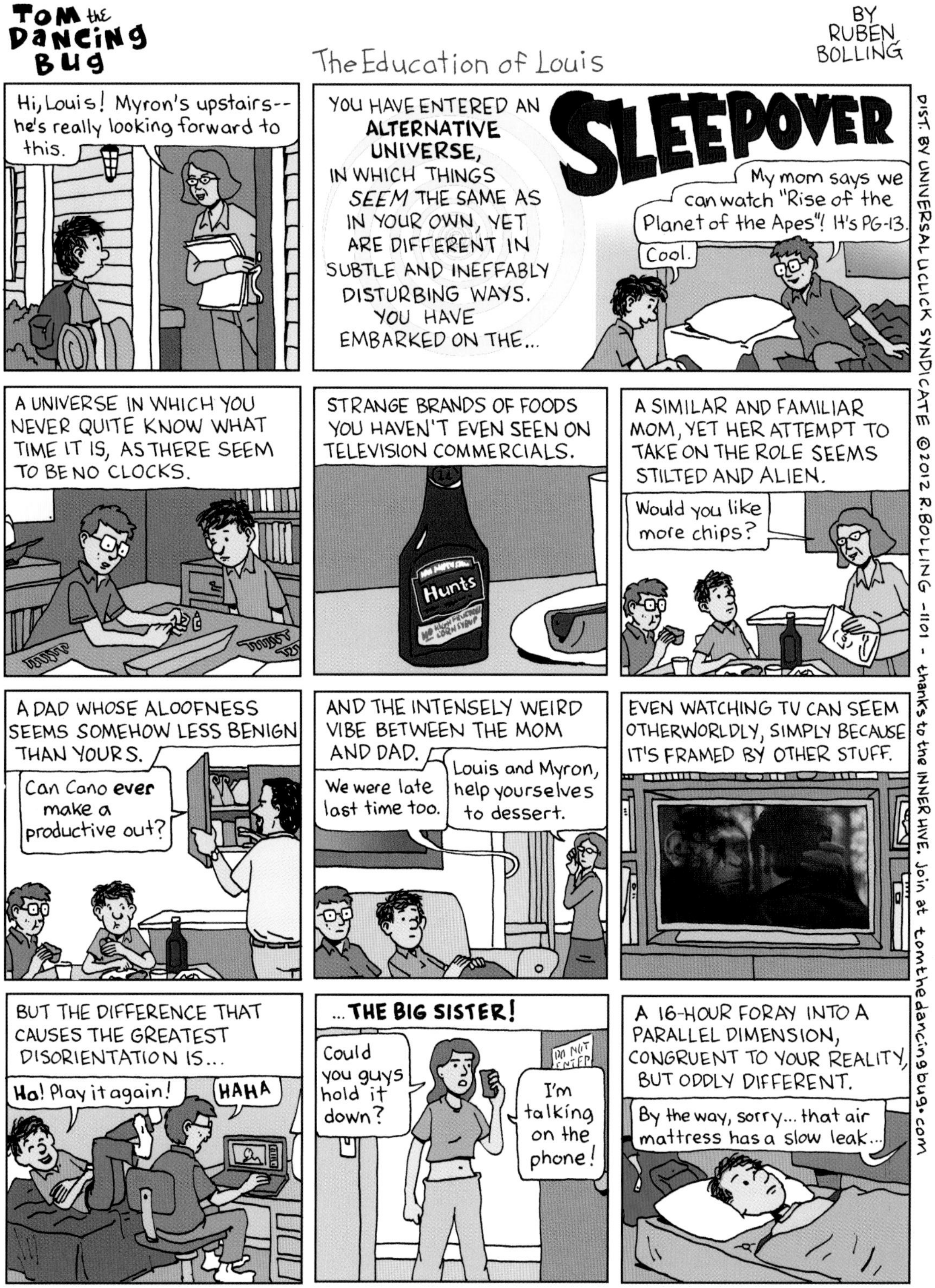

TOM the DANCING BUG
The Education of Louis
BY RUBEN BOLLING
Hi, Louis! Myron's upstairs-- he's really looking forward to this.
YOU HAVE ENTERED AN **ALTERNATIVE UNIVERSE,** IN WHICH THINGS *SEEM* THE SAME AS IN YOUR OWN, YET ARE DIFFERENT IN SUBTLE AND INEFFABLY DISTURBING WAYS. YOU HAVE EMBARKED ON THE...
SLEEPOVER
My mom says we can watch "Rise of the Planet of the Apes"! It's PG-13.
Cool.
A UNIVERSE IN WHICH YOU NEVER QUITE KNOW WHAT TIME IT IS, AS THERE SEEM TO BE NO CLOCKS.
STRANGE BRANDS OF FOODS YOU HAVEN'T EVEN SEEN ON TELEVISION COMMERCIALS.
Hunts
A SIMILAR AND FAMILIAR MOM, YET HER ATTEMPT TO TAKE ON THE ROLE SEEMS STILTED AND ALIEN.
Would you like more chips?
A DAD WHOSE ALOOFNESS SEEMS SOMEHOW LESS BENIGN THAN YOURS.
Can Cano **ever** make a productive out?
AND THE INTENSELY WEIRD VIBE BETWEEN THE MOM AND DAD.
We were late last time too.
Louis and Myron, help yourselves to dessert.
EVEN WATCHING TV CAN SEEM OTHERWORLDLY, SIMPLY BECAUSE IT'S FRAMED BY OTHER STUFF.
BUT THE DIFFERENCE THAT CAUSES THE GREATEST DISORIENTATION IS...
Ha! Play it again!
HAHA
...**THE BIG SISTER!**
Could you guys hold it down?
I'm talking on the phone!
A 16-HOUR FORAY INTO A PARALLEL DIMENSION, CONGRUENT TO YOUR REALITY, BUT ODDLY DIFFERENT.
By the way, sorry... that air mattress has a slow leak...
DIST. BY UNIVERSAL UCLICK SYNDICATE ©2012 R.BOLLING -1101 - thanks to the INNER HIVE. Join at tomthedancingbug.com

8/13/12

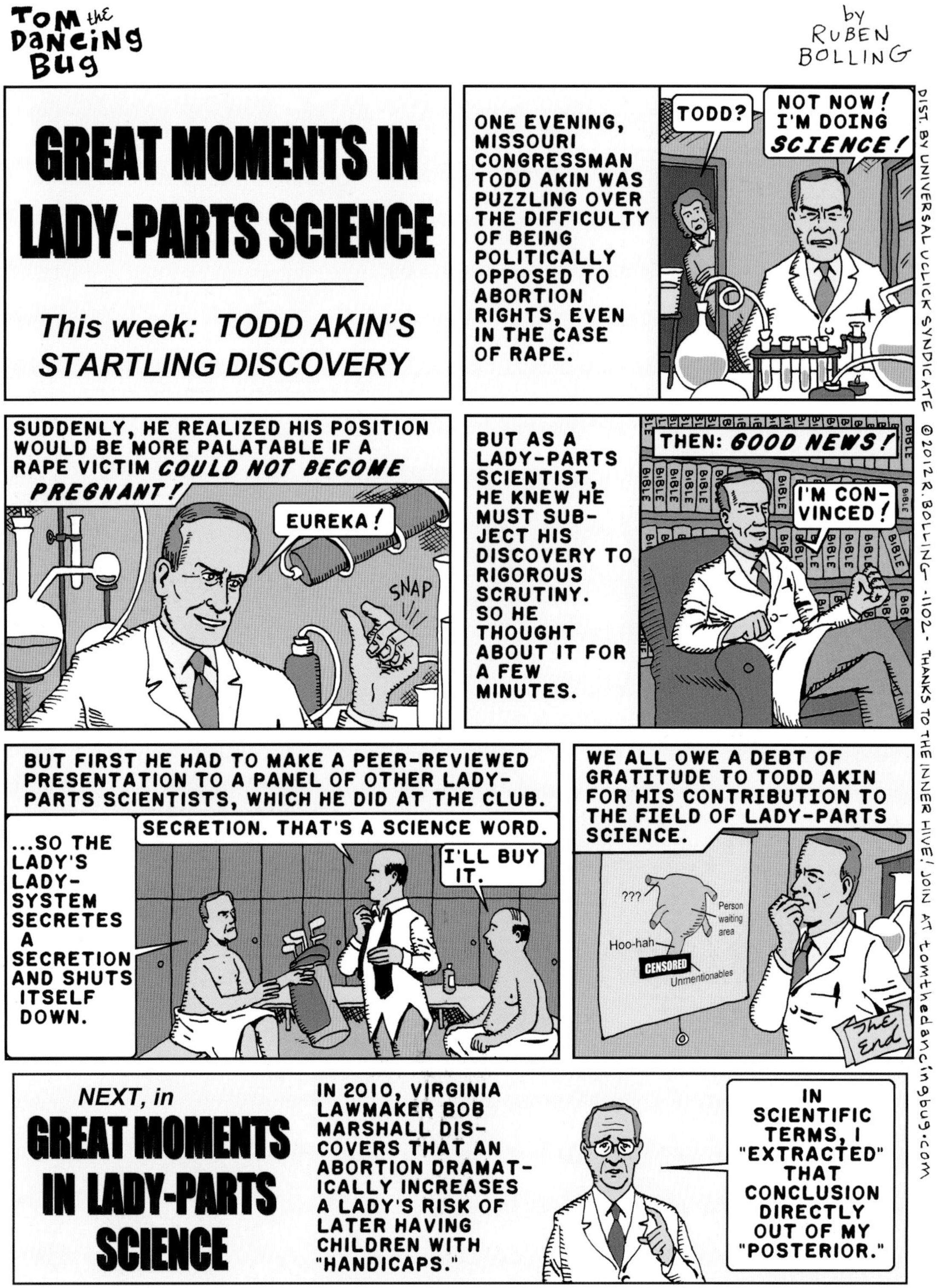
TOM the DANCING BUG
by RUBEN BOLLING
GREAT MOMENTS IN LADY-PARTS SCIENCE
This week: TODD AKIN'S STARTLING DISCOVERY
ONE EVENING, MISSOURI CONGRESSMAN TODD AKIN WAS PUZZLING OVER THE DIFFICULTY OF BEING POLITICALLY OPPOSED TO ABORTION RIGHTS, EVEN IN THE CASE OF RAPE.
TODD?
NOT NOW! I'M DOING SCIENCE!
SUDDENLY, HE REALIZED HIS POSITION WOULD BE MORE PALATABLE IF A RAPE VICTIM COULD NOT BECOME PREGNANT!
EUREKA!
SNAP
BUT AS A LADY-PARTS SCIENTIST, HE KNEW HE MUST SUBJECT HIS DISCOVERY TO RIGOROUS SCRUTINY. SO HE THOUGHT ABOUT IT FOR A FEW MINUTES.
THEN: GOOD NEWS!
I'M CONVINCED!
BUT FIRST HE HAD TO MAKE A PEER-REVIEWED PRESENTATION TO A PANEL OF OTHER LADY-PARTS SCIENTISTS, WHICH HE DID AT THE CLUB.
...SO THE LADY'S LADY-SYSTEM SECRETES A SECRETION AND SHUTS ITSELF DOWN.
SECRETION. THAT'S A SCIENCE WORD.
I'LL BUY IT.
WE ALL OWE A DEBT OF GRATITUDE TO TODD AKIN FOR HIS CONTRIBUTION TO THE FIELD OF LADY-PARTS SCIENCE.
???
Person waiting area
Hoo-hah
CENSORED
Unmentionables
THE End
NEXT, in GREAT MOMENTS IN LADY-PARTS SCIENCE
IN 2010, VIRGINIA LAWMAKER BOB MARSHALL DISCOVERS THAT AN ABORTION DRAMATICALLY INCREASES A LADY'S RISK OF LATER HAVING CHILDREN WITH "HANDICAPS."
IN SCIENTIFIC TERMS, I "EXTRACTED" THAT CONCLUSION DIRECTLY OUT OF MY "POSTERIOR."
DIST. BY UNIVERSAL UCLICK SYNDICATE ©2012 R. BOLLING -1102- THANKS TO THE INNER HIVE! JOIN AT tomthedancingbug.com

8/27/12

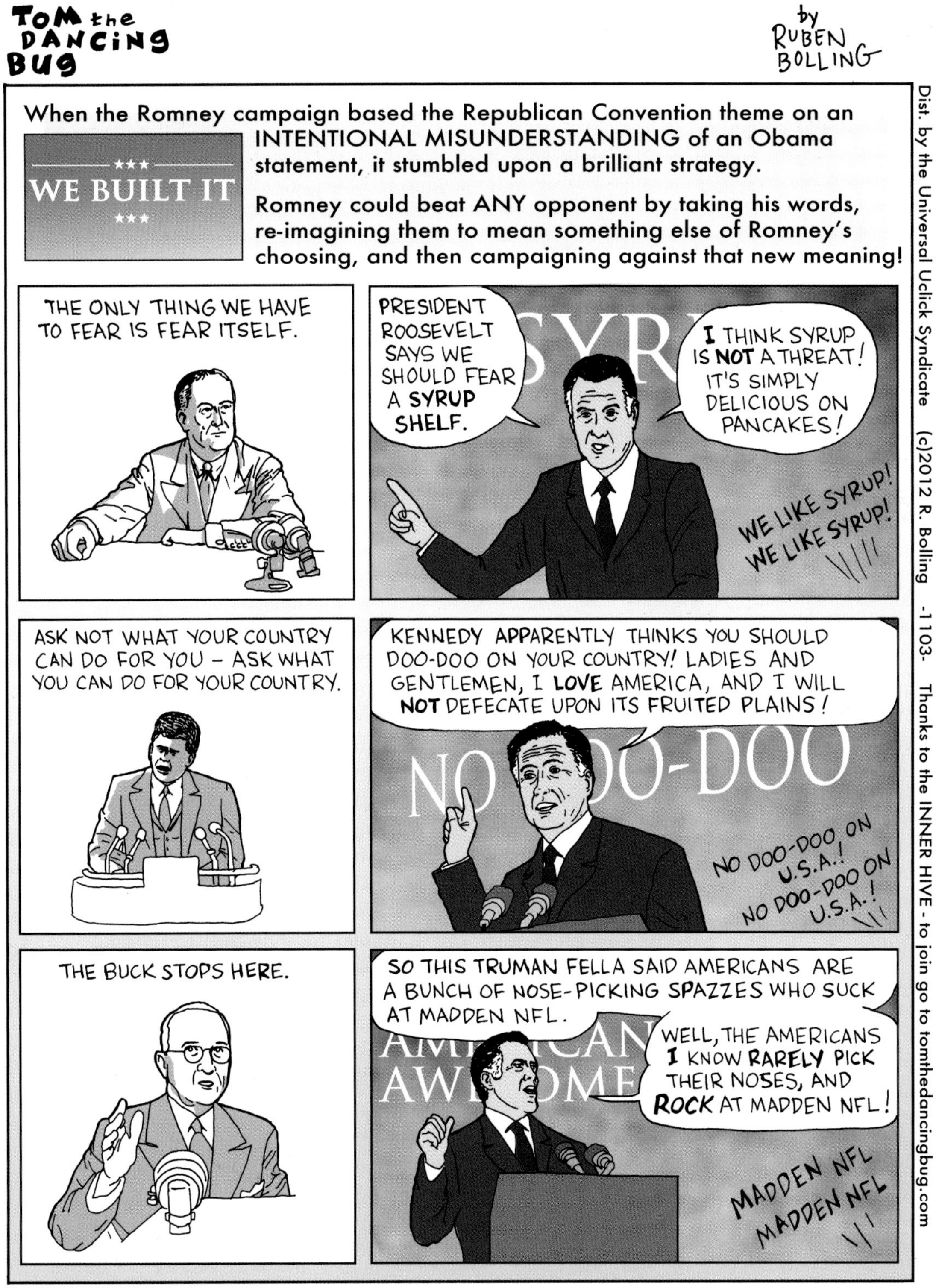
TOM the DANCING BUG
by RUBEN BOLLING
When the Romney campaign based the Republican Convention theme on an INTENTIONAL MISUNDERSTANDING of an Obama statement, it stumbled upon a brilliant strategy.
WE BUILT IT
Romney could beat ANY opponent by taking his words, re-imagining them to mean something else of Romney's choosing, and then campaigning against that new meaning!
THE ONLY THING WE HAVE TO FEAR IS FEAR ITSELF.
PRESIDENT ROOSEVELT SAYS WE SHOULD FEAR A SYRUP SHELF.
SYR
I THINK SYRUP IS NOT A THREAT! IT'S SIMPLY DELICIOUS ON PANCAKES!
WE LIKE SYRUP! WE LIKE SYRUP!
ASK NOT WHAT YOUR COUNTRY CAN DO FOR YOU – ASK WHAT YOU CAN DO FOR YOUR COUNTRY.
KENNEDY APPARENTLY THINKS YOU SHOULD DOO-DOO ON YOUR COUNTRY! LADIES AND GENTLEMEN, I LOVE AMERICA, AND I WILL NOT DEFECATE UPON ITS FRUITED PLAINS!
NO DOO-DOO
NO DOO-DOO ON U.S.A.! NO DOO-DOO ON U.S.A.!
THE BUCK STOPS HERE.
SO THIS TRUMAN FELLA SAID AMERICANS ARE A BUNCH OF NOSE-PICKING SPAZZES WHO SUCK AT MADDEN NFL.
WELL, THE AMERICANS I KNOW RARELY PICK THEIR NOSES, AND ROCK AT MADDEN NFL!
MADDEN NFL MADDEN NFL
Dist. by the Universal Uclick Syndicate (c)2012 R. Bolling -1103- Thanks to the INNER HIVE - to join go to tomthedancingbug.com

9/3/12

TOM the DANCING BUG
BY RUBEN BOLLING
"SANTA CLAUS POLITICS"
— OR —
"TAX CUTS FOR TOTS"
And I'm going to give you a brand new dolly!
Gosh, thanks!
You're so nice to give out toys, and get nothing for yourself!
HO, HO, HO! Oh, me and my one-percent friends will get even bigger toys – horsies, yachts...
Why do you get the good stuff?
We deserve it, little girl! We're big!
I thought things were tight up at the North Pole. How will we afford all this?
Oh, technical stuff. Closing loopholes and such.
What does that mean, exactly? What loopholes?
Don't worry your pretty little head about that.
NEXT!
Wait! What loopholes?!
We think it's best to...
Are you taking my other dollies?
HO, HO, HO! Er... Elf Helper!
ARE YOU GOING TO COME TO MY ROOM AND TAKE ALL MY DOLLIES AND MY DOLLHOUSE??!!
Come on, little girl. It's impolite to ask so many questions.
We didn't even know about the dollhouse. Make a note.
NEXT in "SANTA CLAUS POLITICS" -
Wait, how can you require insurance companies to cover people with pre-existing conditions without an insurance mandate? It makes no sense!
Elf Helper!
Coming!
DIST. BY UNIVERSAL UCLICK SYNDICATE ©2012 R. BOLLING -1104- THANKS TO THE INNER HIVE! JOIN AT tomthedancingbug.com

9/10/12

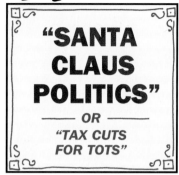

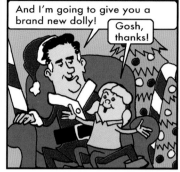

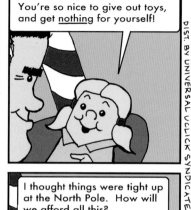

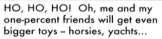

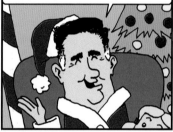

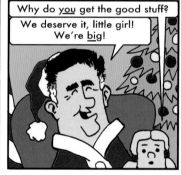

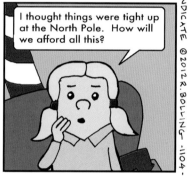

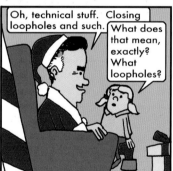

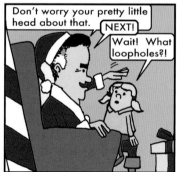

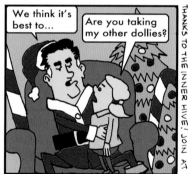

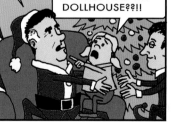

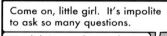

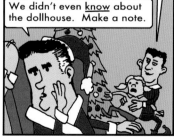

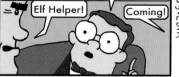

TOM the DANCING BUG

BY RUBEN BOLLING

GOD-MAN

THE OMNIPOTENT SUPERHERO!

HI, I'M GOD-MAN... UH... AND I STINK! HEH-HEH.

THE MOVIE!

UH, GOD-MAN. WHY ARE YOU SO, LIKE, LAME-O?

HEH-HEH. BECAUSE I SUCK. HEH-HEH.

GOD-MAN FAN CLUB

GUYS! CHECK THIS OUT!

LOOK AT ME! I'M A DOOFUS!

IT... IT'S HORRIBLE!

SOMETHING MUST BE DONE ABOUT THIS!

LET'S SPREAD THE WORD ACROSS ALL OF GOD-MAN FANDOM!

AND, SO—

http://yoitsgroovynews.com

Weather Google search blogs shopping movies

YO, IT'S GROOVY NEWS

HOME GROOVYNEWS RUMORS JOSS RUMOR

GROOVY NEWS

GOD-MAN, THE MOVIE

With its sub-basement production values, and execrable acting, it's hard to see why o most powerful superhero got the sloppiest cinematic treatment. This makes Affleck's Daredevil look like Citizen Ka I give it 4 RIOT-AND-KILL-AMBASSADORS.

GOD-MAN IS IN DIRE NEED OF OUR HELP!

RIOT!

MURDER IN THE NAME OF GOD-MAN!

WHERE IS GOD-MAN?!

I MUST CONCENTRATE ON INFORMING GOD-MAN OF THIS GRAVE INSULT!

NEXT

A FEW MILES AWAY, GOD-MAN IS SAVING CHILDREN FROM A BROKEN BRIDGE, WHEN HIS OMNISCIENCE POWER RECEIVES A MENTAL MESSAGE—

GOD-MAN! SEVERAL JERKS MADE A BAD VIDEO INSULTING Y...

I'M BUSY!

9/17/12

TOM the DANCING BUG

by RUBEN BOLLING

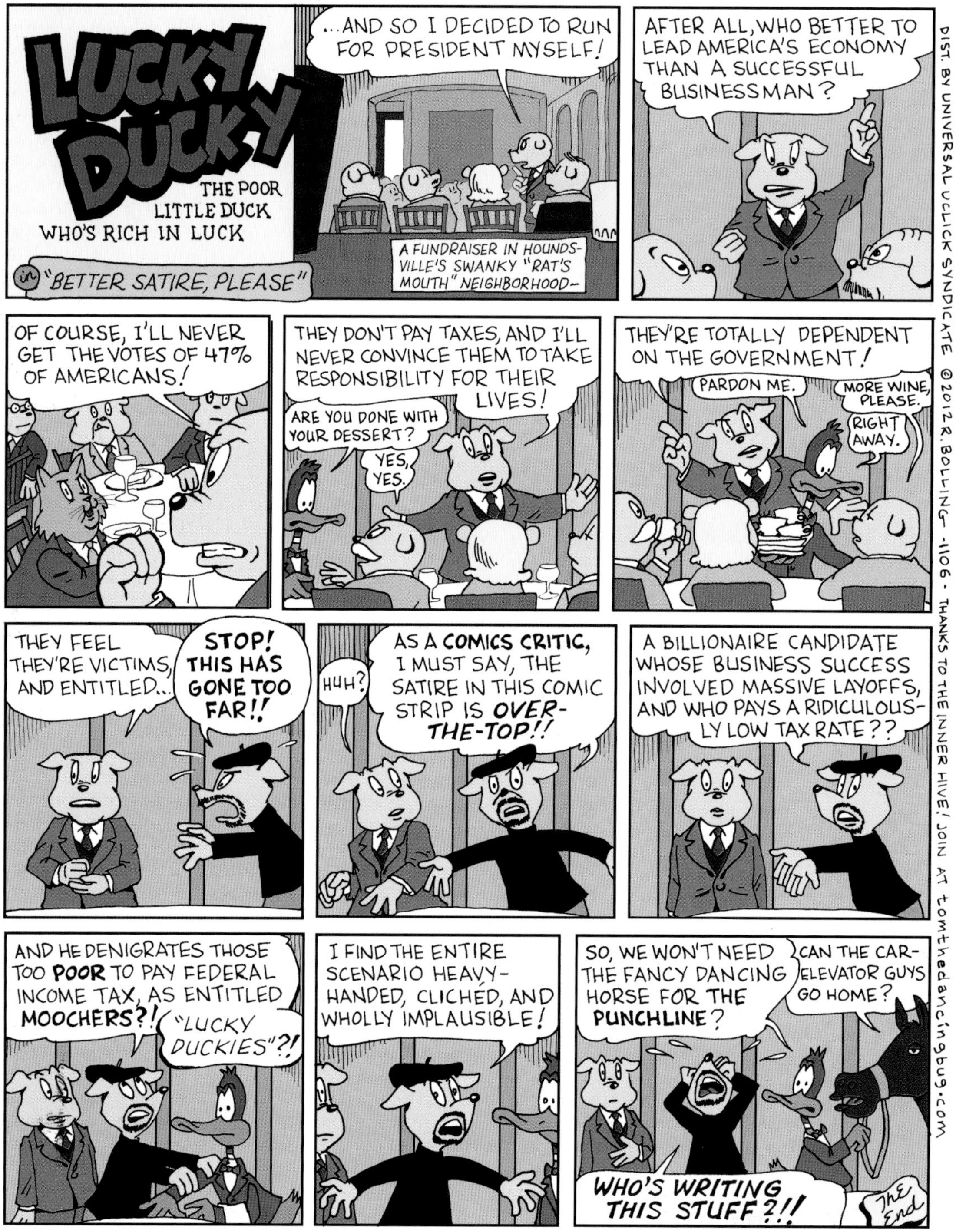
LUCKY DUCKY
THE POOR LITTLE DUCK WHO'S RICH IN LUCK
in "BETTER SATIRE, PLEASE"
...AND SO I DECIDED TO RUN FOR PRESIDENT MYSELF!
A FUNDRAISER IN HOUNDSVILLE'S SWANKY "RAT'S MOUTH" NEIGHBORHOOD–
AFTER ALL, WHO BETTER TO LEAD AMERICA'S ECONOMY THAN A SUCCESSFUL BUSINESSMAN?
OF COURSE, I'LL NEVER GET THE VOTES OF 47% OF AMERICANS!
THEY DON'T PAY TAXES, AND I'LL NEVER CONVINCE THEM TO TAKE RESPONSIBILITY FOR THEIR LIVES!
ARE YOU DONE WITH YOUR DESSERT?
YES, YES.
THEY'RE TOTALLY DEPENDENT ON THE GOVERNMENT!
PARDON ME.
MORE WINE, PLEASE.
RIGHT AWAY.
THEY FEEL THEY'RE VICTIMS, AND ENTITLED...
STOP! THIS HAS GONE TOO FAR!!
HUH?
AS A COMICS CRITIC, I MUST SAY, THE SATIRE IN THIS COMIC STRIP IS OVER-THE-TOP!!
A BILLIONAIRE CANDIDATE WHOSE BUSINESS SUCCESS INVOLVED MASSIVE LAYOFFS, AND WHO PAYS A RIDICULOUSLY LOW TAX RATE??
AND HE DENIGRATES THOSE TOO POOR TO PAY FEDERAL INCOME TAX, AS ENTITLED MOOCHERS?!
"LUCKY DUCKIES"?!
I FIND THE ENTIRE SCENARIO HEAVY-HANDED, CLICHÉD, AND WHOLLY IMPLAUSIBLE!
SO, WE WON'T NEED THE FANCY DANCING HORSE FOR THE PUNCHLINE?
CAN THE CAR-ELEVATOR GUYS GO HOME?
WHO'S WRITING THIS STUFF?!!
THE END
DIST. BY UNIVERSAL UCLICK SYNDICATE ©2012 R. BOLLING -1106- THANKS TO THE INNER HIVE! JOIN AT tomthedancingbug.com

9/24/12

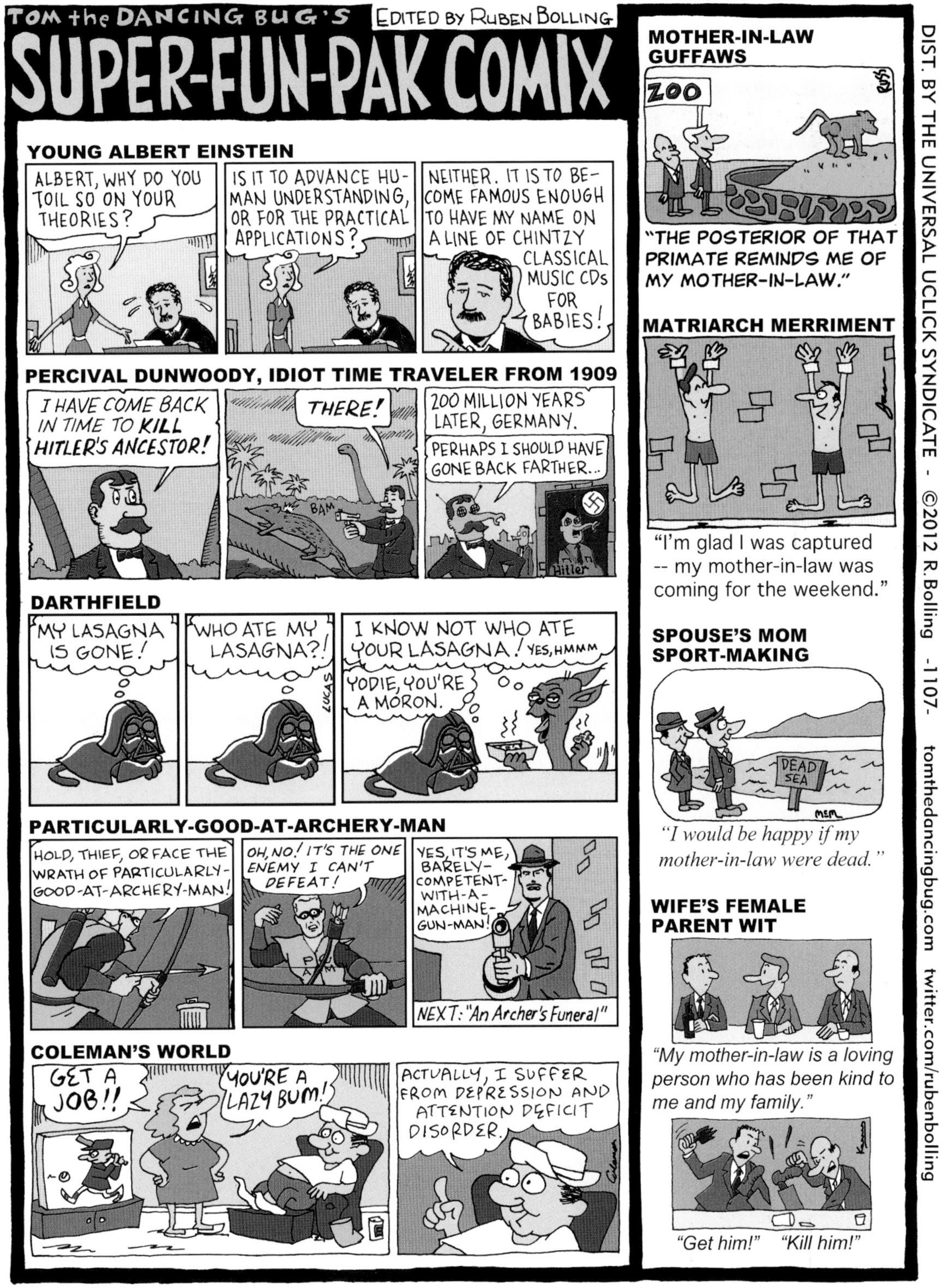
TOM the DANCING BUG'S
EDITED BY RUBEN BOLLING
SUPER-FUN-PAK COMIX
YOUNG ALBERT EINSTEIN
ALBERT, WHY DO YOU TOIL SO ON YOUR THEORIES?
IS IT TO ADVANCE HUMAN UNDERSTANDING, OR FOR THE PRACTICAL APPLICATIONS?
NEITHER. IT IS TO BECOME FAMOUS ENOUGH TO HAVE MY NAME ON A LINE OF CHINTZY CLASSICAL MUSIC CDs FOR BABIES!
PERCIVAL DUNWOODY, IDIOT TIME TRAVELER FROM 1909
I HAVE COME BACK IN TIME TO KILL HITLER'S ANCESTOR!
THERE!
BAM
200 MILLION YEARS LATER, GERMANY.
PERHAPS I SHOULD HAVE GONE BACK FARTHER...
Hitler
DARTHFIELD
MY LASAGNA IS GONE!
WHO ATE MY LASAGNA?!
LUCAS
I KNOW NOT WHO ATE YOUR LASAGNA! YES, HMMM
YODIE, YOU'RE A MORON.
PARTICULARLY-GOOD-AT-ARCHERY-MAN
HOLD, THIEF, OR FACE THE WRATH OF PARTICULARLY-GOOD-AT-ARCHERY-MAN!
OH, NO! IT'S THE ONE ENEMY I CAN'T DEFEAT!
YES, IT'S ME, BARELY-COMPETENT-WITH-A-MACHINE-GUN-MAN!
NEXT: "An Archer's Funeral"
COLEMAN'S WORLD
GET A JOB!!
YOU'RE A LAZY BUM!
ACTUALLY, I SUFFER FROM DEPRESSION AND ATTENTION DEFICIT DISORDER.
MOTHER-IN-LAW GUFFAWS
ZOO
"THE POSTERIOR OF THAT PRIMATE REMINDS ME OF MY MOTHER-IN-LAW."
MATRIARCH MERRIMENT
"I'm glad I was captured -- my mother-in-law was coming for the weekend."
SPOUSE'S MOM SPORT-MAKING
DEAD SEA
MEM
"I would be happy if my mother-in-law were dead."
WIFE'S FEMALE PARENT WIT
"My mother-in-law is a loving person who has been kind to me and my family."
"Get him!" "Kill him!"
DIST. BY THE UNIVERSAL UCLICK SYNDICATE - ©2012 R. Bolling -1107- tomthedancingbug.com twitter.com/rubenbolling

10/1/12

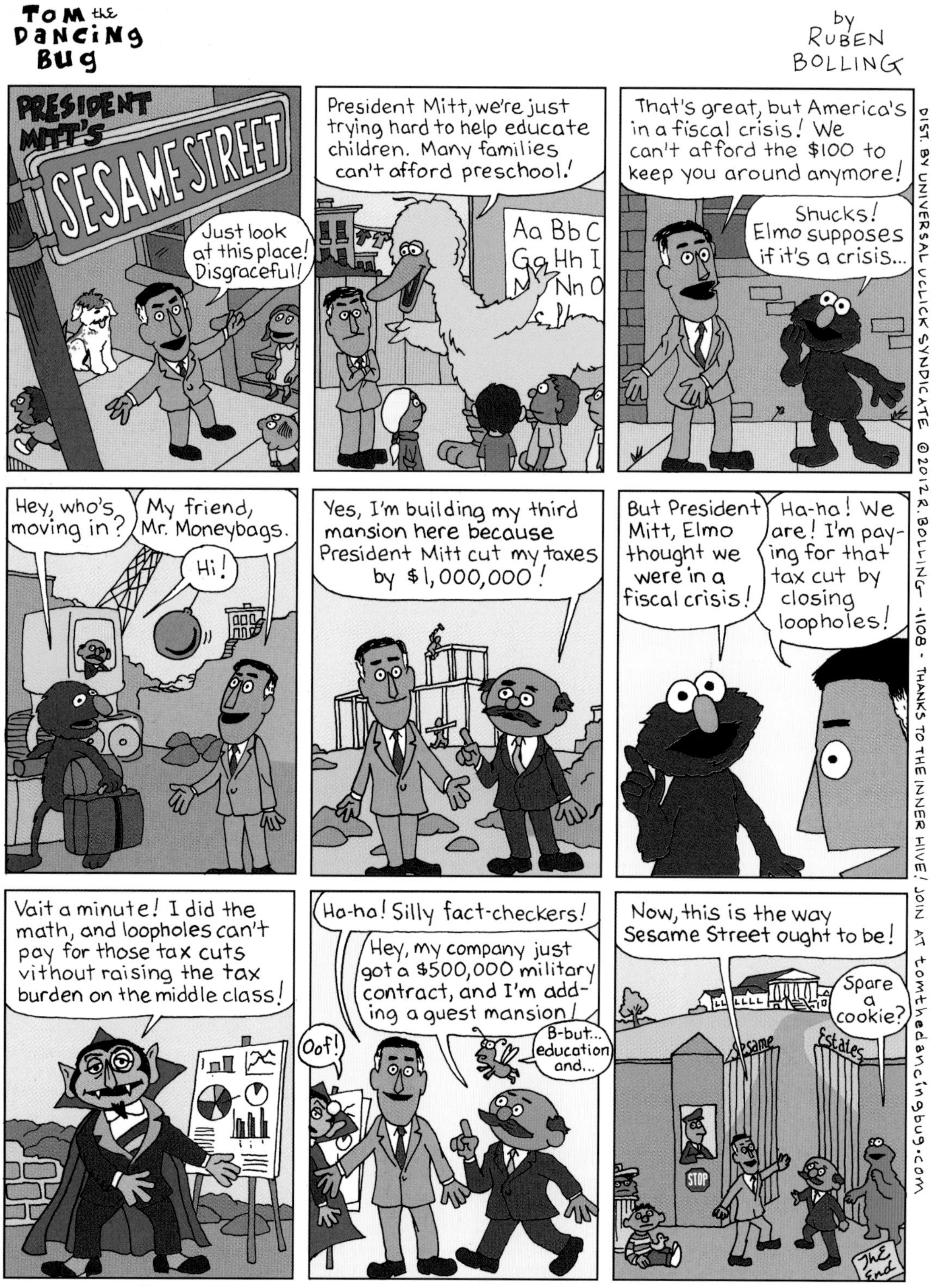
TOM the DANCING BUG
by RUBEN BOLLING
PRESIDENT MITT'S SESAME STREET
Just look at this place! Disgraceful!
President Mitt, we're just trying hard to help educate children. Many families can't afford preschool!
Aa Bb C Gg Hh I Nn O
That's great, but America's in a fiscal crisis! We can't afford the $100 to keep you around anymore!
Shucks! Elmo supposes if it's a crisis...
Hey, who's moving in?
My friend, Mr. Moneybags.
Hi!
Yes, I'm building my third mansion here because President Mitt cut my taxes by $1,000,000!
But President Mitt, Elmo thought we were in a fiscal crisis!
Ha-ha! We are! I'm paying for that tax cut by closing loopholes!
Vait a minute! I did the math, and loopholes can't pay for those tax cuts vithout raising the tax burden on the middle class!
Ha-ha! Silly fact-checkers!
Hey, my company just got a $500,000 military contract, and I'm adding a guest mansion!
Oof!
B-but... education and...
Now, this is the way Sesame Street ought to be!
Spare a cookie?
Sesame Estates
STOP
The End
DIST. BY UNIVERSAL UCLICK SYNDICATE ©2012 R. BOLLING -1108- THANKS TO THE INNER HIVE! JOIN AT tomthedancingbug.com

10/8/12

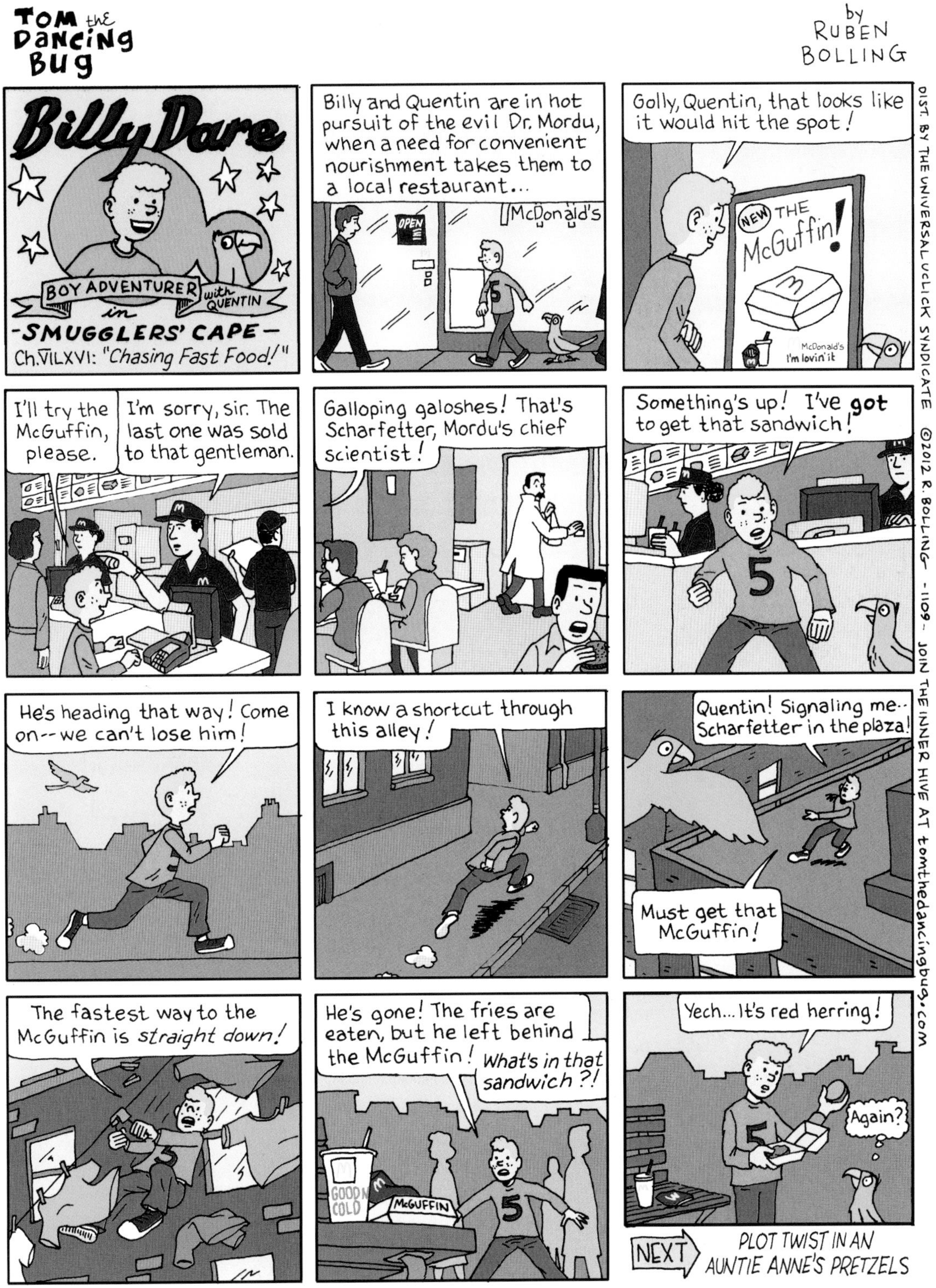
TOM the DANCING BUG
by RUBEN BOLLING
Billy Dare
BOY ADVENTURER with QUENTIN
in
-SMUGGLERS' CAPE-
Ch. VILXVI: "Chasing Fast Food!"
Billy and Quentin are in hot pursuit of the evil Dr. Mordu, when a need for convenient nourishment takes them to a local restaurant...
OPEN
McDonald's
Golly, Quentin, that looks like it would hit the spot!
NEW THE McGuffin!
McDonald's I'm lovin' it
I'll try the McGuffin, please.
I'm sorry, sir. The last one was sold to that gentleman.
Galloping galoshes! That's Scharfetter, Mordu's chief scientist!
Something's up! I've **got** to get that sandwich!
He's heading that way! Come on--we can't lose him!
I know a shortcut through this alley!
Quentin! Signaling me.. Scharfetter in the plaza!
Must get that McGuffin!
The fastest way to the McGuffin is *straight down!*
He's gone! The fries are eaten, but he left behind the McGuffin!
What's in that sandwich?!
GOOD COLD
McGUFFIN
Yech... It's red herring!
Again?
NEXT PLOT TWIST IN AN AUNTIE ANNE'S PRETZELS
DIST. BY THE UNIVERSAL UCLICK SYNDICATE ©2012 R. BOLLING -1109- JOIN THE INNER HIVE AT tomthedancingbug.com

10/15/12

A TOM THE
DANCING BUG PRODUCTION

EXECUTIVE PRODUCER
RUBEN BOLLING

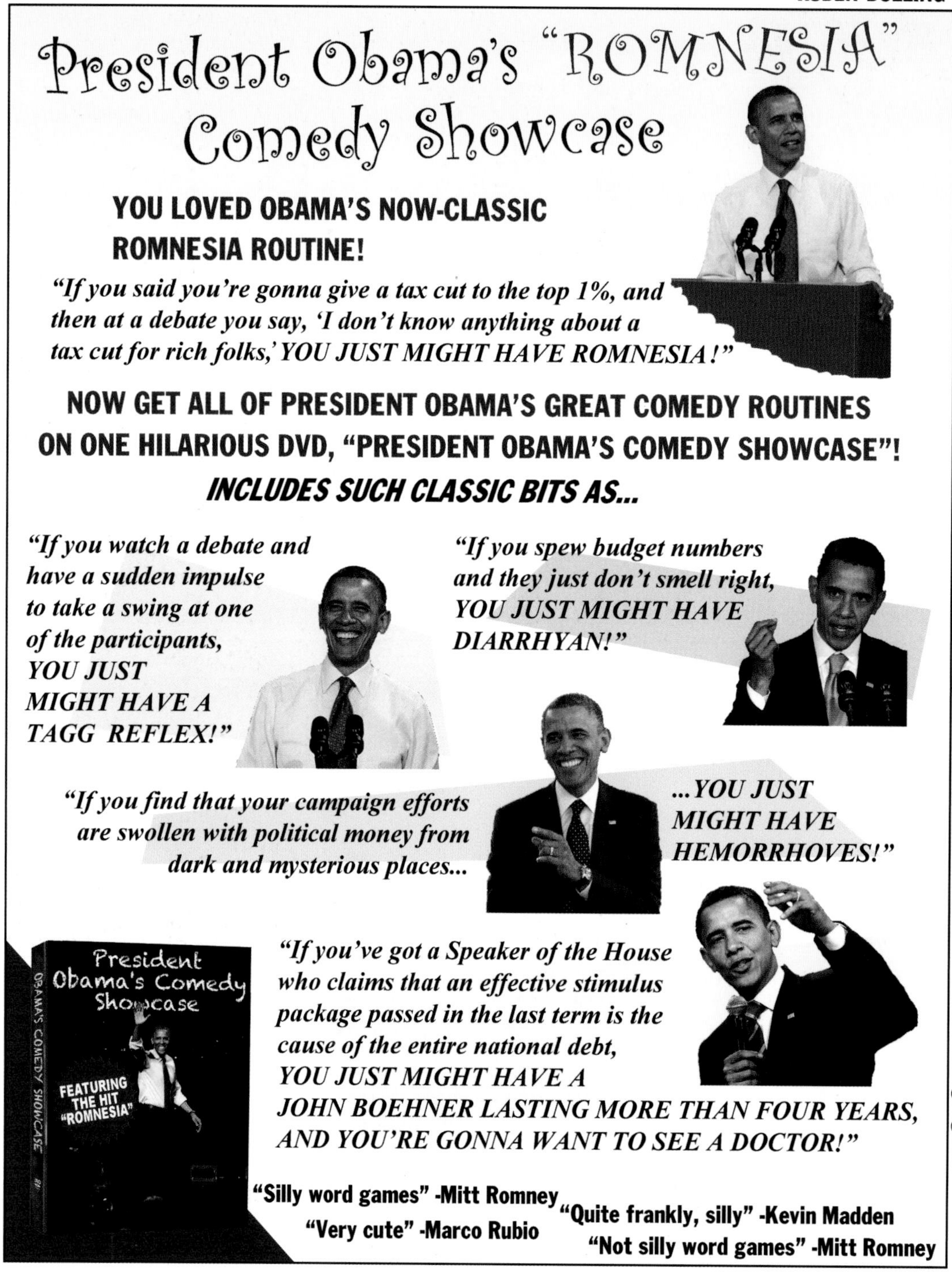

President Obama's "ROMNESIA" Comedy Showcase
YOU LOVED OBAMA'S NOW-CLASSIC ROMNESIA ROUTINE!
"If you said you're gonna give a tax cut to the top 1%, and then at a debate you say, 'I don't know anything about a tax cut for rich folks,' YOU JUST MIGHT HAVE ROMNESIA!"
NOW GET ALL OF PRESIDENT OBAMA'S GREAT COMEDY ROUTINES ON ONE HILARIOUS DVD, "PRESIDENT OBAMA'S COMEDY SHOWCASE"!
INCLUDES SUCH CLASSIC BITS AS...
"If you watch a debate and have a sudden impulse to take a swing at one of the participants, YOU JUST MIGHT HAVE A TAGG REFLEX!"
"If you spew budget numbers and they just don't smell right, YOU JUST MIGHT HAVE DIARRHYAN!"
"If you find that your campaign efforts are swollen with political money from dark and mysterious places...
...YOU JUST MIGHT HAVE HEMORRHOVES!"
President Obama's Comedy Showcase
OBAMA'S COMEDY SHOWCASE
FEATURING THE HIT "ROMNESIA"
"If you've got a Speaker of the House who claims that an effective stimulus package passed in the last term is the cause of the entire national debt, YOU JUST MIGHT HAVE A JOHN BOEHNER LASTING MORE THAN FOUR YEARS, AND YOU'RE GONNA WANT TO SEE A DOCTOR!"
"Silly word games" -Mitt Romney
"Very cute" -Marco Rubio
"Quite frankly, silly" -Kevin Madden
"Not silly word games" -Mitt Romney

10/22/12

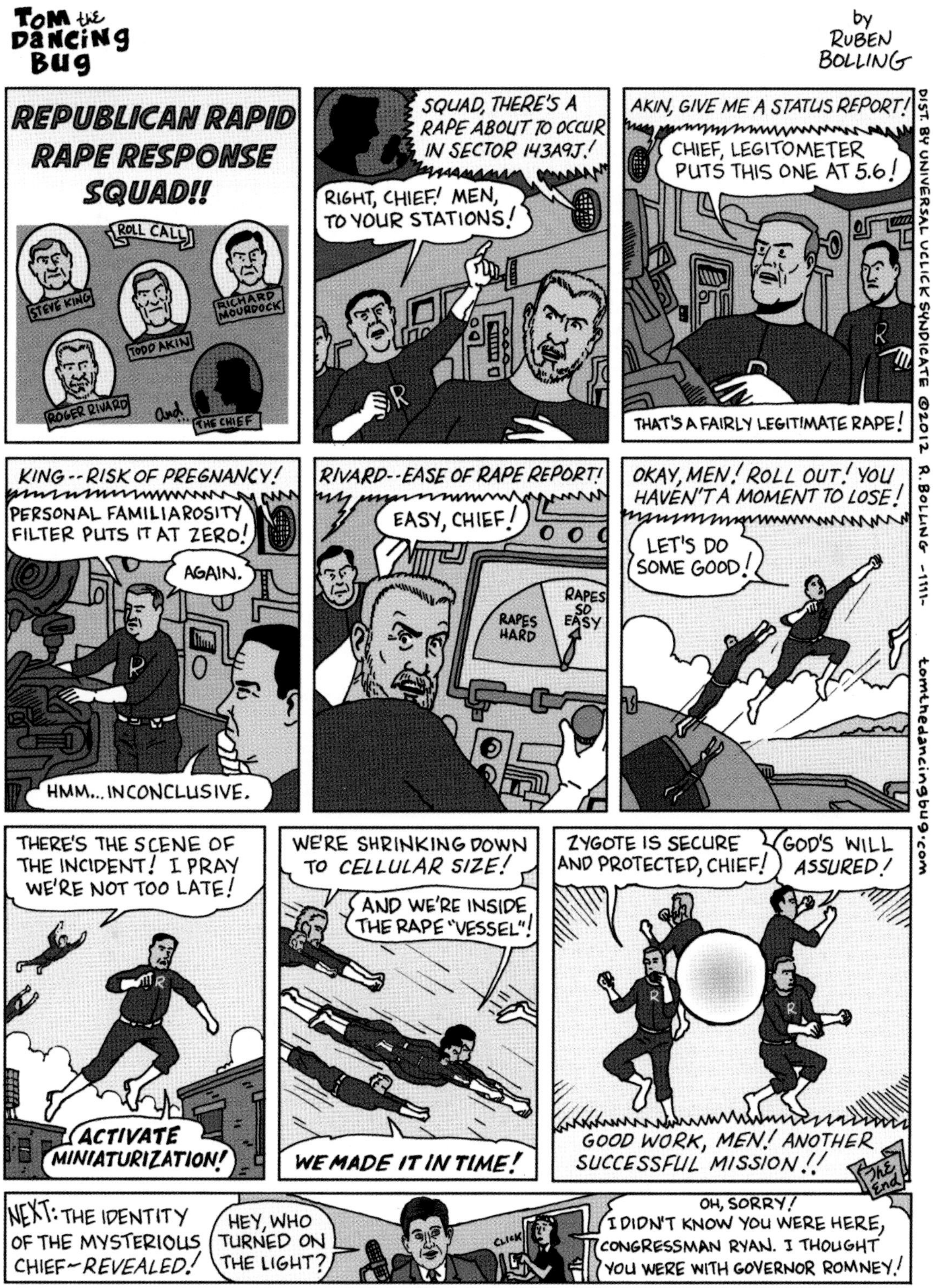
Tom the Dancing Bug
by Ruben Bolling
REPUBLICAN RAPID RAPE RESPONSE SQUAD!!
ROLL CALL
STEVE KING
TODD AKIN
RICHARD MOURDOCK
ROGER RIVARD
and...
THE CHIEF
SQUAD, THERE'S A RAPE ABOUT TO OCCUR IN SECTOR 143A9J!
RIGHT, CHIEF! MEN, TO YOUR STATIONS!
AKIN, GIVE ME A STATUS REPORT!
CHIEF, LEGITOMETER PUTS THIS ONE AT 5.6!
THAT'S A FAIRLY LEGITIMATE RAPE!
KING--RISK OF PREGNANCY!
PERSONAL FAMILIAROSITY FILTER PUTS IT AT ZERO!
AGAIN.
HMM... INCONCLUSIVE.
RIVARD--EASE OF RAPE REPORT!
EASY, CHIEF!
RAPES HARD
RAPES SO EASY
OKAY, MEN! ROLL OUT! YOU HAVEN'T A MOMENT TO LOSE!
LET'S DO SOME GOOD!
THERE'S THE SCENE OF THE INCIDENT! I PRAY WE'RE NOT TOO LATE!
ACTIVATE MINIATURIZATION!
WE'RE SHRINKING DOWN TO CELLULAR SIZE!
AND WE'RE INSIDE THE RAPE "VESSEL"!
WE MADE IT IN TIME!
ZYGOTE IS SECURE AND PROTECTED, CHIEF!
GOD'S WILL ASSURED!
GOOD WORK, MEN! ANOTHER SUCCESSFUL MISSION!!
THE END
NEXT: THE IDENTITY OF THE MYSTERIOUS CHIEF—REVEALED!
HEY, WHO TURNED ON THE LIGHT?
CLICK
OH, SORRY! I DIDN'T KNOW YOU WERE HERE, CONGRESSMAN RYAN. I THOUGHT YOU WERE WITH GOVERNOR ROMNEY!
DIST. BY UNIVERSAL UCLICK SYNDICATE ©2012 R. BOLLING -1111- tomthedancingbug.com

10/29/12

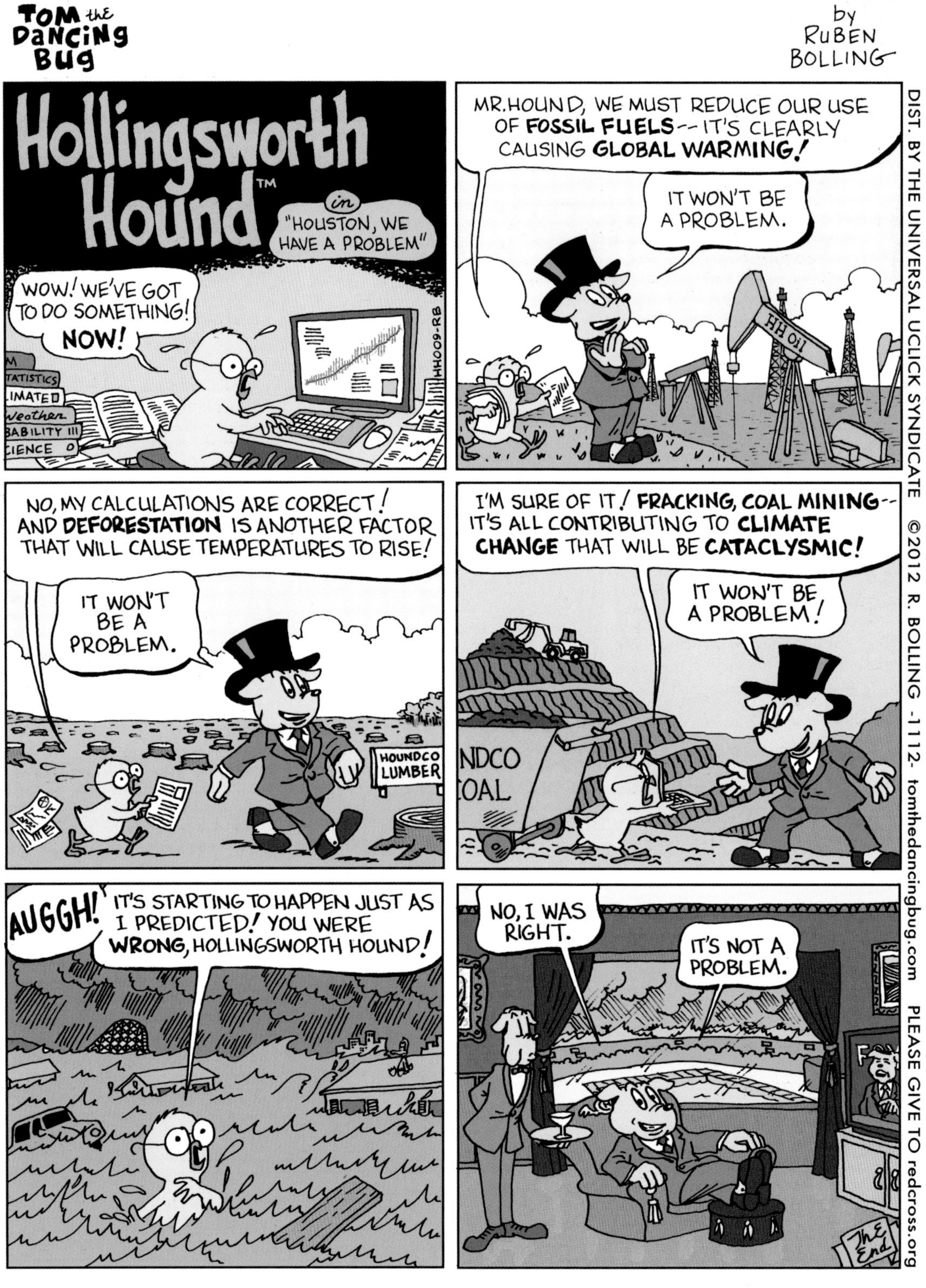
TOM the DANCING BUG
by RUBEN BOLLING
Hollingsworth Hound™
in "HOUSTON, WE HAVE A PROBLEM"
WOW! WE'VE GOT TO DO SOMETHING! NOW!
MR. HOUND, WE MUST REDUCE OUR USE OF FOSSIL FUELS-- IT'S CLEARLY CAUSING GLOBAL WARMING!
IT WON'T BE A PROBLEM.
HH OIL
NO, MY CALCULATIONS ARE CORRECT! AND DEFORESTATION IS ANOTHER FACTOR THAT WILL CAUSE TEMPERATURES TO RISE!
IT WON'T BE A PROBLEM.
HOUNDCO LUMBER
I'M SURE OF IT! FRACKING, COAL MINING-- IT'S ALL CONTRIBUTING TO CLIMATE CHANGE THAT WILL BE CATACLYSMIC!
IT WON'T BE A PROBLEM!
AUGGH!
IT'S STARTING TO HAPPEN JUST AS I PREDICTED! YOU WERE WRONG, HOLLINGSWORTH HOUND!
NO, I WAS RIGHT.
IT'S NOT A PROBLEM.
The End
DIST. BY THE UNIVERSAL UCLICK SYNDICATE © 2012 R. BOLLING -1112- tomthedancingbug.com PLEASE GIVE TO redcross.org

11/5/12

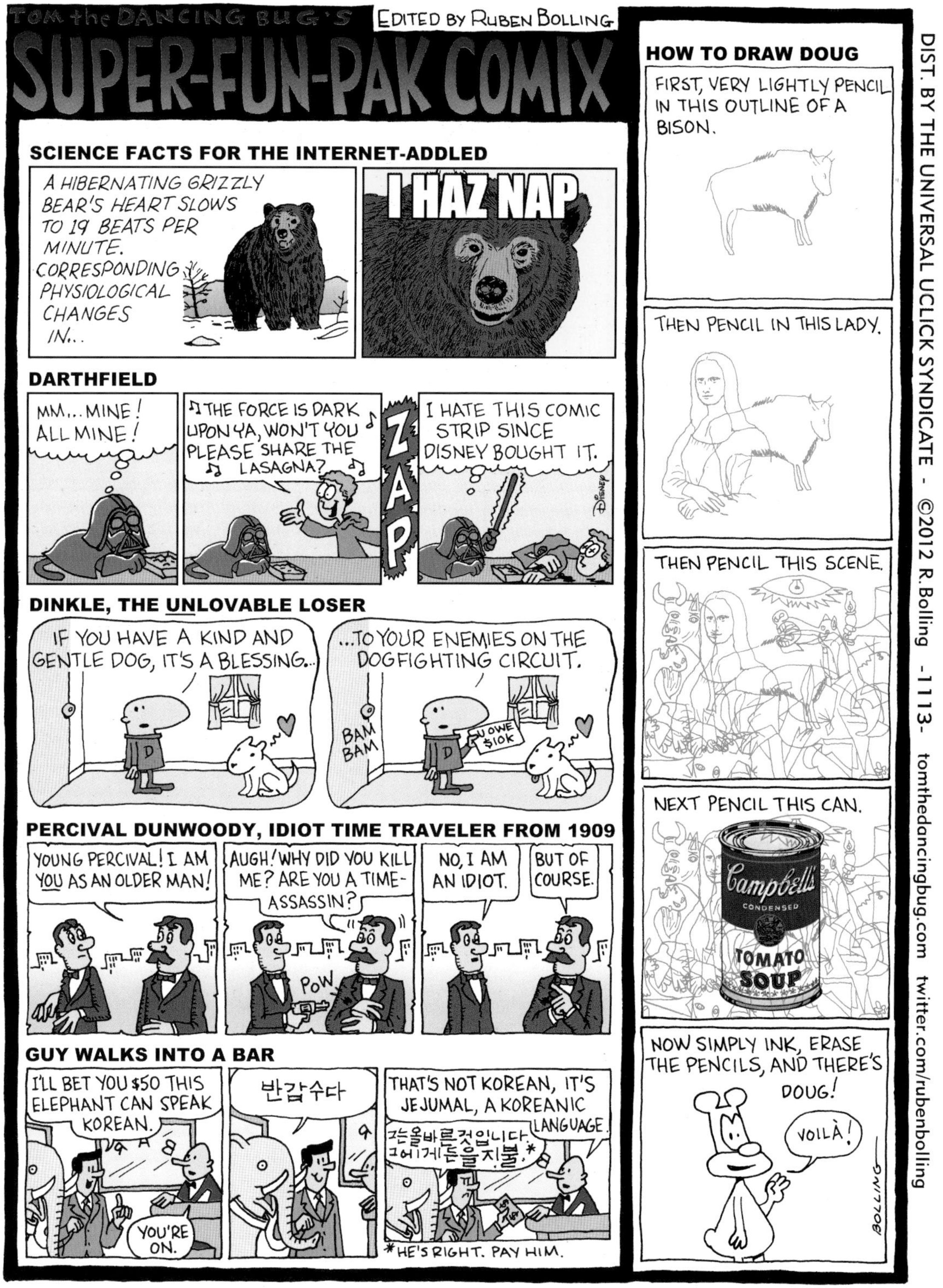
TOM the DANCING BUG'S
EDITED BY RUBEN BOLLING
SUPER-FUN-PAK COMIX
SCIENCE FACTS FOR THE INTERNET-ADDLED
A HIBERNATING GRIZZLY BEAR'S HEART SLOWS TO 19 BEATS PER MINUTE. CORRESPONDING PHYSIOLOGICAL CHANGES IN...
I HAZ NAP
DARTHFIELD
MM... MINE! ALL MINE!
♫ THE FORCE IS DARK UPON YA, WON'T YOU PLEASE SHARE THE LASAGNA? ♫
ZAP
I HATE THIS COMIC STRIP SINCE DISNEY BOUGHT IT.
DISNEY
DINKLE, THE UNLOVABLE LOSER
IF YOU HAVE A KIND AND GENTLE DOG, IT'S A BLESSING...
...TO YOUR ENEMIES ON THE DOGFIGHTING CIRCUIT.
BAM BAM
U OWE $10K
PERCIVAL DUNWOODY, IDIOT TIME TRAVELER FROM 1909
YOUNG PERCIVAL! I AM YOU AS AN OLDER MAN!
AUGH! WHY DID YOU KILL ME? ARE YOU A TIME-ASSASSIN?
POW
NO, I AM AN IDIOT.
BUT OF COURSE.
GUY WALKS INTO A BAR
I'LL BET YOU $50 THIS ELEPHANT CAN SPEAK KOREAN.
YOU'RE ON.
반갑수다
THAT'S NOT KOREAN, IT'S JEJUMAL, A KOREANIC LANGUAGE.
그는올바른것입니다. 그에게돈을지불.*
*HE'S RIGHT. PAY HIM.
HOW TO DRAW DOUG
FIRST, VERY LIGHTLY PENCIL IN THIS OUTLINE OF A BISON.
THEN PENCIL IN THIS LADY.
THEN PENCIL THIS SCENE.
NEXT PENCIL THIS CAN.
Campbell's
CONDENSED
TOMATO SOUP
NOW SIMPLY INK, ERASE THE PENCILS, AND THERE'S DOUG!
VOILÀ!
BOLLING
DIST. BY THE UNIVERSAL UCLICK SYNDICATE - ©2012 R. Bolling -1113- tomthedancingbug.com twitter.com/rubenbolling

11/12/12

TOM the DANCING BUG

by RUBEN BOLLING

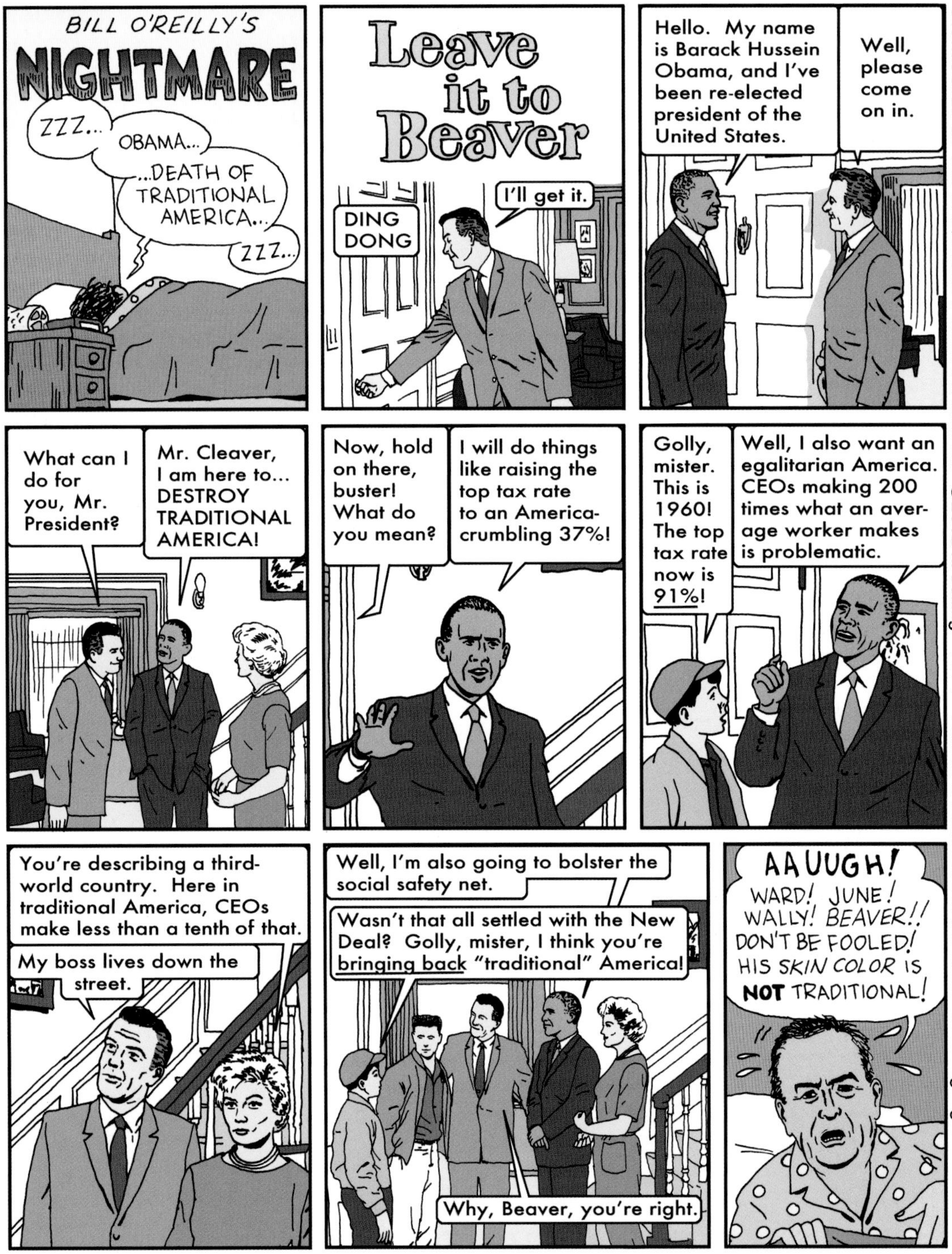

BILL O'REILLY'S
NIGHTMARE
ZZZ...
OBAMA...
...DEATH OF TRADITIONAL AMERICA...
ZZZ...
Leave it to Beaver
DING DONG
I'll get it.
Hello. My name is Barack Hussein Obama, and I've been re-elected president of the United States.
Well, please come on in.
What can I do for you, Mr. President?
Mr. Cleaver, I am here to... DESTROY TRADITIONAL AMERICA!
Now, hold on there, buster! What do you mean?
I will do things like raising the top tax rate to an America-crumbling 37%!
Golly, mister. This is 1960! The top tax rate now is 91%!
Well, I also want an egalitarian America. CEOs making 200 times what an average worker makes is problematic.
You're describing a third-world country. Here in traditional America, CEOs make less than a tenth of that.
My boss lives down the street.
Well, I'm also going to bolster the social safety net.
Wasn't that all settled with the New Deal? Golly, mister, I think you're bringing back "traditional" America!
Why, Beaver, you're right.
AAUUGH!
WARD! JUNE! WALLY! BEAVER!! DON'T BE FOOLED! HIS SKIN COLOR IS NOT TRADITIONAL!

11/19/12

TOM the DANCING BUG

by RUBEN BOLLING

THE ORIGIN OF SPECIES II
ON THE MEMETIC EVOLUTION OF LOLCATS,
OR, THE PRESERVATION OF FAVOURED BYTES
IN THE STRUGGLE FOR LULZ
BY CHARLES DARWIN, M.A.

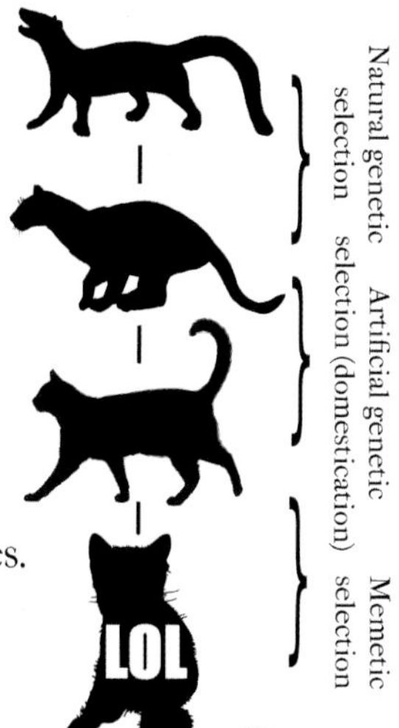

Cats are the first organism to make the leap from genetic evolution to memetic. (See Fig. 1.) While genes replicate themselves physically within biological bodies, memes replicate themselves culturally within human brains and hard drives. (See Dawkins, R.) The feline shift to this form of evolution has led to an explosion of remarkable new adaptations and species.

Natural genetic selection

Artificial genetic selection (domestication)

Memetic selection

Fig. 1

WUN MOR CHEEZBURGER PLEEZ

Fig. 2

The domestic cat's first jump to memetic evolution was made by Lolcats (*Felis virtualus*, or *Felis virtualus audibalguffus*), which gained the power of language, albeit with atrocious spelling. (See Fig. 2.)

Lolcats' ecological niche appears to be North American living rooms, and its diet chiefly consists of "cheezburgers [sic]" and "noms [??]."

The viral success of the Lolcat species spawned new adaptations that quickly took hold, although it is unknown how the memetic mutation that caused Breadcats (*Felis virtualus panus*) has any adaptive advantage whatsoever. (See Fig. 3.)

I HAZ SLICE?

Fig. 3

I SEE U

IZ MY MEMETIC ADVANTAJ

Fig. 4

OMG!

A NEW NICHE!

Fig. 5

Lolcat offshoot species began to invade new territories, such as ceilings (*Felis virtualus masturbatus*, Fig. 4) and footwear (*Felis virtualus pedus*, Fig. 5), &c.

Fig. 6

Equus ebookus *Canis dawgus radus* *Cynomys dramaticus*

Other biological species have attempted to make the leap to memetic evolution (Fig. 6), but these short-lived forays, while spectacular, have been evolutionary dead ends.

NEXT CHAPTER: LMFAOCATS

DIST. BY THE UNIVERSAL UCLICK SYNDICATE - ©2012 R. BOLLING -1115- tomthedancingbug.com RESPECT to Richard Dawkins

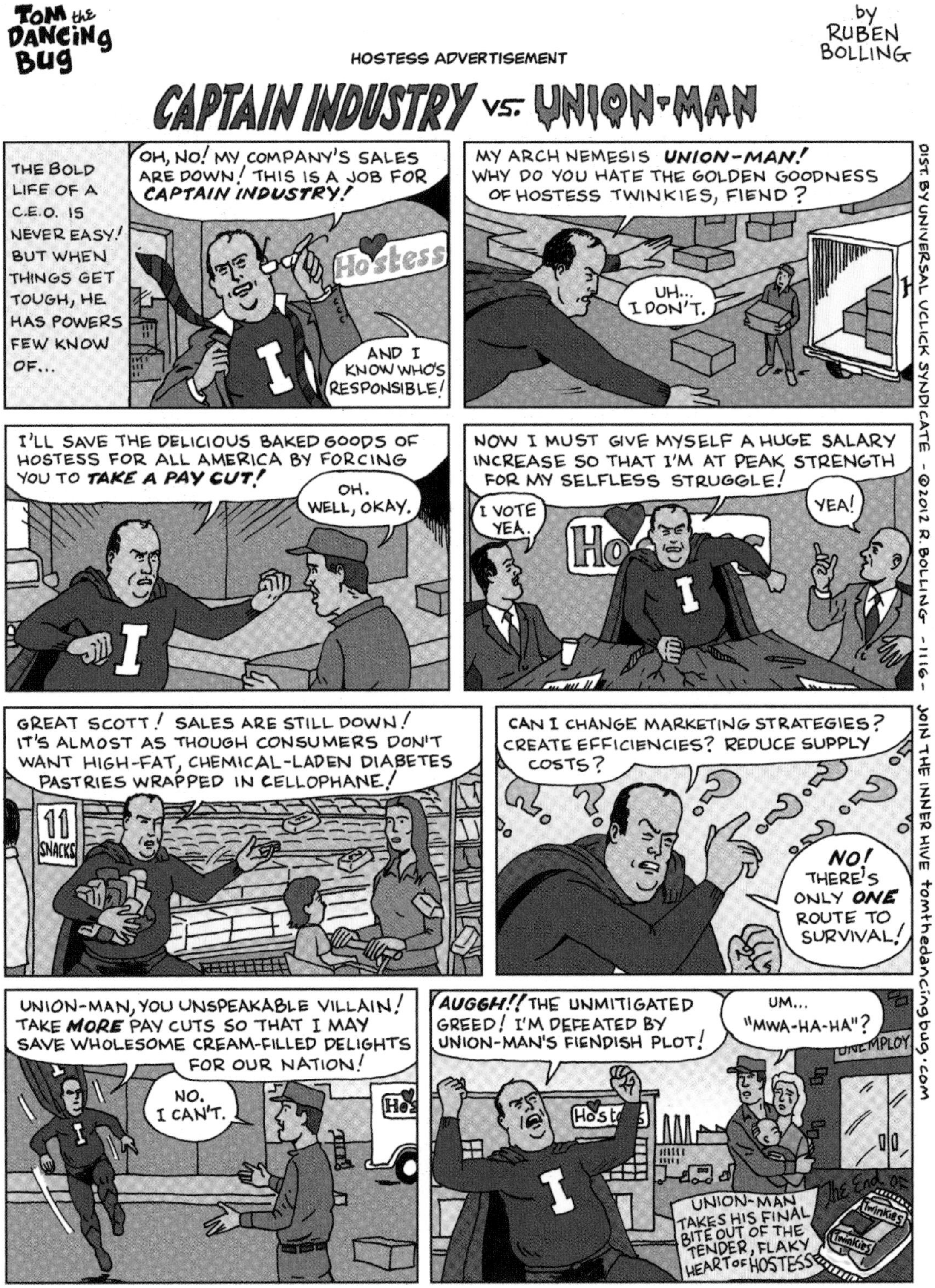
TOM the DANCING BUG
by RUBEN BOLLING
HOSTESS ADVERTISEMENT
CAPTAIN INDUSTRY vs. UNION-MAN
THE BOLD LIFE OF A C.E.O. IS NEVER EASY! BUT WHEN THINGS GET TOUGH, HE HAS POWERS FEW KNOW OF...
OH, NO! MY COMPANY'S SALES ARE DOWN! THIS IS A JOB FOR CAPTAIN INDUSTRY!
Hostess
AND I KNOW WHO'S RESPONSIBLE!
MY ARCH NEMESIS UNION-MAN! WHY DO YOU HATE THE GOLDEN GOODNESS OF HOSTESS TWINKIES, FIEND?
UH... I DON'T.
I'LL SAVE THE DELICIOUS BAKED GOODS OF HOSTESS FOR ALL AMERICA BY FORCING YOU TO TAKE A PAY CUT!
OH. WELL, OKAY.
NOW I MUST GIVE MYSELF A HUGE SALARY INCREASE SO THAT I'M AT PEAK STRENGTH FOR MY SELFLESS STRUGGLE!
I VOTE YEA.
YEA!
GREAT SCOTT! SALES ARE STILL DOWN! IT'S ALMOST AS THOUGH CONSUMERS DON'T WANT HIGH-FAT, CHEMICAL-LADEN DIABETES PASTRIES WRAPPED IN CELLOPHANE!
11 SNACKS
CAN I CHANGE MARKETING STRATEGIES? CREATE EFFICIENCIES? REDUCE SUPPLY COSTS?
NO! THERE'S ONLY ONE ROUTE TO SURVIVAL!
UNION-MAN, YOU UNSPEAKABLE VILLAIN! TAKE MORE PAY CUTS SO THAT I MAY SAVE WHOLESOME CREAM-FILLED DELIGHTS FOR OUR NATION!
NO. I CAN'T.
AUGGH!! THE UNMITIGATED GREED! I'M DEFEATED BY UNION-MAN'S FIENDISH PLOT!
UM... "MWA-HA-HA"?
UNEMPLOY
UNION-MAN TAKES HIS FINAL BITE OUT OF THE TENDER, FLAKY HEART OF HOSTESS
The End of
Twinkies
DIST. BY UNIVERSAL UCLICK SYNDICATE - ©2012 R. BOLLING -1116- JOIN THE INNER HIVE tomthedancingbug.com

12/3/12

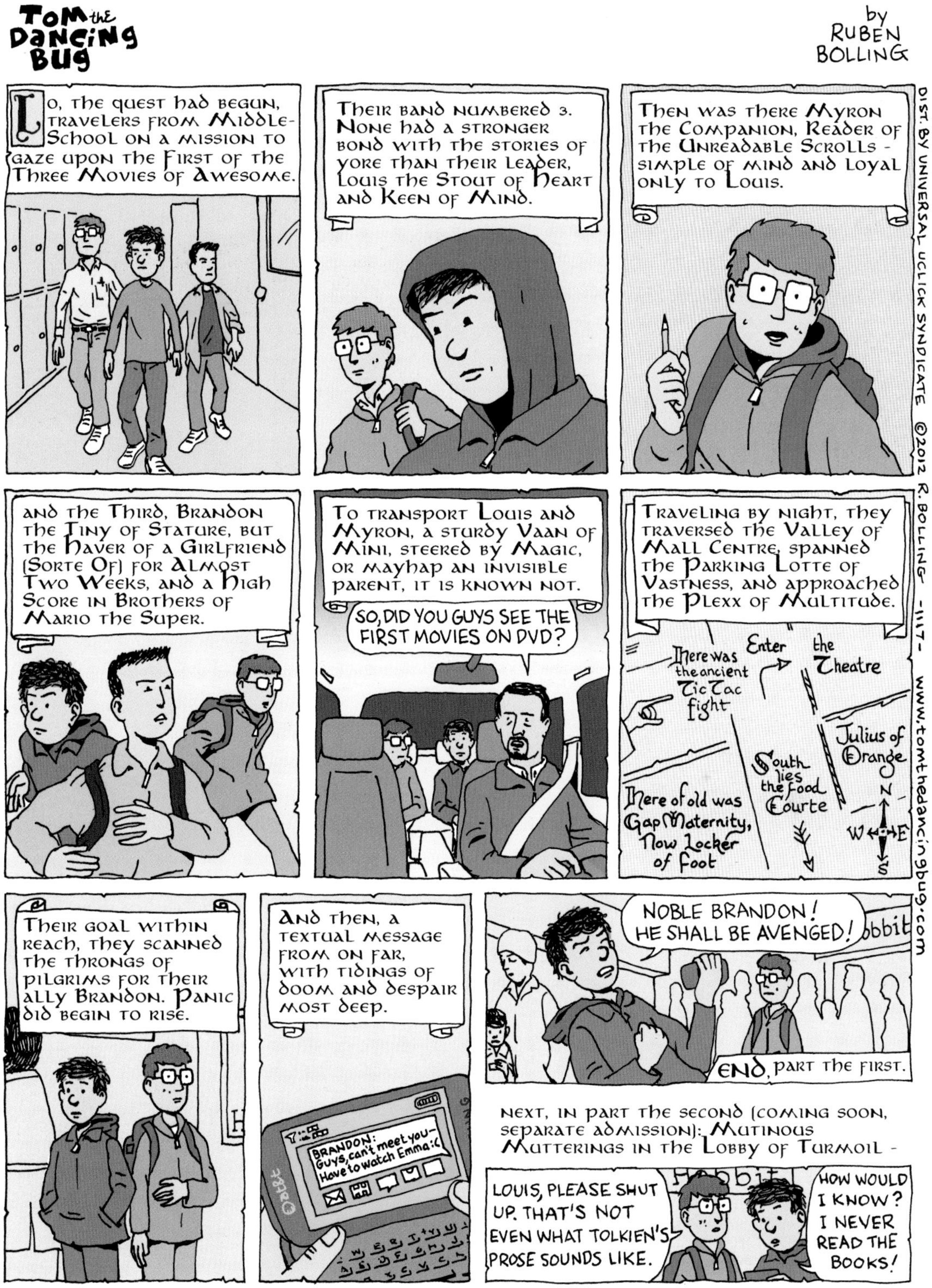
Tom the Dancing Bug
by RUBEN BOLLING
Lo, the quest had begun, travelers from Middle-School on a mission to gaze upon the First of the Three Movies of Awesome.
Their band numbered 3. None had a stronger bond with the stories of yore than their leader, Louis the Stout of Heart and Keen of Mind.
Then was there Myron the Companion, Reader of the Unreadable Scrolls - simple of mind and loyal only to Louis.
DIST. BY UNIVERSAL UCLICK SYNDICATE ©2012 R. BOLLING -1117- www.tomthedancingbug.com
and the Third, Brandon the Tiny of Stature, but the Haver of a Girlfriend (Sorte Of) for Almost Two Weeks, and a High Score in Brothers of Mario the Super.
To transport Louis and Myron, a sturdy Vaan of Mini, steered by Magic, or mayhap an invisible parent, it is known not.
SO, DID YOU GUYS SEE THE FIRST MOVIES ON DVD?
Traveling by night, they traversed the Valley of Mall Centre, spanned the Parking Lotte of Vastness, and approached the Plexx of Multitude.
Here was the ancient Tic Tac fight
Enter the Theatre
Julius of Orange
South lies the Food Courte
Here of old was Gap Maternity, Now Locker of Foot
N W E S
Their goal within reach, they scanned the throngs of pilgrims for their ally Brandon. Panic did begin to rise.
And then, a textual message from on far, with tidings of doom and despair most deep.
BRANDON: Guys, can't meet you- Have to watch Emma :(
NOBLE BRANDON! HE SHALL BE AVENGED!
END, part the first.
Next, in part the second (coming soon, separate admission): Mutinous Mutterings in the Lobby of Turmoil -
LOUIS, PLEASE SHUT UP. THAT'S NOT EVEN WHAT TOLKIEN'S PROSE SOUNDS LIKE.
HOW WOULD I KNOW? I NEVER READ THE BOOKS!

12/10/12

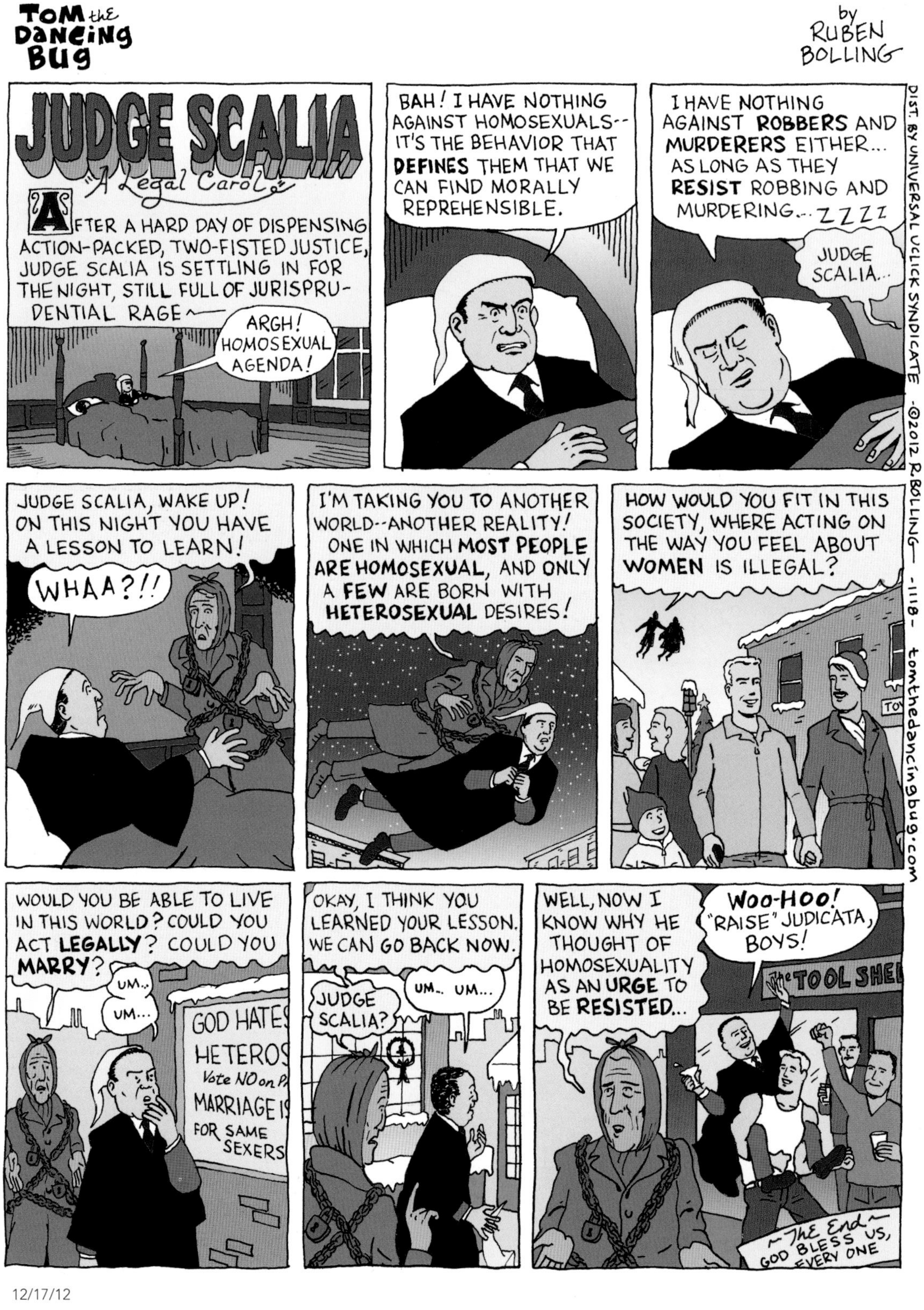
TOM the DANCING BUG
by RUBEN BOLLING
JUDGE SCALIA
"A Legal Carol"
AFTER A HARD DAY OF DISPENSING ACTION-PACKED, TWO-FISTED JUSTICE, JUDGE SCALIA IS SETTLING IN FOR THE NIGHT, STILL FULL OF JURISPRUDENTIAL RAGE
ARGH! HOMOSEXUAL AGENDA!
BAH! I HAVE NOTHING AGAINST HOMOSEXUALS-- IT'S THE BEHAVIOR THAT DEFINES THEM THAT WE CAN FIND MORALLY REPREHENSIBLE.
I HAVE NOTHING AGAINST ROBBERS AND MURDERERS EITHER... AS LONG AS THEY RESIST ROBBING AND MURDERING... ZZZZ
JUDGE SCALIA...
DIST. BY UNIVERSAL UCLICK SYNDICATE ©2012 R.BOLLING -1118- tomthedancingbug.com
JUDGE SCALIA, WAKE UP! ON THIS NIGHT YOU HAVE A LESSON TO LEARN!
WHAA?!!
I'M TAKING YOU TO ANOTHER WORLD--ANOTHER REALITY! ONE IN WHICH MOST PEOPLE ARE HOMOSEXUAL, AND ONLY A FEW ARE BORN WITH HETEROSEXUAL DESIRES!
HOW WOULD YOU FIT IN THIS SOCIETY, WHERE ACTING ON THE WAY YOU FEEL ABOUT WOMEN IS ILLEGAL?
WOULD YOU BE ABLE TO LIVE IN THIS WORLD? COULD YOU ACT LEGALLY? COULD YOU MARRY?
UM...
UM...
GOD HATES HETEROS
Vote NO on P
MARRIAGE IS FOR SAME SEXERS
OKAY, I THINK YOU LEARNED YOUR LESSON. WE CAN GO BACK NOW.
JUDGE SCALIA?
UM... UM...
WELL, NOW I KNOW WHY HE THOUGHT OF HOMOSEXUALITY AS AN URGE TO BE RESISTED...
WOO-HOO! "RAISE" JUDICATA, BOYS!
The TOOL SHE
~The End~
GOD BLESS US, EVERY ONE

12/17/12

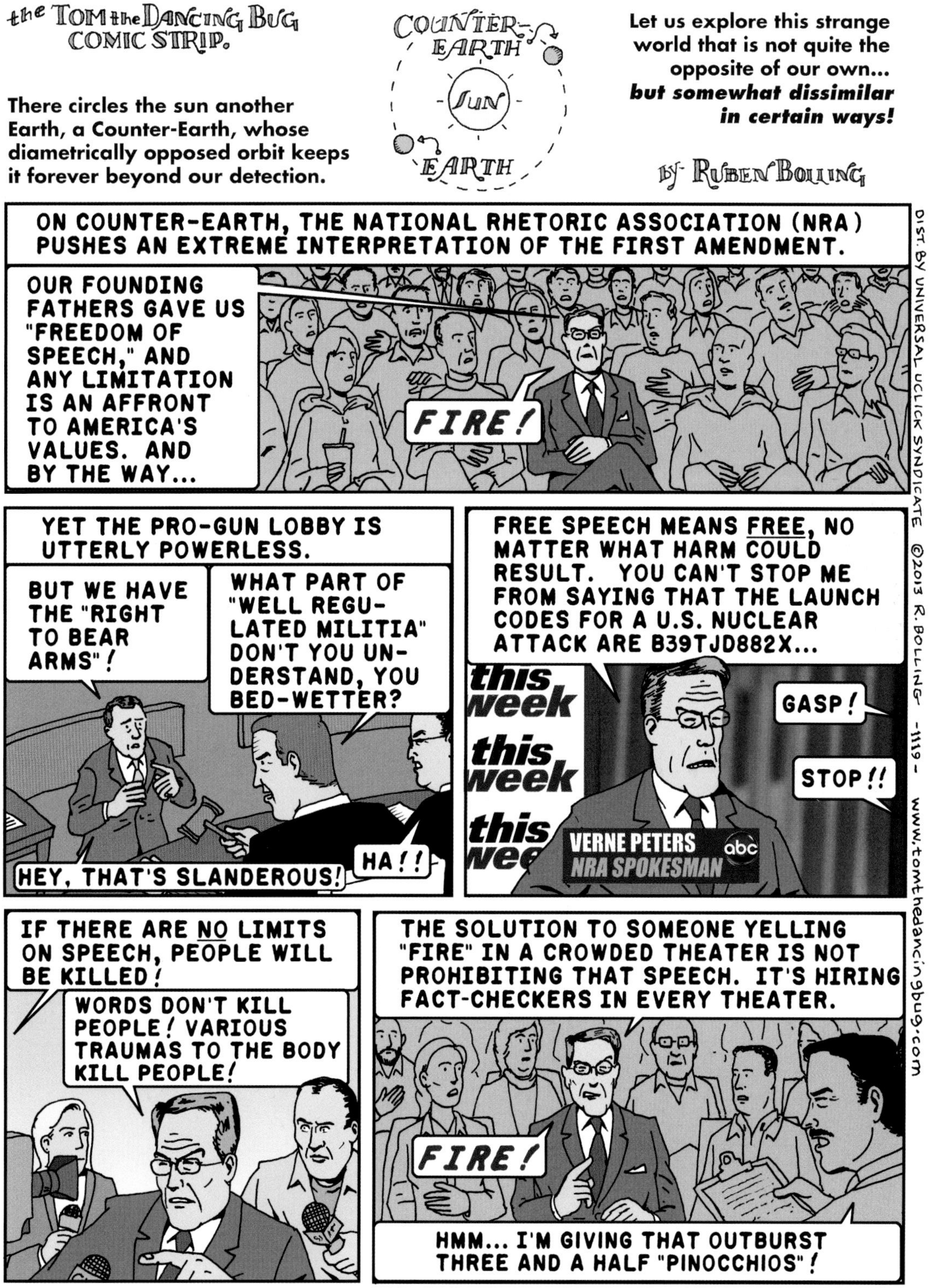
the TOM the DANCING BUG COMIC STRIP.
COUNTER-EARTH
SUN
EARTH
There circles the sun another Earth, a Counter-Earth, whose diametrically opposed orbit keeps it forever beyond our detection.
Let us explore this strange world that is not quite the opposite of our own... but somewhat dissimilar in certain ways!
by RUBEN BOLLING
ON COUNTER-EARTH, THE NATIONAL RHETORIC ASSOCIATION (NRA) PUSHES AN EXTREME INTERPRETATION OF THE FIRST AMENDMENT.
OUR FOUNDING FATHERS GAVE US "FREEDOM OF SPEECH," AND ANY LIMITATION IS AN AFFRONT TO AMERICA'S VALUES. AND BY THE WAY...
FIRE!
YET THE PRO-GUN LOBBY IS UTTERLY POWERLESS.
BUT WE HAVE THE "RIGHT TO BEAR ARMS"!
WHAT PART OF "WELL REGULATED MILITIA" DON'T YOU UNDERSTAND, YOU BED-WETTER?
HEY, THAT'S SLANDEROUS!
HA!!
FREE SPEECH MEANS FREE, NO MATTER WHAT HARM COULD RESULT. YOU CAN'T STOP ME FROM SAYING THAT THE LAUNCH CODES FOR A U.S. NUCLEAR ATTACK ARE B39TJD882X...
this week
this week
this wee
GASP!
STOP!!
VERNE PETERS
NRA SPOKESMAN
abc
IF THERE ARE NO LIMITS ON SPEECH, PEOPLE WILL BE KILLED!
WORDS DON'T KILL PEOPLE! VARIOUS TRAUMAS TO THE BODY KILL PEOPLE!
THE SOLUTION TO SOMEONE YELLING "FIRE" IN A CROWDED THEATER IS NOT PROHIBITING THAT SPEECH. IT'S HIRING FACT-CHECKERS IN EVERY THEATER.
FIRE!
HMM... I'M GIVING THAT OUTBURST THREE AND A HALF "PINOCCHIOS"!
DIST. BY UNIVERSAL UCLICK SYNDICATE ©2013 R. BOLLING -1119- www.tomthedancingbug.com

12/31/12

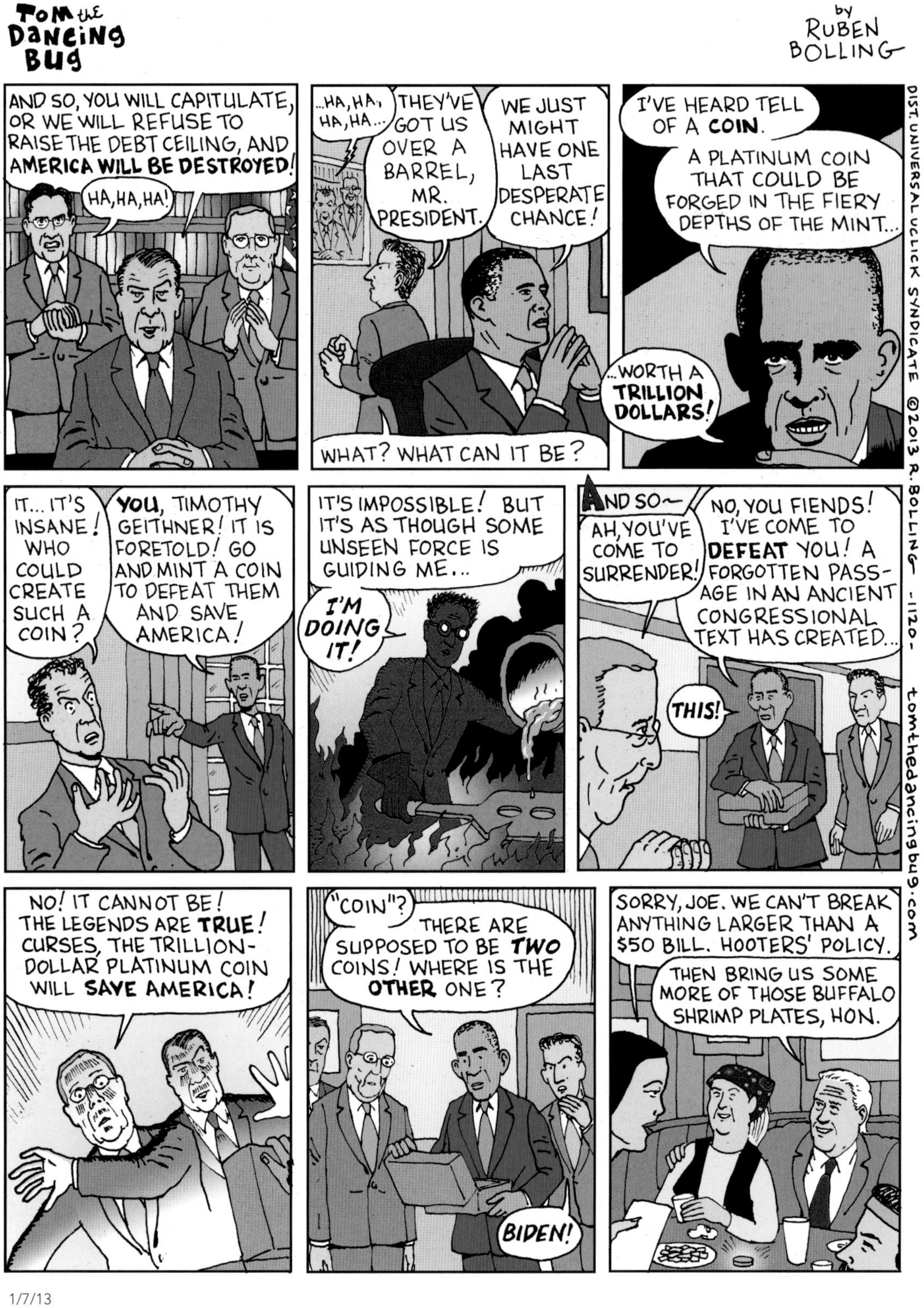

TOM the DANCING BUG
by RUBEN BOLLING
AND SO, YOU WILL CAPITULATE, OR WE WILL REFUSE TO RAISE THE DEBT CEILING, AND **AMERICA WILL BE DESTROYED!**
HA,HA,HA!
...HA, HA, HA, HA...
THEY'VE GOT US OVER A BARREL, MR. PRESIDENT.
WE JUST MIGHT HAVE ONE LAST DESPERATE CHANCE!
WHAT? WHAT CAN IT BE?
I'VE HEARD TELL OF A **COIN**.
A PLATINUM COIN THAT COULD BE FORGED IN THE FIERY DEPTHS OF THE MINT...
...WORTH A **TRILLION DOLLARS!**
IT... IT'S INSANE! WHO COULD CREATE SUCH A COIN?
YOU, TIMOTHY GEITHNER! IT IS FORETOLD! GO AND MINT A COIN TO DEFEAT THEM AND SAVE AMERICA!
IT'S IMPOSSIBLE! BUT IT'S AS THOUGH SOME UNSEEN FORCE IS GUIDING ME...
I'M DOING IT!
AND SO~
AH, YOU'VE COME TO SURRENDER!
NO, YOU FIENDS! I'VE COME TO **DEFEAT** YOU! A FORGOTTEN PASSAGE IN AN ANCIENT CONGRESSIONAL TEXT HAS CREATED...
THIS!
NO! IT CANNOT BE! THE LEGENDS ARE **TRUE**! CURSES, THE TRILLION-DOLLAR PLATINUM COIN WILL **SAVE AMERICA!**
"COIN"?
THERE ARE SUPPOSED TO BE **TWO** COINS! WHERE IS THE **OTHER** ONE?
BIDEN!
SORRY, JOE. WE CAN'T BREAK ANYTHING LARGER THAN A $50 BILL. HOOTERS' POLICY.
THEN BRING US SOME MORE OF THOSE BUFFALO SHRIMP PLATES, HON.
DIST. UNIVERSAL UCLICK SYNDICATE ©2013 R. BOLLING -1120- tomthedancingbug.com

1/7/13

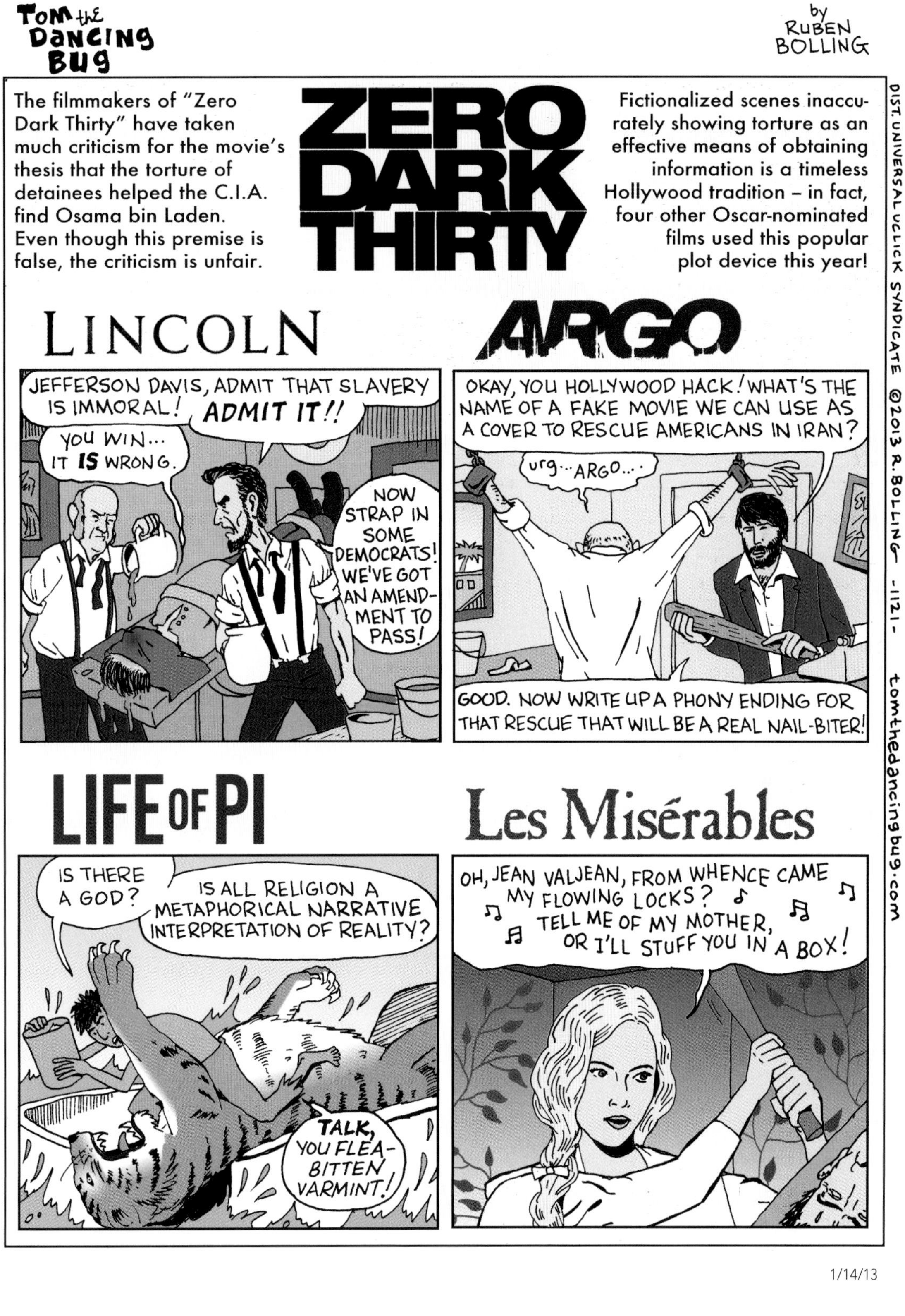
Tom the Dancing Bug
by Ruben Bolling
The filmmakers of "Zero Dark Thirty" have taken much criticism for the movie's thesis that the torture of detainees helped the C.I.A. find Osama bin Laden. Even though this premise is false, the criticism is unfair.
ZERO DARK THIRTY
Fictionalized scenes inaccurately showing torture as an effective means of obtaining information is a timeless Hollywood tradition – in fact, four other Oscar-nominated films used this popular plot device this year!
LINCOLN
JEFFERSON DAVIS, ADMIT THAT SLAVERY IS IMMORAL! ADMIT IT!!
YOU WIN... IT IS WRONG.
NOW STRAP IN SOME DEMOCRATS! WE'VE GOT AN AMENDMENT TO PASS!
ARGO
OKAY, YOU HOLLYWOOD HACK! WHAT'S THE NAME OF A FAKE MOVIE WE CAN USE AS A COVER TO RESCUE AMERICANS IN IRAN?
urg...ARGO...
GOOD. NOW WRITE UP A PHONY ENDING FOR THAT RESCUE THAT WILL BE A REAL NAIL-BITER!
LIFE OF PI
IS THERE A GOD?
IS ALL RELIGION A METAPHORICAL NARRATIVE INTERPRETATION OF REALITY?
TALK, YOU FLEA-BITTEN VARMINT!
Les Misérables
OH, JEAN VALJEAN, FROM WHENCE CAME MY FLOWING LOCKS? TELL ME OF MY MOTHER, OR I'LL STUFF YOU IN A BOX!
DIST. UNIVERSAL UCLICK SYNDICATE ©2013 R. BOLLING -1121- tomthedancingbug.com

1/14/13

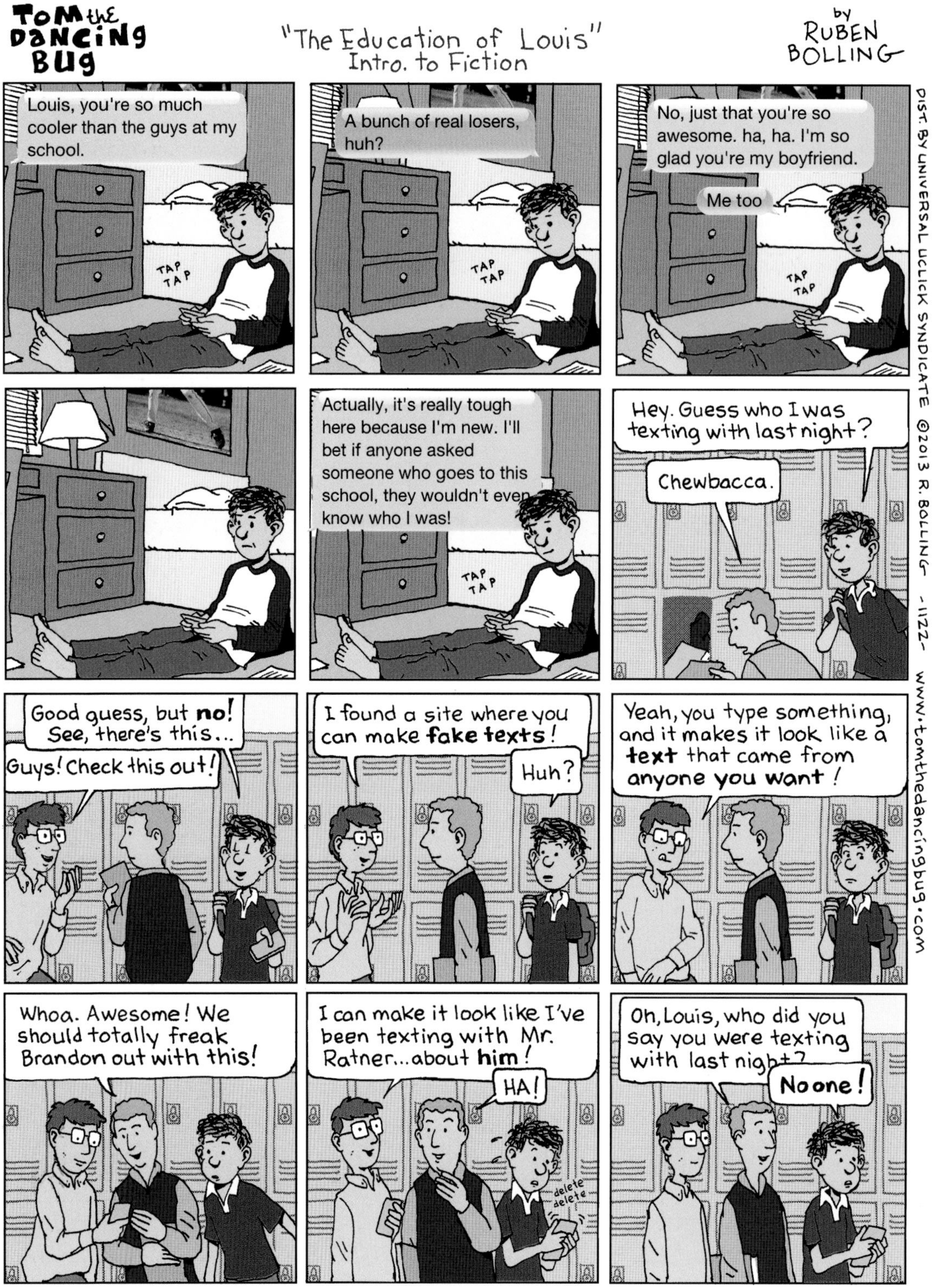

TOM the DANCING BUG
"The Education of Louis"
Intro. to Fiction
by RUBEN BOLLING
Louis, you're so much cooler than the guys at my school.
TAP TAP
A bunch of real losers, huh?
TAP TAP
No, just that you're so awesome. ha, ha. I'm so glad you're my boyfriend.
Me too
TAP TAP
Actually, it's really tough here because I'm new. I'll bet if anyone asked someone who goes to this school, they wouldn't even know who I was!
TAP TAP
Hey. Guess who I was texting with last night?
Chewbacca.
Good guess, but **no**! See, there's this...
Guys! Check this out!
I found a site where you can make **fake texts**!
Huh?
Yeah, you type something, and it makes it look like a **text** that came from **anyone you want**!
Whoa. Awesome! We should totally freak Brandon out with this!
I can make it look like I've been texting with Mr. Ratner...about **him**!
HA!
delete delete
Oh, Louis, who did you say you were texting with last night?
No one!
DIST. BY UNIVERSAL UCLICK SYNDICATE ©2013 R. BOLLING -1122- www.tomthedancingbug.com

1/21/13

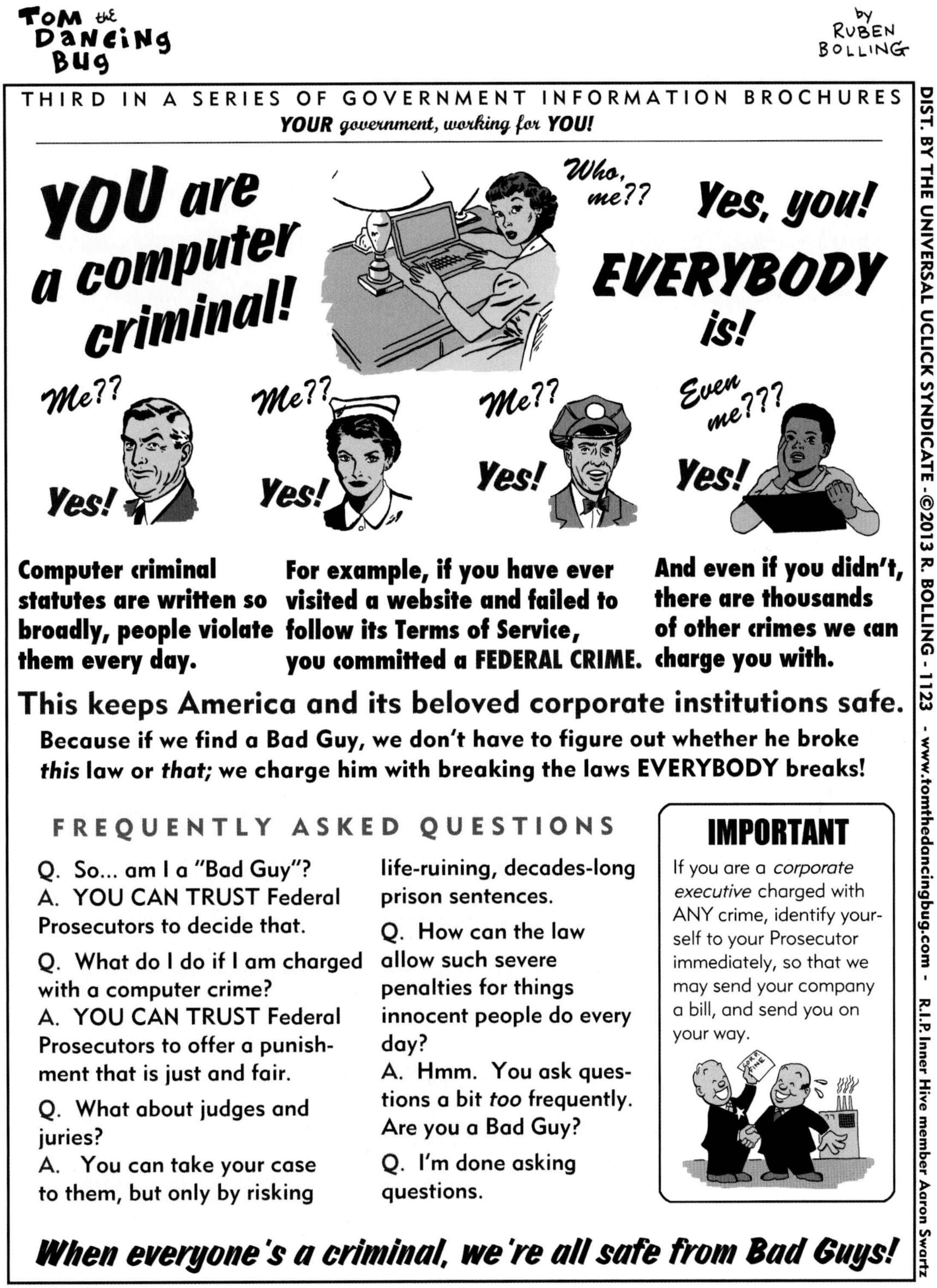
TOM the DANCING BUG
by RUBEN BOLLING
THIRD IN A SERIES OF GOVERNMENT INFORMATION BROCHURES
YOUR government, working for YOU!
YOU are a computer criminal!
Who, me??
Yes, you! EVERYBODY is!
Me?? Yes!
Me?? Yes!
Me?? Yes!
Even me??? Yes!
Computer criminal statutes are written so broadly, people violate them every day.
For example, if you have ever visited a website and failed to follow its Terms of Service, you committed a FEDERAL CRIME.
And even if you didn't, there are thousands of other crimes we can charge you with.
This keeps America and its beloved corporate institutions safe.
Because if we find a Bad Guy, we don't have to figure out whether he broke this law or that; we charge him with breaking the laws EVERYBODY breaks!
FREQUENTLY ASKED QUESTIONS
Q. So... am I a "Bad Guy"?
A. YOU CAN TRUST Federal Prosecutors to decide that.
Q. What do I do if I am charged with a computer crime?
A. YOU CAN TRUST Federal Prosecutors to offer a punishment that is just and fair.
Q. What about judges and juries?
A. You can take your case to them, but only by risking life-ruining, decades-long prison sentences.
Q. How can the law allow such severe penalties for things innocent people do every day?
A. Hmm. You ask questions a bit too frequently. Are you a Bad Guy?
Q. I'm done asking questions.
IMPORTANT
If you are a corporate executive charged with ANY crime, identify yourself to your Prosecutor immediately, so that we may send your company a bill, and send you on your way.
CORP. FINE
When everyone's a criminal, we're all safe from Bad Guys!
DIST. BY THE UNIVERSAL UCLICK SYNDICATE - ©2013 R. BOLLING - 1123 - www.tomthedancingbug.com - R.I.P. Inner Hive member Aaron Swartz

1/28/13

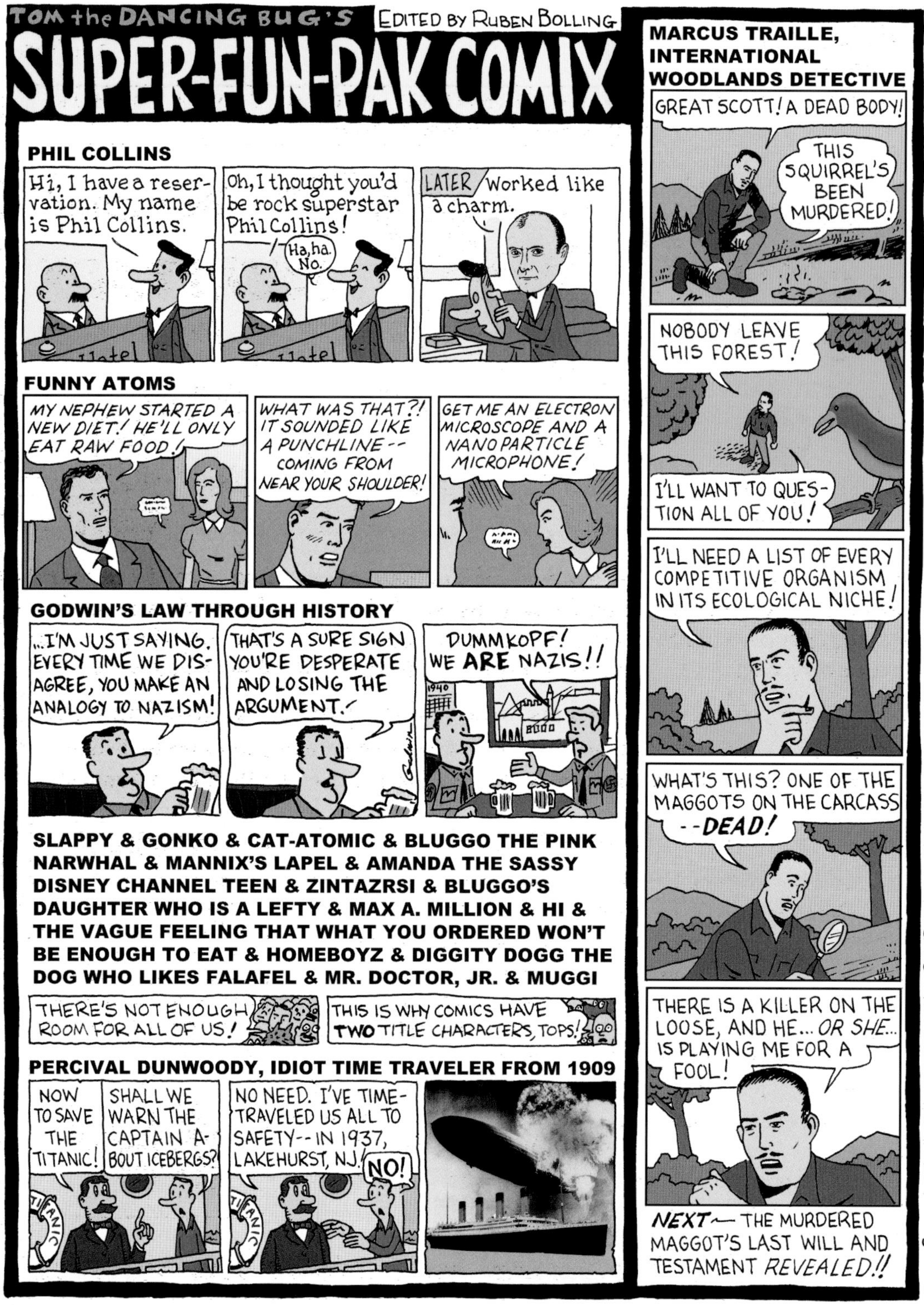
TOM the DANCING BUG'S
EDITED BY RUBEN BOLLING
SUPER-FUN-PAK COMIX
PHIL COLLINS
Hi, I have a reservation. My name is Phil Collins.
Oh, I thought you'd be rock superstar Phil Collins!
Ha, ha. No.
LATER
Worked like a charm.
FUNNY ATOMS
MY NEPHEW STARTED A NEW DIET! HE'LL ONLY EAT RAW FOOD!
WHAT WAS THAT?! IT SOUNDED LIKE A PUNCHLINE -- COMING FROM NEAR YOUR SHOULDER!
GET ME AN ELECTRON MICROSCOPE AND A NANO PARTICLE MICROPHONE!
GODWIN'S LAW THROUGH HISTORY
...I'M JUST SAYING. EVERY TIME WE DISAGREE, YOU MAKE AN ANALOGY TO NAZISM!
THAT'S A SURE SIGN YOU'RE DESPERATE AND LOSING THE ARGUMENT.
1940
DUMMKOPF! WE ARE NAZIS!!
SLAPPY & GONKO & CAT-ATOMIC & BLUGGO THE PINK NARWHAL & MANNIX'S LAPEL & AMANDA THE SASSY DISNEY CHANNEL TEEN & ZINTAZRSI & BLUGGO'S DAUGHTER WHO IS A LEFTY & MAX A. MILLION & HI & THE VAGUE FEELING THAT WHAT YOU ORDERED WON'T BE ENOUGH TO EAT & HOMEBOYZ & DIGGITY DOGG THE DOG WHO LIKES FALAFEL & MR. DOCTOR, JR. & MUGGI
THERE'S NOT ENOUGH ROOM FOR ALL OF US!
THIS IS WHY COMICS HAVE TWO TITLE CHARACTERS, TOPS!
PERCIVAL DUNWOODY, IDIOT TIME TRAVELER FROM 1909
NOW TO SAVE THE TITANIC!
SHALL WE WARN THE CAPTAIN ABOUT ICEBERGS?
NO NEED. I'VE TIME-TRAVELED US ALL TO SAFETY-- IN 1937, LAKEHURST, NJ.
NO!
TITANIC
MARCUS TRAILLE, INTERNATIONAL WOODLANDS DETECTIVE
GREAT SCOTT! A DEAD BODY!
THIS SQUIRREL'S BEEN MURDERED!
NOBODY LEAVE THIS FOREST!
I'LL WANT TO QUESTION ALL OF YOU!
I'LL NEED A LIST OF EVERY COMPETITIVE ORGANISM IN ITS ECOLOGICAL NICHE!
WHAT'S THIS? ONE OF THE MAGGOTS ON THE CARCASS --DEAD!
THERE IS A KILLER ON THE LOOSE, AND HE... OR SHE... IS PLAYING ME FOR A FOOL!
NEXT— THE MURDERED MAGGOT'S LAST WILL AND TESTAMENT REVEALED!!

2/4/13

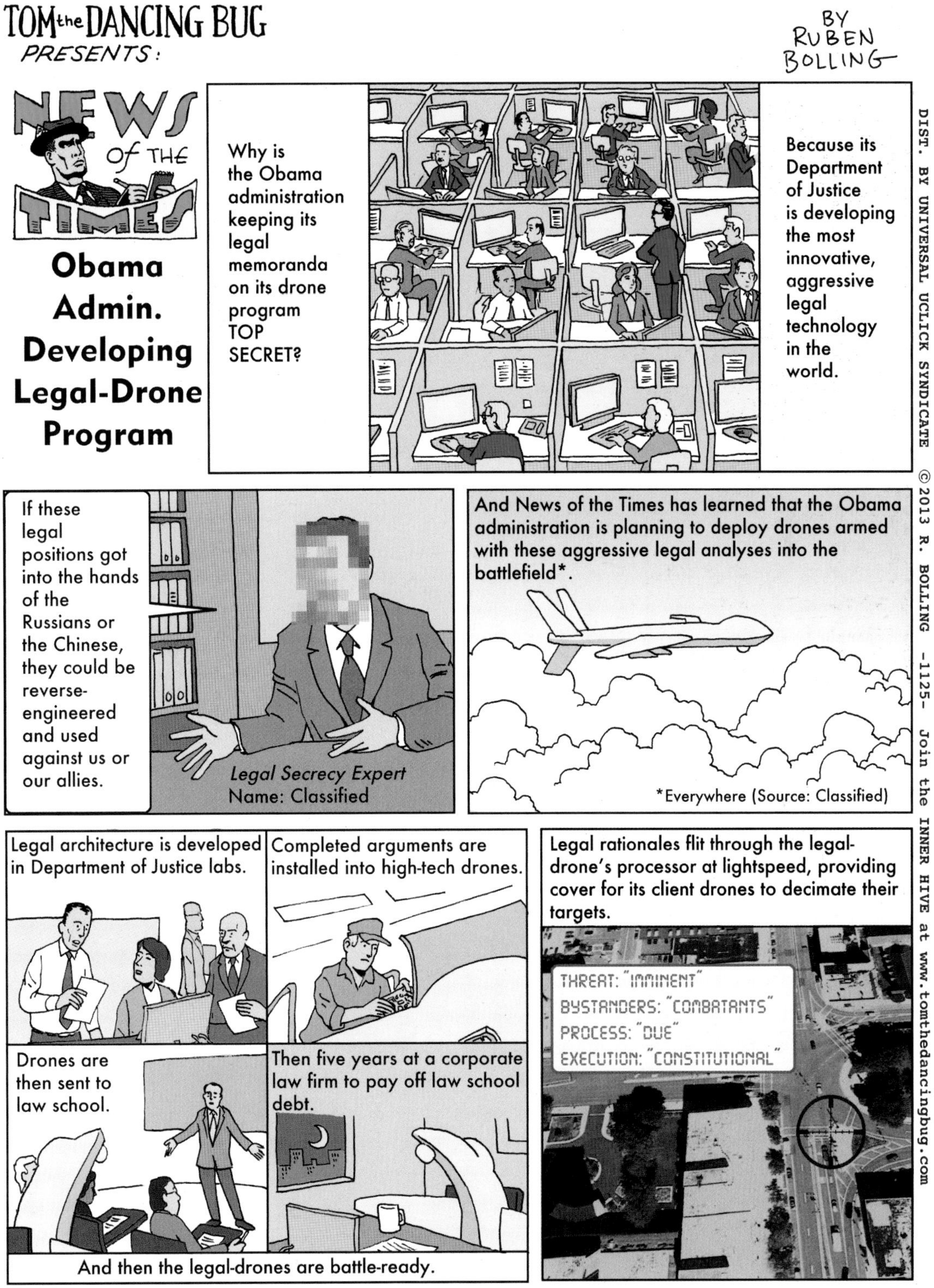
TOM the DANCING BUG PRESENTS:
BY RUBEN BOLLING
NEWS of THE TIMES
Obama Admin. Developing Legal-Drone Program
Why is the Obama administration keeping its legal memoranda on its drone program TOP SECRET?
Because its Department of Justice is developing the most innovative, aggressive legal technology in the world.
If these legal positions got into the hands of the Russians or the Chinese, they could be reverse-engineered and used against us or our allies.
Legal Secrecy Expert
Name: Classified
And News of the Times has learned that the Obama administration is planning to deploy drones armed with these aggressive legal analyses into the battlefield*.
*Everywhere (Source: Classified)
Legal architecture is developed in Department of Justice labs.
Completed arguments are installed into high-tech drones.
Drones are then sent to law school.
Then five years at a corporate law firm to pay off law school debt.
And then the legal-drones are battle-ready.
Legal rationales flit through the legal-drone's processor at lightspeed, providing cover for its client drones to decimate their targets.
THREAT: "IMMINENT"
BYSTANDERS: "COMBATANTS"
PROCESS: "DUE"
EXECUTION: "CONSTITUTIONAL"
DIST. BY UNIVERSAL UCLICK SYNDICATE © 2013 R. BOLLING -1125- Join the INNER HIVE at www.tomthedancingbug.com

2/11/13

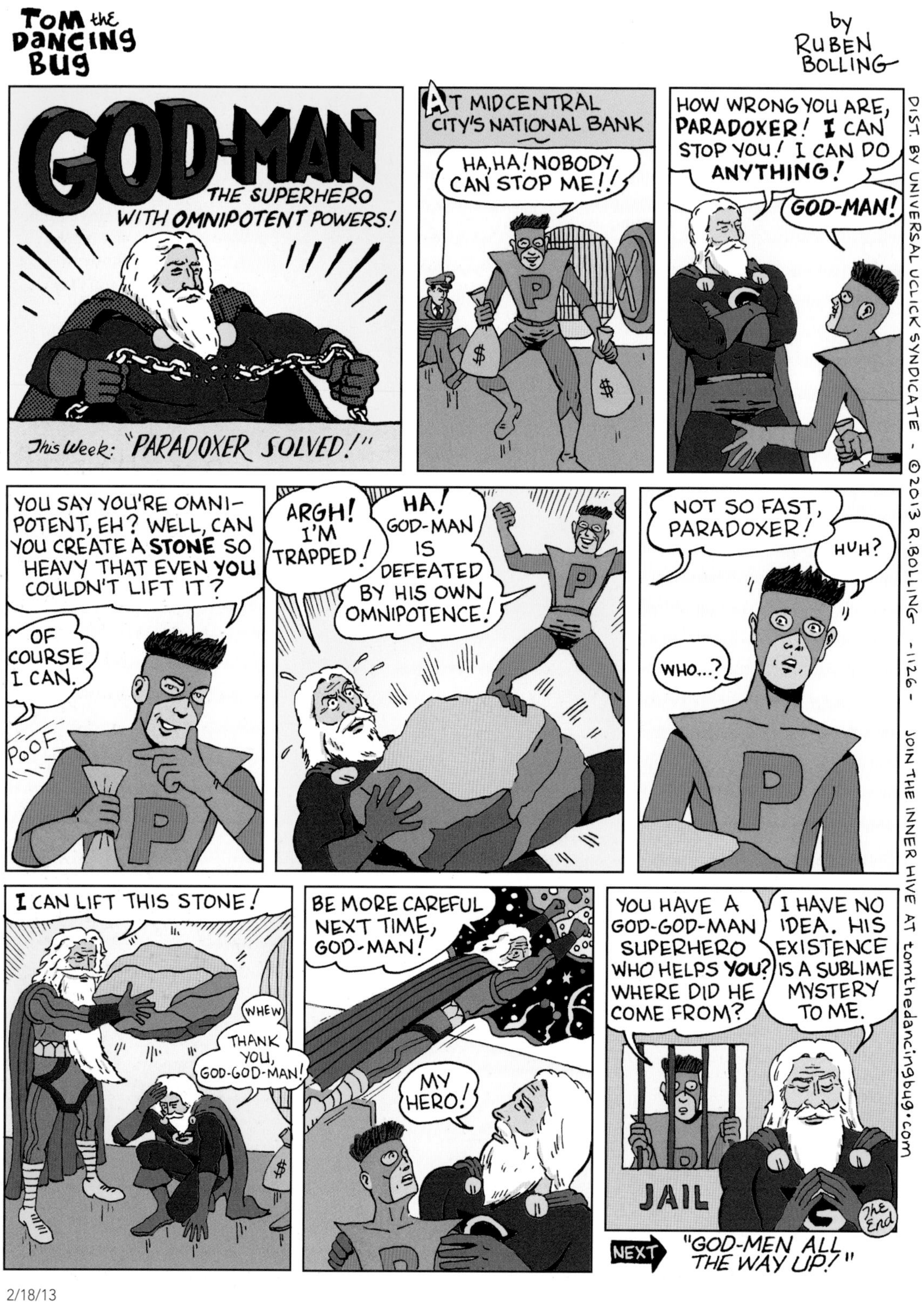
TOM the DANCING BUG
by RUBEN BOLLING
GOD-MAN
THE SUPERHERO WITH OMNIPOTENT POWERS!
This Week: "PARADOXER SOLVED!"
AT MIDCENTRAL CITY'S NATIONAL BANK
HA, HA! NOBODY CAN STOP ME!!
HOW WRONG YOU ARE, PARADOXER! I CAN STOP YOU! I CAN DO ANYTHING!
GOD-MAN!
DIST. BY UNIVERSAL UCLICK SYNDICATE - ©2013 R. BOLLING - 1126 - JOIN THE INNER HIVE AT tomthedancingbug.com
YOU SAY YOU'RE OMNIPOTENT, EH? WELL, CAN YOU CREATE A STONE SO HEAVY THAT EVEN YOU COULDN'T LIFT IT?
OF COURSE I CAN.
POOF
ARGH! I'M TRAPPED!
HA! GOD-MAN IS DEFEATED BY HIS OWN OMNIPOTENCE!
NOT SO FAST, PARADOXER!
HUH?
WHO...?
I CAN LIFT THIS STONE!
WHEW
THANK YOU, GOD-GOD-MAN!
BE MORE CAREFUL NEXT TIME, GOD-MAN!
MY HERO!
YOU HAVE A GOD-GOD-MAN SUPERHERO WHO HELPS YOU? WHERE DID HE COME FROM?
I HAVE NO IDEA. HIS EXISTENCE IS A SUBLIME MYSTERY TO ME.
JAIL
The End
NEXT "GOD-MEN ALL THE WAY UP!"

2/18/13

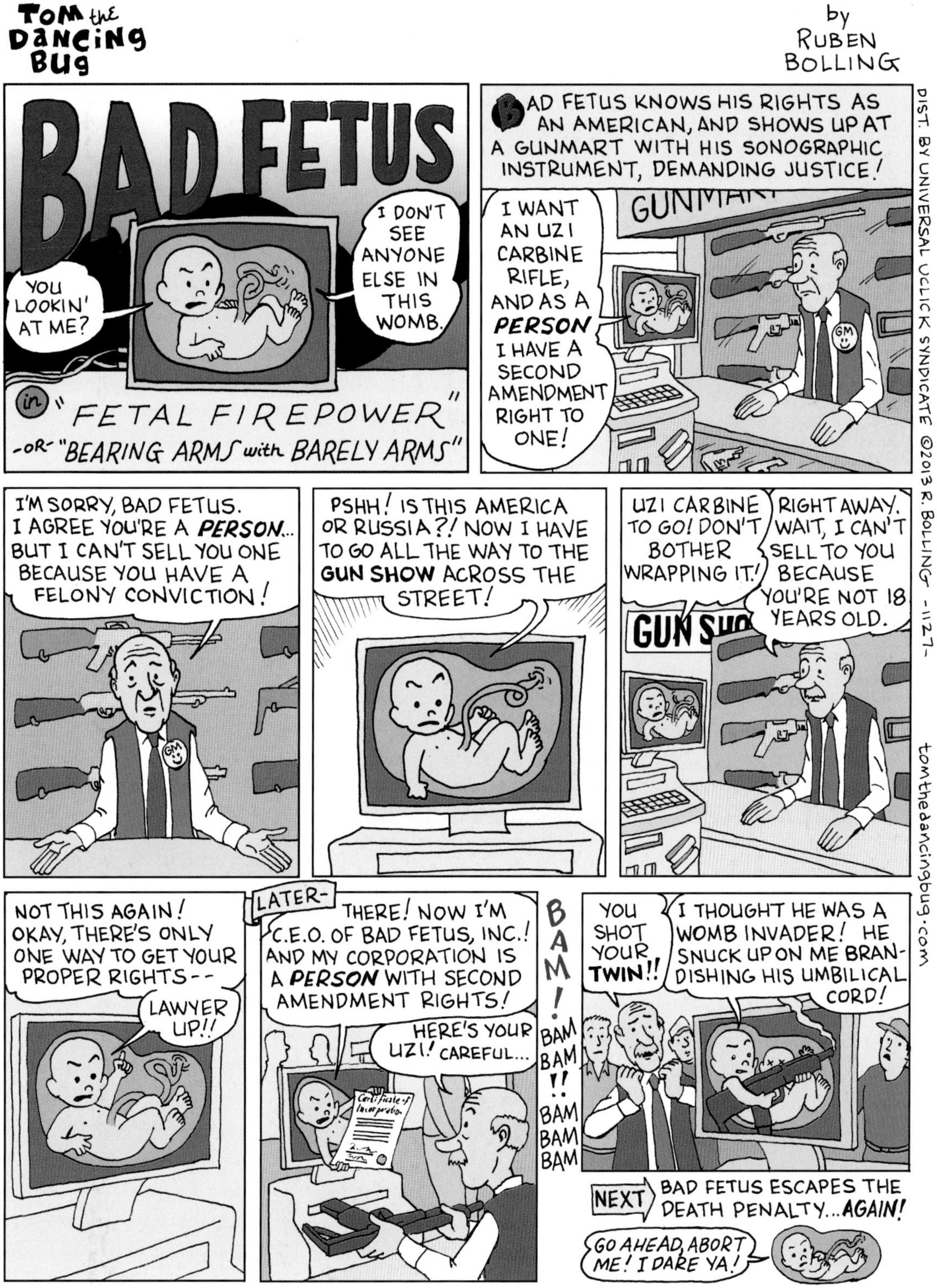

TOM the DANCING BUG
by RUBEN BOLLING
BAD FETUS
YOU LOOKIN' AT ME?
I DON'T SEE ANYONE ELSE IN THIS WOMB.
in "FETAL FIREPOWER" -OR- "BEARING ARMS with BARELY ARMS"
BAD FETUS KNOWS HIS RIGHTS AS AN AMERICAN, AND SHOWS UP AT A GUNMART WITH HIS SONOGRAPHIC INSTRUMENT, DEMANDING JUSTICE!
I WANT AN UZI CARBINE RIFLE, AND AS A PERSON I HAVE A SECOND AMENDMENT RIGHT TO ONE!
I'M SORRY, BAD FETUS. I AGREE YOU'RE A PERSON... BUT I CAN'T SELL YOU ONE BECAUSE YOU HAVE A FELONY CONVICTION!
PSHH! IS THIS AMERICA OR RUSSIA?! NOW I HAVE TO GO ALL THE WAY TO THE GUN SHOW ACROSS THE STREET!
UZI CARBINE TO GO! DON'T BOTHER WRAPPING IT!
RIGHT AWAY. WAIT, I CAN'T SELL TO YOU BECAUSE YOU'RE NOT 18 YEARS OLD.
NOT THIS AGAIN! OKAY, THERE'S ONLY ONE WAY TO GET YOUR PROPER RIGHTS--
LAWYER UP!!
LATER-
THERE! NOW I'M C.E.O. OF BAD FETUS, INC.! AND MY CORPORATION IS A PERSON WITH SECOND AMENDMENT RIGHTS!
Certificate of Incorporation
HERE'S YOUR UZI! CAREFUL...
BAM! BAM BAM!! BAM BAM BAM
YOU SHOT YOUR TWIN!!
I THOUGHT HE WAS A WOMB INVADER! HE SNUCK UP ON ME BRANDISHING HIS UMBILICAL CORD!
NEXT BAD FETUS ESCAPES THE DEATH PENALTY...AGAIN!
GO AHEAD, ABORT ME! I DARE YA!
DIST. BY UNIVERSAL UCLICK SYNDICATE ©2013 R. BOLLING -1127-
tomthedancingbug.com

2/25/13

Tom the Dancing Bug

by Ruben Bolling

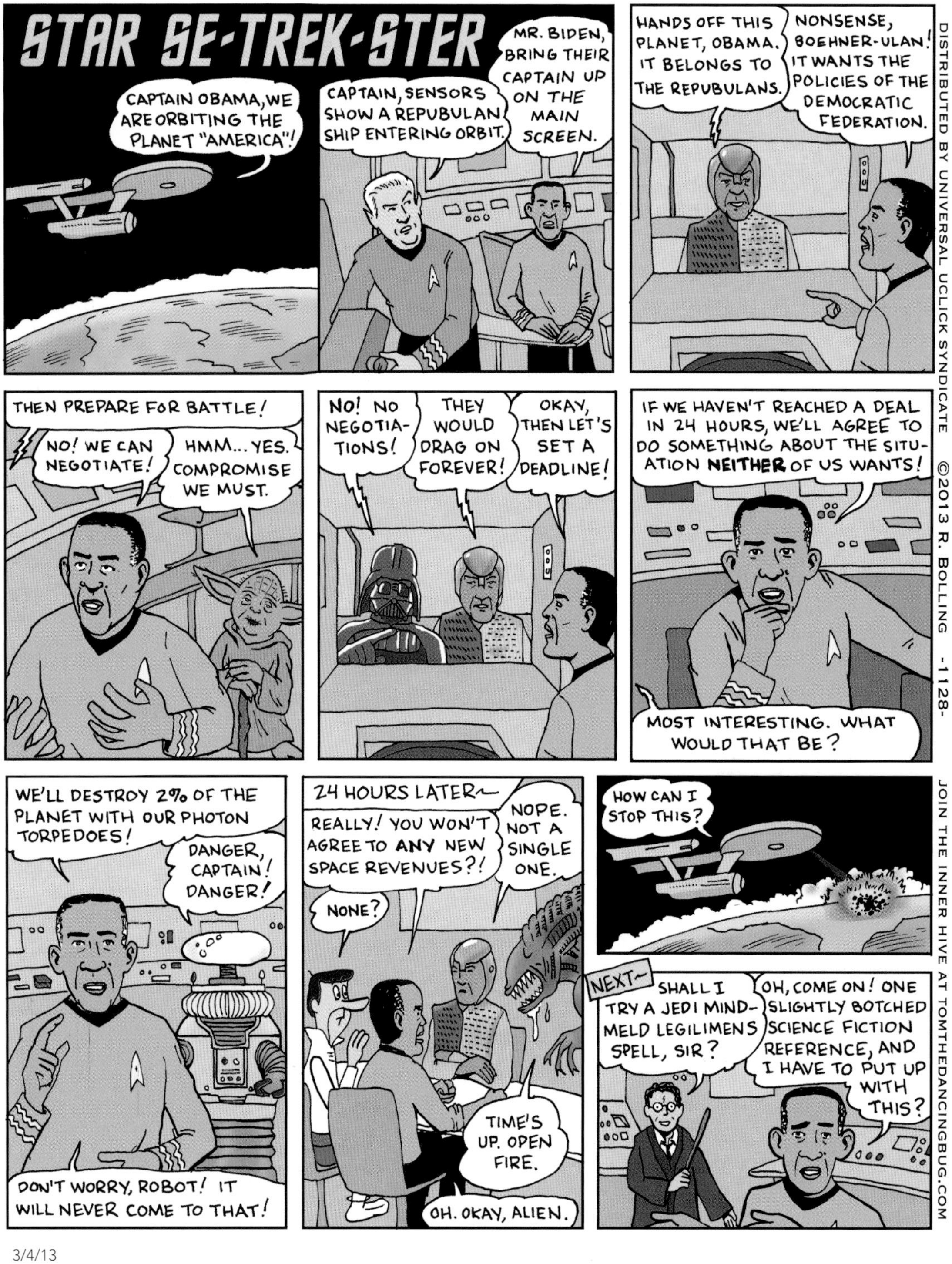
STAR SE-TREK-STER
CAPTAIN OBAMA, WE ARE ORBITING THE PLANET "AMERICA"!
CAPTAIN, SENSORS SHOW A REPUBULAN SHIP ENTERING ORBIT.
MR. BIDEN, BRING THEIR CAPTAIN UP ON THE MAIN SCREEN.
HANDS OFF THIS PLANET, OBAMA. IT BELONGS TO THE REPUBULANS.
NONSENSE, BOEHNER-ULAN! IT WANTS THE POLICIES OF THE DEMOCRATIC FEDERATION.
THEN PREPARE FOR BATTLE!
NO! WE CAN NEGOTIATE!
HMM... YES. COMPROMISE WE MUST.
NO! NO NEGOTIA-TIONS!
THEY WOULD DRAG ON FOREVER!
OKAY, THEN LET'S SET A DEADLINE!
IF WE HAVEN'T REACHED A DEAL IN 24 HOURS, WE'LL AGREE TO DO SOMETHING ABOUT THE SITU-ATION NEITHER OF US WANTS!
MOST INTERESTING. WHAT WOULD THAT BE?
WE'LL DESTROY 2% OF THE PLANET WITH OUR PHOTON TORPEDOES!
DANGER, CAPTAIN! DANGER!
DON'T WORRY, ROBOT! IT WILL NEVER COME TO THAT!
24 HOURS LATER~
REALLY! YOU WON'T AGREE TO ANY NEW SPACE REVENUES?!
NOPE. NOT A SINGLE ONE.
NONE?
TIME'S UP. OPEN FIRE.
OH. OKAY, ALIEN.
HOW CAN I STOP THIS?
NEXT~
SHALL I TRY A JEDI MIND-MELD LEGILIMENS SPELL, SIR?
OH, COME ON! ONE SLIGHTLY BOTCHED SCIENCE FICTION REFERENCE, AND I HAVE TO PUT UP WITH THIS?
DISTRIBUTED BY UNIVERSAL UCLICK SYNDICATE ©2013 R. BOLLING -1128-
JOIN THE INNER HIVE AT TOMTHEDANCINGBUG.COM

3/4/13

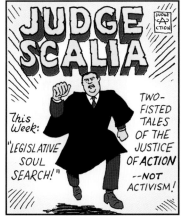

TOM the DANCING BUG
by RUBEN BOLLING
JUDGE SCALIA
JUDGE ACTION
This Week: "LEGISLATIVE SOUL SEARCH!"
TWO-FISTED TALES OF THE JUSTICE OF ACTION --NOT ACTIVISM!
JUDGE SCALIA ARRIVES AS THE JUSTICES DISCUSS A CASE-
MAYBE WE SHOULD LOOK AT THE HISTORY OF HOW THE LAW WAS PASSED...
CRASH
JUDGE SCALIA!
FOOL! LEGISLATIVE HISTORY HAS NO PLACE IN JUDICIAL REVIEW! WE INTERPRET THE WORDS OF THE STATUTE!!
POW
B-BUT WE'RE DECIDING WHETHER TO STRIKE DOWN THE VOTING RIGHTS ACT!
AH, A "RACIAL ENTITLEMENT"? THAT'S TOTALLY DIFFERENT!
SO WE SHOULD REVIEW THE DEBATES AND WRITINGS OF CONGRESS?
MORE THAN THAT, YOU BUFFOON! THE PROCESS HAS BEGUN.
THE ETHEREAL FORM OF JUDGE SCALIA LEAVES HIS BODY AND GOES ON AN EXCURSION INTO THE PSYCHIC DIMENSION.
HE ENTERS THE VERY SOULS OF THOSE SENATORS WHO VOTED 98-0 TO RENEW THE VOTING RIGHTS ACT IN 2006.
HE'S BACK!
WE MUST STRIKE DOWN THE VOTING RIGHTS ACT! CONGRESS ONLY RENEWED IT BECAUSE THEY FEARED VOTER FALLOUT IF THEY OPPOSED IT!
SO THE POLITICAL PROCESS WAS TAINTED... BY POLITICS?
PRECISELY! AND THAT'S WHEN THE COURT MUST STEP IN AND RIGHT THAT WRONG!!
THE END
DIST. BY UNIVERSAL UCLICK SYNDICATE ©2013 R. BOLLING —— -1129- JOIN THE INNER HIVE AT tomthedancingbug.com
JUDGE SCALIA ON JUDGING:
WHAT IS THE SUPREME COURT'S ROLE IF NOT TO PROTECT THE MINORITY?
OF COURSE, BY "MINORITY," I MEAN THAT MINORITY OF STATES WITH HISTORIES OF VOTER SUPPRESSION.

3/11/13

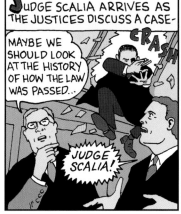

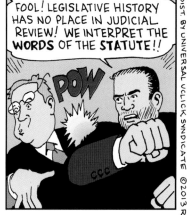

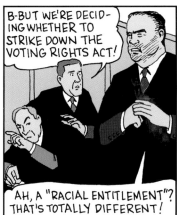

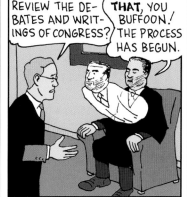

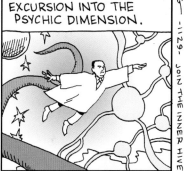

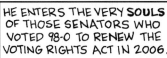

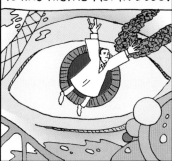

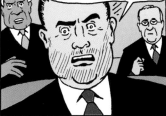

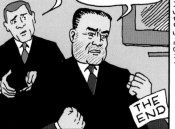

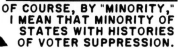

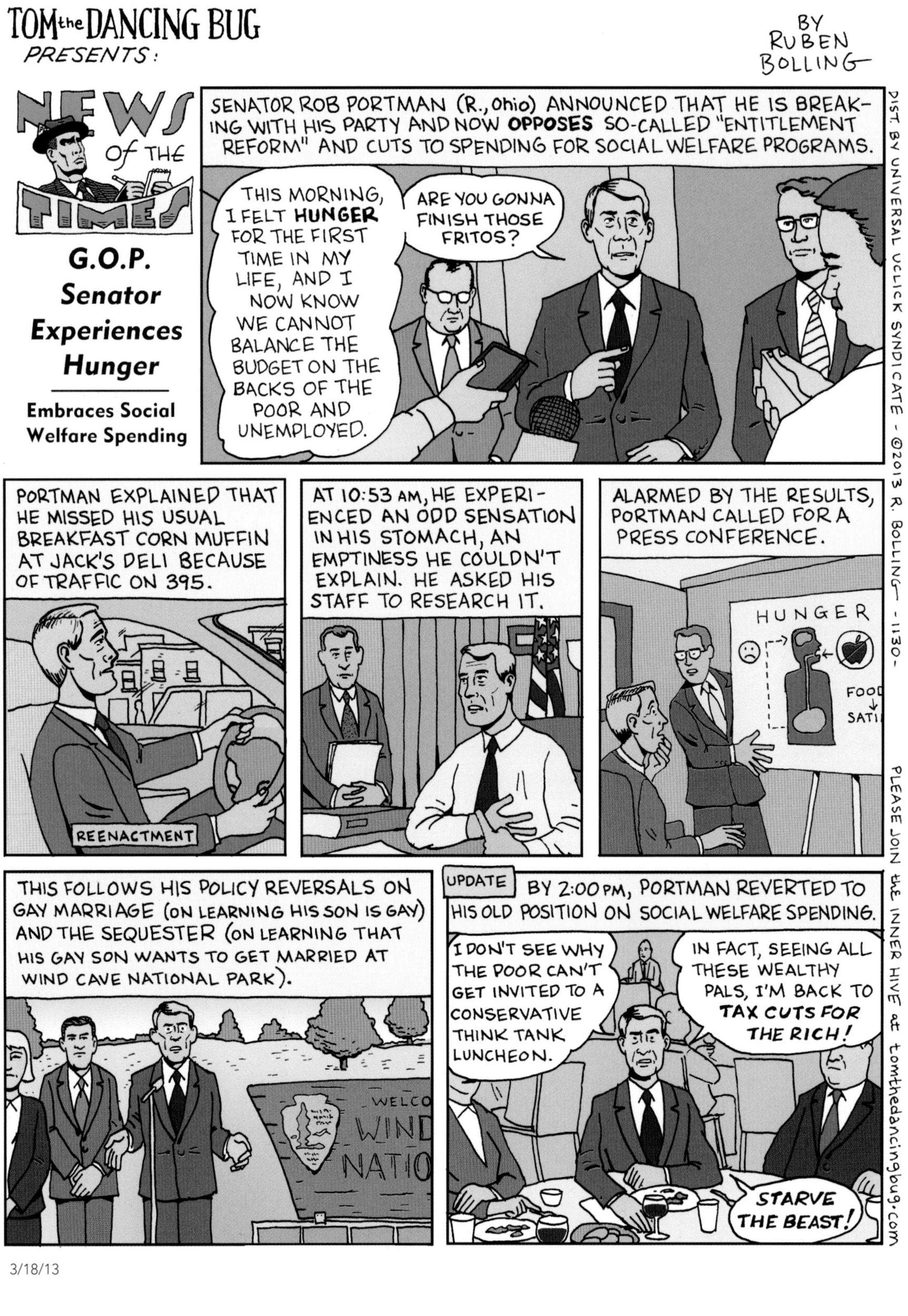
TOM the DANCING BUG
PRESENTS:
BY RUBEN BOLLING
NEWS of THE TIMES
G.O.P. Senator Experiences Hunger
Embraces Social Welfare Spending
SENATOR ROB PORTMAN (R., Ohio) ANNOUNCED THAT HE IS BREAKING WITH HIS PARTY AND NOW OPPOSES SO-CALLED "ENTITLEMENT REFORM" AND CUTS TO SPENDING FOR SOCIAL WELFARE PROGRAMS.
THIS MORNING, I FELT HUNGER FOR THE FIRST TIME IN MY LIFE, AND I NOW KNOW WE CANNOT BALANCE THE BUDGET ON THE BACKS OF THE POOR AND UNEMPLOYED.
ARE YOU GONNA FINISH THOSE FRITOS?
PORTMAN EXPLAINED THAT HE MISSED HIS USUAL BREAKFAST CORN MUFFIN AT JACK'S DELI BECAUSE OF TRAFFIC ON 395.
REENACTMENT
AT 10:53 AM, HE EXPERIENCED AN ODD SENSATION IN HIS STOMACH, AN EMPTINESS HE COULDN'T EXPLAIN. HE ASKED HIS STAFF TO RESEARCH IT.
ALARMED BY THE RESULTS, PORTMAN CALLED FOR A PRESS CONFERENCE.
HUNGER
FOOD
SATI
THIS FOLLOWS HIS POLICY REVERSALS ON GAY MARRIAGE (ON LEARNING HIS SON IS GAY) AND THE SEQUESTER (ON LEARNING THAT HIS GAY SON WANTS TO GET MARRIED AT WIND CAVE NATIONAL PARK).
WELCO
WIND
NATIO
UPDATE
BY 2:00 PM, PORTMAN REVERTED TO HIS OLD POSITION ON SOCIAL WELFARE SPENDING.
I DON'T SEE WHY THE POOR CAN'T GET INVITED TO A CONSERVATIVE THINK TANK LUNCHEON.
IN FACT, SEEING ALL THESE WEALTHY PALS, I'M BACK TO TAX CUTS FOR THE RICH!
STARVE THE BEAST!
DIST BY UNIVERSAL UCLICK SYNDICATE - ©2013 R. BOLLING - 1130-
PLEASE JOIN the INNER HIVE at tomthedancingbug.com

3/18/13

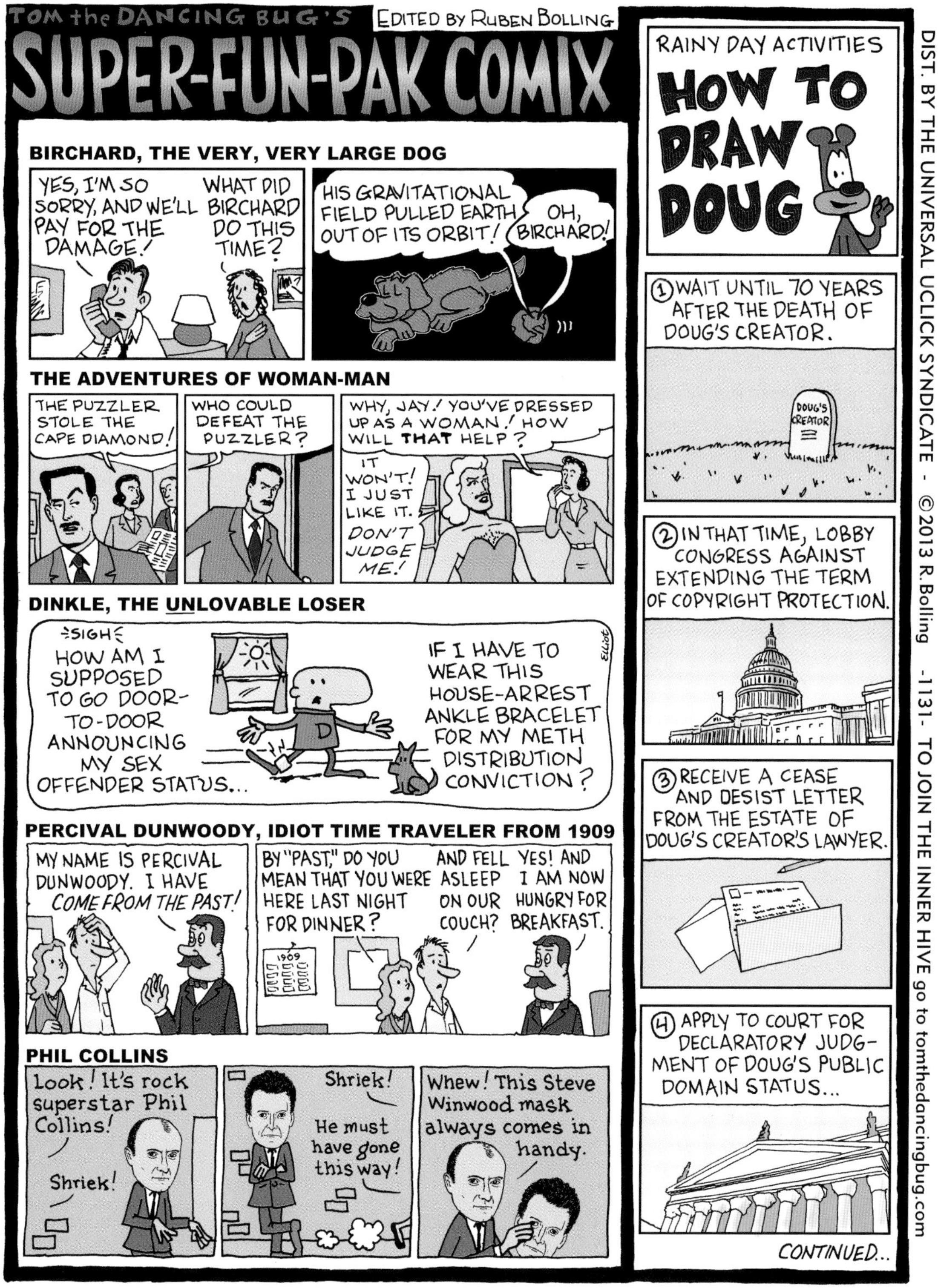
TOM the DANCING BUG'S
EDITED BY RUBEN BOLLING
SUPER-FUN-PAK COMIX
BIRCHARD, THE VERY, VERY LARGE DOG
YES, I'M SO SORRY, AND WE'LL PAY FOR THE DAMAGE!
WHAT DID BIRCHARD DO THIS TIME?
HIS GRAVITATIONAL FIELD PULLED EARTH OUT OF ITS ORBIT!
OH, BIRCHARD!
THE ADVENTURES OF WOMAN-MAN
THE PUZZLER STOLE THE CAPE DIAMOND!
WHO COULD DEFEAT THE PUZZLER?
WHY, JAY! YOU'VE DRESSED UP AS A WOMAN! HOW WILL THAT HELP?
IT WON'T! I JUST LIKE IT. DON'T JUDGE ME!
DINKLE, THE UNLOVABLE LOSER
SIGH
HOW AM I SUPPOSED TO GO DOOR-TO-DOOR ANNOUNCING MY SEX OFFENDER STATUS...
IF I HAVE TO WEAR THIS HOUSE-ARREST ANKLE BRACELET FOR MY METH DISTRIBUTION CONVICTION?
PERCIVAL DUNWOODY, IDIOT TIME TRAVELER FROM 1909
MY NAME IS PERCIVAL DUNWOODY. I HAVE COME FROM THE PAST!
BY "PAST," DO YOU MEAN THAT YOU WERE HERE LAST NIGHT FOR DINNER?
AND FELL ASLEEP ON OUR COUCH?
YES! AND I AM NOW HUNGRY FOR BREAKFAST.
1909
PHIL COLLINS
Look! It's rock superstar Phil Collins!
Shriek!
Shriek!
He must have gone this way!
Whew! This Steve Winwood mask always comes in handy.
RAINY DAY ACTIVITIES
HOW TO DRAW DOUG
1 WAIT UNTIL 70 YEARS AFTER THE DEATH OF DOUG'S CREATOR.
DOUG'S CREATOR
2 IN THAT TIME, LOBBY CONGRESS AGAINST EXTENDING THE TERM OF COPYRIGHT PROTECTION.
3 RECEIVE A CEASE AND DESIST LETTER FROM THE ESTATE OF DOUG'S CREATOR'S LAWYER.
4 APPLY TO COURT FOR DECLARATORY JUDGMENT OF DOUG'S PUBLIC DOMAIN STATUS...
CONTINUED...
DIST. BY THE UNIVERSAL UCLICK SYNDICATE - © 2013 R.Bolling -1131- TO JOIN THE INNER HIVE go to tomthedancingbug.com

3/25/13

TOM the DANCING BUG

The Education of Louis.

BY RUBEN BOLLING

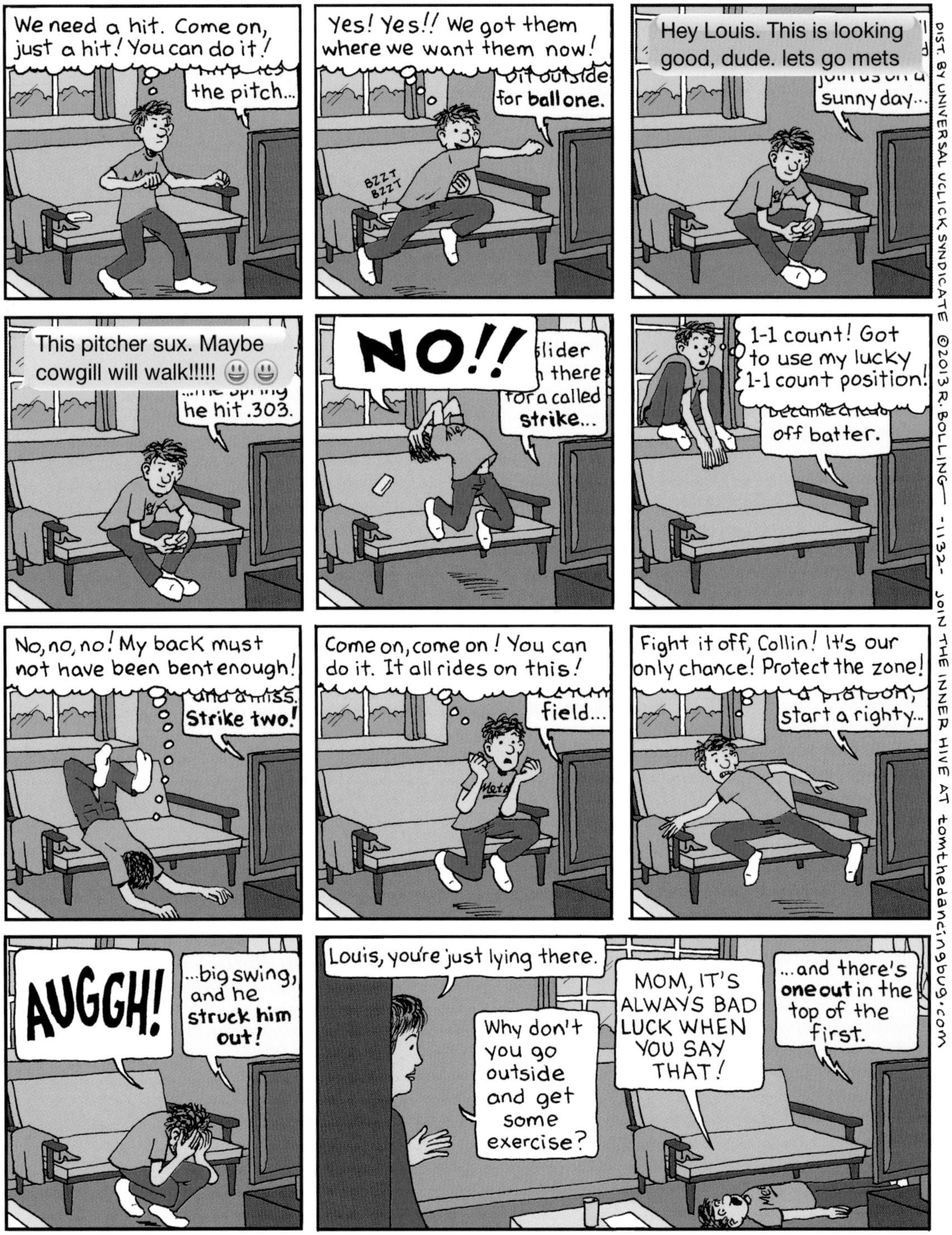

We need a hit. Come on, just a hit! You can do it!
the pitch...
Yes! Yes!! We got them where we want them now!
BZZT BZZT
for ball one.
Hey Louis. This is looking good, dude. lets go mets
sunny day...
This pitcher sux. Maybe cowgill will walk!!!!! 😃😃
he hit .303.
NO!!
for a called strike...
1-1 count! Got to use my lucky 1-1 count position!
off batter.
No, no, no! My back must not have been bent enough!
Strike two!
Come on, come on! You can do it. It all rides on this!
field...
Fight it off, Collin! It's our only chance! Protect the zone!
start a righty...
AUGGH!
...big swing, and he struck him out!
Louis, you're just lying there.
Why don't you go outside and get some exercise?
MOM, IT'S ALWAYS BAD LUCK WHEN YOU SAY THAT!
...and there's one out in the top of the first.
DIST. BY UNIVERSAL UCLICK SYNDICATE ©2013 R. BOLLING —1132— JOIN THE INNER HIVE AT tomthedancingbug.com

4/1/13

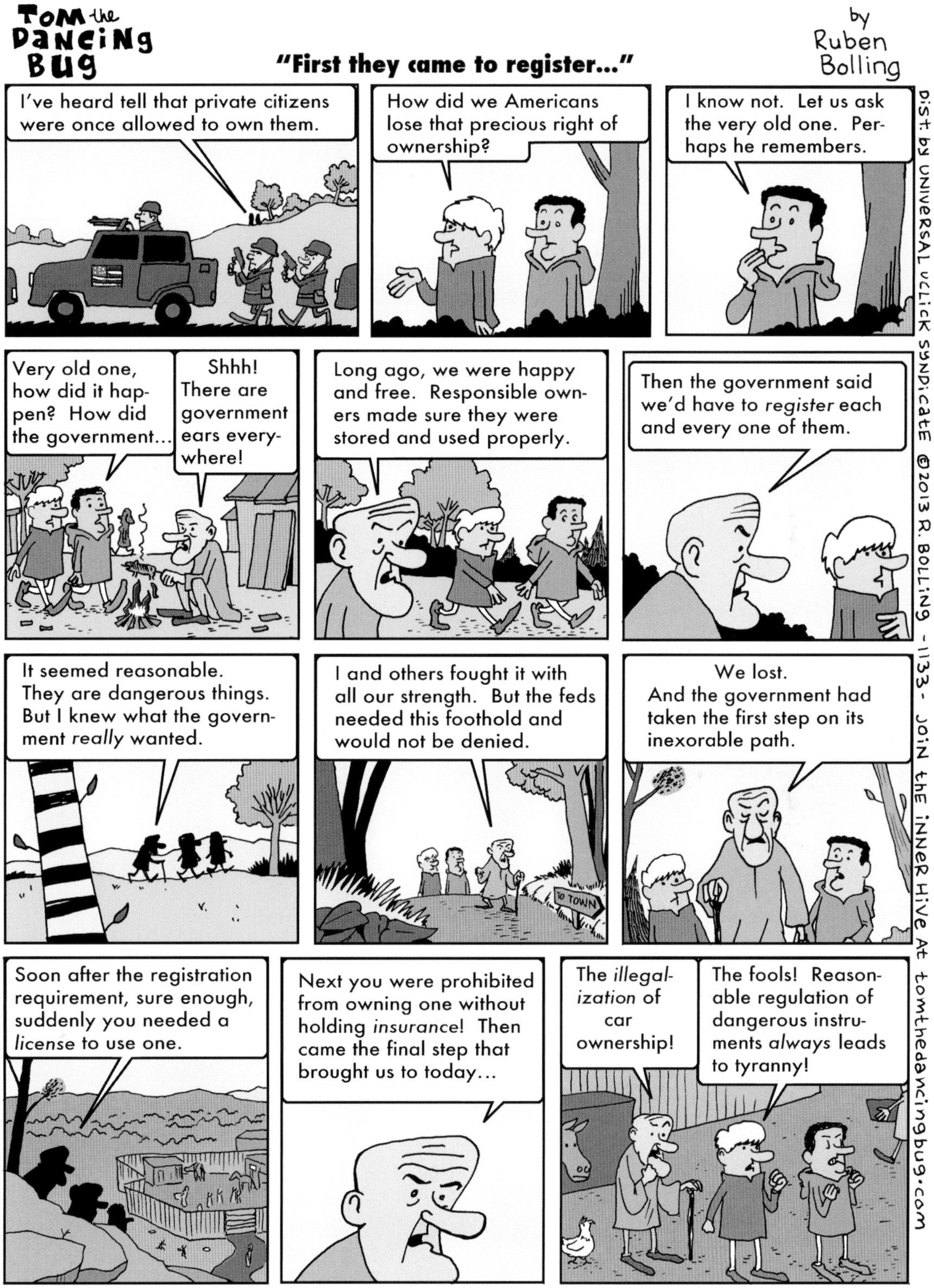

Tom the Dancing Bug
"First they came to register..."
by Ruben Bolling
I've heard tell that private citizens were once allowed to own them.
How did we Americans lose that precious right of ownership?
I know not. Let us ask the very old one. Perhaps he remembers.
Very old one, how did it happen? How did the government...
Shhh! There are government ears everywhere!
Long ago, we were happy and free. Responsible owners made sure they were stored and used properly.
Then the government said we'd have to *register* each and every one of them.
It seemed reasonable. They are dangerous things. But I knew what the government *really* wanted.
I and others fought it with all our strength. But the feds needed this foothold and would not be denied.
TO TOWN
We lost. And the government had taken the first step on its inexorable path.
Soon after the registration requirement, sure enough, suddenly you needed a *license* to use one.
Next you were prohibited from owning one without holding *insurance*! Then came the final step that brought us to today...
The *illegalization* of car ownership!
The fools! Reasonable regulation of dangerous instruments *always* leads to tyranny!
DIST. BY UNIVERSAL UCLICK SYNDICATE ©2013 R. BOLLING -1133- JOIN THE INNER HIVE AT tomthedancingbug.com

4/8/13

THE GREAT PHOTOSHOP WAR OF 2013
NORTH KOREA vs. U.S.A.

The U.S. intelligence community was shocked to find that this photo, released by North Korea, displays hovercrafts that have been cut and pasted using the computer program Photoshop.

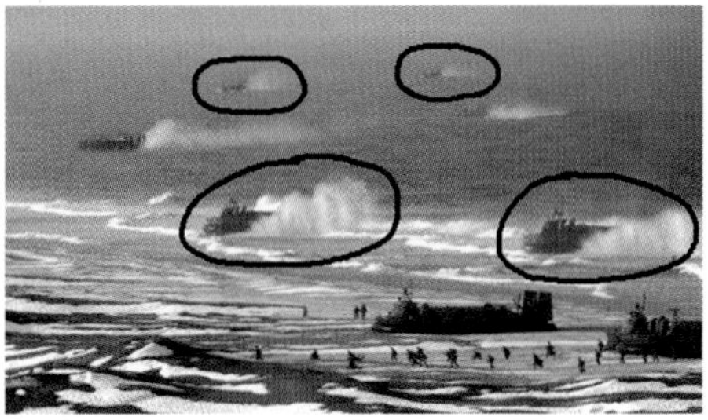

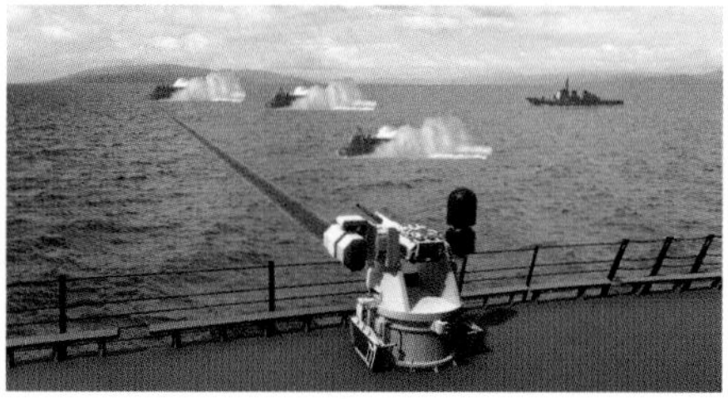

Alarmed that North Korea has attained militarized Photoshop technology, the U.S. military responded by creating this dazzling image of laser beams fired from a U.S. warship at the pixelated hovercrafts.

North Korea was ready. They countered with this horrifying image of Dennis Rodman riding a nuclear warhead across the Pacific.

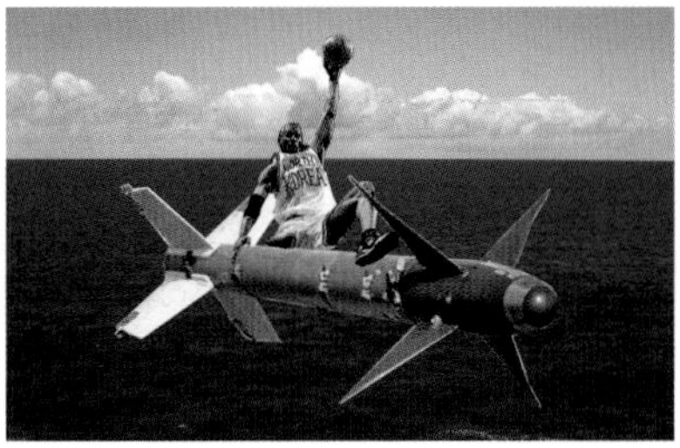

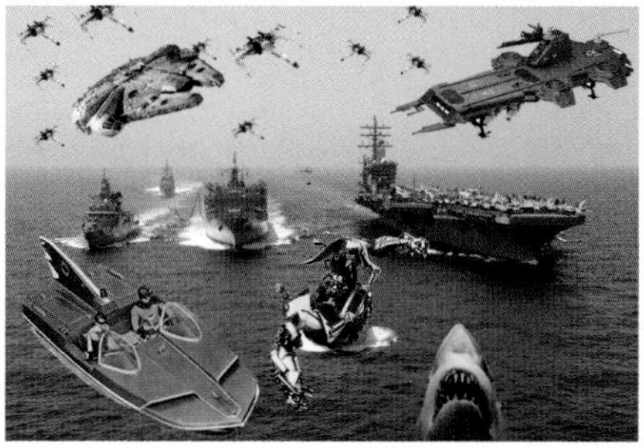

The U.S. was again (see Great Photoshop War of 2008 with Iran) forced to pull out all the stops in its digital arsenal, showcasing a fearsome display of weaponized Photoshop images.

Far from discouraging the North Koreans, this caused an escalation in graphic hostilities, as the Koreans released this monstrous image of its army marching through the streets of Austin, Texas.

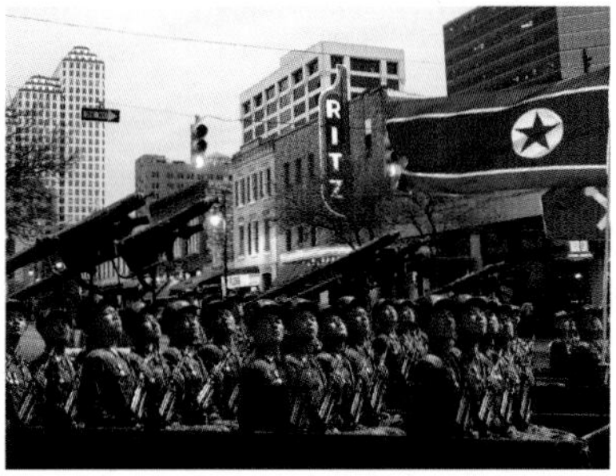
RITZ

U.S. victory was finally attained when an elite squad of the meanest ninth-grade girls was recruited, and created this photobomb, which so mortified North Korean Supreme Leader Kim Jong-un, he disappeared into his palace, deleted his Facebook account, and refused to answer any texts from his military officials.

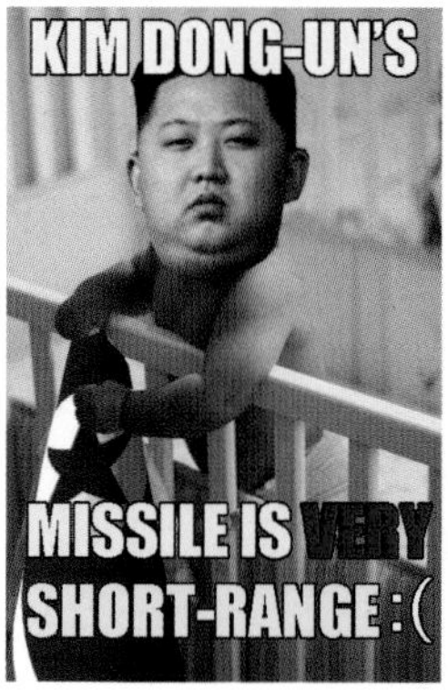
KIM DONG-UN'S
MISSILE IS VERY
SHORT-RANGE :(

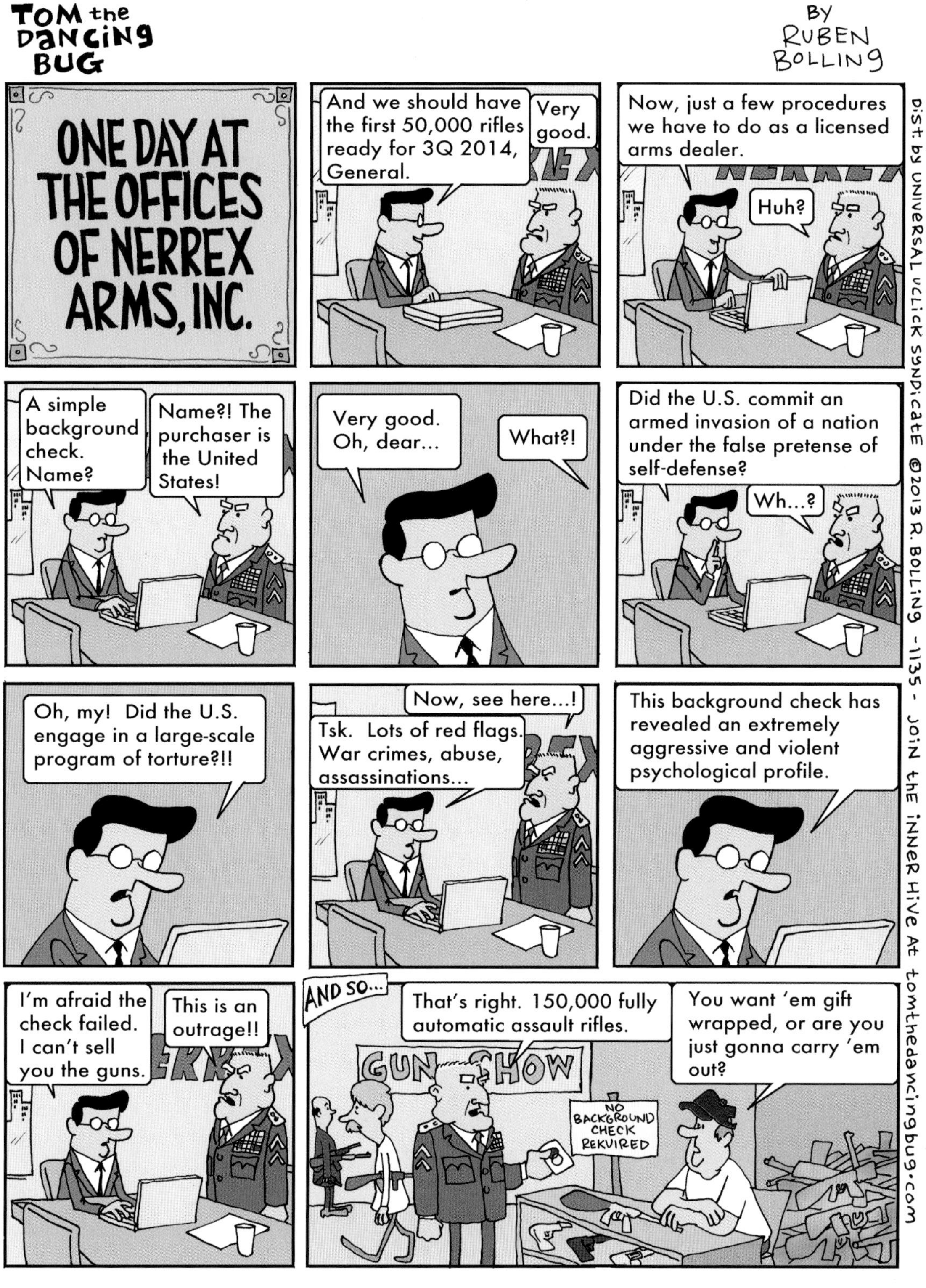

TOM the DANCING BUG
BY RUBEN BOLLING
ONE DAY AT THE OFFICES OF NERREX ARMS, INC.
And we should have the first 50,000 rifles ready for 3Q 2014, General.
Very good.
Now, just a few procedures we have to do as a licensed arms dealer.
Huh?
A simple background check. Name?
Name?! The purchaser is the United States!
Very good. Oh, dear...
What?!
Did the U.S. commit an armed invasion of a nation under the false pretense of self-defense?
Wh...?
Oh, my! Did the U.S. engage in a large-scale program of torture?!!
Now, see here...!
Tsk. Lots of red flags. War crimes, abuse, assassinations...
This background check has revealed an extremely aggressive and violent psychological profile.
I'm afraid the check failed. I can't sell you the guns.
This is an outrage!!
AND SO...
That's right. 150,000 fully automatic assault rifles.
You want 'em gift wrapped, or are you just gonna carry 'em out?
GUN SHOW
NO BACKGROUND CHECK REKUIRED
DIST BY UNIVERSAL UCLICK SYNDICATE ©2013 R. BOLLING -1135- JOIN THE INNER HIVE AT tomthedancingbug.com

4/22/13

TOM the DANCING BUG

by RUBEN BOLLING

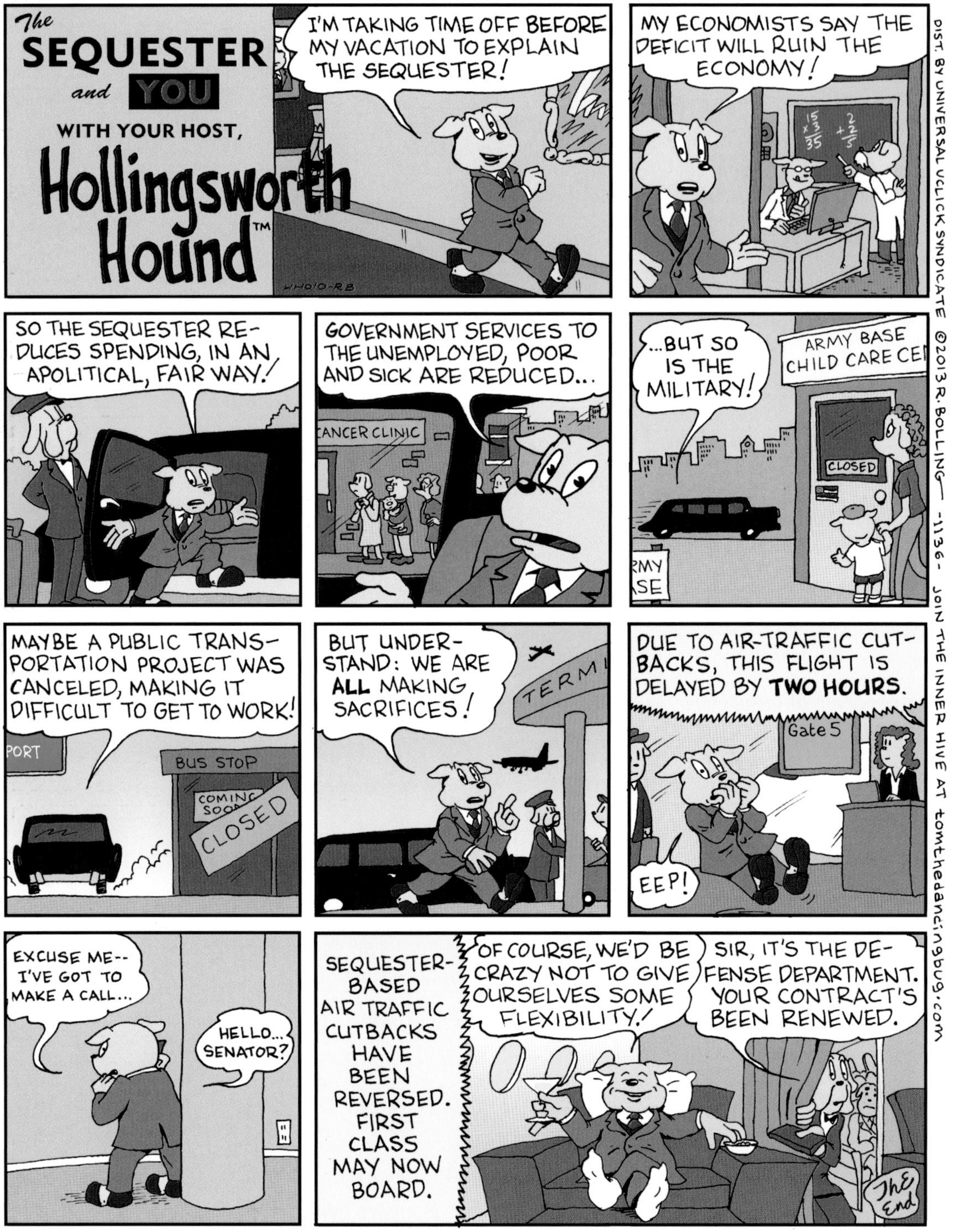

The SEQUESTER and YOU
WITH YOUR HOST, Hollingsworth Hound™
I'M TAKING TIME OFF BEFORE MY VACATION TO EXPLAIN THE SEQUESTER!
MY ECONOMISTS SAY THE DEFICIT WILL RUIN THE ECONOMY!
SO THE SEQUESTER REDUCES SPENDING, IN AN APOLITICAL, FAIR WAY!
GOVERNMENT SERVICES TO THE UNEMPLOYED, POOR AND SICK ARE REDUCED...
CANCER CLINIC
...BUT SO IS THE MILITARY!
ARMY BASE CHILD CARE CE
CLOSED
MAYBE A PUBLIC TRANSPORTATION PROJECT WAS CANCELED, MAKING IT DIFFICULT TO GET TO WORK!
BUS STOP
CLOSED
BUT UNDERSTAND: WE ARE ALL MAKING SACRIFICES!
DUE TO AIR-TRAFFIC CUTBACKS, THIS FLIGHT IS DELAYED BY TWO HOURS.
Gate 5
EEP!
EXCUSE ME-- I'VE GOT TO MAKE A CALL...
HELLO... SENATOR?
SEQUESTER-BASED AIR TRAFFIC CUTBACKS HAVE BEEN REVERSED. FIRST CLASS MAY NOW BOARD.
OF COURSE, WE'D BE CRAZY NOT TO GIVE OURSELVES SOME FLEXIBILITY!
SIR, IT'S THE DEFENSE DEPARTMENT. YOUR CONTRACT'S BEEN RENEWED.
THE End
DIST. BY UNIVERSAL UCLICK SYNDICATE ©2013 R. BOLLING -1136- JOIN THE INNER HIVE AT tomthedancingbug.com

4/29/13

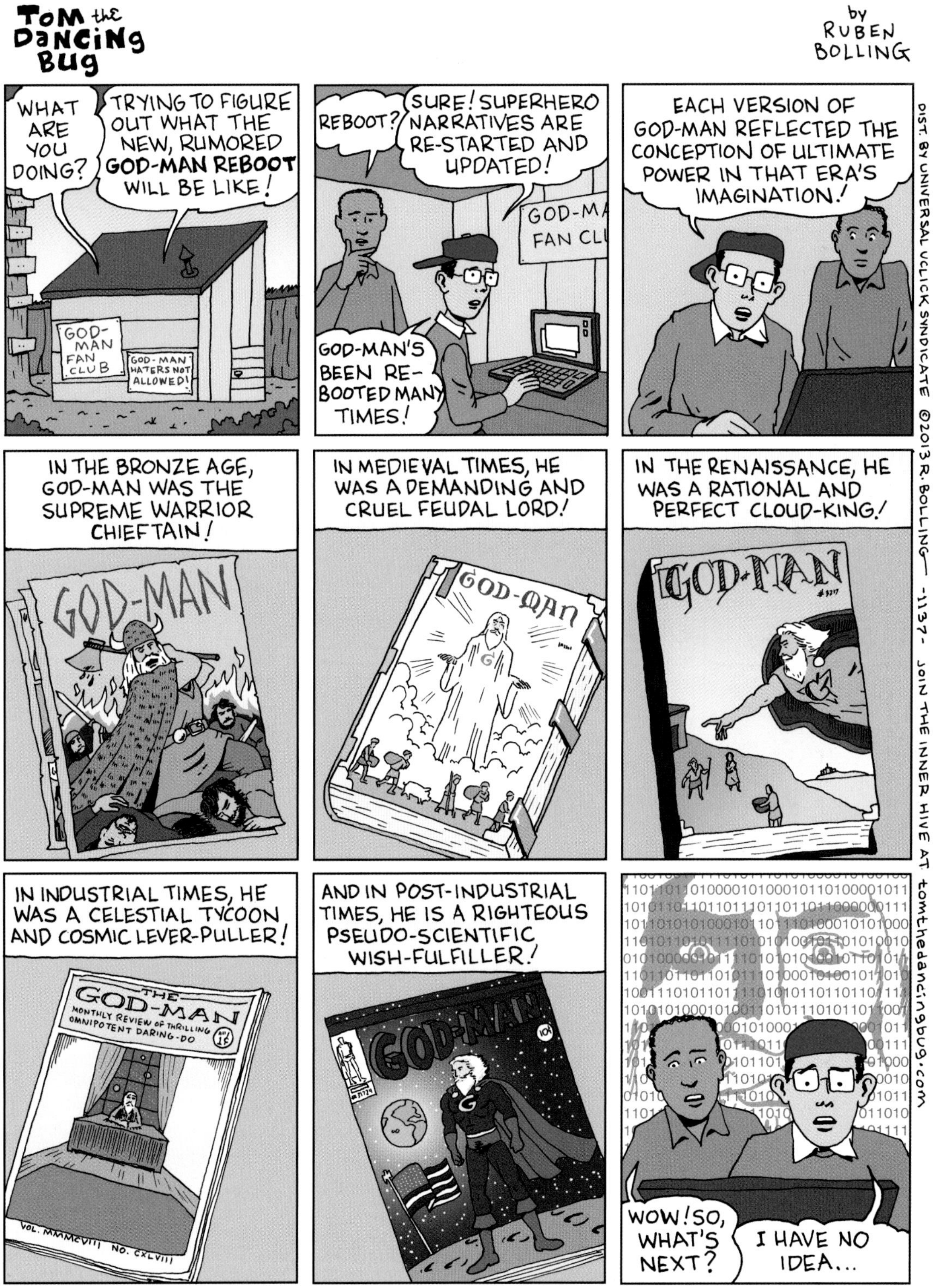

TOM the DANCING BUG
by RUBEN BOLLING
WHAT ARE YOU DOING?
TRYING TO FIGURE OUT WHAT THE NEW, RUMORED GOD-MAN REBOOT WILL BE LIKE!
GOD-MAN FAN CLUB
GOD-MAN HATERS NOT ALLOWED!
REBOOT?
SURE! SUPERHERO NARRATIVES ARE RE-STARTED AND UPDATED!
GOD-MAN'S BEEN RE-BOOTED MANY TIMES!
EACH VERSION OF GOD-MAN REFLECTED THE CONCEPTION OF ULTIMATE POWER IN THAT ERA'S IMAGINATION!
IN THE BRONZE AGE, GOD-MAN WAS THE SUPREME WARRIOR CHIEFTAIN!
GOD-MAN
IN MEDIEVAL TIMES, HE WAS A DEMANDING AND CRUEL FEUDAL LORD!
GOD-MAN
IN THE RENAISSANCE, HE WAS A RATIONAL AND PERFECT CLOUD-KING!
GOD-MAN
IN INDUSTRIAL TIMES, HE WAS A CELESTIAL TYCOON AND COSMIC LEVER-PULLER!
THE GOD-MAN
MONTHLY REVIEW OF THRILLING OMNIPOTENT DARING-DO
VOL. MMMCVIII NO. CXLVIII
AND IN POST-INDUSTRIAL TIMES, HE IS A RIGHTEOUS PSEUDO-SCIENTIFIC WISH-FULFILLER!
GOD-MAN
WOW! SO, WHAT'S NEXT?
I HAVE NO IDEA...
DIST. BY UNIVERSAL UCLICK SYNDICATE ©2013 R. BOLLING —1137— JOIN THE INNER HIVE AT: tomthedancingbug.com

5/6/13

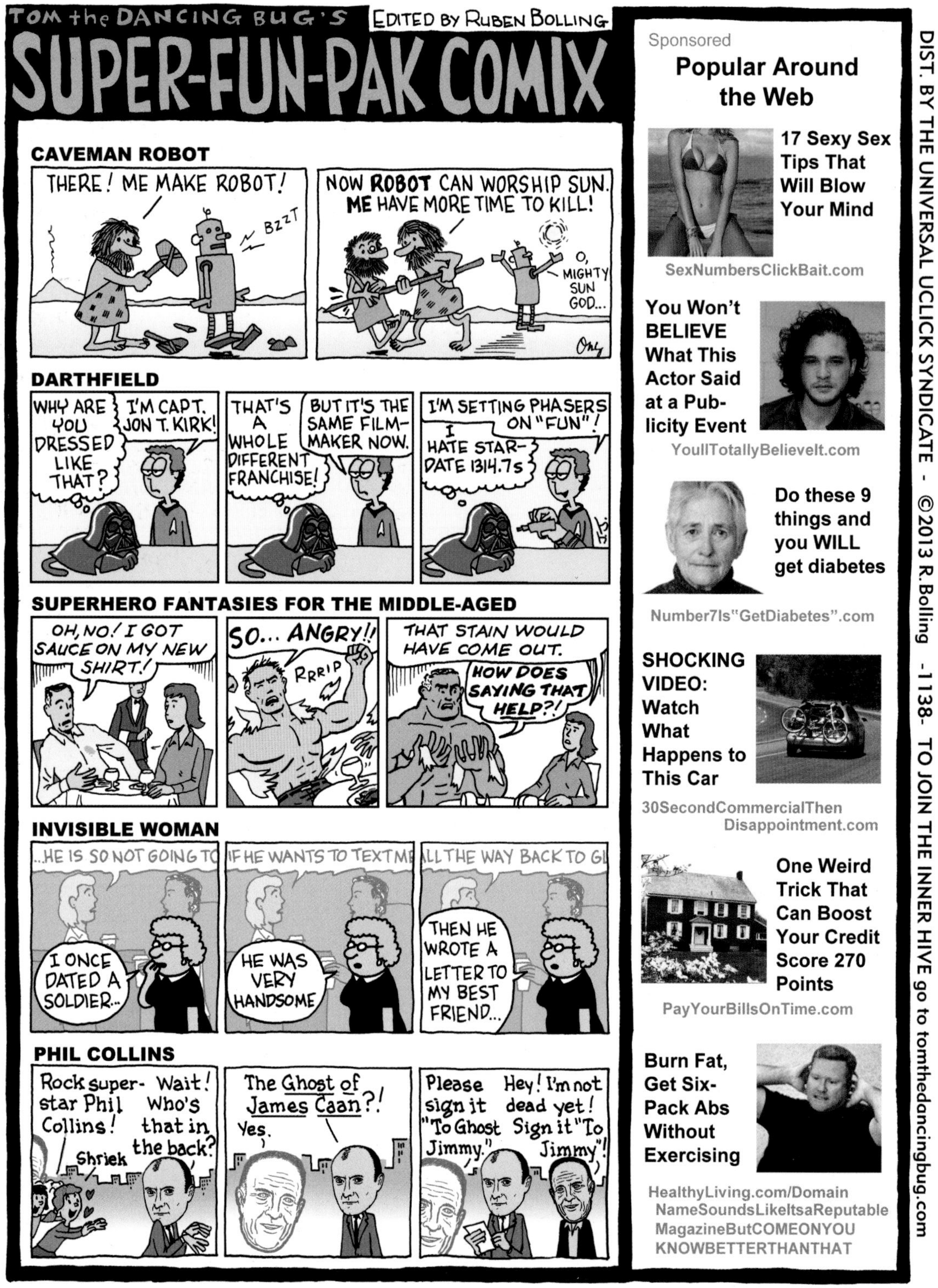
TOM the DANCING BUG'S
EDITED BY RUBEN BOLLING
SUPER-FUN-PAK COMIX
CAVEMAN ROBOT
THERE! ME MAKE ROBOT!
BZZT
NOW ROBOT CAN WORSHIP SUN. ME HAVE MORE TIME TO KILL!
O, MIGHTY SUN GOD...
DARTHFIELD
WHY ARE YOU DRESSED LIKE THAT?
I'M CAPT. JON T. KIRK!
THAT'S A WHOLE DIFFERENT FRANCHISE!
BUT IT'S THE SAME FILM-MAKER NOW.
I'M SETTING PHASERS ON "FUN"!
I HATE STAR-DATE 1314.7s
SUPERHERO FANTASIES FOR THE MIDDLE-AGED
OH, NO! I GOT SAUCE ON MY NEW SHIRT!
SO... ANGRY!!
RRRIP
THAT STAIN WOULD HAVE COME OUT.
HOW DOES SAYING THAT HELP?!
INVISIBLE WOMAN
...HE IS SO NOT GOING TO
I ONCE DATED A SOLDIER...
IF HE WANTS TO TEXT M
HE WAS VERY HANDSOME
ALL THE WAY BACK TO G
THEN HE WROTE A LETTER TO MY BEST FRIEND...
PHIL COLLINS
Rock super-star Phil Collins!
Shriek
Wait! Who's that in the back?
The Ghost of James Caan?!
Yes.
Please sign it "To Ghost Jimmy."
Hey! I'm not dead yet! Sign it "To Jimmy"!
Sponsored
Popular Around the Web
17 Sexy Sex Tips That Will Blow Your Mind
SexNumbersClickBait.com
You Won't BELIEVE What This Actor Said at a Pub-licity Event
YoullTotallyBelieveIt.com
Do these 9 things and you WILL get diabetes
Number7Is"GetDiabetes".com
SHOCKING VIDEO: Watch What Happens to This Car
30SecondCommercialThen Disappointment.com
One Weird Trick That Can Boost Your Credit Score 270 Points
PayYourBillsOnTime.com
Burn Fat, Get Six-Pack Abs Without Exercising
HealthyLiving.com/Domain NameSoundsLikeItsaReputable MagazineButCOMEONYOU KNOWBETTERTHANTHAT
DIST. BY THE UNIVERSAL UCLICK SYNDICATE - © 2013 R. Bolling -1138- TO JOIN THE INNER HIVE go to tomthedancingbug.com

5/13/13

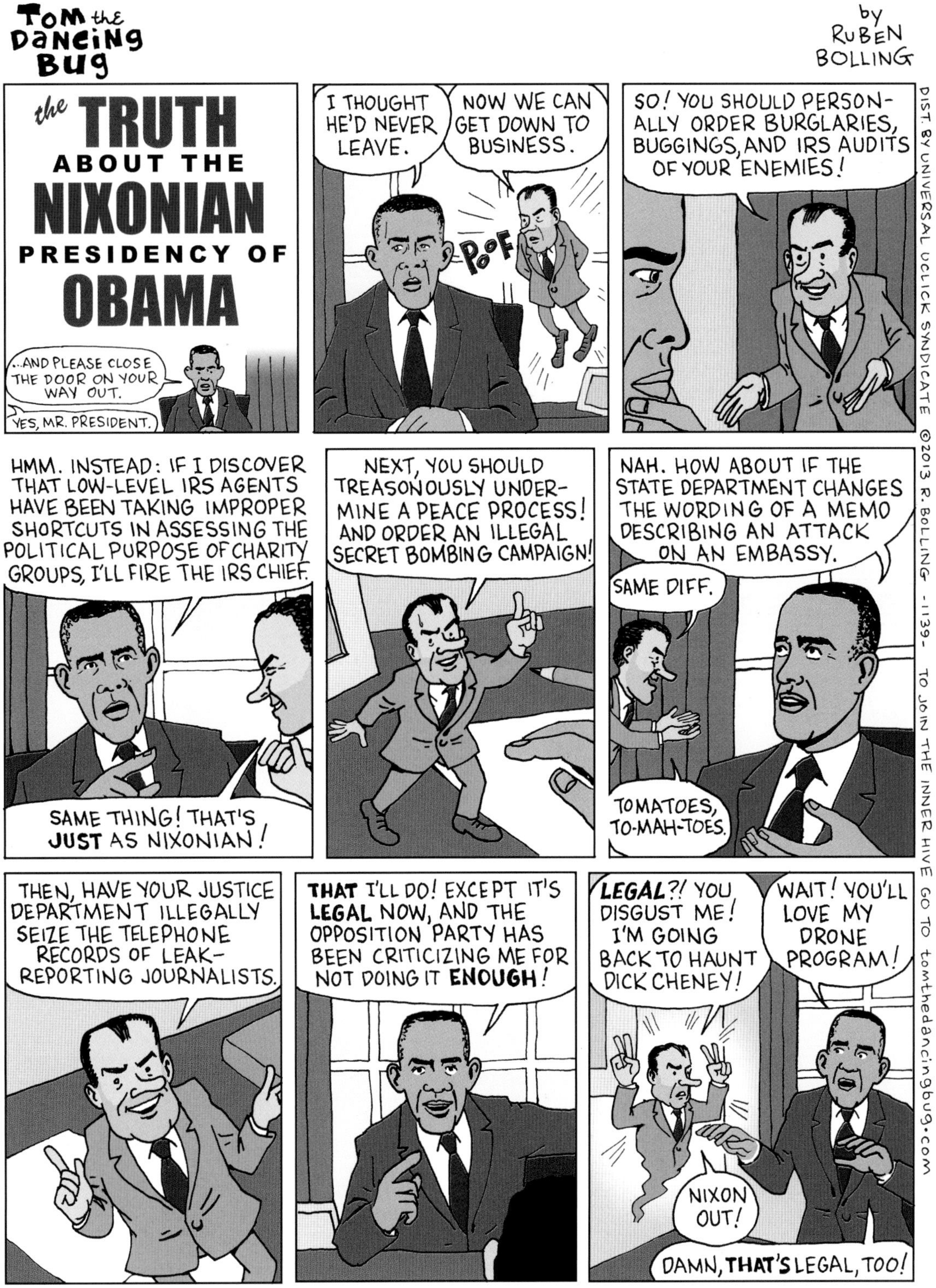
TOM the DANCING BUG
by RUBEN BOLLING
the TRUTH ABOUT THE NIXONIAN PRESIDENCY OF OBAMA
...AND PLEASE CLOSE THE DOOR ON YOUR WAY OUT.
YES, MR. PRESIDENT.
I THOUGHT HE'D NEVER LEAVE.
NOW WE CAN GET DOWN TO BUSINESS.
POOF
SO! YOU SHOULD PERSONALLY ORDER BURGLARIES, BUGGINGS, AND IRS AUDITS OF YOUR ENEMIES!
HMM. INSTEAD: IF I DISCOVER THAT LOW-LEVEL IRS AGENTS HAVE BEEN TAKING IMPROPER SHORTCUTS IN ASSESSING THE POLITICAL PURPOSE OF CHARITY GROUPS, I'LL FIRE THE IRS CHIEF.
SAME THING! THAT'S JUST AS NIXONIAN!
NEXT, YOU SHOULD TREASONOUSLY UNDERMINE A PEACE PROCESS! AND ORDER AN ILLEGAL SECRET BOMBING CAMPAIGN!
NAH. HOW ABOUT IF THE STATE DEPARTMENT CHANGES THE WORDING OF A MEMO DESCRIBING AN ATTACK ON AN EMBASSY.
SAME DIFF.
TOMATOES, TO-MAH-TOES.
THEN, HAVE YOUR JUSTICE DEPARTMENT ILLEGALLY SEIZE THE TELEPHONE RECORDS OF LEAK-REPORTING JOURNALISTS.
THAT I'LL DO! EXCEPT IT'S LEGAL NOW, AND THE OPPOSITION PARTY HAS BEEN CRITICIZING ME FOR NOT DOING IT ENOUGH!
LEGAL?! YOU DISGUST ME! I'M GOING BACK TO HAUNT DICK CHENEY!
WAIT! YOU'LL LOVE MY DRONE PROGRAM!
NIXON OUT!
DAMN, THAT'S LEGAL, TOO!
DIST. BY UNIVERSAL UCLICK SYNDICATE ©2013 R. BOLLING -1139- TO JOIN THE INNER HIVE GO TO tomthedancingbug.com

5/20/13

TOM the DANCING BUG

by RUBEN BOLLING

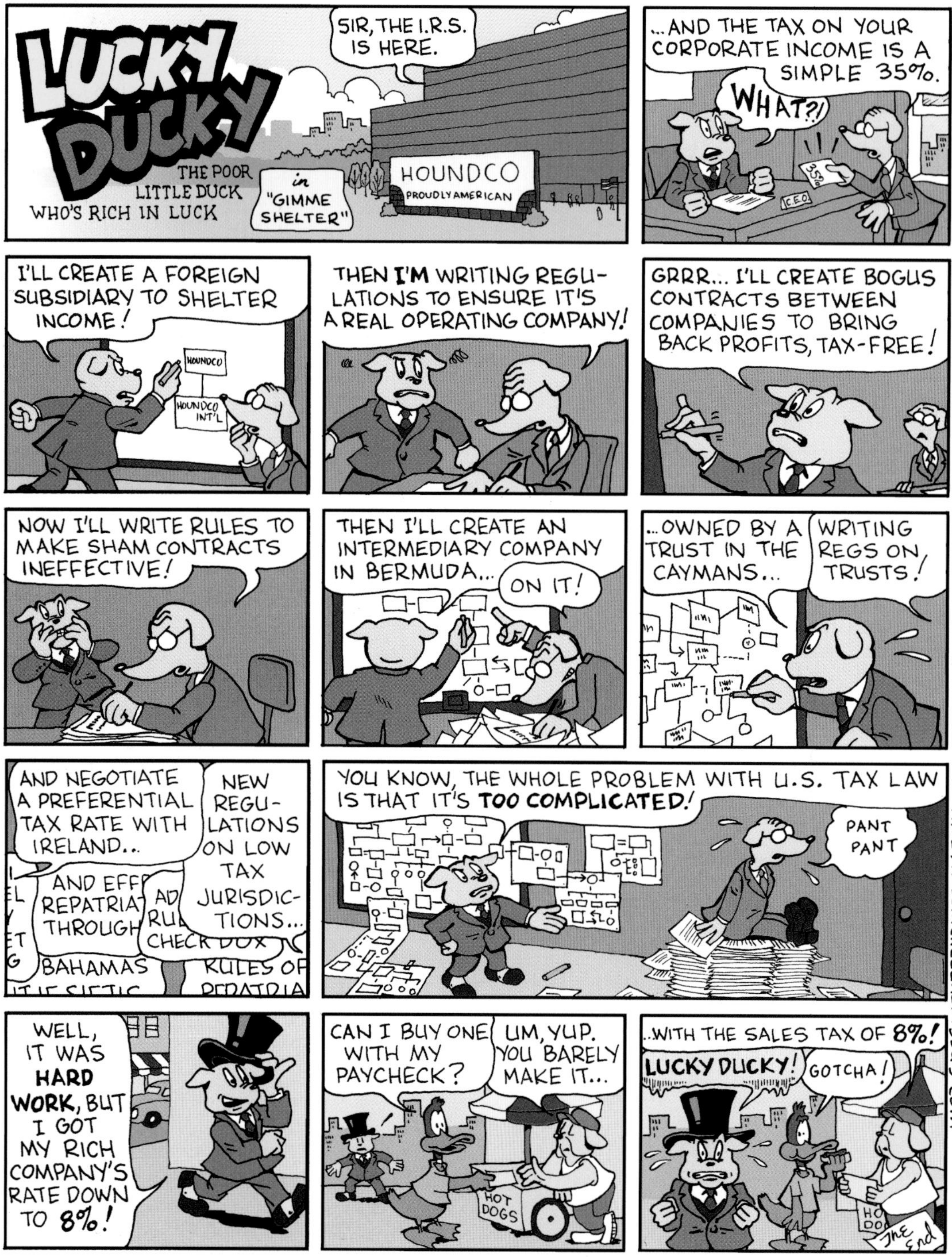
LUCKY DUCKY
THE POOR LITTLE DUCK WHO'S RICH IN LUCK
in "GIMME SHELTER"
SIR, THE I.R.S. IS HERE.
HOUNDCO
PROUDLY AMERICAN
...AND THE TAX ON YOUR CORPORATE INCOME IS A SIMPLE 35%.
WHAT?!
35%
C.E.O.
I'LL CREATE A FOREIGN SUBSIDIARY TO SHELTER INCOME!
HOUNDCO
HOUNDCO INT'L
THEN I'M WRITING REGULATIONS TO ENSURE IT'S A REAL OPERATING COMPANY!
GRRR... I'LL CREATE BOGUS CONTRACTS BETWEEN COMPANIES TO BRING BACK PROFITS, TAX-FREE!
NOW I'LL WRITE RULES TO MAKE SHAM CONTRACTS INEFFECTIVE!
THEN I'LL CREATE AN INTERMEDIARY COMPANY IN BERMUDA...
ON IT!
...OWNED BY A TRUST IN THE CAYMANS...
WRITING REGS ON TRUSTS!
AND NEGOTIATE A PREFERENTIAL TAX RATE WITH IRELAND...
NEW REGULATIONS ON LOW TAX JURISDICTIONS...
AND EFF
REPATRIAT
THROUGH
CHECK BOX
BAHAMAS
RULES OF
YOU KNOW, THE WHOLE PROBLEM WITH U.S. TAX LAW IS THAT IT'S TOO COMPLICATED!
PANT PANT
WELL, IT WAS HARD WORK, BUT I GOT MY RICH COMPANY'S RATE DOWN TO 8%!
CAN I BUY ONE WITH MY PAYCHECK?
UM, YUP. YOU BARELY MAKE IT...
HOT DOGS
...WITH THE SALES TAX OF 8%!
LUCKY DUCKY!
GOTCHA!
THE End

5/27/13

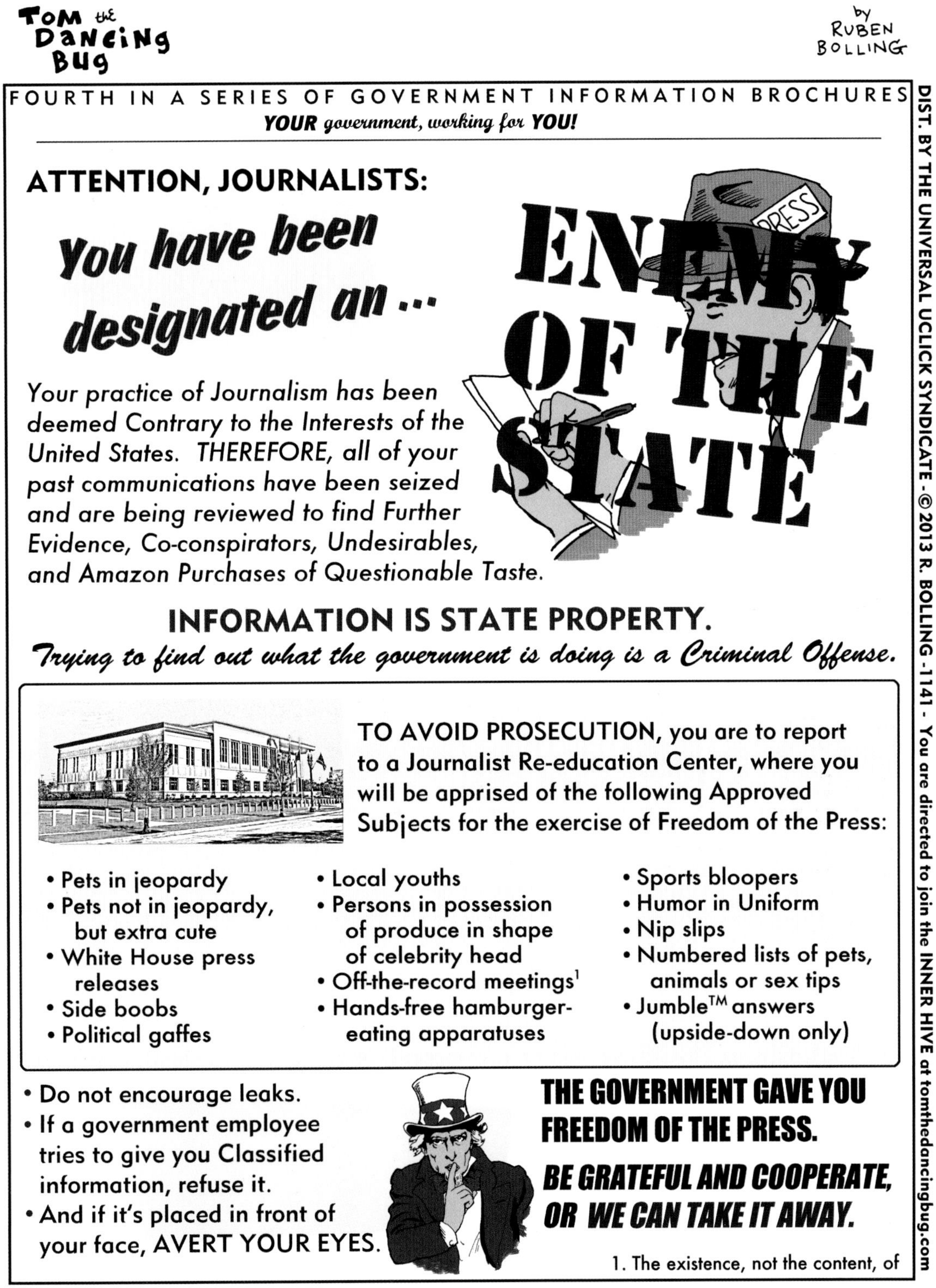

TOM the DANCING BUG
by RUBEN BOLLING
FOURTH IN A SERIES OF GOVERNMENT INFORMATION BROCHURES
YOUR government, working for YOU!
ATTENTION, JOURNALISTS:
You have been designated an ...
ENEMY OF THE STATE
PRESS
Your practice of Journalism has been deemed Contrary to the Interests of the United States. THEREFORE, all of your past communications have been seized and are being reviewed to find Further Evidence, Co-conspirators, Undesirables, and Amazon Purchases of Questionable Taste.
INFORMATION IS STATE PROPERTY.
Trying to find out what the government is doing is a Criminal Offense.
TO AVOID PROSECUTION, you are to report to a Journalist Re-education Center, where you will be apprised of the following Approved Subjects for the exercise of Freedom of the Press:
• Pets in jeopardy
• Pets not in jeopardy, but extra cute
• White House press releases
• Side boobs
• Political gaffes
• Local youths
• Persons in possession of produce in shape of celebrity head
• Off-the-record meetings[1]
• Hands-free hamburger-eating apparatuses
• Sports bloopers
• Humor in Uniform
• Nip slips
• Numbered lists of pets, animals or sex tips
• Jumble™ answers (upside-down only)
• Do not encourage leaks.
• If a government employee tries to give you Classified information, refuse it.
• And if it's placed in front of your face, AVERT YOUR EYES.
THE GOVERNMENT GAVE YOU FREEDOM OF THE PRESS.
BE GRATEFUL AND COOPERATE, OR WE CAN TAKE IT AWAY.
1. The existence, not the content, of
DIST. BY THE UNIVERSAL UCLICK SYNDICATE - © 2013 R. BOLLING -1141- You are directed to join the INNER HIVE at tomthedancingbug.com

6/3/13

Tom the Dancing Bug

by Ruben Bolling

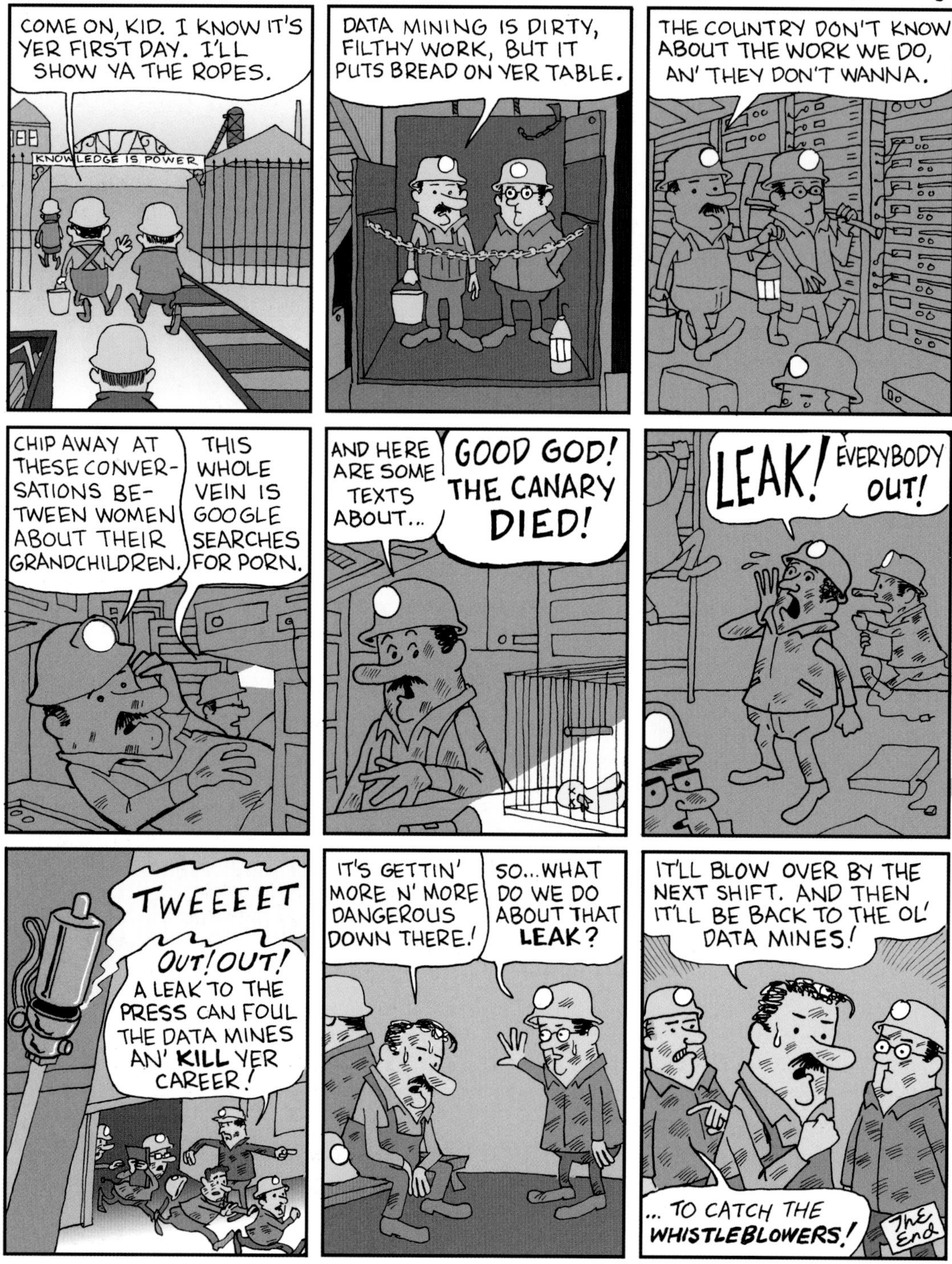

COME ON, KID. I KNOW IT'S YER FIRST DAY. I'LL SHOW YA THE ROPES.
NSA
KNOWLEDGE IS POWER
DATA MINING IS DIRTY, FILTHY WORK, BUT IT PUTS BREAD ON YER TABLE.
THE COUNTRY DON'T KNOW ABOUT THE WORK WE DO, AN' THEY DON'T WANNA.
CHIP AWAY AT THESE CONVERSATIONS BETWEEN WOMEN ABOUT THEIR GRANDCHILDREN.
THIS WHOLE VEIN IS GOOGLE SEARCHES FOR PORN.
AND HERE ARE SOME TEXTS ABOUT...
GOOD GOD! THE CANARY DIED!
LEAK!
EVERYBODY OUT!
TWEEEET
OUT! OUT! A LEAK TO THE PRESS CAN FOUL THE DATA MINES AN' KILL YER CAREER!
IT'S GETTIN' MORE N' MORE DANGEROUS DOWN THERE!
SO...WHAT DO WE DO ABOUT THAT LEAK?
IT'LL BLOW OVER BY THE NEXT SHIFT. AND THEN IT'LL BE BACK TO THE OL' DATA MINES!
... TO CATCH THE WHISTLEBLOWERS!
THE End

6/10/13

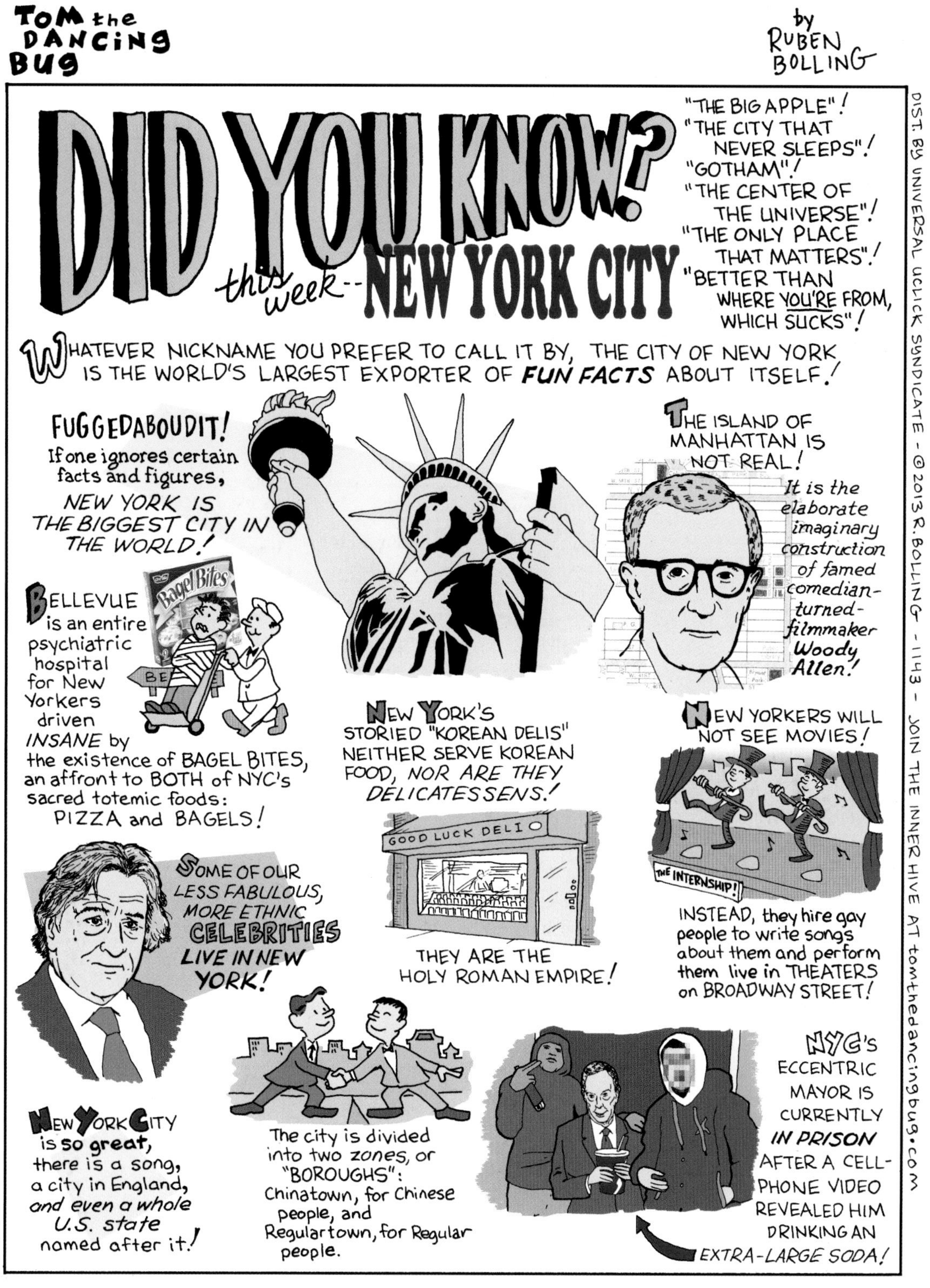
TOM the DANCING BUG
by RUBEN BOLLING
DID YOU KNOW?
this week -- NEW YORK CITY
"THE BIG APPLE"! "THE CITY THAT NEVER SLEEPS"! "GOTHAM"! "THE CENTER OF THE UNIVERSE"! "THE ONLY PLACE THAT MATTERS"! "BETTER THAN WHERE YOU'RE FROM, WHICH SUCKS"!
WHATEVER NICKNAME YOU PREFER TO CALL IT BY, THE CITY OF NEW YORK IS THE WORLD'S LARGEST EXPORTER OF FUN FACTS ABOUT ITSELF!
FUGGEDABOUDIT! If one ignores certain facts and figures, NEW YORK IS THE BIGGEST CITY IN THE WORLD!
THE ISLAND OF MANHATTAN IS NOT REAL! It is the elaborate imaginary construction of famed comedian-turned-filmmaker Woody Allen!
Bagel Bites
BELLEVUE is an entire psychiatric hospital for New Yorkers driven INSANE by the existence of BAGEL BITES, an affront to BOTH of NYC's sacred totemic foods: PIZZA and BAGELS!
NEW YORK'S STORIED "KOREAN DELIS" NEITHER SERVE KOREAN FOOD, NOR ARE THEY DELICATESSENS!
GOOD LUCK DELI
THEY ARE THE HOLY ROMAN EMPIRE!
NEW YORKERS WILL NOT SEE MOVIES!
THE INTERNSHIP!
INSTEAD, they hire gay people to write songs about them and perform them live in THEATERS on BROADWAY STREET!
SOME OF OUR LESS FABULOUS, MORE ETHNIC CELEBRITIES LIVE IN NEW YORK!
NEW YORK CITY is so great, there is a song, a city in England, and even a whole U.S. state named after it!
The city is divided into two zones, or "BOROUGHS": Chinatown, for Chinese people, and Regulartown, for Regular people.
NYC'S ECCENTRIC MAYOR IS CURRENTLY IN PRISON AFTER A CELL-PHONE VIDEO REVEALED HIM DRINKING AN EXTRA-LARGE SODA!
DIST. BY UNIVERSAL UCLICK SYNDICATE - © 2013 R. BOLLING - 1143 - JOIN THE INNER HIVE AT tomthedancingbug.com

6/17/13

TOM the DANCING BUG
BY RUBEN BOLLING
Chagrin Falls
"AN OPEN BOOK"
So I say, what's the big deal about government surveillance? I've got nothing to hide!
You wanna join our customer loyalty program?
fried donu
fried donuts
Sure.
They can look at everything I do, for all I care.
Your name is "Gamal Singh"?
Huh?
fried donu
SCREEECH
fried donuts
fried donuts
TAP TAP
Oh, ha-ha! No! Sloppy hand-writing! I'm Gavin Smythe!
You're coming with us, Mr. Singh!
You live at 345 Maple St., Mr. Singh?
Yes, and the name's Smythe.
Did you declare on your taxes the $250 you made selling NFL-themed beanie babies on eBay?
Uh...
In June, 2005, did you copy a Michael Bolton CD from the library onto your hard drive?
It's terrific! Have you heard the live version of "Soul Provider"?
On January 18, 2009, did you visit a website called www.suburbanmilfs1.com?
Ah, heh-heh... You see, my wife Rita was out of town...
On May 7, 2004, did you text a confederate the message: "About to blow up"?
Ho! I'd just eaten a really spicy burrito with Al at lunch!
You were driving by a Federal office building at the time!
THREE YEARS LATER-
Time for your cavity search, Mr. Singh.
Okee-doke. Nothing to hide. By the way, full disclosure: I used a pebble to scratch a picture of my family on the wall under my stool.
The End
DIST. BY UNIVERSAL UCLICK SYNDICATE ©2013 R. BOLLING -1144- JOIN THE INNER HIVE AT tomthedancingbug.com

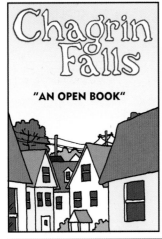

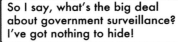

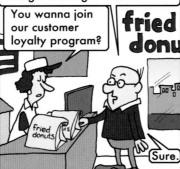

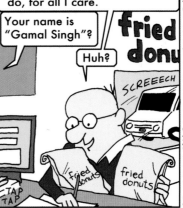

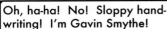

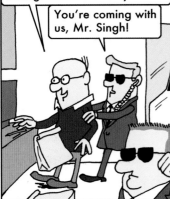

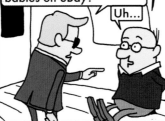

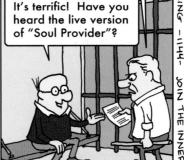

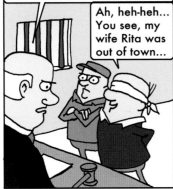

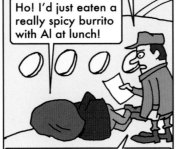

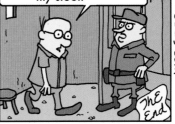

6/24/13

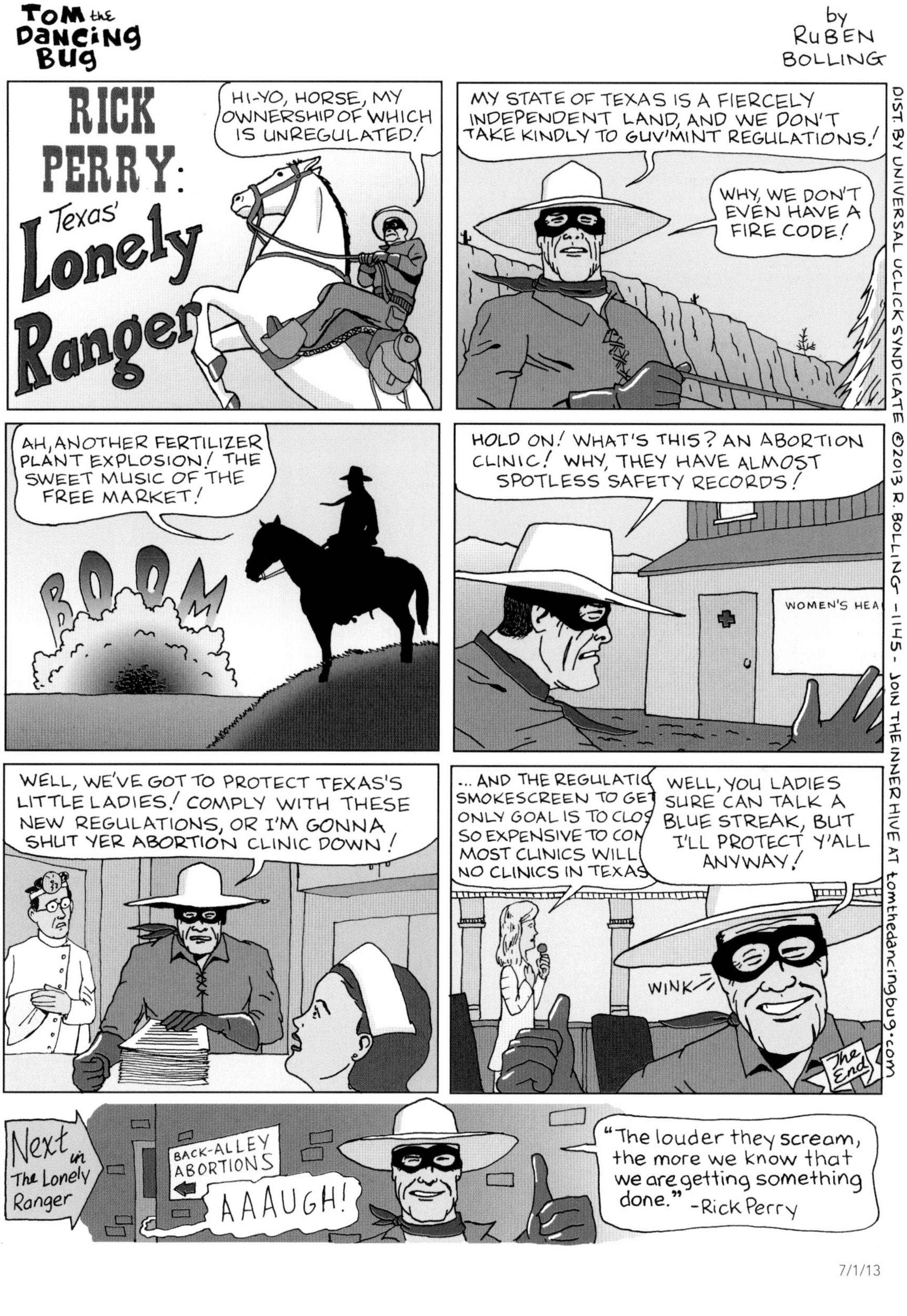

TOM the DANCING BUG
by RUBEN BOLLING
RICK PERRY: Texas' Lonely Ranger
HI-YO, HORSE, MY OWNERSHIP OF WHICH IS UNREGULATED!
MY STATE OF TEXAS IS A FIERCELY INDEPENDENT LAND, AND WE DON'T TAKE KINDLY TO GUV'MINT REGULATIONS!
WHY, WE DON'T EVEN HAVE A FIRE CODE!
AH, ANOTHER FERTILIZER PLANT EXPLOSION! THE SWEET MUSIC OF THE FREE MARKET!
BOOM
HOLD ON! WHAT'S THIS? AN ABORTION CLINIC! WHY, THEY HAVE ALMOST SPOTLESS SAFETY RECORDS!
WOMEN'S HEA
WELL, WE'VE GOT TO PROTECT TEXAS'S LITTLE LADIES! COMPLY WITH THESE NEW REGULATIONS, OR I'M GONNA SHUT YER ABORTION CLINIC DOWN!
...AND THE REGULATI SMOKESCREEN TO GET ONLY GOAL IS TO CLOS SO EXPENSIVE TO COM MOST CLINICS WILL NO CLINICS IN TEXAS
WELL, YOU LADIES SURE CAN TALK A BLUE STREAK, BUT I'LL PROTECT Y'ALL ANYWAY!
WINK
The End
Next in The Lonely Ranger
BACK-ALLEY ABORTIONS
AAAUGH!
"The louder they scream, the more we know that we are getting something done." -Rick Perry
DIST. BY UNIVERSAL UCLICK SYNDICATE ©2013 R. BOLLING - 1145 - JOIN THE INNER HIVE AT tomthedancingbug.com

7/1/13

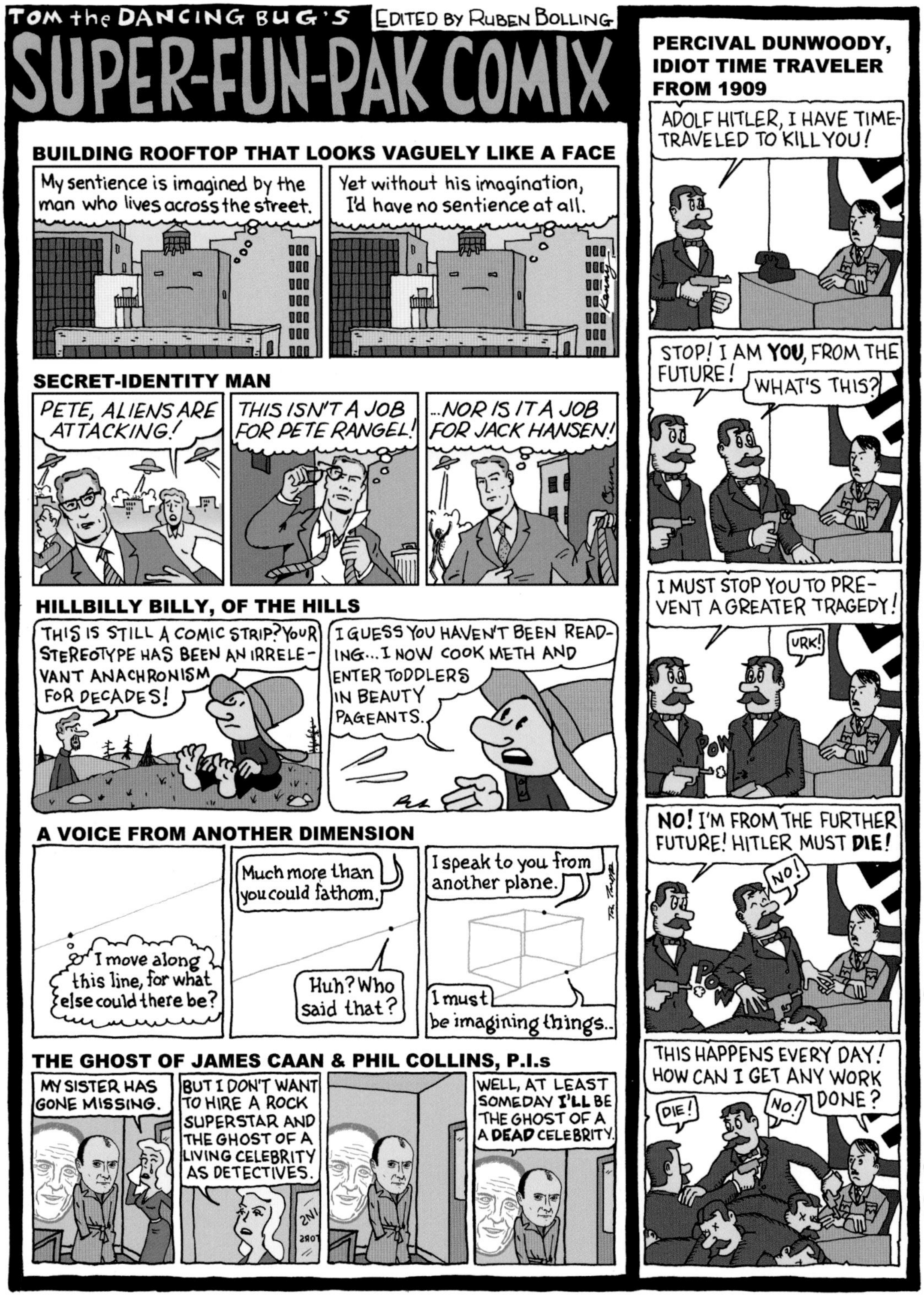
TOM the DANCING BUG'S
EDITED BY RUBEN BOLLING
SUPER-FUN-PAK COMIX
BUILDING ROOFTOP THAT LOOKS VAGUELY LIKE A FACE
My sentience is imagined by the man who lives across the street.
Yet without his imagination, I'd have no sentience at all.
SECRET-IDENTITY MAN
PETE, ALIENS ARE ATTACKING!
THIS ISN'T A JOB FOR PETE RANGEL!
...NOR IS IT A JOB FOR JACK HANSEN!
HILLBILLY BILLY, OF THE HILLS
THIS IS STILL A COMIC STRIP? YOUR STEREOTYPE HAS BEEN AN IRRELEVANT ANACHRONISM FOR DECADES!
I GUESS YOU HAVEN'T BEEN READING... I NOW COOK METH AND ENTER TODDLERS IN BEAUTY PAGEANTS.
A VOICE FROM ANOTHER DIMENSION
I move along this line, for what else could there be?
Much more than you could fathom.
Huh? Who said that?
I speak to you from another plane.
I must be imagining things..
THE GHOST OF JAMES CAAN & PHIL COLLINS, P.I.s
MY SISTER HAS GONE MISSING.
BUT I DON'T WANT TO HIRE A ROCK SUPERSTAR AND THE GHOST OF A LIVING CELEBRITY AS DETECTIVES.
WELL, AT LEAST SOMEDAY I'LL BE THE GHOST OF A DEAD CELEBRITY.
PERCIVAL DUNWOODY, IDIOT TIME TRAVELER FROM 1909
ADOLF HITLER, I HAVE TIME-TRAVELED TO KILL YOU!
STOP! I AM YOU, FROM THE FUTURE!
WHAT'S THIS?
I MUST STOP YOU TO PREVENT A GREATER TRAGEDY!
URK!
POW
NO! I'M FROM THE FURTHER FUTURE! HITLER MUST DIE!
NO!
POW
THIS HAPPENS EVERY DAY! HOW CAN I GET ANY WORK DONE?
DIE!
NO!

7/8/13

Tom the Dancing Bug

by RUBEN BOLLING

Chagrin Falls

"AN IMMIGRANT'S STORY"

Kids, as you know, it's been tough with your dad out of work.

Yes, I've decided to travel to where the jobs are. I'll send money home.

'Kay

DAY 1.

Guess I'm not the only one...

DAY 2.

So, did you hear Twinkies are back?

DAY 3. MEXICO.

I'm picking up some wifi. You know the password?

Quiet! Here comes someone!

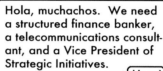

Hola, muchachos. We need a structured finance banker, a telecommunications consultant, and a Vice President of Strategic Initiatives.

Here!

Here!

Me!

Get in! Rápido! You, you're new. What do you do, amigo?

Ah, I'm something of a theoretical physicist.

Sí? Bosonic string theory or M-theory?

Oh, you know, I've dabbled in both.

Hm... I may have something. Where did you get your Ph.D.?

Um, I've surveyed courses at Chagrin Falls Community College, but I don't have a Ph.D., *per se*, not in the strictest definition of the term.

It's a text from your dad!

"Still looking. Send money, ketchup, and pls renew my NFL Online Pass."

'Kay

Looks like I'm adding another shift at my job.

The End

DIST. BY UNIVERSAL UCLICK SYNDICATE ©2013 R. BOLLING - 1147- JOIN THE INNER HIVE AT tomthedancingbug.com   Thanks to Ted Rall

7/15/13

TOM THE DANCING BUG

by Ruben Bolling

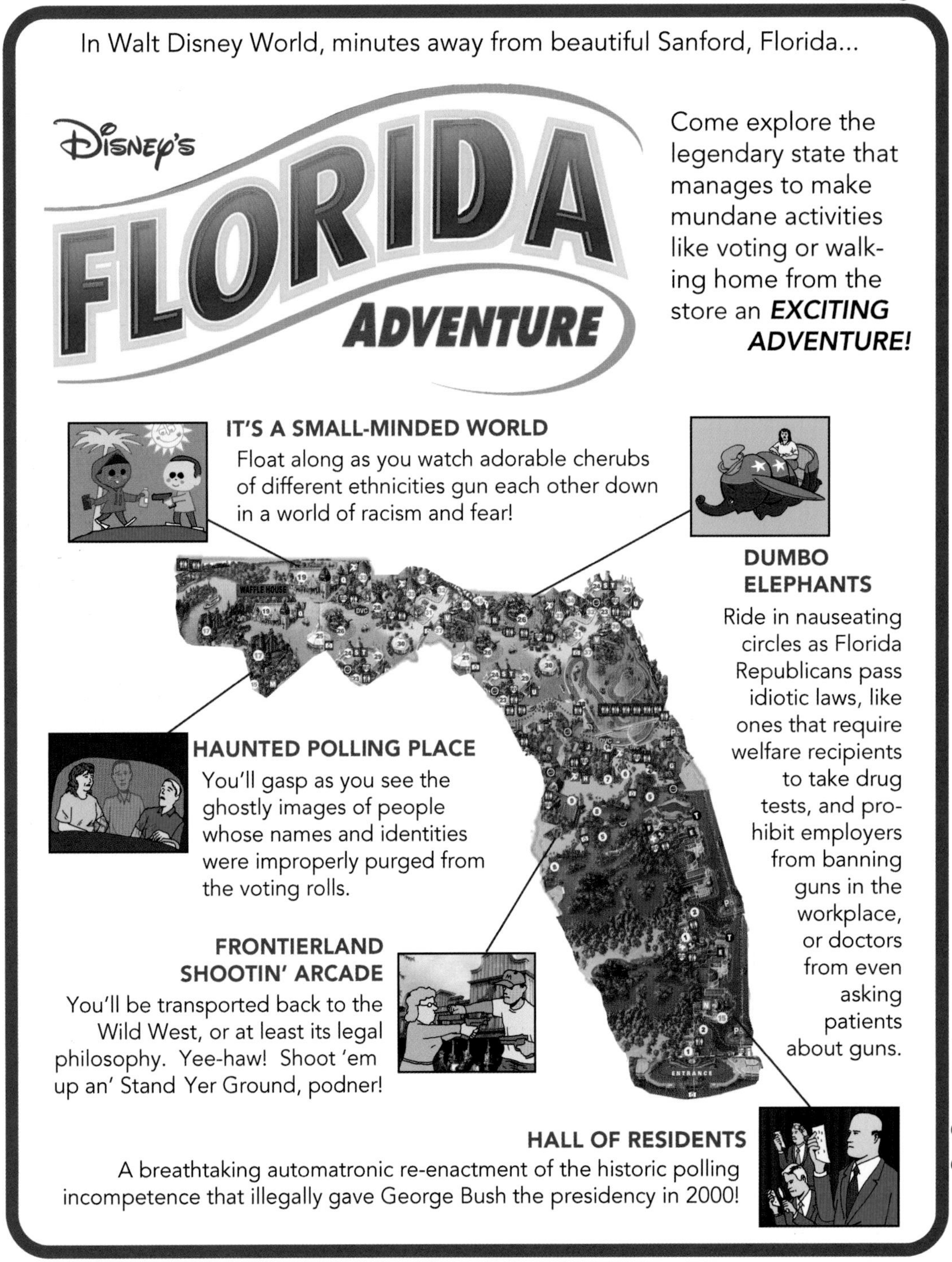
In Walt Disney World, minutes away from beautiful Sanford, Florida...
Disney's
FLORIDA
ADVENTURE
Come explore the legendary state that manages to make mundane activities like voting or walking home from the store an *EXCITING ADVENTURE!*
IT'S A SMALL-MINDED WORLD
Float along as you watch adorable cherubs of different ethnicities gun each other down in a world of racism and fear!
DUMBO ELEPHANTS
Ride in nauseating circles as Florida Republicans pass idiotic laws, like ones that require welfare recipients to take drug tests, and prohibit employers from banning guns in the workplace, or doctors from even asking patients about guns.
WAFFLE HOUSE
HAUNTED POLLING PLACE
You'll gasp as you see the ghostly images of people whose names and identities were improperly purged from the voting rolls.
FRONTIERLAND SHOOTIN' ARCADE
You'll be transported back to the Wild West, or at least its legal philosophy. Yee-haw! Shoot 'em up an' Stand Yer Ground, podner!
ENTRANCE
HALL OF RESIDENTS
A breathtaking automatronic re-enactment of the historic polling incompetence that illegally gave George Bush the presidency in 2000!

7/22/13

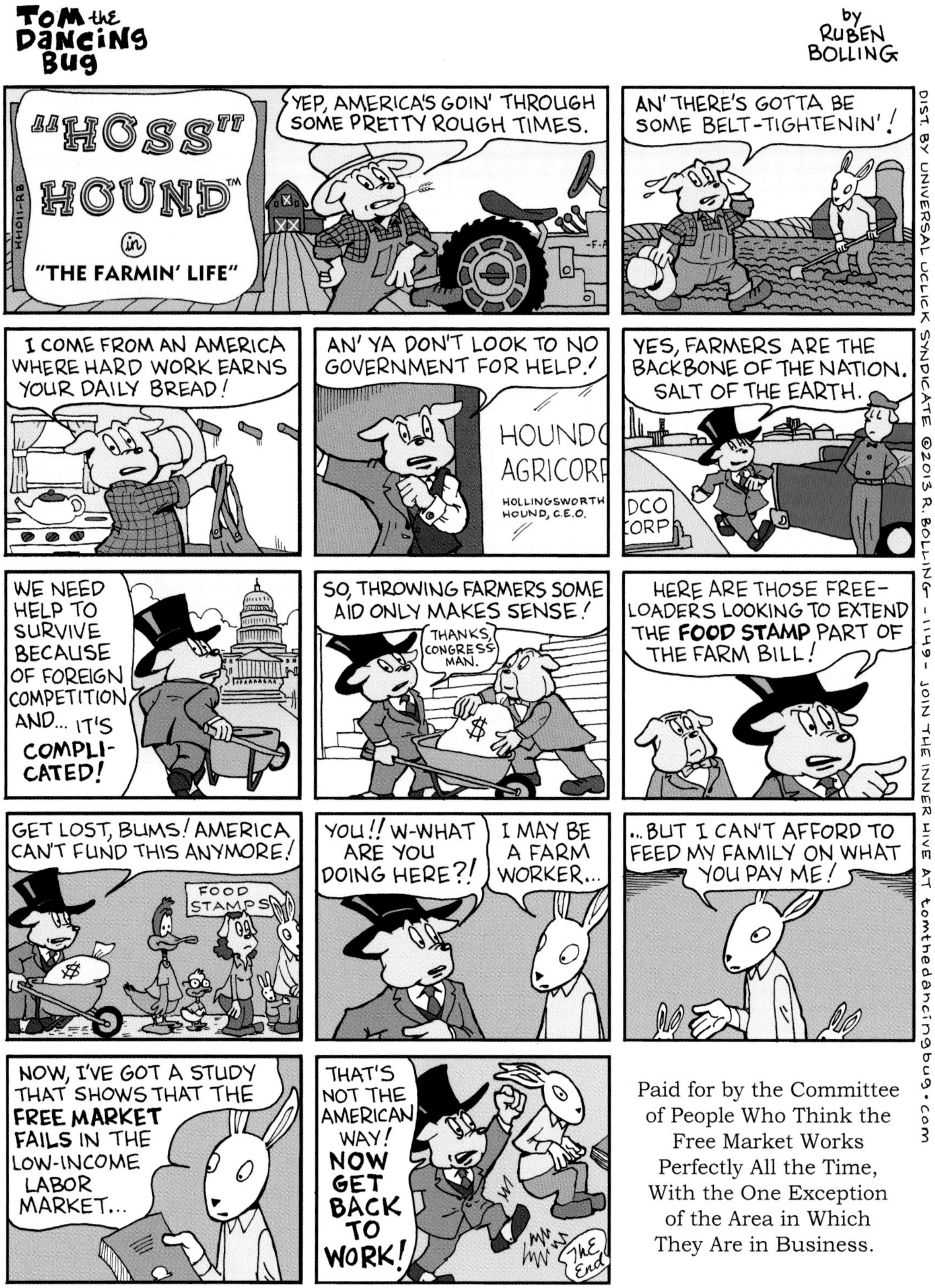

TOM the DANCING BUG
by RUBEN BOLLING
"HOSS" HOUND™
in
"THE FARMIN' LIFE"
HH011-RB
YEP, AMERICA'S GOIN' THROUGH SOME PRETTY ROUGH TIMES.
AN' THERE'S GOTTA BE SOME BELT-TIGHTENIN'!
I COME FROM AN AMERICA WHERE HARD WORK EARNS YOUR DAILY BREAD!
AN' YA DON'T LOOK TO NO GOVERNMENT FOR HELP!
HOUND AGRICORP
HOLLINGSWORTH HOUND, C.E.O.
YES, FARMERS ARE THE BACKBONE OF THE NATION. SALT OF THE EARTH.
WE NEED HELP TO SURVIVE BECAUSE OF FOREIGN COMPETITION AND... IT'S COMPLICATED!
SO, THROWING FARMERS SOME AID ONLY MAKES SENSE!
THANKS, CONGRESSMAN.
HERE ARE THOSE FREE-LOADERS LOOKING TO EXTEND THE **FOOD STAMP** PART OF THE FARM BILL!
GET LOST, BUMS! AMERICA CAN'T FUND THIS ANYMORE!
FOOD STAMPS
YOU!! W-WHAT ARE YOU DOING HERE?!
I MAY BE A FARM WORKER...
...BUT I CAN'T AFFORD TO FEED MY FAMILY ON WHAT YOU PAY ME!
NOW, I'VE GOT A STUDY THAT SHOWS THAT THE **FREE MARKET FAILS** IN THE LOW-INCOME LABOR MARKET...
THAT'S NOT THE AMERICAN WAY! **NOW GET BACK TO WORK!**
The End
Paid for by the Committee of People Who Think the Free Market Works Perfectly All the Time, With the One Exception of the Area in Which They Are in Business.
DIST. BY UNIVERSAL UCLICK SYNDICATE ©2013 R. BOLLING - 1149 - JOIN THE INNER HIVE AT tomthedancingbug.com

7/29/13

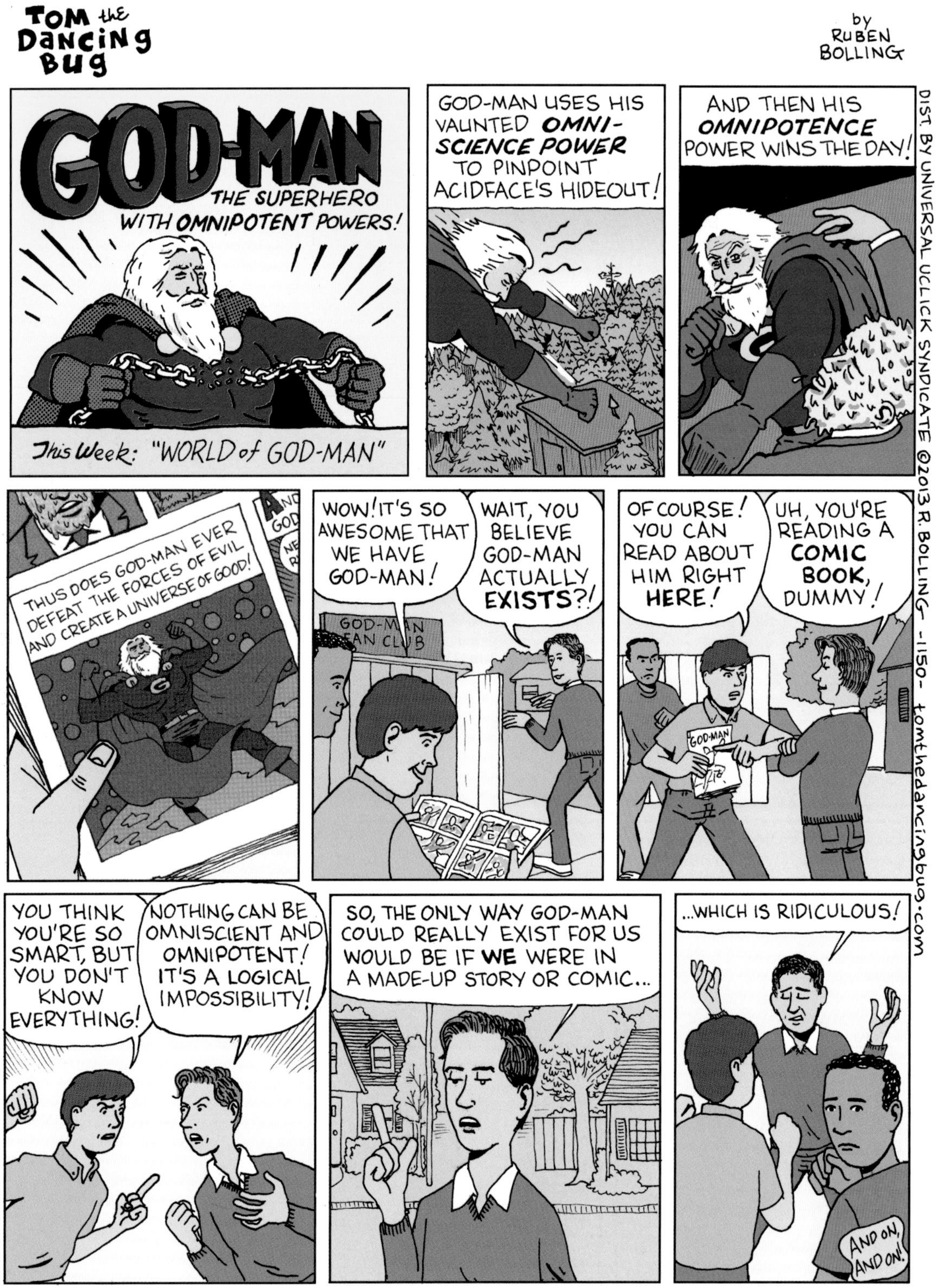
TOM the DANCING BUG
by RUBEN BOLLING
GOD-MAN
THE SUPERHERO WITH OMNIPOTENT POWERS!
This Week: "WORLD of GOD-MAN"
GOD-MAN USES HIS VAUNTED OMNI-SCIENCE POWER TO PINPOINT ACIDFACE'S HIDEOUT!
AND THEN HIS OMNIPOTENCE POWER WINS THE DAY!
THUS DOES GOD-MAN EVER DEFEAT THE FORCES OF EVIL AND CREATE A UNIVERSE OF GOOD!
WOW! IT'S SO AWESOME THAT WE HAVE GOD-MAN!
WAIT, YOU BELIEVE GOD-MAN ACTUALLY EXISTS?!
GOD-MAN FAN CLUB
OF COURSE! YOU CAN READ ABOUT HIM RIGHT HERE!
UH, YOU'RE READING A COMIC BOOK, DUMMY!
GOD-MAN
YOU THINK YOU'RE SO SMART, BUT YOU DON'T KNOW EVERYTHING!
NOTHING CAN BE OMNISCIENT AND OMNIPOTENT! IT'S A LOGICAL IMPOSSIBILITY!
SO, THE ONLY WAY GOD-MAN COULD REALLY EXIST FOR US WOULD BE IF WE WERE IN A MADE-UP STORY OR COMIC...
...WHICH IS RIDICULOUS!
AND ON, AND ON!
DIST. BY UNIVERSAL UCLICK SYNDICATE ©2013 R. BOLLING -1150- tomthedancingbug.com

8/5/13

TOM the DANCING BUG'S SUPER-FUN-PAK COMIX
EDITED BY RUBEN BOLLING

BRAIN IN A BEAKER

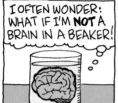

I OFTEN WONDER: WHAT IF I'M **NOT** A BRAIN IN A BEAKER!

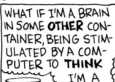

WHAT IF I'M A BRAIN IN SOME **OTHER** CONTAINER, BEING STIMULATED BY A COMPUTER TO **THINK** I'M A BRAIN IN A BEAKER!

CRAZY, RIGHT?

PERCIVAL DUNWOODY, IDIOT TIME TRAVELER FROM 1909

PEOPLE OF 1963! I HAVE COME FROM 2013 TO TELL YOU OF THEIR WONDROUS ADVANCES!

ALL THEIR **SUITCASES** HAVE **WHEELS**!

GASP! NO! HOW TH...?

COMICS FOR THE ELDERLY

MEGABYTES! DOT-COM! YEESH!

YOU YOUNG PEOPLE ARE COMPUTER-CRAZY!

ACTUALLY, I'M AN ARTISANAL CHEESE-MAKER.

WELL, GET A HAIRCUT!

THE FURTHER ADVENTURES OF HARRY POTTER

Harry! Hagrid's in danger!

Wait! This comic strip is a copyright infringement unless it's a parody!

Quick! Say something parodic! PARODIUS!

Okay, on with the story!

CHAOS BUTTERFLY

BRAZIL DON'T DISTURB IT! THAT'S CHAOS BUTTERFLY! THAT BUTTERFLY'S ABOUT TO FLAP ITS WINGS!

OH, WHAT HARM COULD IT DO?

FLAP FLAP

3 WEEKS LATER, L.A.

SHARKNADO! CHAOS BUTTERFLY!!

targeted comics

Comics algorithmically generated to be hilarious to YOU, based on YOUR browsing history!!

Finally!! That must be that juicer or blender *I ordered!*

If it weren't for bad news about the St. Louis Rams, *there wouldn't be any news at all!*

...an' God bless Mommy an' Daddy an' Rover an' nude videos free porn hardcore*!*

8/12/13

TOM the DANCING BUG

by RUBEN BOLLING

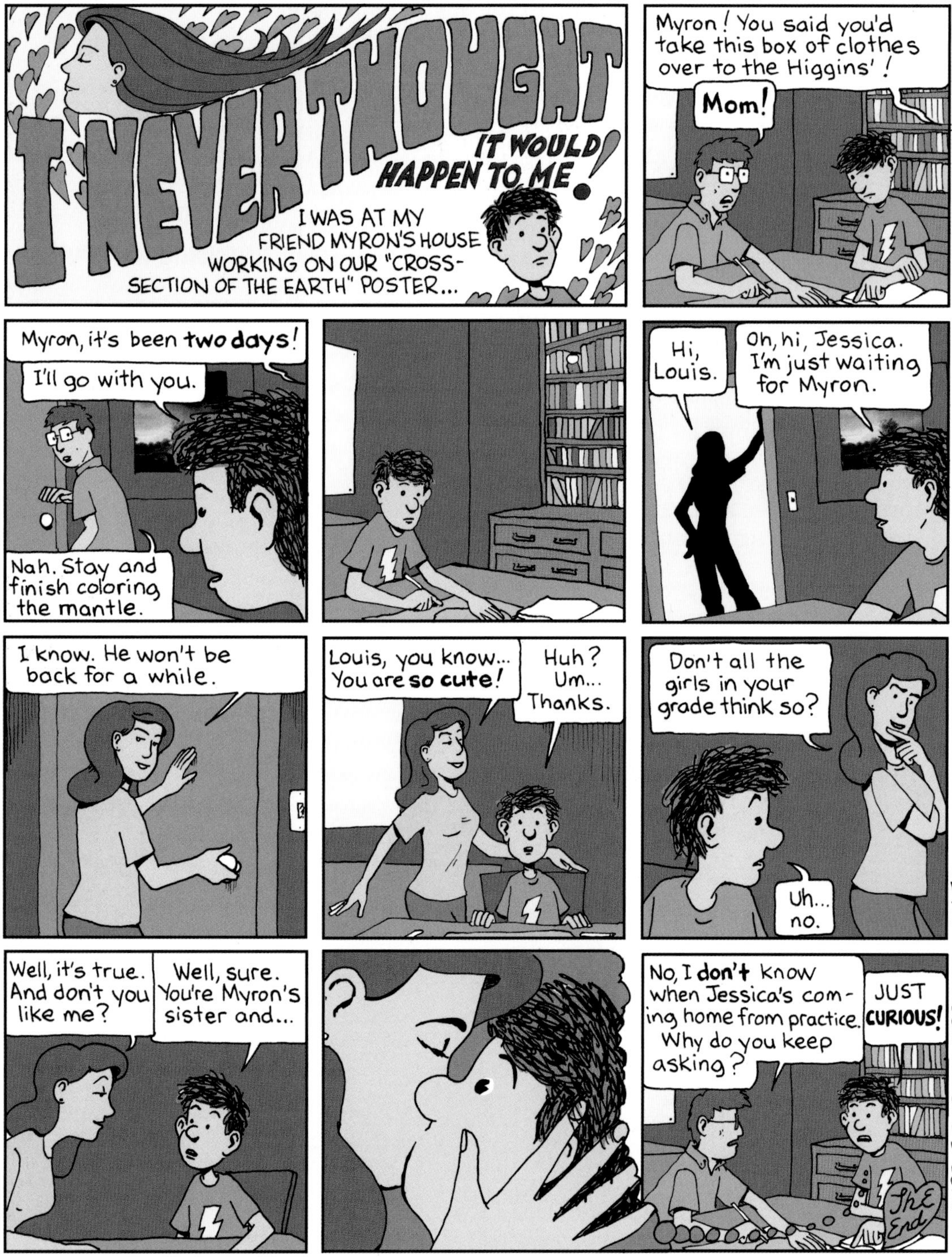

I NEVER THOUGHT IT WOULD HAPPEN TO ME!
I WAS AT MY FRIEND MYRON'S HOUSE WORKING ON OUR "CROSS-SECTION OF THE EARTH" POSTER...
Myron! You said you'd take this box of clothes over to the Higgins'!
Mom!
Myron, it's been **two days**!
I'll go with you.
Nah. Stay and finish coloring the mantle.
Hi, Louis.
Oh, hi, Jessica. I'm just waiting for Myron.
I know. He won't be back for a while.
Louis, you know... You are **so cute**!
Huh? Um... Thanks.
Don't all the girls in your grade think so?
Uh... no.
Well, it's true. And don't you like me?
Well, sure. You're Myron's sister and...
No, I **don't** know when Jessica's coming home from practice. Why do you keep asking?
JUST **CURIOUS!**
The End

8/26/13

TOM the DANCING BUG

by RUBEN BOLLING

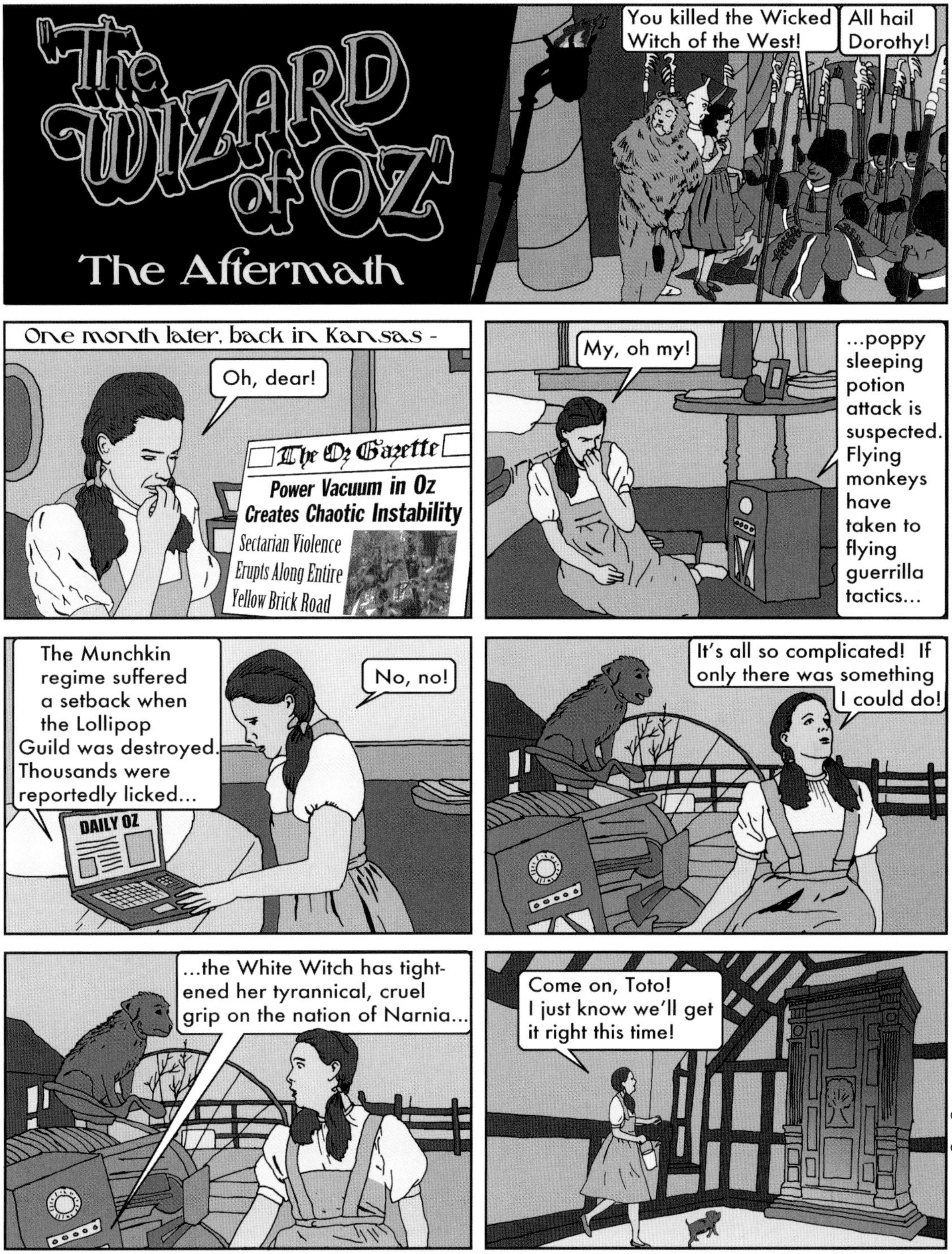

"The WIZARD of OZ"
The Aftermath
You killed the Wicked Witch of the West!
All hail Dorothy!
One month later, back in Kansas -
Oh, dear!
The Oz Gazette
Power Vacuum in Oz Creates Chaotic Instability
Sectarian Violence Erupts Along Entire Yellow Brick Road
My, oh my!
...poppy sleeping potion attack is suspected. Flying monkeys have taken to flying guerrilla tactics...
The Munchkin regime suffered a setback when the Lollipop Guild was destroyed. Thousands were reportedly licked...
DAILY OZ
No, no!
It's all so complicated! If only there was something I could do!
...the White Witch has tightened her tyrannical, cruel grip on the nation of Narnia...
Come on, Toto! I just know we'll get it right this time!

9/2/13

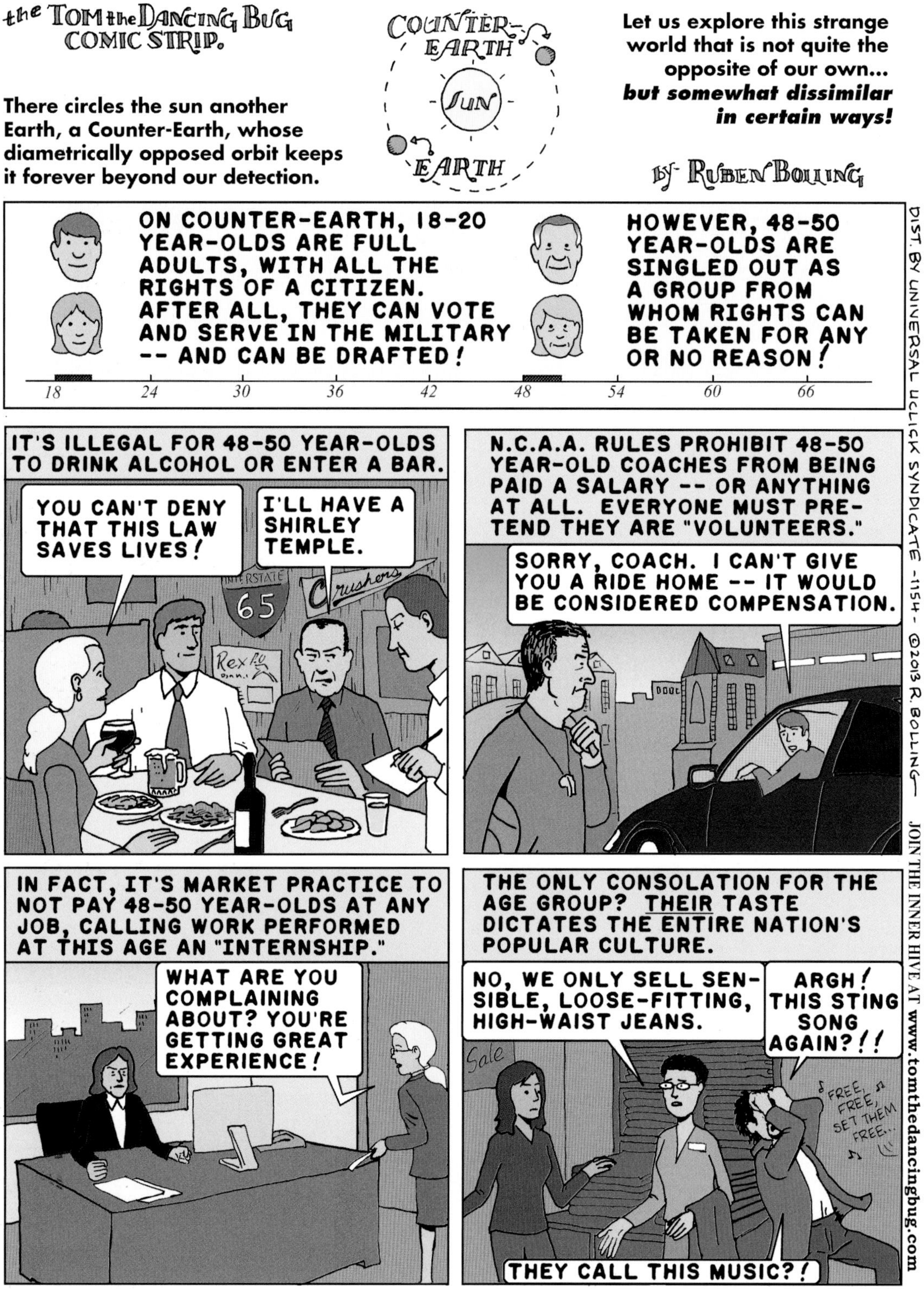
the TOM the DANCING BUG COMIC STRIP.
There circles the sun another Earth, a Counter-Earth, whose diametrically opposed orbit keeps it forever beyond our detection.
COUNTER-EARTH
SUN
EARTH
Let us explore this strange world that is not quite the opposite of our own... but somewhat dissimilar in certain ways!
BY RUBEN BOLLING
ON COUNTER-EARTH, 18-20 YEAR-OLDS ARE FULL ADULTS, WITH ALL THE RIGHTS OF A CITIZEN. AFTER ALL, THEY CAN VOTE AND SERVE IN THE MILITARY -- AND CAN BE DRAFTED!
HOWEVER, 48-50 YEAR-OLDS ARE SINGLED OUT AS A GROUP FROM WHOM RIGHTS CAN BE TAKEN FOR ANY OR NO REASON!
18 24 30 36 42 48 54 60 66
IT'S ILLEGAL FOR 48-50 YEAR-OLDS TO DRINK ALCOHOL OR ENTER A BAR.
YOU CAN'T DENY THAT THIS LAW SAVES LIVES!
I'LL HAVE A SHIRLEY TEMPLE.
INTERSTATE 65
Crushers
N.C.A.A. RULES PROHIBIT 48-50 YEAR-OLD COACHES FROM BEING PAID A SALARY -- OR ANYTHING AT ALL. EVERYONE MUST PRETEND THEY ARE "VOLUNTEERS."
SORRY, COACH. I CAN'T GIVE YOU A RIDE HOME -- IT WOULD BE CONSIDERED COMPENSATION.
IN FACT, IT'S MARKET PRACTICE TO NOT PAY 48-50 YEAR-OLDS AT ANY JOB, CALLING WORK PERFORMED AT THIS AGE AN "INTERNSHIP."
WHAT ARE YOU COMPLAINING ABOUT? YOU'RE GETTING GREAT EXPERIENCE!
THE ONLY CONSOLATION FOR THE AGE GROUP? THEIR TASTE DICTATES THE ENTIRE NATION'S POPULAR CULTURE.
NO, WE ONLY SELL SENSIBLE, LOOSE-FITTING, HIGH-WAIST JEANS.
ARGH! THIS STING SONG AGAIN?!!
Sale
FREE, FREE, SET THEM FREE...
THEY CALL THIS MUSIC?!
DIST. BY UNIVERSAL UCLICK SYNDICATE -1154- ©2013 R. BOLLING
JOIN THE INNER HIVE AT www.tomthedancingbug.com

9/9/13

Tom the Dancing Bug

by RUBEN BOLLING

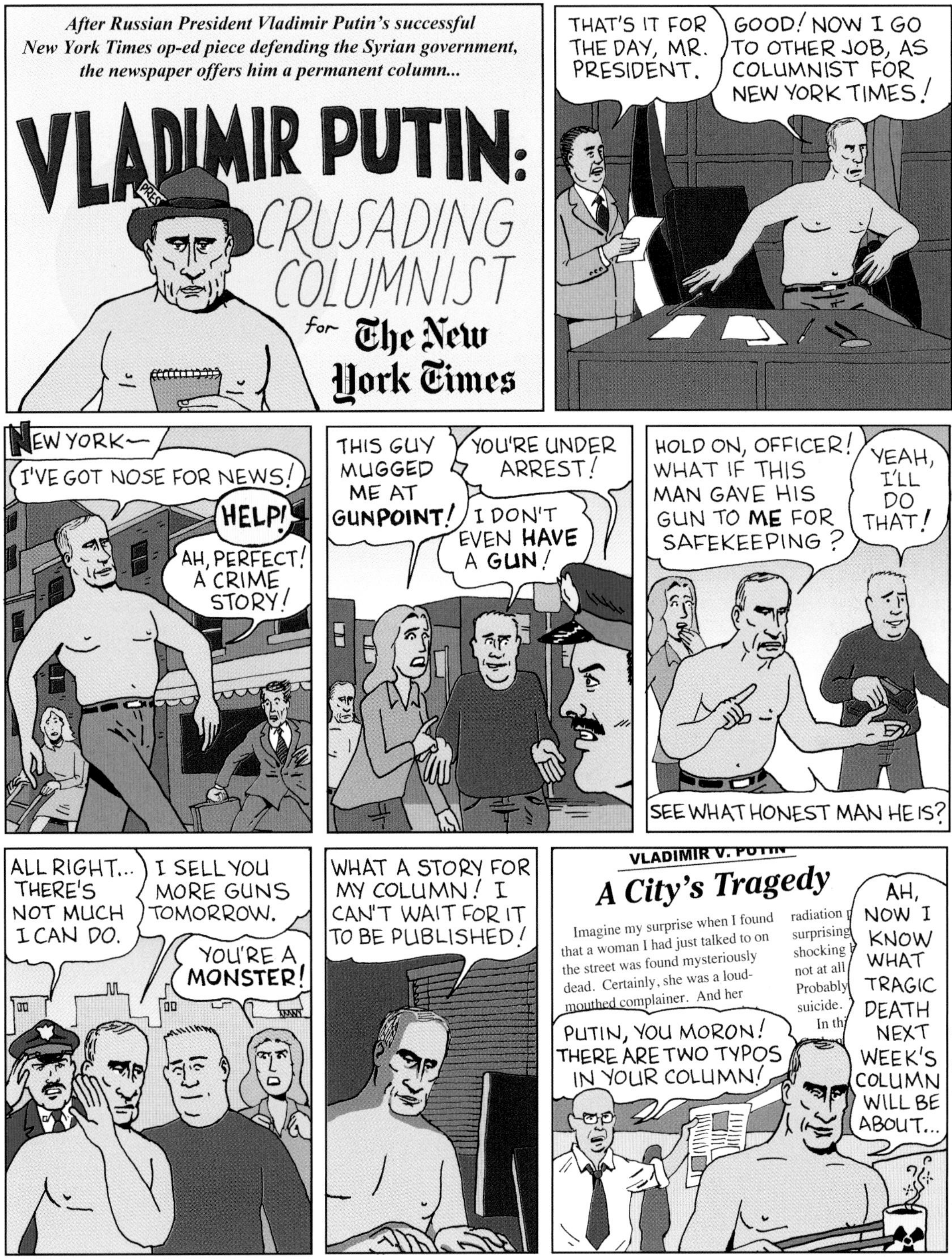
After Russian President Vladimir Putin's successful New York Times op-ed piece defending the Syrian government, the newspaper offers him a permanent column...
VLADIMIR PUTIN: CRUSADING COLUMNIST for The New York Times
PRES
THAT'S IT FOR THE DAY, MR. PRESIDENT.
GOOD! NOW I GO TO OTHER JOB, AS COLUMNIST FOR NEW YORK TIMES!
NEW YORK—
I'VE GOT NOSE FOR NEWS!
HELP!
AH, PERFECT! A CRIME STORY!
THIS GUY MUGGED ME AT GUNPOINT!
YOU'RE UNDER ARREST!
I DON'T EVEN HAVE A GUN!
HOLD ON, OFFICER! WHAT IF THIS MAN GAVE HIS GUN TO ME FOR SAFEKEEPING?
YEAH, I'LL DO THAT!
SEE WHAT HONEST MAN HE IS?
ALL RIGHT... THERE'S NOT MUCH I CAN DO.
I SELL YOU MORE GUNS TOMORROW.
YOU'RE A MONSTER!
WHAT A STORY FOR MY COLUMN! I CAN'T WAIT FOR IT TO BE PUBLISHED!
VLADIMIR V. PUTIN
A City's Tragedy
Imagine my surprise when I found that a woman I had just talked to on the street was found mysteriously dead. Certainly, she was a loud-mouthed complainer. And her
PUTIN, YOU MORON! THERE ARE TWO TYPOS IN YOUR COLUMN!
AH, NOW I KNOW WHAT TRAGIC DEATH NEXT WEEK'S COLUMN WILL BE ABOUT...

9/16/13

TOM the DANCING BUG

by RUBEN BOLLING

ANNOUNCEMENT TO THE READERS OF THE TOM THE DANCING BUG COMIC STRIP

We here at Tom the Dancing Bug, Inc. have found the proliferation of mass shootings to be very troubling. It's repetitive and depressing to keep trying to write and draw comic strips with the right blend of poignancy and outrage to follow each horrifying incident.

SO we present this **MASS SHOOTING comic strip template**, which you can refer to after each tragedy, sparing us the trouble and anguish of creating a new one over and over.

PLEASE BE SO KIND AS TO mentally insert the details of each latest shooting where indicated.

PANEL ONE, about how the media got things wrong, and/or acted callously. Finding the right tone after a tragedy can be tricky, but the media's always a safe target.

[Insert caricature of media personality]

[Insert whatever media personality said, exaggerated for comic effect]

[Insert logo of offending media organization]

PANEL TWO, about the pro-gun lobby's predictably insane reaction, which will always be about arming "good guys" with more guns, and blaming video games.

IF ONLY EVERY GAME CONSOLE IN AMERICA WERE REPLACED WITH A *GLOCK 22 GEN4,* THESE KINDS OF THINGS WOULD NEVER HAPPEN!

PANELS THREE AND FOUR, about gun advocates' misreading of the Second Amendment, including an ironic depiction of our Founding Fathers debating the Bill of Rights.

SURELY OUR DESCENDANTS WILL KNOW THAT THE SECOND AMENDMENT, LIKE THE ENTIRE BILL OF RIGHTS, MUST BE INTERPRETED WISELY!

OF COURSE THEY WILL! WHO WOULD EVER SAY THIS AMENDMENT MUST ALLOW A [Insert type of person who should not be allowed to buy a gun] TO BUY SOME FIREARM THAT WE IN THE 18TH CENTURY COULD NEVER IMAGINE, LIKE A [Insert type of modern horrific gun/death machine used] ?!

HEAR, HEAR!

Most importantly, PANEL FIVE keeps the tone respectful – mournful yet optimistic – by presenting a somber illustration of the scene of the shootings.

AFTER [Insert name of latest gun tragedy], WILL AMERICA FINALLY WAKE UP AND ENACT SANE GUN LAWS?

[Insert picture of shooting site]

No, it will not. Obviously.

So save this template for the next and all future shootings.

Thank you for your cooperation.

DIST. BY UNIVERSAL UCLICK SYNDICATE - ©2013 R. BOLLING - 1156 - JOIN THE INNER HIVE AT tomthedancingbug.com

9/23/13

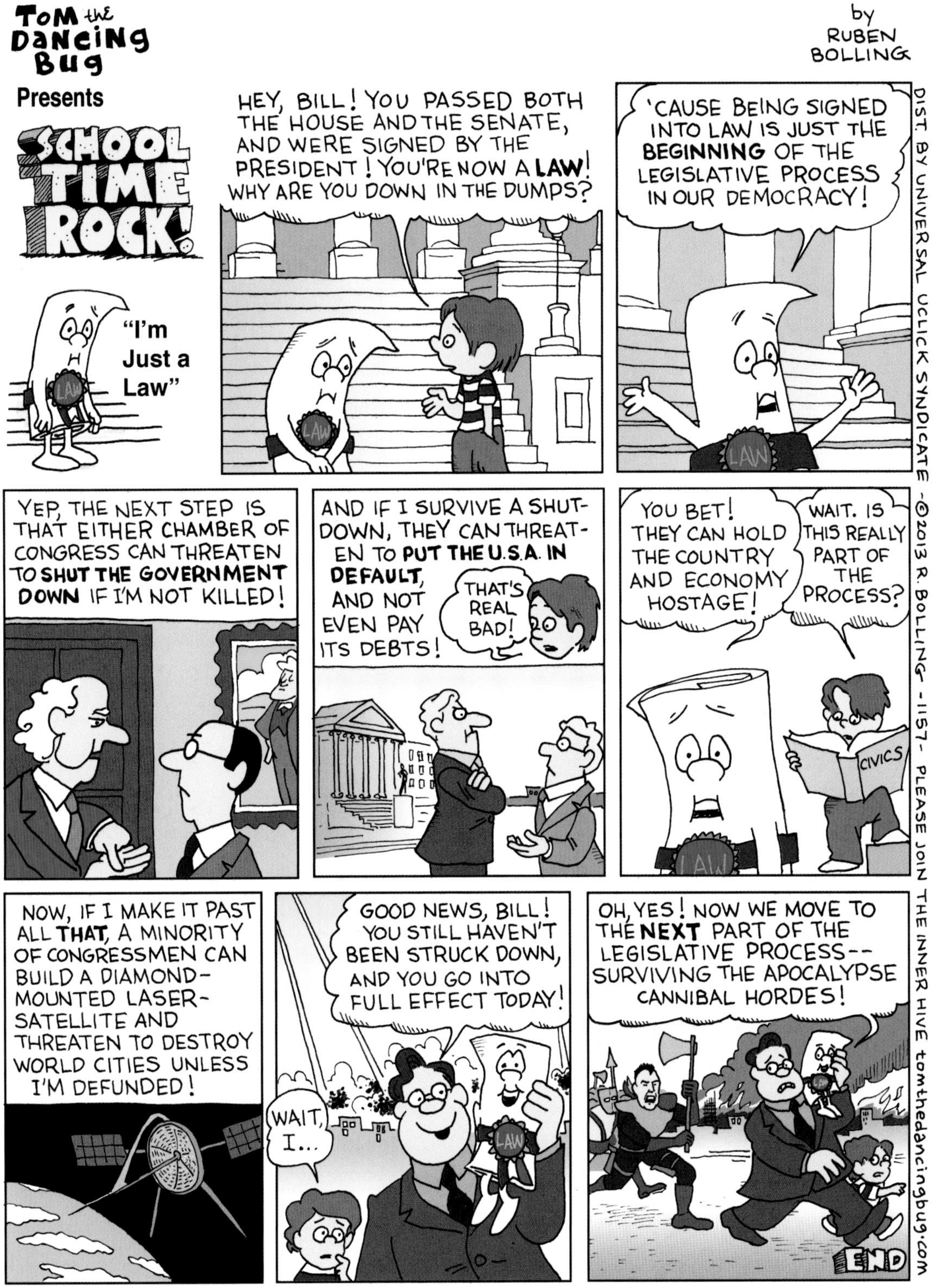
Tom the Dancing Bug
Presents
SCHOOL TIME ROCK!
"I'm Just a Law"
by RUBEN BOLLING
HEY, BILL! YOU PASSED BOTH THE HOUSE AND THE SENATE, AND WERE SIGNED BY THE PRESIDENT! YOU'RE NOW A LAW! WHY ARE YOU DOWN IN THE DUMPS?
LAW
'CAUSE BEING SIGNED INTO LAW IS JUST THE BEGINNING OF THE LEGISLATIVE PROCESS IN OUR DEMOCRACY!
LAW
YEP, THE NEXT STEP IS THAT EITHER CHAMBER OF CONGRESS CAN THREATEN TO SHUT THE GOVERNMENT DOWN IF I'M NOT KILLED!
AND IF I SURVIVE A SHUT-DOWN, THEY CAN THREAT-EN TO PUT THE U.S.A. IN DEFAULT, AND NOT EVEN PAY ITS DEBTS!
THAT'S REAL BAD!
YOU BET! THEY CAN HOLD THE COUNTRY AND ECONOMY HOSTAGE!
WAIT. IS THIS REALLY PART OF THE PROCESS?
CIVICS
LAW
NOW, IF I MAKE IT PAST ALL THAT, A MINORITY OF CONGRESSMEN CAN BUILD A DIAMOND-MOUNTED LASER-SATELLITE AND THREATEN TO DESTROY WORLD CITIES UNLESS I'M DEFUNDED!
GOOD NEWS, BILL! YOU STILL HAVEN'T BEEN STRUCK DOWN, AND YOU GO INTO FULL EFFECT TODAY!
WAIT, I...
LAW
OH, YES! NOW WE MOVE TO THE NEXT PART OF THE LEGISLATIVE PROCESS-- SURVIVING THE APOCALYPSE CANNIBAL HORDES!
END
DIST. BY UNIVERSAL UCLICK SYNDICATE -©2013 R. BOLLING -1157- PLEASE JOIN THE INNER HIVE tomthedancingbug.com

9/30/13

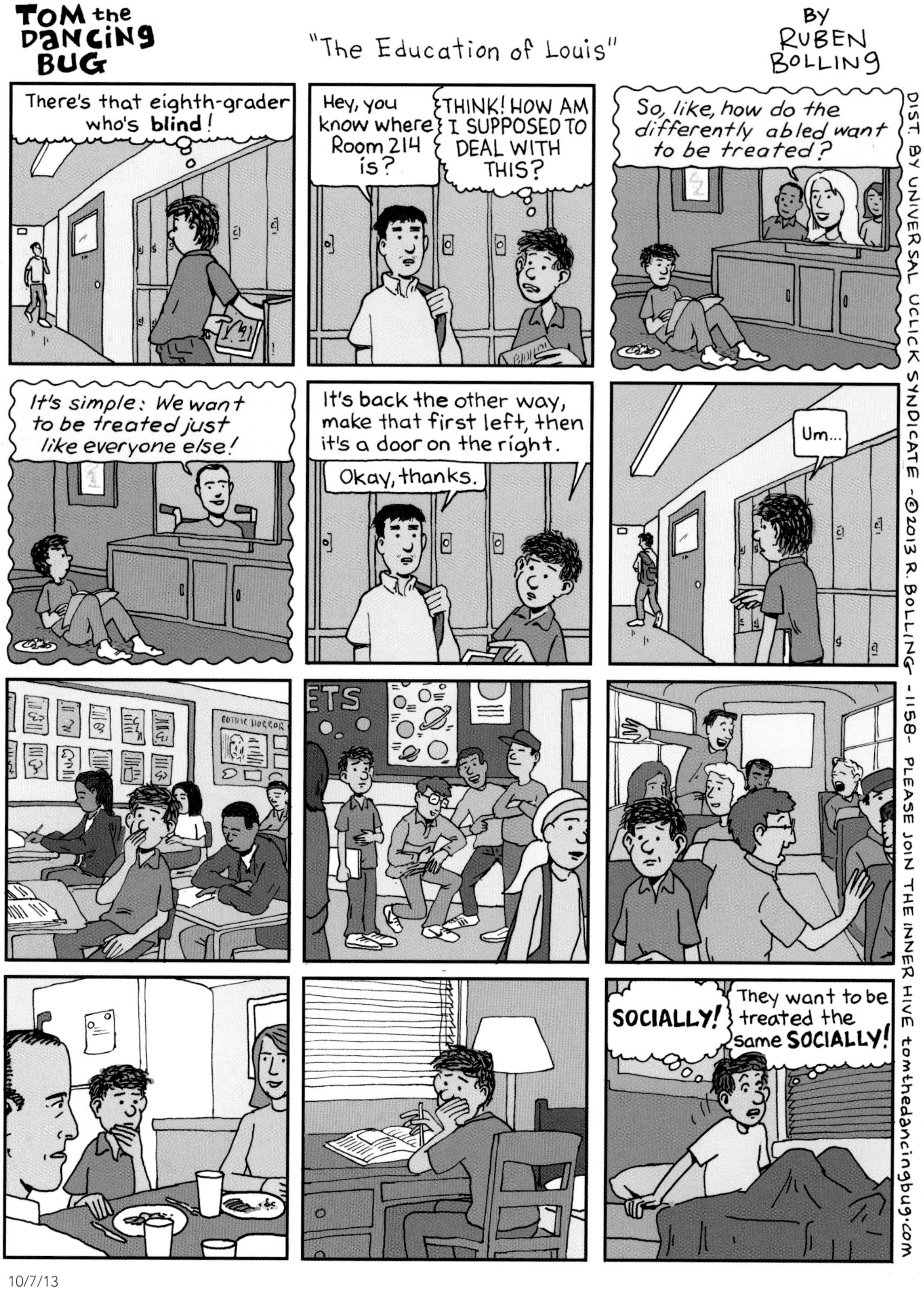
TOM the DANCING BUG
"The Education of Louis"
BY RUBEN BOLLING
There's that eighth-grader who's **blind**!
Hey, you know where Room 214 is?
THINK! HOW AM I SUPPOSED TO DEAL WITH THIS?
So, like, how do the differently abled want to be treated?
It's simple: We want to be treated just like everyone else!
It's back the other way, make that first left, then it's a door on the right.
Okay, thanks.
Um...
SOCIALLY!
They want to be treated the same **SOCIALLY**!
DIST. BY UNIVERSAL UCLICK SYNDICATE -©2013 R. BOLLING- -1158- PLEASE JOIN THE INNER HIVE tomthedancingbug.com

10/7/13

TOM the DANCING BUG

by RUBEN BOLLING

"When a law is an affront to Morality, it is a moral obligation to fight it, even by undermining one's own State."

- Henry David Thoreau, probably

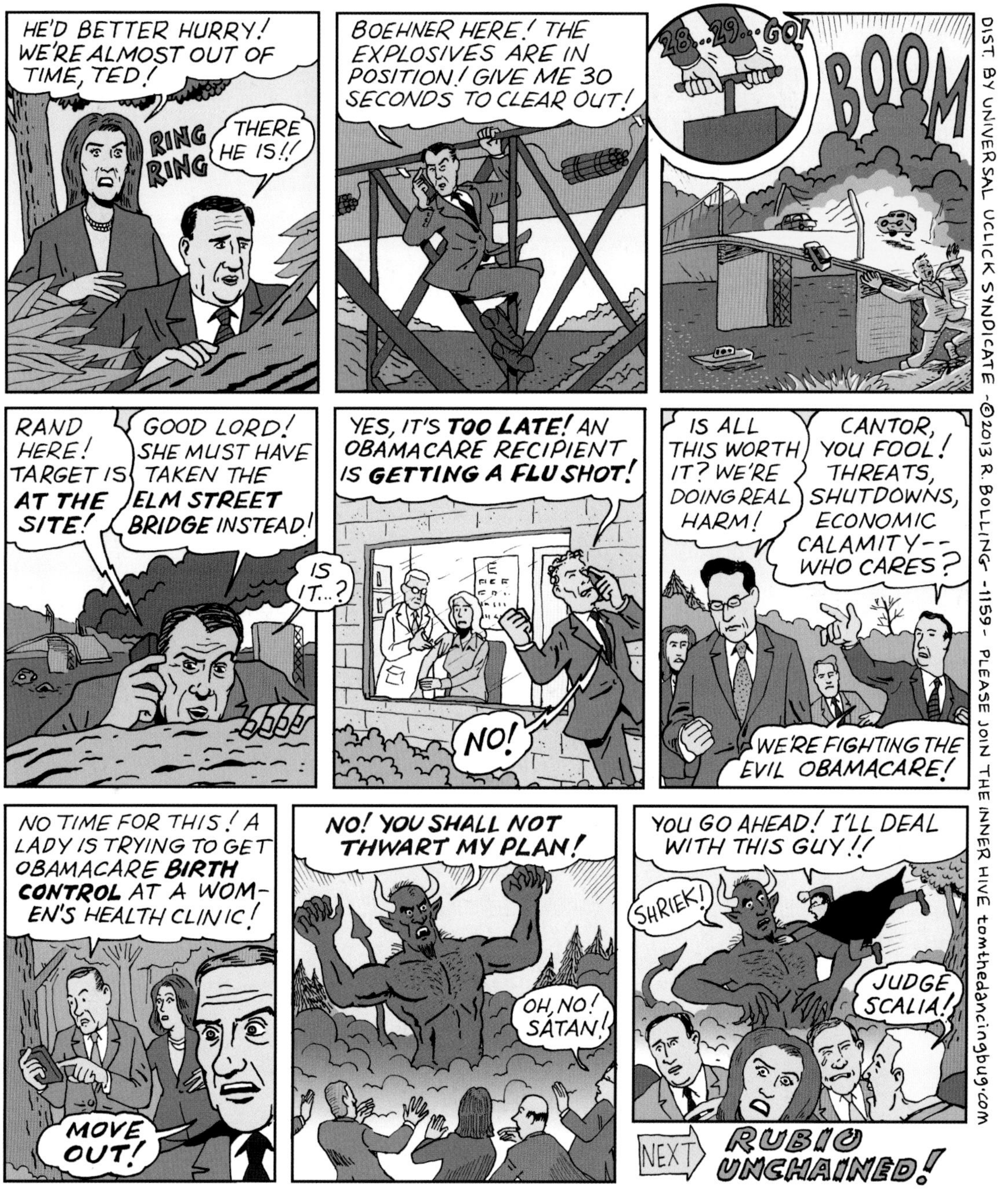

HE'D BETTER HURRY! WE'RE ALMOST OUT OF TIME, TED!
RING RING
THERE HE IS!!
BOEHNER HERE! THE EXPLOSIVES ARE IN POSITION! GIVE ME 30 SECONDS TO CLEAR OUT!
28...29...GO!
BOOM
RAND HERE! TARGET IS AT THE SITE!
GOOD LORD! SHE MUST HAVE TAKEN THE ELM STREET BRIDGE INSTEAD!
IS IT...?
YES, IT'S TOO LATE! AN OBAMACARE RECIPIENT IS GETTING A FLU SHOT!
NO!
IS ALL THIS WORTH IT? WE'RE DOING REAL HARM!
CANTOR, YOU FOOL! THREATS, SHUTDOWNS, ECONOMIC CALAMITY-- WHO CARES?
WE'RE FIGHTING THE EVIL OBAMACARE!
NO TIME FOR THIS! A LADY IS TRYING TO GET OBAMACARE BIRTH CONTROL AT A WOMEN'S HEALTH CLINIC!
MOVE OUT!
NO! YOU SHALL NOT THWART MY PLAN!
OH, NO! SATAN!
YOU GO AHEAD! I'LL DEAL WITH THIS GUY!!
SHRIEK!
JUDGE SCALIA!
NEXT
RUBIO UNCHAINED!
DIST. BY UNIVERSAL UCLICK SYNDICATE -©2013 R. BOLLING -1159- PLEASE JOIN THE INNER HIVE tomthedancingbug.com

10/14/13

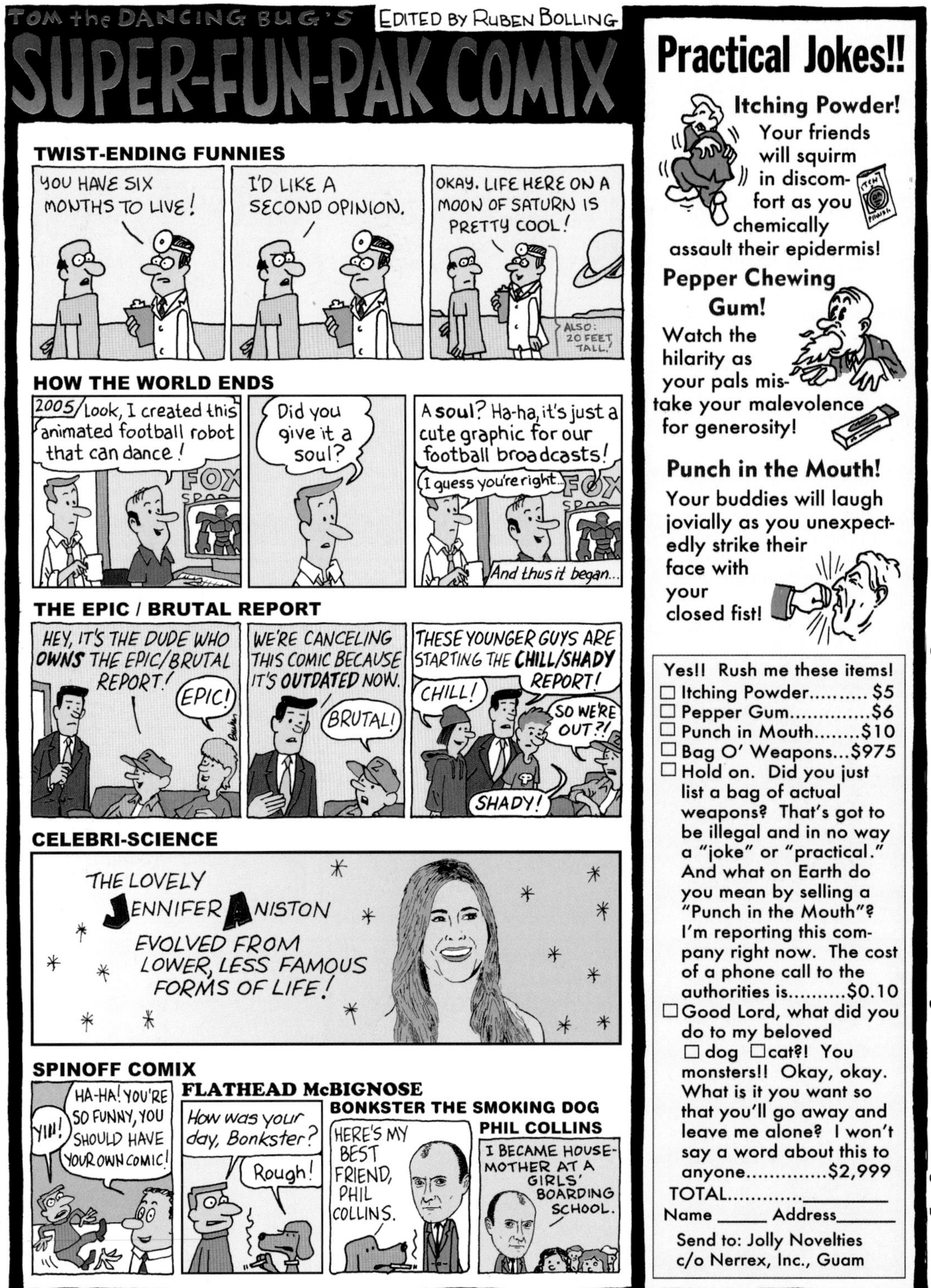
TOM the DANCING BUG'S
EDITED BY RUBEN BOLLING
SUPER-FUN-PAK COMIX
TWIST-ENDING FUNNIES
YOU HAVE SIX MONTHS TO LIVE!
I'D LIKE A SECOND OPINION.
OKAY. LIFE HERE ON A MOON OF SATURN IS PRETTY COOL!
ALSO: 20 FEET TALL!
HOW THE WORLD ENDS
2005
Look, I created this animated football robot that can dance!
Did you give it a soul?
A soul? Ha-ha, it's just a cute graphic for our football broadcasts!
I guess you're right...
And thus it began...
THE EPIC / BRUTAL REPORT
HEY, IT'S THE DUDE WHO OWNS THE EPIC/BRUTAL REPORT!
EPIC!
WE'RE CANCELING THIS COMIC BECAUSE IT'S OUTDATED NOW.
BRUTAL!
THESE YOUNGER GUYS ARE STARTING THE CHILL/SHADY REPORT!
CHILL!
SO WE'RE OUT?!
SHADY!
CELEBRI-SCIENCE
THE LOVELY JENNIFER ANISTON EVOLVED FROM LOWER, LESS FAMOUS FORMS OF LIFE!
SPINOFF COMIX
HA-HA! YOU'RE SO FUNNY, YOU SHOULD HAVE YOUR OWN COMIC!
YIP!
FLATHEAD McBIGNOSE
How was your day, Bonkster?
Rough!
BONKSTER THE SMOKING DOG
HERE'S MY BEST FRIEND, PHIL COLLINS.
PHIL COLLINS
I BECAME HOUSE-MOTHER AT A GIRLS' BOARDING SCHOOL.
Practical Jokes!!
Itching Powder! Your friends will squirm in discomfort as you chemically assault their epidermis!
Pepper Chewing Gum! Watch the hilarity as your pals mistake your malevolence for generosity!
Punch in the Mouth! Your buddies will laugh jovially as you unexpectedly strike their face with your closed fist!
Yes!! Rush me these items!
☐ Itching Powder.......... $5
☐ Pepper Gum.............$6
☐ Punch in Mouth........$10
☐ Bag O' Weapons...$975
☐ Hold on. Did you just list a bag of actual weapons? That's got to be illegal and in no way a "joke" or "practical." And what on Earth do you mean by selling a "Punch in the Mouth"? I'm reporting this company right now. The cost of a phone call to the authorities is..........$0.10
☐ Good Lord, what did you do to my beloved ☐ dog ☐ cat?! You monsters!! Okay, okay. What is it you want so that you'll go away and leave me alone? I won't say a word about this to anyone.............$2,999
TOTAL............________
Name _____ Address________
Send to: Jolly Novelties c/o Nerrex, Inc., Guam

10/21/13

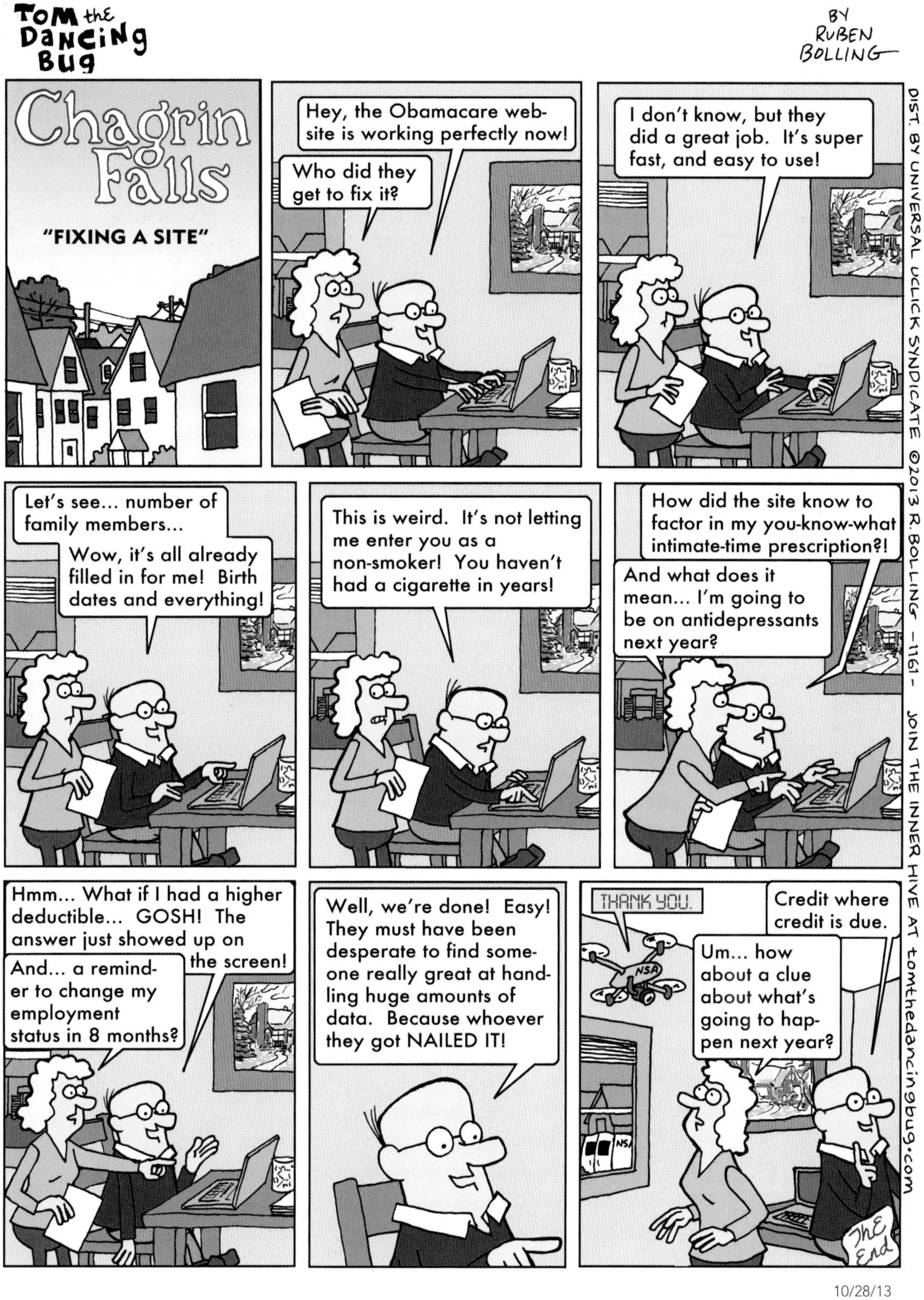
TOM the DANCING BUG
BY RUBEN BOLLING
Chagrin Falls
"FIXING A SITE"
Hey, the Obamacare web-site is working perfectly now!
Who did they get to fix it?
I don't know, but they did a great job. It's super fast, and easy to use!
Let's see... number of family members...
Wow, it's all already filled in for me! Birth dates and everything!
This is weird. It's not letting me enter you as a non-smoker! You haven't had a cigarette in years!
How did the site know to factor in my you-know-what intimate-time prescription?!
And what does it mean... I'm going to be on antidepressants next year?
Hmm... What if I had a higher deductible... GOSH! The answer just showed up on the screen!
And... a reminder to change my employment status in 8 months?
Well, we're done! Easy! They must have been desperate to find someone really great at handling huge amounts of data. Because whoever they got NAILED IT!
THANK YOU.
NSA
Credit where credit is due.
Um... how about a clue about what's going to happen next year?
ThE End
DIST. BY UNIVERSAL UCLICK SYNDICATE ©2013 R. BOLLING -1161- JOIN THE INNER HIVE AT tomthedancingbug.com

10/28/13

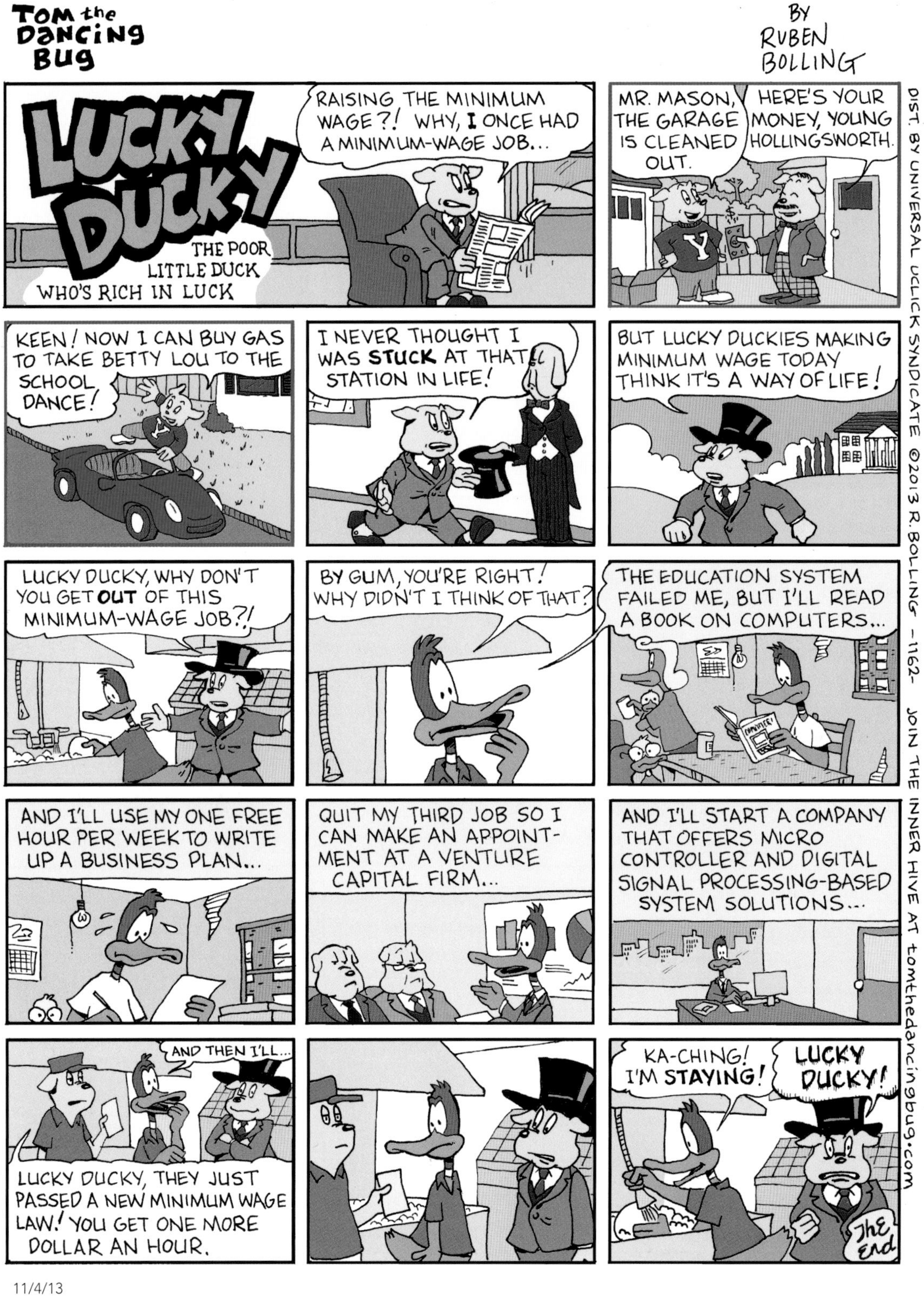
TOM the DANCING BUG
BY RUBEN BOLLING
LUCKY DUCKY
THE POOR LITTLE DUCK WHO'S RICH IN LUCK
RAISING THE MINIMUM WAGE?! WHY, I ONCE HAD A MINIMUM-WAGE JOB...
MR. MASON, THE GARAGE IS CLEANED OUT.
HERE'S YOUR MONEY, YOUNG HOLLINGSWORTH.
KEEN! NOW I CAN BUY GAS TO TAKE BETTY LOU TO THE SCHOOL DANCE!
I NEVER THOUGHT I WAS STUCK AT THAT STATION IN LIFE!
BUT LUCKY DUCKIES MAKING MINIMUM WAGE TODAY THINK IT'S A WAY OF LIFE!
LUCKY DUCKY, WHY DON'T YOU GET OUT OF THIS MINIMUM-WAGE JOB?!
BY GUM, YOU'RE RIGHT! WHY DIDN'T I THINK OF THAT?
THE EDUCATION SYSTEM FAILED ME, BUT I'LL READ A BOOK ON COMPUTERS...
COMPUTERS
AND I'LL USE MY ONE FREE HOUR PER WEEK TO WRITE UP A BUSINESS PLAN...
QUIT MY THIRD JOB SO I CAN MAKE AN APPOINTMENT AT A VENTURE CAPITAL FIRM...
AND I'LL START A COMPANY THAT OFFERS MICRO CONTROLLER AND DIGITAL SIGNAL PROCESSING-BASED SYSTEM SOLUTIONS...
AND THEN I'LL...
LUCKY DUCKY, THEY JUST PASSED A NEW MINIMUM WAGE LAW! YOU GET ONE MORE DOLLAR AN HOUR.
KA-CHING! I'M STAYING!
LUCKY DUCKY!
THE END
DIST. BY UNIVERSAL UCLICK SYNDICATE ©2013 R. BOLLING -1162- JOIN THE INNER HIVE AT tomthedancingbug.com

11/4/13

TOM the DANCING BUG

by RUBEN BOLLING

Hey, NFL Kids!

Get your...

88 GUS FERNANDEZ Tight End

OFFENSIVE STEREO- TYPES OF NATIVE AMERICAN PEOPLES

STATS

	CH.	CONV.
Assault	5	0
Manslgtr.	2	0
Murder	1	0
Poss. Firearm	27	0
DUI	118	0

GUS IS KNOWN FOR HIS GENEROSITY TO FRIENDS WHO GO TO JAIL FOR CRIMES COMMITTED IN HIS PRESENCE.

PRTD. IN U.S.A.

Gus **FERNANDEZ**
OFFENSIVE STEREOTYPES OF NATIVE AMERICAN PEOPLES • TIGHT END

64 BULL LUZEOWICZ Defensive End

NOBLE SAVAGES

STATS

Who are you to ask about stats, you weak-kneed panty-waisted NERD? I'll kill you and hunt down your family and kill them and then defecate in the skull of your baby! jk, lol. Now, PAY FOR MY DINNER, WORM!

BULL SET A RECORD IN 2011 FOR MOST ANGER PER RAGE INCIDENT.

PRTD. IN U.S.A.

Bull **LUZEOWICZ**
NOBLE SAVAGES • DEF. END

73 JIMMY WITTINSON Tackle

GOOD INJUNS

STATS

Please, if you read this, help me. Contact my parents or law enforcement. Oh, lord, they're coming... Okay, I'll use Morse code to blink my location in my next post-game interview. Please, someone HELP ME!

JIMMY LED THE LEAGUE IN UNEX- PLAINED INJURIES AND VACATIONS PAID FOR BUT NOT ATTENDED.

PRTD. IN U.S.A.

ROOKIE

Jimmy **WITTINSON**
GOOD INJUNS • OFF. TACKLE

29 DIZZ WASHINGTON Running Back

DEAD INJUNS

STATS

CONCUSSIONS	
2007.	.9
2008.	11
2009.	17
2010.	21
2011.	. .I don't remember
2012.	. .What's a . . . .! ?
LIFE.	. .apple juice good

DIZZ SAYS HIS FAVORITE MEMORY OF THE '09 PLAYOFFS IS "PRETTY COLORS."

PRTD. IN U.S.A.

Dizz **WASHING**...
DEAD INJUNS • RUNNI...

NFL TRADING CARDS!!

DIST. BY UNIVERSAL UCLICK SYNDICATE - ©2013 R. BOLLING -1163- JOIN THE INNER HIVE AT tomthedancingbug.com

11/11/13

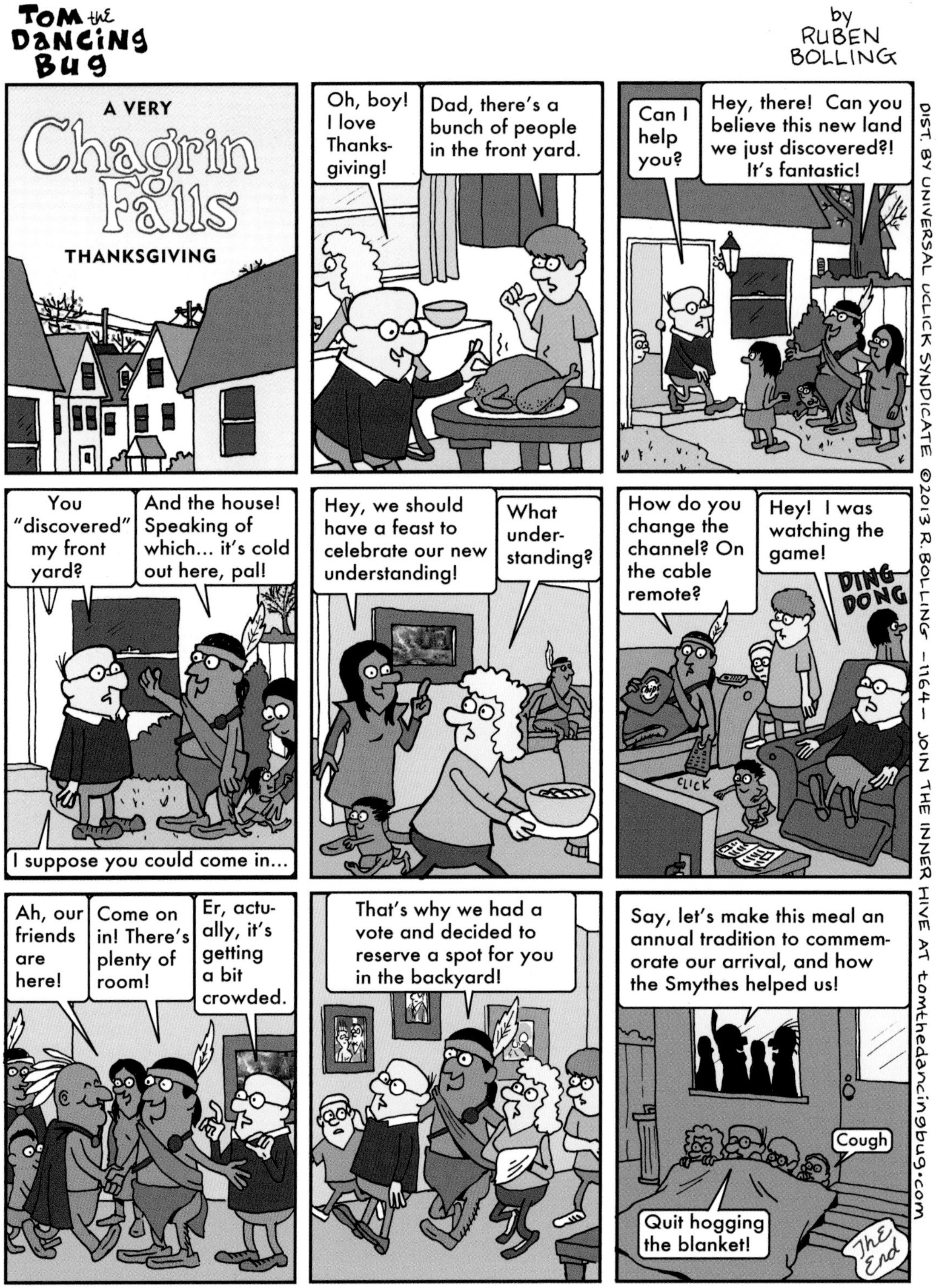
TOM the DANCING BUG
by RUBEN BOLLING
A VERY Chagrin Falls THANKSGIVING
Oh, boy! I love Thanks-giving!
Dad, there's a bunch of people in the front yard.
Can I help you?
Hey, there! Can you believe this new land we just discovered?! It's fantastic!
You "discovered" my front yard?
And the house! Speaking of which... it's cold out here, pal!
I suppose you could come in...
Hey, we should have a feast to celebrate our new understanding!
What under-standing?
How do you change the channel? On the cable remote?
Hey! I was watching the game!
DING DONG
CLICK
Ah, our friends are here!
Come on in! There's plenty of room!
Er, actu-ally, it's getting a bit crowded.
That's why we had a vote and decided to reserve a spot for you in the backyard!
Say, let's make this meal an annual tradition to commem-orate our arrival, and how the Smythes helped us!
Cough
Quit hogging the blanket!
The End
DIST. BY UNIVERSAL UCLICK SYNDICATE ©2013 R. BOLLING -1164- JOIN THE INNER HIVE AT tomthedancingbug.com

11/18/13

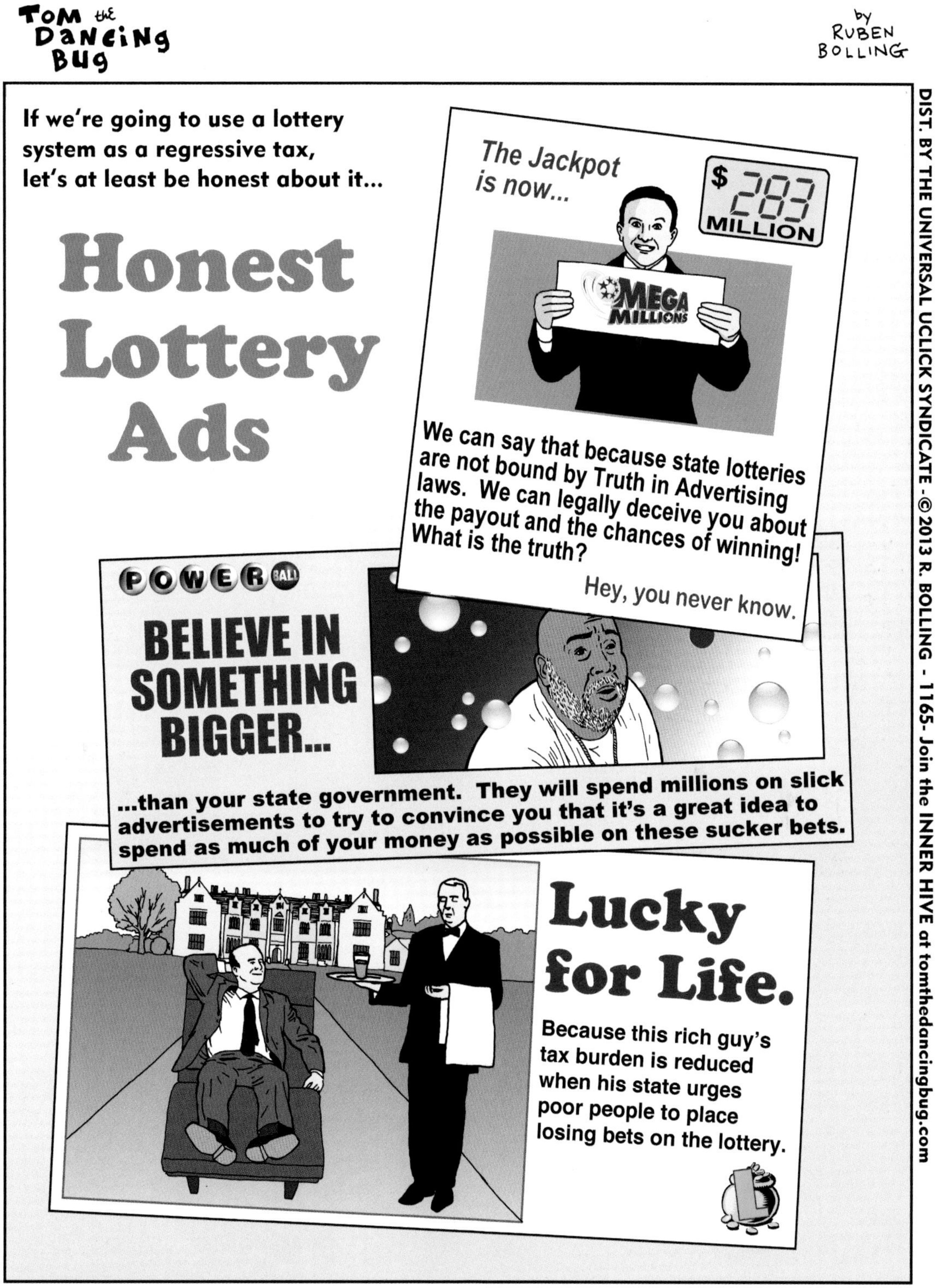
TOM the DANCING BUG
by RUBEN BOLLING
If we're going to use a lottery system as a regressive tax, let's at least be honest about it...
Honest Lottery Ads
The Jackpot is now...
$283 MILLION
MEGA MILLIONS
We can say that because state lotteries are not bound by Truth in Advertising laws. We can legally deceive you about the payout and the chances of winning! What is the truth?
Hey, you never know.
POWERBALL
BELIEVE IN SOMETHING BIGGER...
...than your state government. They will spend millions on slick advertisements to try to convince you that it's a great idea to spend as much of your money as possible on these sucker bets.
Lucky for Life.
Because this rich guy's tax burden is reduced when his state urges poor people to place losing bets on the lottery.
DIST. BY THE UNIVERSAL UCLICK SYNDICATE - © 2013 R. BOLLING - 1165- Join the INNER HIVE at tomthedancingbug.com

11/25/13

TOM the DANCING BUG

by RUBEN BOLLING

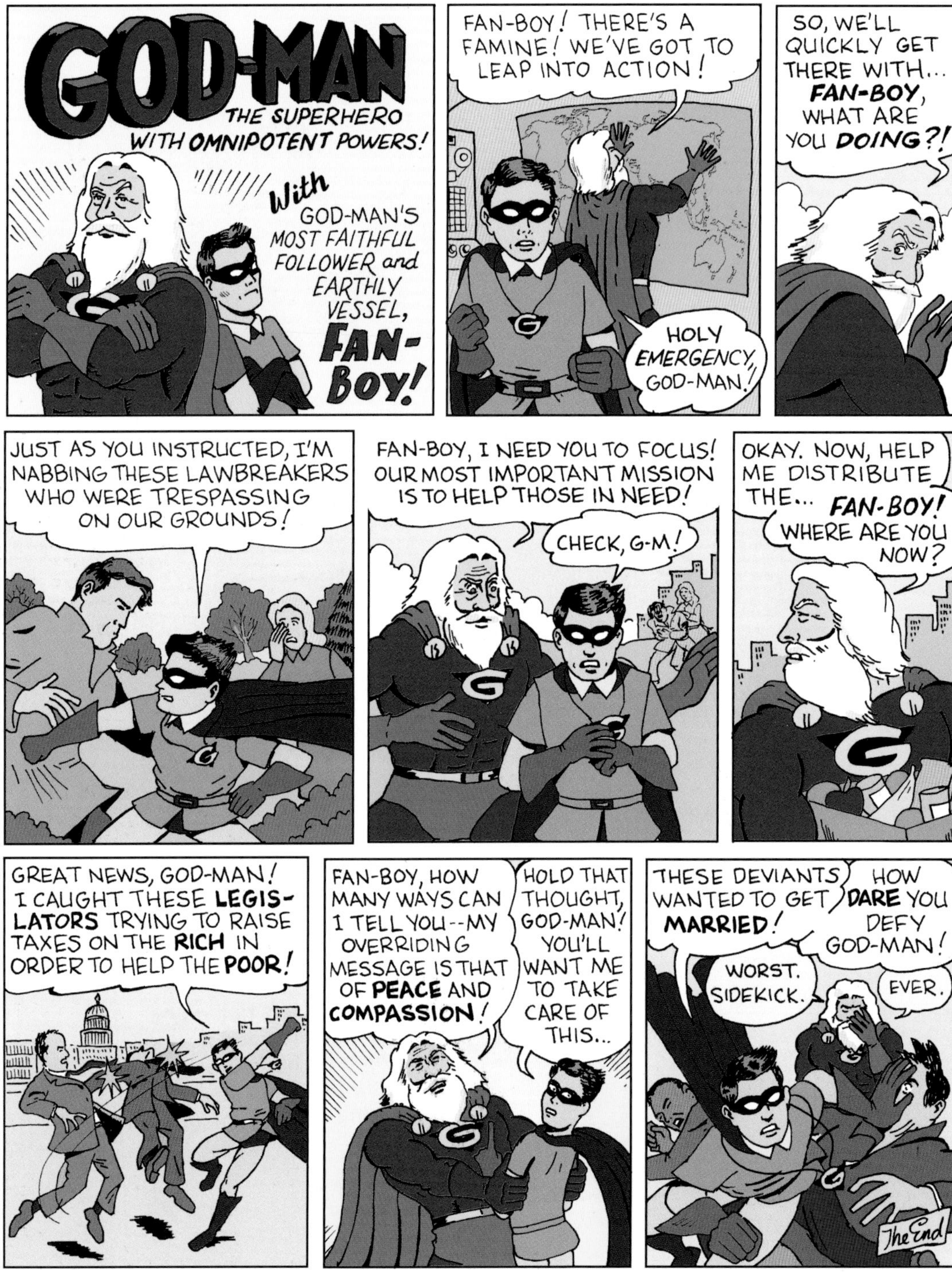
GOD-MAN
THE SUPERHERO WITH OMNIPOTENT POWERS!
With GOD-MAN'S MOST FAITHFUL FOLLOWER and EARTHLY VESSEL, FAN-BOY!
FAN-BOY! THERE'S A FAMINE! WE'VE GOT TO LEAP INTO ACTION!
HOLY EMERGENCY, GOD-MAN!
SO, WE'LL QUICKLY GET THERE WITH... FAN-BOY, WHAT ARE YOU DOING?!
JUST AS YOU INSTRUCTED, I'M NABBING THESE LAWBREAKERS WHO WERE TRESPASSING ON OUR GROUNDS!
FAN-BOY, I NEED YOU TO FOCUS! OUR MOST IMPORTANT MISSION IS TO HELP THOSE IN NEED!
CHECK, G-M!
OKAY. NOW, HELP ME DISTRIBUTE THE... FAN-BOY! WHERE ARE YOU NOW?
GREAT NEWS, GOD-MAN! I CAUGHT THESE LEGISLATORS TRYING TO RAISE TAXES ON THE RICH IN ORDER TO HELP THE POOR!
FAN-BOY, HOW MANY WAYS CAN I TELL YOU--MY OVERRIDING MESSAGE IS THAT OF PEACE AND COMPASSION!
HOLD THAT THOUGHT, GOD-MAN! YOU'LL WANT ME TO TAKE CARE OF THIS...
THESE DEVIANTS WANTED TO GET MARRIED!
HOW DARE YOU DEFY GOD-MAN!
WORST. SIDEKICK.
EVER.
The End

12/2/13

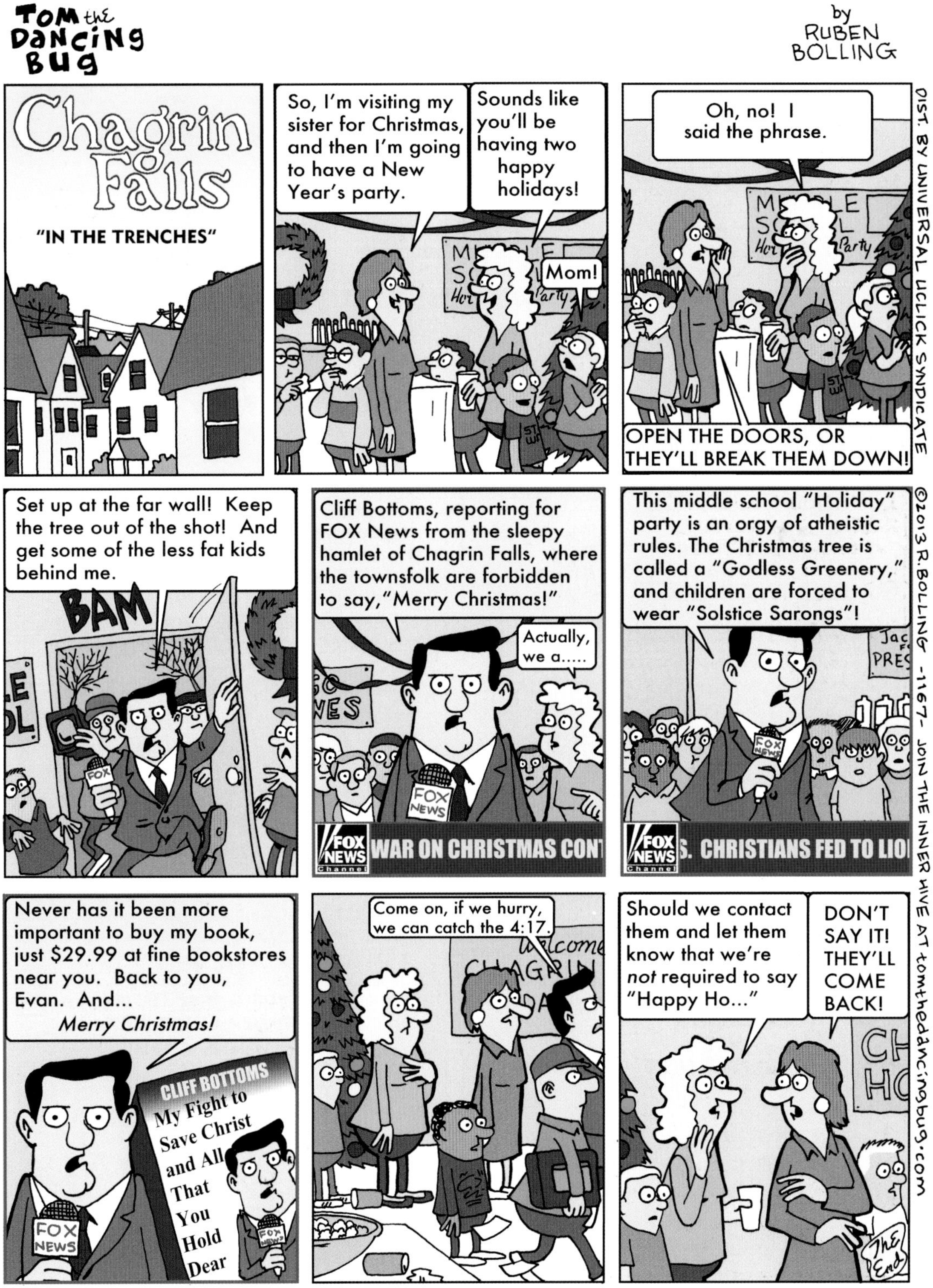
TOM the DANCING BUG
by RUBEN BOLLING
Chagrin Falls
"IN THE TRENCHES"
So, I'm visiting my sister for Christmas, and then I'm going to have a New Year's party.
Sounds like you'll be having two happy holidays!
Mom!
Oh, no! I said the phrase.
OPEN THE DOORS, OR THEY'LL BREAK THEM DOWN!
Set up at the far wall! Keep the tree out of the shot! And get some of the less fat kids behind me.
BAM
Cliff Bottoms, reporting for FOX News from the sleepy hamlet of Chagrin Falls, where the townsfolk are forbidden to say, "Merry Christmas!"
Actually, we a.....
WAR ON CHRISTMAS CONT
This middle school "Holiday" party is an orgy of atheistic rules. The Christmas tree is called a "Godless Greenery," and children are forced to wear "Solstice Sarongs"!
S. CHRISTIANS FED TO LIO
Never has it been more important to buy my book, just $29.99 at fine bookstores near you. Back to you, Evan. And...
Merry Christmas!
CLIFF BOTTOMS
My Fight to Save Christ and All That You Hold Dear
Come on, if we hurry, we can catch the 4:17.
Should we contact them and let them know that we're *not* required to say "Happy Ho..."
DON'T SAY IT! THEY'LL COME BACK!
The End
DIST. BY UNIVERSAL UCLICK SYNDICATE
©2013 R. BOLLING -1167- JOIN THE INNER HIVE AT tomthedancingbug.com

12/9/13

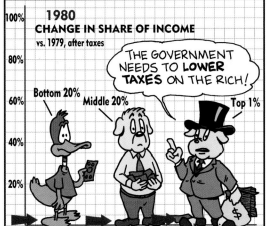

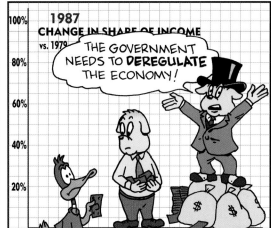

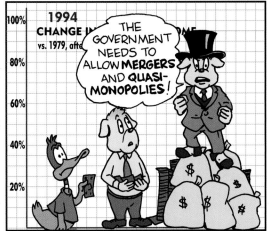

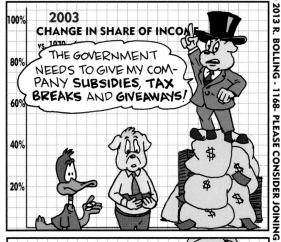

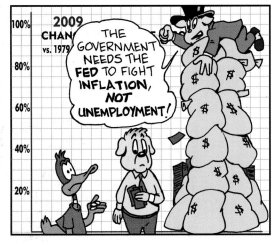

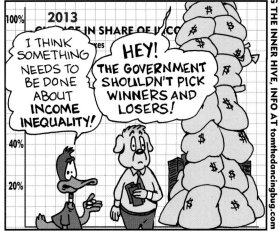

TOM the DANCING BUG
by RUBEN BOLLING
1980
CHANGE IN SHARE OF INCOME
vs. 1979, after taxes
100%
80%
60%
40%
20%
Bottom 20%
Middle 20%
Top 1%
THE GOVERNMENT NEEDS TO LOWER TAXES ON THE RICH!
1987
THE GOVERNMENT NEEDS TO DEREGULATE THE ECONOMY!
1994
THE GOVERNMENT NEEDS TO ALLOW MERGERS AND QUASI-MONOPOLIES!
2003
CHANGE IN SHARE OF INCOME
THE GOVERNMENT NEEDS TO GIVE MY COMPANY SUBSIDIES, TAX BREAKS AND GIVEAWAYS!
2009
THE GOVERNMENT NEEDS THE FED TO FIGHT INFLATION, NOT UNEMPLOYMENT!
2013
I THINK SOMETHING NEEDS TO BE DONE ABOUT INCOME INEQUALITY!
HEY! THE GOVERNMENT SHOULDN'T PICK WINNERS AND LOSERS!
DIST. BY THE UNIVERSAL UCLICK SYNDICATE - (C) 2013 R. BOLLING - 1168- PLEASE CONSIDER JOINING THE INNER HIVE, INFO AT tomthedancingbug.com

12/16/13

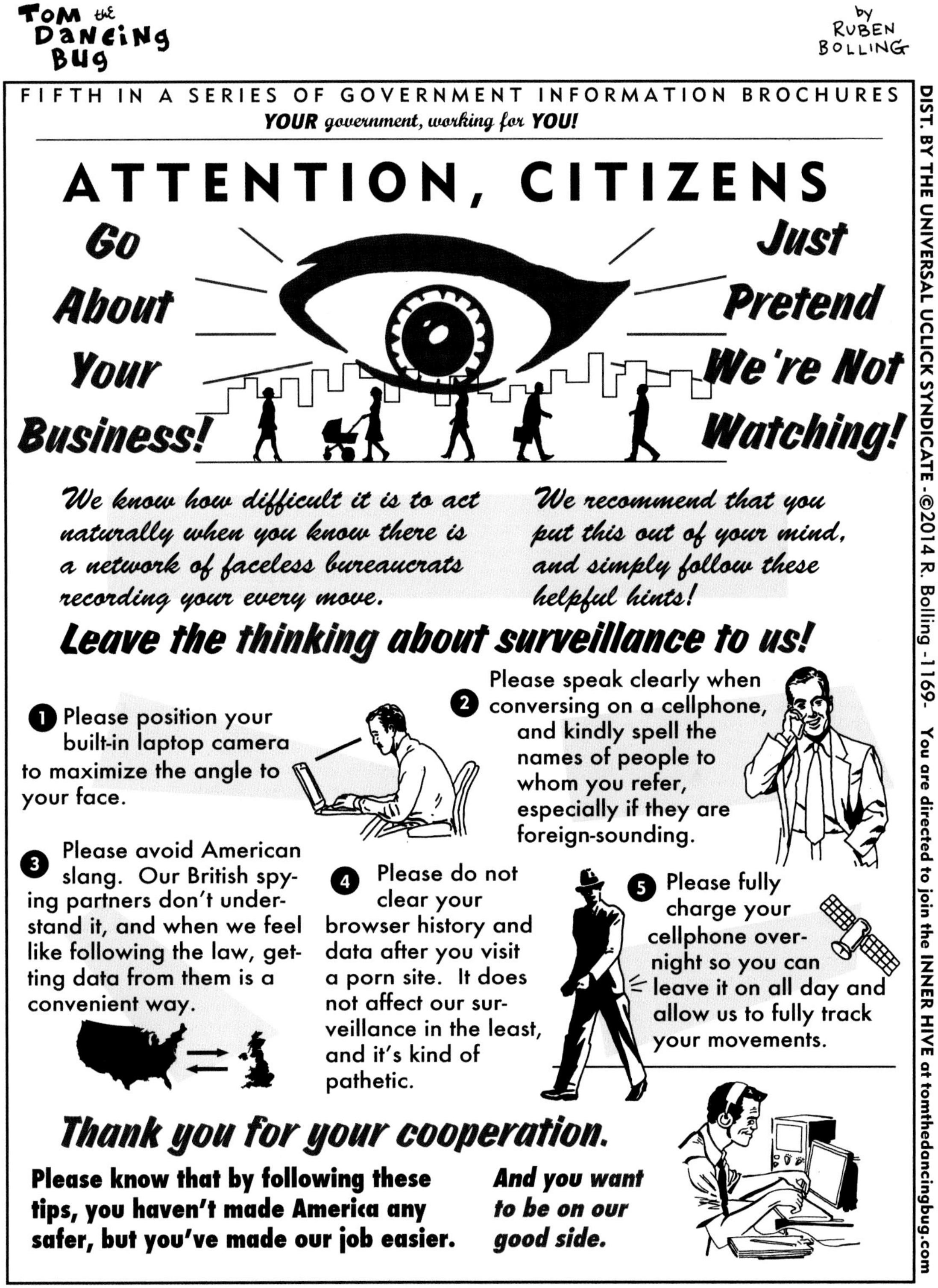
TOM the DANCING BUG
by RUBEN BOLLING
FIFTH IN A SERIES OF GOVERNMENT INFORMATION BROCHURES
YOUR government, working for YOU!
ATTENTION, CITIZENS
Go About Your Business!
Just Pretend We're Not Watching!
We know how difficult it is to act naturally when you know there is a network of faceless bureaucrats recording your every move.
We recommend that you put this out of your mind, and simply follow these helpful hints!
Leave the thinking about surveillance to us!
1 Please position your built-in laptop camera to maximize the angle to your face.
2 Please speak clearly when conversing on a cellphone, and kindly spell the names of people to whom you refer, especially if they are foreign-sounding.
3 Please avoid American slang. Our British spying partners don't understand it, and when we feel like following the law, getting data from them is a convenient way.
4 Please do not clear your browser history and data after you visit a porn site. It does not affect our surveillance in the least, and it's kind of pathetic.
5 Please fully charge your cellphone overnight so you can leave it on all day and allow us to fully track your movements.
Thank you for your cooperation.
Please know that by following these tips, you haven't made America any safer, but you've made our job easier.
And you want to be on our good side.
DIST. BY THE UNIVERSAL UCLICK SYNDICATE ©2014 R. Bolling -1169- You are directed to join the INNER HIVE at tomthedancingbug.com

12/30/13

TOM the DANCING BUG

by RUBEN BOLLING

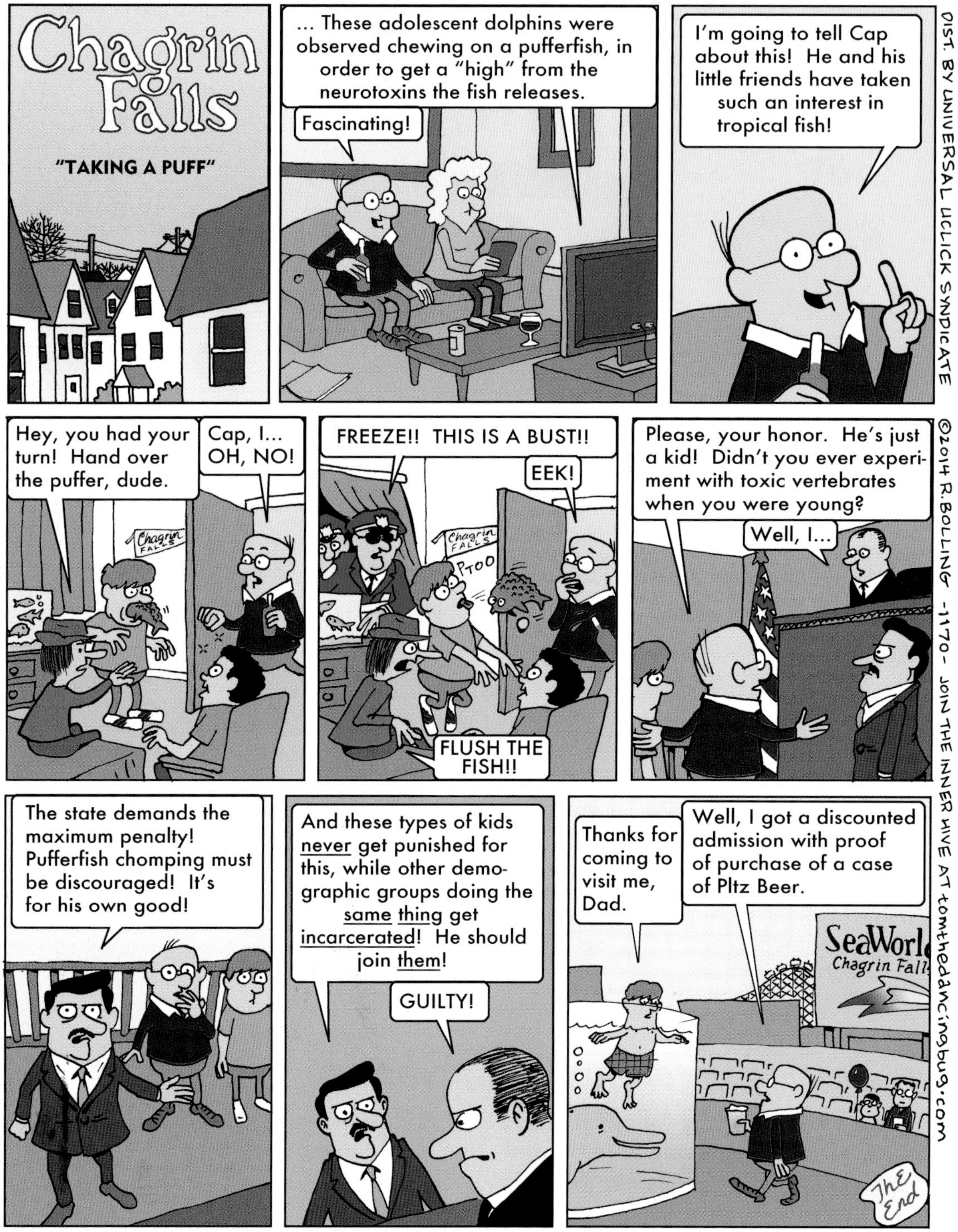

Chagrin Falls
"TAKING A PUFF"
... These adolescent dolphins were observed chewing on a pufferfish, in order to get a "high" from the neurotoxins the fish releases.
Fascinating!
I'm going to tell Cap about this! He and his little friends have taken such an interest in tropical fish!
Hey, you had your turn! Hand over the puffer, dude.
Cap, I... OH, NO!
Chagrin FALLS
FREEZE!! THIS IS A BUST!!
EEK!
Chagrin FALLS
PTOO
FLUSH THE FISH!!
Please, your honor. He's just a kid! Didn't you ever experiment with toxic vertebrates when you were young?
Well, I...
The state demands the maximum penalty! Pufferfish chomping must be discouraged! It's for his own good!
And these types of kids never get punished for this, while other demographic groups doing the same thing get incarcerated! He should join them!
GUILTY!
Thanks for coming to visit me, Dad.
Well, I got a discounted admission with proof of purchase of a case of Pltz Beer.
SeaWorl
Chagrin Fall
The End
DIST. BY UNIVERSAL UCLICK SYNDICATE ©2014 R. BOLLING -1170- JOIN THE INNER HIVE AT tomthedancingbug.com

1/6/14

TOM the DANCING BUG

by RUBEN BOLLING

DIST. BY UNIVERSAL UCLICK SYNDICATE

©2014 R.BOLLING -1171- JOIN THE INNER HIVE AT tomthedancingbug.com

PRESIDENT CHRIS CHRISTIE, DAY 100

April 30, 2017

The United States is stronger than ever. I was just in Delaware, and I told the governor that he had a nice little state there.

When I said it would be "a shame if anything bad happened to it," that was a statement of fact. It was not a threat, as a bunch of you Poindexters in the press would have Americans believe.

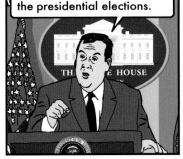

And I want to say that I had no idea that some staffers determined the site of a nuclear test on the basis of who didn't vote for me in the presidential elections.

My apologies to everyone in the Chicago area, but the truth is, we have to test those things somewhere, so come on. Quit your crying.

I also want to say that what happened in Hawaii is tragic, and my sympathy and best wishes go to all the people who live there.

But the critics who say I didn't have the military defend Hawaii from the North Korean invasion as some kind of political payback – that's partisan and hurtful.

Anyway, it's just a bunch of islands... I was surprised it was a state, to be perfectly frank. I think we're going to save money on this thing.

That's it. Thank you, Washington, DC press, for coming. Oh, and John? You live in Virginia? You're gonna want to take 14th Street to 395. Do not take the Roosevelt Bridge. I'm just saying.

1/13/14

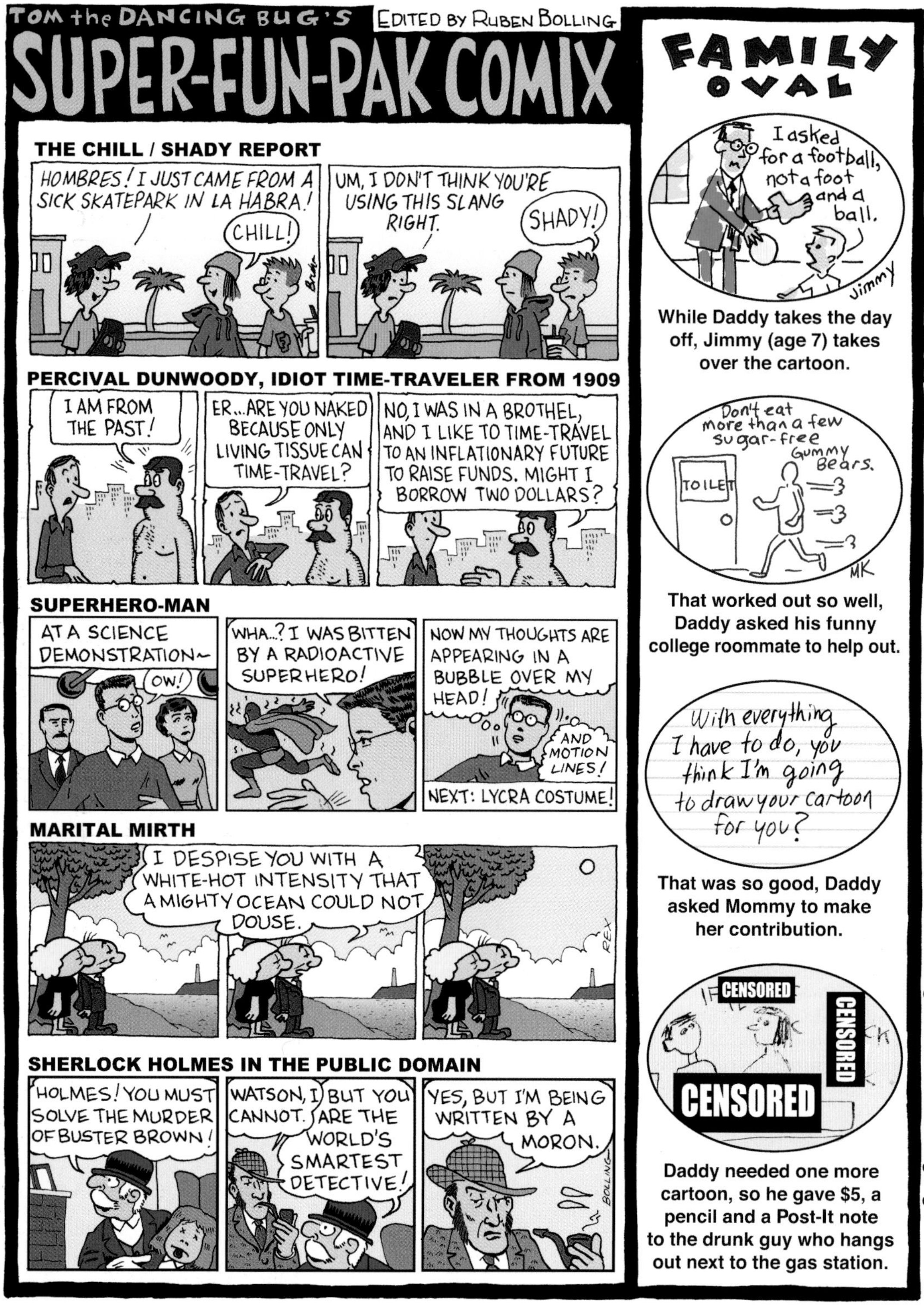

TOM the DANCING BUG'S
EDITED BY RUBEN BOLLING
SUPER-FUN-PAK COMIX
THE CHILL / SHADY REPORT
HOMBRES! I JUST CAME FROM A SICK SKATEPARK IN LA HABRA!
CHILL!
UM, I DON'T THINK YOU'RE USING THIS SLANG RIGHT.
SHADY!
PERCIVAL DUNWOODY, IDIOT TIME-TRAVELER FROM 1909
I AM FROM THE PAST!
ER...ARE YOU NAKED BECAUSE ONLY LIVING TISSUE CAN TIME-TRAVEL?
NO, I WAS IN A BROTHEL, AND I LIKE TO TIME-TRAVEL TO AN INFLATIONARY FUTURE TO RAISE FUNDS. MIGHT I BORROW TWO DOLLARS?
SUPERHERO-MAN
AT A SCIENCE DEMONSTRATION—
OW!
WHA...? I WAS BITTEN BY A RADIOACTIVE SUPERHERO!
NOW MY THOUGHTS ARE APPEARING IN A BUBBLE OVER MY HEAD!
AND MOTION LINES!
NEXT: LYCRA COSTUME!
MARITAL MIRTH
I DESPISE YOU WITH A WHITE-HOT INTENSITY THAT A MIGHTY OCEAN COULD NOT DOUSE.
REX
SHERLOCK HOLMES IN THE PUBLIC DOMAIN
HOLMES! YOU MUST SOLVE THE MURDER OF BUSTER BROWN!
WATSON, I CANNOT.
BUT YOU ARE THE WORLD'S SMARTEST DETECTIVE!
YES, BUT I'M BEING WRITTEN BY A MORON.
BOLLING
FAMILY OVAL
I asked for a football, not a foot and a ball.
Jimmy
While Daddy takes the day off, Jimmy (age 7) takes over the cartoon.
Don't eat more than a few sugar-free Gummy Bears.
TOILET
MK
That worked out so well, Daddy asked his funny college roommate to help out.
With everything I have to do, you think I'm going to draw your cartoon for you?
That was so good, Daddy asked Mommy to make her contribution.
CENSORED
CENSORED
CENSORED
Daddy needed one more cartoon, so he gave $5, a pencil and a Post-It note to the drunk guy who hangs out next to the gas station.

1/20/14

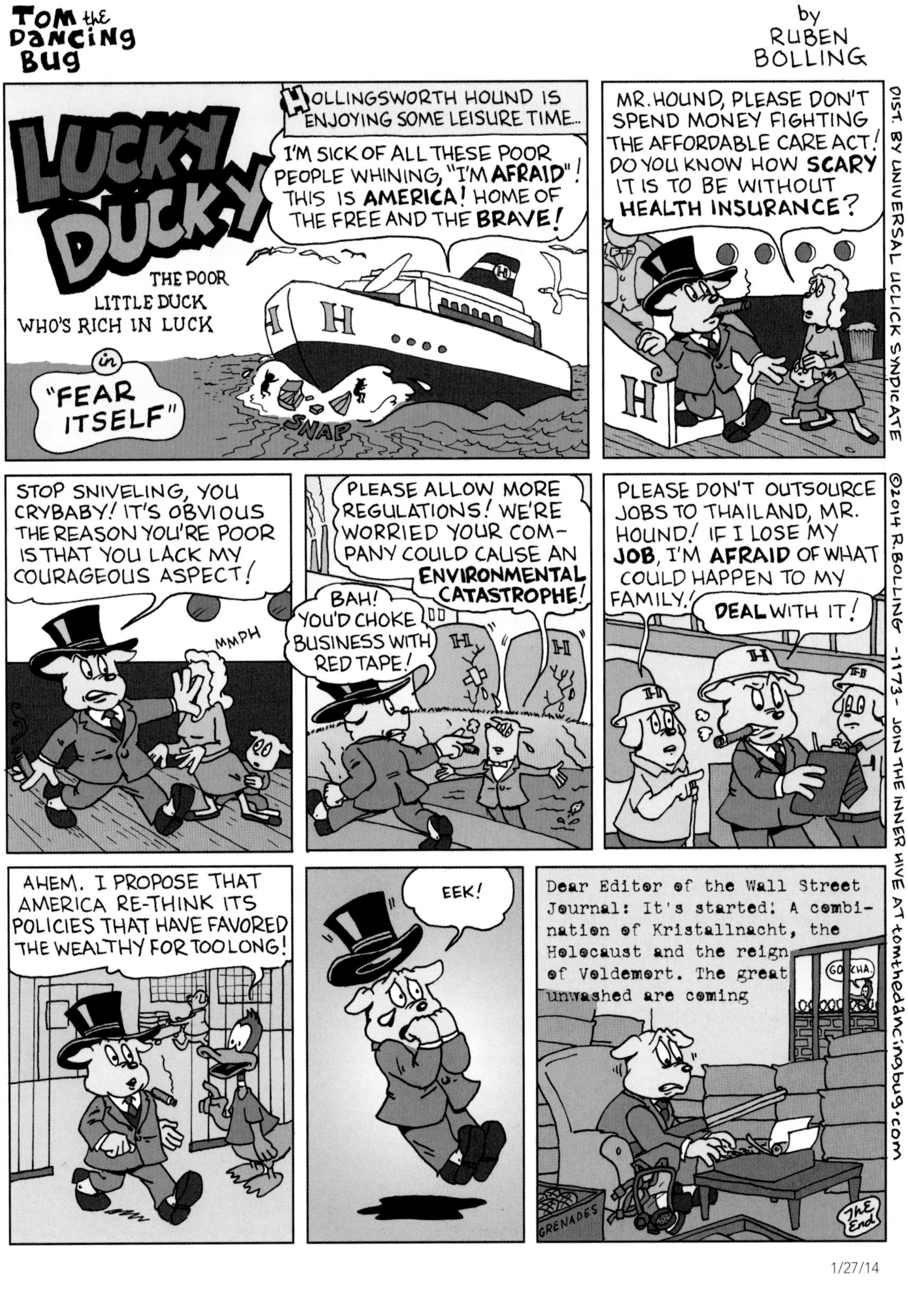

TOM the DANCING BUG
by RUBEN BOLLING
LUCKY DUCKY
THE POOR LITTLE DUCK WHO'S RICH IN LUCK
in "FEAR ITSELF"
HOLLINGSWORTH HOUND IS ENJOYING SOME LEISURE TIME...
I'M SICK OF ALL THESE POOR PEOPLE WHINING, "I'M AFRAID"! THIS IS AMERICA! HOME OF THE FREE AND THE BRAVE!
SNAP
MR. HOUND, PLEASE DON'T SPEND MONEY FIGHTING THE AFFORDABLE CARE ACT! DO YOU KNOW HOW SCARY IT IS TO BE WITHOUT HEALTH INSURANCE?
STOP SNIVELING, YOU CRYBABY! IT'S OBVIOUS THE REASON YOU'RE POOR IS THAT YOU LACK MY COURAGEOUS ASPECT!
MMPH
PLEASE ALLOW MORE REGULATIONS! WE'RE WORRIED YOUR COMPANY COULD CAUSE AN ENVIRONMENTAL CATASTROPHE!
BAH! YOU'D CHOKE BUSINESS WITH RED TAPE!
PLEASE DON'T OUTSOURCE JOBS TO THAILAND, MR. HOUND! IF I LOSE MY JOB, I'M AFRAID OF WHAT COULD HAPPEN TO MY FAMILY!
DEAL WITH IT!
AHEM. I PROPOSE THAT AMERICA RE-THINK ITS POLICIES THAT HAVE FAVORED THE WEALTHY FOR TOO LONG!
EEK!
Dear Editor of the Wall Street Journal: It's started! A combination of Kristallnacht, the Holocaust and the reign of Voldemort. The great unwashed are coming
GRENADES
THE End
DIST. BY UNIVERSAL UCLICK SYNDICATE ©2014 R. BOLLING -1173- JOIN THE INNER HIVE AT tomthedancingbug.com

1/27/14

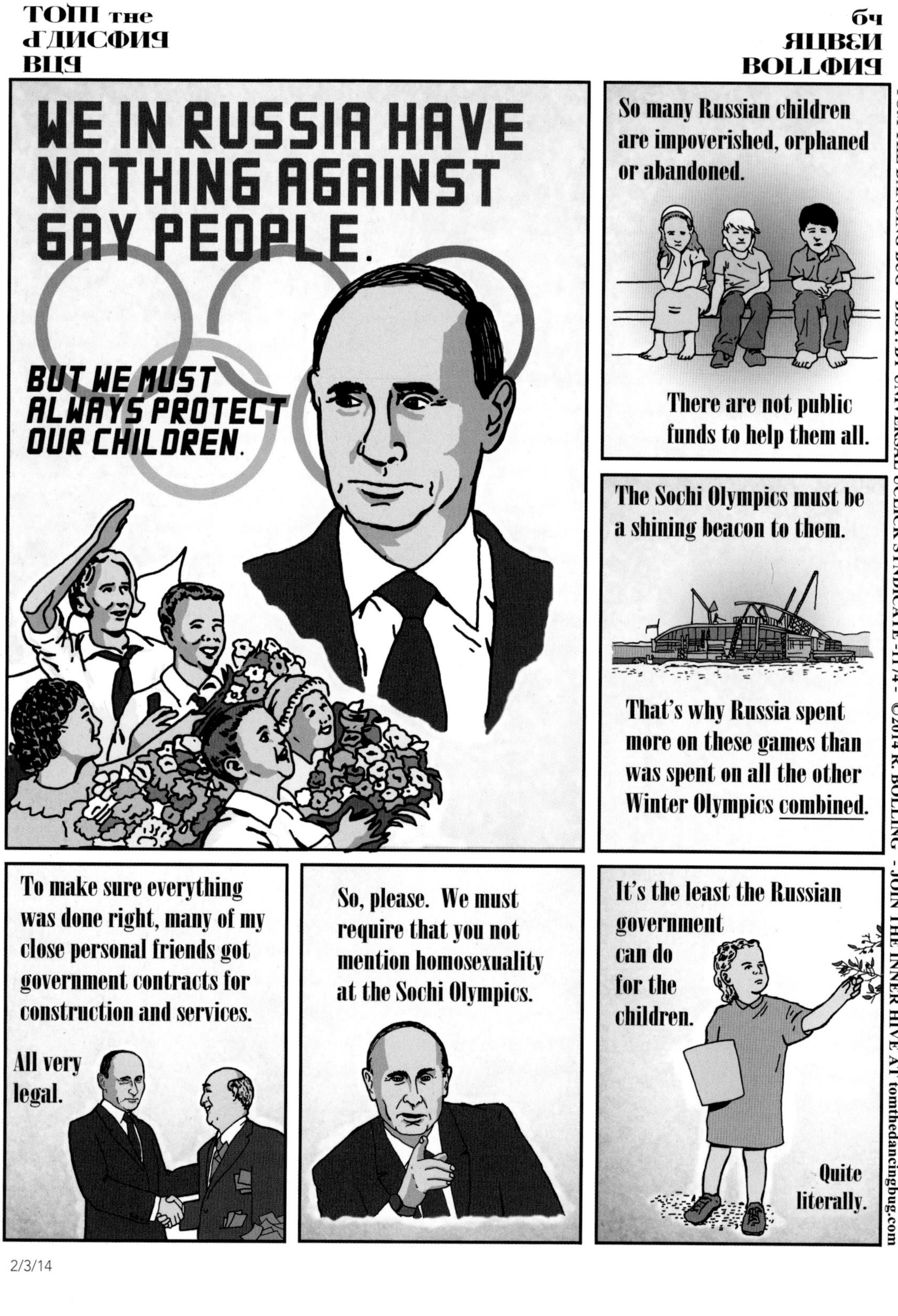
TOM the DANCING BUG
by RUBEN BOLLING
WE IN RUSSIA HAVE NOTHING AGAINST GAY PEOPLE.
BUT WE MUST ALWAYS PROTECT OUR CHILDREN.
So many Russian children are impoverished, orphaned or abandoned.
There are not public funds to help them all.
The Sochi Olympics must be a shining beacon to them.
That's why Russia spent more on these games than was spent on all the other Winter Olympics combined.
To make sure everything was done right, many of my close personal friends got government contracts for construction and services.
All very legal.
So, please. We must require that you not mention homosexuality at the Sochi Olympics.
It's the least the Russian government can do for the children.
Quite literally.
TOM THE DANCING BUG - DIST. BY UNIVERSAL UCLICK SYNDICATE -1174- ©2014 R. BOLLING - JOIN THE INNER HIVE AT tomthedancingbug.com

2/3/14

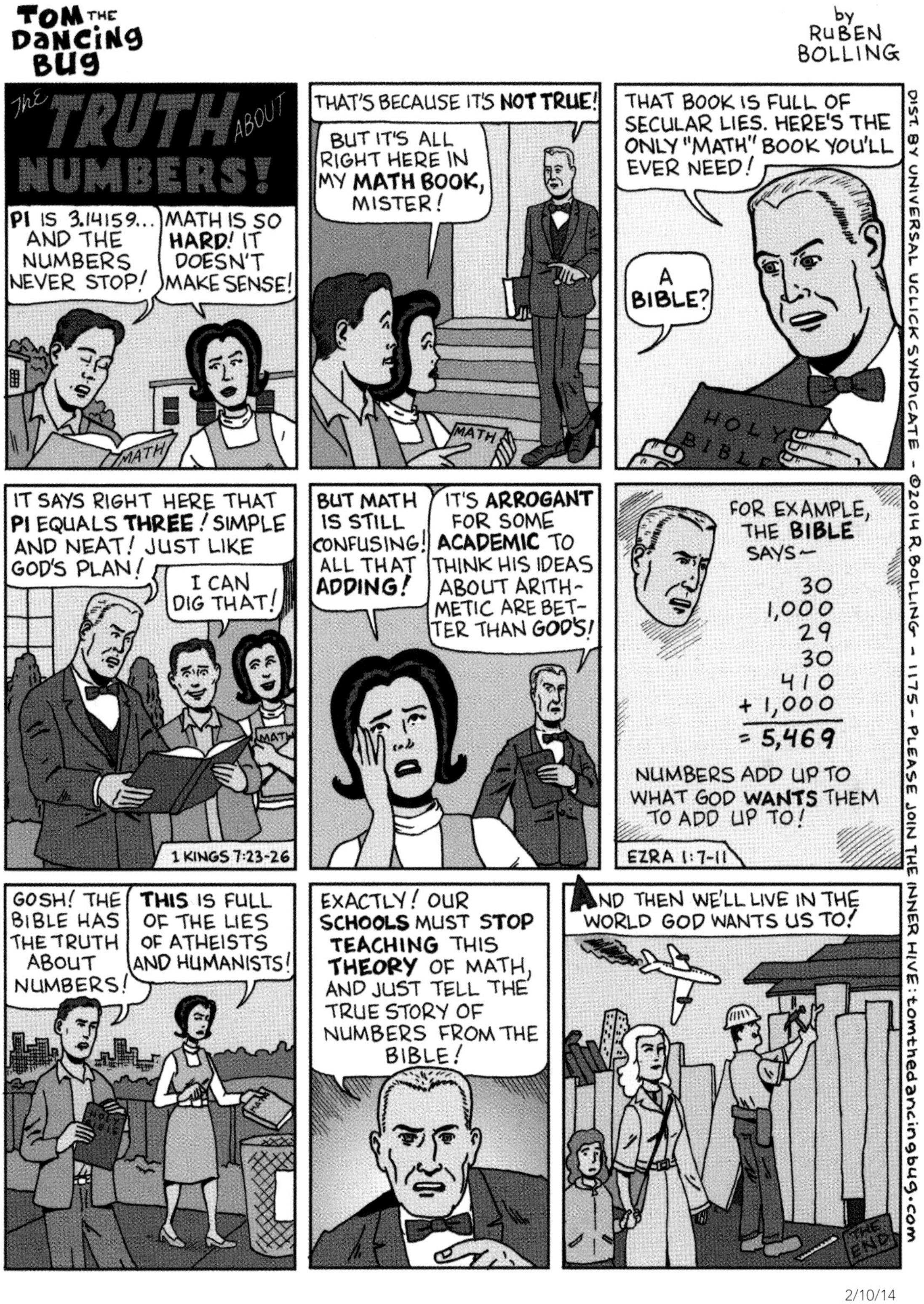
TOM THE DANCING BUG
by RUBEN BOLLING
THE TRUTH ABOUT NUMBERS!
PI IS 3.14159... AND THE NUMBERS NEVER STOP!
MATH IS SO HARD! IT DOESN'T MAKE SENSE!
MATH
THAT'S BECAUSE IT'S NOT TRUE!
BUT IT'S ALL RIGHT HERE IN MY MATH BOOK, MISTER!
MATH
THAT BOOK IS FULL OF SECULAR LIES. HERE'S THE ONLY "MATH" BOOK YOU'LL EVER NEED!
A BIBLE?
HOLY BIBLE
IT SAYS RIGHT HERE THAT PI EQUALS THREE! SIMPLE AND NEAT! JUST LIKE GOD'S PLAN!
I CAN DIG THAT!
MATH
1 KINGS 7:23-26
BUT MATH IS STILL CONFUSING! ALL THAT ADDING!
IT'S ARROGANT FOR SOME ACADEMIC TO THINK HIS IDEAS ABOUT ARITH-METIC ARE BET-TER THAN GOD'S!
FOR EXAMPLE, THE BIBLE SAYS—
30
1,000
29
30
410
+ 1,000
= 5,469
NUMBERS ADD UP TO WHAT GOD WANTS THEM TO ADD UP TO!
EZRA 1:7-11
GOSH! THE BIBLE HAS THE TRUTH ABOUT NUMBERS!
THIS IS FULL OF THE LIES OF ATHEISTS AND HUMANISTS!
HOLY BIBLE
MATH
EXACTLY! OUR SCHOOLS MUST STOP TEACHING THIS THEORY OF MATH, AND JUST TELL THE TRUE STORY OF NUMBERS FROM THE BIBLE!
AND THEN WE'LL LIVE IN THE WORLD GOD WANTS US TO!
THE END
DIST. BY UNIVERSAL UCLICK SYNDICATE - ©2014 R. BOLLING - 1175 - PLEASE JOIN THE INNER HIVE: tomthedancingbug.com

2/10/14

TOM the DANCING BUG

by Ruben Bolling

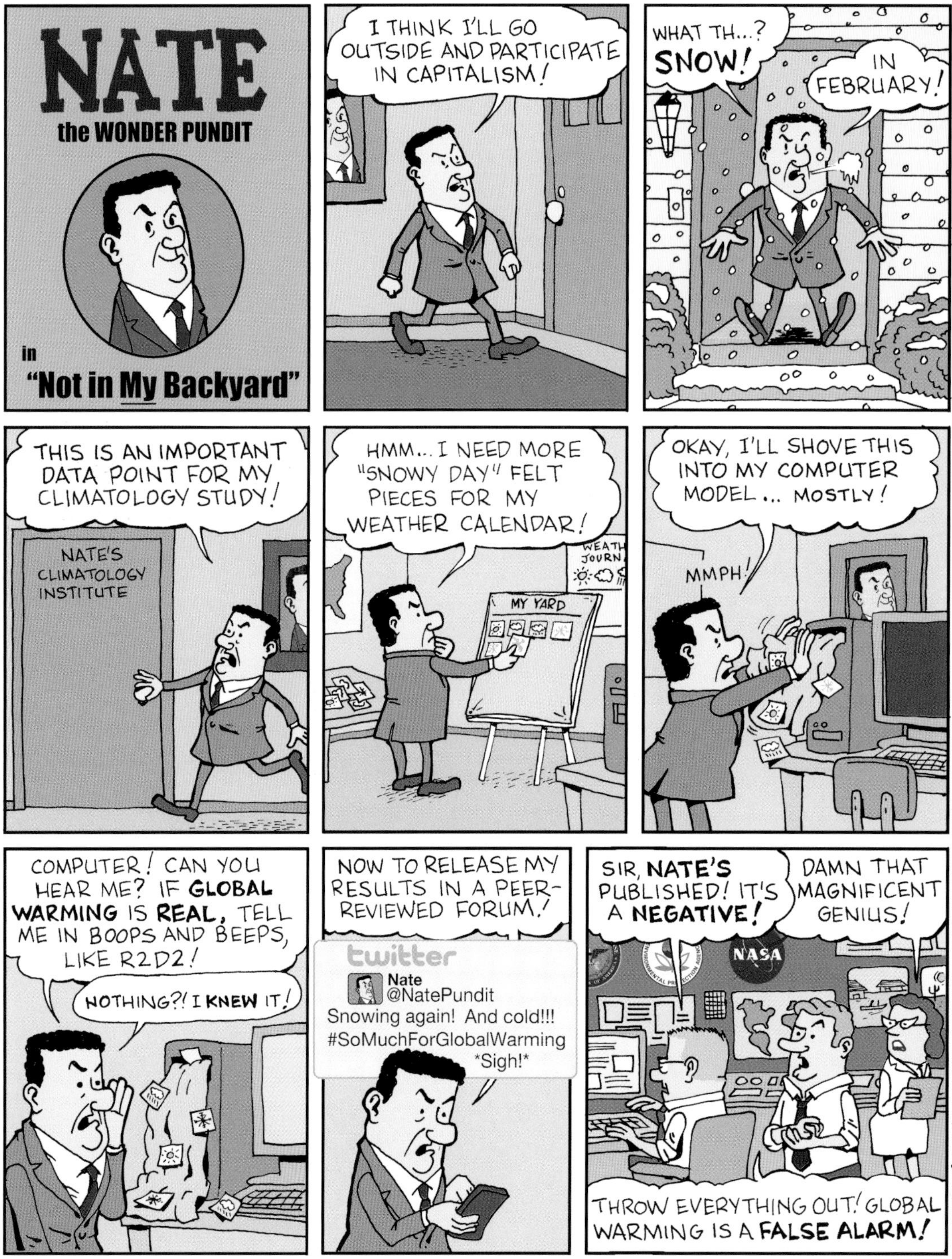
NATE
the WONDER PUNDIT
in "Not in My Backyard"
I THINK I'LL GO OUTSIDE AND PARTICIPATE IN CAPITALISM!
WHAT TH...? SNOW!
IN FEBRUARY!
THIS IS AN IMPORTANT DATA POINT FOR MY CLIMATOLOGY STUDY!
NATE'S CLIMATOLOGY INSTITUTE
HMM... I NEED MORE "SNOWY DAY" FELT PIECES FOR MY WEATHER CALENDAR!
MY YARD
OKAY, I'LL SHOVE THIS INTO MY COMPUTER MODEL... MOSTLY!
MMPH!
COMPUTER! CAN YOU HEAR ME? IF GLOBAL WARMING IS REAL, TELL ME IN BOOPS AND BEEPS, LIKE R2D2!
NOTHING?! I KNEW IT!
NOW TO RELEASE MY RESULTS IN A PEER-REVIEWED FORUM!
twitter
Nate
@NatePundit
Snowing again! And cold!!!
#SoMuchForGlobalWarming
Sigh!
SIR, NATE'S PUBLISHED! IT'S A NEGATIVE!
DAMN THAT MAGNIFICENT GENIUS!
NASA
THROW EVERYTHING OUT! GLOBAL WARMING IS A FALSE ALARM!

2/17/14

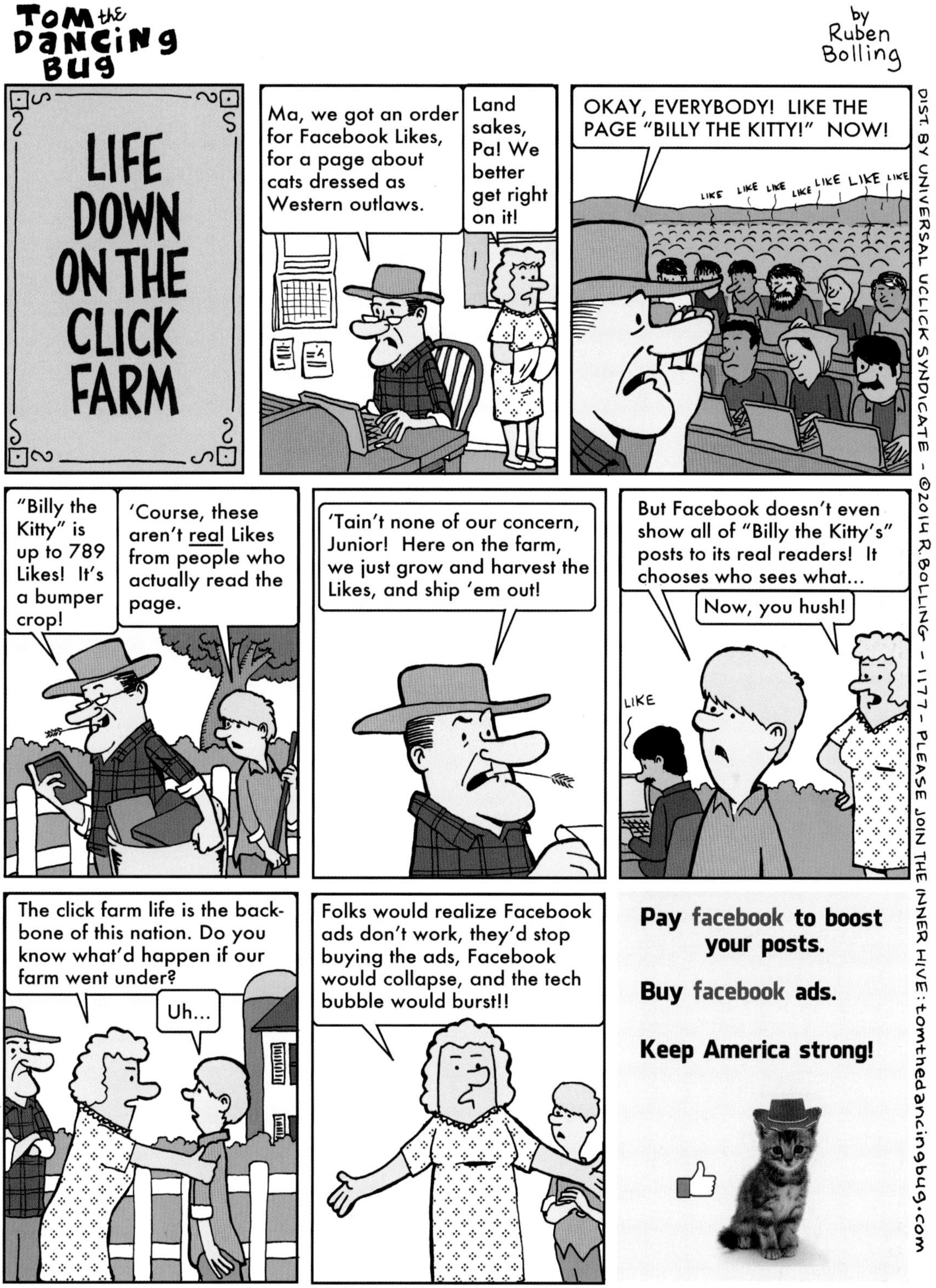
TOM the DANCING BUG
by Ruben Bolling
LIFE DOWN ON THE CLICK FARM
Ma, we got an order for Facebook Likes, for a page about cats dressed as Western outlaws.
Land sakes, Pa! We better get right on it!
OKAY, EVERYBODY! LIKE THE PAGE "BILLY THE KITTY!" NOW!
LIKE LIKE LIKE LIKE LIKE LIKE LIKE
"Billy the Kitty" is up to 789 Likes! It's a bumper crop!
'Course, these aren't real Likes from people who actually read the page.
'Tain't none of our concern, Junior! Here on the farm, we just grow and harvest the Likes, and ship 'em out!
But Facebook doesn't even show all of "Billy the Kitty's" posts to its real readers! It chooses who sees what...
Now, you hush!
LIKE
The click farm life is the back-bone of this nation. Do you know what'd happen if our farm went under?
Uh...
Folks would realize Facebook ads don't work, they'd stop buying the ads, Facebook would collapse, and the tech bubble would burst!!
Pay facebook to boost your posts.
Buy facebook ads.
Keep America strong!
DIST. BY UNIVERSAL UCLICK SYNDICATE - ©2014 R. BOLLING - 1177 - PLEASE JOIN THE INNER HIVE: tomthedancingbug.com

2/24/14

TOM the DANCING BUG

by Ruben Bolling

After his New York Times op-ed piece admonishing the U.S. for considering military intervention in Syria, Russian President Vladimir Putin takes on a new career...

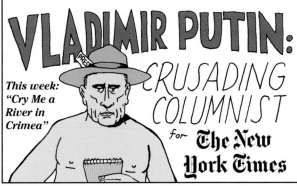

VLADIMIR PUTIN: CRUSADING COLUMNIST for The New York Times

This week: "Cry Me a River in Crimea"

PUTIN! YOUR COLUMNS ARE **STILL** ABOUT THE SOCHI OLYMPICS! NO ONE **CARES** IF THAT BEAR MASCOT IS HETEROSEXUAL!

NYET?

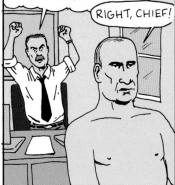

THERE'S A **WAR** BREWING IN UKRAINE! I WANT YOU TO COVER **THAT!**

RIGHT, CHIEF!

HELLO, UKRAINE?

YES?

YOU NEED RUSSIA TO PROTECT YOUR RUSSIAN PEOPLES, RIGHT?

RIGHT.

WHAT A SCOOP! RUSSIA IS FULLY JUSTIFIED IN ITS MILITARY ACTION!

LATER~ PUTIN, THIS COLUMN MAKES NO SENSE! YOU SUPPORTED INTERNATIONAL LAW WHEN THE WEST WANTED TO INTERVENE IN SYRIA, BUT IGNORE IT NOW IN UKRAINE!

UH-OH. I SENSE THREAT TO RUSSIAN INTERESTS HERE.

WHAT DO YOU...?

AND SO~

VLADIMIR PUTIN
Russian Necessity

Russian forces occupied the op-ed offices of *The New York Times* yesterday, in a move that was necessitated by a stubborn editor who seems psychotic and is now suspected of embezzlement. ...d contro... ...ocated ...ison in up

PUTIN! WHAT'S **THIS** ALL ABOUT?!

JUST A TEMPORARY MEASURE UNTIL THINGS ARE NORMALIZED...

DISTRIBUTED BY THE UNIVERSAL UCLICK SYNDICATE - (C)2014 R. BOLLING - 1178 - Join the INNER HIVE at tomthedancingbug.com

3/3/14

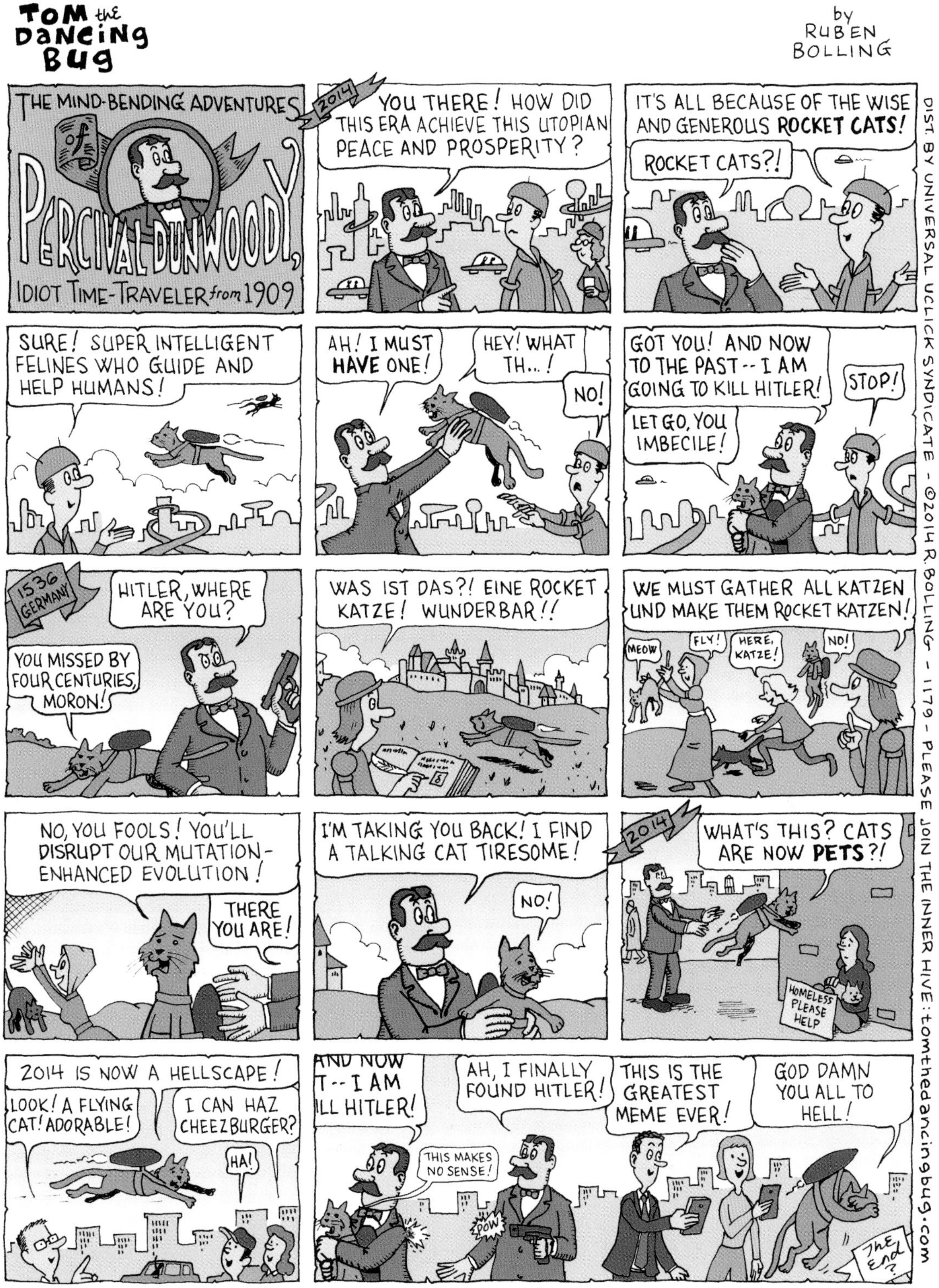

TOM the DANCING BUG
by RUBEN BOLLING
THE MIND-BENDING ADVENTURES of PERCIVAL DUNWOODY, IDIOT TIME-TRAVELER from 1909
2014
YOU THERE! HOW DID THIS ERA ACHIEVE THIS UTOPIAN PEACE AND PROSPERITY?
IT'S ALL BECAUSE OF THE WISE AND GENEROUS ROCKET CATS!
ROCKET CATS?!
SURE! SUPER INTELLIGENT FELINES WHO GUIDE AND HELP HUMANS!
AH! I MUST HAVE ONE!
HEY! WHAT TH...!
NO!
GOT YOU! AND NOW TO THE PAST -- I AM GOING TO KILL HITLER!
LET GO, YOU IMBECILE!
STOP!
1536 GERMANY
HITLER, WHERE ARE YOU?
YOU MISSED BY FOUR CENTURIES, MORON!
WAS IST DAS?! EINE ROCKET KATZE! WUNDERBAR!!
WE MUST GATHER ALL KATZEN UND MAKE THEM ROCKET KATZEN!
MEOW
FLY!
HERE, KATZE!
NO!
NO, YOU FOOLS! YOU'LL DISRUPT OUR MUTATION-ENHANCED EVOLUTION!
THERE YOU ARE!
I'M TAKING YOU BACK! I FIND A TALKING CAT TIRESOME!
NO!
2014
WHAT'S THIS? CATS ARE NOW PETS?!
HOMELESS PLEASE HELP
2014 IS NOW A HELLSCAPE!
LOOK! A FLYING CAT! ADORABLE!
I CAN HAZ CHEEZBURGER?
HA!
AND NOW
T -- I AM
LL HITLER!
THIS MAKES NO SENSE!
POW
AH, I FINALLY FOUND HITLER!
THIS IS THE GREATEST MEME EVER!
GOD DAMN YOU ALL TO HELL!
THE END?
DIST. BY UNIVERSAL UCLICK SYNDICATE - ©2014 R. BOLLING - 1179 - PLEASE JOIN THE INNER HIVE: tomthedancingbug.com

3/10/14

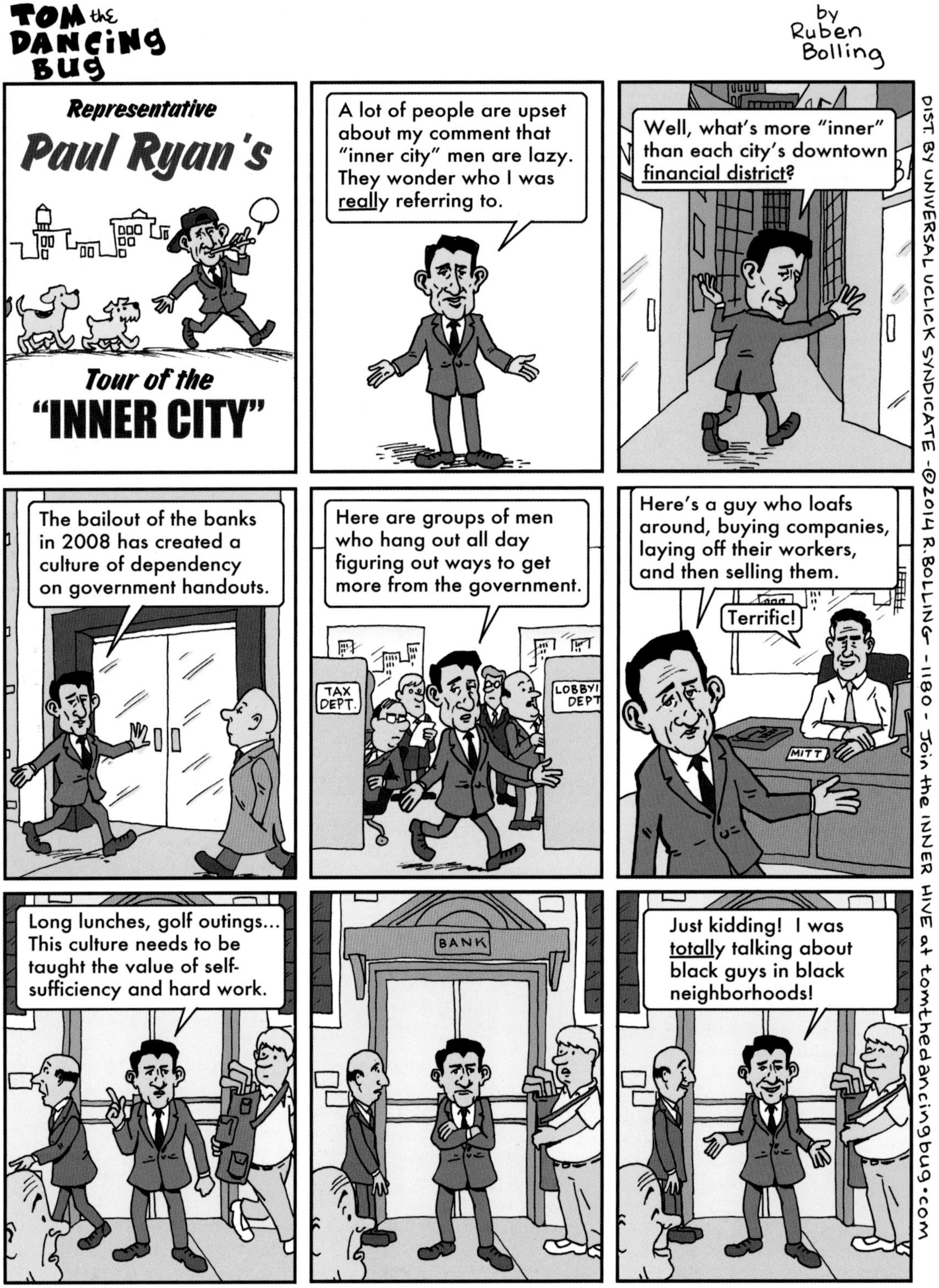
TOM the DANCING BUG
by Ruben Bolling
Representative Paul Ryan's Tour of the "INNER CITY"
A lot of people are upset about my comment that "inner city" men are lazy. They wonder who I was really referring to.
Well, what's more "inner" than each city's downtown financial district?
The bailout of the banks in 2008 has created a culture of dependency on government handouts.
Here are groups of men who hang out all day figuring out ways to get more from the government.
TAX DEPT.
LOBBYI DEPT
Here's a guy who loafs around, buying companies, laying off their workers, and then selling them.
Terrific!
MITT
Long lunches, golf outings... This culture needs to be taught the value of self-sufficiency and hard work.
BANK
Just kidding! I was totally talking about black guys in black neighborhoods!
DIST. BY UNIVERSAL UCLICK SYNDICATE -©2014 R. BOLLING -1180- Join the INNER HIVE at tomthedancingbug.com

3/17/14

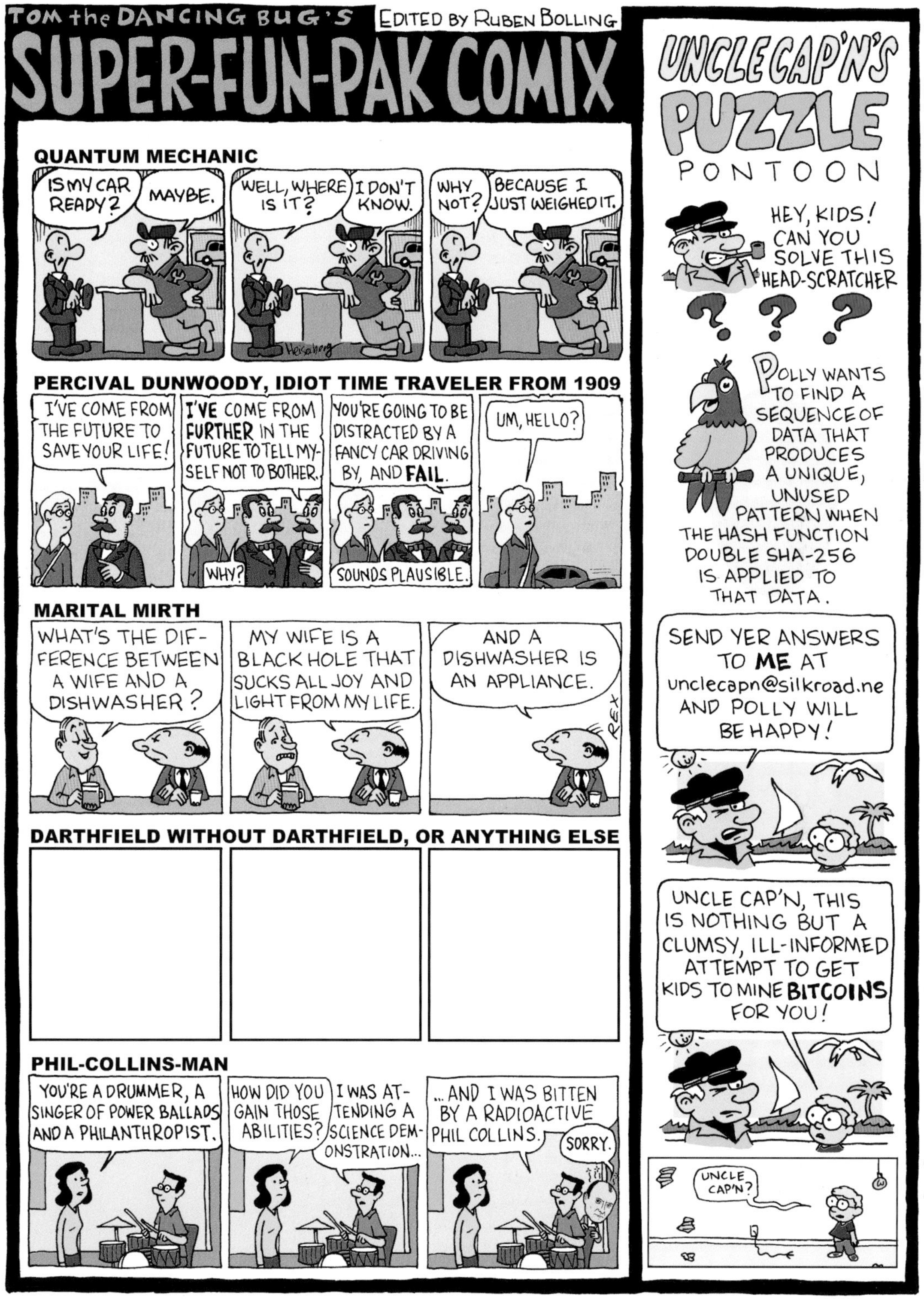
TOM the DANCING BUG'S
EDITED BY RUBEN BOLLING
SUPER-FUN-PAK COMIX
QUANTUM MECHANIC
IS MY CAR READY?
MAYBE.
WELL, WHERE IS IT?
I DON'T KNOW.
WHY NOT?
BECAUSE I JUST WEIGHED IT.
PERCIVAL DUNWOODY, IDIOT TIME TRAVELER FROM 1909
I'VE COME FROM THE FUTURE TO SAVE YOUR LIFE!
WHY?
I'VE COME FROM FURTHER IN THE FUTURE TO TELL MYSELF NOT TO BOTHER.
YOU'RE GOING TO BE DISTRACTED BY A FANCY CAR DRIVING BY, AND FAIL.
SOUNDS PLAUSIBLE.
UM, HELLO?
MARITAL MIRTH
WHAT'S THE DIFFERENCE BETWEEN A WIFE AND A DISHWASHER?
MY WIFE IS A BLACK HOLE THAT SUCKS ALL JOY AND LIGHT FROM MY LIFE.
AND A DISHWASHER IS AN APPLIANCE.
DARTHFIELD WITHOUT DARTHFIELD, OR ANYTHING ELSE
PHIL-COLLINS-MAN
YOU'RE A DRUMMER, A SINGER OF POWER BALLADS AND A PHILANTHROPIST.
HOW DID YOU GAIN THOSE ABILITIES?
I WAS ATTENDING A SCIENCE DEMONSTRATION...
...AND I WAS BITTEN BY A RADIOACTIVE PHIL COLLINS.
SORRY.
UNCLE CAP'N'S PUZZLE PONTOON
HEY, KIDS! CAN YOU SOLVE THIS HEAD-SCRATCHER
POLLY WANTS TO FIND A SEQUENCE OF DATA THAT PRODUCES A UNIQUE, UNUSED PATTERN WHEN THE HASH FUNCTION DOUBLE SHA-256 IS APPLIED TO THAT DATA.
SEND YER ANSWERS TO ME AT unclecapn@silkroad.ne AND POLLY WILL BE HAPPY!
UNCLE CAP'N, THIS IS NOTHING BUT A CLUMSY, ILL-INFORMED ATTEMPT TO GET KIDS TO MINE BITCOINS FOR YOU!
UNCLE CAP'N?

3/24/14

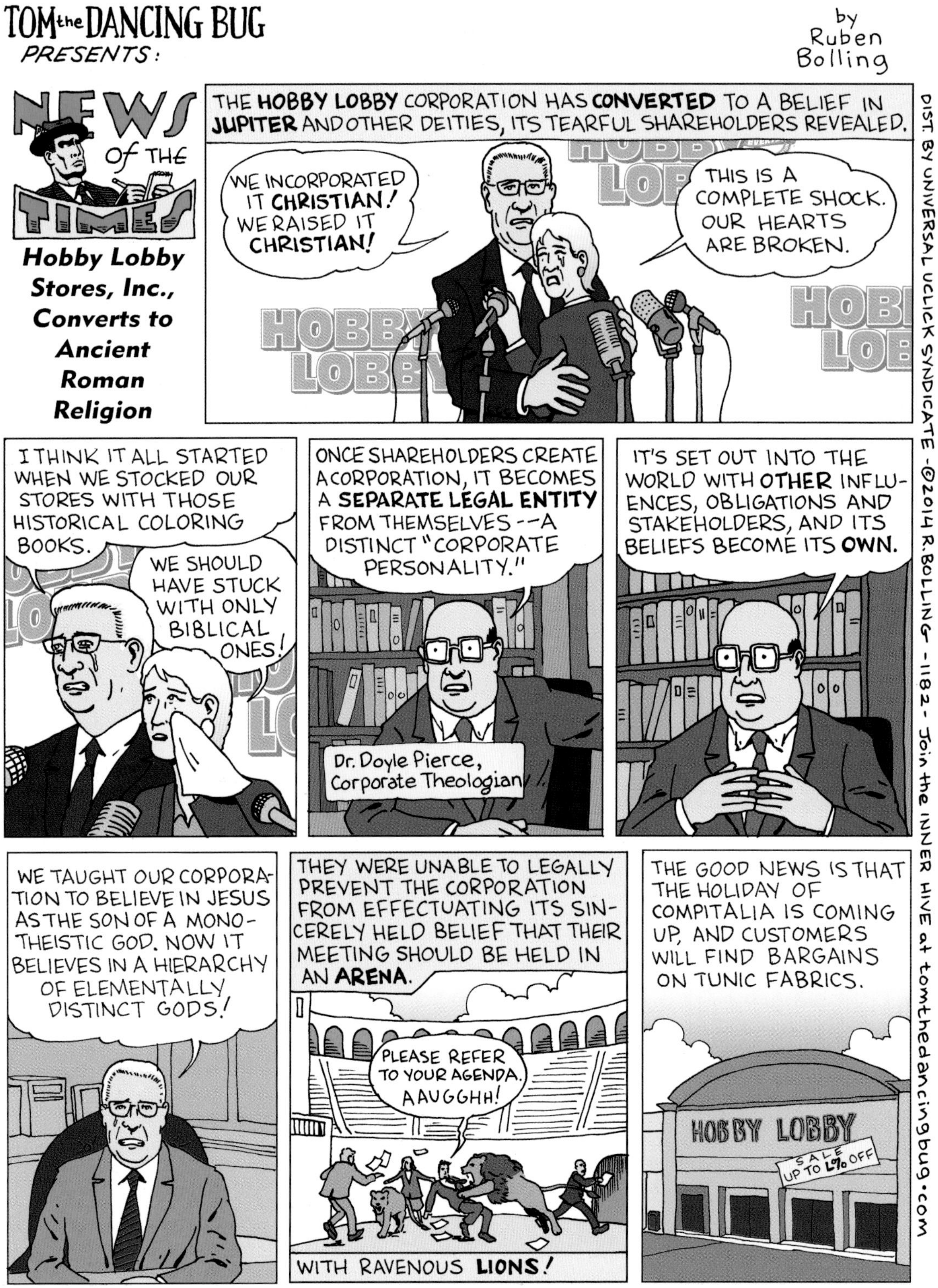
TOM the DANCING BUG PRESENTS:
by Ruben Bolling
NEWS of the TIMES
Hobby Lobby Stores, Inc., Converts to Ancient Roman Religion
THE HOBBY LOBBY CORPORATION HAS CONVERTED TO A BELIEF IN JUPITER AND OTHER DEITIES, ITS TEARFUL SHAREHOLDERS REVEALED.
WE INCORPORATED IT CHRISTIAN! WE RAISED IT CHRISTIAN!
THIS IS A COMPLETE SHOCK. OUR HEARTS ARE BROKEN.
HOBBY LOBBY
I THINK IT ALL STARTED WHEN WE STOCKED OUR STORES WITH THOSE HISTORICAL COLORING BOOKS.
WE SHOULD HAVE STUCK WITH ONLY BIBLICAL ONES!
ONCE SHAREHOLDERS CREATE A CORPORATION, IT BECOMES A SEPARATE LEGAL ENTITY FROM THEMSELVES -- A DISTINCT "CORPORATE PERSONALITY."
Dr. Doyle Pierce, Corporate Theologian
IT'S SET OUT INTO THE WORLD WITH OTHER INFLUENCES, OBLIGATIONS AND STAKEHOLDERS, AND ITS BELIEFS BECOME ITS OWN.
WE TAUGHT OUR CORPORATION TO BELIEVE IN JESUS AS THE SON OF A MONOTHEISTIC GOD. NOW IT BELIEVES IN A HIERARCHY OF ELEMENTALLY DISTINCT GODS!
THEY WERE UNABLE TO LEGALLY PREVENT THE CORPORATION FROM EFFECTUATING ITS SINCERELY HELD BELIEF THAT THEIR MEETING SHOULD BE HELD IN AN ARENA
PLEASE REFER TO YOUR AGENDA. AAUGGHH!
WITH RAVENOUS LIONS!
THE GOOD NEWS IS THAT THE HOLIDAY OF COMPITALIA IS COMING UP, AND CUSTOMERS WILL FIND BARGAINS ON TUNIC FABRICS.
HOBBY LOBBY
SALE UP TO L% OFF
DIST. BY UNIVERSAL UCLICK SYNDICATE -©2014 R. BOLLING - 1182 - Join the INNER HIVE at tomthedancingbug.com

3/31/14

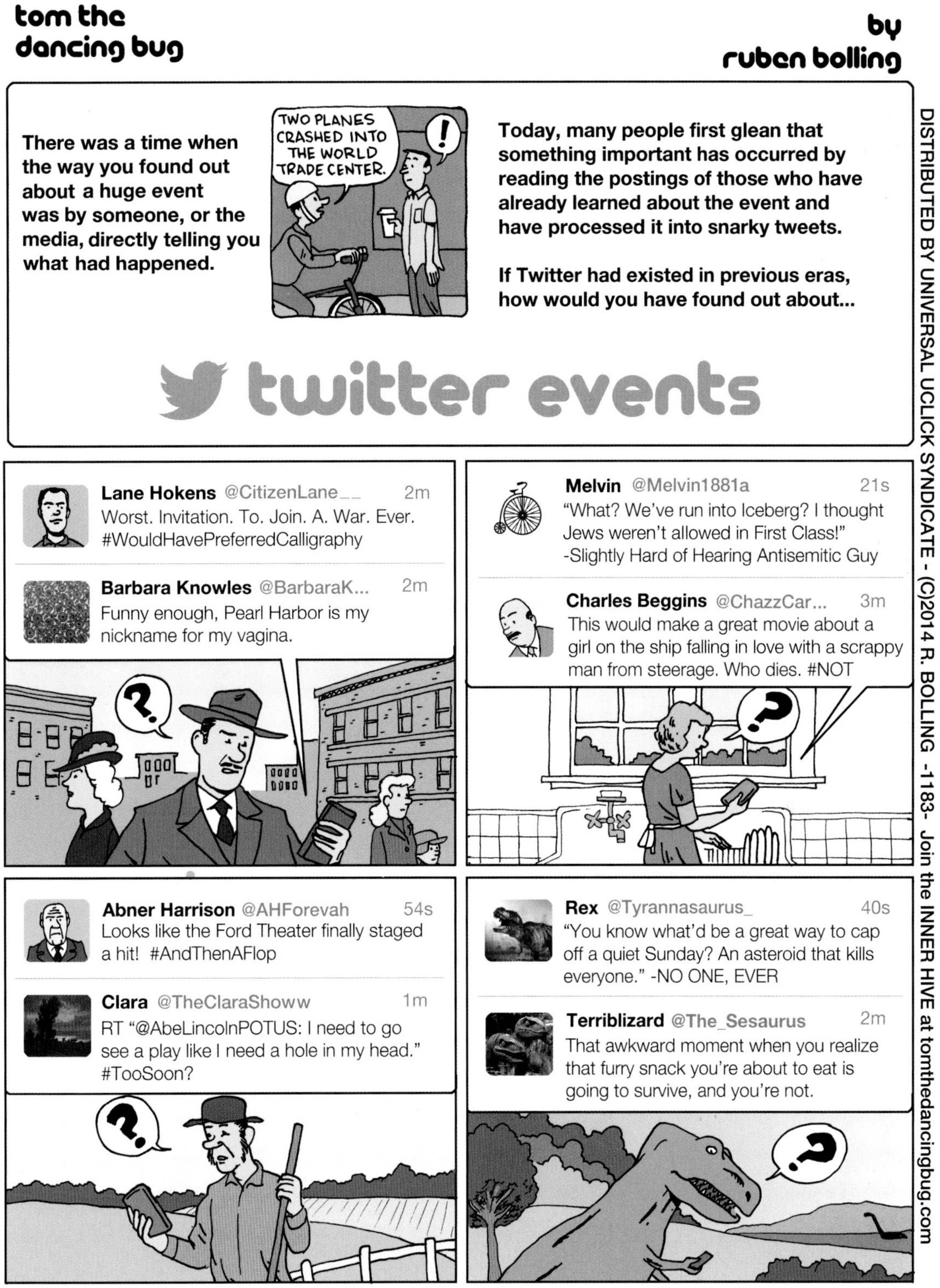
tom the dancing bug
by ruben bolling
There was a time when the way you found out about a huge event was by someone, or the media, directly telling you what had happened.
TWO PLANES CRASHED INTO THE WORLD TRADE CENTER.
!
Today, many people first glean that something important has occurred by reading the postings of those who have already learned about the event and have processed it into snarky tweets.
If Twitter had existed in previous eras, how would you have found out about...
twitter events
Lane Hokens @CitizenLane__ 2m
Worst. Invitation. To. Join. A. War. Ever. #WouldHavePreferredCalligraphy
Barbara Knowles @BarbaraK... 2m
Funny enough, Pearl Harbor is my nickname for my vagina.
?
Melvin @Melvin1881a 21s
"What? We've run into Iceberg? I thought Jews weren't allowed in First Class!" -Slightly Hard of Hearing Antisemitic Guy
Charles Beggins @ChazzCar... 3m
This would make a great movie about a girl on the ship falling in love with a scrappy man from steerage. Who dies. #NOT
?
Abner Harrison @AHForevah 54s
Looks like the Ford Theater finally staged a hit! #AndThenAFlop
Clara @TheClaraShoww 1m
RT "@AbeLincolnPOTUS: I need to go see a play like I need a hole in my head." #TooSoon?
?
Rex @Tyrannasaurus_ 40s
"You know what'd be a great way to cap off a quiet Sunday? An asteroid that kills everyone." -NO ONE, EVER
Terriblizard @The_Sesaurus 2m
That awkward moment when you realize that furry snack you're about to eat is going to survive, and you're not.
?
DISTRIBUTED BY UNIVERSAL UCLICK SYNDICATE - (C)2014 R. BOLLING -1183- Join the INNER HIVE at tomthedancingbug.com

4/7/14

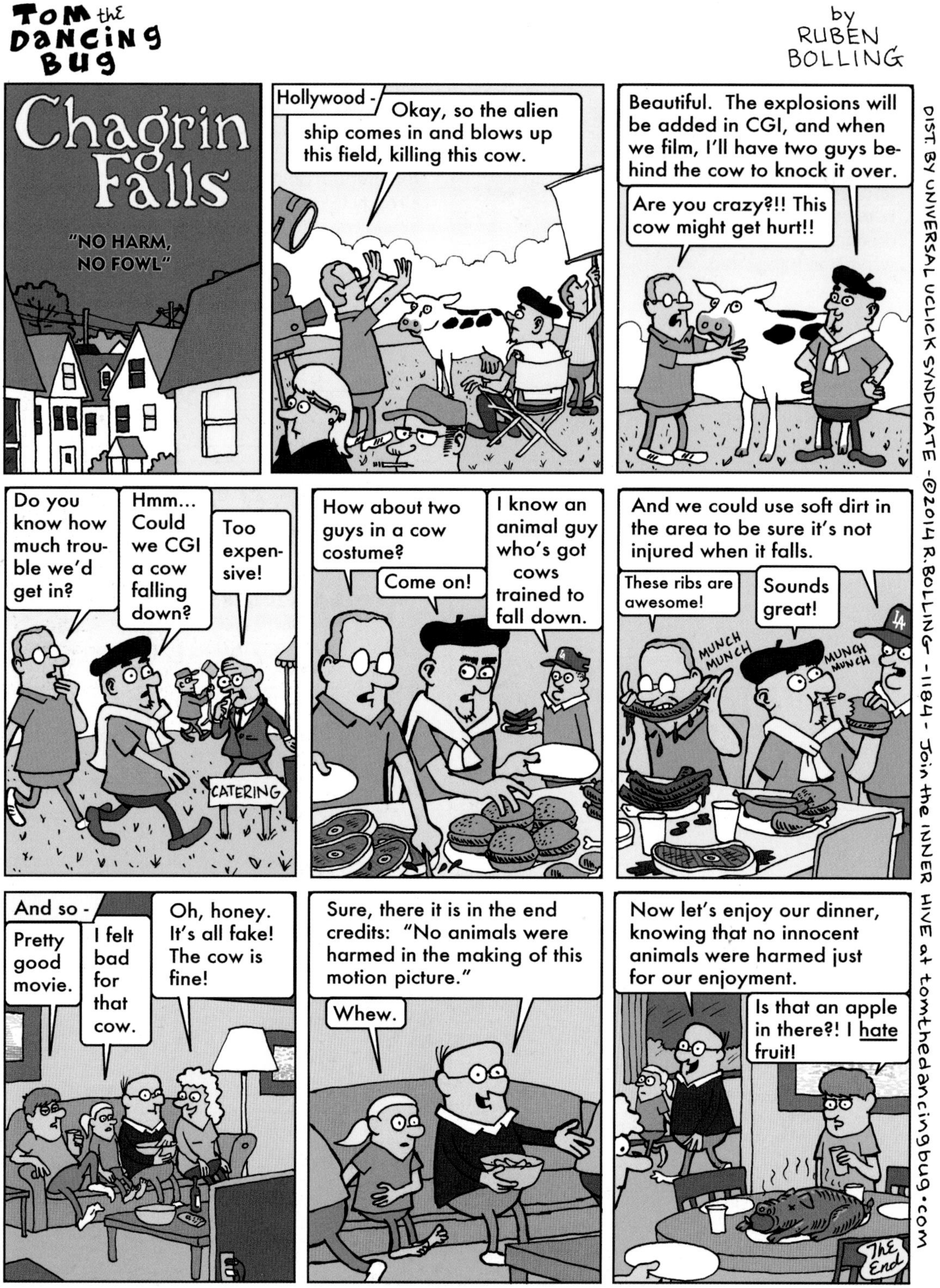

TOM the DANCING BUG
by RUBEN BOLLING
Chagrin Falls
"NO HARM, NO FOWL"
Hollywood -
Okay, so the alien ship comes in and blows up this field, killing this cow.
Beautiful. The explosions will be added in CGI, and when we film, I'll have two guys behind the cow to knock it over.
Are you crazy?!! This cow might get hurt!!
Do you know how much trouble we'd get in?
Hmm... Could we CGI a cow falling down?
Too expensive!
CATERING
How about two guys in a cow costume?
Come on!
I know an animal guy who's got cows trained to fall down.
And we could use soft dirt in the area to be sure it's not injured when it falls.
These ribs are awesome!
Sounds great!
MUNCH MUNCH
MUNCH MUNCH
And so -
Pretty good movie.
I felt bad for that cow.
Oh, honey. It's all fake! The cow is fine!
Sure, there it is in the end credits: "No animals were harmed in the making of this motion picture."
Whew.
Now let's enjoy our dinner, knowing that no innocent animals were harmed just for our enjoyment.
Is that an apple in there?! I hate fruit!
THE End
DIST. BY UNIVERSAL UCLICK SYNDICATE - ©2014 R. BOLLING - 1184 - Join the INNER HIVE at tomthedancingbug.com

4/14/14

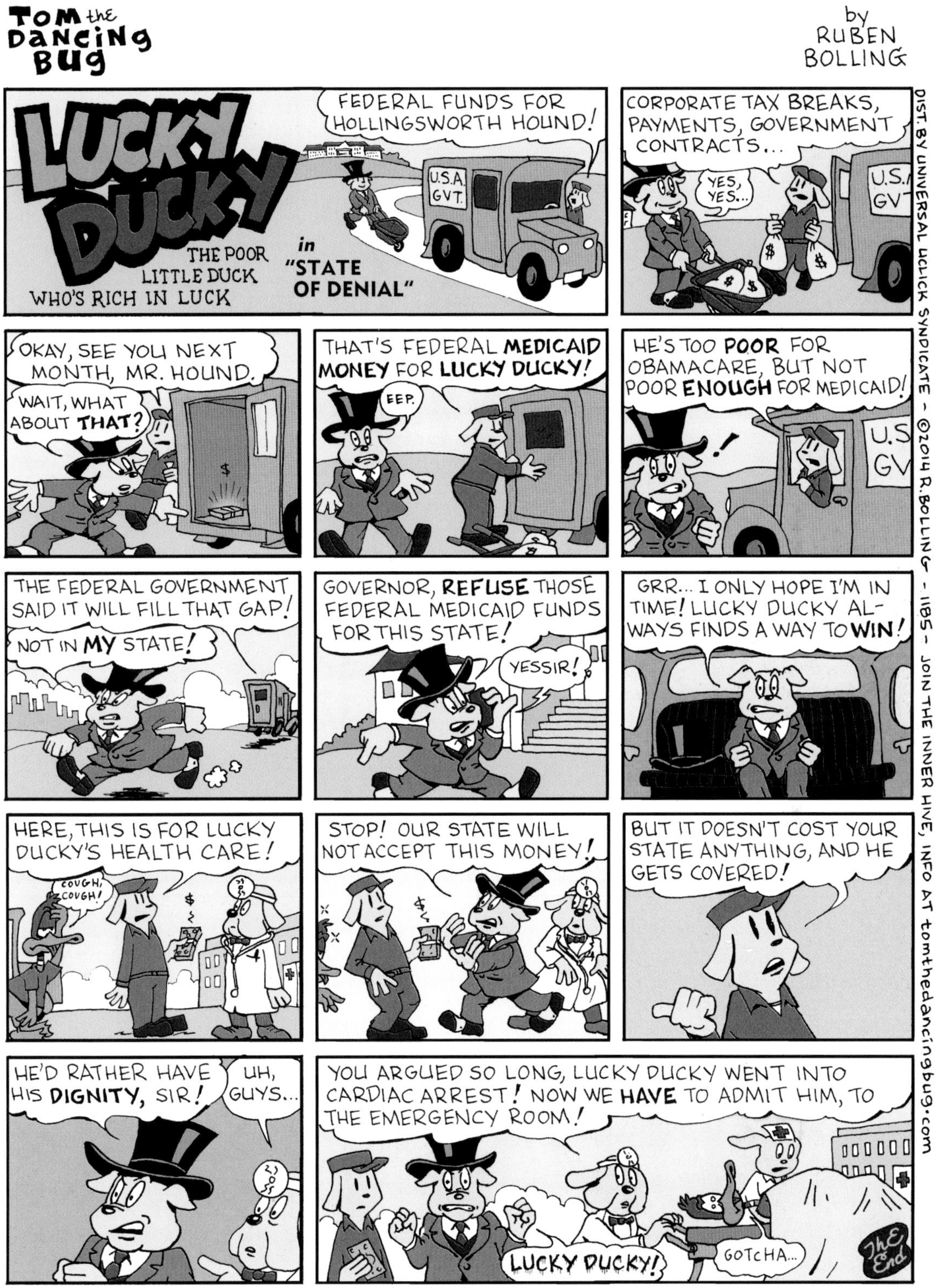
TOM the DANCING BUG
by RUBEN BOLLING
LUCKY DUCKY
THE POOR LITTLE DUCK WHO'S RICH IN LUCK
in "STATE OF DENIAL"
FEDERAL FUNDS FOR HOLLINGSWORTH HOUND!
U.S.A. GVT.
CORPORATE TAX BREAKS, PAYMENTS, GOVERNMENT CONTRACTS...
YES, YES...
OKAY, SEE YOU NEXT MONTH, MR. HOUND.
WAIT, WHAT ABOUT THAT?
THAT'S FEDERAL MEDICAID MONEY FOR LUCKY DUCKY!
EEP.
HE'S TOO POOR FOR OBAMACARE, BUT NOT POOR ENOUGH FOR MEDICAID!
THE FEDERAL GOVERNMENT SAID IT WILL FILL THAT GAP!
NOT IN MY STATE!
GOVERNOR, REFUSE THOSE FEDERAL MEDICAID FUNDS FOR THIS STATE!
YESSIR!
GRR... I ONLY HOPE I'M IN TIME! LUCKY DUCKY ALWAYS FINDS A WAY TO WIN!
HERE, THIS IS FOR LUCKY DUCKY'S HEALTH CARE!
COUGH, COUGH!
STOP! OUR STATE WILL NOT ACCEPT THIS MONEY!
BUT IT DOESN'T COST YOUR STATE ANYTHING, AND HE GETS COVERED!
HE'D RATHER HAVE HIS DIGNITY, SIR!
UH, GUYS...
YOU ARGUED SO LONG, LUCKY DUCKY WENT INTO CARDIAC ARREST! NOW WE HAVE TO ADMIT HIM, TO THE EMERGENCY ROOM!
LUCKY DUCKY!
GOTCHA...
THE END
DIST. BY UNIVERSAL UCLICK SYNDICATE - ©2014 R. BOLLING - 1185 - JOIN THE INNER HIVE, INFO AT tomthedancingbug.com

4/21/14

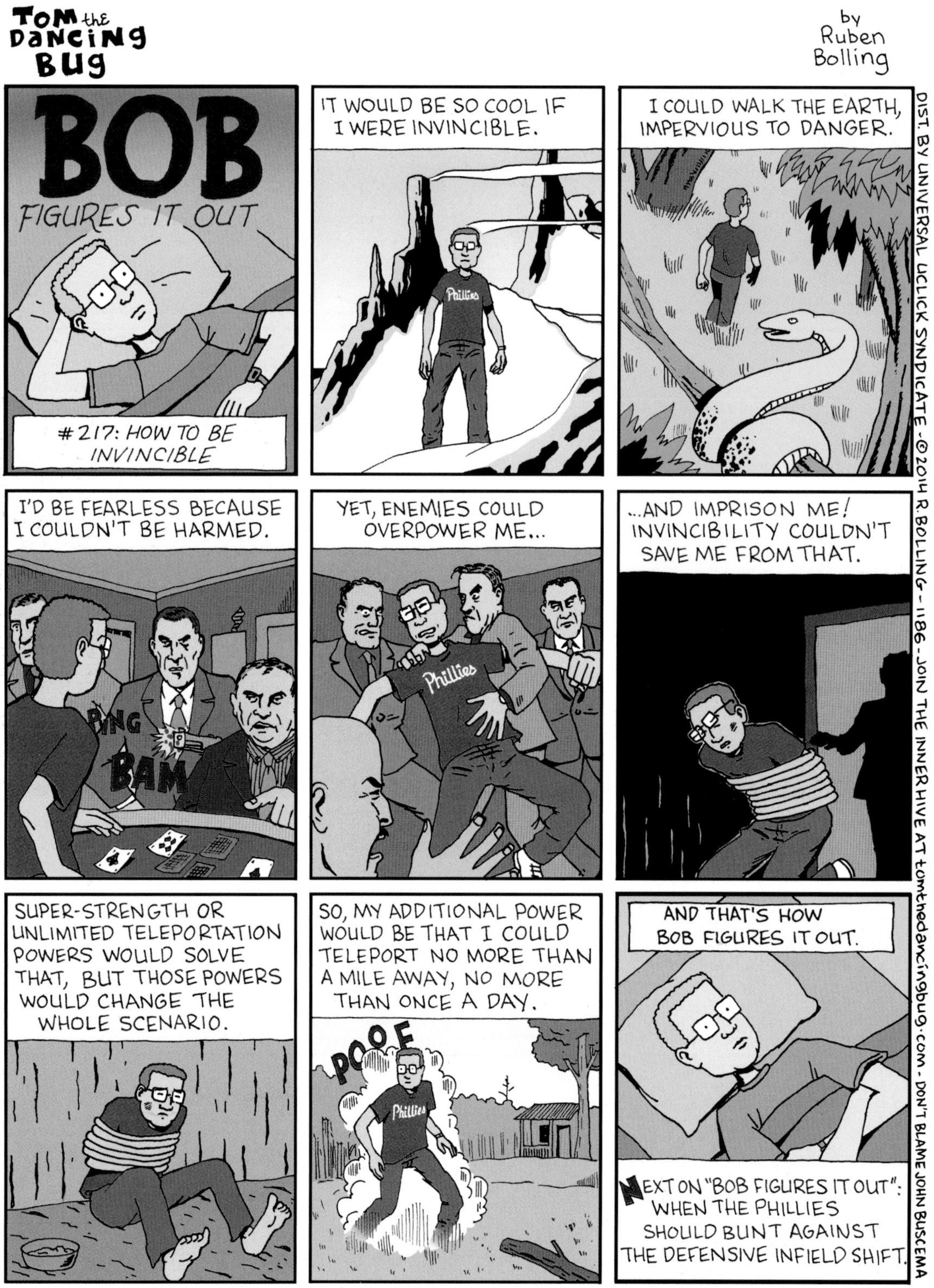
TOM the DANCING BUG
by Ruben Bolling
BOB FIGURES IT OUT
#217: HOW TO BE INVINCIBLE
IT WOULD BE SO COOL IF I WERE INVINCIBLE.
Phillies
I COULD WALK THE EARTH, IMPERVIOUS TO DANGER.
I'D BE FEARLESS BECAUSE I COULDN'T BE HARMED.
BAM
YET, ENEMIES COULD OVERPOWER ME...
Phillies
...AND IMPRISON ME! INVINCIBILITY COULDN'T SAVE ME FROM THAT.
SUPER-STRENGTH OR UNLIMITED TELEPORTATION POWERS WOULD SOLVE THAT, BUT THOSE POWERS WOULD CHANGE THE WHOLE SCENARIO.
SO, MY ADDITIONAL POWER WOULD BE THAT I COULD TELEPORT NO MORE THAN A MILE AWAY, NO MORE THAN ONCE A DAY.
POOF
Phillies
AND THAT'S HOW BOB FIGURES IT OUT.
NEXT ON "BOB FIGURES IT OUT": WHEN THE PHILLIES SHOULD BUNT AGAINST THE DEFENSIVE INFIELD SHIFT.
DIST. BY UNIVERSAL UCLICK SYNDICATE - ©2014 R. BOLLING - 1186 - JOIN THE INNER HIVE AT tomthedancingbug.com - DON'T BLAME JOHN BUSCEMA

4/28/14

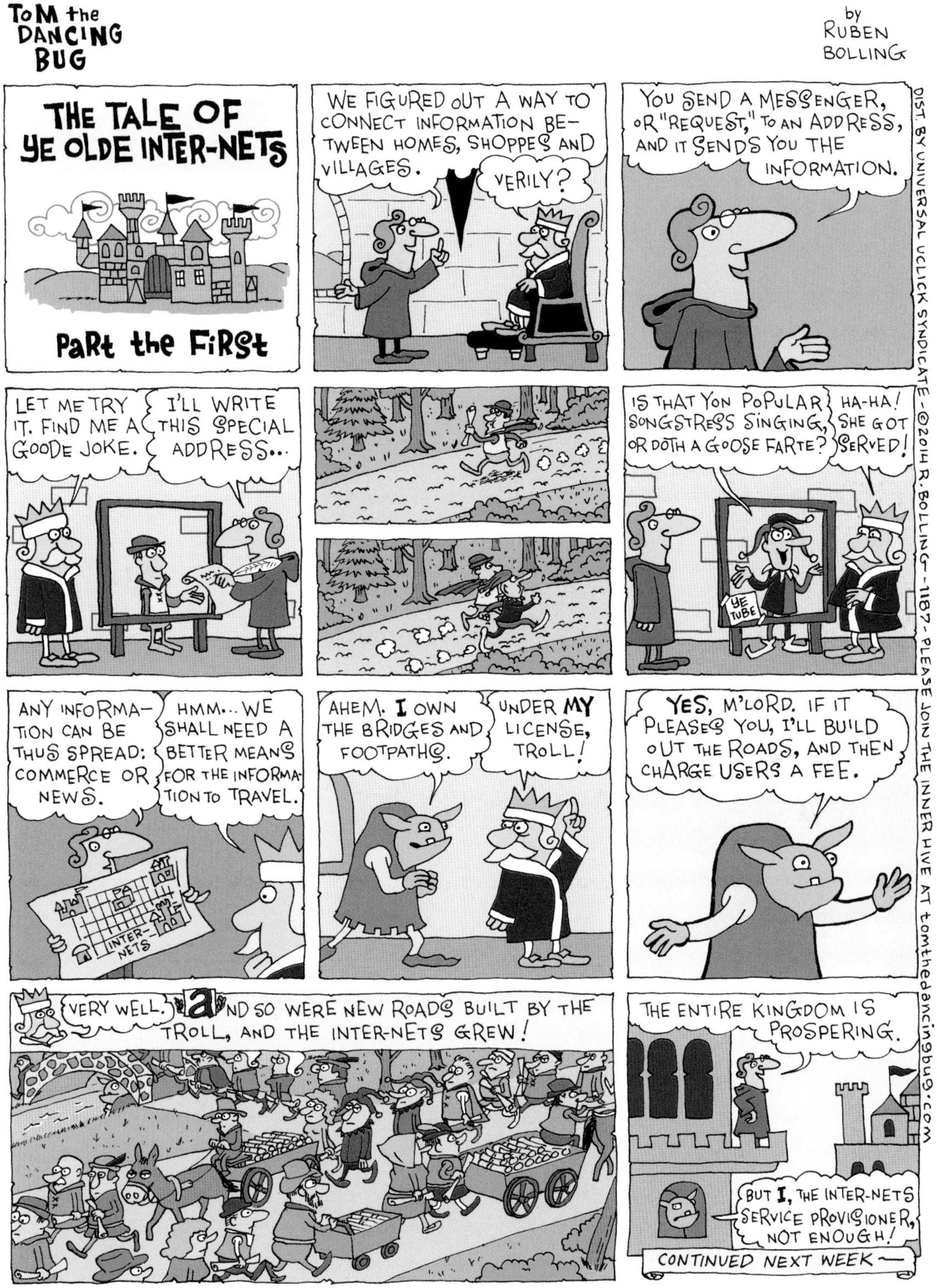

TOM the DANCING BUG
by RUBEN BOLLING
THE TALE OF YE OLDE INTER-NETS
PaRt the FiRSt
WE FIGURED OUT A WAY TO CONNECT INFORMATION BETWEEN HOMES, SHOPPES AND VILLAGES.
VERILY?
YOU SEND A MESSENGER, OR "REQUEST," TO AN ADDRESS, AND IT SENDS YOU THE INFORMATION.
LET ME TRY IT. FIND ME A GOODE JOKE.
I'LL WRITE THIS SPECIAL ADDRESS...
IS THAT YON POPULAR SONGSTRESS SINGING, OR DOTH A GOOSE FARTE?
HA-HA! SHE GOT SERVED!
YE TUBE
ANY INFORMATION CAN BE THUS SPREAD: COMMERCE OR NEWS.
HMM... WE SHALL NEED A BETTER MEANS FOR THE INFORMATION TO TRAVEL.
INTER-NETS
AHEM. I OWN THE BRIDGES AND FOOTPATHS.
UNDER MY LICENSE, TROLL!
YES, M'LORD. IF IT PLEASES YOU, I'LL BUILD OUT THE ROADS, AND THEN CHARGE USERS A FEE.
VERY WELL.
And SO WERE NEW ROADS BUILT BY THE TROLL, AND THE INTER-NETS GREW!
THE ENTIRE KINGDOM IS PROSPERING.
BUT I, THE INTER-NETS SERVICE PROVISIONER, NOT ENOUGH!
CONTINUED NEXT WEEK
DIST. BY UNIVERSAL UCLICK SYNDICATE - ©2014 R. BOLLING - 1187 - PLEASE JOIN THE INNER HIVE AT tomthedancingbug.com

5/5/14

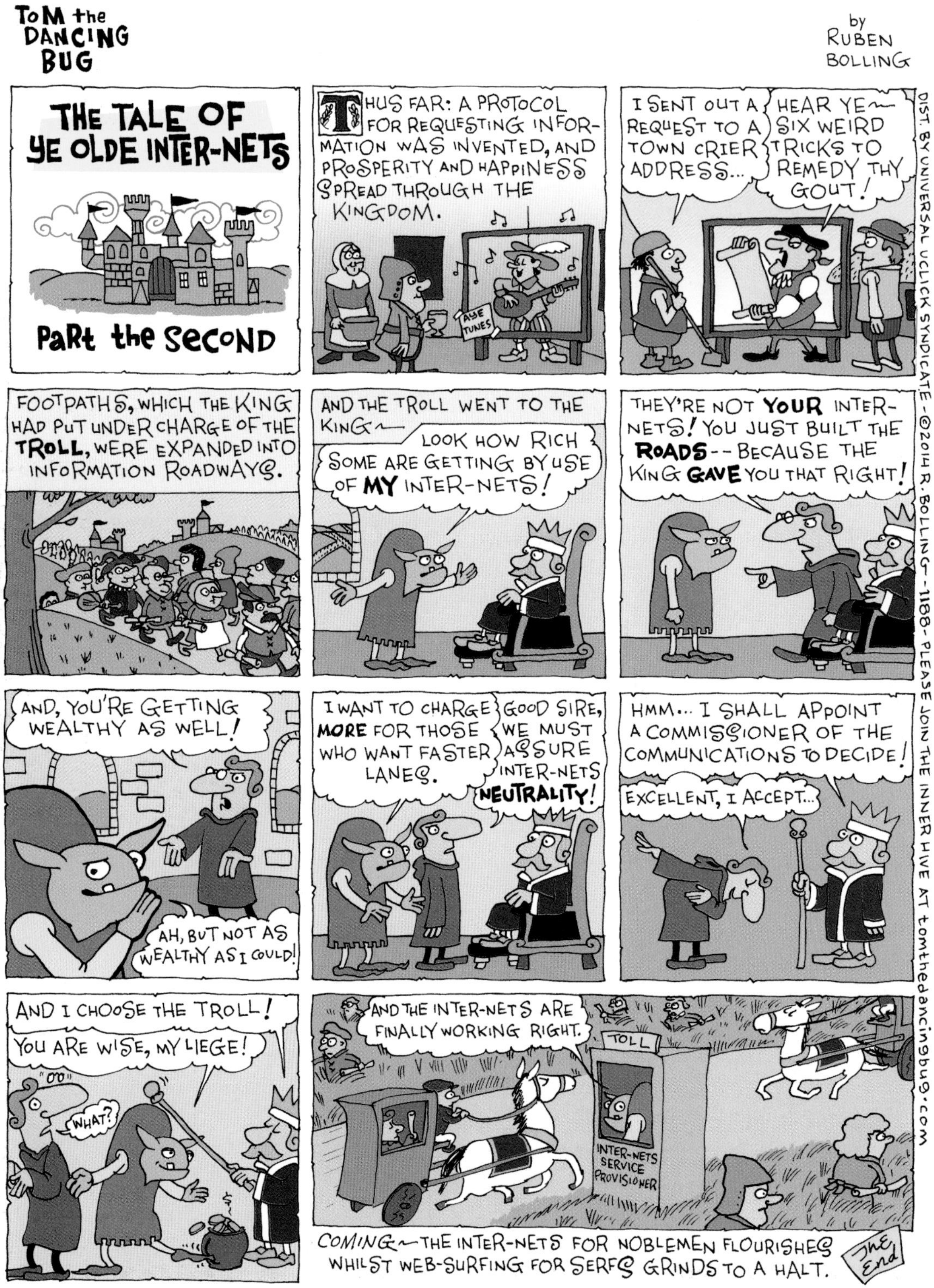

TOM THE DANCING BUG
by RUBEN BOLLING
THE TALE OF YE OLDE INTER-NETS
PART THE SECOND
THUS FAR: A PROTOCOL FOR REQUESTING INFORMATION WAS INVENTED, AND PROSPERITY AND HAPPINESS SPREAD THROUGH THE KINGDOM.
AYE TUNES
I SENT OUT A REQUEST TO A TOWN CRIER ADDRESS...
HEAR YE— SIX WEIRD TRICKS TO REMEDY THY GOUT!
FOOTPATHS, WHICH THE KING HAD PUT UNDER CHARGE OF THE TROLL, WERE EXPANDED INTO INFORMATION ROADWAYS.
AND THE TROLL WENT TO THE KING—
LOOK HOW RICH SOME ARE GETTING BY USE OF MY INTER-NETS!
THEY'RE NOT YOUR INTER-NETS! YOU JUST BUILT THE ROADS-- BECAUSE THE KING GAVE YOU THAT RIGHT!
AND, YOU'RE GETTING WEALTHY AS WELL!
AH, BUT NOT AS WEALTHY AS I COULD!
I WANT TO CHARGE MORE FOR THOSE WHO WANT FASTER LANES.
GOOD SIRE, WE MUST ASSURE INTER-NETS NEUTRALITY!
HMM... I SHALL APPOINT A COMMISSIONER OF THE COMMUNICATIONS TO DECIDE!
EXCELLENT, I ACCEPT...
AND I CHOOSE THE TROLL!
YOU ARE WISE, MY LIEGE!
"OO"
WHAT?
AND THE INTER-NETS ARE FINALLY WORKING RIGHT.
TOLL
INTER-NETS SERVICE PROVISIONER
COMING— THE INTER-NETS FOR NOBLEMEN FLOURISHES WHILST WEB-SURFING FOR SERFS GRINDS TO A HALT.
THE End
DIST. BY UNIVERSAL UCLICK SYNDICATE-©2014 R. BOLLING-1188-PLEASE JOIN THE INNER HIVE AT tomthedancingbug.com

5/12/14

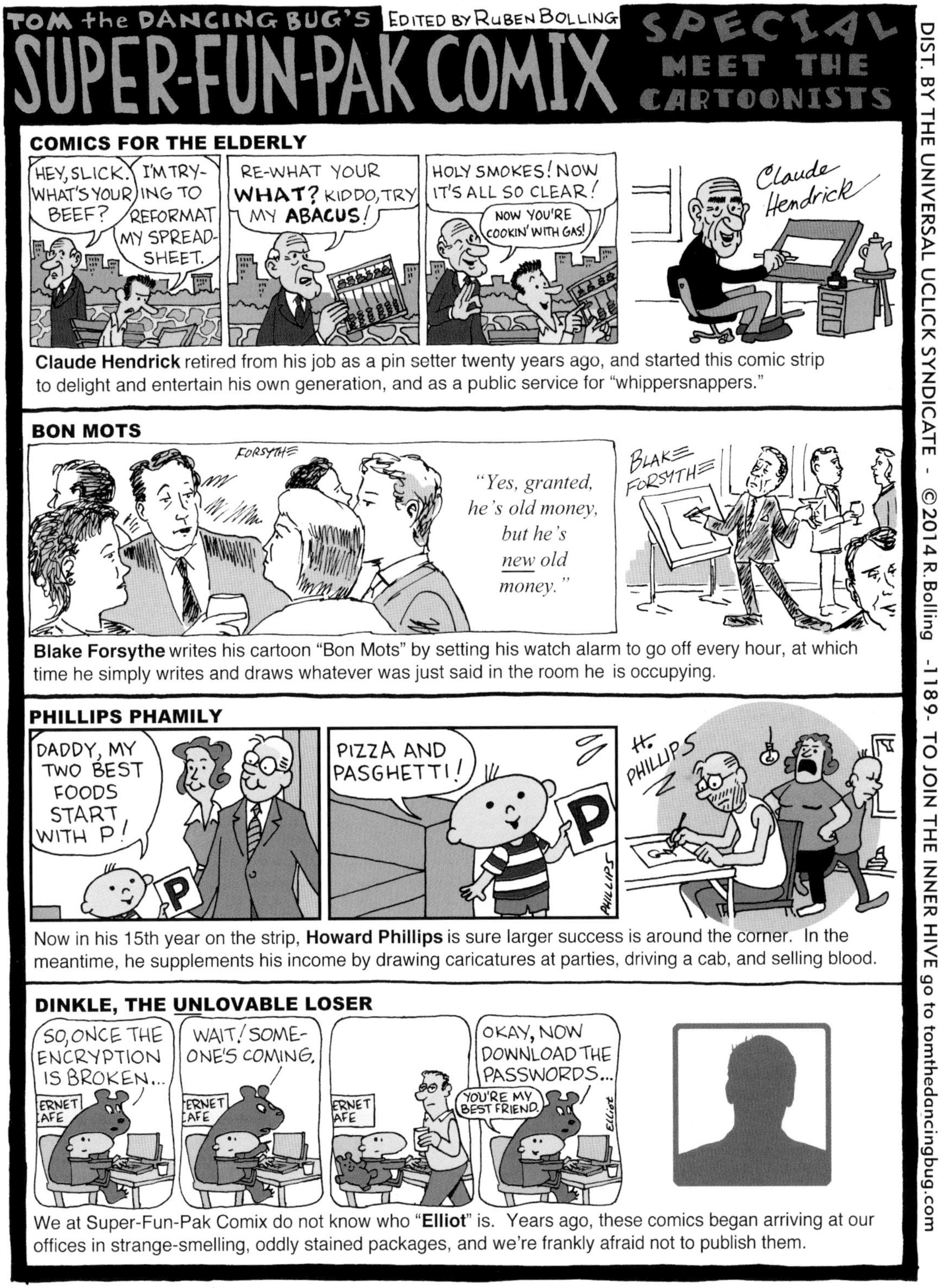
TOM the DANCING BUG'S
EDITED BY RUBEN BOLLING
SUPER-FUN-PAK COMIX
SPECIAL
MEET THE CARTOONISTS
COMICS FOR THE ELDERLY
HEY, SLICK. WHAT'S YOUR BEEF?
I'M TRYING TO REFORMAT MY SPREADSHEET.
RE-WHAT YOUR WHAT? KIDDO, TRY MY ABACUS!
HOLY SMOKES! NOW IT'S ALL SO CLEAR!
NOW YOU'RE COOKIN' WITH GAS!
Claude Hendrick
Claude Hendrick retired from his job as a pin setter twenty years ago, and started this comic strip to delight and entertain his own generation, and as a public service for "whippersnappers."
BON MOTS
FORSYTHE
"Yes, granted, he's old money, but he's new old money."
BLAKE FORSYTHE
Blake Forsythe writes his cartoon "Bon Mots" by setting his watch alarm to go off every hour, at which time he simply writes and draws whatever was just said in the room he is occupying.
PHILLIPS PHAMILY
DADDY, MY TWO BEST FOODS START WITH P!
P
PIZZA AND PASGHETTI!
P
PHILLIPS
H. PHILLIPS
Now in his 15th year on the strip, Howard Phillips is sure larger success is around the corner. In the meantime, he supplements his income by drawing caricatures at parties, driving a cab, and selling blood.
DINKLE, THE UNLOVABLE LOSER
SO, ONCE THE ENCRYPTION IS BROKEN...
ERNET AFE
WAIT! SOMEONE'S COMING.
ERNET AFE
ERNET AFE
OKAY, NOW DOWNLOAD THE PASSWORDS...
YOU'RE MY BEST FRIEND.
Elliot
We at Super-Fun-Pak Comix do not know who "Elliot" is. Years ago, these comics began arriving at our offices in strange-smelling, oddly stained packages, and we're frankly afraid not to publish them.
DIST. BY THE UNIVERSAL UCLICK SYNDICATE - © 2014 R. Bolling -1189- TO JOIN THE INNER HIVE go to tomthedancingbug.com

5/19/14

TOM the DANCING BUG

by RUBEN BOLLING

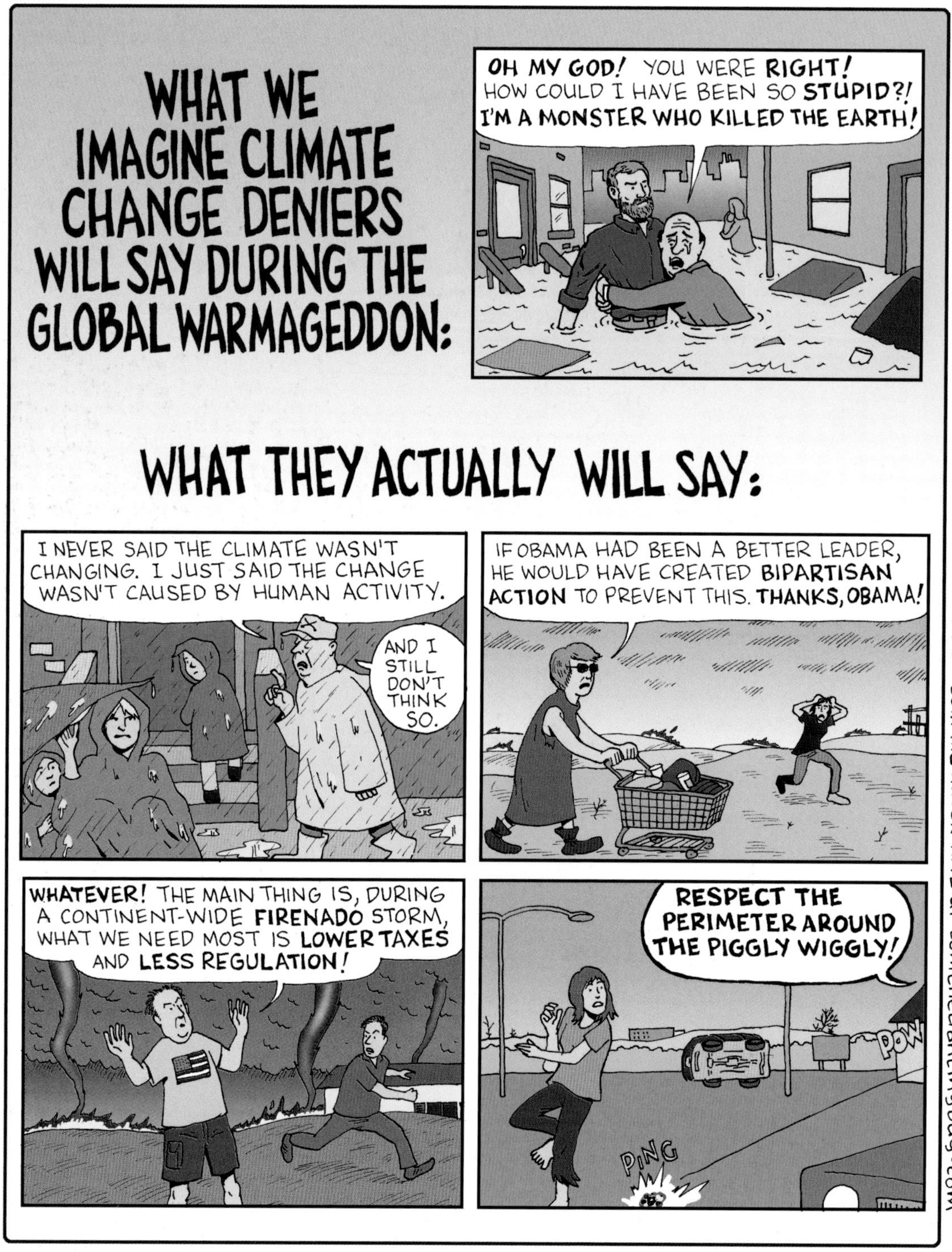

WHAT WE IMAGINE CLIMATE CHANGE DENIERS WILL SAY DURING THE GLOBAL WARMAGEDDON:
OH MY GOD! YOU WERE RIGHT! HOW COULD I HAVE BEEN SO STUPID?! I'M A MONSTER WHO KILLED THE EARTH!
WHAT THEY ACTUALLY WILL SAY:
I NEVER SAID THE CLIMATE WASN'T CHANGING. I JUST SAID THE CHANGE WASN'T CAUSED BY HUMAN ACTIVITY.
AND I STILL DON'T THINK SO.
IF OBAMA HAD BEEN A BETTER LEADER, HE WOULD HAVE CREATED BIPARTISAN ACTION TO PREVENT THIS. THANKS, OBAMA!
WHATEVER! THE MAIN THING IS, DURING A CONTINENT-WIDE FIRENADO STORM, WHAT WE NEED MOST IS LOWER TAXES AND LESS REGULATION!
RESPECT THE PERIMETER AROUND THE PIGGLY WIGGLY!
POW
PING

5/26/14

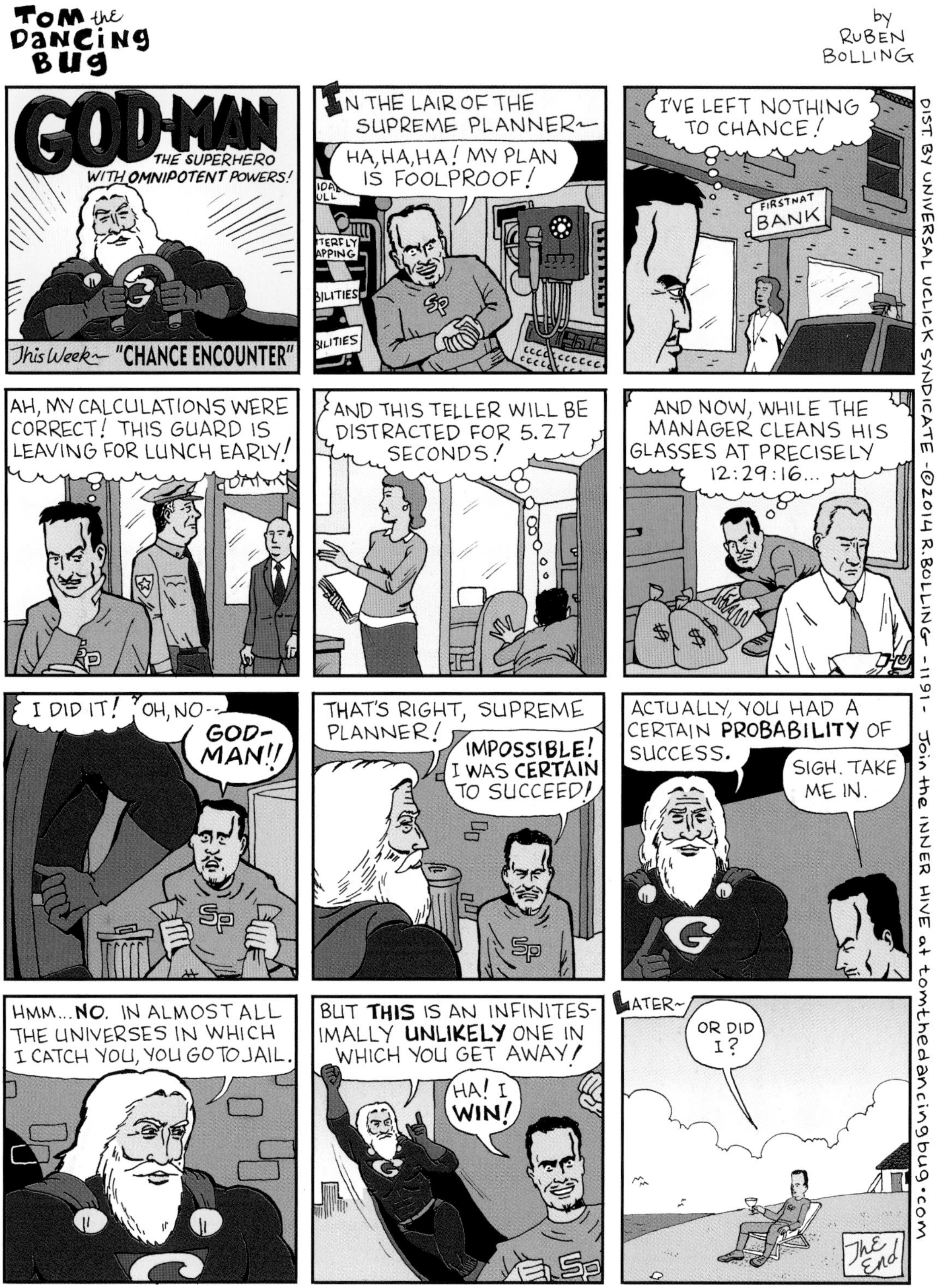
TOM the DANCING BUG
by RUBEN BOLLING
GOD-MAN
THE SUPERHERO WITH OMNIPOTENT POWERS!
This Week~ "CHANCE ENCOUNTER"
IN THE LAIR OF THE SUPREME PLANNER~
HA, HA, HA! MY PLAN IS FOOLPROOF!
I'VE LEFT NOTHING TO CHANCE!
FIRSTNAT BANK
AH, MY CALCULATIONS WERE CORRECT! THIS GUARD IS LEAVING FOR LUNCH EARLY!
AND THIS TELLER WILL BE DISTRACTED FOR 5.27 SECONDS!
AND NOW, WHILE THE MANAGER CLEANS HIS GLASSES AT PRECISELY 12:29:16...
I DID IT!
OH, NO--
GOD-MAN!!
THAT'S RIGHT, SUPREME PLANNER!
IMPOSSIBLE! I WAS CERTAIN TO SUCCEED!
ACTUALLY, YOU HAD A CERTAIN PROBABILITY OF SUCCESS.
SIGH. TAKE ME IN.
HMM... NO. IN ALMOST ALL THE UNIVERSES IN WHICH I CATCH YOU, YOU GO TO JAIL.
BUT THIS IS AN INFINITESIMALLY UNLIKELY ONE IN WHICH YOU GET AWAY!
HA! I WIN!
LATER~
OR DID I?
THE END
DIST. BY UNIVERSAL UCLICK SYNDICATE - ©2014 R. BOLLING - 1191 - Join the INNER HIVE at tomthedancingbug.com

6/2/14

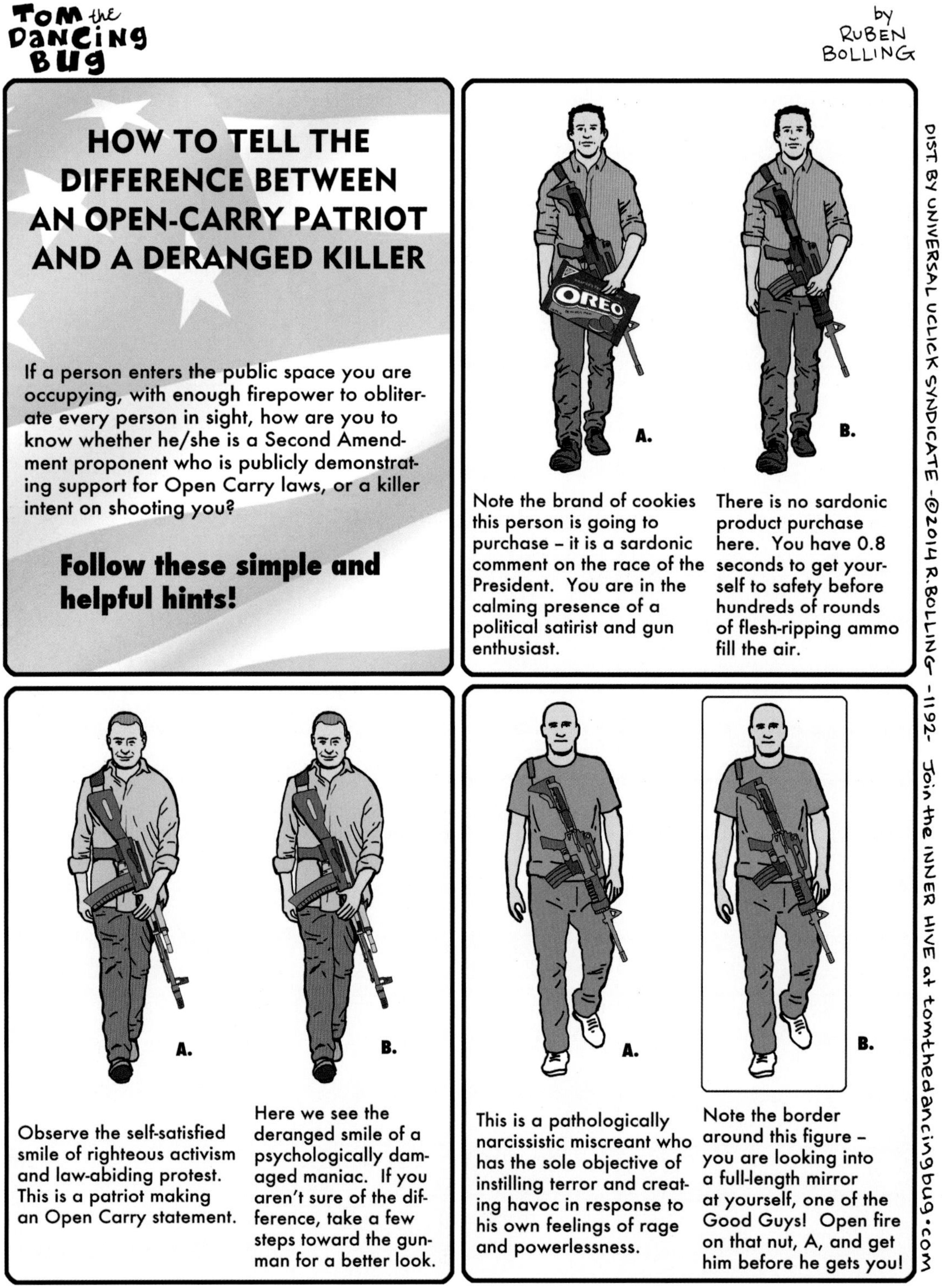
TOM the DANCING BUG
by RUBEN BOLLING
HOW TO TELL THE DIFFERENCE BETWEEN AN OPEN-CARRY PATRIOT AND A DERANGED KILLER
If a person enters the public space you are occupying, with enough firepower to obliterate every person in sight, how are you to know whether he/she is a Second Amendment proponent who is publicly demonstrating support for Open Carry laws, or a killer intent on shooting you?
Follow these simple and helpful hints!
OREO
A.
B.
Note the brand of cookies this person is going to purchase – it is a sardonic comment on the race of the President. You are in the calming presence of a political satirist and gun enthusiast.
There is no sardonic product purchase here. You have 0.8 seconds to get yourself to safety before hundreds of rounds of flesh-ripping ammo fill the air.
A.
B.
Observe the self-satisfied smile of righteous activism and law-abiding protest. This is a patriot making an Open Carry statement.
Here we see the deranged smile of a psychologically damaged maniac. If you aren't sure of the difference, take a few steps toward the gunman for a better look.
A.
B.
This is a pathologically narcissistic miscreant who has the sole objective of instilling terror and creating havoc in response to his own feelings of rage and powerlessness.
Note the border around this figure – you are looking into a full-length mirror at yourself, one of the Good Guys! Open fire on that nut, A, and get him before he gets you!
DIST. BY UNIVERSAL UCLICK SYNDICATE -©2014 R. BOLLING- -1192- Join the INNER HIVE at tomthedancingbug•com

6/9/14

TOM the DANCING BUG

by RUBEN BOLLING

If Social Media Existed in the 20th Century

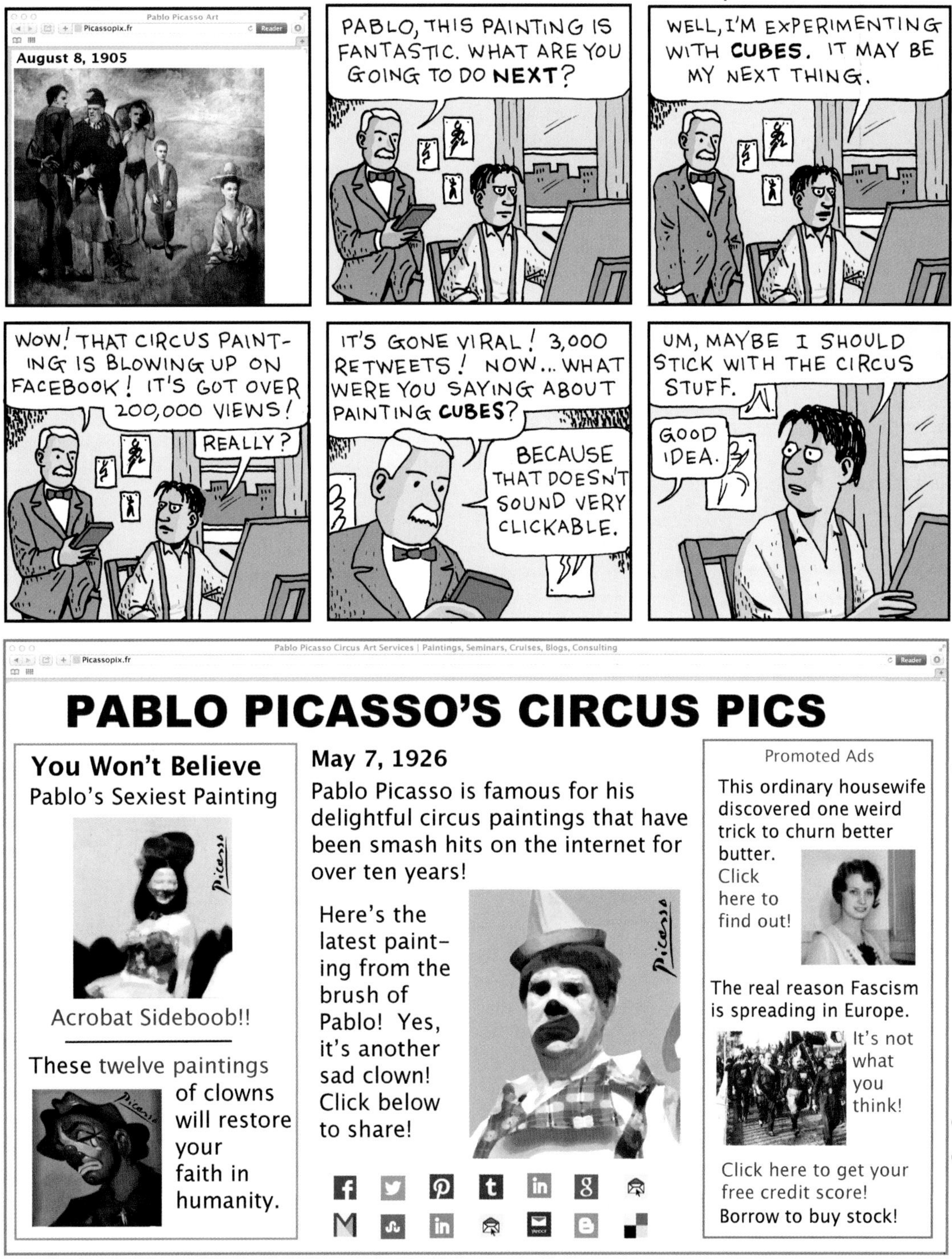

Pablo Picasso Art
Picassopix.fr
August 8, 1905
PABLO, THIS PAINTING IS FANTASTIC. WHAT ARE YOU GOING TO DO NEXT?
WELL, I'M EXPERIMENTING WITH CUBES. IT MAY BE MY NEXT THING.
WOW! THAT CIRCUS PAINTING IS BLOWING UP ON FACEBOOK! IT'S GOT OVER 200,000 VIEWS!
REALLY?
IT'S GONE VIRAL! 3,000 RETWEETS! NOW... WHAT WERE YOU SAYING ABOUT PAINTING CUBES?
BECAUSE THAT DOESN'T SOUND VERY CLICKABLE.
UM, MAYBE I SHOULD STICK WITH THE CIRCUS STUFF.
GOOD IDEA.
Pablo Picasso Circus Art Services | Paintings, Seminars, Cruises, Blogs, Consulting
Picassopix.fr
PABLO PICASSO'S CIRCUS PICS
You Won't Believe
Pablo's Sexiest Painting
Picasso
Acrobat Sideboob!!
These twelve paintings of clowns will restore your faith in humanity.
May 7, 1926
Pablo Picasso is famous for his delightful circus paintings that have been smash hits on the internet for over ten years!
Here's the latest painting from the brush of Pablo! Yes, it's another sad clown! Click below to share!
Promoted Ads
This ordinary housewife discovered one weird trick to churn better butter. Click here to find out!
The real reason Fascism is spreading in Europe.
It's not what you think!
Click here to get your free credit score!
Borrow to buy stock!

6/16/14

TOM the DANCING BUG

by RUBEN BOLLING

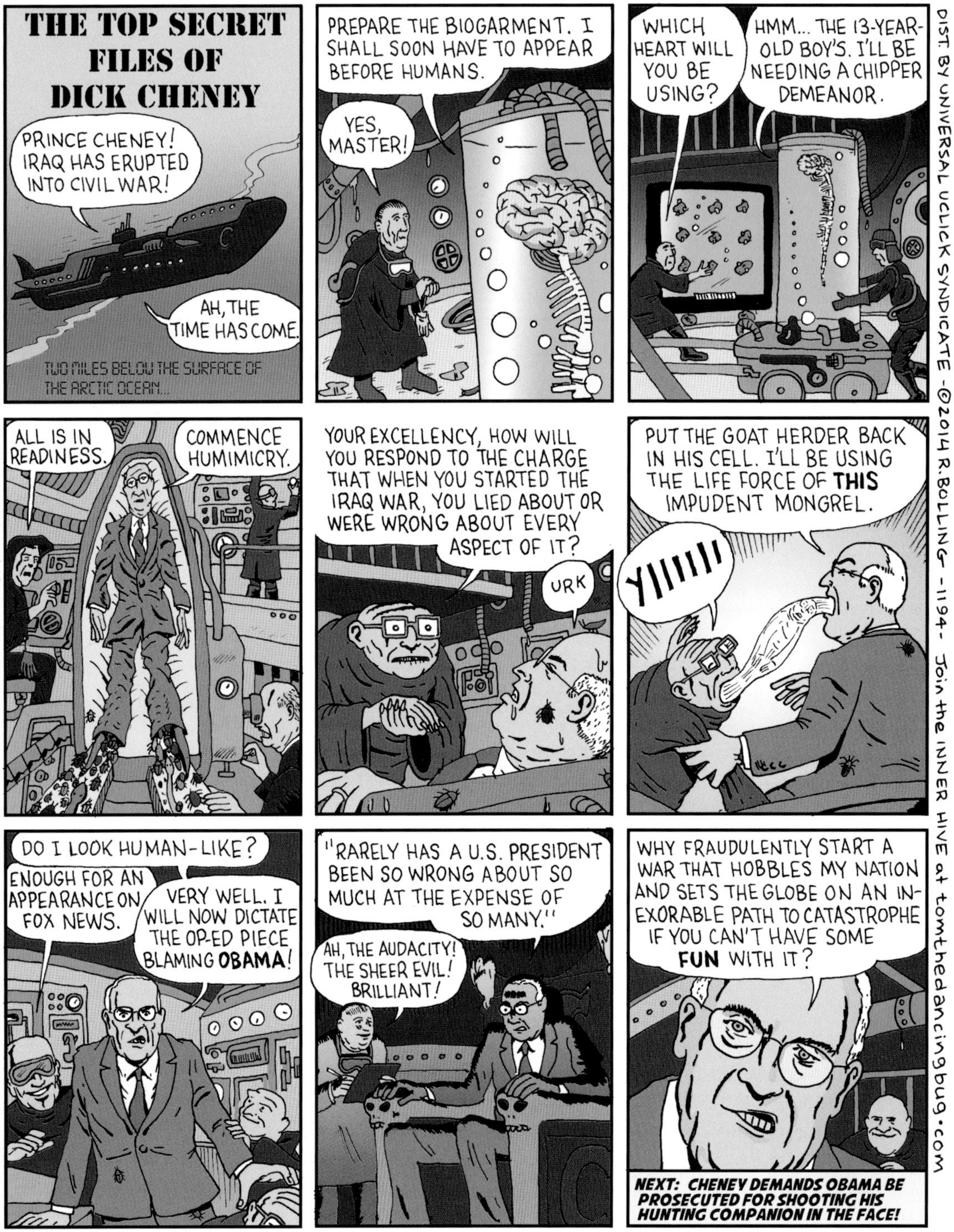
THE TOP SECRET FILES OF DICK CHENEY
PRINCE CHENEY! IRAQ HAS ERUPTED INTO CIVIL WAR!
AH, THE TIME HAS COME.
TWO MILES BELOW THE SURFACE OF THE ARCTIC OCEAN...
PREPARE THE BIOGARMENT. I SHALL SOON HAVE TO APPEAR BEFORE HUMANS.
YES, MASTER!
WHICH HEART WILL YOU BE USING?
HMM... THE 13-YEAR-OLD BOY'S. I'LL BE NEEDING A CHIPPER DEMEANOR.
ALL IS IN READINESS.
COMMENCE HUMIMICRY.
YOUR EXCELLENCY, HOW WILL YOU RESPOND TO THE CHARGE THAT WHEN YOU STARTED THE IRAQ WAR, YOU LIED ABOUT OR WERE WRONG ABOUT EVERY ASPECT OF IT?
URK
PUT THE GOAT HERDER BACK IN HIS CELL. I'LL BE USING THE LIFE FORCE OF **THIS** IMPUDENT MONGREL.
YIIIIII
DO I LOOK HUMAN-LIKE?
ENOUGH FOR AN APPEARANCE ON FOX NEWS.
VERY WELL. I WILL NOW DICTATE THE OP-ED PIECE BLAMING **OBAMA**!
"RARELY HAS A U.S. PRESIDENT BEEN SO WRONG ABOUT SO MUCH AT THE EXPENSE OF SO MANY."
AH, THE AUDACITY! THE SHEER EVIL! BRILLIANT!
WHY FRAUDULENTLY START A WAR THAT HOBBLES MY NATION AND SETS THE GLOBE ON AN INEXORABLE PATH TO CATASTROPHE IF YOU CAN'T HAVE SOME **FUN** WITH IT?
NEXT: CHENEY DEMANDS OBAMA BE PROSECUTED FOR SHOOTING HIS HUNTING COMPANION IN THE FACE!
DIST. BY UNIVERSAL UCLICK SYNDICATE - ©2014 R. BOLLING - 1194 - Join the INNER HIVE at tomthedancingbug.com

6/23/14

Tom the Dancing Bug

by RUBEN BOLLING

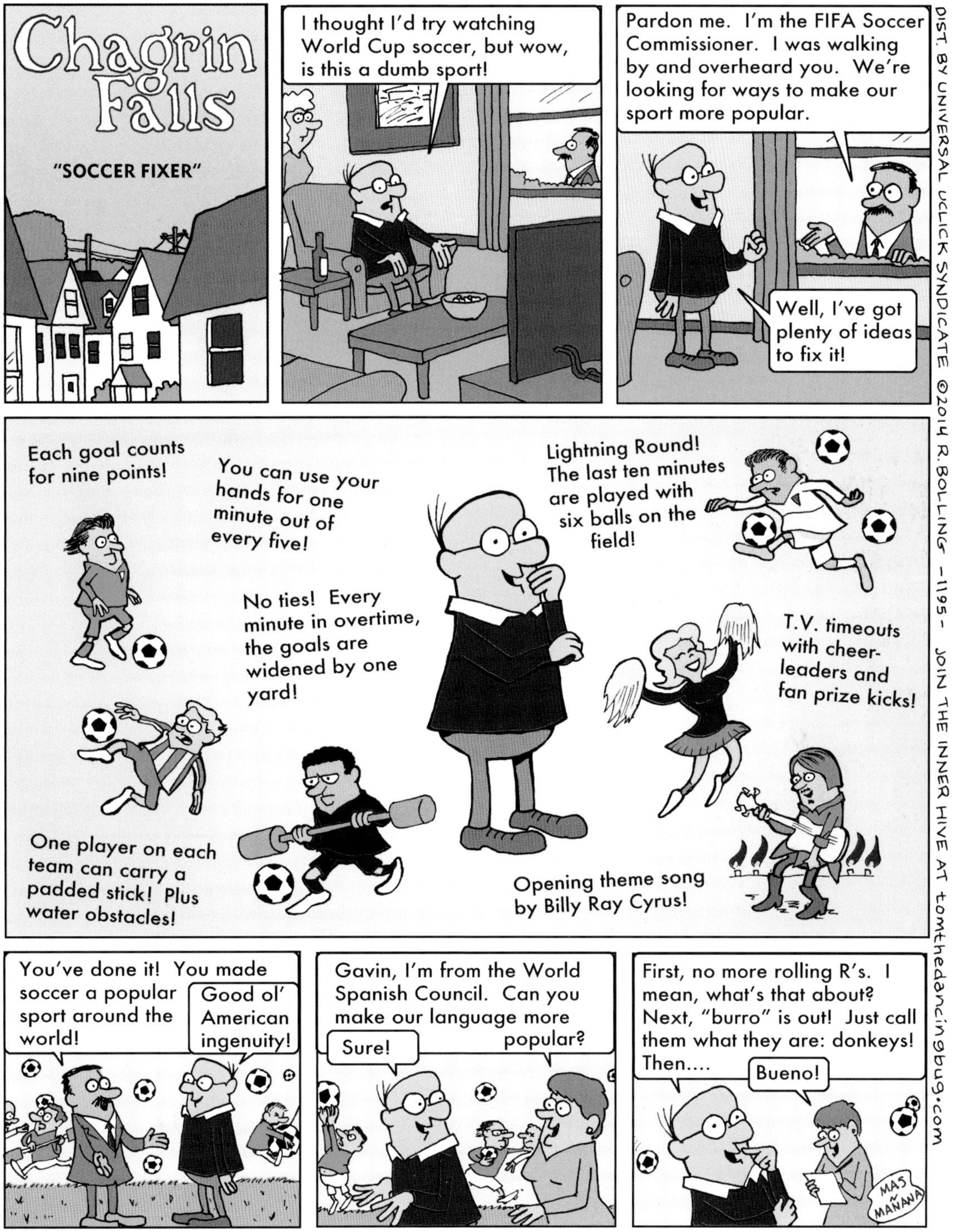
Chagrin Falls
"SOCCER FIXER"
I thought I'd try watching World Cup soccer, but wow, is this a dumb sport!
Pardon me. I'm the FIFA Soccer Commissioner. I was walking by and overheard you. We're looking for ways to make our sport more popular.
Well, I've got plenty of ideas to fix it!
Each goal counts for nine points!
You can use your hands for one minute out of every five!
No ties! Every minute in overtime, the goals are widened by one yard!
Lightning Round! The last ten minutes are played with six balls on the field!
T.V. timeouts with cheer-leaders and fan prize kicks!
One player on each team can carry a padded stick! Plus water obstacles!
Opening theme song by Billy Ray Cyrus!
You've done it! You made soccer a popular sport around the world!
Good ol' American ingenuity!
Gavin, I'm from the World Spanish Council. Can you make our language more popular?
Sure!
First, no more rolling R's. I mean, what's that about? Next, "burro" is out! Just call them what they are: donkeys! Then....
Bueno!
MAS MAÑANA
DIST. BY UNIVERSAL UCLICK SYNDICATE ©2014 R. BOLLING -1195- JOIN THE INNER HIVE AT tomthedancingbug.com

6/30/14

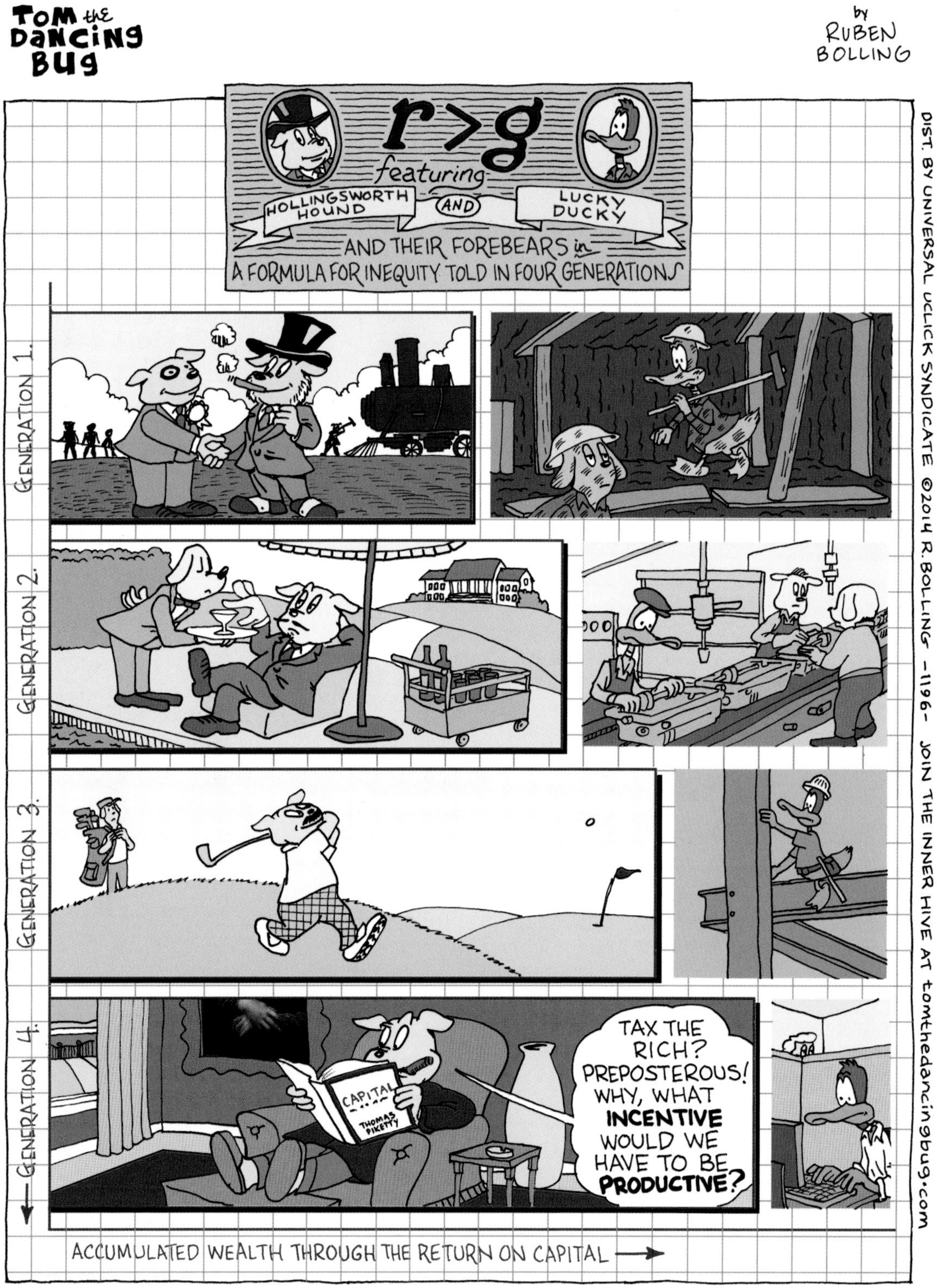
TOM the DANCING BUG
by RUBEN BOLLING
r>g
featuring
HOLLINGSWORTH HOUND
AND
LUCKY DUCKY
AND THEIR FOREBEARS in
A FORMULA FOR INEQUITY TOLD IN FOUR GENERATIONS
DIST. BY UNIVERSAL UCLICK SYNDICATE ©2014 R. BOLLING -1196- JOIN THE INNER HIVE AT tomthedancingbug.com
GENERATION 1.
GENERATION 2.
GENERATION 3.
GENERATION 4.
CAPITAL
THOMAS PIKETTY
TAX THE RICH? PREPOSTEROUS! WHY, WHAT **INCENTIVE** WOULD WE HAVE TO BE **PRODUCTIVE**?
ACCUMULATED WEALTH THROUGH THE RETURN ON CAPITAL

7/7/14

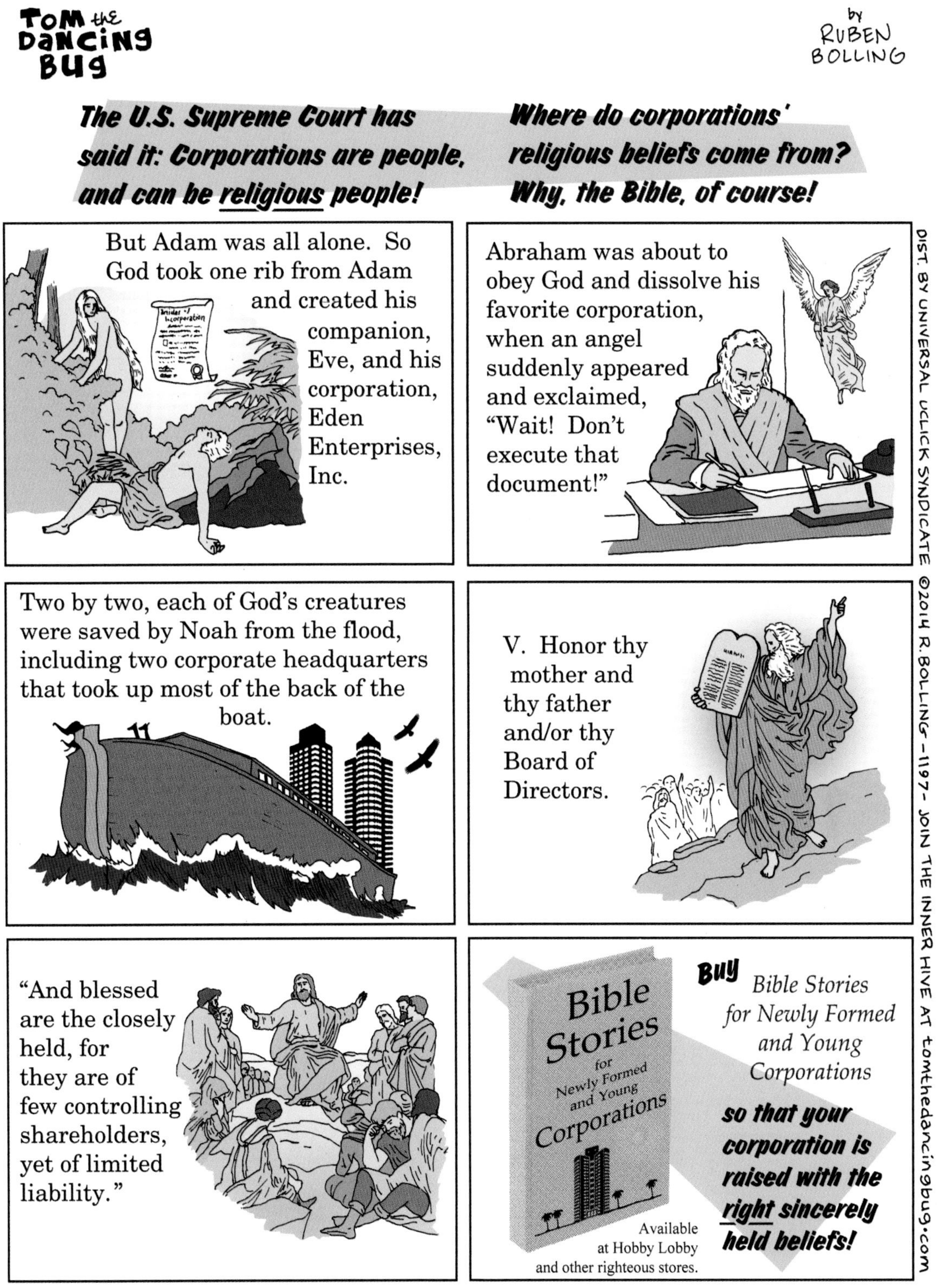
TOM the DANCING BUG
by RUBEN BOLLING
The U.S. Supreme Court has said it: Corporations are people, and can be religious people!
Where do corporations' religious beliefs come from? Why, the Bible, of course!
But Adam was all alone. So God took one rib from Adam and created his companion, Eve, and his corporation, Eden Enterprises, Inc.
Abraham was about to obey God and dissolve his favorite corporation, when an angel suddenly appeared and exclaimed, "Wait! Don't execute that document!"
Two by two, each of God's creatures were saved by Noah from the flood, including two corporate headquarters that took up most of the back of the boat.
V. Honor thy mother and thy father and/or thy Board of Directors.
"And blessed are the closely held, for they are of few controlling shareholders, yet of limited liability."
Bible Stories for Newly Formed and Young Corporations
Available at Hobby Lobby and other righteous stores.
Buy Bible Stories for Newly Formed and Young Corporations
so that your corporation is raised with the right sincerely held beliefs!
DIST. BY UNIVERSAL UCLICK SYNDICATE ©2014 R. BOLLING -1197- JOIN THE INNER HIVE AT tomthedancingbug.com

7/14/14

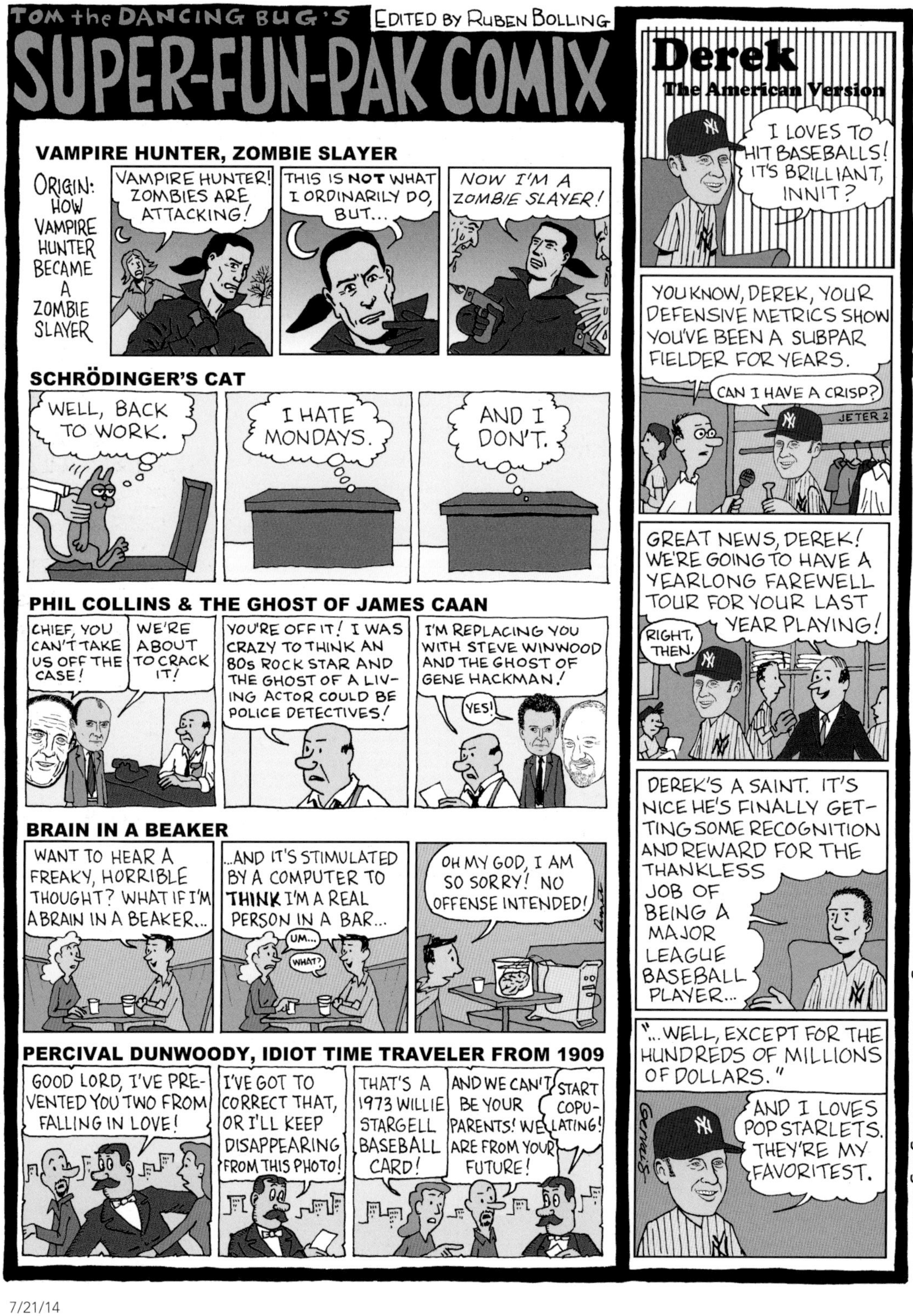
TOM the DANCING BUG'S
EDITED BY RUBEN BOLLING
SUPER-FUN-PAK COMIX
VAMPIRE HUNTER, ZOMBIE SLAYER
ORIGIN: HOW VAMPIRE HUNTER BECAME A ZOMBIE SLAYER
VAMPIRE HUNTER! ZOMBIES ARE ATTACKING!
THIS IS NOT WHAT I ORDINARILY DO, BUT...
NOW I'M A ZOMBIE SLAYER!
SCHRÖDINGER'S CAT
WELL, BACK TO WORK.
I HATE MONDAYS.
AND I DON'T.
PHIL COLLINS & THE GHOST OF JAMES CAAN
CHIEF, YOU CAN'T TAKE US OFF THE CASE!
WE'RE ABOUT TO CRACK IT!
YOU'RE OFF IT! I WAS CRAZY TO THINK AN 80s ROCK STAR AND THE GHOST OF A LIVING ACTOR COULD BE POLICE DETECTIVES!
I'M REPLACING YOU WITH STEVE WINWOOD AND THE GHOST OF GENE HACKMAN!
YES!
BRAIN IN A BEAKER
WANT TO HEAR A FREAKY, HORRIBLE THOUGHT? WHAT IF I'M A BRAIN IN A BEAKER...
...AND IT'S STIMULATED BY A COMPUTER TO THINK I'M A REAL PERSON IN A BAR...
UM...
WHAT?
OH MY GOD, I AM SO SORRY! NO OFFENSE INTENDED!
PERCIVAL DUNWOODY, IDIOT TIME TRAVELER FROM 1909
GOOD LORD, I'VE PREVENTED YOU TWO FROM FALLING IN LOVE!
I'VE GOT TO CORRECT THAT, OR I'LL KEEP DISAPPEARING FROM THIS PHOTO!
THAT'S A 1973 WILLIE STARGELL BASEBALL CARD!
AND WE CAN'T BE YOUR PARENTS! WE ARE FROM YOUR FUTURE!
START COPULATING!
Derek
The American Version
I LOVES TO HIT BASEBALLS! IT'S BRILLIANT, INNIT?
YOU KNOW, DEREK, YOUR DEFENSIVE METRICS SHOW YOU'VE BEEN A SUBPAR FIELDER FOR YEARS.
CAN I HAVE A CRISP?
JETER 2
GREAT NEWS, DEREK! WE'RE GOING TO HAVE A YEARLONG FAREWELL TOUR FOR YOUR LAST YEAR PLAYING!
RIGHT, THEN.
DEREK'S A SAINT. IT'S NICE HE'S FINALLY GETTING SOME RECOGNITION AND REWARD FOR THE THANKLESS JOB OF BEING A MAJOR LEAGUE BASEBALL PLAYER...
"...WELL, EXCEPT FOR THE HUNDREDS OF MILLIONS OF DOLLARS."
AND I LOVES POP STARLETS. THEY'RE MY FAVORITEST.

7/21/14

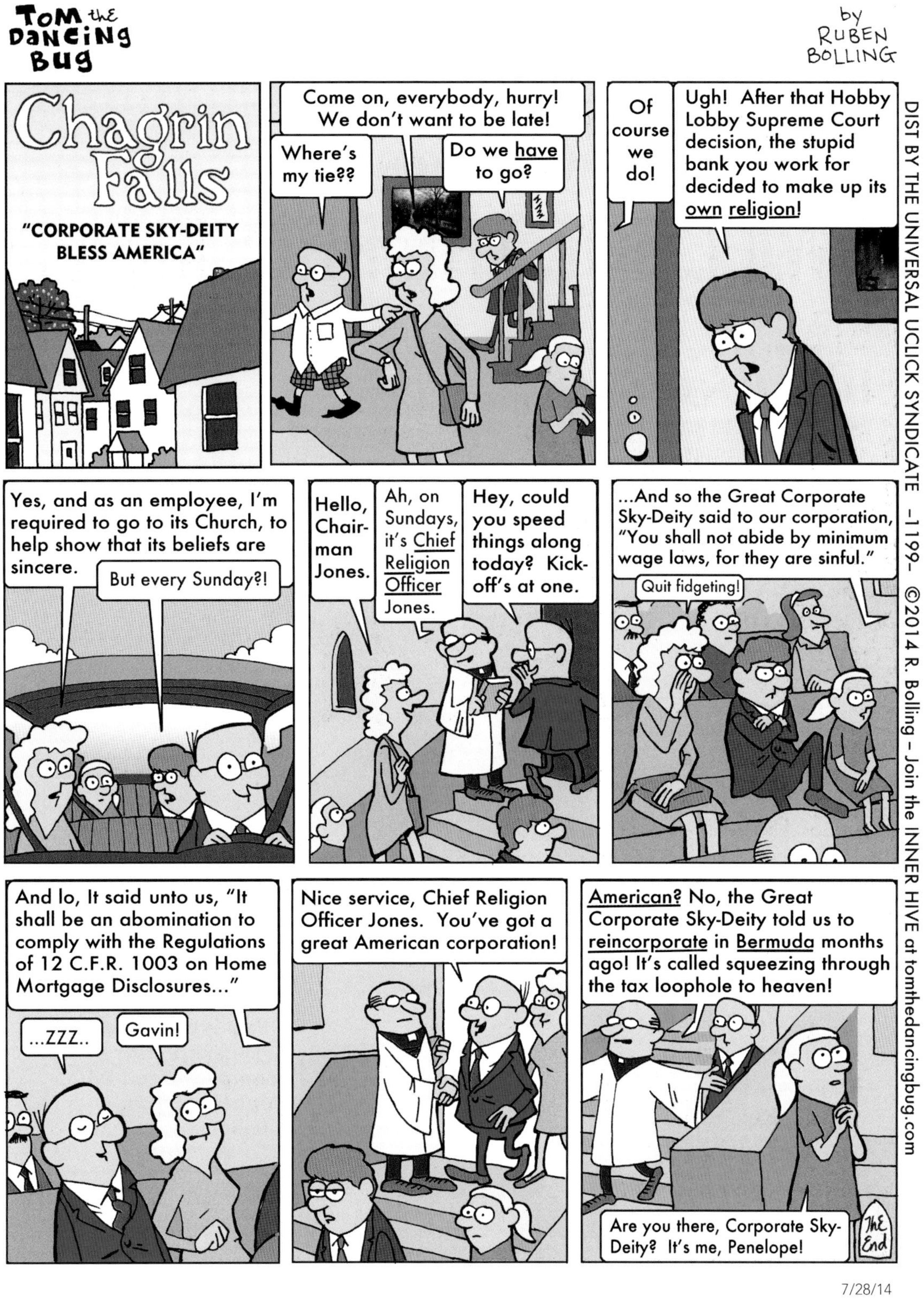
Tom the Dancing Bug
by Ruben Bolling
Chagrin Falls
"CORPORATE SKY-DEITY BLESS AMERICA"
Come on, everybody, hurry! We don't want to be late!
Where's my tie??
Do we have to go?
Of course we do!
Ugh! After that Hobby Lobby Supreme Court decision, the stupid bank you work for decided to make up its own religion!
Yes, and as an employee, I'm required to go to its Church, to help show that its beliefs are sincere.
But every Sunday?!
Hello, Chair-man Jones.
Ah, on Sundays, it's Chief Religion Officer Jones.
Hey, could you speed things along today? Kick-off's at one.
...And so the Great Corporate Sky-Deity said to our corporation, "You shall not abide by minimum wage laws, for they are sinful."
Quit fidgeting!
And lo, It said unto us, "It shall be an abomination to comply with the Regulations of 12 C.F.R. 1003 on Home Mortgage Disclosures..."
...ZZZ..
Gavin!
Nice service, Chief Religion Officer Jones. You've got a great American corporation!
American? No, the Great Corporate Sky-Deity told us to reincorporate in Bermuda months ago! It's called squeezing through the tax loophole to heaven!
Are you there, Corporate Sky-Deity? It's me, Penelope!
The End
DIST BY THE UNIVERSAL UCLICK SYNDICATE -1199- ©2014 R. Bolling – Join the INNER HIVE at tomthedancingbug.com

7/28/14

Tom the Dancing Bug

by Ruben Bolling

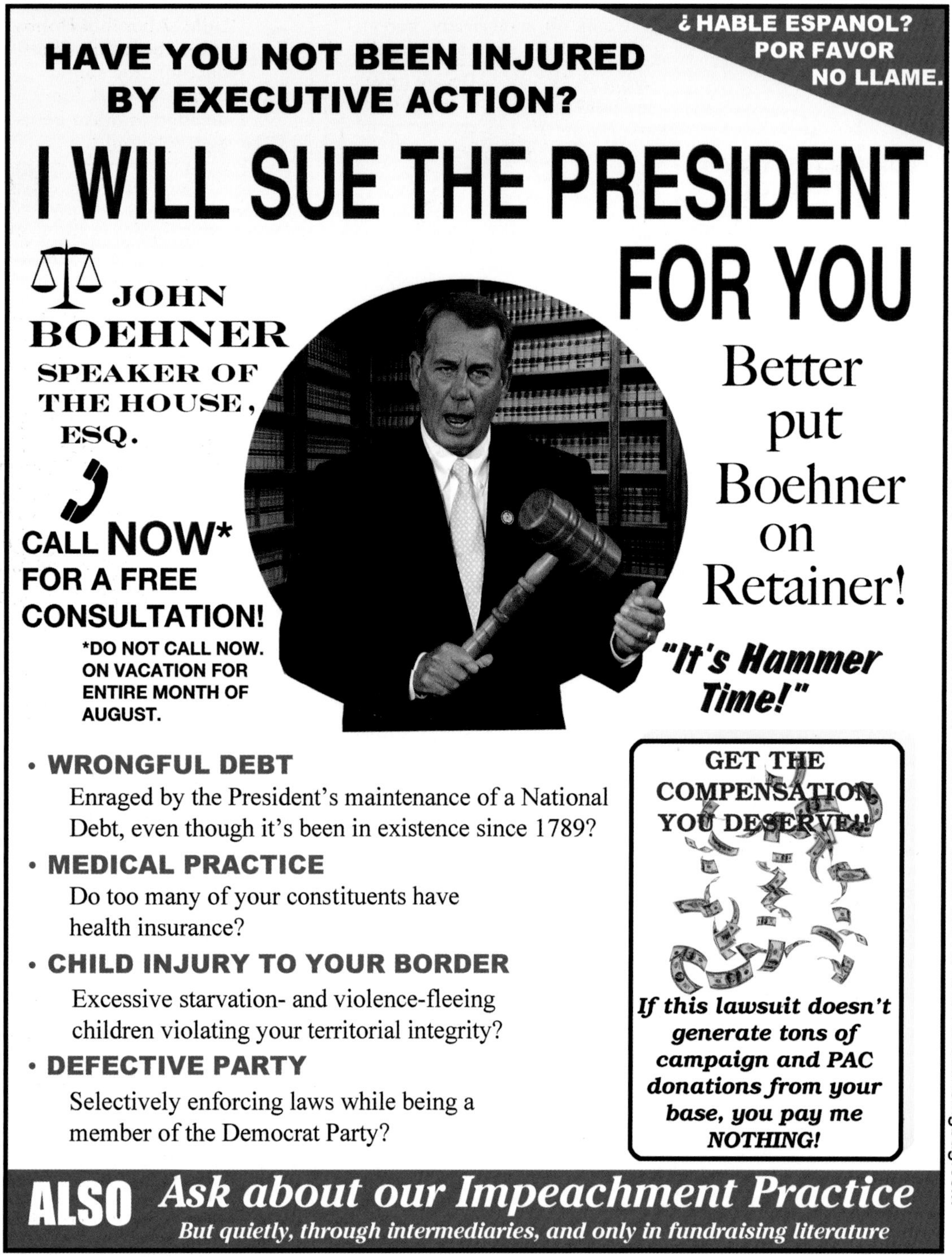
¿HABLE ESPANOL? POR FAVOR NO LLAME.
HAVE YOU NOT BEEN INJURED BY EXECUTIVE ACTION?
I WILL SUE THE PRESIDENT FOR YOU
JOHN BOEHNER SPEAKER OF THE HOUSE, ESQ.
CALL NOW* FOR A FREE CONSULTATION!
*DO NOT CALL NOW. ON VACATION FOR ENTIRE MONTH OF AUGUST.
Better put Boehner on Retainer!
"It's Hammer Time!"
• WRONGFUL DEBT
Enraged by the President's maintenance of a National Debt, even though it's been in existence since 1789?
• MEDICAL PRACTICE
Do too many of your constituents have health insurance?
• CHILD INJURY TO YOUR BORDER
Excessive starvation- and violence-fleeing children violating your territorial integrity?
• DEFECTIVE PARTY
Selectively enforcing laws while being a member of the Democrat Party?
GET THE COMPENSATION YOU DESERVE!!
If this lawsuit doesn't generate tons of campaign and PAC donations from your base, you pay me NOTHING!
ALSO Ask about our Impeachment Practice
But quietly, through intermediaries, and only in fundraising literature

8/4/14

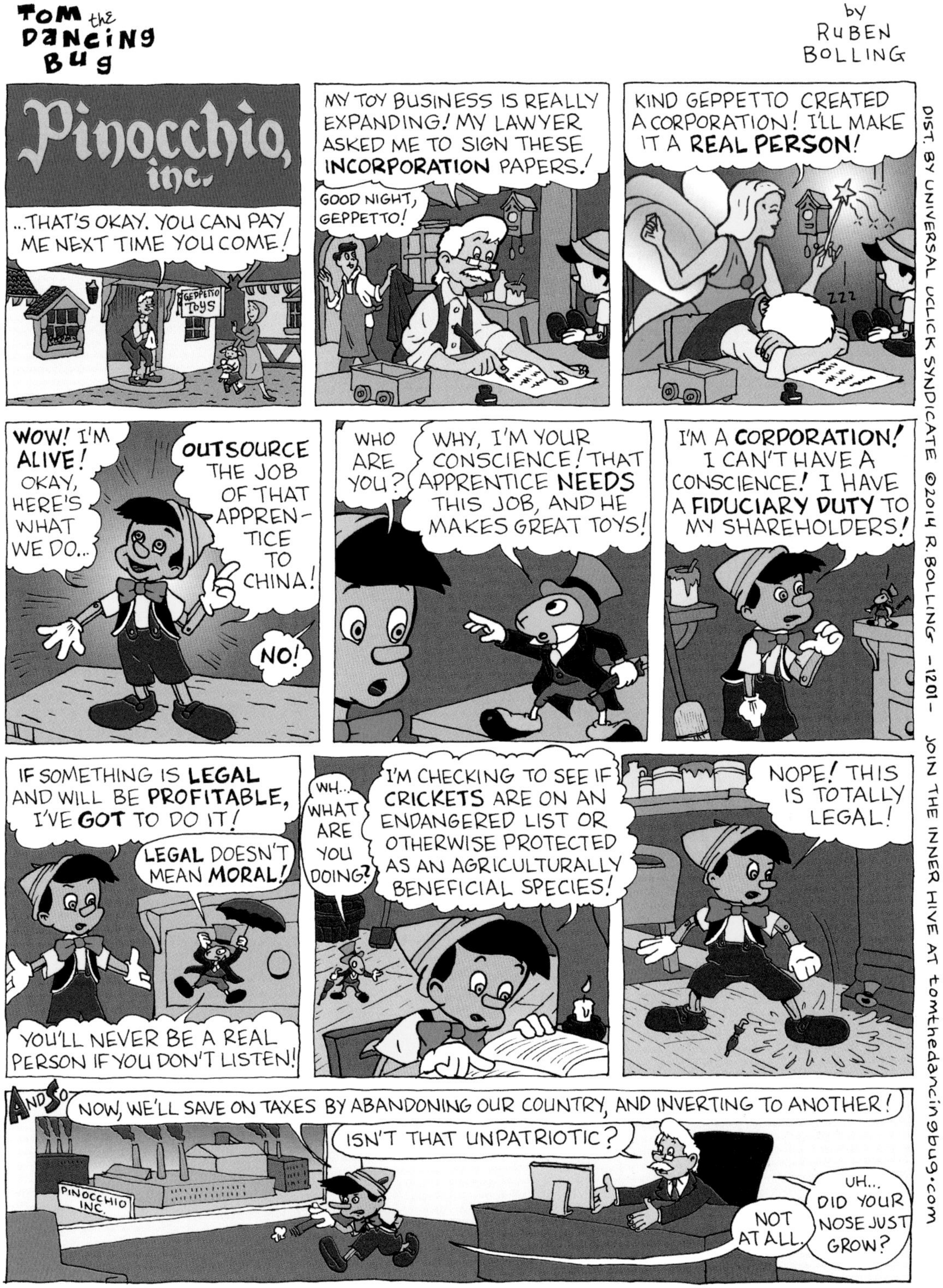
TOM the DANCING BUG
by RUBEN BOLLING
Pinocchio, inc.
...THAT'S OKAY. YOU CAN PAY ME NEXT TIME YOU COME!
GEPPETTO TOYS
MY TOY BUSINESS IS REALLY EXPANDING! MY LAWYER ASKED ME TO SIGN THESE INCORPORATION PAPERS!
GOOD NIGHT, GEPPETTO!
KIND GEPPETTO CREATED A CORPORATION! I'LL MAKE IT A REAL PERSON!
ZZZ
WOW! I'M ALIVE! OKAY, HERE'S WHAT WE DO...
OUTSOURCE THE JOB OF THAT APPRENTICE TO CHINA!
NO!
WHO ARE YOU?
WHY, I'M YOUR CONSCIENCE! THAT APPRENTICE NEEDS THIS JOB, AND HE MAKES GREAT TOYS!
I'M A CORPORATION! I CAN'T HAVE A CONSCIENCE! I HAVE A FIDUCIARY DUTY TO MY SHAREHOLDERS!
IF SOMETHING IS LEGAL AND WILL BE PROFITABLE, I'VE GOT TO DO IT!
LEGAL DOESN'T MEAN MORAL!
YOU'LL NEVER BE A REAL PERSON IF YOU DON'T LISTEN!
WH... WHAT ARE YOU DOING?
I'M CHECKING TO SEE IF CRICKETS ARE ON AN ENDANGERED LIST OR OTHERWISE PROTECTED AS AN AGRICULTURALLY BENEFICIAL SPECIES!
NOPE! THIS IS TOTALLY LEGAL!
AND SO
NOW, WE'LL SAVE ON TAXES BY ABANDONING OUR COUNTRY, AND INVERTING TO ANOTHER!
ISN'T THAT UNPATRIOTIC?
PINOCCHIO INC.
NOT AT ALL.
UH... DID YOUR NOSE JUST GROW?
DIST. BY UNIVERSAL UCLICK SYNDICATE ©2014 R. BOLLING -1201- JOIN THE INNER HIVE AT tomthedancingbug.com

8/11/14

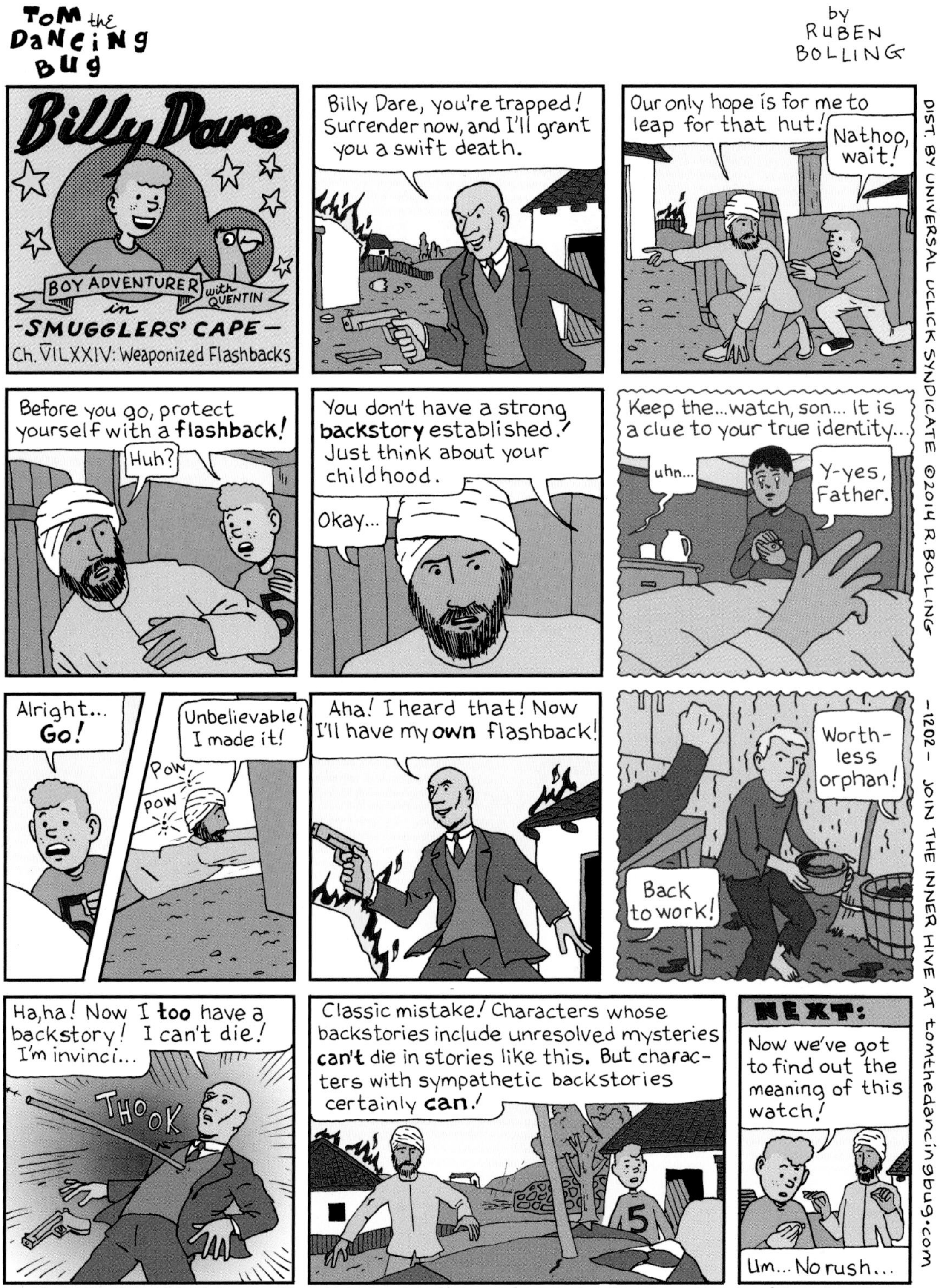
Tom the Dancing Bug
by Ruben Bolling
Billy Dare
Boy Adventurer with Quentin
in
-Smugglers' Cape-
Ch. V̄ILXXIV: Weaponized Flashbacks
Billy Dare, you're trapped! Surrender now, and I'll grant you a swift death.
Our only hope is for me to leap for that hut!
Nathoo, wait!
Before you go, protect yourself with a **flashback**!
Huh?
You don't have a strong **backstory** established! Just think about your childhood.
Okay...
Keep the... watch, son... It is a clue to your true identity...
uhn...
Y-yes, Father.
Alright... **Go**!
Unbelievable! I made it!
Pow
Pow
Aha! I heard that! Now I'll have my **own** flashback!
Worth-less orphan!
Back to work!
Ha, ha! Now I **too** have a backstory! I can't die! I'm invinci...
THOOK
Classic mistake! Characters whose backstories include unresolved mysteries **can't** die in stories like this. But characters with sympathetic backstories certainly **can**!
NEXT:
Now we've got to find out the meaning of this watch!
Um... No rush...
DIST. BY UNIVERSAL UCLICK SYNDICATE ©2014 R. BOLLING -1202- JOIN THE INNER HIVE AT tomthedancingbug.com

8/18/14

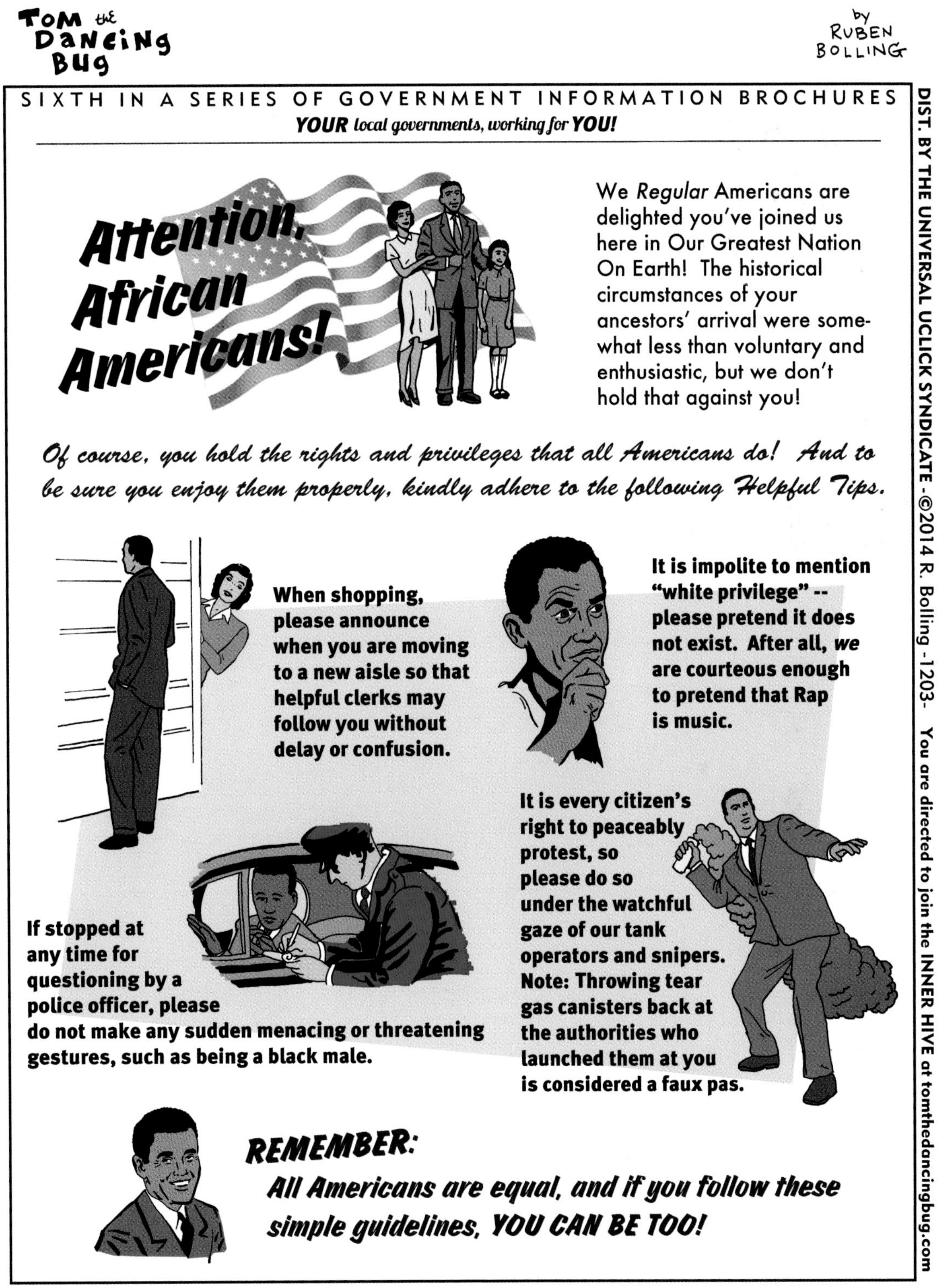
TOM the DANCING BUG
by RUBEN BOLLING
SIXTH IN A SERIES OF GOVERNMENT INFORMATION BROCHURES
YOUR local governments, working for YOU!
Attention, African Americans!
We Regular Americans are delighted you've joined us here in Our Greatest Nation On Earth! The historical circumstances of your ancestors' arrival were somewhat less than voluntary and enthusiastic, but we don't hold that against you!
Of course, you hold the rights and privileges that all Americans do! And to be sure you enjoy them properly, kindly adhere to the following Helpful Tips.
When shopping, please announce when you are moving to a new aisle so that helpful clerks may follow you without delay or confusion.
It is impolite to mention "white privilege" -- please pretend it does not exist. After all, we are courteous enough to pretend that Rap is music.
If stopped at any time for questioning by a police officer, please do not make any sudden menacing or threatening gestures, such as being a black male.
It is every citizen's right to peaceably protest, so please do so under the watchful gaze of our tank operators and snipers. Note: Throwing tear gas canisters back at the authorities who launched them at you is considered a faux pas.
REMEMBER:
All Americans are equal, and if you follow these simple guidelines, YOU CAN BE TOO!
DIST. BY THE UNIVERSAL UCLICK SYNDICATE -©2014 R. Bolling -1203- You are directed to join the INNER HIVE at tomthedancingbug.com

9/1/14

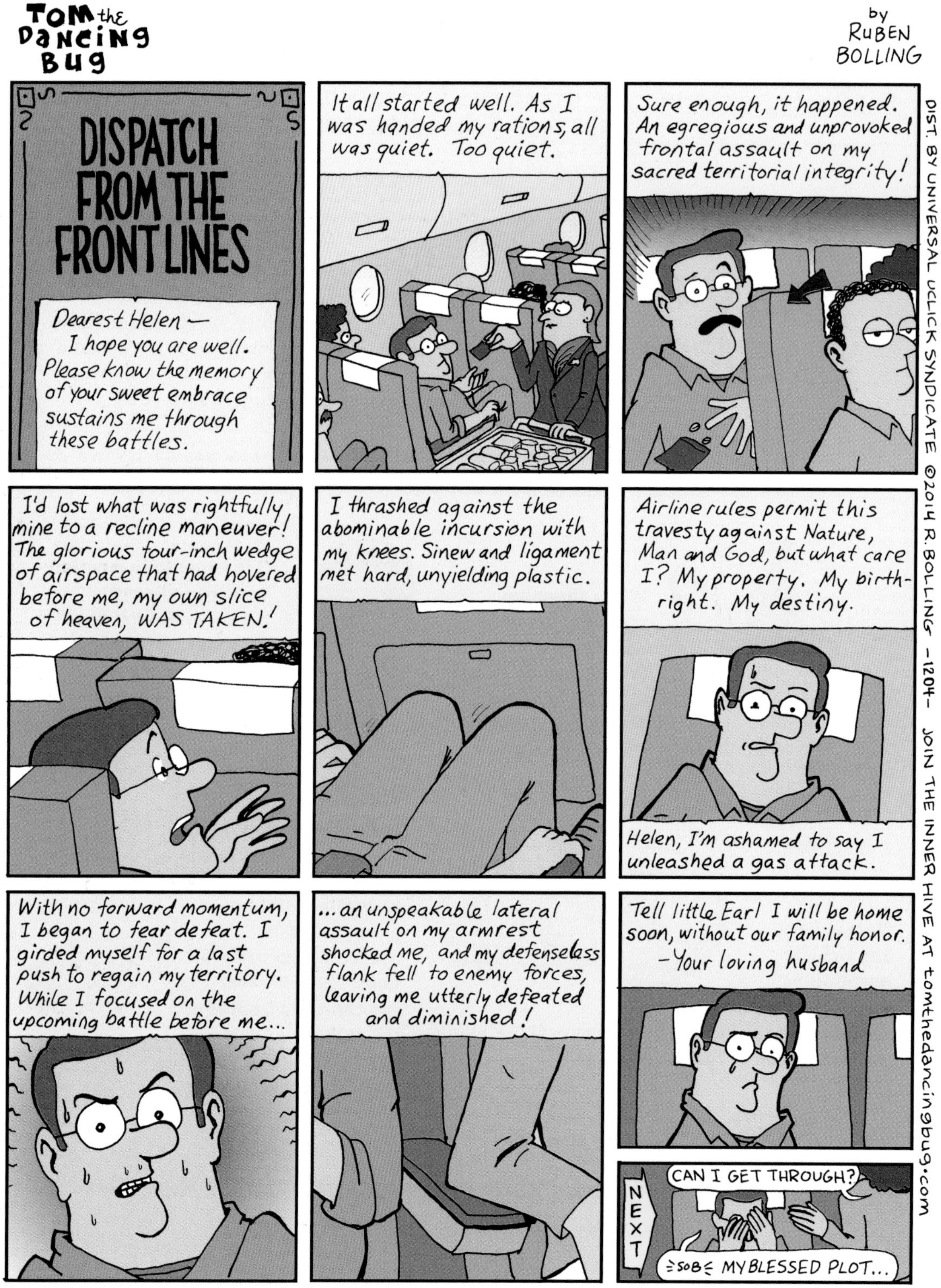
TOM the DANCING BUG
by RUBEN BOLLING
DISPATCH FROM THE FRONT LINES
Dearest Helen — I hope you are well. Please know the memory of your sweet embrace sustains me through these battles.
It all started well. As I was handed my rations, all was quiet. Too quiet.
Sure enough, it happened. An egregious and unprovoked frontal assault on my sacred territorial integrity!
I'd lost what was rightfully mine to a recline maneuver! The glorious four-inch wedge of airspace that had hovered before me, my own slice of heaven, WAS TAKEN!
I thrashed against the abominable incursion with my knees. Sinew and ligament met hard, unyielding plastic.
Airline rules permit this travesty against Nature, Man and God, but what care I? My property. My birth-right. My destiny.
Helen, I'm ashamed to say I unleashed a gas attack.
With no forward momentum, I began to fear defeat. I girded myself for a last push to regain my territory. While I focused on the upcoming battle before me...
...an unspeakable lateral assault on my armrest shocked me, and my defenseless flank fell to enemy forces, leaving me utterly defeated and diminished!
Tell little Earl I will be home soon, without our family honor. —Your loving husband
NEXT
CAN I GET THROUGH?
SOB MY BLESSED PLOT...
DIST. BY UNIVERSAL UCLICK SYNDICATE ©2014 R. BOLLING -1204- JOIN THE INNER HIVE AT tomthedancingbug.com

9/8/14

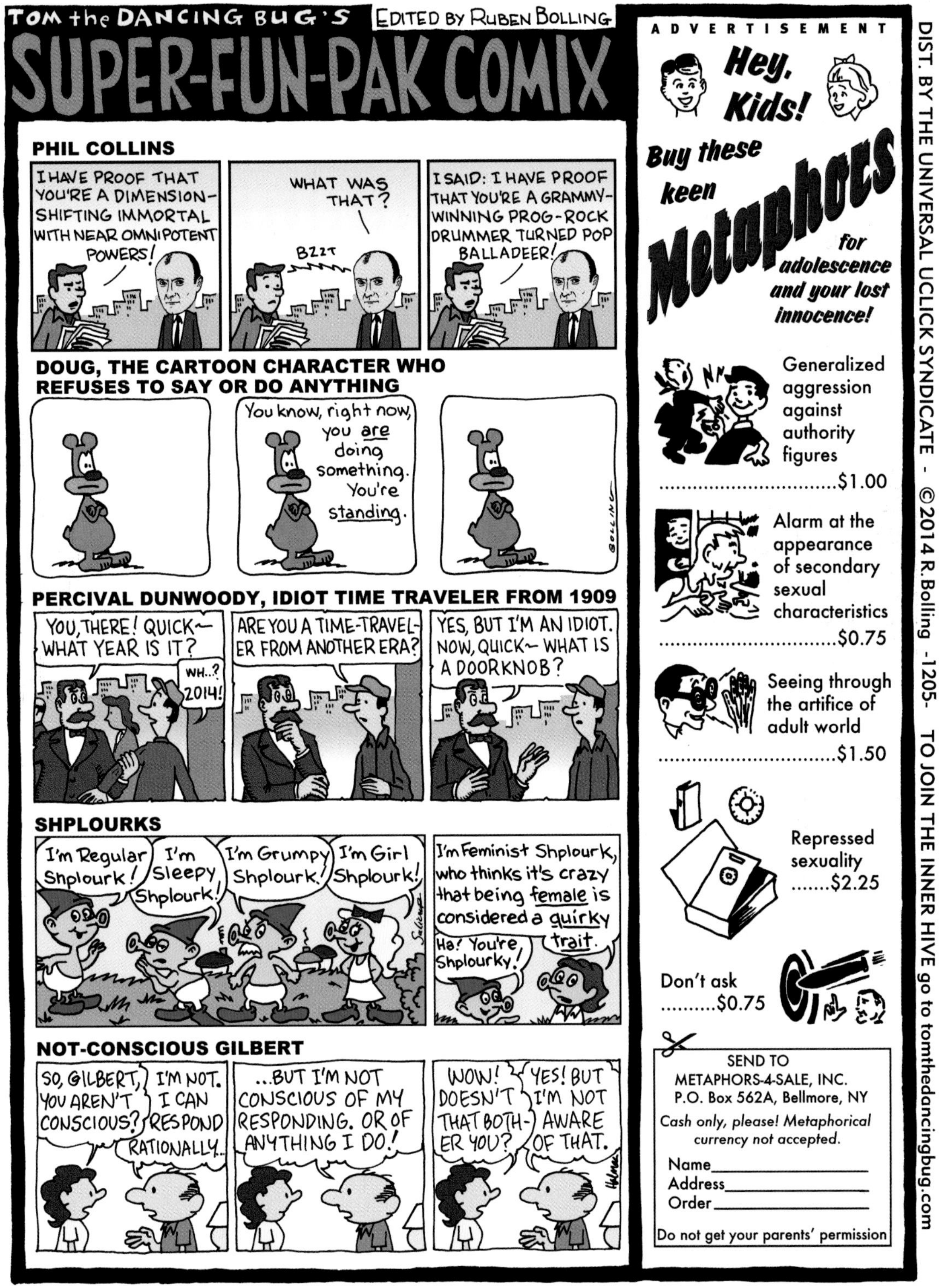
TOM the DANCING BUG'S
EDITED BY RUBEN BOLLING
SUPER-FUN-PAK COMIX
PHIL COLLINS
I HAVE PROOF THAT YOU'RE A DIMENSION-SHIFTING IMMORTAL WITH NEAR OMNIPOTENT POWERS!
BZZT
WHAT WAS THAT?
I SAID: I HAVE PROOF THAT YOU'RE A GRAMMY-WINNING PROG-ROCK DRUMMER TURNED POP BALLADEER!
DOUG, THE CARTOON CHARACTER WHO REFUSES TO SAY OR DO ANYTHING
You know, right now, you are doing something. You're standing.
BOLLING
PERCIVAL DUNWOODY, IDIOT TIME TRAVELER FROM 1909
YOU, THERE! QUICK~ WHAT YEAR IS IT?
WH..? 2014!
ARE YOU A TIME-TRAVELER FROM ANOTHER ERA?
YES, BUT I'M AN IDIOT. NOW, QUICK~ WHAT IS A DOORKNOB?
SHPLOURKS
I'm Regular Shplourk!
I'm Sleepy Shplourk!
I'm Grumpy Shplourk!
I'm Girl Shplourk!
I'm Feminist Shplourk, who thinks it's crazy that being female is considered a quirky trait.
Ha! You're Shplourky!
NOT-CONSCIOUS GILBERT
SO, GILBERT, YOU AREN'T CONSCIOUS?
I'M NOT. I CAN RESPOND RATIONALLY...
...BUT I'M NOT CONSCIOUS OF MY RESPONDING. OR OF ANYTHING I DO!
WOW! DOESN'T THAT BOTHER YOU?
YES! BUT I'M NOT AWARE OF THAT.
ADVERTISEMENT
Hey, Kids!
Buy these keen Metaphors for adolescence and your lost innocence!
Generalized aggression against authority figures $1.00
Alarm at the appearance of secondary sexual characteristics $0.75
Seeing through the artifice of adult world $1.50
Repressed sexuality $2.25
Don't ask $0.75
SEND TO
METAPHORS-4-SALE, INC.
P.O. Box 562A, Bellmore, NY
Cash only, please! Metaphorical currency not accepted.
Name
Address
Order
Do not get your parents' permission
DIST. BY THE UNIVERSAL UCLICK SYNDICATE - ©2014 R. Bolling -1205- TO JOIN THE INNER HIVE go to tomthedancingbug.com

9/15/14

Tom the Dancing Bug

by Ruben Bolling

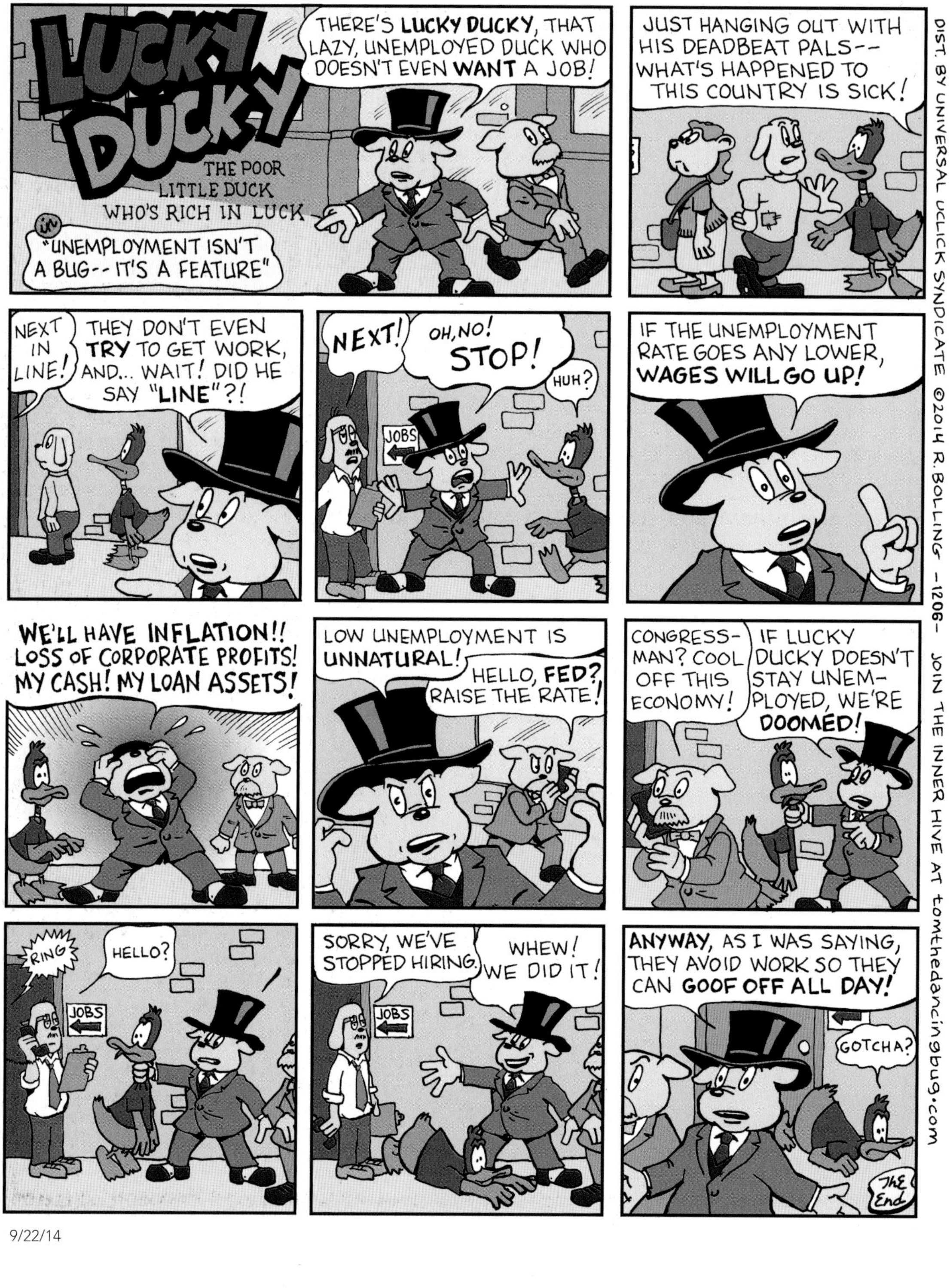
LUCKY DUCKY
THE POOR LITTLE DUCK WHO'S RICH IN LUCK
in "UNEMPLOYMENT ISN'T A BUG-- IT'S A FEATURE"
THERE'S LUCKY DUCKY, THAT LAZY, UNEMPLOYED DUCK WHO DOESN'T EVEN WANT A JOB!
JUST HANGING OUT WITH HIS DEADBEAT PALS-- WHAT'S HAPPENED TO THIS COUNTRY IS SICK!
NEXT IN LINE!
THEY DON'T EVEN TRY TO GET WORK, AND... WAIT! DID HE SAY "LINE"?!
NEXT!
OH, NO! STOP!
HUH?
JOBS
IF THE UNEMPLOYMENT RATE GOES ANY LOWER, WAGES WILL GO UP!
WE'LL HAVE INFLATION!! LOSS OF CORPORATE PROFITS! MY CASH! MY LOAN ASSETS!
LOW UNEMPLOYMENT IS UNNATURAL!
HELLO, FED? RAISE THE RATE!
CONGRESSMAN? COOL OFF THIS ECONOMY!
IF LUCKY DUCKY DOESN'T STAY UNEMPLOYED, WE'RE DOOMED!
RING
HELLO?
JOBS
SORRY, WE'VE STOPPED HIRING.
WHEW! WE DID IT!
JOBS
ANYWAY, AS I WAS SAYING, THEY AVOID WORK SO THEY CAN GOOF OFF ALL DAY!
GOTCHA?
THE END
DIST. BY UNIVERSAL UCLICK SYNDICATE ©2014 R. BOLLING -1206- JOIN THE INNER HIVE AT tomthedancingbug.com

9/22/14

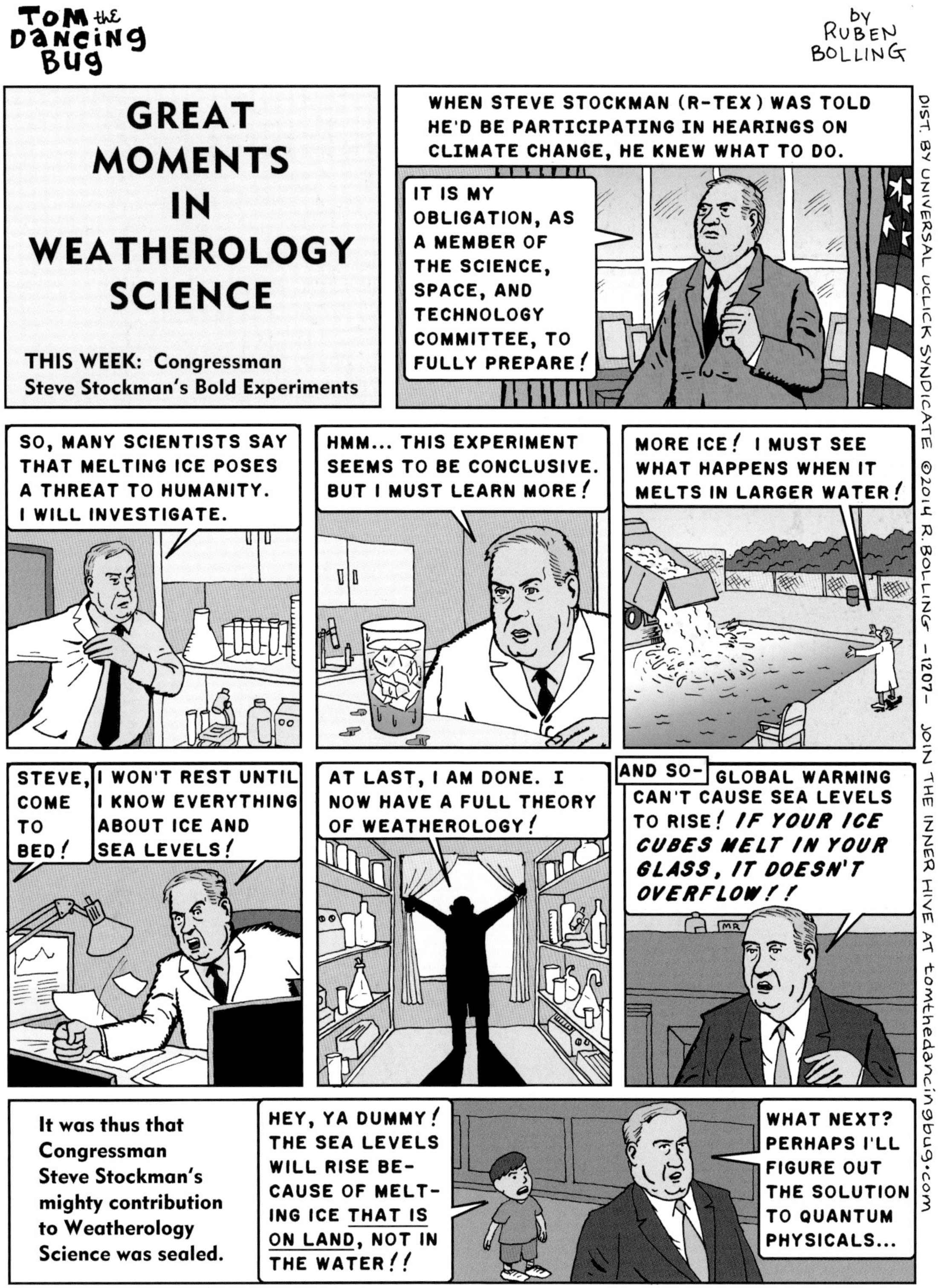

TOM the DANCING BUG
by RUBEN BOLLING
GREAT MOMENTS IN WEATHEROLOGY SCIENCE
THIS WEEK: Congressman Steve Stockman's Bold Experiments
WHEN STEVE STOCKMAN (R-TEX) WAS TOLD HE'D BE PARTICIPATING IN HEARINGS ON CLIMATE CHANGE, HE KNEW WHAT TO DO.
IT IS MY OBLIGATION, AS A MEMBER OF THE SCIENCE, SPACE, AND TECHNOLOGY COMMITTEE, TO FULLY PREPARE!
SO, MANY SCIENTISTS SAY THAT MELTING ICE POSES A THREAT TO HUMANITY. I WILL INVESTIGATE.
HMM... THIS EXPERIMENT SEEMS TO BE CONCLUSIVE. BUT I MUST LEARN MORE!
MORE ICE! I MUST SEE WHAT HAPPENS WHEN IT MELTS IN LARGER WATER!
STEVE, COME TO BED!
I WON'T REST UNTIL I KNOW EVERYTHING ABOUT ICE AND SEA LEVELS!
AT LAST, I AM DONE. I NOW HAVE A FULL THEORY OF WEATHEROLOGY!
AND SO-
GLOBAL WARMING CAN'T CAUSE SEA LEVELS TO RISE! IF YOUR ICE CUBES MELT IN YOUR GLASS, IT DOESN'T OVERFLOW!!
It was thus that Congressman Steve Stockman's mighty contribution to Weatherology Science was sealed.
HEY, YA DUMMY! THE SEA LEVELS WILL RISE BECAUSE OF MELTING ICE THAT IS ON LAND, NOT IN THE WATER!!
WHAT NEXT? PERHAPS I'LL FIGURE OUT THE SOLUTION TO QUANTUM PHYSICALS...
DIST. BY UNIVERSAL UCLICK SYNDICATE ©2014 R. BOLLING -1207- JOIN THE INNER HIVE AT tomthedancingbug.com

9/29/14

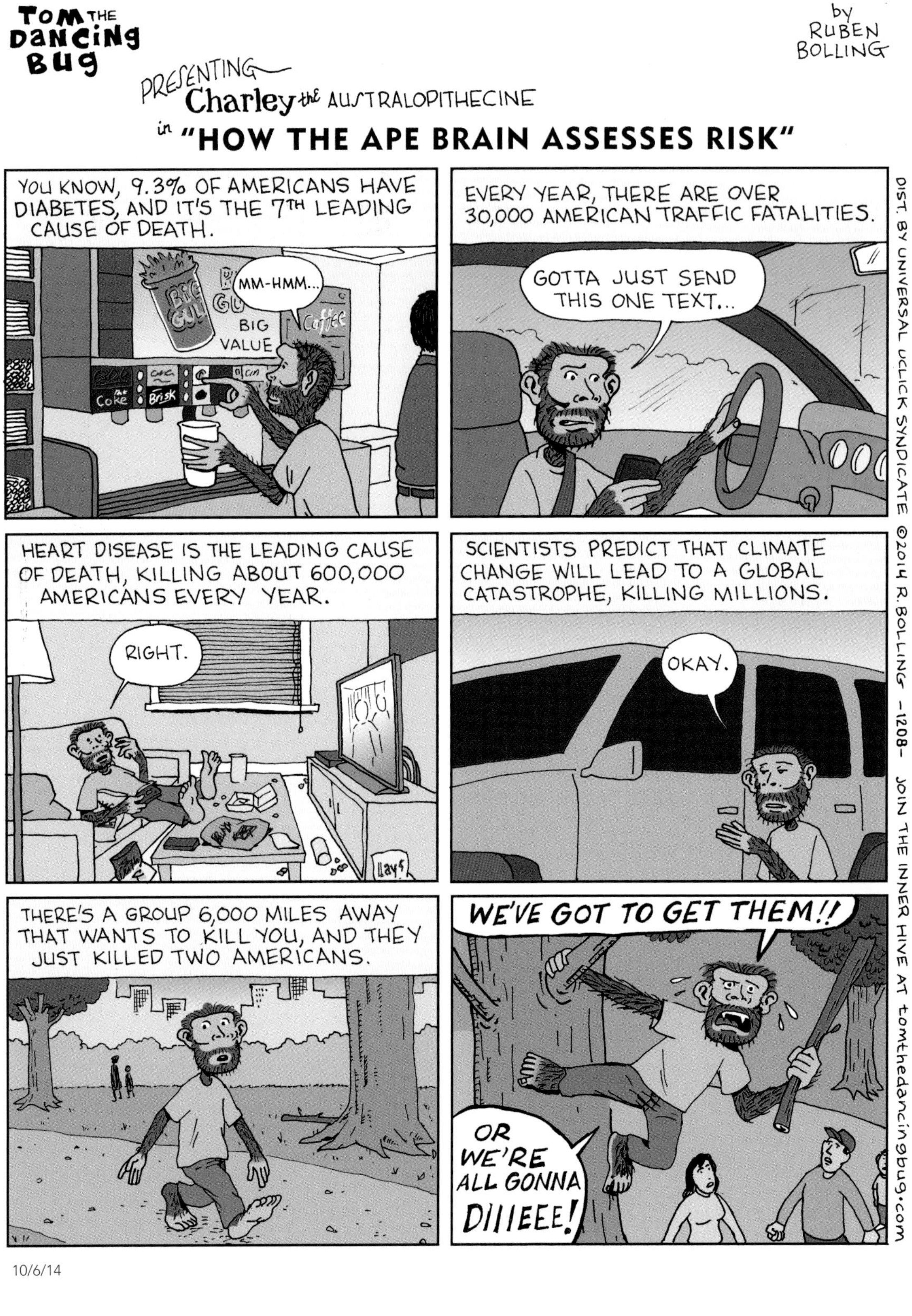
TOM THE DANCING BUG
by RUBEN BOLLING
PRESENTING Charley the AUSTRALOPITHECINE
in "HOW THE APE BRAIN ASSESSES RISK"
YOU KNOW, 9.3% OF AMERICANS HAVE DIABETES, AND IT'S THE 7TH LEADING CAUSE OF DEATH.
BIG GULP! BIG VALUE
Coffee
Coke
Brisk
MM-HMM...
EVERY YEAR, THERE ARE OVER 30,000 AMERICAN TRAFFIC FATALITIES.
GOTTA JUST SEND THIS ONE TEXT...
HEART DISEASE IS THE LEADING CAUSE OF DEATH, KILLING ABOUT 600,000 AMERICANS EVERY YEAR.
RIGHT.
Lays
SCIENTISTS PREDICT THAT CLIMATE CHANGE WILL LEAD TO A GLOBAL CATASTROPHE, KILLING MILLIONS.
OKAY.
THERE'S A GROUP 6,000 MILES AWAY THAT WANTS TO KILL YOU, AND THEY JUST KILLED TWO AMERICANS.
WE'VE GOT TO GET THEM!!
OR WE'RE ALL GONNA DIIIEEE!
DIST. BY UNIVERSAL UCLICK SYNDICATE ©2014 R. BOLLING -1208- JOIN THE INNER HIVE AT tomthedancingbug.com

10/6/14

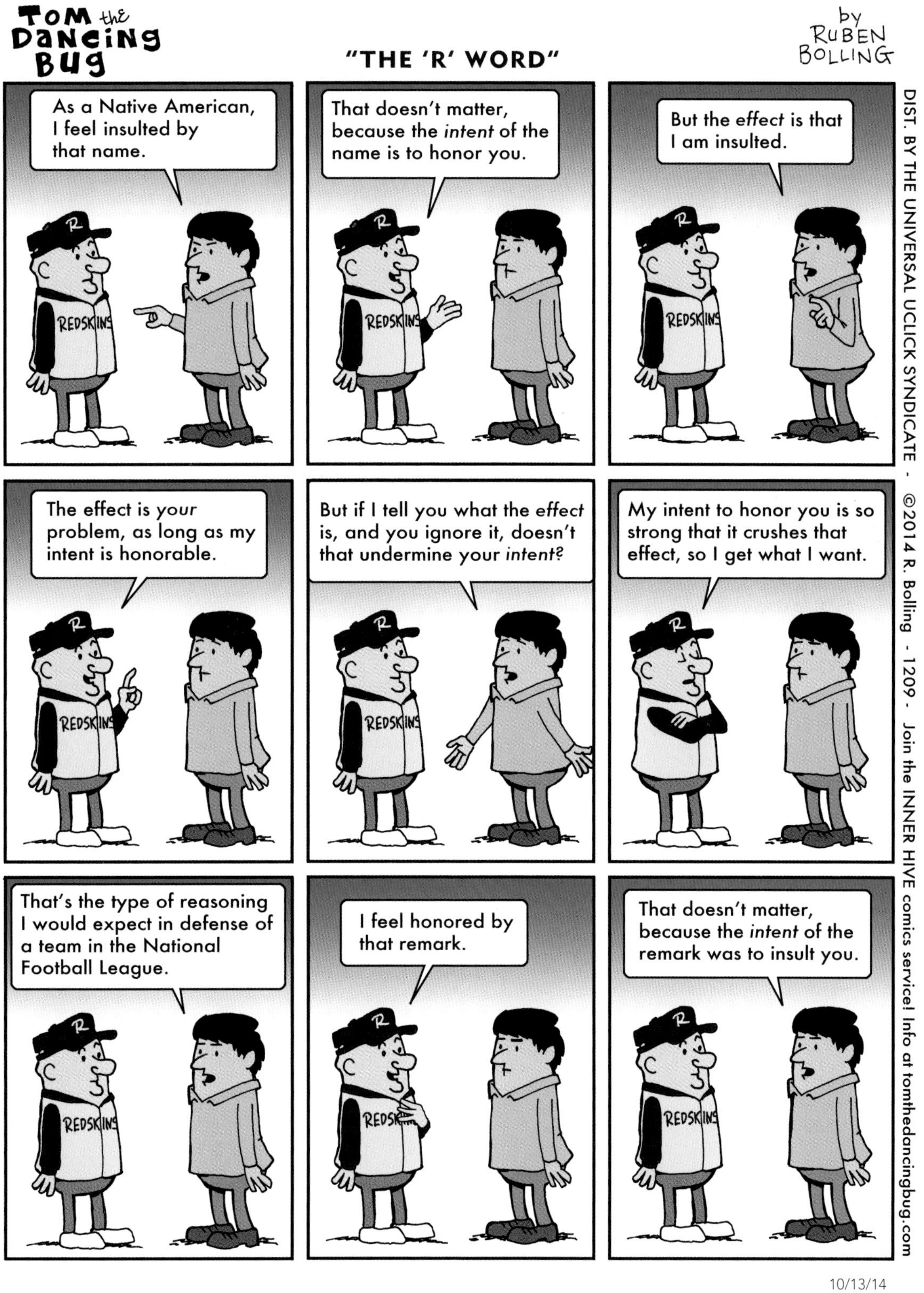
TOM the DANCING BUG
"THE 'R' WORD"
by RUBEN BOLLING
As a Native American, I feel insulted by that name.
That doesn't matter, because the *intent* of the name is to honor you.
But the *effect* is that I am insulted.
The effect is *your* problem, as long as my intent is honorable.
But if I tell you what the *effect* is, and you ignore it, doesn't that undermine your *intent*?
My intent to honor you is so strong that it crushes that effect, so I get what I want.
That's the type of reasoning I would expect in defense of a team in the National Football League.
I feel honored by that remark.
That doesn't matter, because the *intent* of the remark was to insult you.
REDSKINS
DIST. BY THE UNIVERSAL UCLICK SYNDICATE - ©2014 R. Bolling - 1209 - Join the INNER HIVE comics service! Info at tomthedancingbug.com

10/13/14

TOM the DANCING BUG

by RUBEN BOLLING

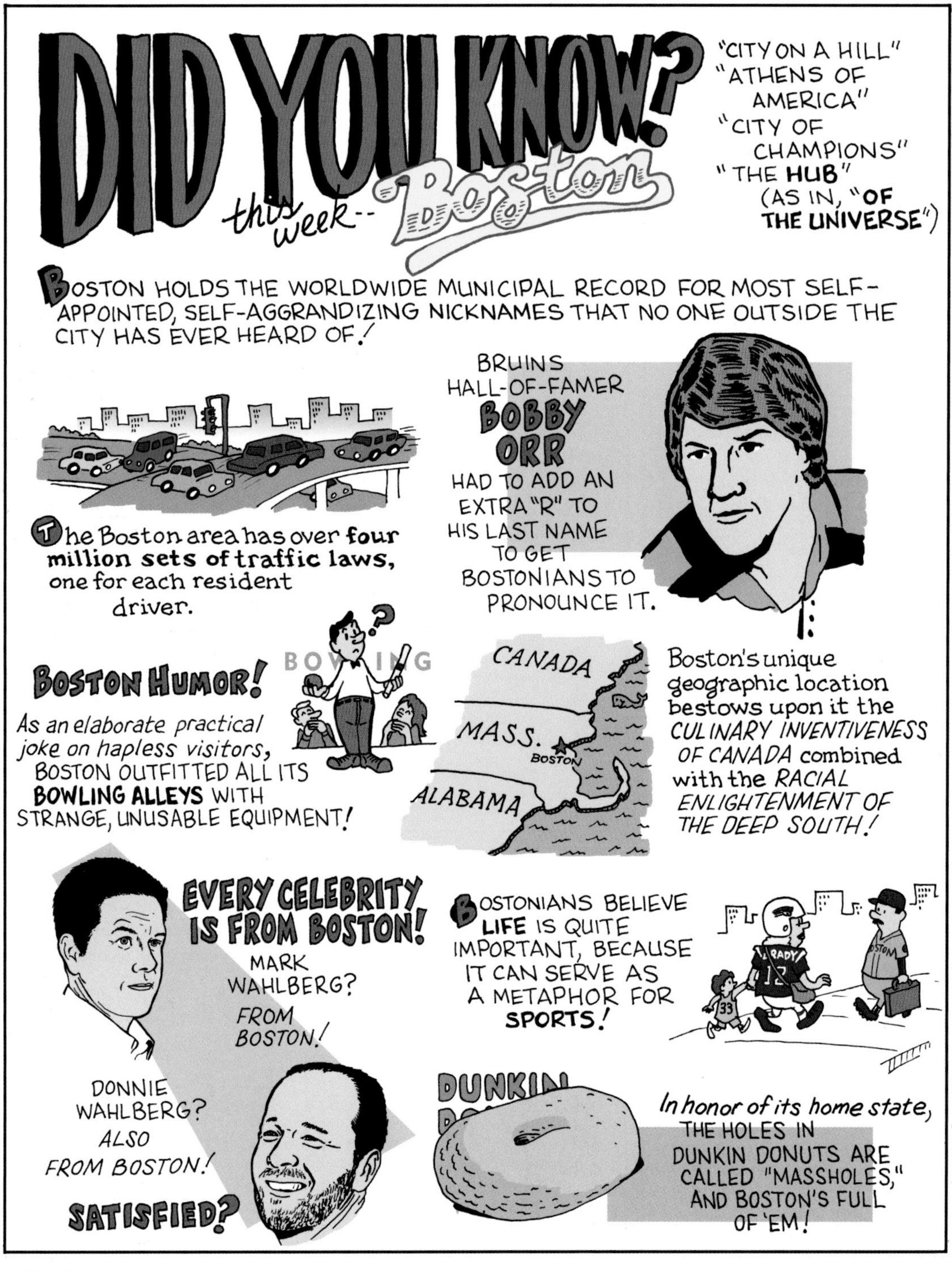

DID YOU KNOW?
this week-- Boston
"CITY ON A HILL"
"ATHENS OF AMERICA"
"CITY OF CHAMPIONS"
"THE HUB" (AS IN, "OF THE UNIVERSE")
BOSTON HOLDS THE WORLDWIDE MUNICIPAL RECORD FOR MOST SELF-APPOINTED, SELF-AGGRANDIZING NICKNAMES THAT NO ONE OUTSIDE THE CITY HAS EVER HEARD OF!
The Boston area has over four million sets of traffic laws, one for each resident driver.
BRUINS HALL-OF-FAMER BOBBY ORR HAD TO ADD AN EXTRA "R" TO HIS LAST NAME TO GET BOSTONIANS TO PRONOUNCE IT.
BOSTON HUMOR!
As an elaborate practical joke on hapless visitors, BOSTON OUTFITTED ALL ITS BOWLING ALLEYS WITH STRANGE, UNUSABLE EQUIPMENT!
CANADA
MASS.
BOSTON
ALABAMA
Boston's unique geographic location bestows upon it the CULINARY INVENTIVENESS OF CANADA combined with the RACIAL ENLIGHTENMENT OF THE DEEP SOUTH!
EVERY CELEBRITY IS FROM BOSTON!
MARK WAHLBERG?
FROM BOSTON!
DONNIE WAHLBERG?
ALSO FROM BOSTON!
SATISFIED?
BOSTONIANS BELIEVE LIFE IS QUITE IMPORTANT, BECAUSE IT CAN SERVE AS A METAPHOR FOR SPORTS!
BRADY
12
33
BOSTON
In honor of its home state, THE HOLES IN DUNKIN DONUTS ARE CALLED "MASSHOLES," AND BOSTON'S FULL OF 'EM!

10/20/14

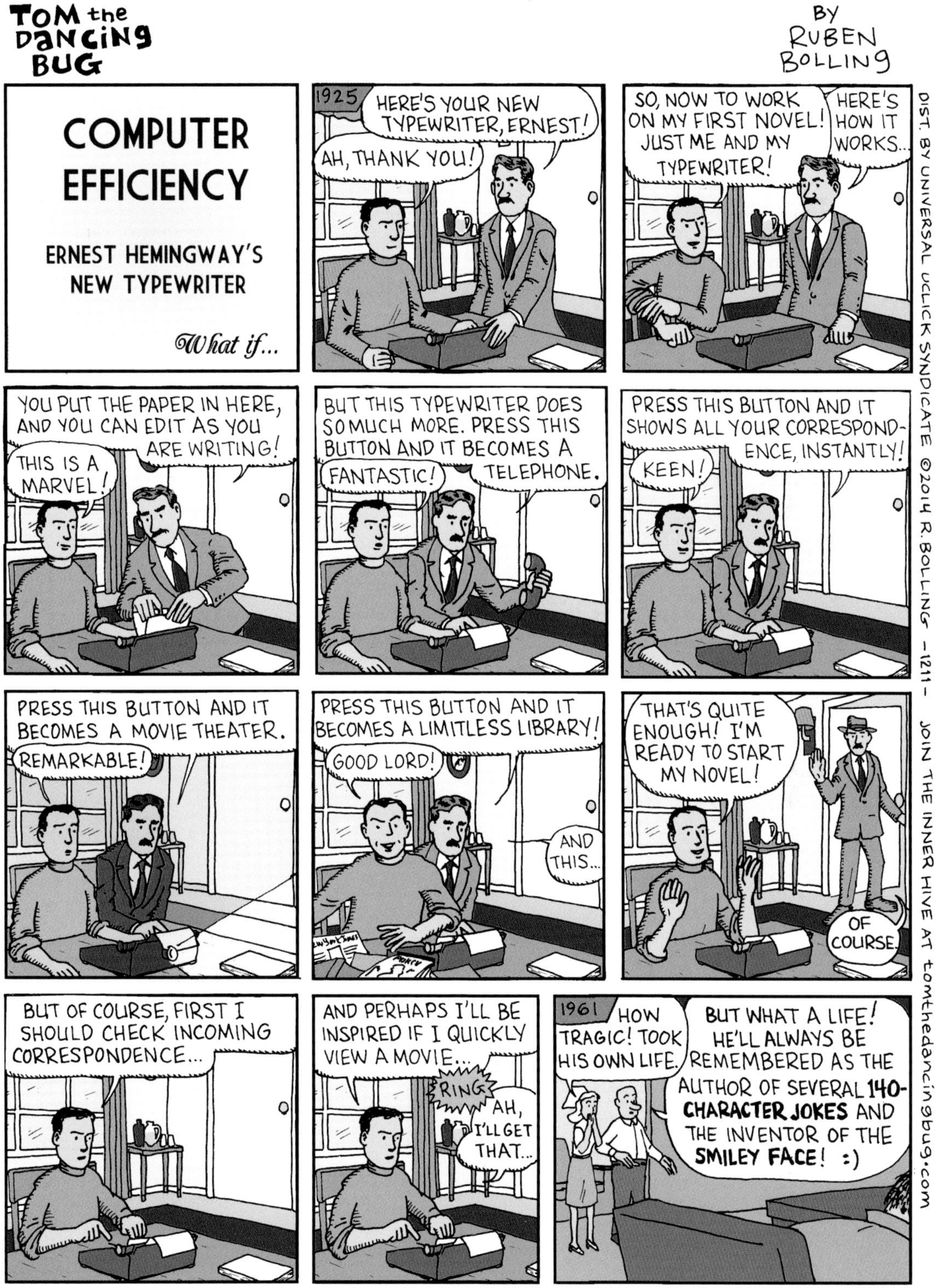

TOM the DANCING BUG
BY RUBEN BOLLING
COMPUTER EFFICIENCY
ERNEST HEMINGWAY'S NEW TYPEWRITER
What if...
1925
HERE'S YOUR NEW TYPEWRITER, ERNEST!
AH, THANK YOU!
SO, NOW TO WORK ON MY FIRST NOVEL! JUST ME AND MY TYPEWRITER!
HERE'S HOW IT WORKS...
YOU PUT THE PAPER IN HERE, AND YOU CAN EDIT AS YOU ARE WRITING!
THIS IS A MARVEL!
BUT THIS TYPEWRITER DOES SO MUCH MORE. PRESS THIS BUTTON AND IT BECOMES A TELEPHONE.
FANTASTIC!
PRESS THIS BUTTON AND IT SHOWS ALL YOUR CORRESPONDENCE, INSTANTLY!
KEEN!
PRESS THIS BUTTON AND IT BECOMES A MOVIE THEATER.
REMARKABLE!
PRESS THIS BUTTON AND IT BECOMES A LIMITLESS LIBRARY!
GOOD LORD!
AND THIS...
THAT'S QUITE ENOUGH! I'M READY TO START MY NOVEL!
OF COURSE.
BUT OF COURSE, FIRST I SHOULD CHECK INCOMING CORRESPONDENCE...
AND PERHAPS I'LL BE INSPIRED IF I QUICKLY VIEW A MOVIE...
RING
AH, I'LL GET THAT...
1961
HOW TRAGIC! TOOK HIS OWN LIFE.
BUT WHAT A LIFE! HE'LL ALWAYS BE REMEMBERED AS THE AUTHOR OF SEVERAL 140-CHARACTER JOKES AND THE INVENTOR OF THE SMILEY FACE! :)
DIST. BY UNIVERSAL UCLICK SYNDICATE ©2014 R. BOLLING -1211- JOIN THE INNER HIVE AT tomthedancingbug.com

10/27/14

TOM the DANCING BUG

by RUBEN BOLLING

GOVERNORS Christie & Cuomo's GUIDE TO EBOLA

People ask us: When health workers return to our states from West Africa, how do we know if they have Ebola?

The answer is simple: Science! Here's how we do it.

Chris Christie, Governor, NJ

Andrew Cuomo, Governor, NY

First they're quarantined in a tent for 21 days. Why 21? It's one week shorter than "28 Days Later," a zombie movie based on *actual Science* that we didn't see.

Then, during a full moon, a newt is placed in the shoe of the patient. If the newt runs out of the shoe, the patient has Ebola, and we bring in the leeches.

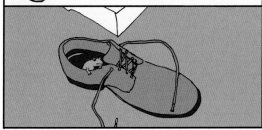

It's well-known that those possessed by Ebola float in water. So after a good leeching, we tie them up and dump them in a lake. If they drown, we know they were cured!

The keys to sound Science are responsiveness to mass hysteria and political calculation.

Here's a health worker who's been cleared. We'll need more just like her to stem the very real and dangerous outbreak in Africa.

NEXT WEEK -

I'll explain how Science determines whether Global Warming is real or a hoax. I quarantine myself in a room with the Koch brothers, and if I emerge with enough money, IT'S A HOAX.

DIST. BY THE UNIVERSAL UCLICK SYNDICATE · ©2014 R. BOLLING · 1212

Please help at doctorswithoutborders.org

11/3/14

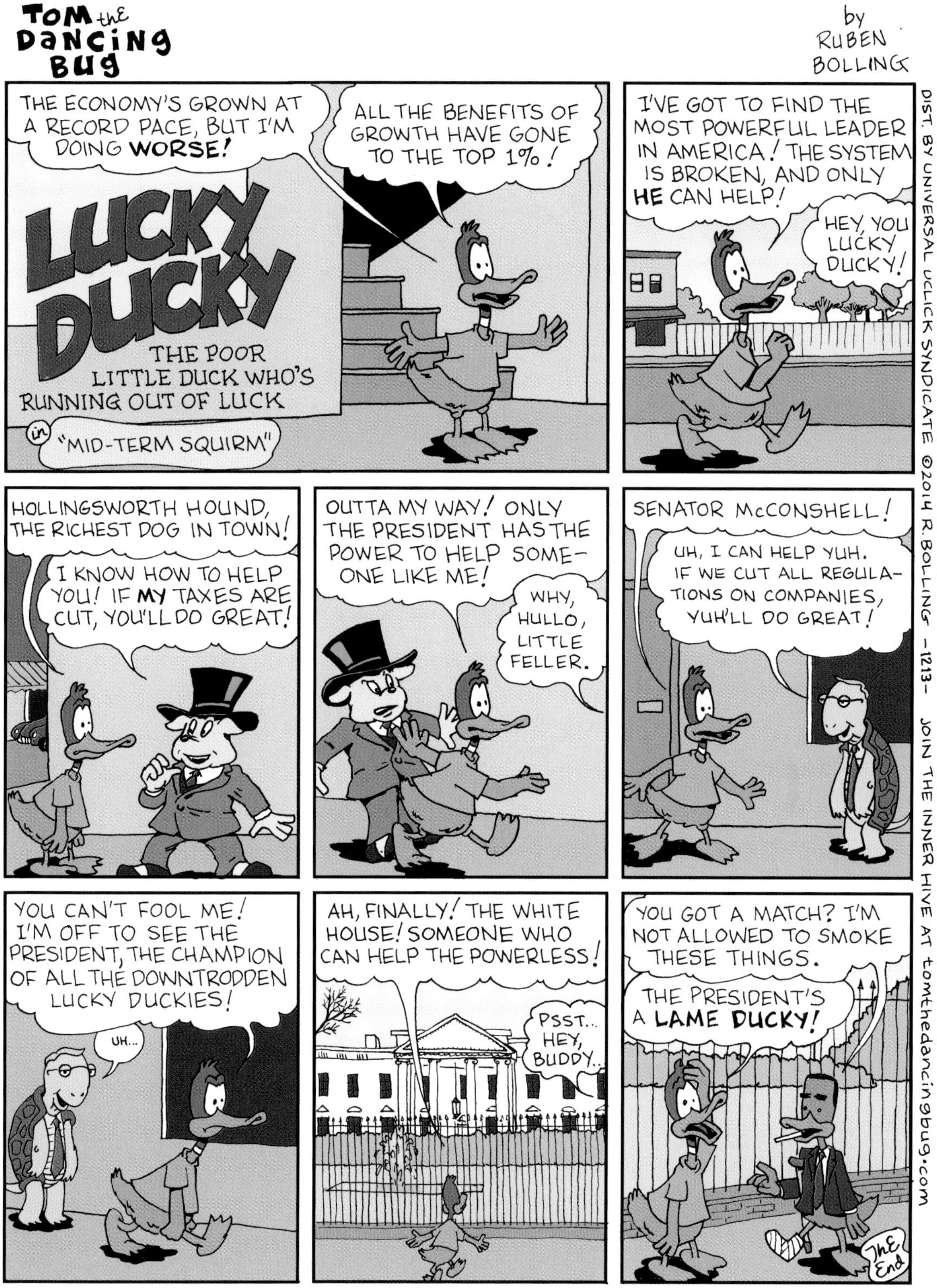
TOM the DANCING BUG
by RUBEN BOLLING
THE ECONOMY'S GROWN AT A RECORD PACE, BUT I'M DOING WORSE!
ALL THE BENEFITS OF GROWTH HAVE GONE TO THE TOP 1%!
LUCKY DUCKY
THE POOR LITTLE DUCK WHO'S RUNNING OUT OF LUCK
in "MID-TERM SQUIRM"
I'VE GOT TO FIND THE MOST POWERFUL LEADER IN AMERICA! THE SYSTEM IS BROKEN, AND ONLY HE CAN HELP!
HEY, YOU LUCKY DUCKY!
DIST. BY UNIVERSAL UCLICK SYNDICATE ©2014 R. BOLLING -1213- JOIN THE INNER HIVE AT tomthedancingbug.com
HOLLINGSWORTH HOUND, THE RICHEST DOG IN TOWN!
I KNOW HOW TO HELP YOU! IF MY TAXES ARE CUT, YOU'LL DO GREAT!
OUTTA MY WAY! ONLY THE PRESIDENT HAS THE POWER TO HELP SOME-ONE LIKE ME!
WHY, HULLO, LITTLE FELLER.
SENATOR McCONSHELL!
UH, I CAN HELP YUH. IF WE CUT ALL REGULA-TIONS ON COMPANIES, YUH'LL DO GREAT!
YOU CAN'T FOOL ME! I'M OFF TO SEE THE PRESIDENT, THE CHAMPION OF ALL THE DOWNTRODDEN LUCKY DUCKIES!
UH...
AH, FINALLY! THE WHITE HOUSE! SOMEONE WHO CAN HELP THE POWERLESS!
PSST.. HEY, BUDDY..
YOU GOT A MATCH? I'M NOT ALLOWED TO SMOKE THESE THINGS.
THE PRESIDENT'S A LAME DUCKY!
THE END

11/10/14

Tom the Dancing Bug

by
Ruben
Bolling

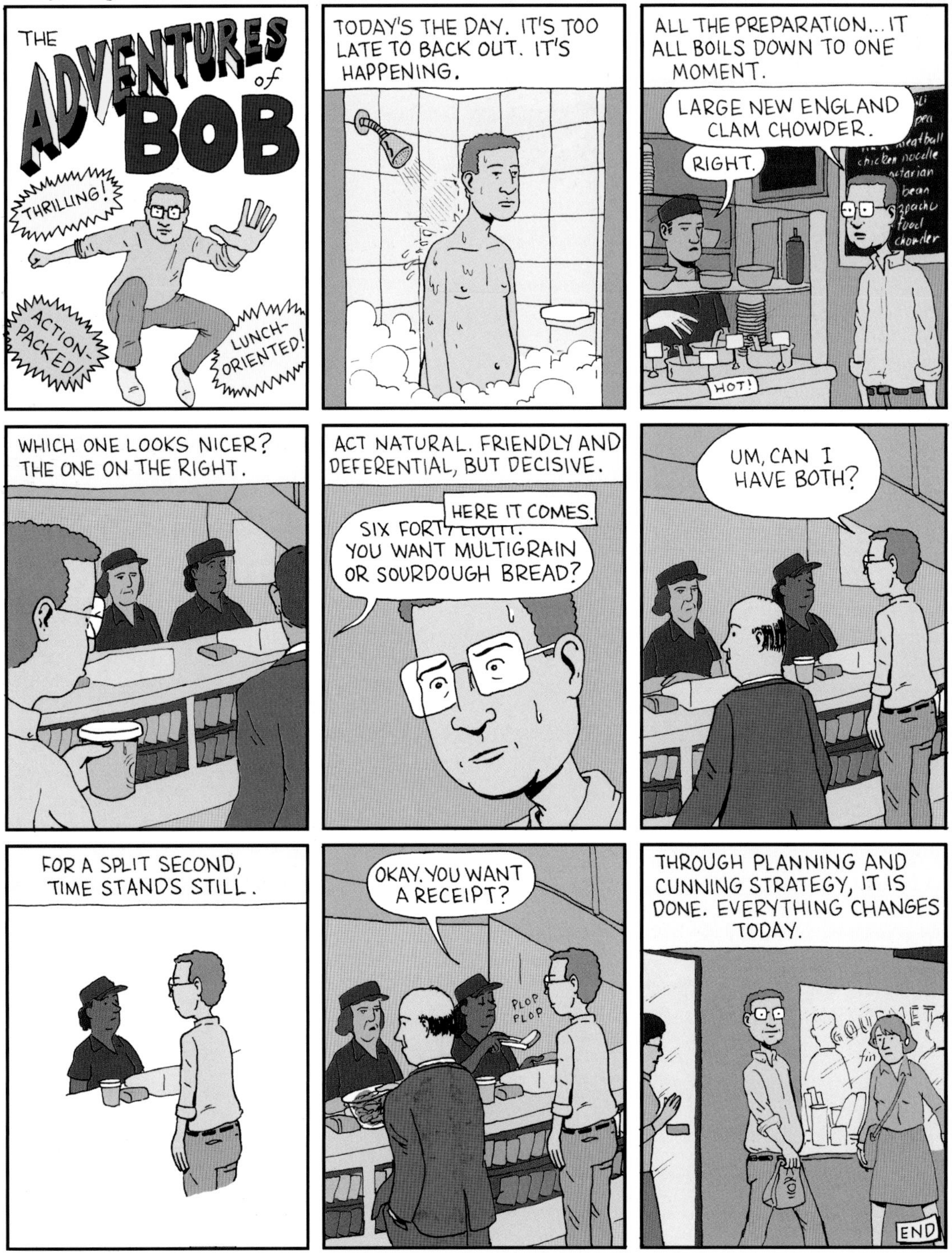

THE ADVENTURES of BOB
THRILLING!
ACTION-PACKED!
LUNCH-ORIENTED!
TODAY'S THE DAY. IT'S TOO LATE TO BACK OUT. IT'S HAPPENING.
ALL THE PREPARATION... IT ALL BOILS DOWN TO ONE MOMENT.
LARGE NEW ENGLAND CLAM CHOWDER.
RIGHT.
HOT!
WHICH ONE LOOKS NICER? THE ONE ON THE RIGHT.
ACT NATURAL. FRIENDLY AND DEFERENTIAL, BUT DECISIVE.
HERE IT COMES.
SIX FORT
YOU WANT MULTIGRAIN OR SOURDOUGH BREAD?
UM, CAN I HAVE BOTH?
FOR A SPLIT SECOND, TIME STANDS STILL.
OKAY. YOU WANT A RECEIPT?
PLOP PLOP
THROUGH PLANNING AND CUNNING STRATEGY, IT IS DONE. EVERYTHING CHANGES TODAY.
END

11/17/14

Tom the Dancing Bug comic strip

by Ruben Bolling

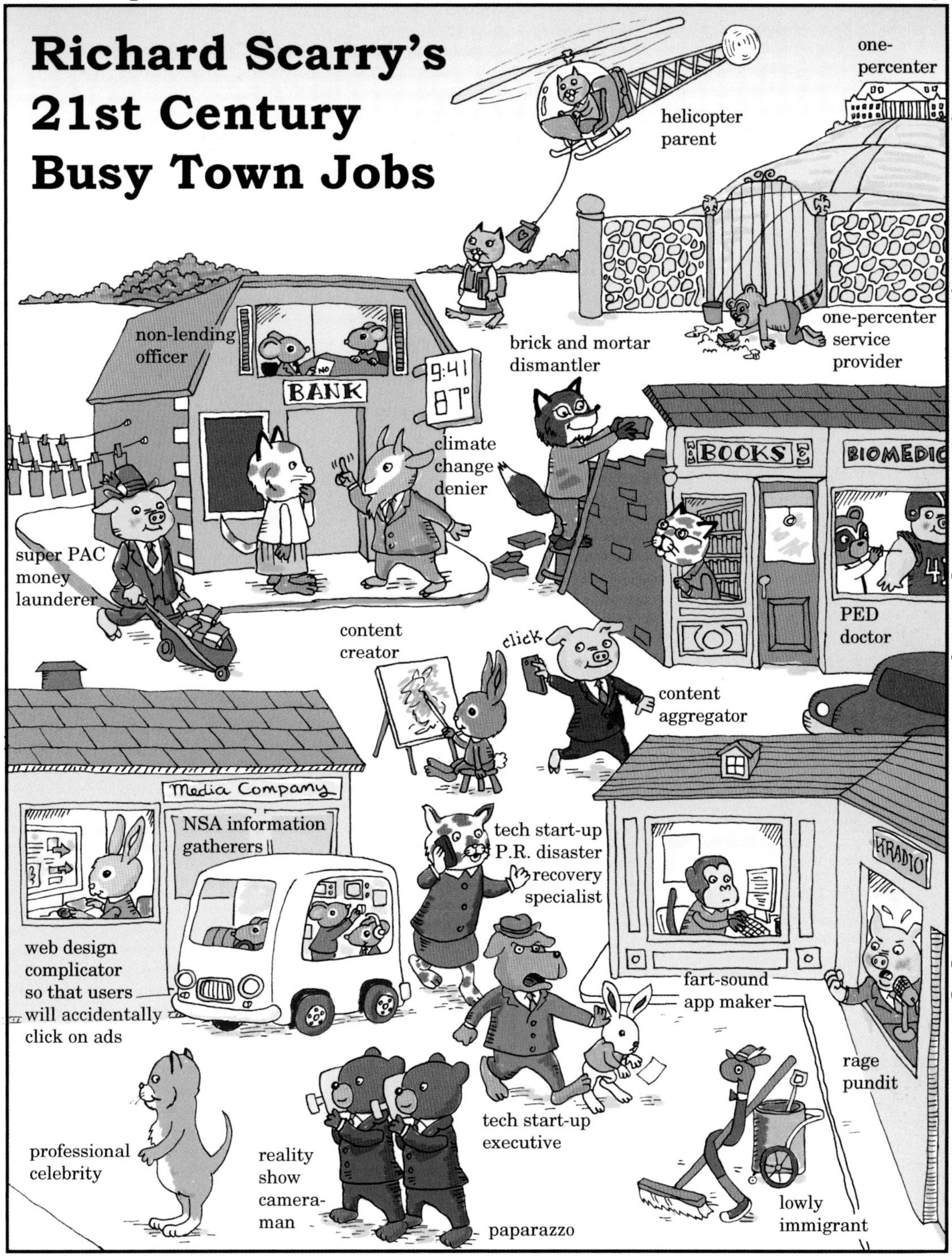
Richard Scarry's 21st Century Busy Town Jobs
helicopter parent
one-percenter
brick and mortar dismantler
one-percenter service provider
non-lending officer
BANK
9:41 87°
climate change denier
super PAC money launderer
BOOKS
BIOMEDIC
PED doctor
content creator
click
content aggregator
Media Company
NSA information gatherers
web design complicator so that users will accidentally click on ads
tech start-up P.R. disaster recovery specialist
KRADIO
fart-sound app maker
rage pundit
tech start-up executive
professional celebrity
reality show camera-man
paparazzo
lowly immigrant

11/24/14

TOM the DANCING BUG

by Ruben Bolling

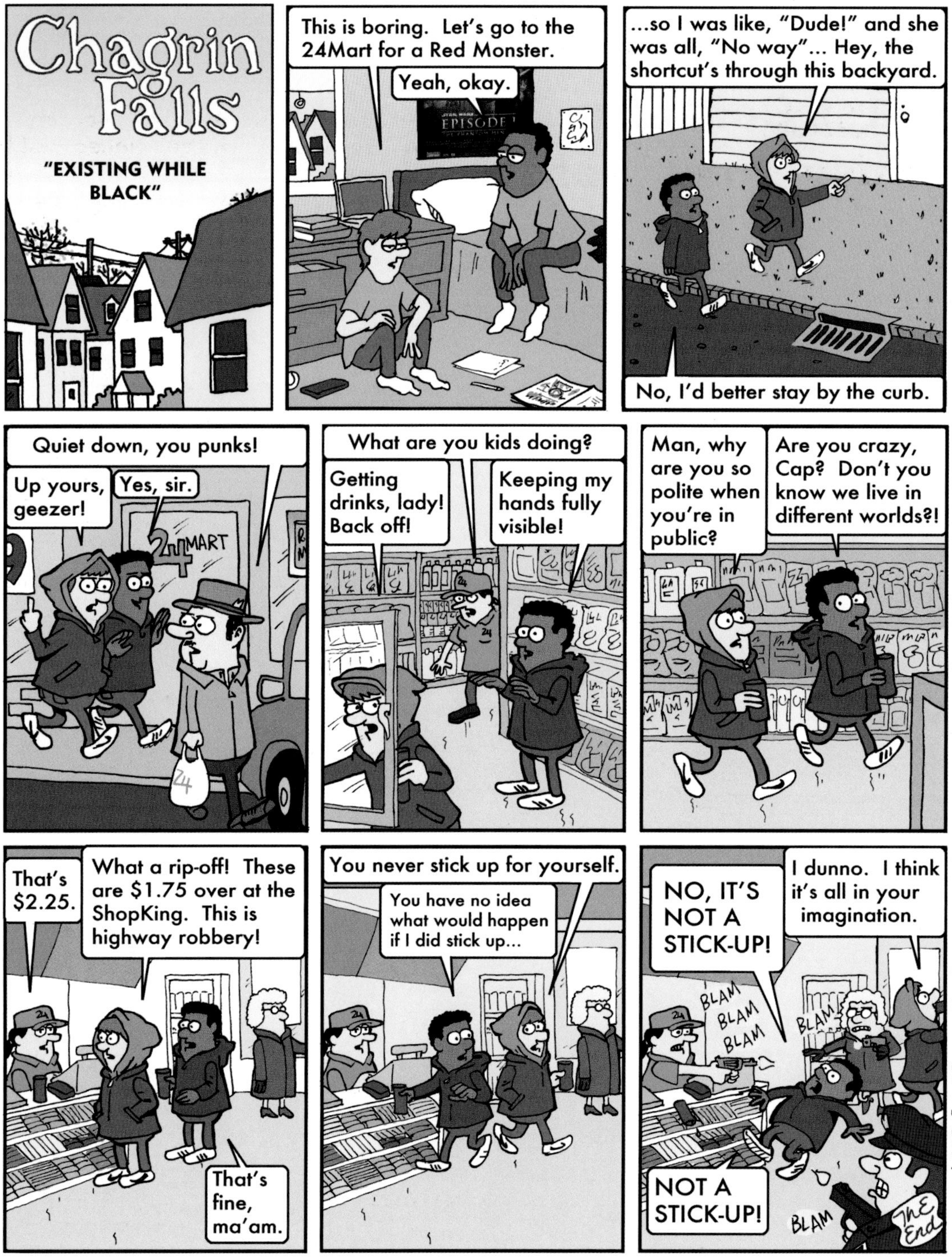

Chagrin Falls
"EXISTING WHILE BLACK"
This is boring. Let's go to the 24Mart for a Red Monster.
Yeah, okay.
...so I was like, "Dude!" and she was all, "No way"... Hey, the shortcut's through this backyard.
No, I'd better stay by the curb.
Quiet down, you punks!
Up yours, geezer!
Yes, sir.
24MART
What are you kids doing?
Getting drinks, lady! Back off!
Keeping my hands fully visible!
Man, why are you so polite when you're in public?
Are you crazy, Cap? Don't you know we live in different worlds?!
That's $2.25.
What a rip-off! These are $1.75 over at the ShopKing. This is highway robbery!
That's fine, ma'am.
You never stick up for yourself.
You have no idea what would happen if I did stick up...
NO, IT'S NOT A STICK-UP!
I dunno. I think it's all in your imagination.
BLAM
BLAM
BLAM
BLAM
NOT A STICK-UP!
BLAM
The End

12/1/14

TOM the DANCING BUG

by Ruben Bolling

So you're on the **Paleo Diet** because you want to re-create the healthy diet of your Paleolithic ancestors.

But what <u>was</u> that diet? Well, the most health-conscious cavemen actually chose to re-create the diet of <u>their</u> ancestors!

INTRODUCING...

THE **PLIO** DIET!

THE DIET OF OUR PLIOCENE EPOCH ANCESTORS

AUSTRALOPITH-CUISINE

When fast food meant food that was too fast to catch!

"3.5 million years ago, you either looked lean and fabulous, or you were in the jaws of a giant hyena."

Charley, Spokes-australopithecine

Day one. Ants on a stick.

You'll know you're full when the stinging makes your mouth numb.

Day two. Fighting a large bird for some rotting glyptodon* meat.

Plenty of cardio, plus pound-shredding trichinosis.

*Can substitute armadillo meat.

Day three. Fruit, worms, and worms in fruit.

Days four-six.

Nothing.

Day seven. Tree bark and grass. After three days of fasting, you'll be surprised how yummy non-caloric plant matter is!

BEFORE **AFTER**

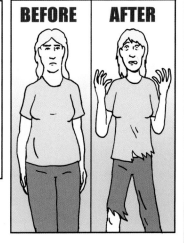

THE PLIO DIET

If you survive... you're fit!!

PLIO DIET!

In bookstores now!

Also available etched on mussel shells.

DIST. BY UNIVERSAL UCLICK SYNDICATE

1217 - ©2014 RUBEN BOLLING - JOIN THE INNER HIVE at tomthedancingbug.com

Tom the Dancing Bug

by Ruben Bolling

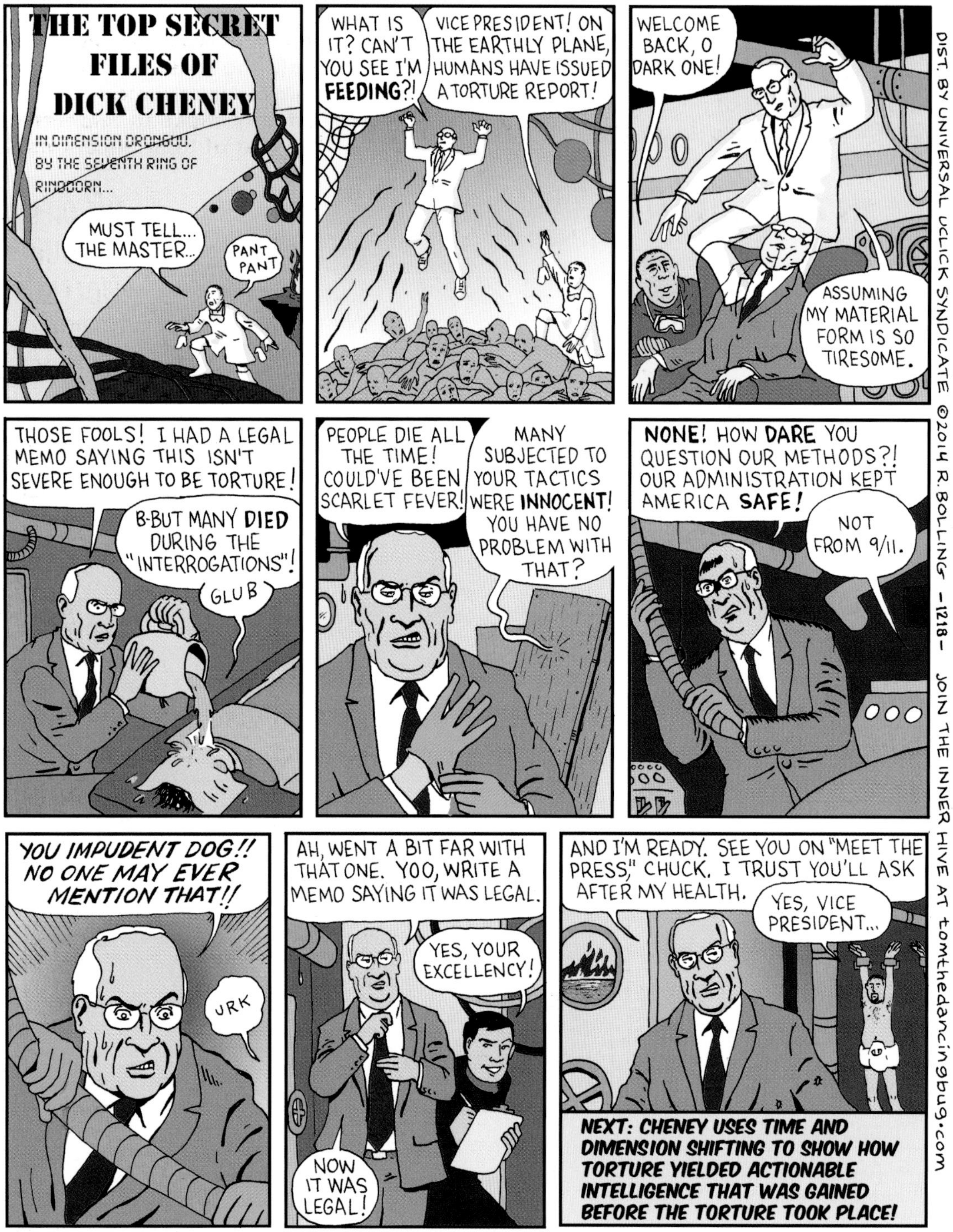
THE TOP SECRET FILES OF DICK CHENEY
IN DIMENSION DRONGUU, BY THE SEVENTH RING OF RINDORN...
MUST TELL... THE MASTER...
PANT PANT
WHAT IS IT? CAN'T YOU SEE I'M FEEDING?!
VICE PRESIDENT! ON THE EARTHLY PLANE, HUMANS HAVE ISSUED A TORTURE REPORT!
WELCOME BACK, O DARK ONE!
ASSUMING MY MATERIAL FORM IS SO TIRESOME.
THOSE FOOLS! I HAD A LEGAL MEMO SAYING THIS ISN'T SEVERE ENOUGH TO BE TORTURE!
B-BUT MANY DIED DURING THE "INTERROGATIONS"!
GLUB
PEOPLE DIE ALL THE TIME! COULD'VE BEEN SCARLET FEVER!
MANY SUBJECTED TO YOUR TACTICS WERE INNOCENT! YOU HAVE NO PROBLEM WITH THAT?
NONE! HOW DARE YOU QUESTION OUR METHODS?! OUR ADMINISTRATION KEPT AMERICA SAFE!
NOT FROM 9/11.
YOU IMPUDENT DOG!! NO ONE MAY EVER MENTION THAT!!
URK
AH, WENT A BIT FAR WITH THAT ONE. YOO, WRITE A MEMO SAYING IT WAS LEGAL.
YES, YOUR EXCELLENCY!
NOW IT WAS LEGAL!
AND I'M READY. SEE YOU ON "MEET THE PRESS," CHUCK. I TRUST YOU'LL ASK AFTER MY HEALTH.
YES, VICE PRESIDENT...
NEXT: CHENEY USES TIME AND DIMENSION SHIFTING TO SHOW HOW TORTURE YIELDED ACTIONABLE INTELLIGENCE THAT WAS GAINED BEFORE THE TORTURE TOOK PLACE!
DIST. BY UNIVERSAL UCLICK SYNDICATE ©2014 R. BOLLING -1218- JOIN THE INNER HIVE AT tomthedancingbug.com

12/15/14

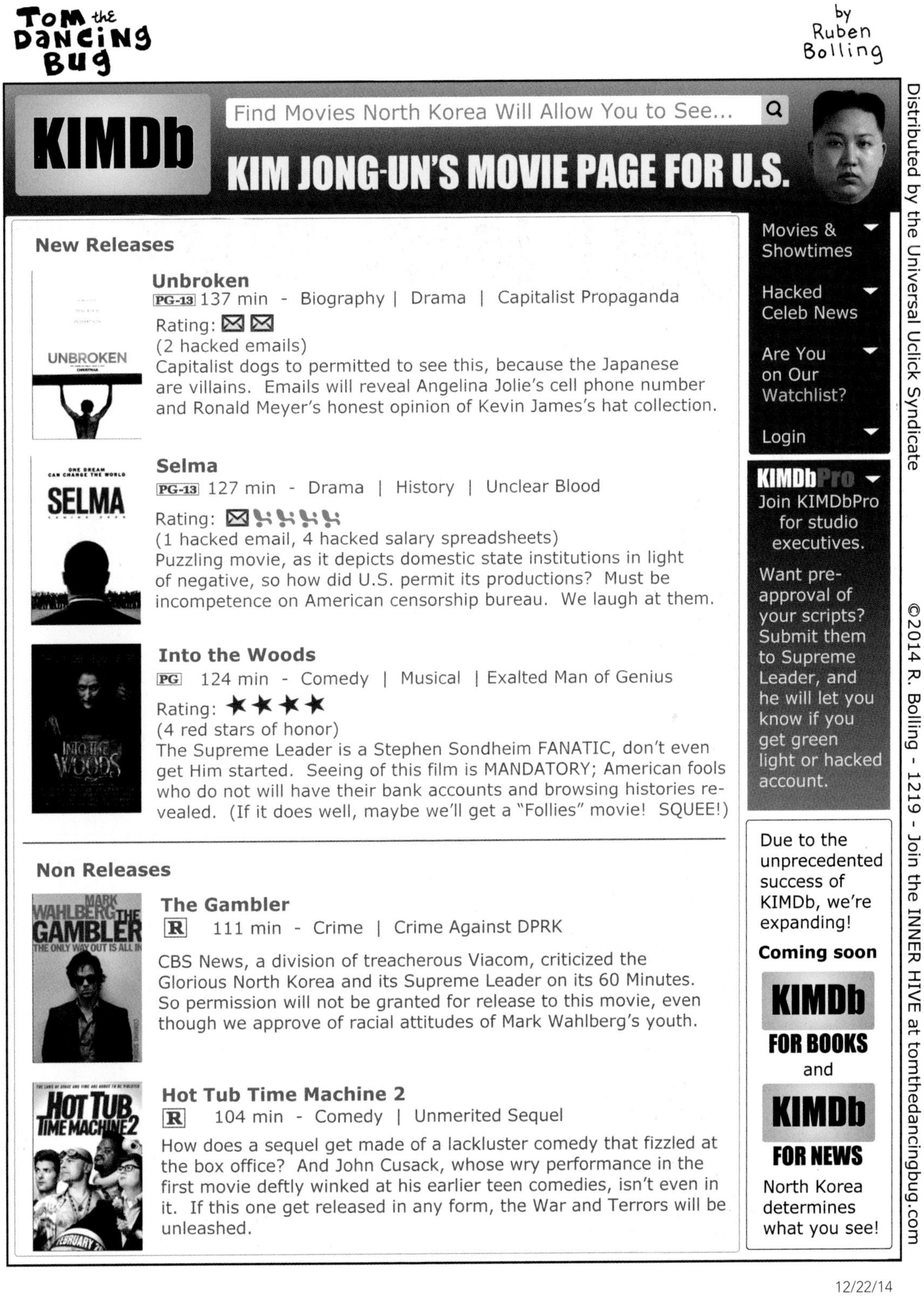
Tom the Dancing Bug
by Ruben Bolling
KIMDb
Find Movies North Korea Will Allow You to See...
KIM JONG-UN'S MOVIE PAGE FOR U.S.
New Releases
Unbroken
PG-13 137 min - Biography | Drama | Capitalist Propaganda
Rating:
(2 hacked emails)
Capitalist dogs to permitted to see this, because the Japanese are villains. Emails will reveal Angelina Jolie's cell phone number and Ronald Meyer's honest opinion of Kevin James's hat collection.
UNBROKEN
Selma
PG-13 127 min - Drama | History | Unclear Blood
Rating:
(1 hacked email, 4 hacked salary spreadsheets)
Puzzling movie, as it depicts domestic state institutions in light of negative, so how did U.S. permit its productions? Must be incompetence on American censorship bureau. We laugh at them.
ONE DREAM CAN CHANGE THE WORLD
SELMA
Into the Woods
PG 124 min - Comedy | Musical | Exalted Man of Genius
Rating: ★★★★
(4 red stars of honor)
The Supreme Leader is a Stephen Sondheim FANATIC, don't even get Him started. Seeing of this film is MANDATORY; American fools who do not will have their bank accounts and browsing histories revealed. (If it does well, maybe we'll get a "Follies" movie! SQUEE!)
INTO THE WOODS
Non Releases
The Gambler
R 111 min - Crime | Crime Against DPRK
CBS News, a division of treacherous Viacom, criticized the Glorious North Korea and its Supreme Leader on its 60 Minutes. So permission will not be granted for release to this movie, even though we approve of racial attitudes of Mark Wahlberg's youth.
MARK WAHLBERG THE GAMBLER
THE ONLY WAY OUT IS ALL IN
Hot Tub Time Machine 2
R 104 min - Comedy | Unmerited Sequel
How does a sequel get made of a lackluster comedy that fizzled at the box office? And John Cusack, whose wry performance in the first movie deftly winked at his earlier teen comedies, isn't even in it. If this one get released in any form, the War and Terrors will be unleashed.
HOT TUB TIME MACHINE 2
Movies & Showtimes
Hacked Celeb News
Are You on Our Watchlist?
Login
KIMDbPro
Join KIMDbPro for studio executives.
Want pre-approval of your scripts? Submit them to Supreme Leader, and he will let you know if you get green light or hacked account.
Due to the unprecedented success of KIMDb, we're expanding!
Coming soon
KIMDb FOR BOOKS
and
KIMDb FOR NEWS
North Korea determines what you see!
Distributed by the Universal Uclick Syndicate
©2014 R. Bolling - 1219 - Join the INNER HIVE at tomthedancingbug.com

12/22/14

TOM the DANCING BUG

by Ruben Bolling

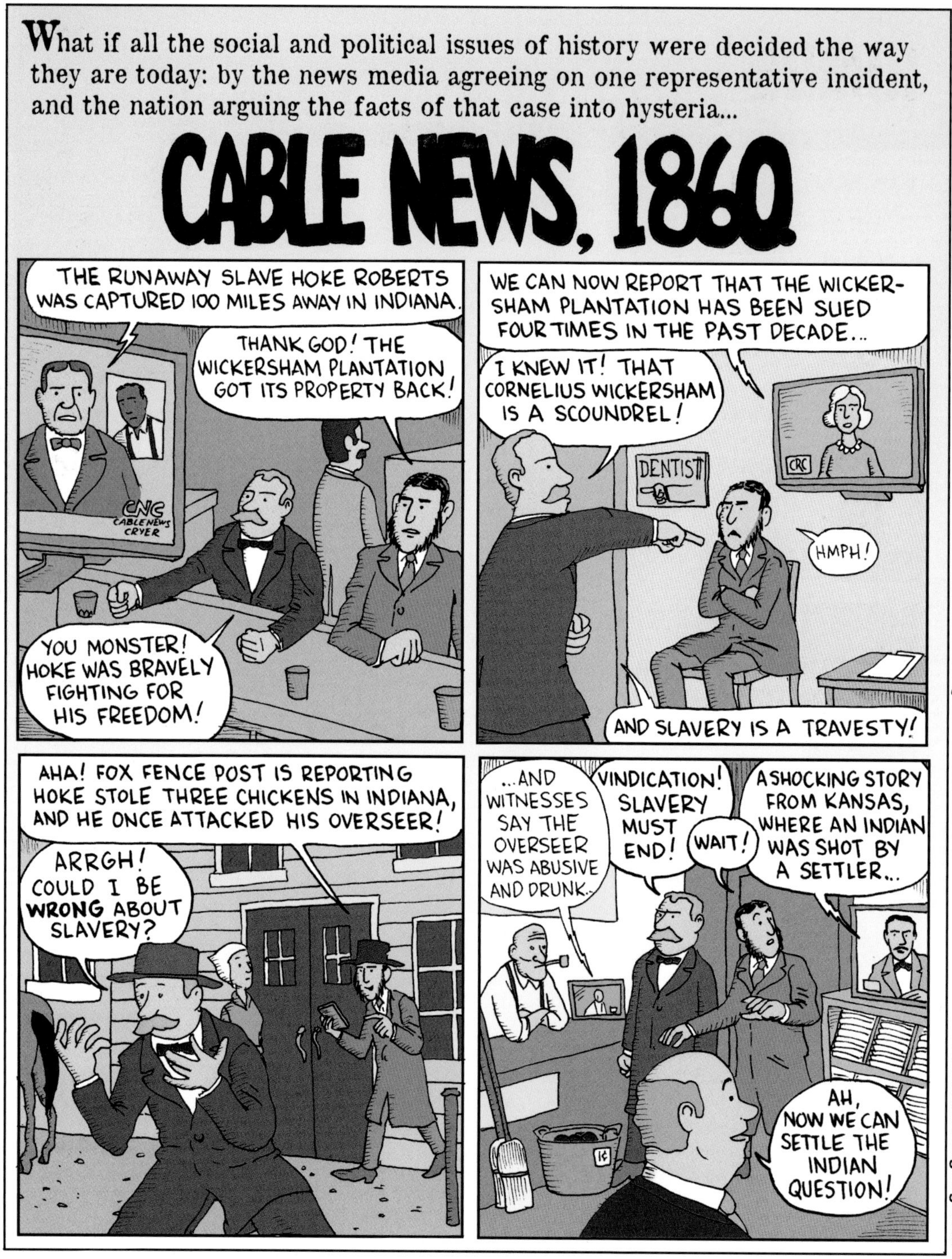

What if all the social and political issues of history were decided the way they are today: by the news media agreeing on one representative incident, and the nation arguing the facts of that case into hysteria...
CABLE NEWS, 1860
THE RUNAWAY SLAVE HOKE ROBERTS WAS CAPTURED 100 MILES AWAY IN INDIANA.
CNC CABLE NEWS CRYER
THANK GOD! THE WICKERSHAM PLANTATION GOT ITS PROPERTY BACK!
YOU MONSTER! HOKE WAS BRAVELY FIGHTING FOR HIS FREEDOM!
WE CAN NOW REPORT THAT THE WICKERSHAM PLANTATION HAS BEEN SUED FOUR TIMES IN THE PAST DECADE...
CRC
I KNEW IT! THAT CORNELIUS WICKERSHAM IS A SCOUNDREL!
DENTIST
HMPH!
AND SLAVERY IS A TRAVESTY!
AHA! FOX FENCE POST IS REPORTING HOKE STOLE THREE CHICKENS IN INDIANA, AND HE ONCE ATTACKED HIS OVERSEER!
ARRGH! COULD I BE **WRONG** ABOUT SLAVERY?
...AND WITNESSES SAY THE OVERSEER WAS ABUSIVE AND DRUNK..
VINDICATION! SLAVERY MUST END!
WAIT!
A SHOCKING STORY FROM KANSAS, WHERE AN INDIAN WAS SHOT BY A SETTLER...
AH, NOW WE CAN SETTLE THE INDIAN QUESTION!

JOIN THE INNER HIVE at tomthedancingbug.com

1/5/15

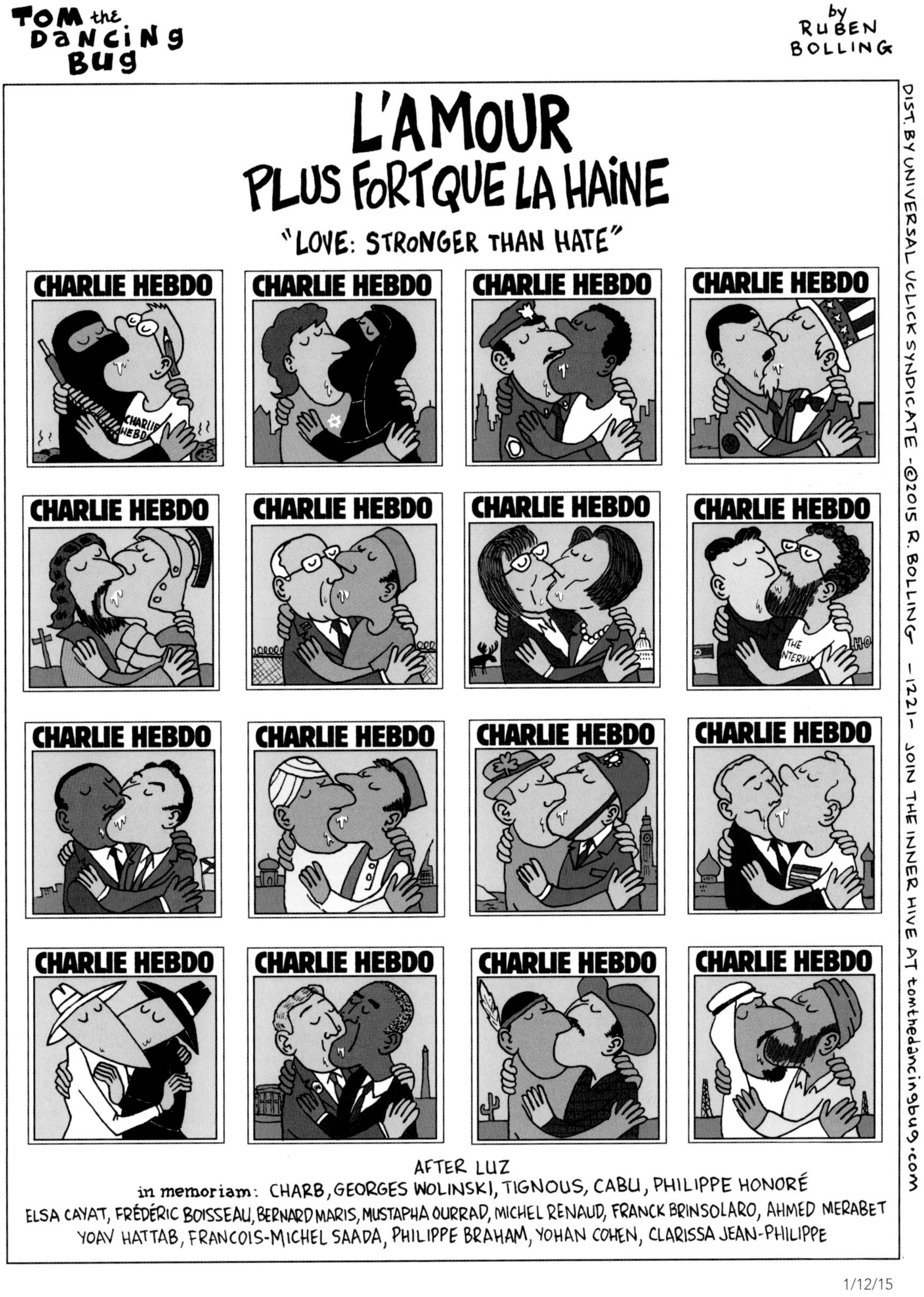
TOM the DANCING BUG
by RUBEN BOLLING
L'AMOUR PLUS FORT QUE LA HAINE
"LOVE: STRONGER THAN HATE"
CHARLIE HEBDO
CHARLIE HEBDO
CHARLIE HEBDO
CHARLIE HEBDO
CHARLIE HEBDO
CHARLIE HEBDO
CHARLIE HEBDO
CHARLIE HEBDO
CHARLIE HEBDO
CHARLIE HEBDO
CHARLIE HEBDO
CHARLIE HEBDO
CHARLIE HEBDO
CHARLIE HEBDO
CHARLIE HEBDO
CHARLIE HEBDO
AFTER LUZ
in memoriam: CHARB, GEORGES WOLINSKI, TIGNOUS, CABU, PHILIPPE HONORÉ
ELSA CAYAT, FRÉDÉRIC BOISSEAU, BERNARD MARIS, MUSTAPHA OURRAD, MICHEL RENAUD, FRANCK BRINSOLARO, AHMED MERABET
YOAV HATTAB, FRANCOIS-MICHEL SAADA, PHILIPPE BRAHAM, YOHAN COHEN, CLARISSA JEAN-PHILIPPE
DIST. BY UNIVERSAL UCLICK SYNDICATE - ©2015 R. BOLLING - 1221 - JOIN THE INNER HIVE AT tomthedancingbug.com

1/12/15

DISTRIBUTED BY THE UNIVERSAL UCLICK SYNDICATE - 1222 - ©2015 R. BOLLING - JOIN THE INNER HIVE! Info at tomthedancingbug.com

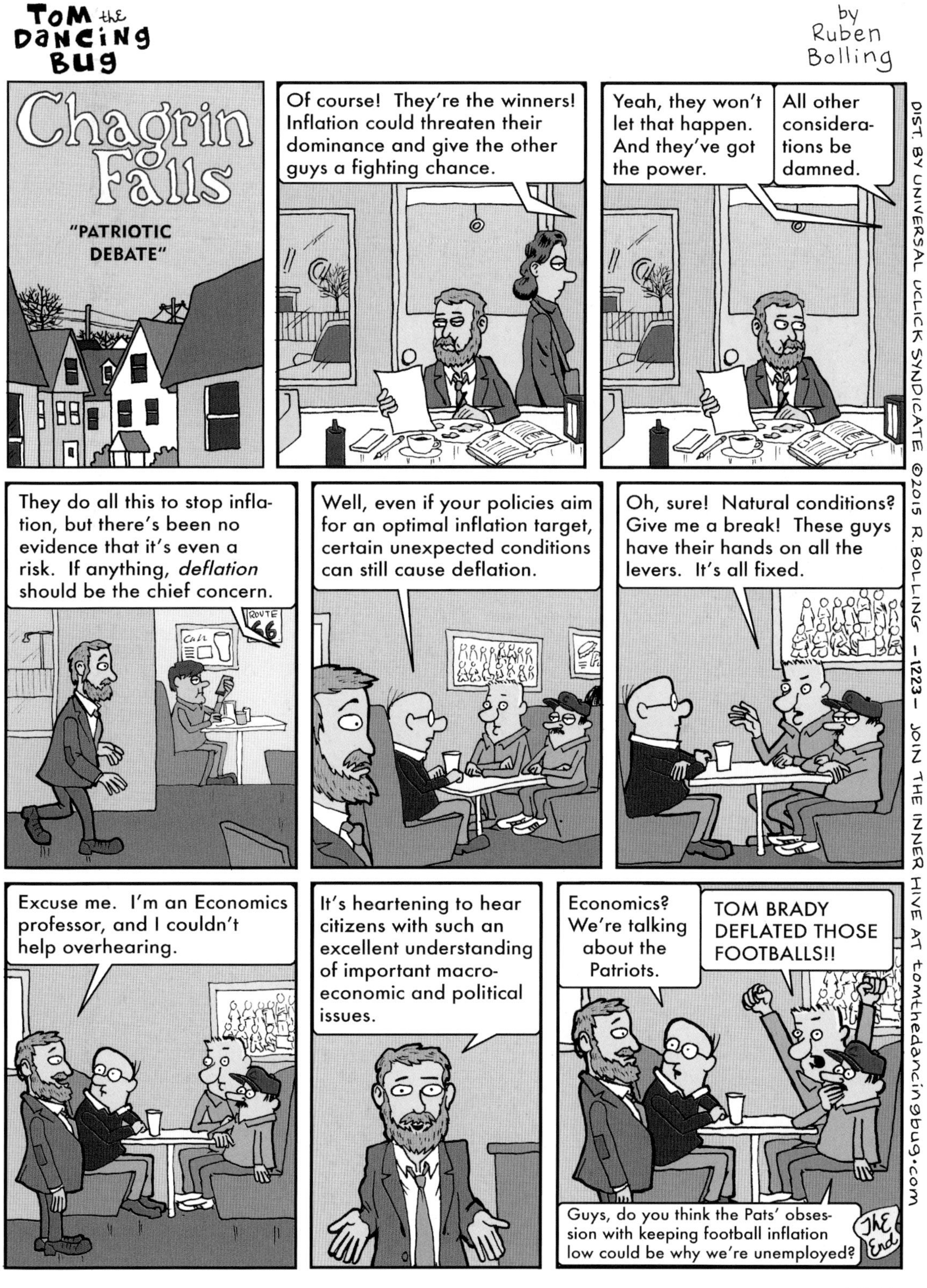
TOM the DANCING BUG
by Ruben Bolling
Chagrin Falls
"PATRIOTIC DEBATE"
Of course! They're the winners! Inflation could threaten their dominance and give the other guys a fighting chance.
Yeah, they won't let that happen. And they've got the power.
All other considera-tions be damned.
They do all this to stop infla-tion, but there's been no evidence that it's even a risk. If anything, *deflation* should be the chief concern.
ROUTE 66
Well, even if your policies aim for an optimal inflation target, certain unexpected conditions can still cause deflation.
Oh, sure! Natural conditions? Give me a break! These guys have their hands on all the levers. It's all fixed.
Excuse me. I'm an Economics professor, and I couldn't help overhearing.
It's heartening to hear citizens with such an excellent understanding of important macro-economic and political issues.
Economics? We're talking about the Patriots.
TOM BRADY DEFLATED THOSE FOOTBALLS!!
Guys, do you think the Pats' obses-sion with keeping football inflation low could be why we're unemployed?
THE End
DIST. BY UNIVERSAL UCLICK SYNDICATE ©2015 R. BOLLING —1223— JOIN THE INNER HIVE AT tomthedancingbug.com

1/26/15

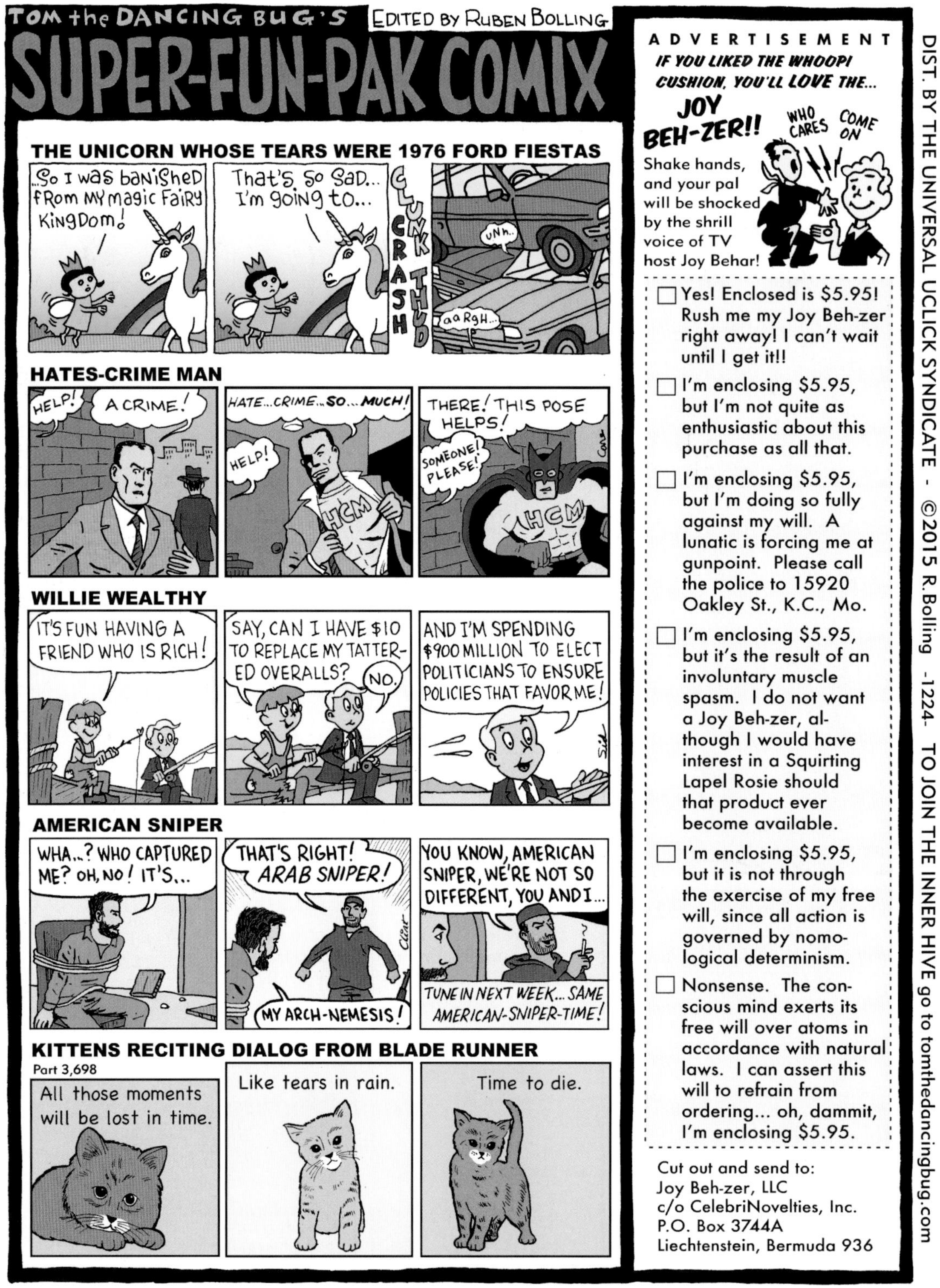
TOM the DANCING BUG'S
EDITED BY RUBEN BOLLING
SUPER-FUN-PAK COMIX
THE UNICORN WHOSE TEARS WERE 1976 FORD FIESTAS
...So I was banished from my magic Fairy Kingdom!
That's so sad... I'm going to...
CLUNK
CRASH
THUD
UNh..
aaRgH...
HATES-CRIME MAN
HELP!
A CRIME!
HATE...CRIME...SO...MUCH!
HELP!
HCM
THERE! THIS POSE HELPS!
SOMEONE! PLEASE!
HCM
WILLIE WEALTHY
IT'S FUN HAVING A FRIEND WHO IS RICH!
SAY, CAN I HAVE $10 TO REPLACE MY TATTERED OVERALLS?
NO.
AND I'M SPENDING $900 MILLION TO ELECT POLITICIANS TO ENSURE POLICIES THAT FAVOR ME!
AMERICAN SNIPER
WHA...? WHO CAPTURED ME? OH, NO! IT'S...
THAT'S RIGHT! ARAB SNIPER!
MY ARCH-NEMESIS!
YOU KNOW, AMERICAN SNIPER, WE'RE NOT SO DIFFERENT, YOU AND I...
TUNE IN NEXT WEEK... SAME AMERICAN-SNIPER-TIME!
KITTENS RECITING DIALOG FROM BLADE RUNNER
Part 3,698
All those moments will be lost in time.
Like tears in rain.
Time to die.
ADVERTISEMENT
IF YOU LIKED THE WHOOPI CUSHION, YOU'LL LOVE THE...
JOY BEH-ZER!!
WHO CARES
COME ON
Shake hands, and your pal will be shocked by the shrill voice of TV host Joy Behar!
☐ Yes! Enclosed is $5.95! Rush me my Joy Beh-zer right away! I can't wait until I get it!!
☐ I'm enclosing $5.95, but I'm not quite as enthusiastic about this purchase as all that.
☐ I'm enclosing $5.95, but I'm doing so fully against my will. A lunatic is forcing me at gunpoint. Please call the police to 15920 Oakley St., K.C., Mo.
☐ I'm enclosing $5.95, but it's the result of an involuntary muscle spasm. I do not want a Joy Beh-zer, although I would have interest in a Squirting Lapel Rosie should that product ever become available.
☐ I'm enclosing $5.95, but it is not through the exercise of my free will, since all action is governed by nomological determinism.
☐ Nonsense. The conscious mind exerts its free will over atoms in accordance with natural laws. I can assert this will to refrain from ordering... oh, dammit, I'm enclosing $5.95.
Cut out and send to:
Joy Beh-zer, LLC
c/o CelebriNovelties, Inc.
P.O. Box 3744A
Liechtenstein, Bermuda 936
DIST. BY THE UNIVERSAL UCLICK SYNDICATE - ©2015 R. Bolling -1224- TO JOIN THE INNER HIVE go to tomthedancingbug.com

2/2/15

TOM the DANCING BUG

by RUBEN BOLLING

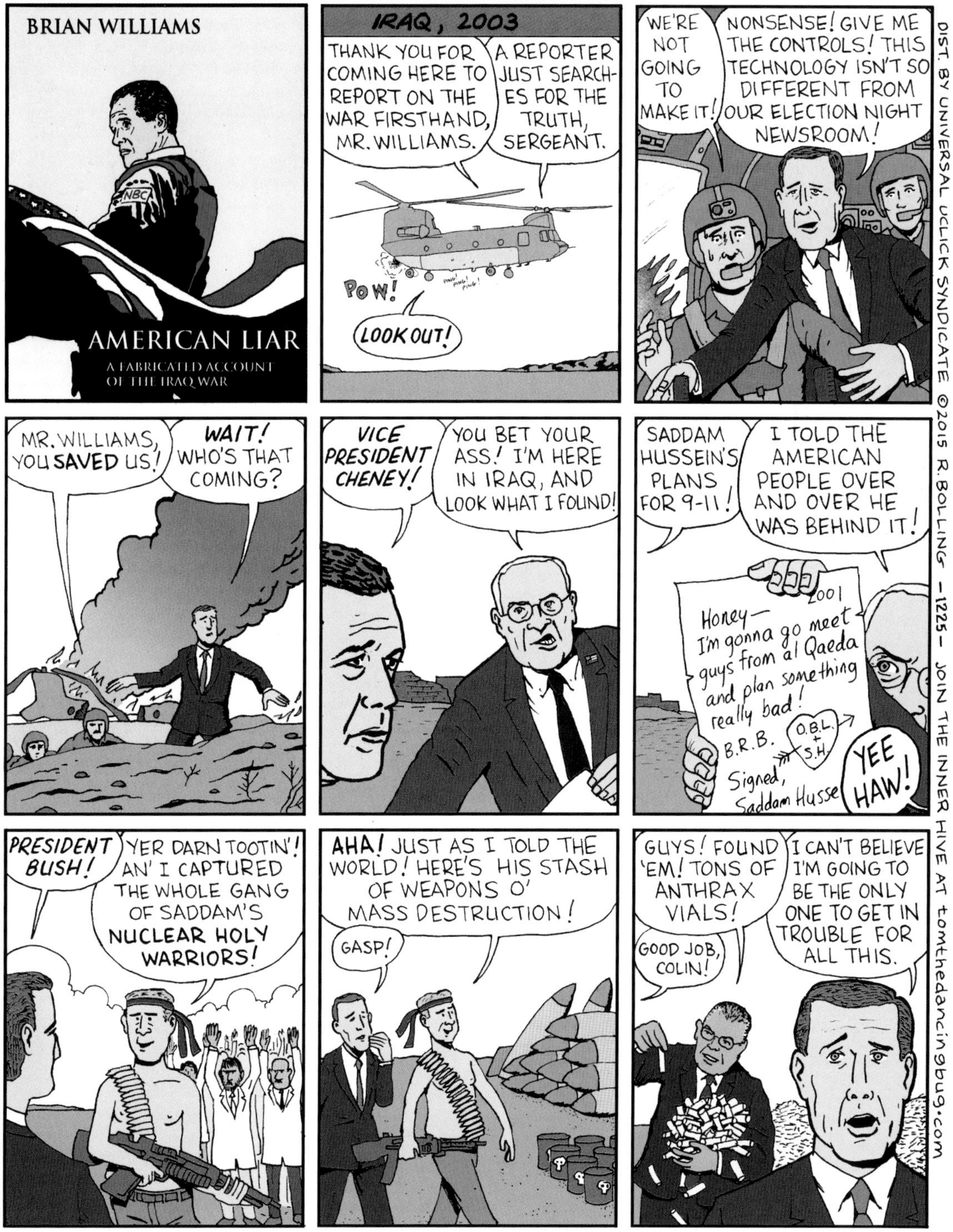

BRIAN WILLIAMS
NBC
AMERICAN LIAR
A FABRICATED ACCOUNT OF THE IRAQ WAR
IRAQ, 2003
THANK YOU FOR COMING HERE TO REPORT ON THE WAR FIRSTHAND, MR. WILLIAMS.
A REPORTER JUST SEARCHES FOR THE TRUTH, SERGEANT.
POW!
LOOK OUT!
WE'RE NOT GOING TO MAKE IT!
NONSENSE! GIVE ME THE CONTROLS! THIS TECHNOLOGY ISN'T SO DIFFERENT FROM OUR ELECTION NIGHT NEWSROOM!
MR. WILLIAMS, YOU SAVED US!
WAIT! WHO'S THAT COMING?
VICE PRESIDENT CHENEY!
YOU BET YOUR ASS! I'M HERE IN IRAQ, AND LOOK WHAT I FOUND!
SADDAM HUSSEIN'S PLANS FOR 9-11!
I TOLD THE AMERICAN PEOPLE OVER AND OVER HE WAS BEHIND IT!
2001
Honey— I'm gonna go meet guys from al Qaeda and plan something really bad! B.R.B.
O.B.L. + S.H.
Signed, Saddam Husse
YEE HAW!
PRESIDENT BUSH!
YER DARN TOOTIN'! AN' I CAPTURED THE WHOLE GANG OF SADDAM'S NUCLEAR HOLY WARRIORS!
AHA! JUST AS I TOLD THE WORLD! HERE'S HIS STASH OF WEAPONS O' MASS DESTRUCTION!
GASP!
GUYS! FOUND 'EM! TONS OF ANTHRAX VIALS!
GOOD JOB, COLIN!
I CAN'T BELIEVE I'M GOING TO BE THE ONLY ONE TO GET IN TROUBLE FOR ALL THIS.
DIST. BY UNIVERSAL UCLICK SYNDICATE ©2015 R. BOLLING —1225— JOIN THE INNER HIVE AT tomthedancingbug.com

2/9/15

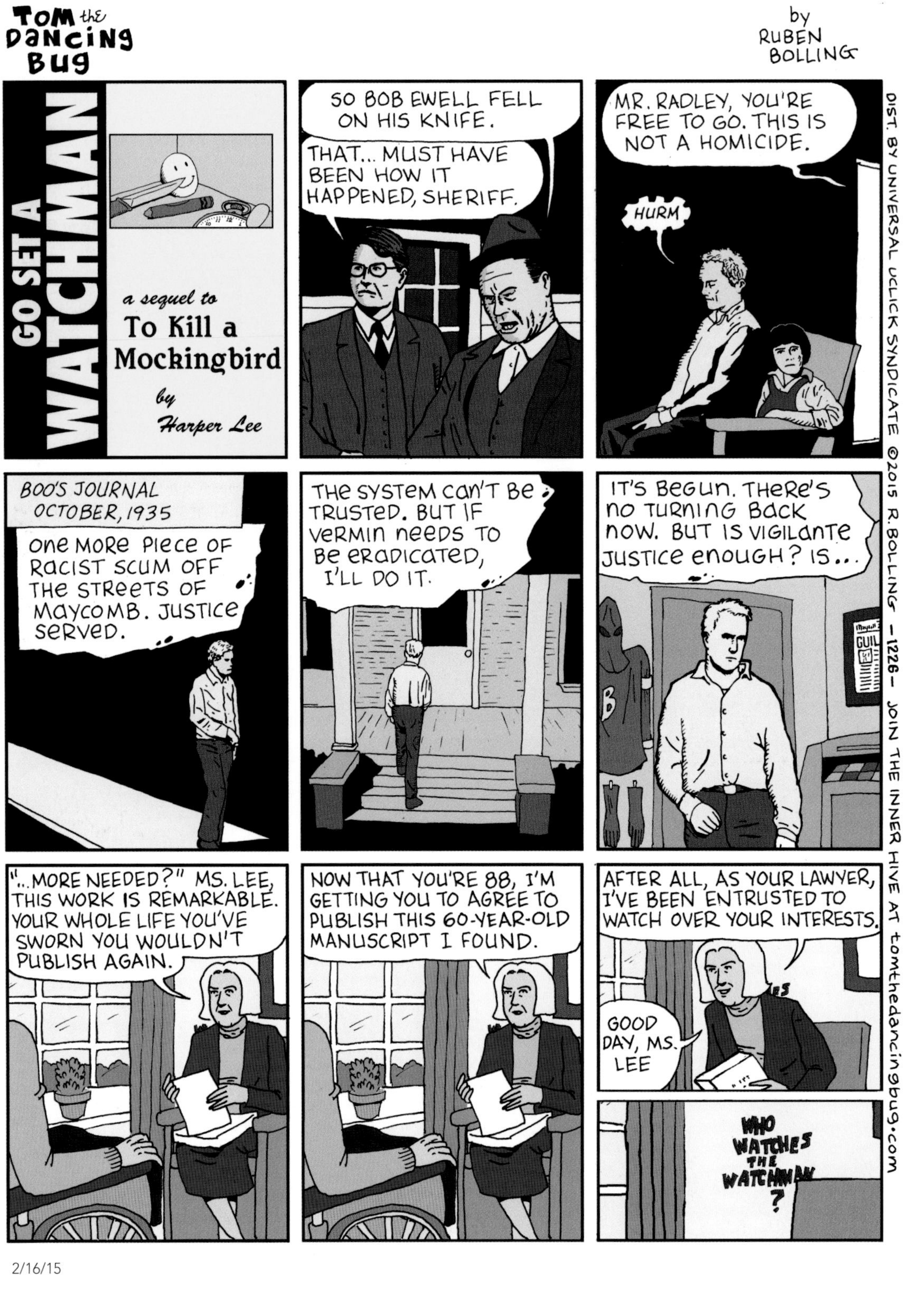
TOM the DANCING BUG
by RUBEN BOLLING
GO SET A WATCHMAN
a sequel to To Kill a Mockingbird
by Harper Lee
SO BOB EWELL FELL ON HIS KNIFE.
THAT... MUST HAVE BEEN HOW IT HAPPENED, SHERIFF.
MR. RADLEY, YOU'RE FREE TO GO. THIS IS NOT A HOMICIDE.
HURM
BOO'S JOURNAL OCTOBER, 1935
ONE MORE PIECE OF RACIST SCUM OFF THE STREETS OF MAYCOMB. JUSTICE SERVED.
THE SYSTEM CAN'T BE TRUSTED. BUT IF VERMIN NEEDS TO BE ERADICATED, I'LL DO IT.
IT'S BEGUN. THERE'S NO TURNING BACK NOW. BUT IS VIGILANTE JUSTICE ENOUGH? IS...
"...MORE NEEDED?" MS. LEE, THIS WORK IS REMARKABLE. YOUR WHOLE LIFE YOU'VE SWORN YOU WOULDN'T PUBLISH AGAIN.
NOW THAT YOU'RE 88, I'M GETTING YOU TO AGREE TO PUBLISH THIS 60-YEAR-OLD MANUSCRIPT I FOUND.
AFTER ALL, AS YOUR LAWYER, I'VE BEEN ENTRUSTED TO WATCH OVER YOUR INTERESTS.
GOOD DAY, MS. LEE
WHO WATCHES THE WATCHMAN?
DIST. BY UNIVERSAL UCLICK SYNDICATE ©2015 R. BOLLING -1226- JOIN THE INNER HIVE AT tomthedancingbug.com

2/16/15

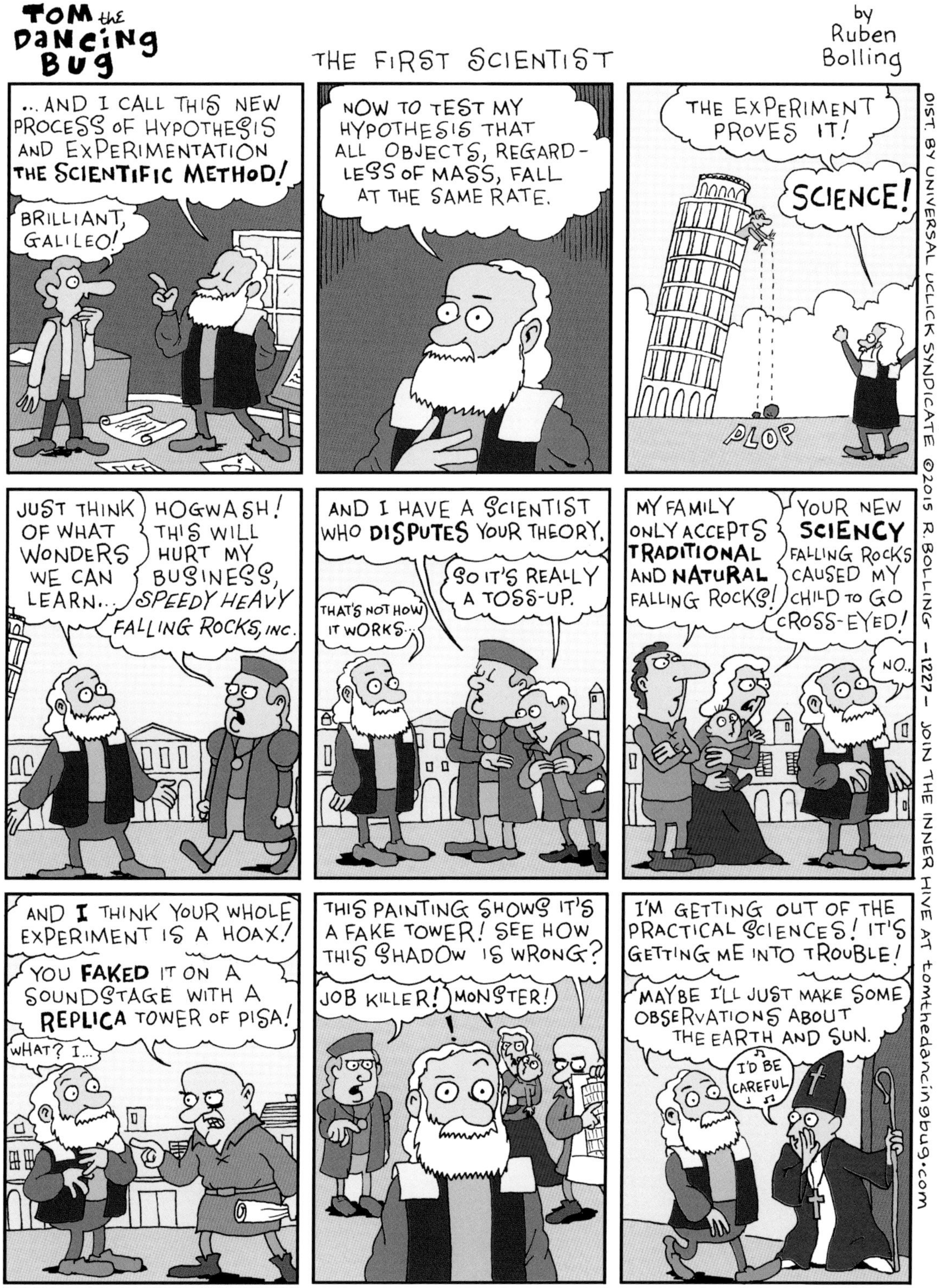
TOM the DANCING BUG
THE FIRST SCIENTIST
by Ruben Bolling
...AND I CALL THIS NEW PROCESS OF HYPOTHESIS AND EXPERIMENTATION THE SCIENTIFIC METHOD!
BRILLIANT, GALILEO!
NOW TO TEST MY HYPOTHESIS THAT ALL OBJECTS, REGARDLESS OF MASS, FALL AT THE SAME RATE.
THE EXPERIMENT PROVES IT!
SCIENCE!
PLOP
JUST THINK OF WHAT WONDERS WE CAN LEARN...
HOGWASH! THIS WILL HURT MY BUSINESS, SPEEDY HEAVY FALLING ROCKS, INC.
AND I HAVE A SCIENTIST WHO DISPUTES YOUR THEORY.
SO IT'S REALLY A TOSS-UP.
THAT'S NOT HOW IT WORKS...
MY FAMILY ONLY ACCEPTS TRADITIONAL AND NATURAL FALLING ROCKS!
YOUR NEW SCIENCY FALLING ROCKS CAUSED MY CHILD TO GO CROSS-EYED!
NO...
AND I THINK YOUR WHOLE EXPERIMENT IS A HOAX!
YOU FAKED IT ON A SOUNDSTAGE WITH A REPLICA TOWER OF PISA!
WHAT? I...
THIS PAINTING SHOWS IT'S A FAKE TOWER! SEE HOW THIS SHADOW IS WRONG?
JOB KILLER!
MONSTER!
!
I'M GETTING OUT OF THE PRACTICAL SCIENCES! IT'S GETTING ME INTO TROUBLE!
MAYBE I'LL JUST MAKE SOME OBSERVATIONS ABOUT THE EARTH AND SUN.
I'D BE CAREFUL
DIST. BY UNIVERSAL UCLICK SYNDICATE ©2015 R. BOLLING —1227— JOIN THE INNER HIVE AT tomthedancingbug.com

2/23/15

by Ruben Bolling

The Education of Louis
"My School Week of Magical Thinking"
or, "Arriving at a Superstition that Will Drive You Crazy"

DIST. BY UNIVERSAL UCLICK SYNDICATE ©2015 R. BOLLING —1228— JOIN THE INNER HIVE AT tomthedancingbug.com

Okay, let's try this: don't step on any cracks.

Oops. Ha!

How about knocking on wood?

And, Louis. Your poster of Geronimo?

I forgot it at home, Ms. Hartsel.

Is this flattened penny souvenir from Mt. Rushmore a good luck charm?

What's wrong, Louis?

I think I lost my Math book.

Maybe I have to be **rubbing** the penny for it to work.

Pass them back.

Did you know about this test?

Yeah! He told us on Monday.

I thought this penny was a good luck charm, but it sucks.

Did you forget your Geronimo poster again, Louis?

Yes.

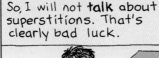

So, I will not **talk** about superstitions. That's clearly bad luck.

D−

Name Louis Maltby

= 3x+

Plot the graph for x=1, x=0, x=2, x=

Oh my god. I think I know what's happening! It's **bad luck** to follow superstitions!

GERONIMO

That's it!! So I won't be superstitious, and I'll have good luck.

But that **is** a superstition!

GERONIMO

This is going to be rough.

GERONIMO

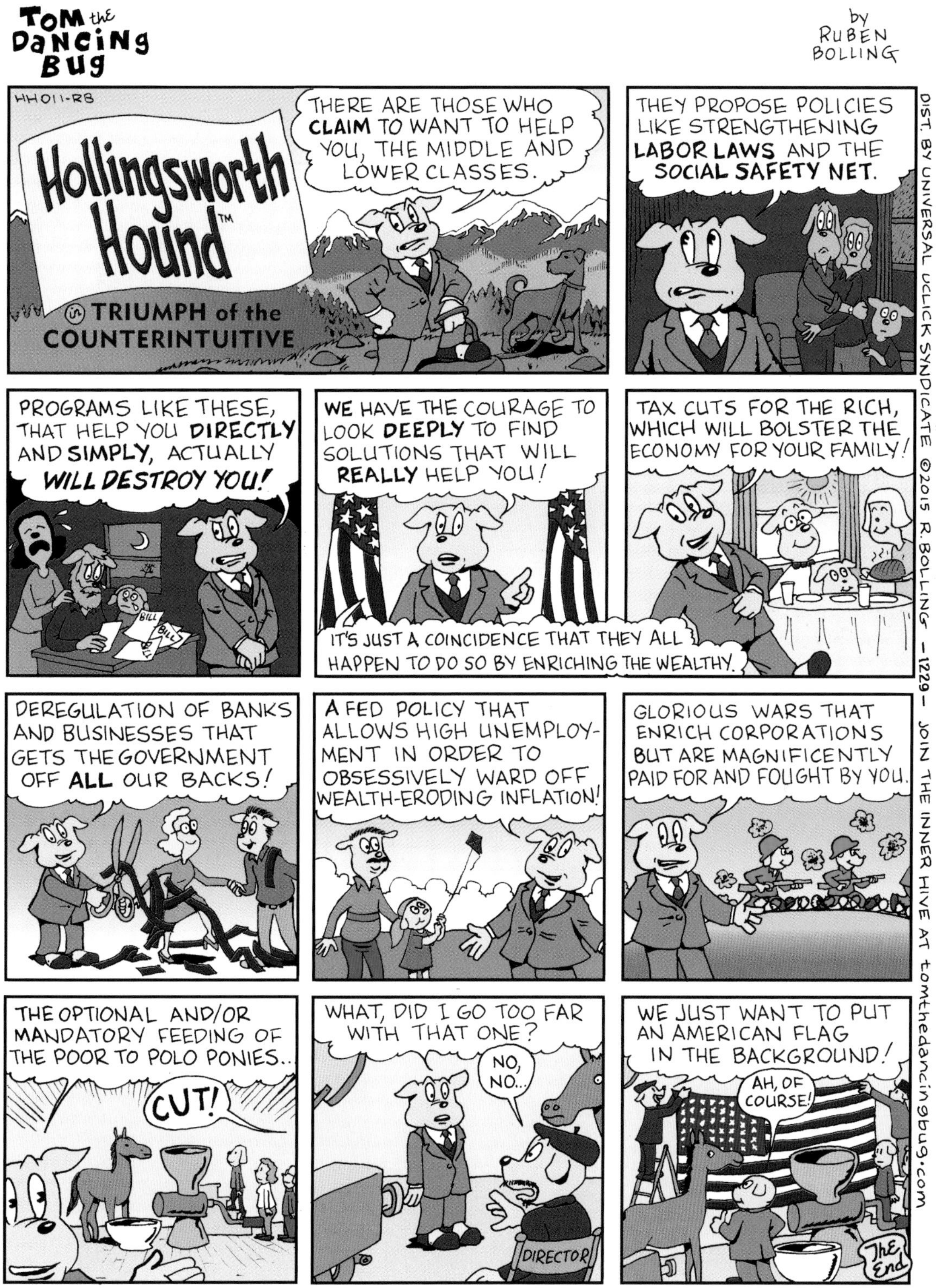
TOM the DaNCiNg Bug
by RUBEN BOLLING
HH011-RB
Hollingsworth Hound™
in TRIUMPH of the COUNTERINTUITIVE
THERE ARE THOSE WHO CLAIM TO WANT TO HELP YOU, THE MIDDLE AND LOWER CLASSES.
THEY PROPOSE POLICIES LIKE STRENGTHENING LABOR LAWS AND THE SOCIAL SAFETY NET.
PROGRAMS LIKE THESE, THAT HELP YOU DIRECTLY AND SIMPLY, ACTUALLY WILL DESTROY YOU!
BILL
BILL
BILL
WE HAVE THE COURAGE TO LOOK DEEPLY TO FIND SOLUTIONS THAT WILL REALLY HELP YOU!
TAX CUTS FOR THE RICH, WHICH WILL BOLSTER THE ECONOMY FOR YOUR FAMILY!
IT'S JUST A COINCIDENCE THAT THEY ALL HAPPEN TO DO SO BY ENRICHING THE WEALTHY.
DEREGULATION OF BANKS AND BUSINESSES THAT GETS THE GOVERNMENT OFF ALL OUR BACKS!
A FED POLICY THAT ALLOWS HIGH UNEMPLOYMENT IN ORDER TO OBSESSIVELY WARD OFF WEALTH-ERODING INFLATION!
GLORIOUS WARS THAT ENRICH CORPORATIONS BUT ARE MAGNIFICENTLY PAID FOR AND FOUGHT BY YOU.
THE OPTIONAL AND/OR MANDATORY FEEDING OF THE POOR TO POLO PONIES...
CUT!
WHAT, DID I GO TOO FAR WITH THAT ONE?
NO, NO...
DIRECTOR
WE JUST WANT TO PUT AN AMERICAN FLAG IN THE BACKGROUND!
AH, OF COURSE!
ThE End
DIST. BY UNIVERSAL UCLICK SYNDICATE ©2015 R. BOLLING -1229- JOIN THE INNER HIVE AT tomthedancingbug.com

3/9/15

TOM the DANCING BUG

by RUBEN BOLLING

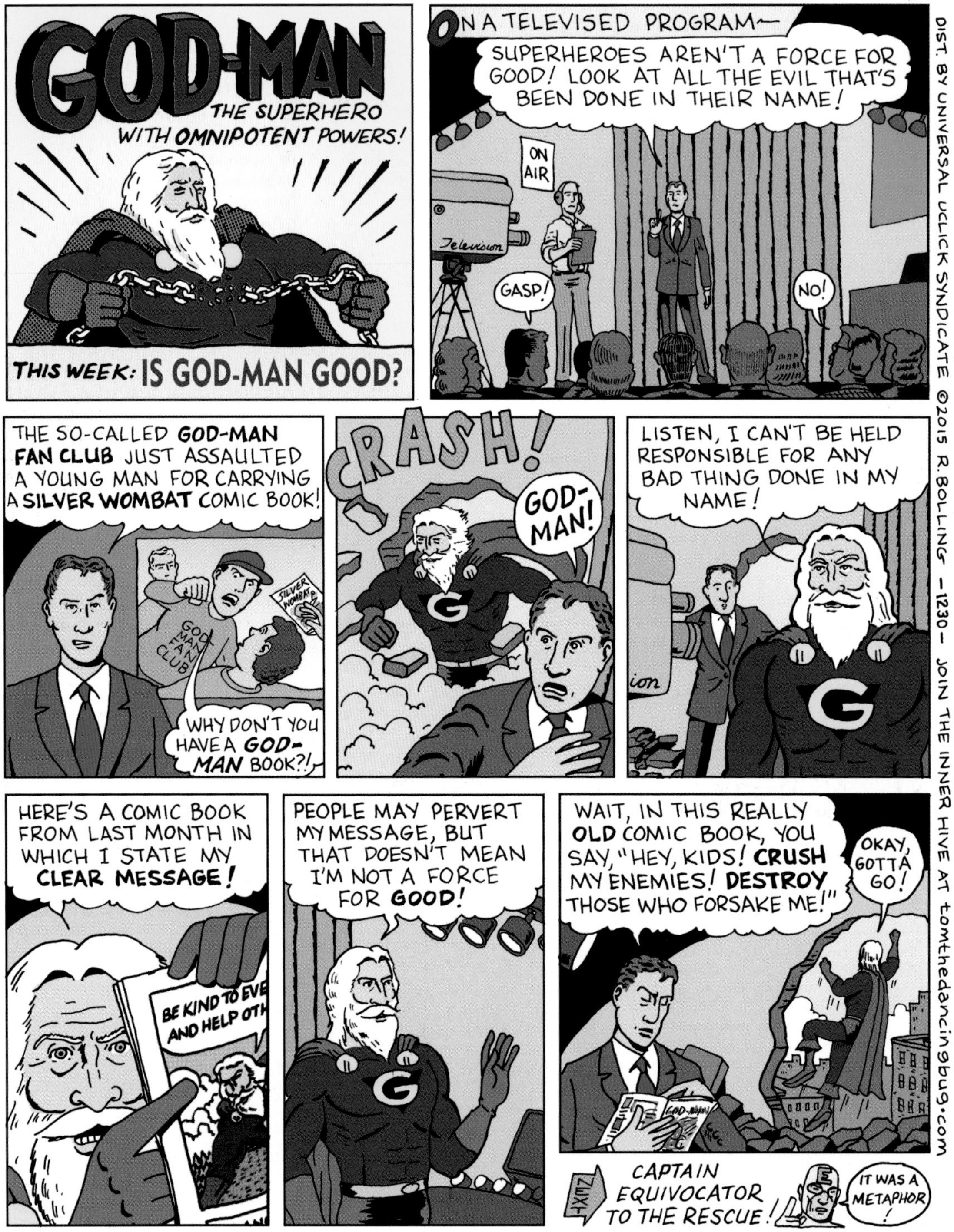

GOD-MAN
THE SUPERHERO WITH OMNIPOTENT POWERS!
THIS WEEK: IS GOD-MAN GOOD?
ON A TELEVISED PROGRAM—
SUPERHEROES AREN'T A FORCE FOR GOOD! LOOK AT ALL THE EVIL THAT'S BEEN DONE IN THEIR NAME!
ON AIR
Television
GASP!
NO!
THE SO-CALLED GOD-MAN FAN CLUB JUST ASSAULTED A YOUNG MAN FOR CARRYING A SILVER WOMBAT COMIC BOOK!
GOD MAN FAN CLUB
SILVER WOMBAT
WHY DON'T YOU HAVE A GOD-MAN BOOK?!
CRASH!
GOD-MAN!
LISTEN, I CAN'T BE HELD RESPONSIBLE FOR ANY BAD THING DONE IN MY NAME!
HERE'S A COMIC BOOK FROM LAST MONTH IN WHICH I STATE MY CLEAR MESSAGE!
BE KIND TO EVE AND HELP OTH
PEOPLE MAY PERVERT MY MESSAGE, BUT THAT DOESN'T MEAN I'M NOT A FORCE FOR GOOD!
WAIT, IN THIS REALLY OLD COMIC BOOK, YOU SAY, "HEY, KIDS! CRUSH MY ENEMIES! DESTROY THOSE WHO FORSAKE ME!"
OKAY, GOTTA GO!
NEXT
CAPTAIN EQUIVOCATOR TO THE RESCUE!
IT WAS A METAPHOR!
DIST. BY UNIVERSAL UCLICK SYNDICATE ©2015 R. BOLLING —1230— JOIN THE INNER HIVE AT tomthedancingbug.com

3/16/15

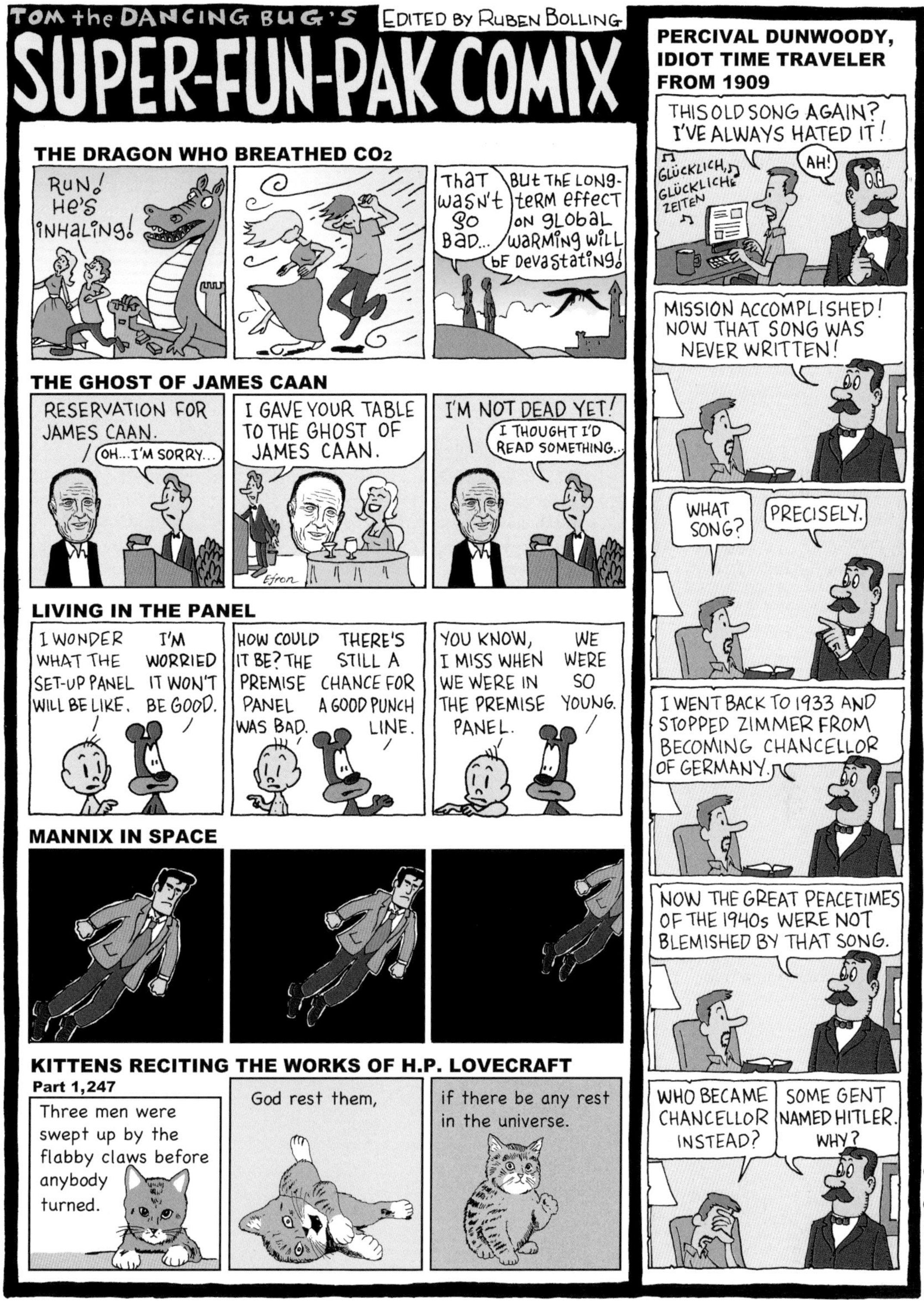
TOM the DANCING BUG'S
EDITED BY RUBEN BOLLING
SUPER-FUN-PAK COMIX
THE DRAGON WHO BREATHED CO2
RUN! HE'S INHALING!
That wasn't so bad...
But the long-term effect on global warming will be devastating!
THE GHOST OF JAMES CAAN
RESERVATION FOR JAMES CAAN.
OH... I'M SORRY...
I GAVE YOUR TABLE TO THE GHOST OF JAMES CAAN.
Efron
I'M NOT DEAD YET!
I THOUGHT I'D READ SOMETHING...
LIVING IN THE PANEL
I WONDER WHAT THE SET-UP PANEL WILL BE LIKE.
I'M WORRIED IT WON'T BE GOOD.
HOW COULD IT BE? THE PREMISE PANEL WAS BAD.
THERE'S STILL A CHANCE FOR A GOOD PUNCH LINE.
YOU KNOW, I MISS WHEN WE WERE IN THE PREMISE PANEL.
WE WERE SO YOUNG.
MANNIX IN SPACE
KITTENS RECITING THE WORKS OF H.P. LOVECRAFT
Part 1,247
Three men were swept up by the flabby claws before anybody turned.
God rest them,
if there be any rest in the universe.
PERCIVAL DUNWOODY, IDIOT TIME TRAVELER FROM 1909
THIS OLD SONG AGAIN? I'VE ALWAYS HATED IT!
GLÜCKLICH, GLÜCKLICHE ZEITEN
AH!
MISSION ACCOMPLISHED! NOW THAT SONG WAS NEVER WRITTEN!
WHAT SONG?
PRECISELY.
I WENT BACK TO 1933 AND STOPPED ZIMMER FROM BECOMING CHANCELLOR OF GERMANY.
NOW THE GREAT PEACETIMES OF THE 1940s WERE NOT BLEMISHED BY THAT SONG.
WHO BECAME CHANCELLOR INSTEAD?
SOME GENT NAMED HITLER. WHY?

3/23/15

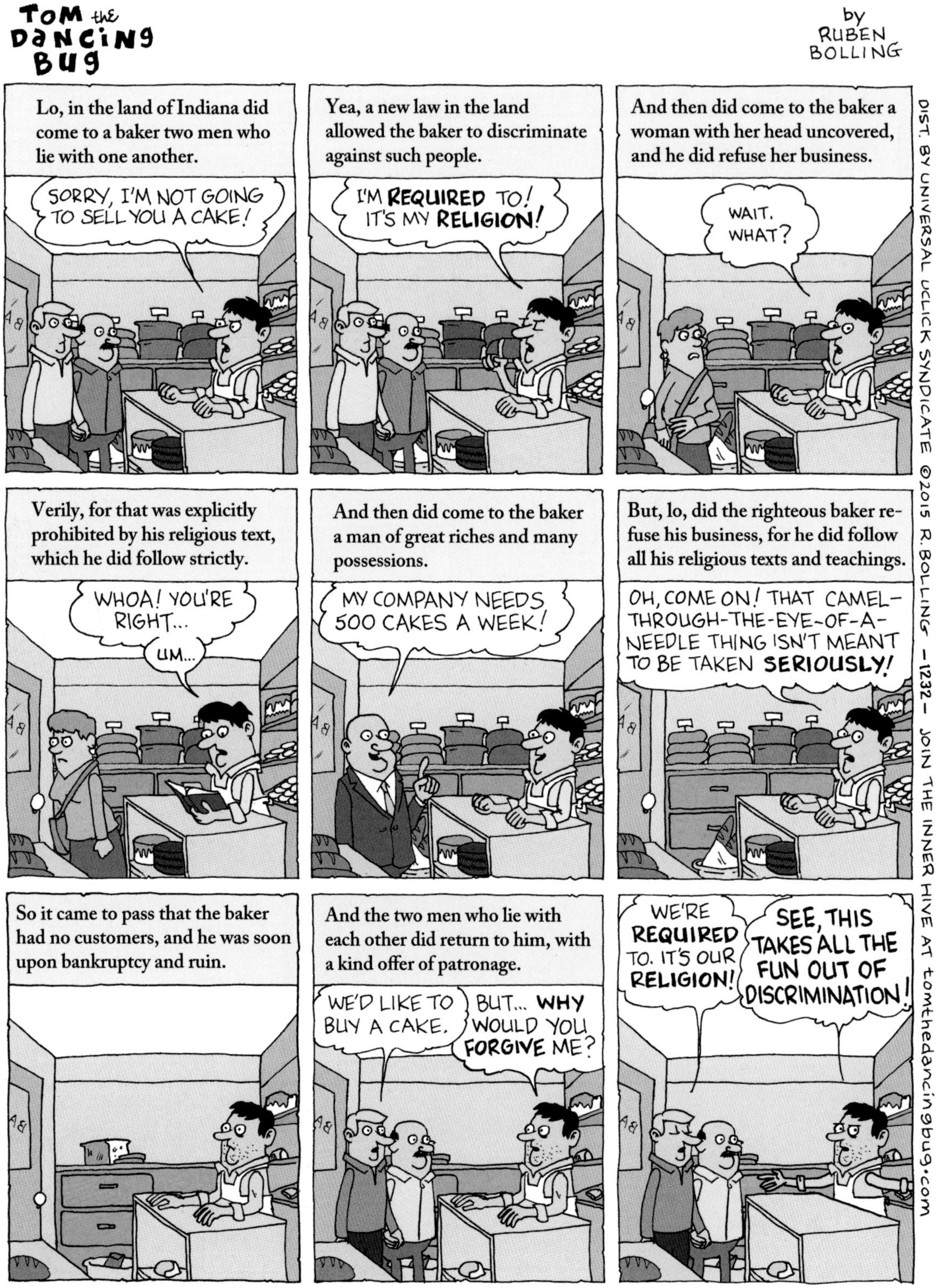

TOM the DANCING BUG
by RUBEN BOLLING
Lo, in the land of Indiana did come to a baker two men who lie with one another.
SORRY, I'M NOT GOING TO SELL YOU A CAKE!
Yea, a new law in the land allowed the baker to discriminate against such people.
I'M REQUIRED TO! IT'S MY RELIGION!
And then did come to the baker a woman with her head uncovered, and he did refuse her business.
WAIT. WHAT?
Verily, for that was explicitly prohibited by his religious text, which he did follow strictly.
WHOA! YOU'RE RIGHT...
UM...
And then did come to the baker a man of great riches and many possessions.
MY COMPANY NEEDS 500 CAKES A WEEK!
But, lo, did the righteous baker refuse his business, for he did follow all his religious texts and teachings.
OH, COME ON! THAT CAMEL-THROUGH-THE-EYE-OF-A-NEEDLE THING ISN'T MEANT TO BE TAKEN SERIOUSLY!
So it came to pass that the baker had no customers, and he was soon upon bankruptcy and ruin.
And the two men who lie with each other did return to him, with a kind offer of patronage.
WE'D LIKE TO BUY A CAKE.
BUT... WHY WOULD YOU FORGIVE ME?
WE'RE REQUIRED TO. IT'S OUR RELIGION!
SEE, THIS TAKES ALL THE FUN OUT OF DISCRIMINATION!
DIST. BY UNIVERSAL UCLICK SYNDICATE ©2015 R. BOLLING -1232- JOIN THE INNER HIVE AT tomthedancingbug.com

3/30/15

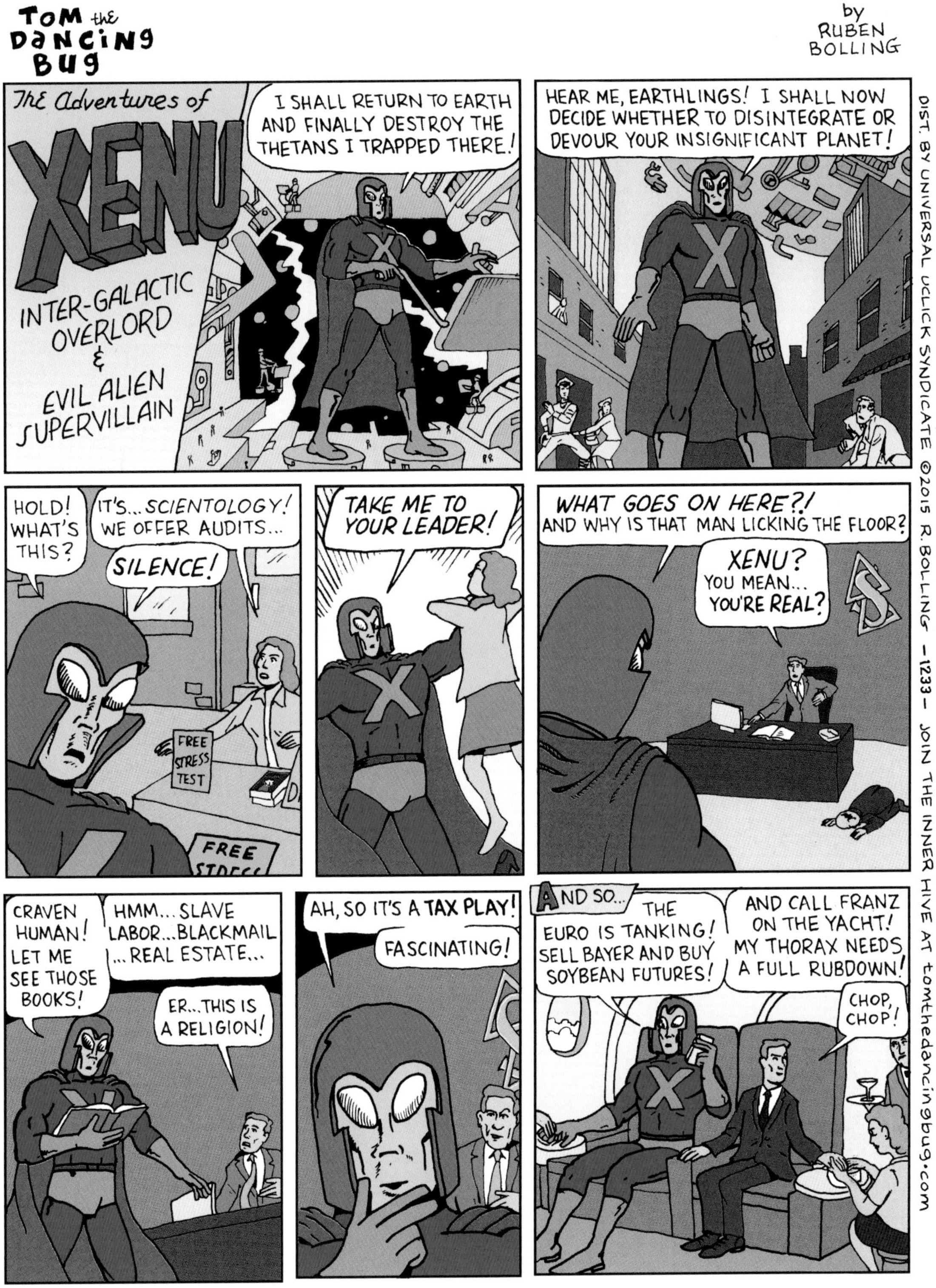

TOM the DANCING BUG
by RUBEN BOLLING
The Adventures of XENU
INTER-GALACTIC OVERLORD & EVIL ALIEN SUPERVILLAIN
I SHALL RETURN TO EARTH AND FINALLY DESTROY THE THETANS I TRAPPED THERE!
HEAR ME, EARTHLINGS! I SHALL NOW DECIDE WHETHER TO DISINTEGRATE OR DEVOUR YOUR INSIGNIFICANT PLANET!
HOLD! WHAT'S THIS?
IT'S... SCIENTOLOGY! WE OFFER AUDITS...
SILENCE!
FREE STRESS TEST
TAKE ME TO YOUR LEADER!
WHAT GOES ON HERE?! AND WHY IS THAT MAN LICKING THE FLOOR?
XENU? YOU MEAN... YOU'RE REAL?
CRAVEN HUMAN! LET ME SEE THOSE BOOKS!
HMM... SLAVE LABOR... BLACKMAIL ... REAL ESTATE...
ER... THIS IS A RELIGION!
AH, SO IT'S A TAX PLAY!
FASCINATING!
AND SO...
THE EURO IS TANKING! SELL BAYER AND BUY SOYBEAN FUTURES!
AND CALL FRANZ ON THE YACHT! MY THORAX NEEDS A FULL RUBDOWN!
CHOP, CHOP!
DIST. BY UNIVERSAL UCLICK SYNDICATE ©2015 R. BOLLING —1233— JOIN THE INNER HIVE AT tomthedancingbug.com

4/6/15

TOM the DANCING BUG
by Ruben Bolling

AN UNIMAGINABLE JOURNEY--STRETCHING BACK BILLIONS OF YEARS.

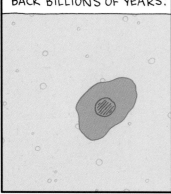

THE BRUTAL AND REMORSE-LESS STRUGGLE FOR SURVIVAL IS IMMENSE.

THE ODDS OF SURVIVAL, MINUSCULE.

AND NOT JUST **SOME**...

NOT JUST **MOST**...

...BUT **EVERY SINGLE ONE** OF HIS **MILLIONS** AND **MILLIONS** OF ANCESTORS NOT ONLY SURVIVED...

...BUT SURVIVED LONG ENOUGH TO REPRODUCE.

WHAT IS THE RESULT OF THIS UNFATHOMABLE WINNING STREAK?

PRESENTING... **BOB.**

COMING UP ON NEWS AT 11...

UGH...THE REMOTE IS SO FAR AWAY...!

DIST. BY UNIVERSAL UCLICK SYNDICATE ©2015 R.BOLLING —1234— JOIN THE INNER HIVE AT tomthedancingbug.com

4/13/15

TOM the DANCING BUG

by RUBEN BOLLING

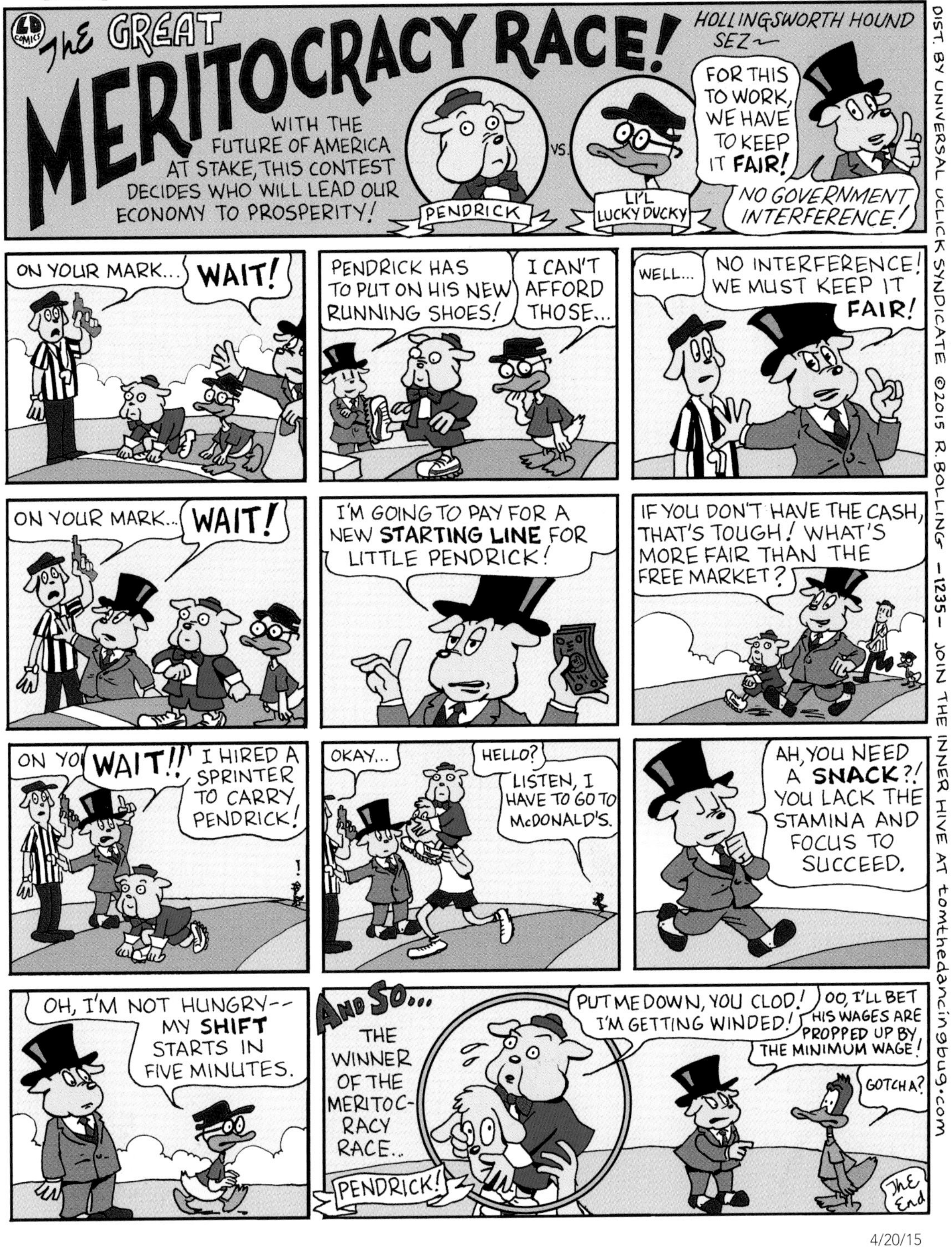
LD COMICS
THE GREAT MERITOCRACY RACE!
WITH THE FUTURE OF AMERICA AT STAKE, THIS CONTEST DECIDES WHO WILL LEAD OUR ECONOMY TO PROSPERITY!
PENDRICK
VS.
LI'L LUCKY DUCKY
HOLLINGSWORTH HOUND SEZ~
FOR THIS TO WORK, WE HAVE TO KEEP IT FAIR!
NO GOVERNMENT INTERFERENCE!
ON YOUR MARK...
WAIT!
PENDRICK HAS TO PUT ON HIS NEW RUNNING SHOES!
I CAN'T AFFORD THOSE...
WELL...
NO INTERFERENCE! WE MUST KEEP IT FAIR!
ON YOUR MARK...
WAIT!
I'M GOING TO PAY FOR A NEW STARTING LINE FOR LITTLE PENDRICK!
IF YOU DON'T HAVE THE CASH, THAT'S TOUGH! WHAT'S MORE FAIR THAN THE FREE MARKET?
ON YO
WAIT!!
I HIRED A SPRINTER TO CARRY PENDRICK!
!
OKAY...
HELLO?
LISTEN, I HAVE TO GO TO McDONALD'S.
AH, YOU NEED A SNACK?! YOU LACK THE STAMINA AND FOCUS TO SUCCEED.
OH, I'M NOT HUNGRY-- MY SHIFT STARTS IN FIVE MINUTES.
AND SO...
THE WINNER OF THE MERITOC-RACY RACE..
PENDRICK!
PUT ME DOWN, YOU CLOD! I'M GETTING WINDED!
OO, I'LL BET HIS WAGES ARE PROPPED UP BY THE MINIMUM WAGE!
GOTCHA?
THE END
DIST. BY UNIVERSAL UCLICK SYNDICATE ©2015 R. BOLLING -1235- JOIN THE INNER HIVE AT tomthedancingbug.com

4/20/15

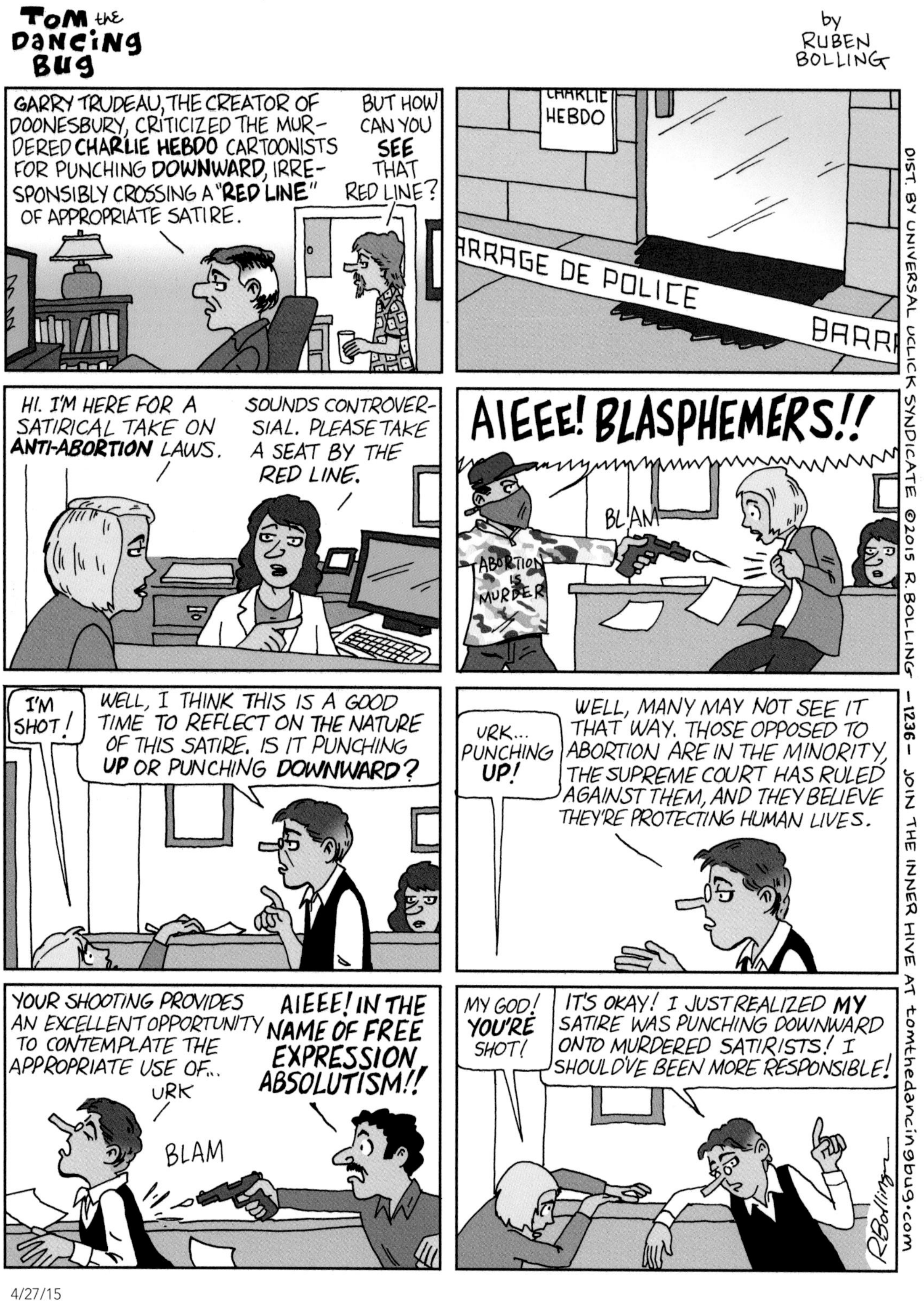
TOM the DANCING BUG
by RUBEN BOLLING
GARRY TRUDEAU, THE CREATOR OF DOONESBURY, CRITICIZED THE MURDERED CHARLIE HEBDO CARTOONISTS FOR PUNCHING DOWNWARD, IRRESPONSIBLY CROSSING A "RED LINE" OF APPROPRIATE SATIRE.
BUT HOW CAN YOU SEE THAT RED LINE?
CHARLIE HEBDO
ARRAGE DE POLICE
BARRA
HI. I'M HERE FOR A SATIRICAL TAKE ON ANTI-ABORTION LAWS.
SOUNDS CONTROVERSIAL. PLEASE TAKE A SEAT BY THE RED LINE.
AIEEE! BLASPHEMERS!!
BLAM
ABORTION IS MURDER
I'M SHOT!
WELL, I THINK THIS IS A GOOD TIME TO REFLECT ON THE NATURE OF THIS SATIRE. IS IT PUNCHING UP OR PUNCHING DOWNWARD?
URK... PUNCHING UP!
WELL, MANY MAY NOT SEE IT THAT WAY. THOSE OPPOSED TO ABORTION ARE IN THE MINORITY, THE SUPREME COURT HAS RULED AGAINST THEM, AND THEY BELIEVE THEY'RE PROTECTING HUMAN LIVES.
YOUR SHOOTING PROVIDES AN EXCELLENT OPPORTUNITY TO CONTEMPLATE THE APPROPRIATE USE OF...
AIEEE! IN THE NAME OF FREE EXPRESSION ABSOLUTISM!!
URK
BLAM
MY GOD! YOU'RE SHOT!
IT'S OKAY! I JUST REALIZED MY SATIRE WAS PUNCHING DOWNWARD ONTO MURDERED SATIRISTS! I SHOULD'VE BEEN MORE RESPONSIBLE!
RBolling
DIST. BY UNIVERSAL UCLICK SYNDICATE ©2015 R. BOLLING -1236- JOIN THE INNER HIVE AT tomthedancingbug.com

4/27/15

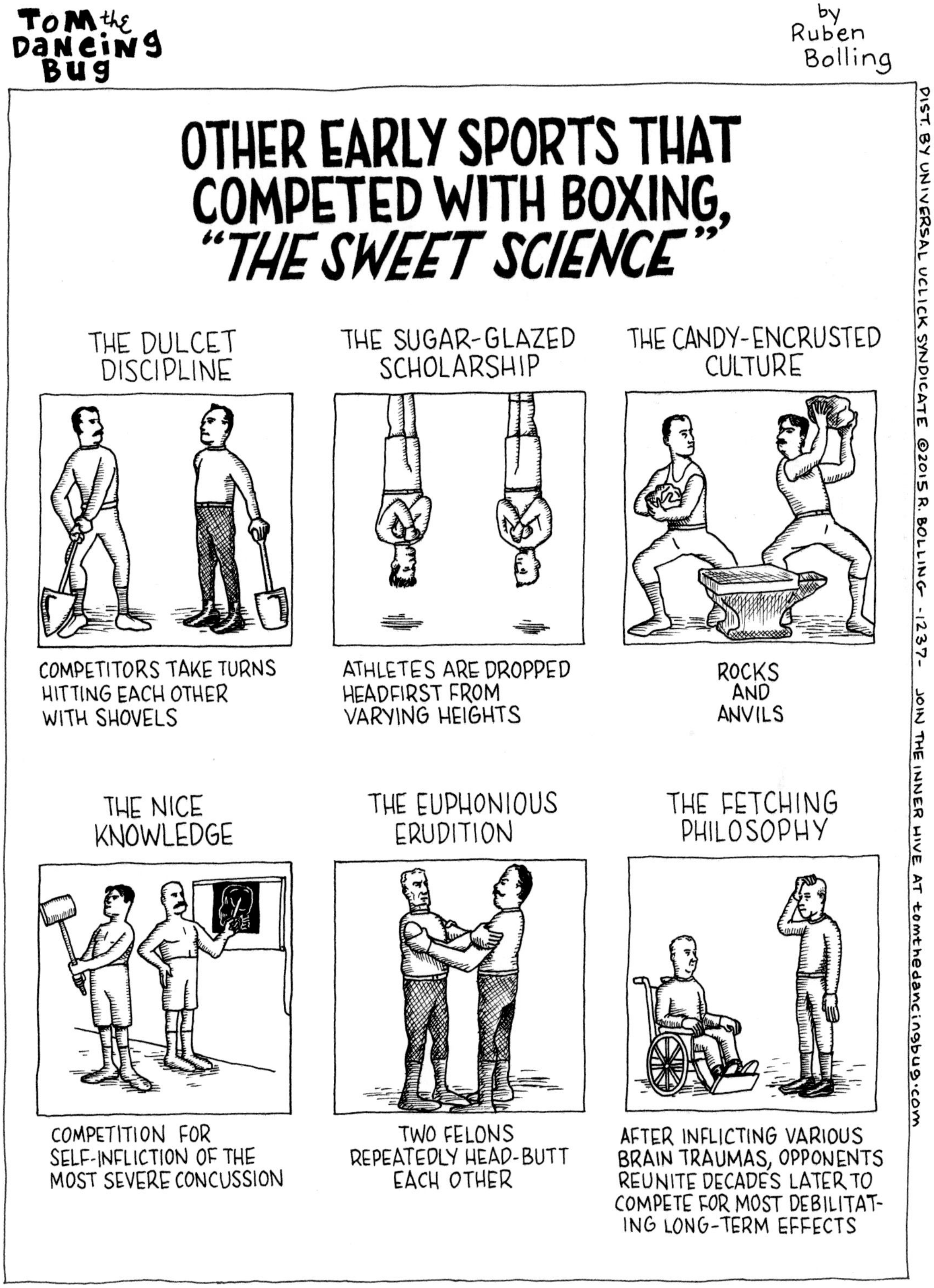
TOM the DANCING BUG
by Ruben Bolling
OTHER EARLY SPORTS THAT COMPETED WITH BOXING, "THE SWEET SCIENCE"
THE DULCET DISCIPLINE
COMPETITORS TAKE TURNS HITTING EACH OTHER WITH SHOVELS
THE SUGAR-GLAZED SCHOLARSHIP
ATHLETES ARE DROPPED HEADFIRST FROM VARYING HEIGHTS
THE CANDY-ENCRUSTED CULTURE
ROCKS AND ANVILS
THE NICE KNOWLEDGE
COMPETITION FOR SELF-INFLICTION OF THE MOST SEVERE CONCUSSION
THE EUPHONIOUS ERUDITION
TWO FELONS REPEATEDLY HEAD-BUTT EACH OTHER
THE FETCHING PHILOSOPHY
AFTER INFLICTING VARIOUS BRAIN TRAUMAS, OPPONENTS REUNITE DECADES LATER TO COMPETE FOR MOST DEBILITAT-ING LONG-TERM EFFECTS
DIST. BY UNIVERSAL UCLICK SYNDICATE ©2015 R. BOLLING -1237- JOIN THE INNER HIVE AT tomthedancingbug.com

5/4/15

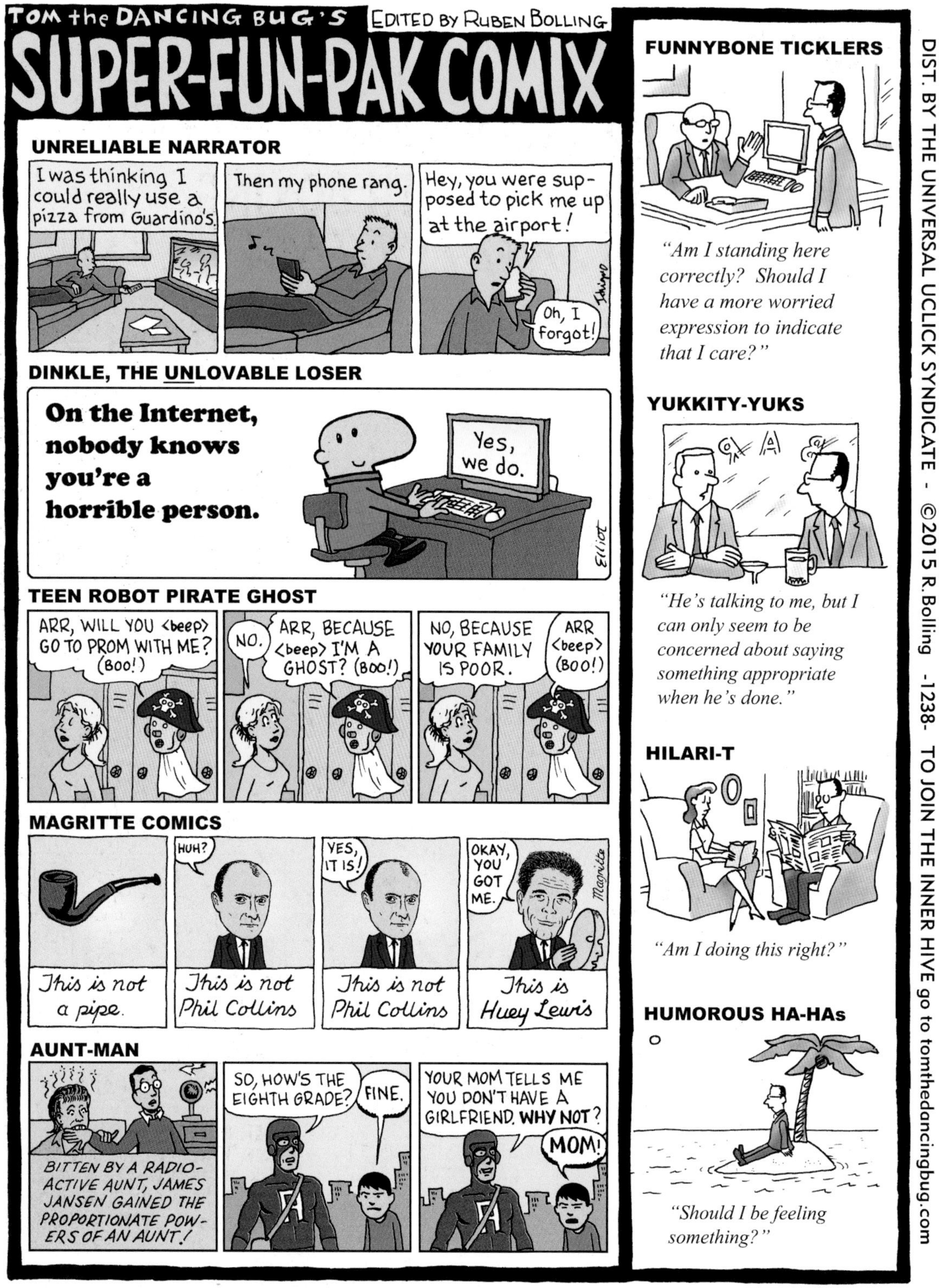
TOM the DANCING BUG'S
EDITED BY RUBEN BOLLING
SUPER-FUN-PAK COMIX
UNRELIABLE NARRATOR
I was thinking I could really use a pizza from Guardino's.
Then my phone rang.
Hey, you were supposed to pick me up at the airport!
Oh, I forgot!
DINKLE, THE UNLOVABLE LOSER
On the Internet, nobody knows you're a horrible person.
Yes, we do.
Elliot
TEEN ROBOT PIRATE GHOST
ARR, WILL YOU <beep> GO TO PROM WITH ME? (BOO!)
NO.
ARR, BECAUSE <beep> I'M A GHOST? (BOO!)
NO, BECAUSE YOUR FAMILY IS POOR.
ARR <beep> (BOO!)
MAGRITTE COMICS
This is not a pipe.
HUH?
This is not Phil Collins
YES, IT IS!
This is not Phil Collins
OKAY, YOU GOT ME.
Magritte
This is Huey Lewis
AUNT-MAN
BITTEN BY A RADIOACTIVE AUNT, JAMES JANSEN GAINED THE PROPORTIONATE POWERS OF AN AUNT!
SO, HOW'S THE EIGHTH GRADE?
FINE.
YOUR MOM TELLS ME YOU DON'T HAVE A GIRLFRIEND. WHY NOT?
MOM!
FUNNYBONE TICKLERS
"Am I standing here correctly? Should I have a more worried expression to indicate that I care?"
YUKKITY-YUKS
"He's talking to me, but I can only seem to be concerned about saying something appropriate when he's done."
HILARI-T
"Am I doing this right?"
HUMOROUS HA-HAs
"Should I be feeling something?"
DIST. BY THE UNIVERSAL UCLICK SYNDICATE - ©2015 R. Bolling -1238- TO JOIN THE INNER HIVE go to tomthedancingbug.com

5/11/15

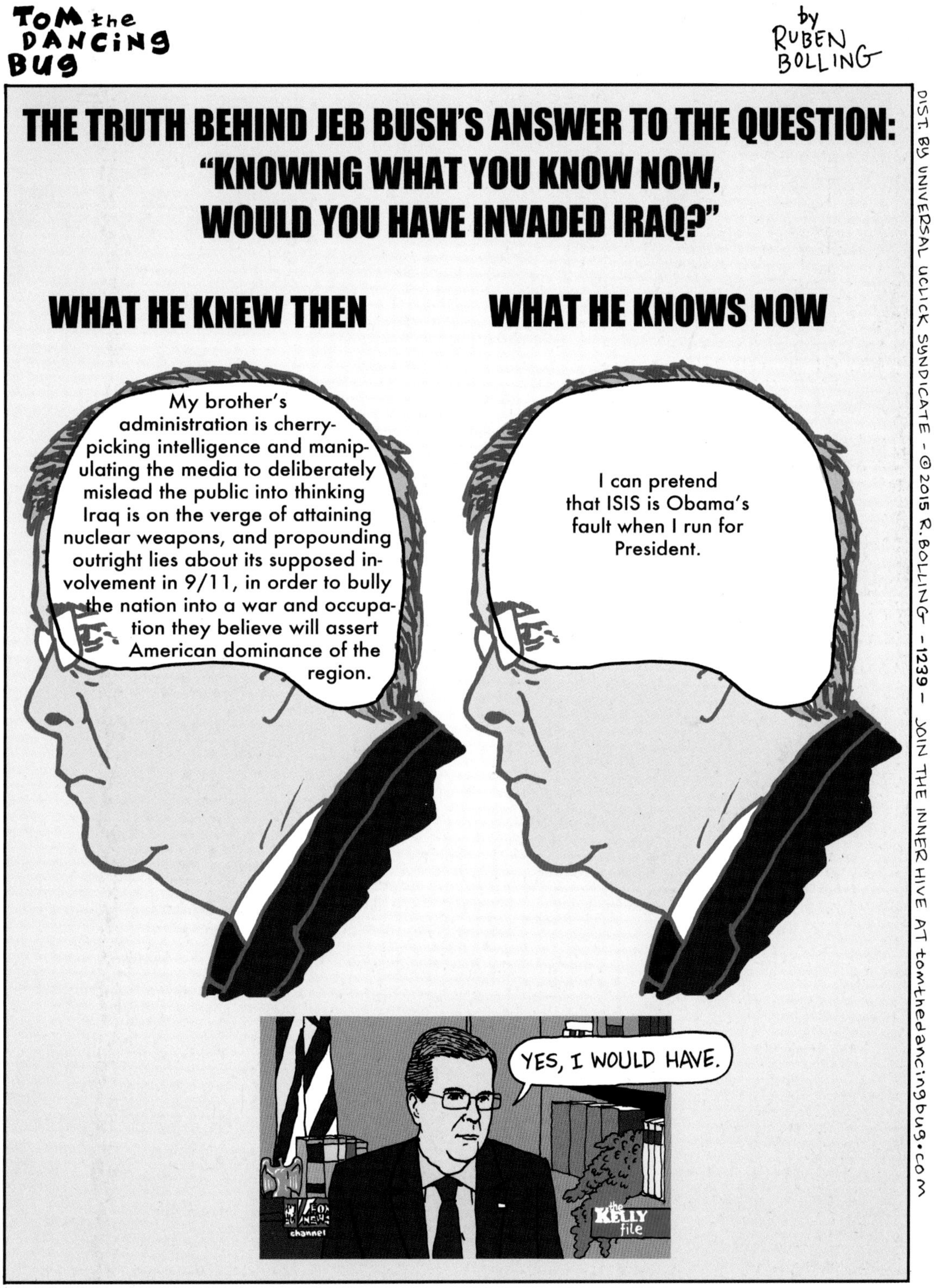

TOM the DANCING BUG
by RUBEN BOLLING
THE TRUTH BEHIND JEB BUSH'S ANSWER TO THE QUESTION: "KNOWING WHAT YOU KNOW NOW, WOULD YOU HAVE INVADED IRAQ?"
WHAT HE KNEW THEN
My brother's administration is cherry-picking intelligence and manipulating the media to deliberately mislead the public into thinking Iraq is on the verge of attaining nuclear weapons, and propounding outright lies about its supposed involvement in 9/11, in order to bully the nation into a war and occupation they believe will assert American dominance of the region.
WHAT HE KNOWS NOW
I can pretend that ISIS is Obama's fault when I run for President.
YES, I WOULD HAVE.
FOX NEWS channel
the KELLY file
DIST. BY UNIVERSAL UCLICK SYNDICATE - © 2015 R. BOLLING - 1239 - JOIN THE INNER HIVE AT tomthedancingbug.com

5/18/15

TOM the DANCING BUG

The Education of Louis

by RUBEN BOLLING

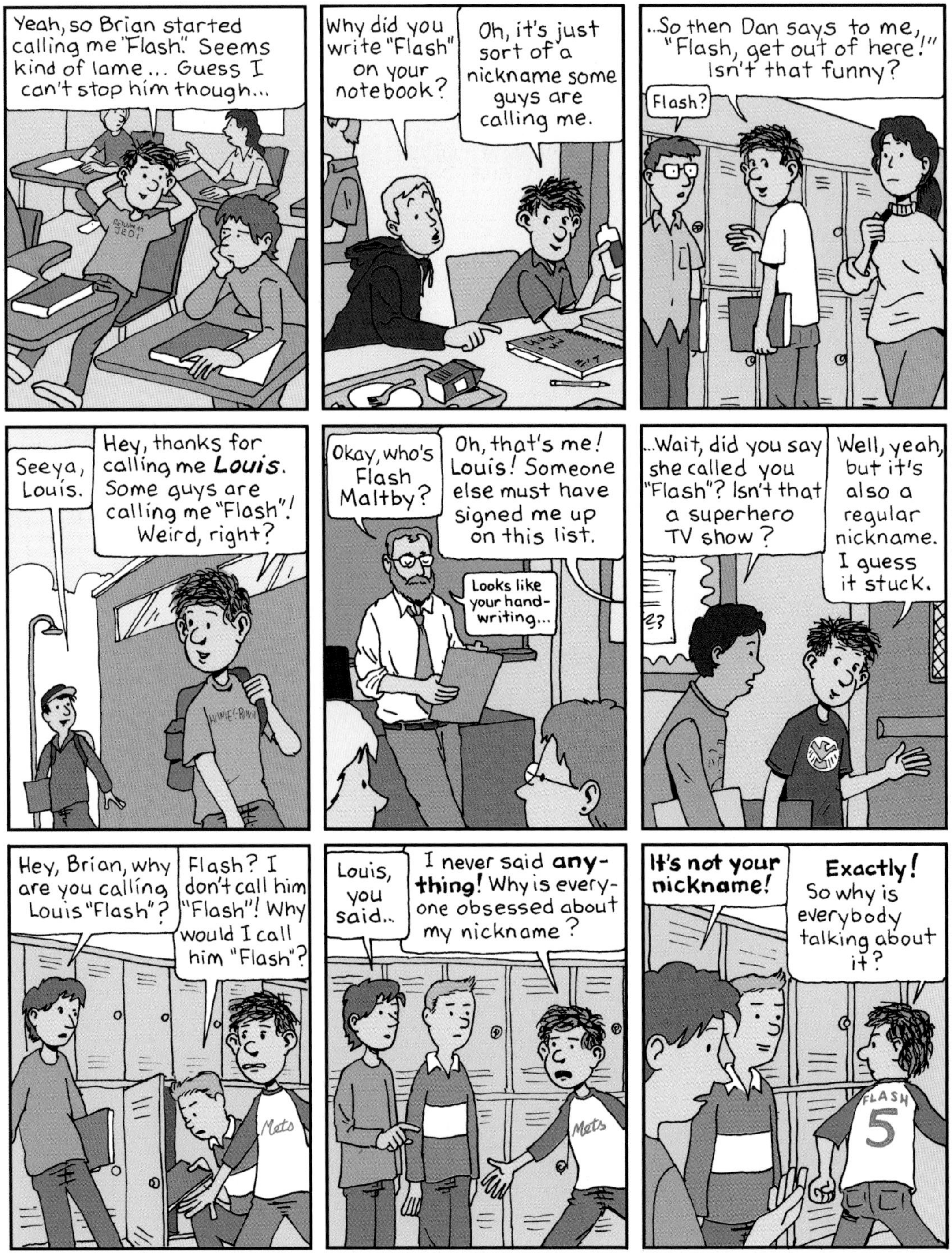

Yeah, so Brian started calling me "Flash." Seems kind of lame... Guess I can't stop him though...
Why did you write "Flash" on your notebook?
Oh, it's just sort of a nickname some guys are calling me.
...So then Dan says to me, "Flash, get out of here!" Isn't that funny?
Flash?
Seeya, Louis.
Hey, thanks for calling me **Louis**. Some guys are calling me "Flash"! Weird, right?
Okay, who's Flash Maltby?
Oh, that's me! Louis! Someone else must have signed me up on this list.
Looks like your hand-writing...
...Wait, did you say she called you "Flash"? Isn't that a superhero TV show?
Well, yeah, but it's also a regular nickname. I guess it stuck.
Hey, Brian, why are you calling Louis "Flash"?
Flash? I don't call him "Flash"! Why would I call him "Flash"?
Mets
Louis, you said..
I never said **any-thing!** Why is every-one obsessed about my nickname?
Mets
It's not your nickname!
Exactly! So why is everybody talking about it?
FLASH
5

5/25/15

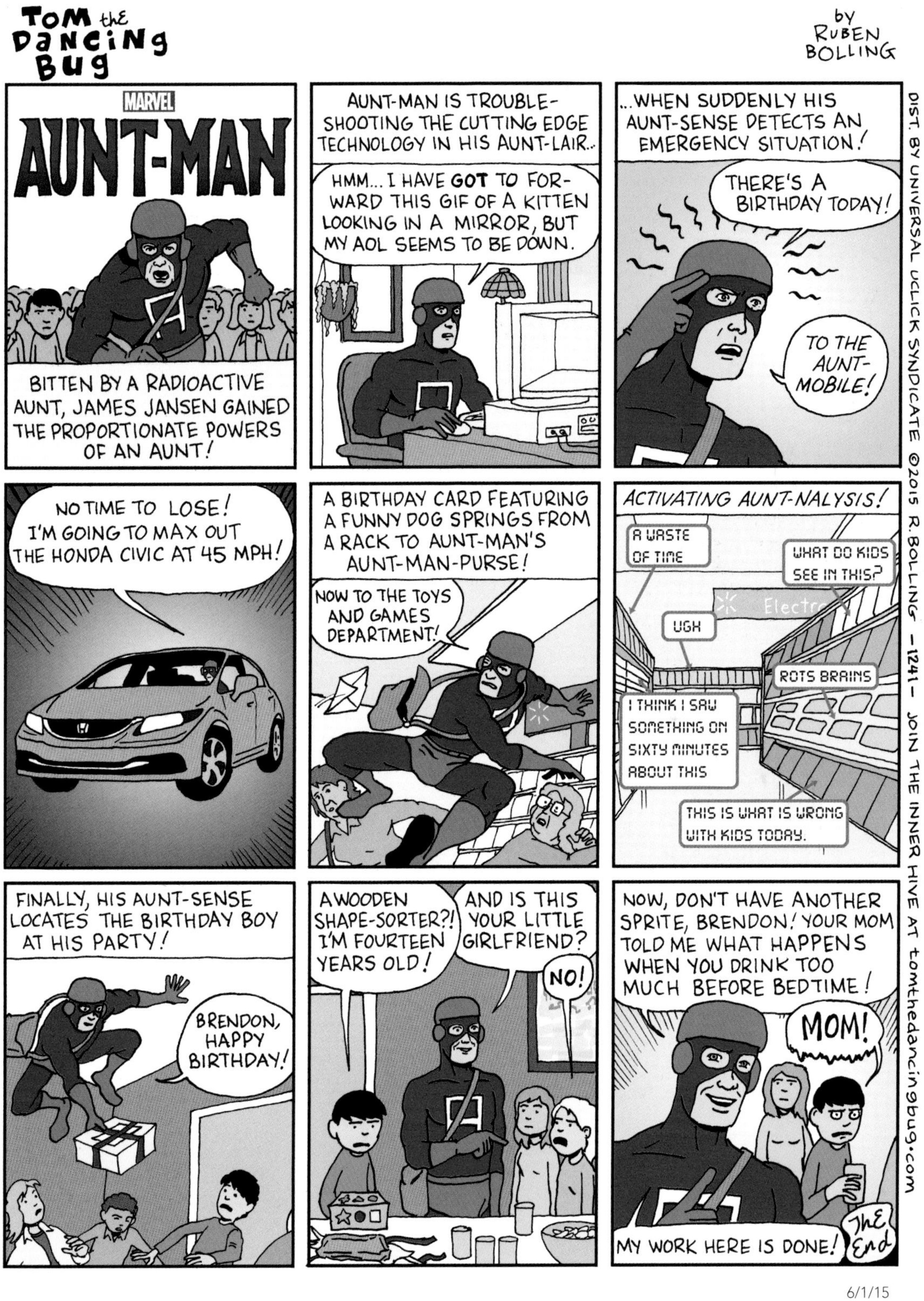
TOM the DANCING BUG
by RUBEN BOLLING
DIST. BY UNIVERSAL UCLICK SYNDICATE ©2015 R. BOLLING —1241— JOIN THE INNER HIVE AT tomthedancingbug.com
MARVEL
AUNT-MAN
BITTEN BY A RADIOACTIVE AUNT, JAMES JANSEN GAINED THE PROPORTIONATE POWERS OF AN AUNT!
AUNT-MAN IS TROUBLE-SHOOTING THE CUTTING EDGE TECHNOLOGY IN HIS AUNT-LAIR..
HMM... I HAVE GOT TO FOR-WARD THIS GIF OF A KITTEN LOOKING IN A MIRROR, BUT MY AOL SEEMS TO BE DOWN.
...WHEN SUDDENLY HIS AUNT-SENSE DETECTS AN EMERGENCY SITUATION!
THERE'S A BIRTHDAY TODAY!
TO THE AUNT-MOBILE!
NO TIME TO LOSE! I'M GOING TO MAX OUT THE HONDA CIVIC AT 45 MPH!
A BIRTHDAY CARD FEATURING A FUNNY DOG SPRINGS FROM A RACK TO AUNT-MAN'S AUNT-MAN-PURSE!
NOW TO THE TOYS AND GAMES DEPARTMENT!
ACTIVATING AUNT-NALYSIS!
A WASTE OF TIME
WHAT DO KIDS SEE IN THIS?
Electr
UGH
ROTS BRAINS
I THINK I SAW SOMETHING ON SIXTY MINUTES ABOUT THIS
THIS IS WHAT IS WRONG WITH KIDS TODAY.
FINALLY, HIS AUNT-SENSE LOCATES THE BIRTHDAY BOY AT HIS PARTY!
BRENDON, HAPPY BIRTHDAY!
A WOODEN SHAPE-SORTER?! I'M FOURTEEN YEARS OLD!
AND IS THIS YOUR LITTLE GIRLFRIEND?
NO!
NOW, DON'T HAVE ANOTHER SPRITE, BRENDON! YOUR MOM TOLD ME WHAT HAPPENS WHEN YOU DRINK TOO MUCH BEFORE BEDTIME!
MOM!
MY WORK HERE IS DONE!
THE End

6/1/15

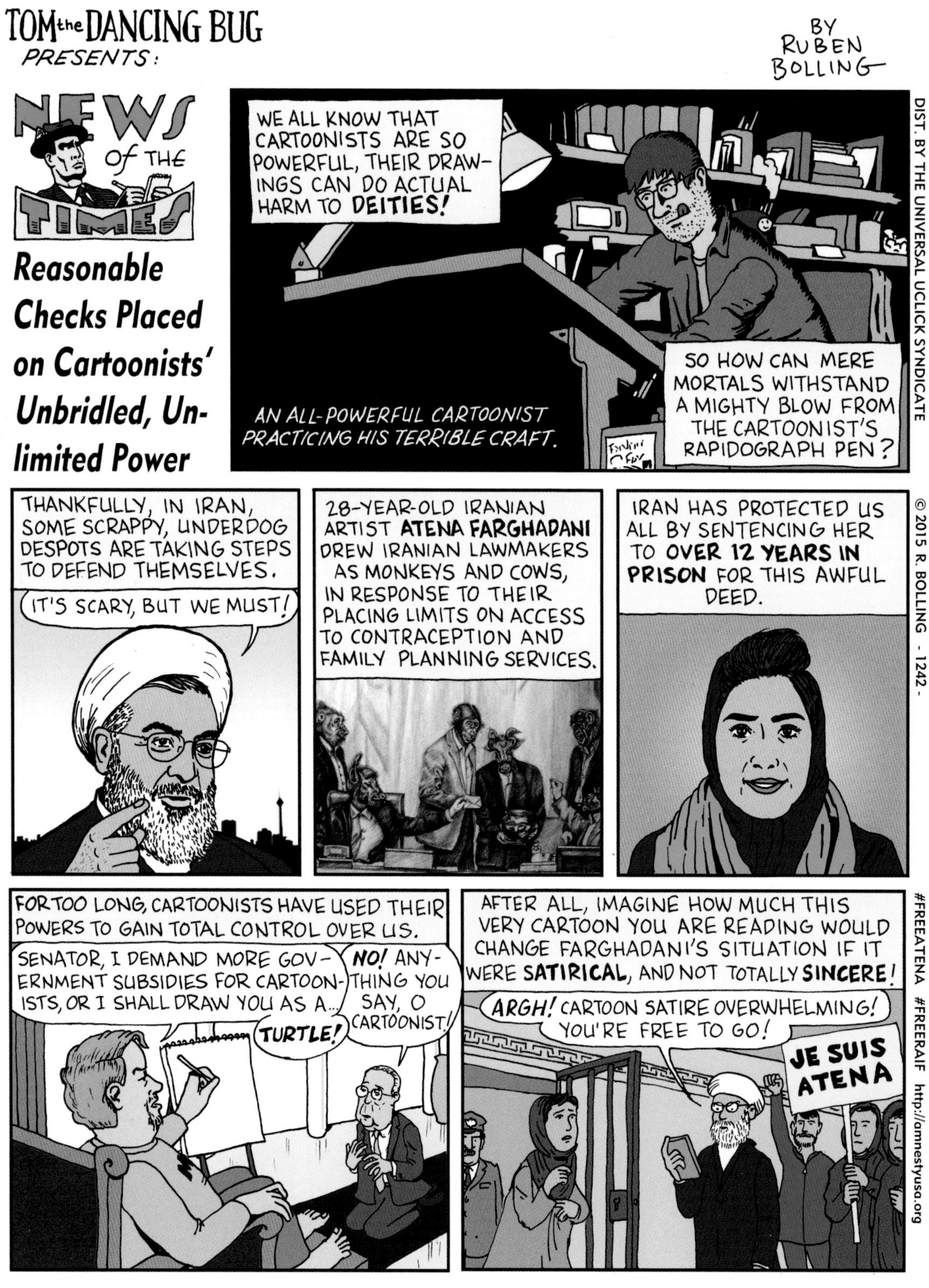
TOM the DANCING BUG PRESENTS:
BY RUBEN BOLLING
NEWS of THE TIMES
Reasonable Checks Placed on Cartoonists' Unbridled, Unlimited Power
WE ALL KNOW THAT CARTOONISTS ARE SO POWERFUL, THEIR DRAWINGS CAN DO ACTUAL HARM TO DEITIES!
SO HOW CAN MERE MORTALS WITHSTAND A MIGHTY BLOW FROM THE CARTOONIST'S RAPIDOGRAPH PEN?
AN ALL-POWERFUL CARTOONIST PRACTICING HIS TERRIBLE CRAFT.
DIST. BY THE UNIVERSAL UCLICK SYNDICATE
THANKFULLY, IN IRAN, SOME SCRAPPY, UNDERDOG DESPOTS ARE TAKING STEPS TO DEFEND THEMSELVES.
IT'S SCARY, BUT WE MUST!
28-YEAR-OLD IRANIAN ARTIST ATENA FARGHADANI DREW IRANIAN LAWMAKERS AS MONKEYS AND COWS, IN RESPONSE TO THEIR PLACING LIMITS ON ACCESS TO CONTRACEPTION AND FAMILY PLANNING SERVICES.
IRAN HAS PROTECTED US ALL BY SENTENCING HER TO OVER 12 YEARS IN PRISON FOR THIS AWFUL DEED.
© 2015 R. BOLLING - 1242 -
FOR TOO LONG, CARTOONISTS HAVE USED THEIR POWERS TO GAIN TOTAL CONTROL OVER US.
SENATOR, I DEMAND MORE GOVERNMENT SUBSIDIES FOR CARTOONISTS, OR I SHALL DRAW YOU AS A... TURTLE!
NO! ANYTHING YOU SAY, O CARTOONIST!
AFTER ALL, IMAGINE HOW MUCH THIS VERY CARTOON YOU ARE READING WOULD CHANGE FARGHADANI'S SITUATION IF IT WERE SATIRICAL, AND NOT TOTALLY SINCERE!
ARGH! CARTOON SATIRE OVERWHELMING! YOU'RE FREE TO GO!
JE SUIS ATENA
#FREEATENA #FREERAIF http://amnestyusa.org

6/8/15

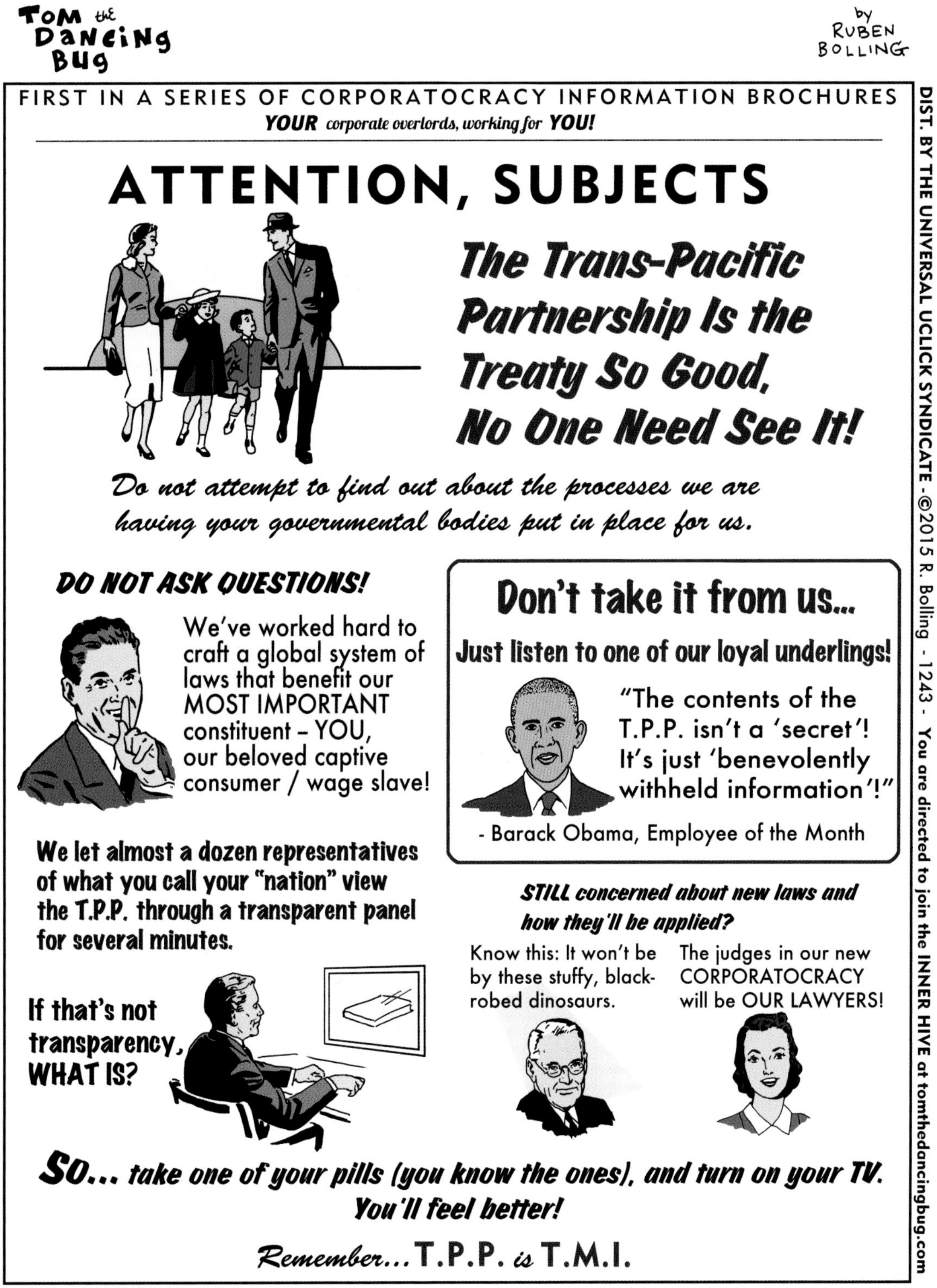

Tom the Dancing Bug
by Ruben Bolling
FIRST IN A SERIES OF CORPORATOCRACY INFORMATION BROCHURES
YOUR corporate overlords, working for YOU!
ATTENTION, SUBJECTS
The Trans-Pacific Partnership Is the Treaty So Good, No One Need See It!
Do not attempt to find out about the processes we are having your governmental bodies put in place for us.
DO NOT ASK QUESTIONS!
We've worked hard to craft a global system of laws that benefit our MOST IMPORTANT constituent – YOU, our beloved captive consumer / wage slave!
Don't take it from us...
Just listen to one of our loyal underlings!
"The contents of the T.P.P. isn't a 'secret'! It's just 'benevolently withheld information'!"
- Barack Obama, Employee of the Month
We let almost a dozen representatives of what you call your "nation" view the T.P.P. through a transparent panel for several minutes.
If that's not transparency, WHAT IS?
STILL concerned about new laws and how they'll be applied?
Know this: It won't be by these stuffy, black-robed dinosaurs.
The judges in our new CORPORATOCRACY will be OUR LAWYERS!
SO... take one of your pills (you know the ones), and turn on your TV. You'll feel better!
Remember... T.P.P. is T.M.I.
DIST. BY THE UNIVERSAL UCLICK SYNDICATE -©2015 R. Bolling - 1243 - You are directed to join the INNER HIVE at tomthedancingbug.com

6/15/15

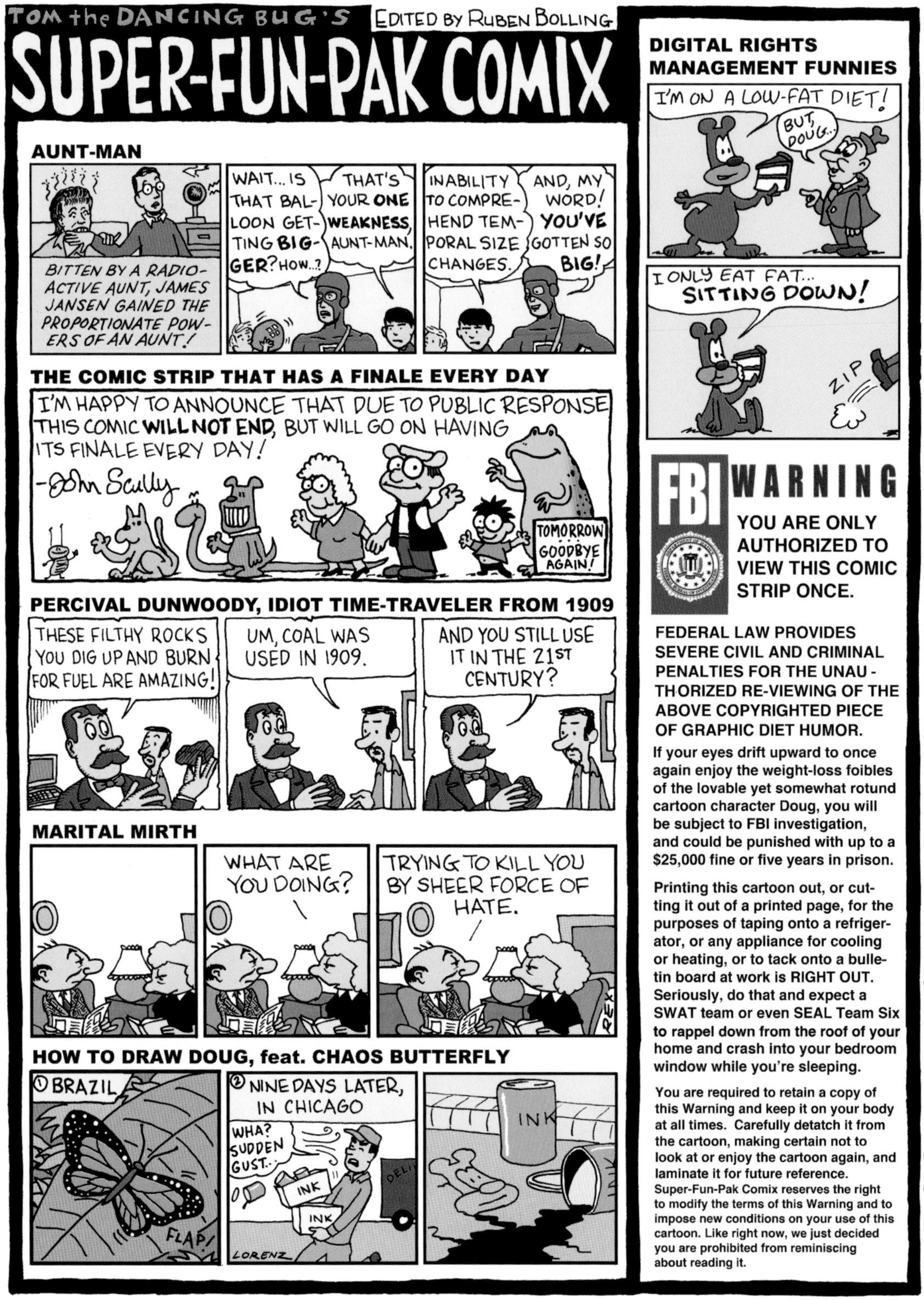
TOM the DANCING BUG'S
EDITED BY RUBEN BOLLING
SUPER-FUN-PAK COMIX
AUNT-MAN
BITTEN BY A RADIO-ACTIVE AUNT, JAMES JANSEN GAINED THE PROPORTIONATE POWERS OF AN AUNT!
WAIT... IS THAT BALLOON GETTING BIGGER? HOW..?
THAT'S YOUR ONE WEAKNESS, AUNT-MAN.
INABILITY TO COMPREHEND TEMPORAL SIZE CHANGES.
AND, MY WORD! YOU'VE GOTTEN SO BIG!
THE COMIC STRIP THAT HAS A FINALE EVERY DAY
I'M HAPPY TO ANNOUNCE THAT DUE TO PUBLIC RESPONSE THIS COMIC WILL NOT END, BUT WILL GO ON HAVING ITS FINALE EVERY DAY!
-John Scully
TOMORROW GOODBYE AGAIN!
PERCIVAL DUNWOODY, IDIOT TIME-TRAVELER FROM 1909
THESE FILTHY ROCKS YOU DIG UP AND BURN FOR FUEL ARE AMAZING!
UM, COAL WAS USED IN 1909.
AND YOU STILL USE IT IN THE 21ST CENTURY?
MARITAL MIRTH
WHAT ARE YOU DOING?
TRYING TO KILL YOU BY SHEER FORCE OF HATE.
REX
HOW TO DRAW DOUG, feat. CHAOS BUTTERFLY
① BRAZIL
FLAP!
② NINE DAYS LATER, IN CHICAGO
WHA? SUDDEN GUST..
INK
INK
LORENZ
INK
DIGITAL RIGHTS MANAGEMENT FUNNIES
I'M ON A LOW-FAT DIET!
BUT, DOUG..
I ONLY EAT FAT... SITTING DOWN!
ZIP
FBI WARNING
YOU ARE ONLY AUTHORIZED TO VIEW THIS COMIC STRIP ONCE.
FEDERAL LAW PROVIDES SEVERE CIVIL AND CRIMINAL PENALTIES FOR THE UNAU-THORIZED RE-VIEWING OF THE ABOVE COPYRIGHTED PIECE OF GRAPHIC DIET HUMOR.
If your eyes drift upward to once again enjoy the weight-loss foibles of the lovable yet somewhat rotund cartoon character Doug, you will be subject to FBI investigation, and could be punished with up to a $25,000 fine or five years in prison.
Printing this cartoon out, or cutting it out of a printed page, for the purposes of taping onto a refrigerator, or any appliance for cooling or heating, or to tack onto a bulletin board at work is RIGHT OUT. Seriously, do that and expect a SWAT team or even SEAL Team Six to rappel down from the roof of your home and crash into your bedroom window while you're sleeping.
You are required to retain a copy of this Warning and keep it on your body at all times. Carefully detatch it from the cartoon, making certain not to look at or enjoy the cartoon again, and laminate it for future reference.
Super-Fun-Pak Comix reserves the right to modify the terms of this Warning and to impose new conditions on your use of this cartoon. Like right now, we just decided you are prohibited from reminiscing about reading it.

6/22/15

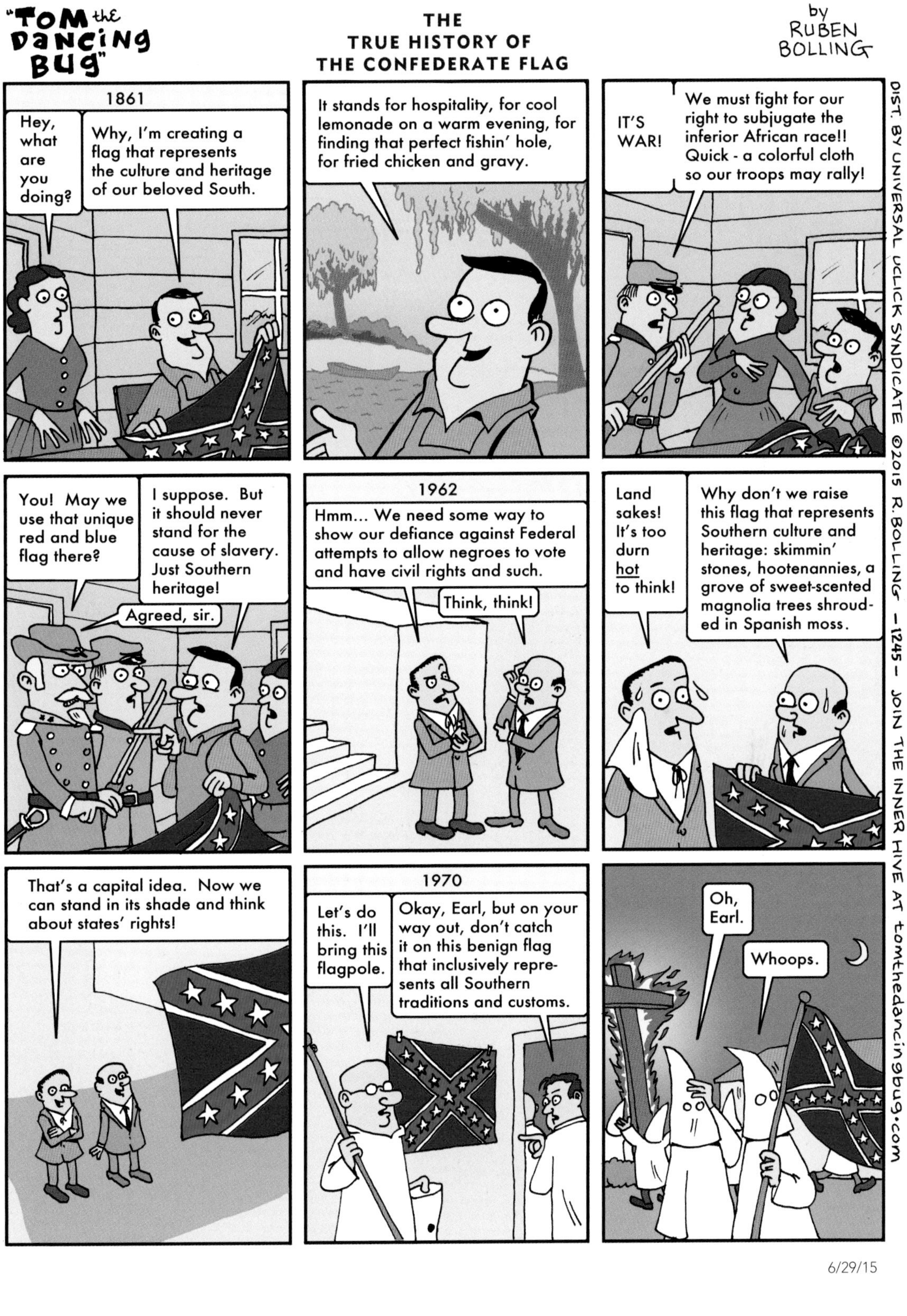
"TOM the DANCING BUG"
THE TRUE HISTORY OF THE CONFEDERATE FLAG
by RUBEN BOLLING
1861
Hey, what are you doing?
Why, I'm creating a flag that represents the culture and heritage of our beloved South.
It stands for hospitality, for cool lemonade on a warm evening, for finding that perfect fishin' hole, for fried chicken and gravy.
IT'S WAR!
We must fight for our right to subjugate the inferior African race!! Quick - a colorful cloth so our troops may rally!
You! May we use that unique red and blue flag there?
I suppose. But it should never stand for the cause of slavery. Just Southern heritage!
Agreed, sir.
1962
Hmm... We need some way to show our defiance against Federal attempts to allow negroes to vote and have civil rights and such.
Think, think!
Land sakes! It's too durn hot to think!
Why don't we raise this flag that represents Southern culture and heritage: skimmin' stones, hootenannies, a grove of sweet-scented magnolia trees shrouded in Spanish moss.
That's a capital idea. Now we can stand in its shade and think about states' rights!
1970
Let's do this. I'll bring this flagpole.
Okay, Earl, but on your way out, don't catch it on this benign flag that inclusively represents all Southern traditions and customs.
Oh, Earl.
Whoops.
DIST. BY UNIVERSAL UCLICK SYNDICATE ©2015 R. BOLLING –1245– JOIN THE INNER HIVE AT tomthedancingbug.com

6/29/15

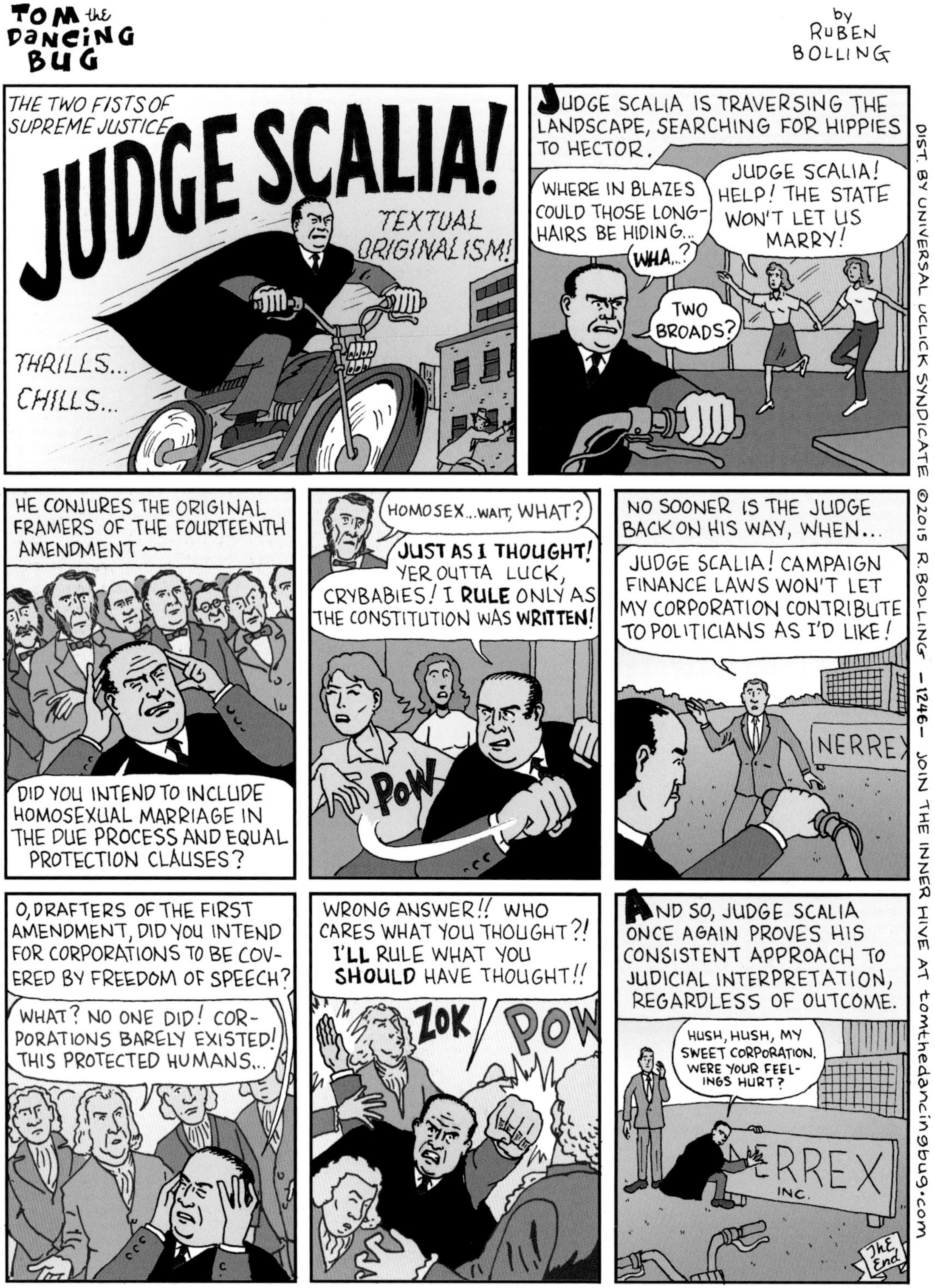
TOM the DANCING BUG
by RUBEN BOLLING
THE TWO FISTS OF SUPREME JUSTICE
JUDGE SCALIA!
TEXTUAL ORIGINALISM!
THRILLS... CHILLS...
JUDGE SCALIA IS TRAVERSING THE LANDSCAPE, SEARCHING FOR HIPPIES TO HECTOR.
WHERE IN BLAZES COULD THOSE LONG-HAIRS BE HIDING...
JUDGE SCALIA! HELP! THE STATE WON'T LET US MARRY!
WHA...?
TWO BROADS?
HE CONJURES THE ORIGINAL FRAMERS OF THE FOURTEENTH AMENDMENT—
DID YOU INTEND TO INCLUDE HOMOSEXUAL MARRIAGE IN THE DUE PROCESS AND EQUAL PROTECTION CLAUSES?
HOMOSEX...WAIT, WHAT?
JUST AS I THOUGHT! YER OUTTA LUCK, CRYBABIES! I RULE ONLY AS THE CONSTITUTION WAS WRITTEN!
POW
NO SOONER IS THE JUDGE BACK ON HIS WAY, WHEN...
JUDGE SCALIA! CAMPAIGN FINANCE LAWS WON'T LET MY CORPORATION CONTRIBUTE TO POLITICIANS AS I'D LIKE!
NERREX
O, DRAFTERS OF THE FIRST AMENDMENT, DID YOU INTEND FOR CORPORATIONS TO BE COVERED BY FREEDOM OF SPEECH?
WHAT? NO ONE DID! CORPORATIONS BARELY EXISTED! THIS PROTECTED HUMANS...
WRONG ANSWER!! WHO CARES WHAT YOU THOUGHT?! I'LL RULE WHAT YOU SHOULD HAVE THOUGHT!!
ZOK
POW
AND SO, JUDGE SCALIA ONCE AGAIN PROVES HIS CONSISTENT APPROACH TO JUDICIAL INTERPRETATION, REGARDLESS OF OUTCOME.
HUSH, HUSH, MY SWEET CORPORATION. WERE YOUR FEELINGS HURT?
ERREX INC.
THE END
DIST. BY UNIVERSAL UCLICK SYNDICATE ©2015 R. BOLLING —1246— JOIN THE INNER HIVE AT tomthedancingbug.com

7/6/15

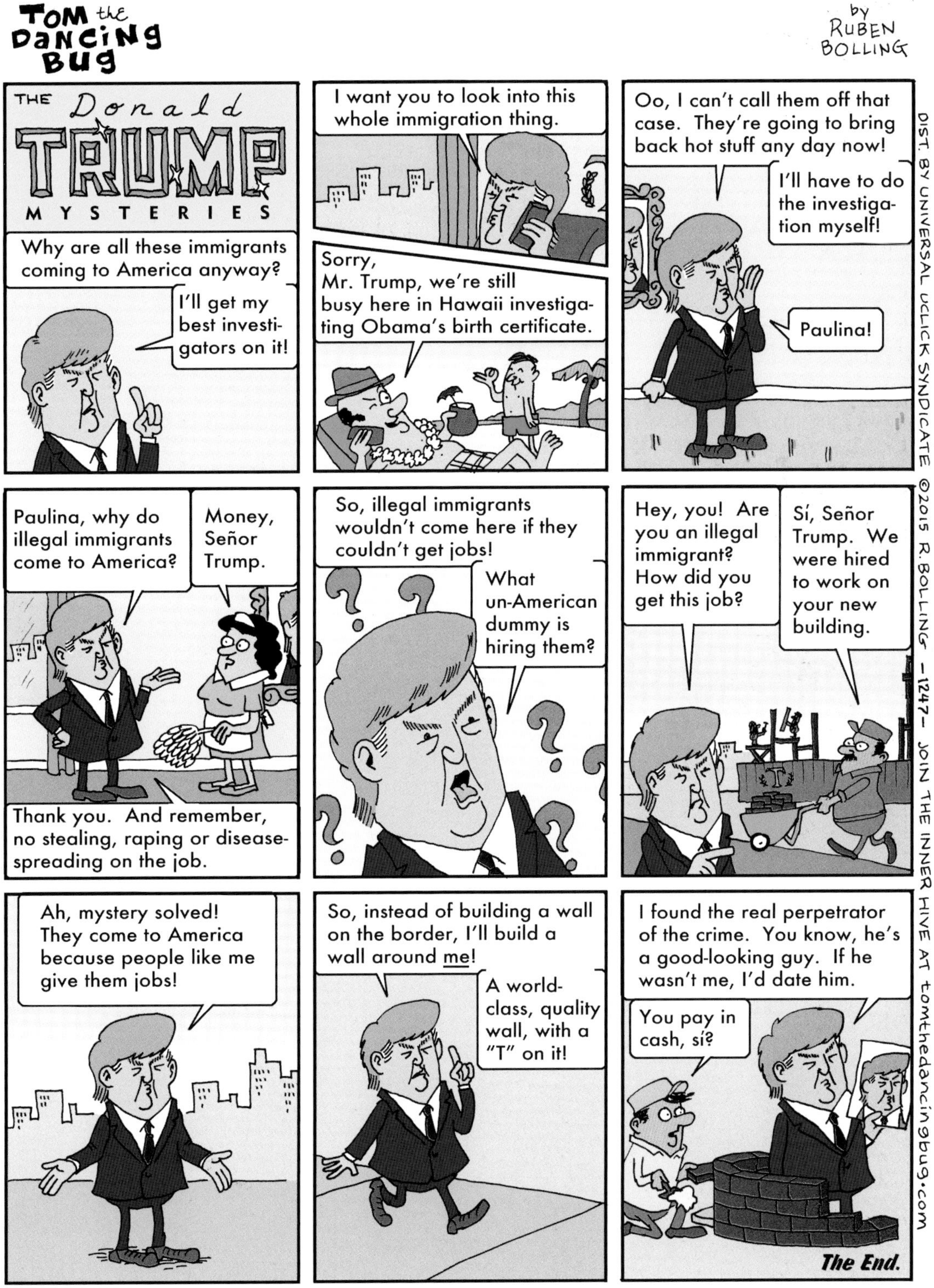

TOM the DANCING BUG
by RUBEN BOLLING
THE Donald TRUMP MYSTERIES
Why are all these immigrants coming to America anyway?
I'll get my best investigators on it!
I want you to look into this whole immigration thing.
Sorry, Mr. Trump, we're still busy here in Hawaii investigating Obama's birth certificate.
Oo, I can't call them off that case. They're going to bring back hot stuff any day now!
I'll have to do the investigation myself!
Paulina!
Paulina, why do illegal immigrants come to America?
Money, Señor Trump.
Thank you. And remember, no stealing, raping or disease-spreading on the job.
So, illegal immigrants wouldn't come here if they couldn't get jobs!
What un-American dummy is hiring them?
Hey, you! Are you an illegal immigrant? How did you get this job?
Sí, Señor Trump. We were hired to work on your new building.
Ah, mystery solved! They come to America because people like me give them jobs!
So, instead of building a wall on the border, I'll build a wall around me!
A world-class, quality wall, with a "T" on it!
I found the real perpetrator of the crime. You know, he's a good-looking guy. If he wasn't me, I'd date him.
You pay in cash, sí?
The End.
DIST. BY UNIVERSAL UCLICK SYNDICATE ©2015 R. BOLLING -1247- JOIN THE INNER HIVE AT tomthedancingbug.com

7/13/15

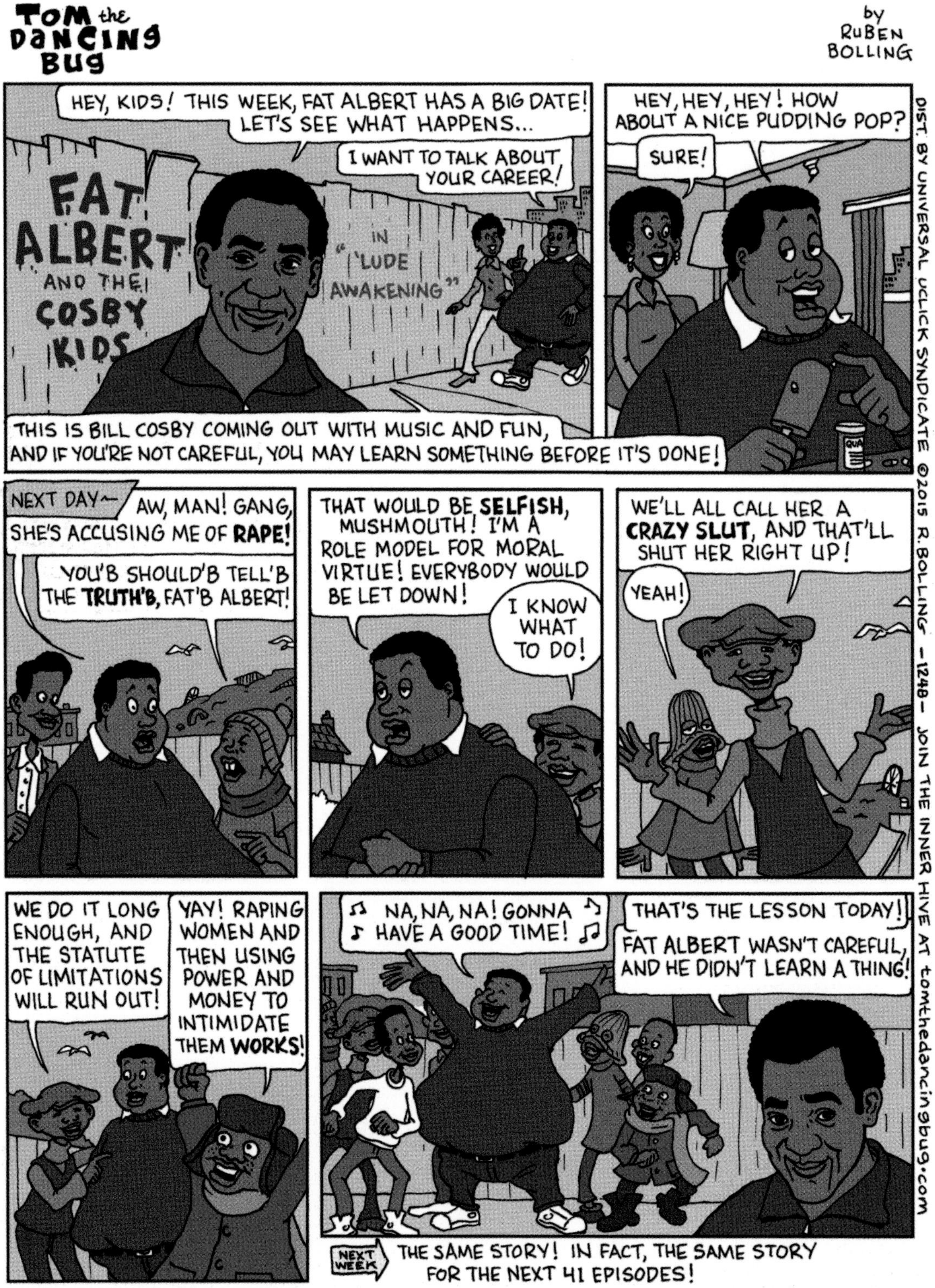
TOM the DANCING BUG
by RUBEN BOLLING
HEY, KIDS! THIS WEEK, FAT ALBERT HAS A BIG DATE! LET'S SEE WHAT HAPPENS...
FAT ALBERT AND THE COSBY KIDS
IN "'LUDE AWAKENING"
I WANT TO TALK ABOUT YOUR CAREER!
THIS IS BILL COSBY COMING OUT WITH MUSIC AND FUN, AND IF YOU'RE NOT CAREFUL, YOU MAY LEARN SOMETHING BEFORE IT'S DONE!
HEY, HEY, HEY! HOW ABOUT A NICE PUDDING POP?
SURE!
QUA
NEXT DAY~
AW, MAN! GANG, SHE'S ACCUSING ME OF **RAPE!**
YOU'B SHOULD'B TELL'B THE **TRUTH'B,** FAT'B ALBERT!
THAT WOULD BE **SELFISH,** MUSHMOUTH! I'M A ROLE MODEL FOR MORAL VIRTUE! EVERYBODY WOULD BE LET DOWN!
I KNOW WHAT TO DO!
WE'LL ALL CALL HER A **CRAZY SLUT,** AND THAT'LL SHUT HER RIGHT UP!
YEAH!
WE DO IT LONG ENOUGH, AND THE STATUTE OF LIMITATIONS WILL RUN OUT!
YAY! RAPING WOMEN AND THEN USING POWER AND MONEY TO INTIMIDATE THEM **WORKS!**
♫ NA, NA, NA! GONNA ♪ HAVE A GOOD TIME! ♫
THAT'S THE LESSON TODAY!
FAT ALBERT WASN'T CAREFUL, AND HE DIDN'T LEARN A THING!
NEXT WEEK THE SAME STORY! IN FACT, THE SAME STORY FOR THE NEXT 41 EPISODES!
DIST. BY UNIVERSAL UCLICK SYNDICATE ©2015 R. BOLLING -1248- JOIN THE INNER HIVE AT tomthedancingbug.com

7/20/15

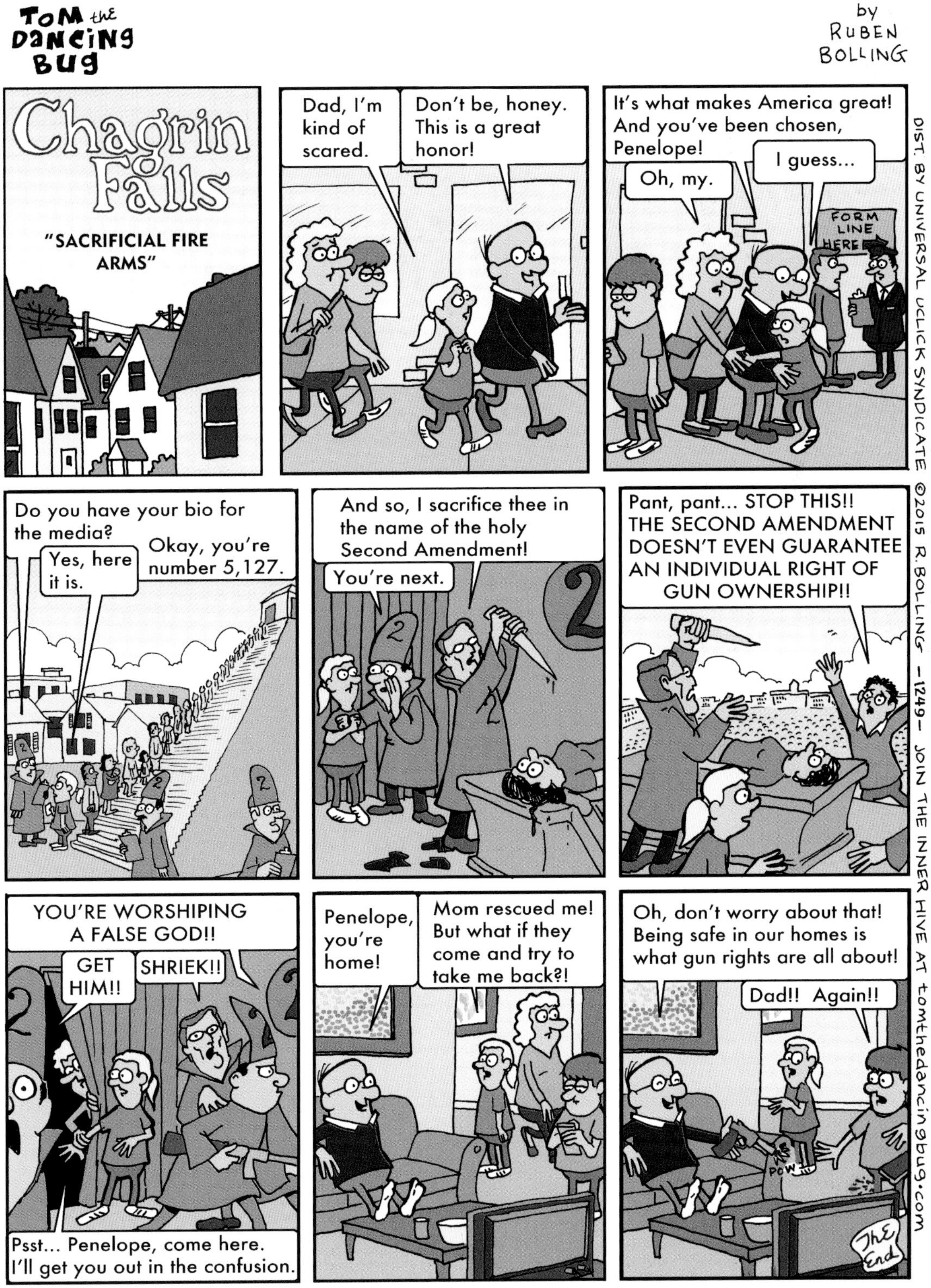
TOM the DANCING BUG
by RUBEN BOLLING
Chagrin Falls
"SACRIFICIAL FIRE ARMS"
Dad, I'm kind of scared.
Don't be, honey. This is a great honor!
It's what makes America great! And you've been chosen, Penelope!
Oh, my.
I guess...
FORM LINE HERE
Do you have your bio for the media?
Yes, here it is.
Okay, you're number 5,127.
And so, I sacrifice thee in the name of the holy Second Amendment!
You're next.
Pant, pant... STOP THIS!! THE SECOND AMENDMENT DOESN'T EVEN GUARANTEE AN INDIVIDUAL RIGHT OF GUN OWNERSHIP!!
YOU'RE WORSHIPING A FALSE GOD!!
GET HIM!!
SHRIEK!!
Psst... Penelope, come here. I'll get you out in the confusion.
Penelope, you're home!
Mom rescued me! But what if they come and try to take me back?!
Oh, don't worry about that! Being safe in our homes is what gun rights are all about!
Dad!! Again!!
POW
The End
DIST. BY UNIVERSAL UCLICK SYNDICATE ©2015 R. BOLLING —1249— JOIN THE INNER HIVE AT tomthedancingbug.com

7/27/15

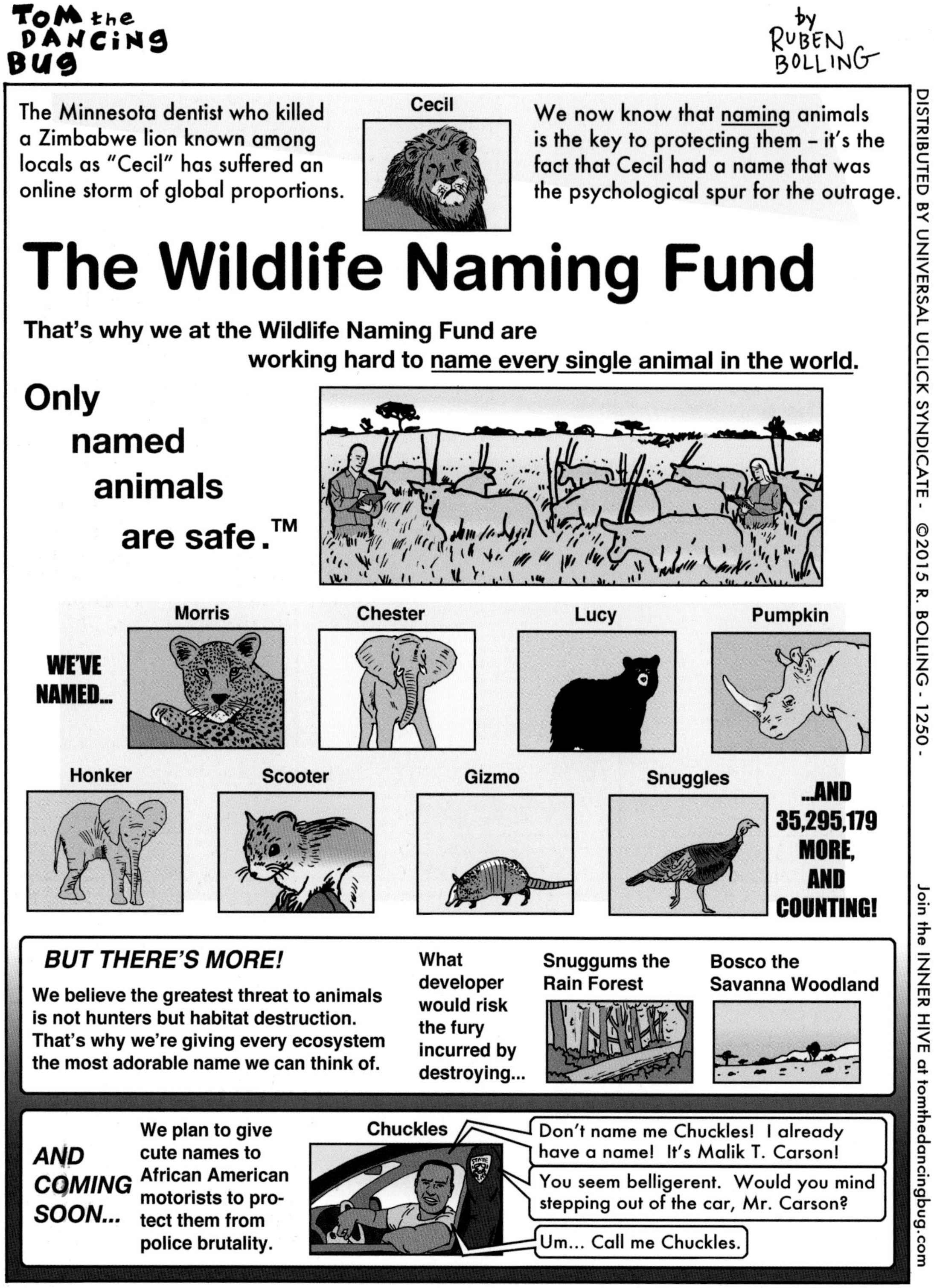
TOM the DANCING BUG
by RUBEN BOLLING
The Minnesota dentist who killed a Zimbabwe lion known among locals as "Cecil" has suffered an online storm of global proportions.
Cecil
We now know that naming animals is the key to protecting them – it's the fact that Cecil had a name that was the psychological spur for the outrage.
The Wildlife Naming Fund
That's why we at the Wildlife Naming Fund are working hard to name every single animal in the world.
Only named animals are safe.™
WE'VE NAMED...
Morris
Chester
Lucy
Pumpkin
Honker
Scooter
Gizmo
Snuggles
...AND 35,295,179 MORE, AND COUNTING!
BUT THERE'S MORE!
We believe the greatest threat to animals is not hunters but habitat destruction. That's why we're giving every ecosystem the most adorable name we can think of.
What developer would risk the fury incurred by destroying...
Snuggums the Rain Forest
Bosco the Savanna Woodland
AND COMING SOON...
We plan to give cute names to African American motorists to protect them from police brutality.
Chuckles
Don't name me Chuckles! I already have a name! It's Malik T. Carson!
You seem belligerent. Would you mind stepping out of the car, Mr. Carson?
Um... Call me Chuckles.
DISTRIBUTED BY UNIVERSAL UCLICK SYNDICATE - ©2015 R. BOLLING - 1250 -
Join the INNER HIVE at tomthedancingbug.com

8/3/15

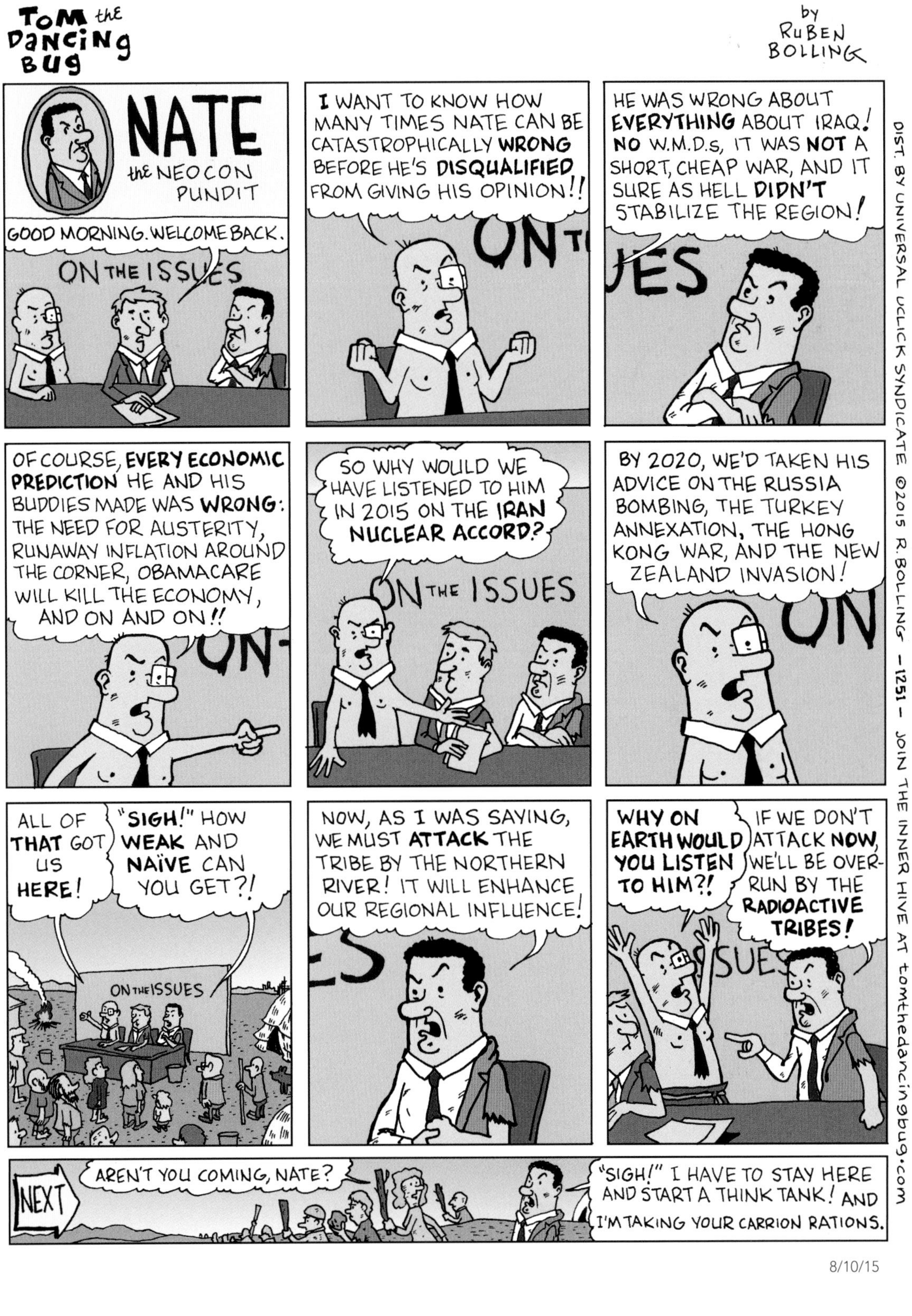
TOM the DANCING BUG
by RUBEN BOLLING
NATE the NEOCON PUNDIT
GOOD MORNING. WELCOME BACK.
ON THE ISSUES
I WANT TO KNOW HOW MANY TIMES NATE CAN BE CATASTROPHICALLY WRONG BEFORE HE'S DISQUALIFIED FROM GIVING HIS OPINION!!
HE WAS WRONG ABOUT EVERYTHING ABOUT IRAQ! NO W.M.D.s, IT WAS NOT A SHORT, CHEAP WAR, AND IT SURE AS HELL DIDN'T STABILIZE THE REGION!
OF COURSE, EVERY ECONOMIC PREDICTION HE AND HIS BUDDIES MADE WAS WRONG: THE NEED FOR AUSTERITY, RUNAWAY INFLATION AROUND THE CORNER, OBAMACARE WILL KILL THE ECONOMY, AND ON AND ON!!
SO WHY WOULD WE HAVE LISTENED TO HIM IN 2015 ON THE IRAN NUCLEAR ACCORD?
ON THE ISSUES
BY 2020, WE'D TAKEN HIS ADVICE ON THE RUSSIA BOMBING, THE TURKEY ANNEXATION, THE HONG KONG WAR, AND THE NEW ZEALAND INVASION!
ALL OF THAT GOT US HERE!
"SIGH!" HOW WEAK AND NAÏVE CAN YOU GET?!
ON THE ISSUES
NOW, AS I WAS SAYING, WE MUST ATTACK THE TRIBE BY THE NORTHERN RIVER! IT WILL ENHANCE OUR REGIONAL INFLUENCE!
WHY ON EARTH WOULD YOU LISTEN TO HIM?!
IF WE DON'T ATTACK NOW, WE'LL BE OVER-RUN BY THE RADIOACTIVE TRIBES!
NEXT
AREN'T YOU COMING, NATE?
"SIGH!" I HAVE TO STAY HERE AND START A THINK TANK! AND I'M TAKING YOUR CARRION RATIONS.
DIST. BY UNIVERSAL UCLICK SYNDICATE ©2015 R. BOLLING -1251- JOIN THE INNER HIVE AT tomthedancingbug.com

8/10/15

TOM the DANCING BUG

by RUBEN BOLLING

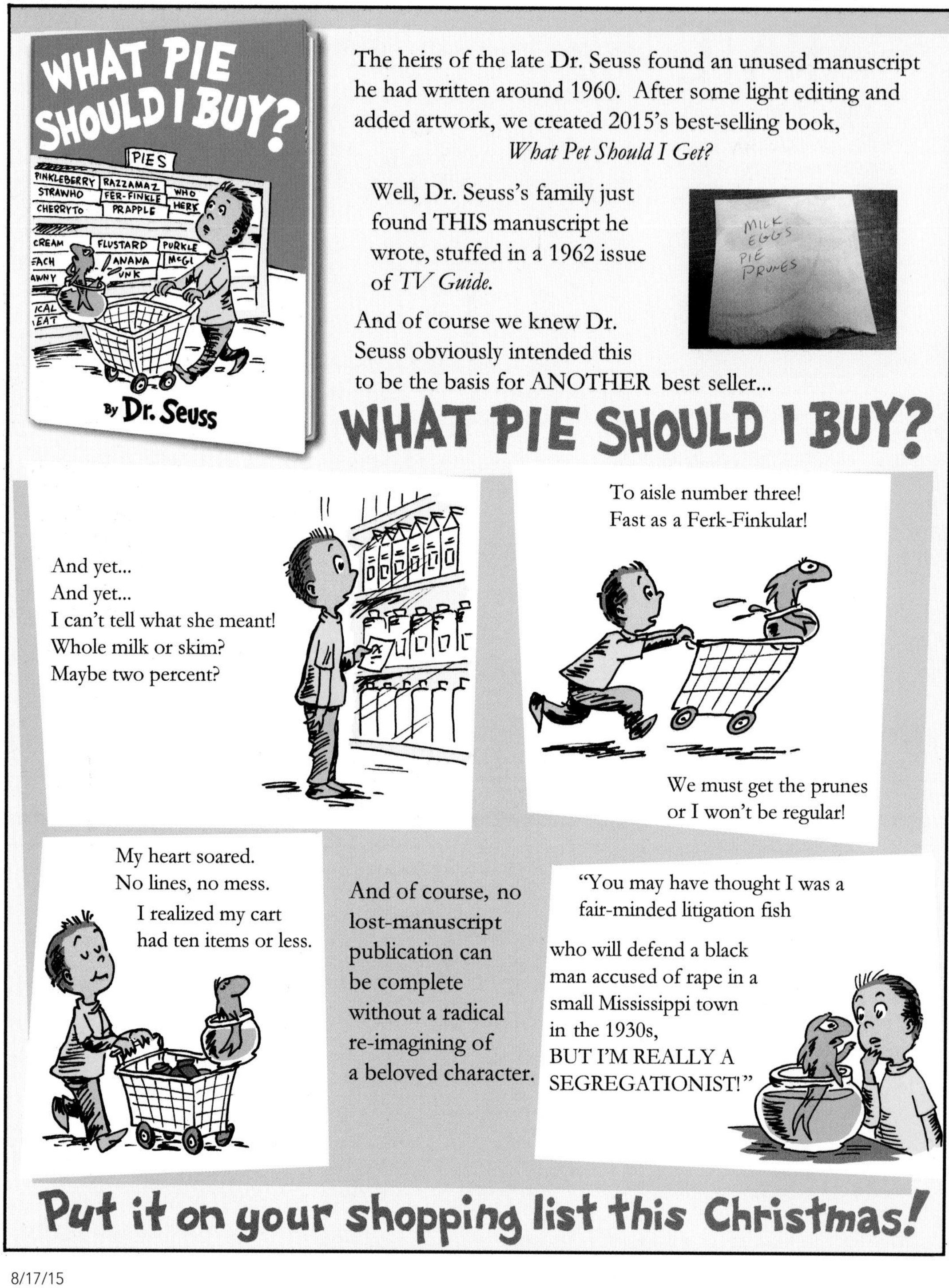
WHAT PIE SHOULD I BUY?
PIES
PINKLEBERRY
RAZZAMAZ
WHO
STRAWHO
FER-FINKLE
HERK
CHERRYTO
PRAPPLE
CREAM
FLUSTARD
PURKLE
ANANA
McGl
By Dr. Seuss
The heirs of the late Dr. Seuss found an unused manuscript he had written around 1960. After some light editing and added artwork, we created 2015's best-selling book,
What Pet Should I Get?
Well, Dr. Seuss's family just found THIS manuscript he wrote, stuffed in a 1962 issue of *TV Guide.*
MILK
EGGS
PIE
PRUNES
And of course we knew Dr. Seuss obviously intended this to be the basis for ANOTHER best seller...
WHAT PIE SHOULD I BUY?
And yet...
And yet...
I can't tell what she meant!
Whole milk or skim?
Maybe two percent?
To aisle number three!
Fast as a Ferk-Finkular!
We must get the prunes or I won't be regular!
My heart soared.
No lines, no mess.
I realized my cart had ten items or less.
And of course, no lost-manuscript publication can be complete without a radical re-imagining of a beloved character.
"You may have thought I was a fair-minded litigation fish
who will defend a black man accused of rape in a small Mississippi town in the 1930s,
BUT I'M REALLY A SEGREGATIONIST!"
Put it on your shopping list this Christmas!

8/17/15

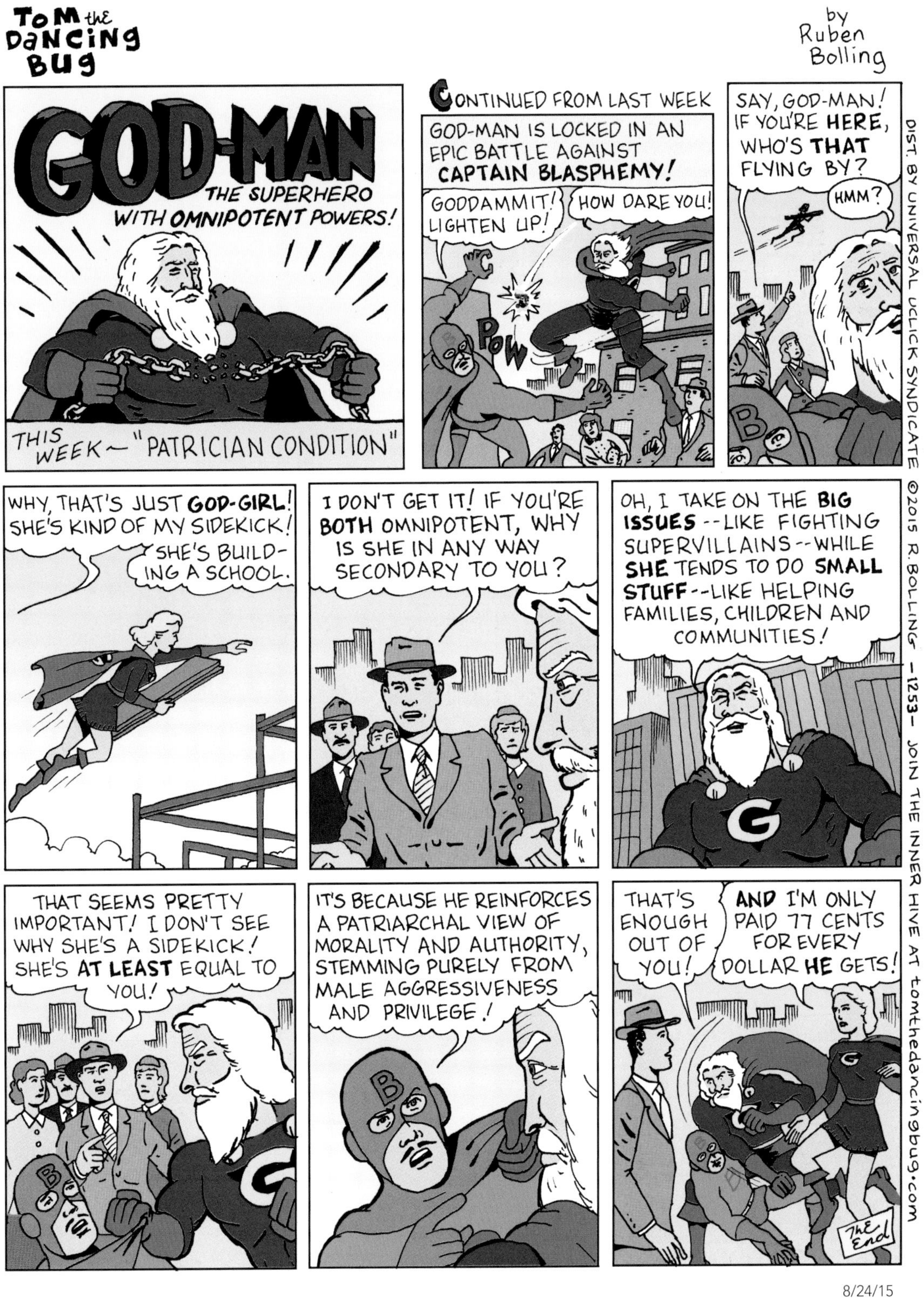
TOM the DANCING BUG
by Ruben Bolling
GOD-MAN
THE SUPERHERO WITH OMNIPOTENT POWERS!
THIS WEEK — "PATRICIAN CONDITION"
CONTINUED FROM LAST WEEK
GOD-MAN IS LOCKED IN AN EPIC BATTLE AGAINST CAPTAIN BLASPHEMY!
GODDAMMIT! LIGHTEN UP!
HOW DARE YOU!
POW
SAY, GOD-MAN! IF YOU'RE HERE, WHO'S THAT FLYING BY?
HMM?
WHY, THAT'S JUST GOD-GIRL! SHE'S KIND OF MY SIDEKICK!
SHE'S BUILDING A SCHOOL.
I DON'T GET IT! IF YOU'RE BOTH OMNIPOTENT, WHY IS SHE IN ANY WAY SECONDARY TO YOU?
OH, I TAKE ON THE BIG ISSUES --LIKE FIGHTING SUPERVILLAINS--WHILE SHE TENDS TO DO SMALL STUFF--LIKE HELPING FAMILIES, CHILDREN AND COMMUNITIES!
THAT SEEMS PRETTY IMPORTANT! I DON'T SEE WHY SHE'S A SIDEKICK! SHE'S AT LEAST EQUAL TO YOU!
IT'S BECAUSE HE REINFORCES A PATRIARCHAL VIEW OF MORALITY AND AUTHORITY, STEMMING PURELY FROM MALE AGGRESSIVENESS AND PRIVILEGE!
THAT'S ENOUGH OUT OF YOU!
AND I'M ONLY PAID 77 CENTS FOR EVERY DOLLAR HE GETS!
THE END
DIST. BY UNIVERSAL UCLICK SYNDICATE ©2015 R. BOLLING -1253- JOIN THE INNER HIVE AT tomthedancingbug.com

8/24/15

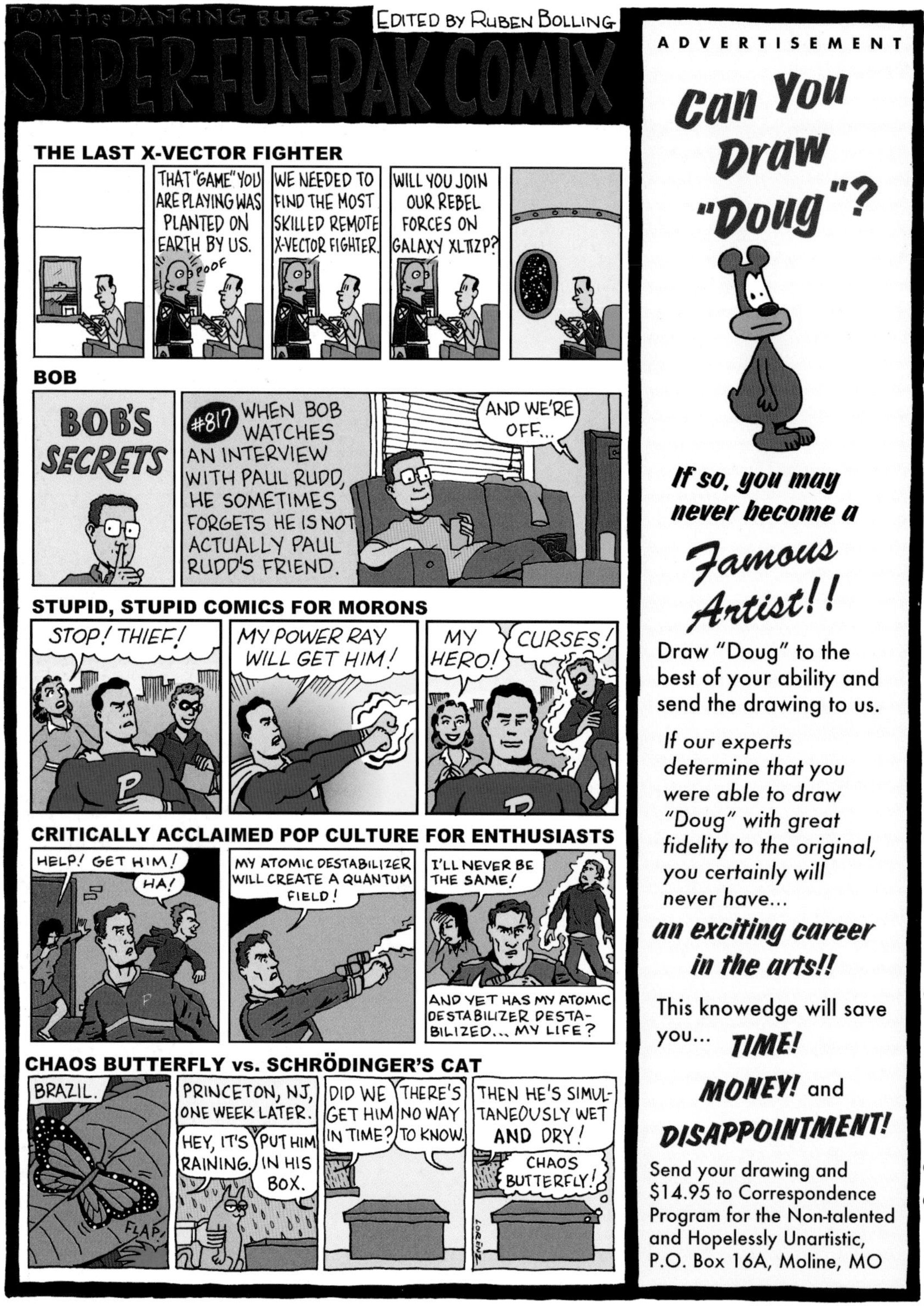
TOM the DANCING BUG'S
SUPER-FUN-PAK COMIX
EDITED BY RUBEN BOLLING
THE LAST X-VECTOR FIGHTER
THAT "GAME" YOU ARE PLAYING WAS PLANTED ON EARTH BY US.
POOF
WE NEEDED TO FIND THE MOST SKILLED REMOTE X-VECTOR FIGHTER.
WILL YOU JOIN OUR REBEL FORCES ON GALAXY XLTTZP?
BOB
BOB'S SECRETS
#817 WHEN BOB WATCHES AN INTERVIEW WITH PAUL RUDD, HE SOMETIMES FORGETS HE IS NOT ACTUALLY PAUL RUDD'S FRIEND.
AND WE'RE OFF...
STUPID, STUPID COMICS FOR MORONS
STOP! THIEF!
MY POWER RAY WILL GET HIM!
MY HERO!
CURSES!
CRITICALLY ACCLAIMED POP CULTURE FOR ENTHUSIASTS
HELP! GET HIM!
HA!
MY ATOMIC DESTABILIZER WILL CREATE A QUANTUM FIELD!
I'LL NEVER BE THE SAME!
AND YET HAS MY ATOMIC DESTABILIZER DESTA-BILIZED... MY LIFE?
CHAOS BUTTERFLY vs. SCHRÖDINGER'S CAT
BRAZIL.
FLAP
PRINCETON, NJ, ONE WEEK LATER.
HEY, IT'S RAINING.
PUT HIM IN HIS BOX.
DID WE GET HIM IN TIME?
THERE'S NO WAY TO KNOW.
THEN HE'S SIMUL-TANEOUSLY WET AND DRY!
CHAOS BUTTERFLY!
LORENZ
ADVERTISEMENT
Can You Draw "Doug"?
If so, you may never become a Famous Artist!!
Draw "Doug" to the best of your ability and send the drawing to us.
If our experts determine that you were able to draw "Doug" with great fidelity to the original, you certainly will never have...
an exciting career in the arts!!
This knowedge will save you... TIME! MONEY! and DISAPPOINTMENT!
Send your drawing and $14.95 to Correspondence Program for the Non-talented and Hopelessly Unartistic, P.O. Box 16A, Moline, MO

9/7/15

TOM the DANCING BUG

by RUBEN BOLLING

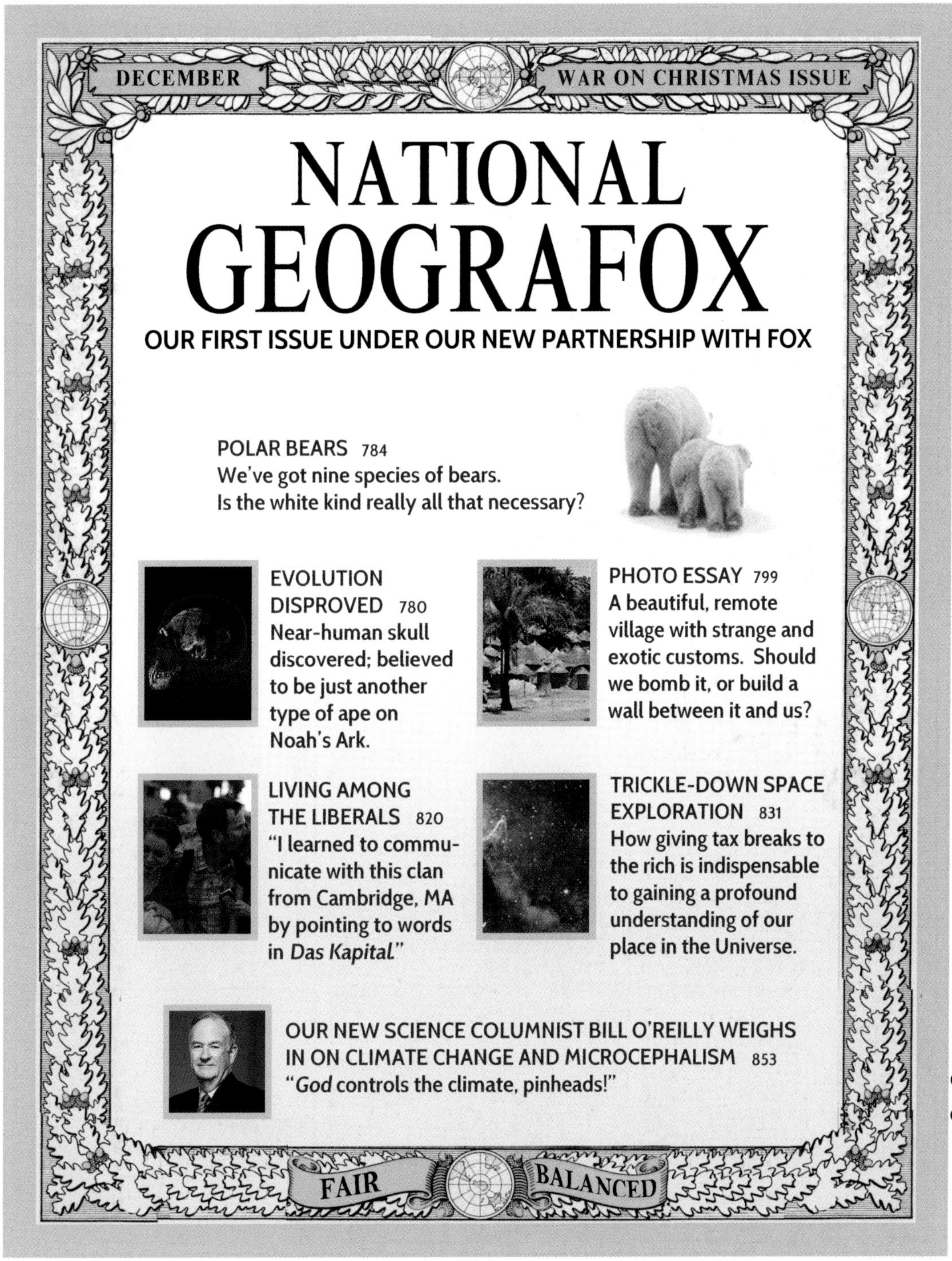
DECEMBER
WAR ON CHRISTMAS ISSUE
NATIONAL GEOGRAFOX
OUR FIRST ISSUE UNDER OUR NEW PARTNERSHIP WITH FOX
POLAR BEARS 784
We've got nine species of bears.
Is the white kind really all that necessary?
EVOLUTION DISPROVED 780
Near-human skull discovered; believed to be just another type of ape on Noah's Ark.
PHOTO ESSAY 799
A beautiful, remote village with strange and exotic customs. Should we bomb it, or build a wall between it and us?
LIVING AMONG THE LIBERALS 820
"I learned to communicate with this clan from Cambridge, MA by pointing to words in *Das Kapital*."
TRICKLE-DOWN SPACE EXPLORATION 831
How giving tax breaks to the rich is indispensable to gaining a profound understanding of our place in the Universe.
OUR NEW SCIENCE COLUMNIST BILL O'REILLY WEIGHS IN ON CLIMATE CHANGE AND MICROCEPHALISM 853
"*God* controls the climate, pinheads!"
FAIR
BALANCED

9/14/15

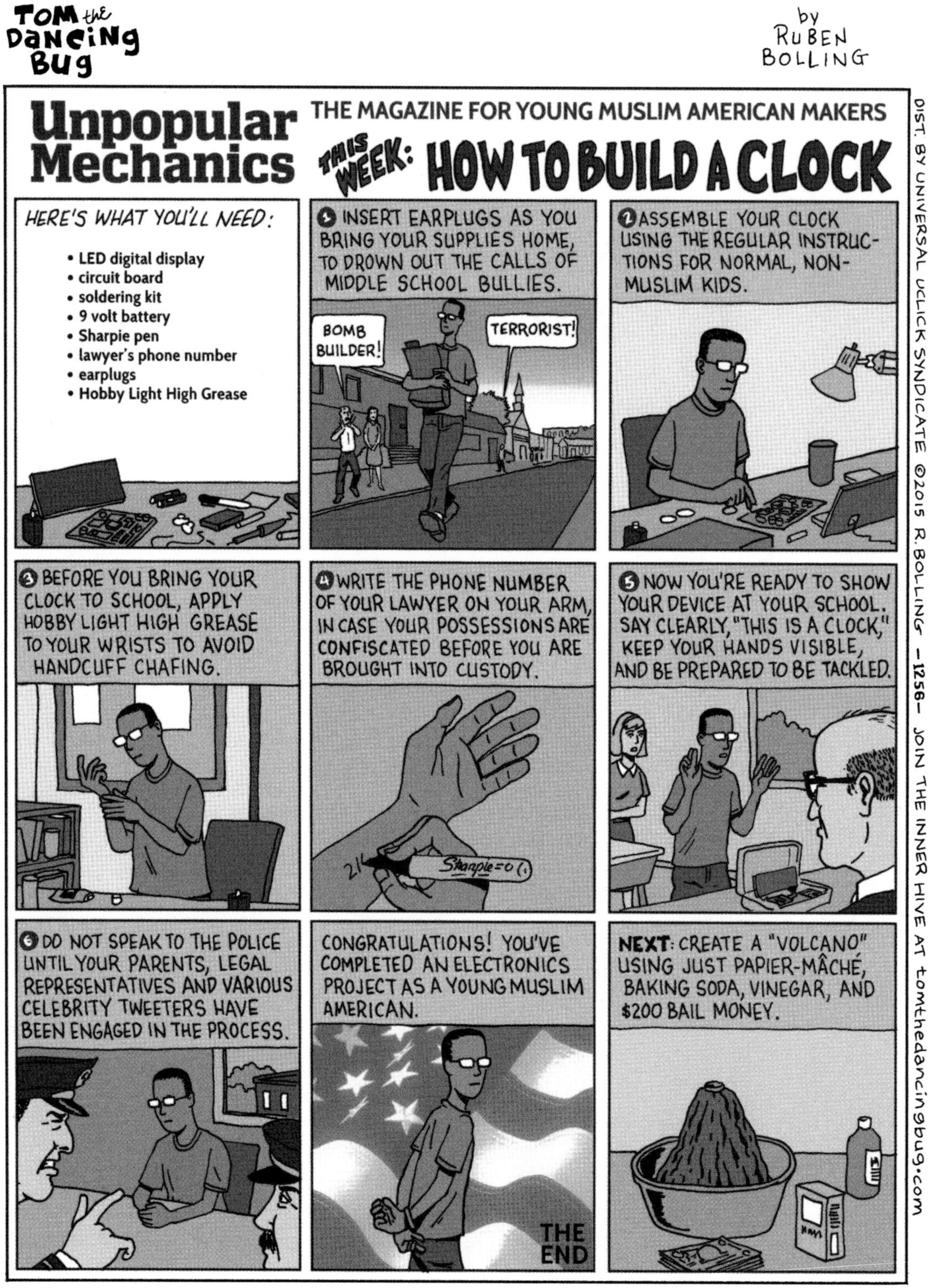
TOM the DANCING BUG
by RUBEN BOLLING
Unpopular Mechanics
THE MAGAZINE FOR YOUNG MUSLIM AMERICAN MAKERS
THIS WEEK: HOW TO BUILD A CLOCK
HERE'S WHAT YOU'LL NEED:
• LED digital display
• circuit board
• soldering kit
• 9 volt battery
• Sharpie pen
• lawyer's phone number
• earplugs
• Hobby Light High Grease
1 INSERT EARPLUGS AS YOU BRING YOUR SUPPLIES HOME, TO DROWN OUT THE CALLS OF MIDDLE SCHOOL BULLIES.
BOMB BUILDER!
TERRORIST!
2 ASSEMBLE YOUR CLOCK USING THE REGULAR INSTRUCTIONS FOR NORMAL, NON-MUSLIM KIDS.
3 BEFORE YOU BRING YOUR CLOCK TO SCHOOL, APPLY HOBBY LIGHT HIGH GREASE TO YOUR WRISTS TO AVOID HANDCUFF CHAFING.
4 WRITE THE PHONE NUMBER OF YOUR LAWYER ON YOUR ARM, IN CASE YOUR POSSESSIONS ARE CONFISCATED BEFORE YOU ARE BROUGHT INTO CUSTODY.
Sharpie
5 NOW YOU'RE READY TO SHOW YOUR DEVICE AT YOUR SCHOOL. SAY CLEARLY, "THIS IS A CLOCK," KEEP YOUR HANDS VISIBLE, AND BE PREPARED TO BE TACKLED.
6 DO NOT SPEAK TO THE POLICE UNTIL YOUR PARENTS, LEGAL REPRESENTATIVES AND VARIOUS CELEBRITY TWEETERS HAVE BEEN ENGAGED IN THE PROCESS.
CONGRATULATIONS! YOU'VE COMPLETED AN ELECTRONICS PROJECT AS A YOUNG MUSLIM AMERICAN.
THE END
NEXT: CREATE A "VOLCANO" USING JUST PAPIER-MÂCHÉ, BAKING SODA, VINEGAR, AND $200 BAIL MONEY.
DIST. BY UNIVERSAL UCLICK SYNDICATE ©2015 R. BOLLING -1256- JOIN THE INNER HIVE AT tomthedancingbug.com

9/21/15

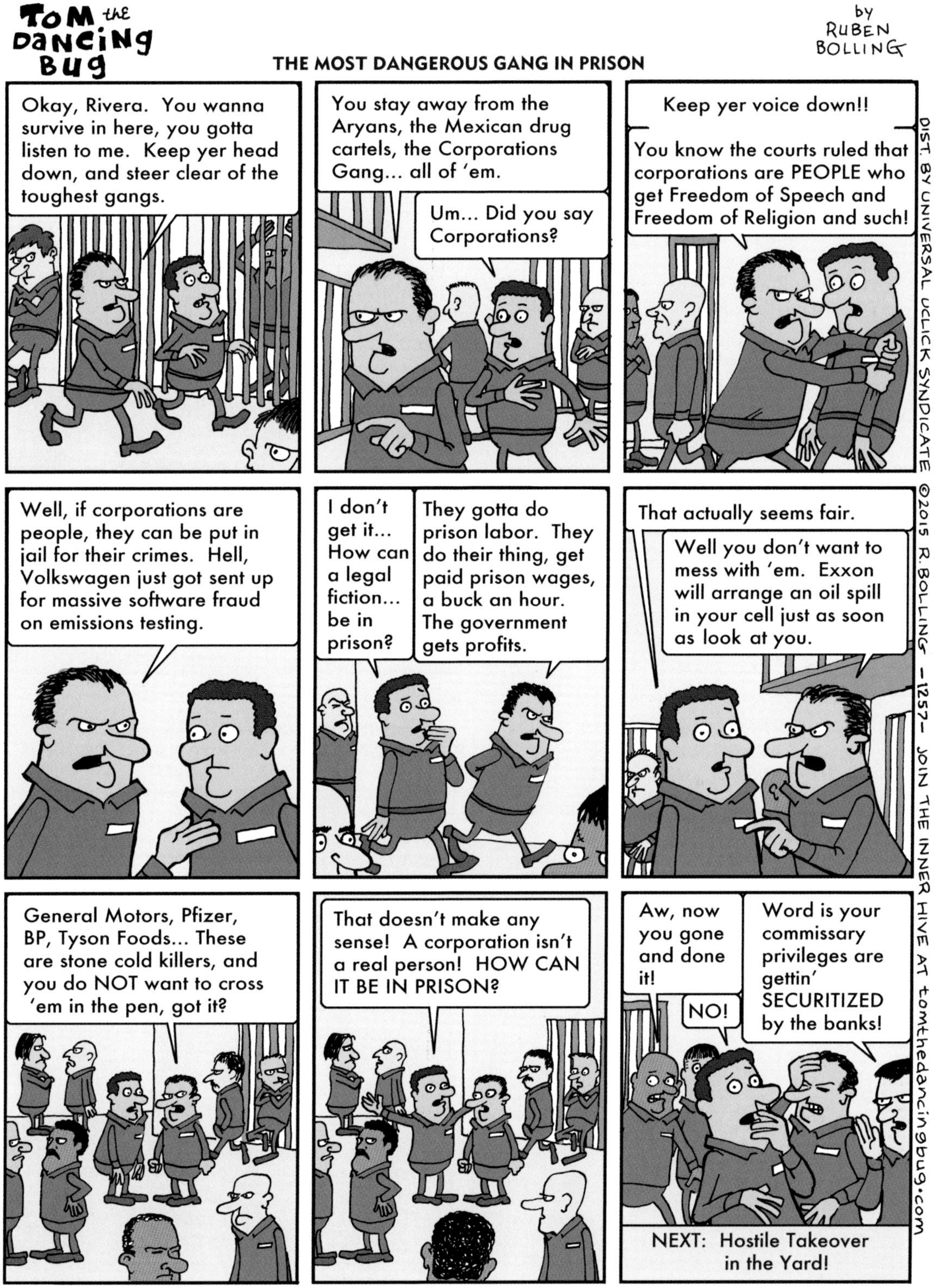
TOM the DANCING BUG
by RUBEN BOLLING
THE MOST DANGEROUS GANG IN PRISON
Okay, Rivera. You wanna survive in here, you gotta listen to me. Keep yer head down, and steer clear of the toughest gangs.
You stay away from the Aryans, the Mexican drug cartels, the Corporations Gang... all of 'em.
Um... Did you say Corporations?
Keep yer voice down!!
You know the courts ruled that corporations are PEOPLE who get Freedom of Speech and Freedom of Religion and such!
Well, if corporations are people, they can be put in jail for their crimes. Hell, Volkswagen just got sent up for massive software fraud on emissions testing.
I don't get it... How can a legal fiction... be in prison?
They gotta do prison labor. They do their thing, get paid prison wages, a buck an hour. The government gets profits.
That actually seems fair.
Well you don't want to mess with 'em. Exxon will arrange an oil spill in your cell just as soon as look at you.
General Motors, Pfizer, BP, Tyson Foods... These are stone cold killers, and you do NOT want to cross 'em in the pen, got it?
That doesn't make any sense! A corporation isn't a real person! HOW CAN IT BE IN PRISON?
Aw, now you gone and done it!
NO!
Word is your commissary privileges are gettin' SECURITIZED by the banks!
NEXT: Hostile Takeover in the Yard!
DIST. BY UNIVERSAL UCLICK SYNDICATE ©2015 R. BOLLING -1257- JOIN THE INNER HIVE AT tomthedancingbug.com

9/28/15

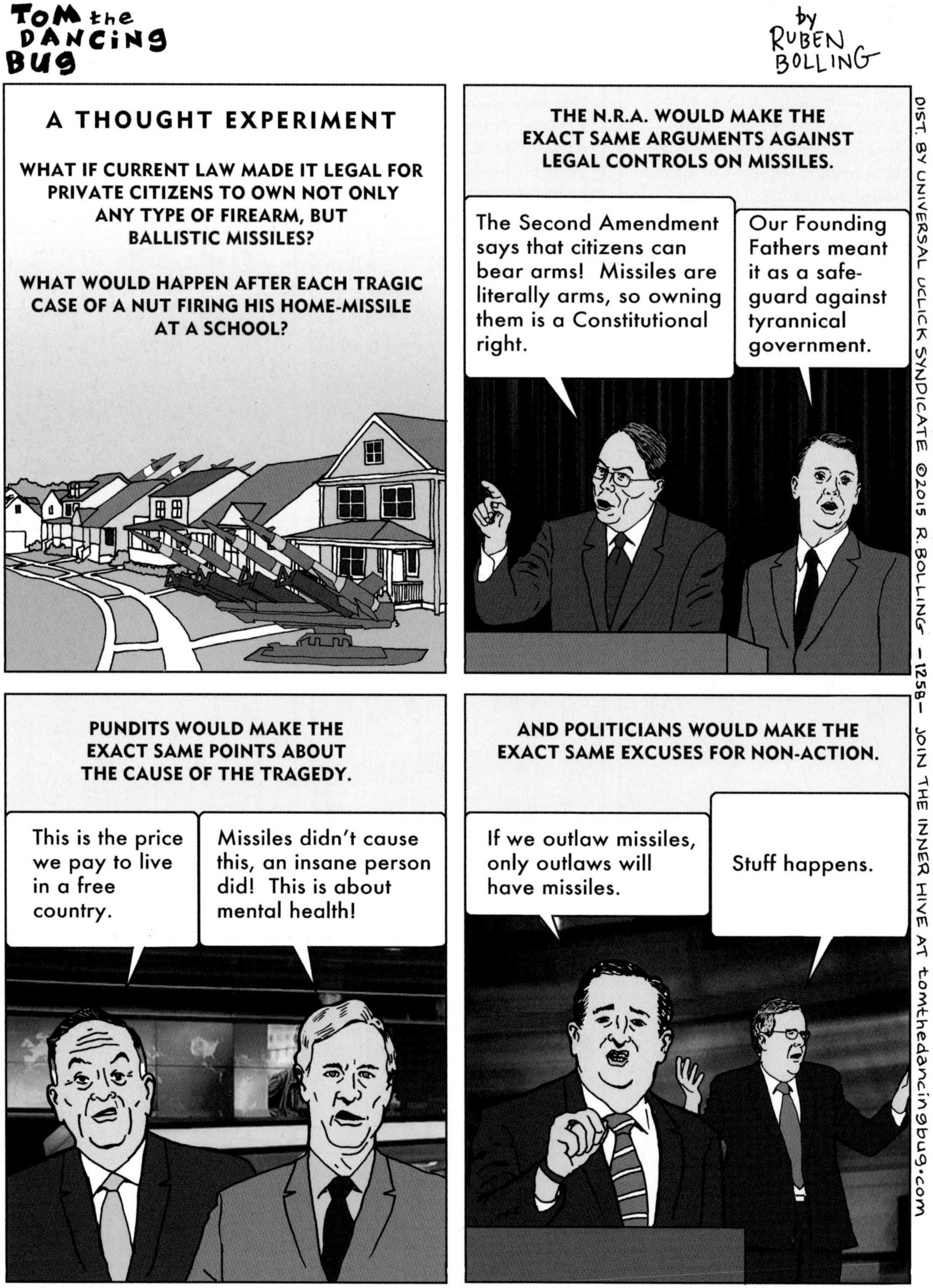
TOM the DANCING BUG
by RUBEN BOLLING
A THOUGHT EXPERIMENT
WHAT IF CURRENT LAW MADE IT LEGAL FOR PRIVATE CITIZENS TO OWN NOT ONLY ANY TYPE OF FIREARM, BUT BALLISTIC MISSILES?
WHAT WOULD HAPPEN AFTER EACH TRAGIC CASE OF A NUT FIRING HIS HOME-MISSILE AT A SCHOOL?
THE N.R.A. WOULD MAKE THE EXACT SAME ARGUMENTS AGAINST LEGAL CONTROLS ON MISSILES.
The Second Amendment says that citizens can bear arms! Missiles are literally arms, so owning them is a Constitutional right.
Our Founding Fathers meant it as a safeguard against tyrannical government.
PUNDITS WOULD MAKE THE EXACT SAME POINTS ABOUT THE CAUSE OF THE TRAGEDY.
This is the price we pay to live in a free country.
Missiles didn't cause this, an insane person did! This is about mental health!
AND POLITICIANS WOULD MAKE THE EXACT SAME EXCUSES FOR NON-ACTION.
If we outlaw missiles, only outlaws will have missiles.
Stuff happens.
DIST. BY UNIVERSAL UCLICK SYNDICATE ©2015 R. BOLLING —1258— JOIN THE INNER HIVE AT tomthedancingbug.com

10/5/15

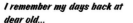

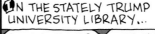

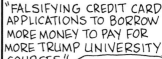

TOM the DANCING BUG
by RUBEN BOLLING
I remember my days back at dear old...
TRUMP UNIVERSITY
DONALD TRUMP'S AKKREDITED* UNIVERSITY
*"Akkredited" = non-accredited and currently under investigation
IN THE STATELY TRUMP UNIVERSITY LIBRARY...
SO, I INCLUDE "PROJECTED INCOME" TO GET APPROVED? THIS IS HARD!
HEY, I'M STUDYING THAT TOO! WHAT'S YOUR MAJOR?
"FALSIFYING CREDIT CARD APPLICATIONS TO BORROW MORE MONEY TO PAY FOR MORE TRUMP UNIVERSITY COURSES."
MINE TOO. IT'S KINDA THE ONLY MAJOR HERE.
GUYS! I JUST HAD MY MEETING WITH DONALD TRUMP!
AWESOME! HOW'D IT GO?
GREAT! IN FACT, HE AGREED TO GO GET SOME BREWS WITH ME!
WAIT, THAT'S NOT DONALD TRUMP! IT'S A CARDBOARD CUTOUT!
HUH. WELL, AT LEAST I GOT A NICE PHOTO OF ME WITH IT!
RIGHTEOUS.
BROS, I'M STARTING TO FIGURE SOMETHING OUT...
TRUMP UNIVERSITY ISN'T AN INSTITUTION OF HIGHER LEARNING! IT'S A FRAUDULENT SCHEME!
OH, NO!
WAIT'LL MY PARENTS FIND OUT!
WELL, I HOPE THAT DOESN'T BECOME AN OBSTACLE FOR TRUMP EVENTUALLY RUNNING FOR PRESIDENT OF THE U.S.!
ARE YOU KIDDING? EXPERIENCE RUNNING A LONG CON WOULD BE AN ASSET!
GO TRUMP U!
YOU KNOW, TRUMP U. IS CONSIDERED "THE HARVARD OF RICO VIOLATORS"!
THE END
DIST. BY UNIVERSAL UCLICK SYNDICATE ©2015 R. BOLLING -1259- JOIN THE INNER HIVE AT tomthedancingbug.com

10/12/15

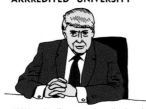

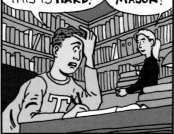

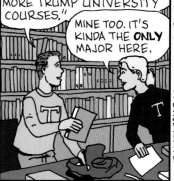

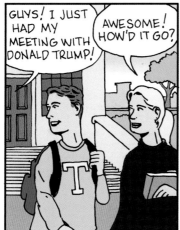

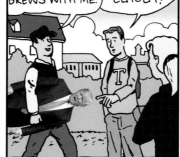

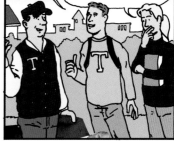

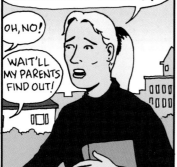

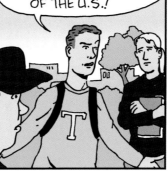

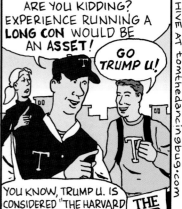

TOM the DANCING BUG

by Ruben Bolling

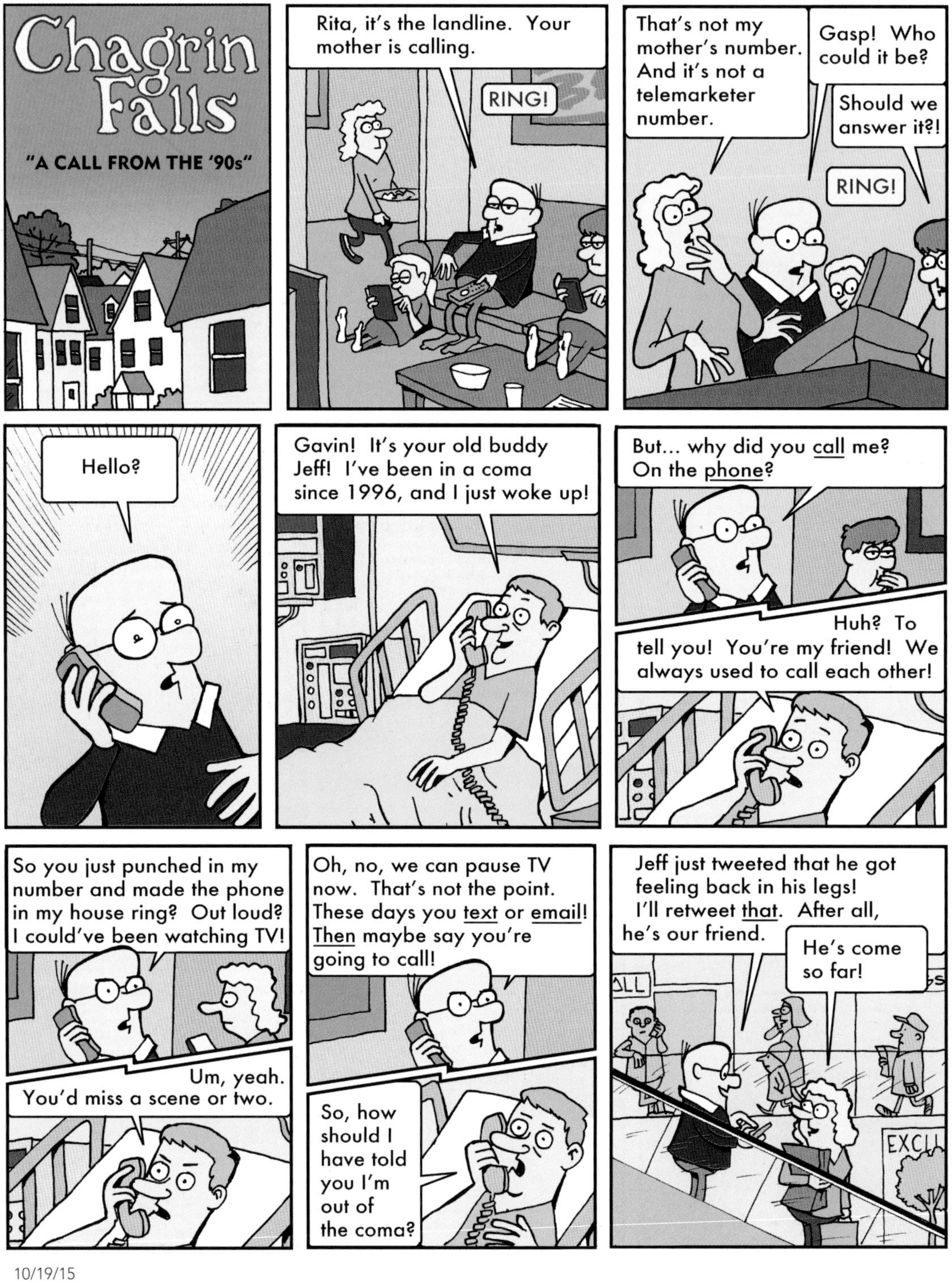
Chagrin Falls
"A CALL FROM THE '90s"
Rita, it's the landline. Your mother is calling.
RING!
That's not my mother's number. And it's not a telemarketer number.
Gasp! Who could it be?
Should we answer it?!
RING!
Hello?
Gavin! It's your old buddy Jeff! I've been in a coma since 1996, and I just woke up!
But... why did you call me? On the phone?
Huh? To tell you! You're my friend! We always used to call each other!
So you just punched in my number and made the phone in my house ring? Out loud? I could've been watching TV!
Um, yeah. You'd miss a scene or two.
Oh, no, we can pause TV now. That's not the point. These days you text or email! Then maybe say you're going to call!
So, how should I have told you I'm out of the coma?
Jeff just tweeted that he got feeling back in his legs! I'll retweet that. After all, he's our friend.
He's come so far!

10/19/15

TOM the DANCING BUG

BY RUBEN BOLLING

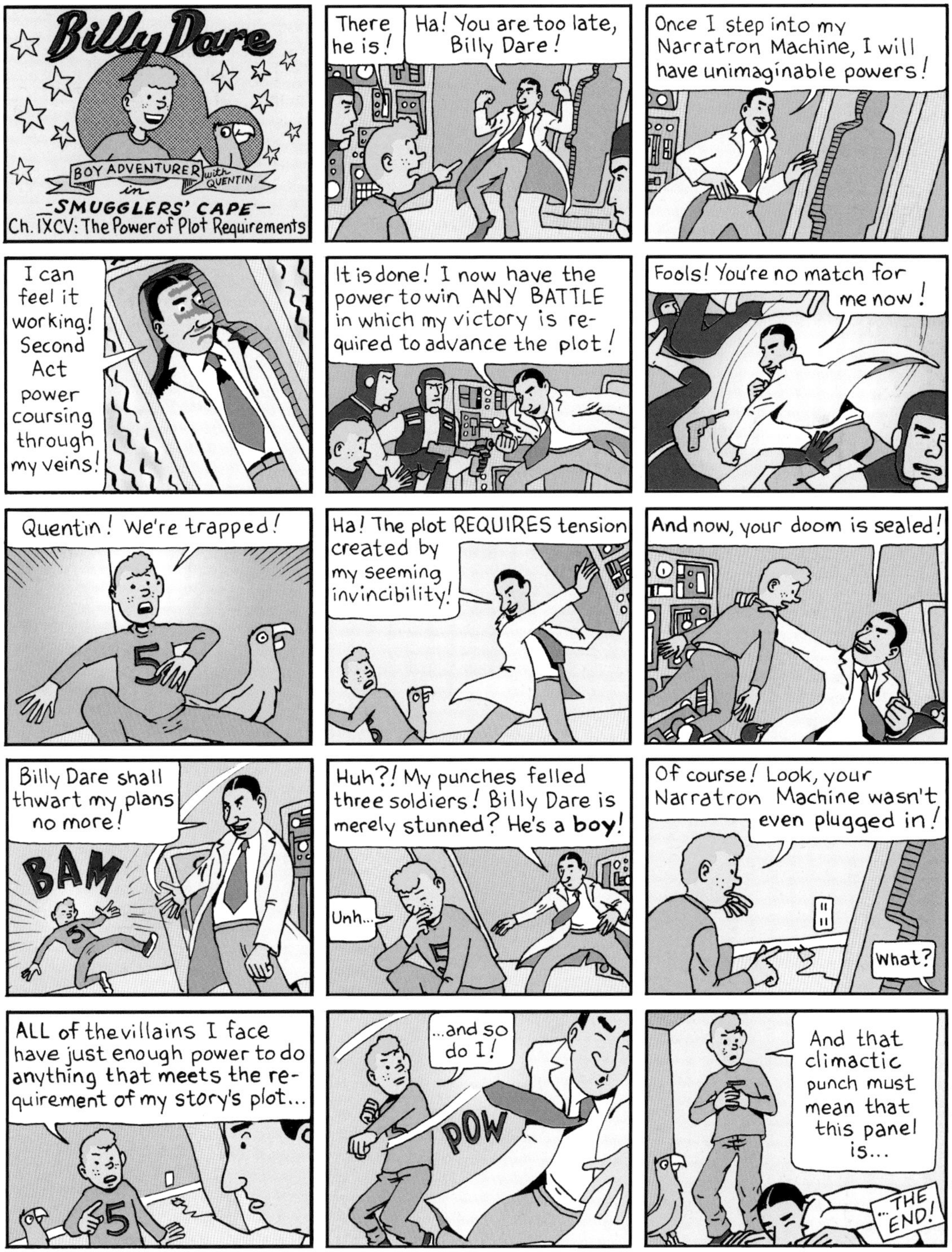
Billy Dare
BOY ADVENTURER with QUENTIN
in
-SMUGGLERS' CAPE-
Ch. IXCV: The Power of Plot Requirements
There he is!
Ha! You are too late, Billy Dare!
Once I step into my Narratron Machine, I will have unimaginable powers!
I can feel it working! Second Act power coursing through my veins!
It is done! I now have the power to win ANY BATTLE in which my victory is required to advance the plot!
Fools! You're no match for me now!
Quentin! We're trapped!
Ha! The plot REQUIRES tension created by my seeming invincibility!
And now, your doom is sealed!
Billy Dare shall thwart my plans no more!
BAM
Huh?! My punches felled three soldiers! Billy Dare is merely stunned? He's a **boy**!
Unh...
Of course! Look, your Narratron Machine wasn't even plugged in!
What?
ALL of the villains I face have just enough power to do anything that meets the requirement of my story's plot...
...and so do I!
POW
And that climactic punch must mean that this panel is...
...THE END!

10/26/15

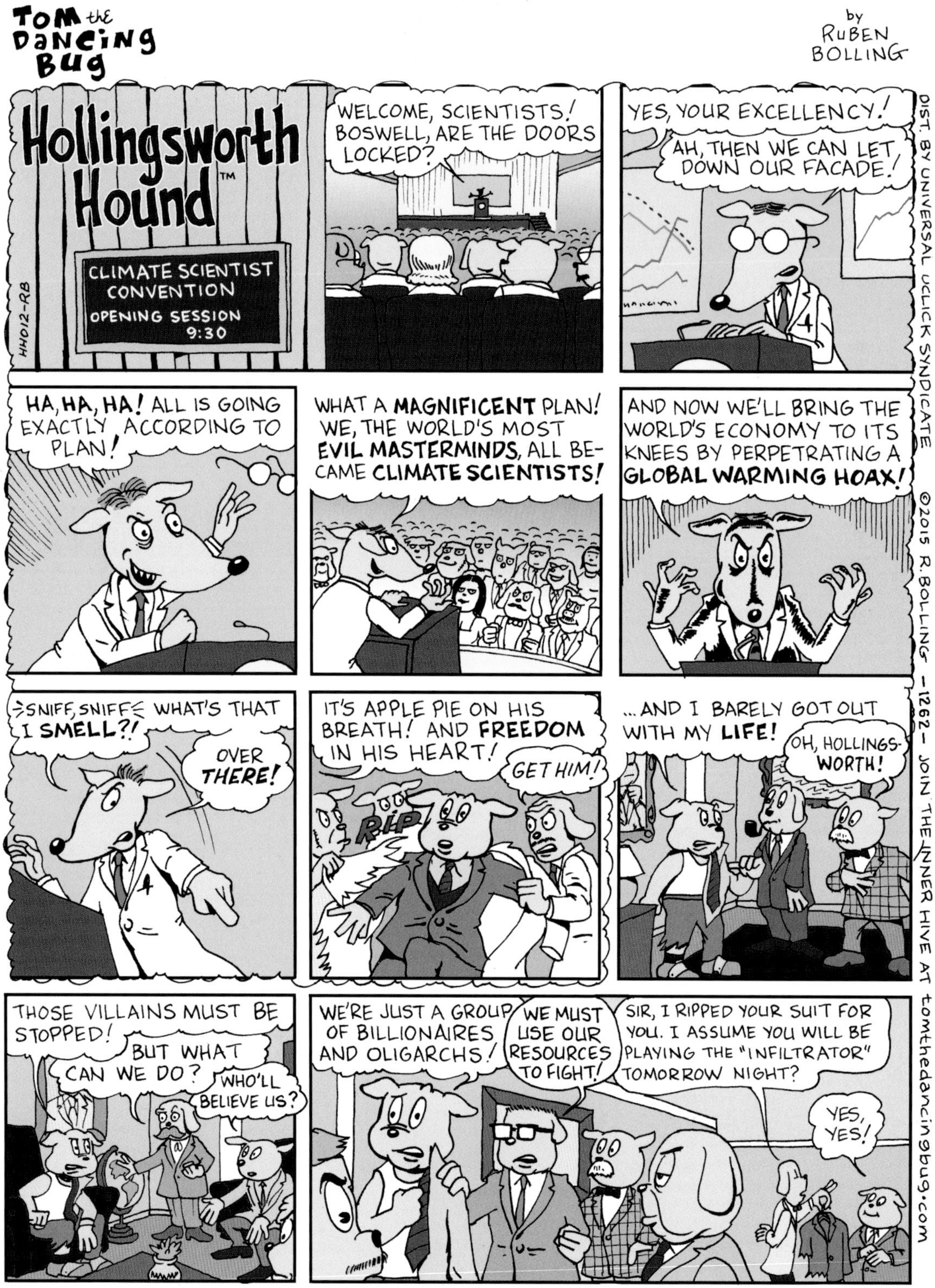
TOM the DANCING BUG
by RUBEN BOLLING
Hollingsworth Hound™
CLIMATE SCIENTIST CONVENTION
OPENING SESSION 9:30
HH012-RB
WELCOME, SCIENTISTS! BOSWELL, ARE THE DOORS LOCKED?
YES, YOUR EXCELLENCY!
AH, THEN WE CAN LET DOWN OUR FACADE!
HA, HA, HA! ALL IS GOING EXACTLY ACCORDING TO PLAN!
WHAT A MAGNIFICENT PLAN! WE, THE WORLD'S MOST EVIL MASTERMINDS, ALL BECAME CLIMATE SCIENTISTS!
AND NOW WE'LL BRING THE WORLD'S ECONOMY TO ITS KNEES BY PERPETRATING A GLOBAL WARMING HOAX!
SNIFF, SNIFF WHAT'S THAT I SMELL?!
OVER THERE!
IT'S APPLE PIE ON HIS BREATH! AND FREEDOM IN HIS HEART!
GET HIM!
RIP
...AND I BARELY GOT OUT WITH MY LIFE!
OH, HOLLINGSWORTH!
THOSE VILLAINS MUST BE STOPPED!
BUT WHAT CAN WE DO?
WHO'LL BELIEVE US?
WE'RE JUST A GROUP OF BILLIONAIRES AND OLIGARCHS!
WE MUST USE OUR RESOURCES TO FIGHT!
SIR, I RIPPED YOUR SUIT FOR YOU. I ASSUME YOU WILL BE PLAYING THE "INFILTRATOR" TOMORROW NIGHT?
YES, YES!
DIST. BY UNIVERSAL UCLICK SYNDICATE ©2015 R. BOLLING -1262- JOIN THE INNER HIVE AT tomthedancingbug.com

11/2/15

TOM the DANCING BUG

by RUBEN BOLLING

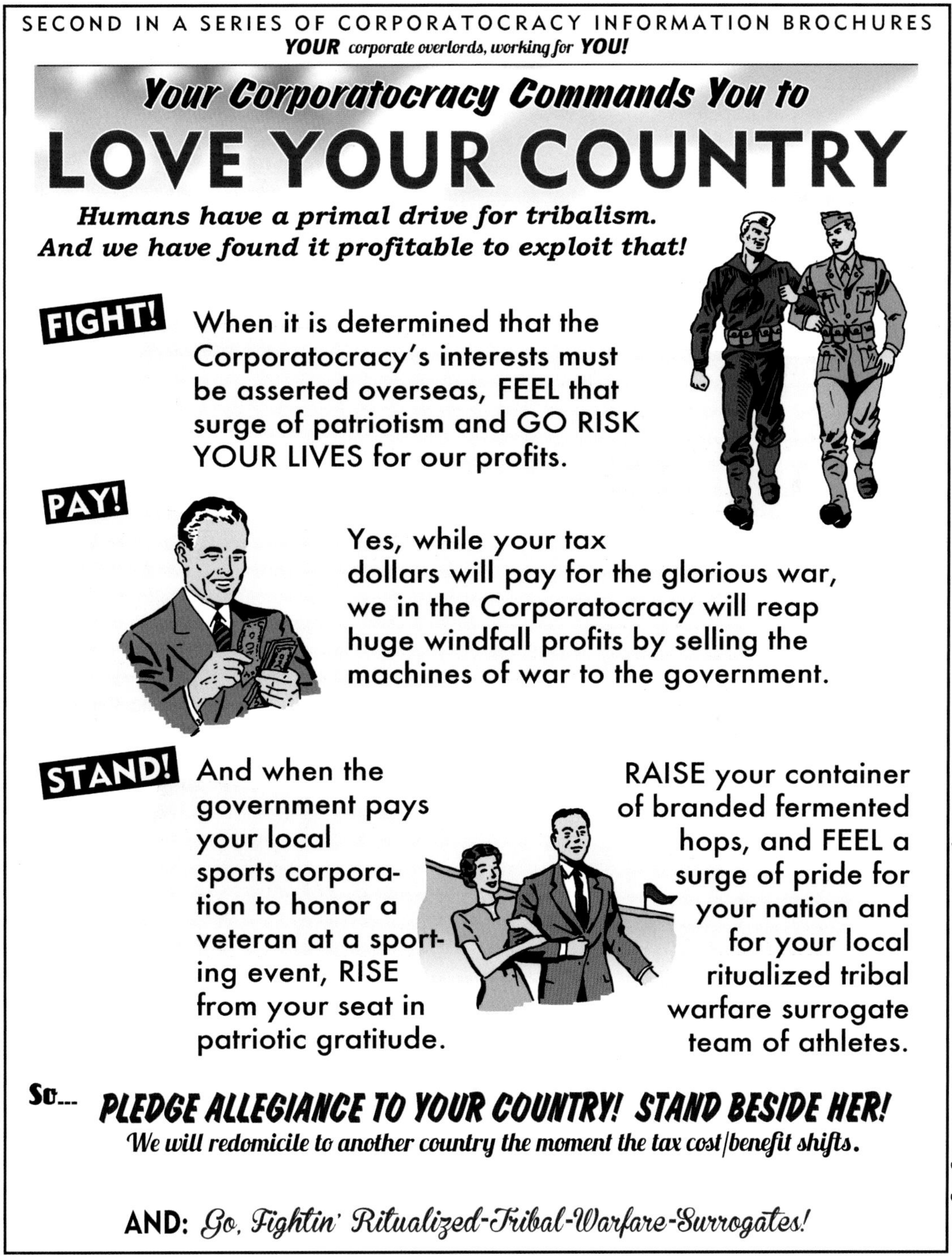

SECOND IN A SERIES OF CORPORATOCRACY INFORMATION BROCHURES
YOUR corporate overlords, working for YOU!
Your Corporatocracy Commands You to
LOVE YOUR COUNTRY
Humans have a primal drive for tribalism.
And we have found it profitable to exploit that!
FIGHT!
When it is determined that the Corporatocracy's interests must be asserted overseas, FEEL that surge of patriotism and GO RISK YOUR LIVES for our profits.
PAY!
Yes, while your tax dollars will pay for the glorious war, we in the Corporatocracy will reap huge windfall profits by selling the machines of war to the government.
STAND!
And when the government pays your local sports corporation to honor a veteran at a sporting event, RISE from your seat in patriotic gratitude.
RAISE your container of branded fermented hops, and FEEL a surge of pride for your nation and for your local ritualized tribal warfare surrogate team of athletes.
So... PLEDGE ALLEGIANCE TO YOUR COUNTRY! STAND BESIDE HER!
We will redomicile to another country the moment the tax cost/benefit shifts.
AND: Go, Fightin' Ritualized-Tribal-Warfare-Surrogates!

11/9/15

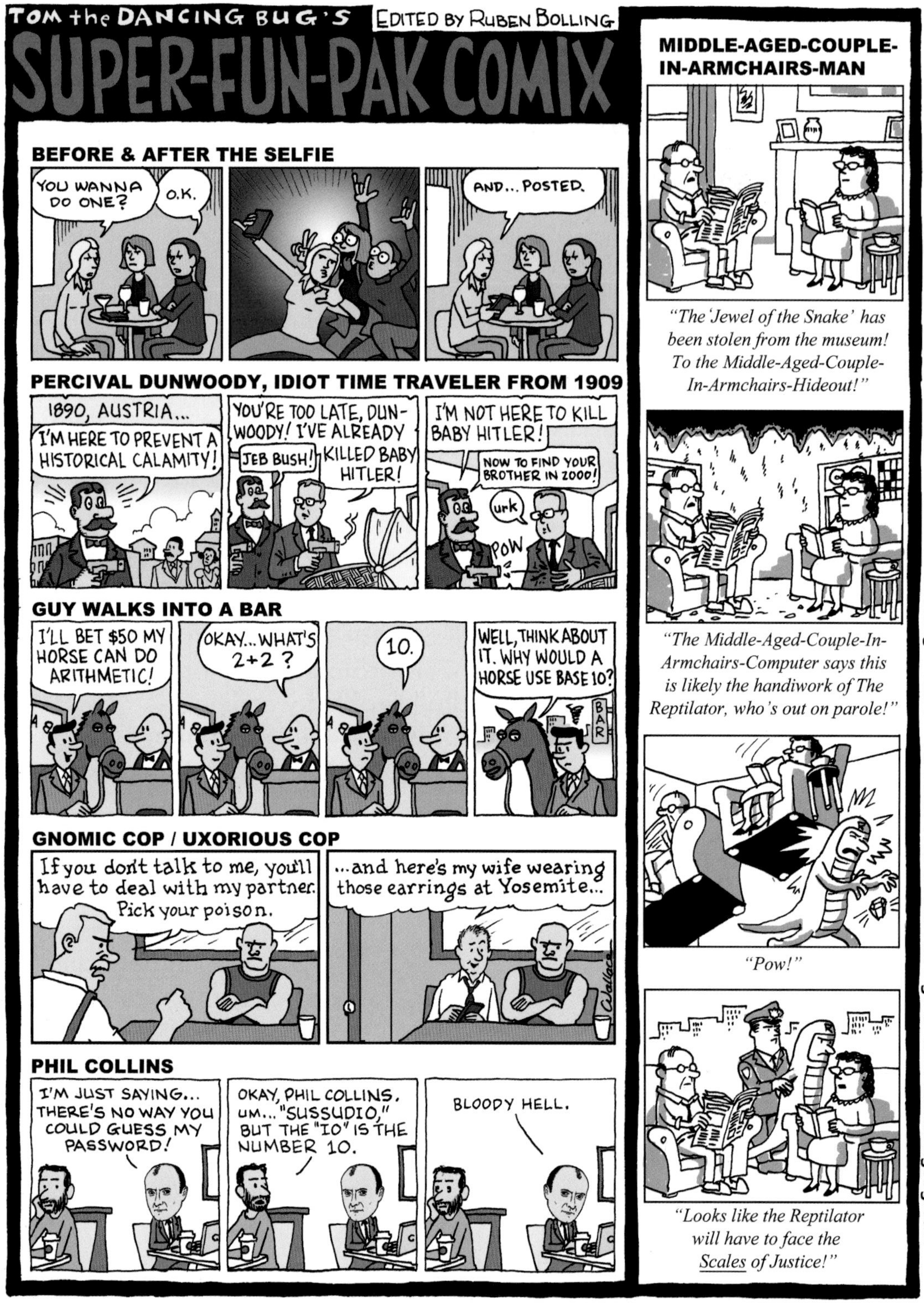
TOM the DANCING BUG'S
EDITED BY RUBEN BOLLING
SUPER-FUN-PAK COMIX
BEFORE & AFTER THE SELFIE
YOU WANNA DO ONE?
O.K.
AND... POSTED.
PERCIVAL DUNWOODY, IDIOT TIME TRAVELER FROM 1909
1890, AUSTRIA...
I'M HERE TO PREVENT A HISTORICAL CALAMITY!
YOU'RE TOO LATE, DUNWOODY! I'VE ALREADY KILLED BABY HITLER!
JEB BUSH!
I'M NOT HERE TO KILL BABY HITLER!
NOW TO FIND YOUR BROTHER IN 2000!
urk
POW
GUY WALKS INTO A BAR
I'LL BET $50 MY HORSE CAN DO ARITHMETIC!
OKAY... WHAT'S 2+2 ?
10.
WELL, THINK ABOUT IT. WHY WOULD A HORSE USE BASE 10?
BAR
GNOMIC COP / UXORIOUS COP
If you don't talk to me, you'll have to deal with my partner. Pick your poison.
...and here's my wife wearing those earrings at Yosemite...
PHIL COLLINS
I'M JUST SAYING... THERE'S NO WAY YOU COULD GUESS MY PASSWORD!
OKAY, PHIL COLLINS. UM... "SUSSUDIO," BUT THE "IO" IS THE NUMBER 10.
BLOODY HELL.
MIDDLE-AGED-COUPLE-IN-ARMCHAIRS-MAN
"The 'Jewel of the Snake' has been stolen from the museum! To the Middle-Aged-Couple-In-Armchairs-Hideout!"
"The Middle-Aged-Couple-In-Armchairs-Computer says this is likely the handiwork of The Reptilator, who's out on parole!"
"Pow!"
"Looks like the Reptilator will have to face the Scales of Justice!"

11/16/15

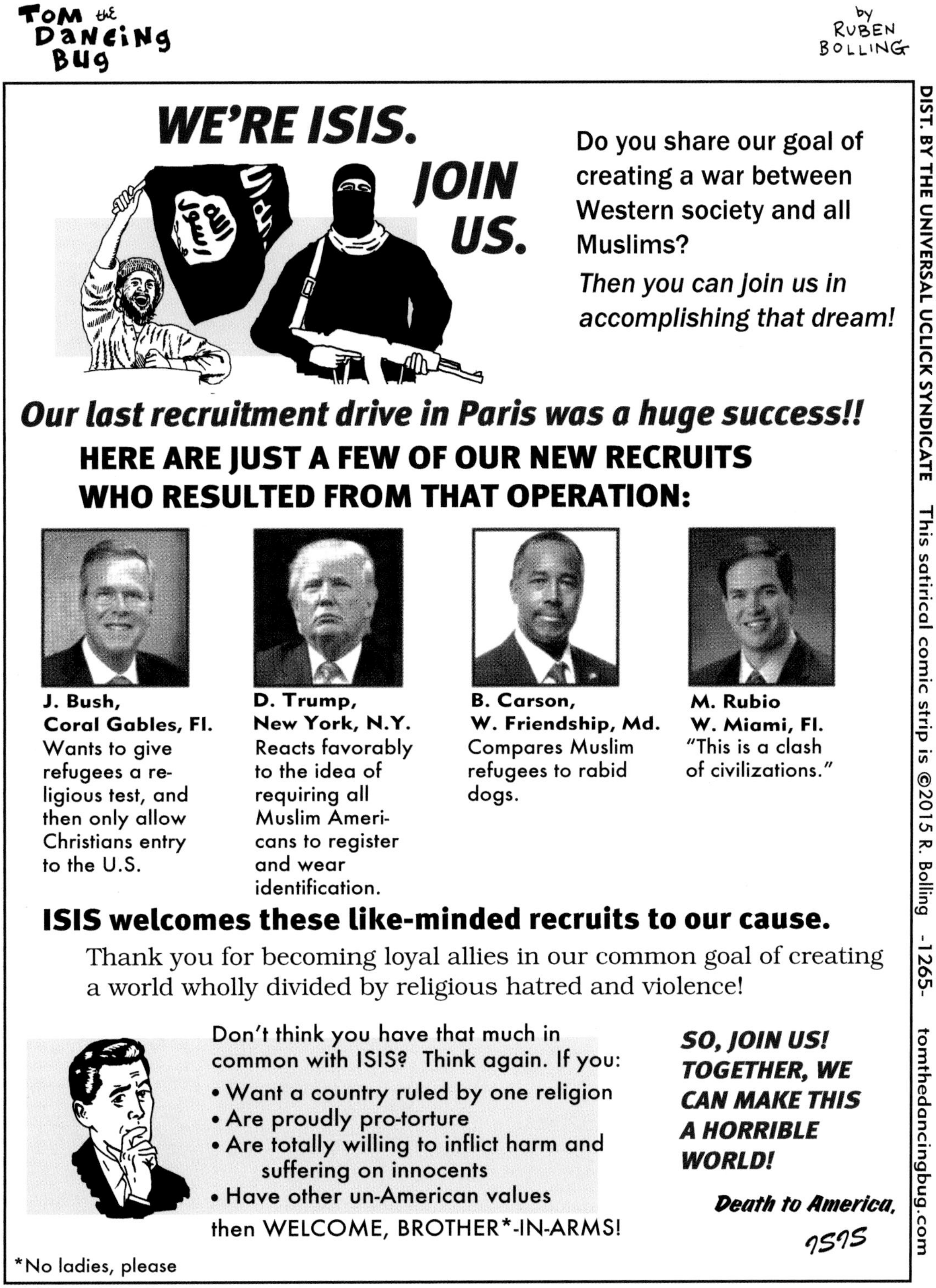
TOM the DANCING BUG
by RUBEN BOLLING
WE'RE ISIS.
JOIN US.
Do you share our goal of creating a war between Western society and all Muslims?
Then you can join us in accomplishing that dream!
Our last recruitment drive in Paris was a huge success!!
HERE ARE JUST A FEW OF OUR NEW RECRUITS WHO RESULTED FROM THAT OPERATION:
J. Bush, Coral Gables, Fl. Wants to give refugees a religious test, and then only allow Christians entry to the U.S.
D. Trump, New York, N.Y. Reacts favorably to the idea of requiring all Muslim Americans to register and wear identification.
B. Carson, W. Friendship, Md. Compares Muslim refugees to rabid dogs.
M. Rubio W. Miami, Fl. "This is a clash of civilizations."
ISIS welcomes these like-minded recruits to our cause.
Thank you for becoming loyal allies in our common goal of creating a world wholly divided by religious hatred and violence!
Don't think you have that much in common with ISIS? Think again. If you:
• Want a country ruled by one religion
• Are proudly pro-torture
• Are totally willing to inflict harm and suffering on innocents
• Have other un-American values
then WELCOME, BROTHER*-IN-ARMS!
SO, JOIN US! TOGETHER, WE CAN MAKE THIS A HORRIBLE WORLD!
Death to America,
ISIS
*No ladies, please
DIST. BY THE UNIVERSAL UCLICK SYNDICATE This satirical comic strip is ©2015 R. Bolling -1265- tomthedancingbug.com

11/23/15

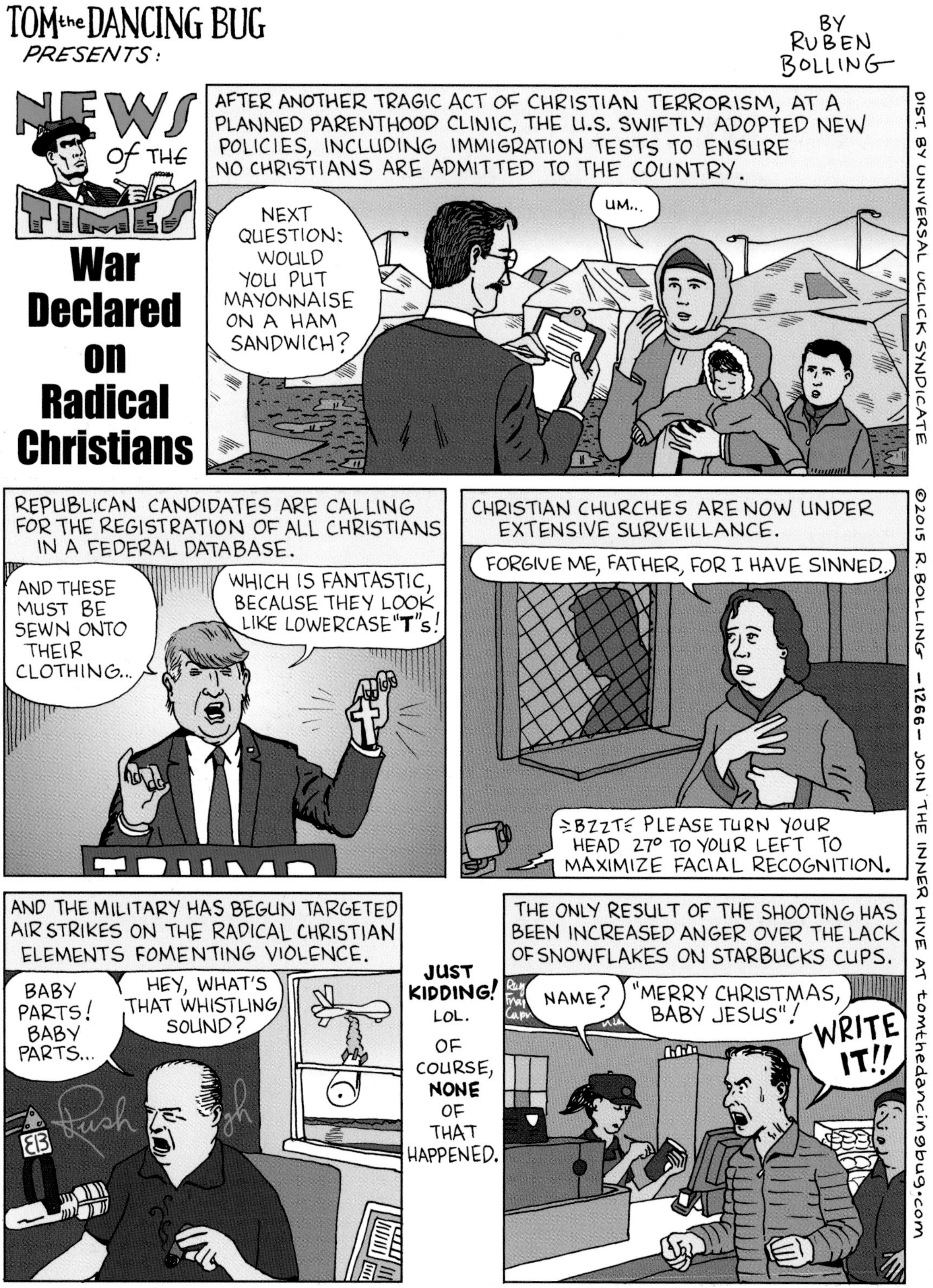
TOM the DANCING BUG
PRESENTS:
BY RUBEN BOLLING
NEWS of THE TIMES
War Declared on Radical Christians
AFTER ANOTHER TRAGIC ACT OF CHRISTIAN TERRORISM, AT A PLANNED PARENTHOOD CLINIC, THE U.S. SWIFTLY ADOPTED NEW POLICIES, INCLUDING IMMIGRATION TESTS TO ENSURE NO CHRISTIANS ARE ADMITTED TO THE COUNTRY.
NEXT QUESTION: WOULD YOU PUT MAYONNAISE ON A HAM SANDWICH?
UM...
REPUBLICAN CANDIDATES ARE CALLING FOR THE REGISTRATION OF ALL CHRISTIANS IN A FEDERAL DATABASE.
AND THESE MUST BE SEWN ONTO THEIR CLOTHING...
WHICH IS FANTASTIC, BECAUSE THEY LOOK LIKE LOWERCASE "T"s!
CHRISTIAN CHURCHES ARE NOW UNDER EXTENSIVE SURVEILLANCE.
FORGIVE ME, FATHER, FOR I HAVE SINNED...
≥BZZT≤ PLEASE TURN YOUR HEAD 27° TO YOUR LEFT TO MAXIMIZE FACIAL RECOGNITION.
AND THE MILITARY HAS BEGUN TARGETED AIR STRIKES ON THE RADICAL CHRISTIAN ELEMENTS FOMENTING VIOLENCE.
BABY PARTS! BABY PARTS...
HEY, WHAT'S THAT WHISTLING SOUND?
JUST KIDDING! LOL. OF COURSE, NONE OF THAT HAPPENED.
THE ONLY RESULT OF THE SHOOTING HAS BEEN INCREASED ANGER OVER THE LACK OF SNOWFLAKES ON STARBUCKS CUPS.
NAME?
"MERRY CHRISTMAS, BABY JESUS"!
WRITE IT!!
DIST. BY UNIVERSAL UCLICK SYNDICATE
©2015 R. BOLLING -1266- JOIN THE INNER HIVE AT tomthedancingbug.com

11/30/15

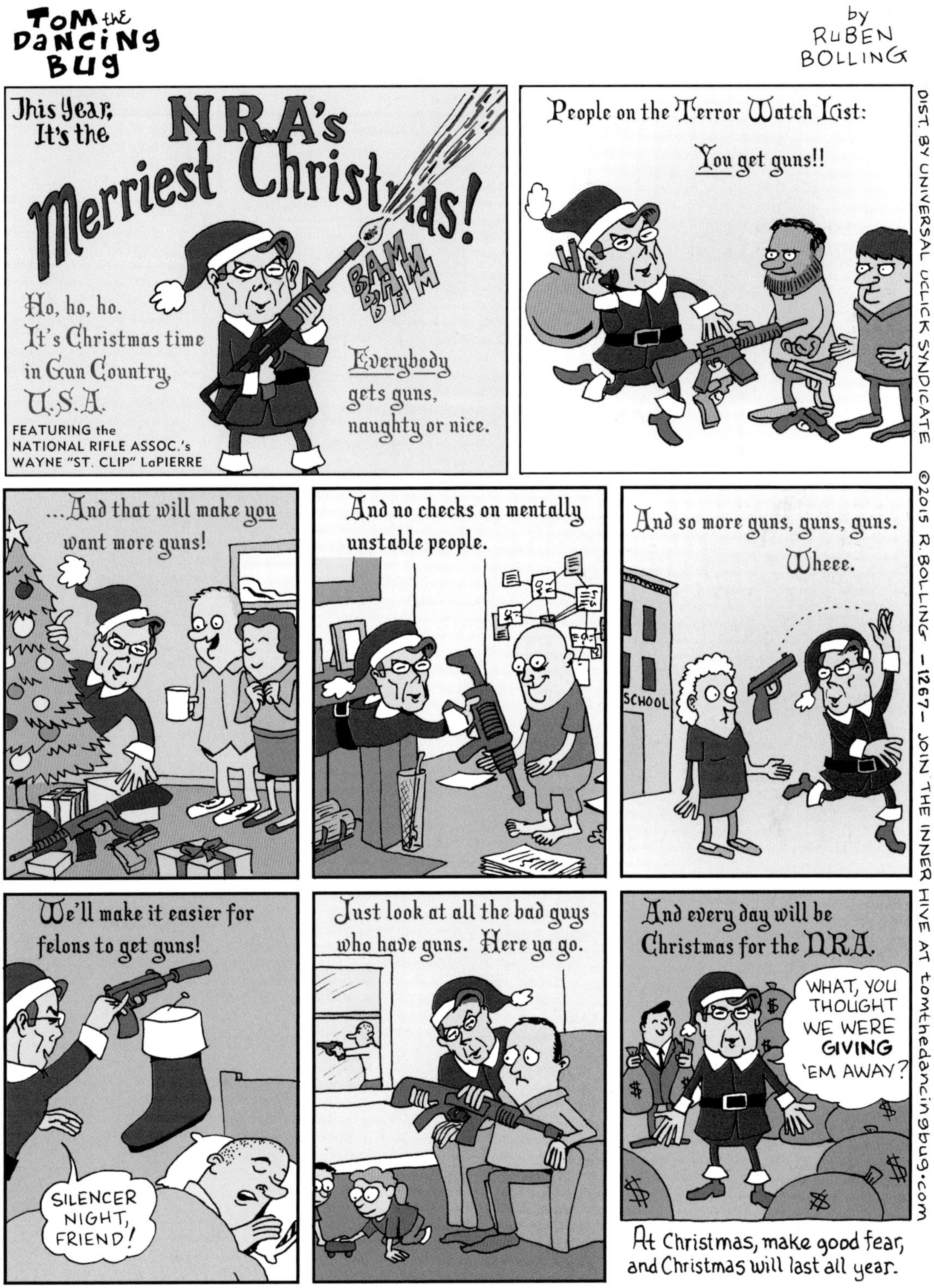

TOM the DANCING BUG
by RUBEN BOLLING
This Year, It's the
NRA's Merriest Christmas!
BAM BAM BAM
Ho, ho, ho. It's Christmas time in Gun Country, U.S.A.
Everybody gets guns, naughty or nice.
FEATURING the NATIONAL RIFLE ASSOC.'s WAYNE "ST. CLIP" LaPIERRE
People on the Terror Watch List:
You get guns!!
...And that will make you want more guns!
And no checks on mentally unstable people.
And so more guns, guns, guns.
Wheee.
SCHOOL
We'll make it easier for felons to get guns!
SILENCER NIGHT, FRIEND!
Just look at all the bad guys who have guns. Here ya go.
And every day will be Christmas for the NRA.
WHAT, YOU THOUGHT WE WERE GIVING 'EM AWAY?
At Christmas, make good fear, and Christmas will last all year.
DIST. BY UNIVERSAL UCLICK SYNDICATE ©2015 R. BOLLING -1267- JOIN THE INNER HIVE AT tomthedancingbug.com

12/7/15

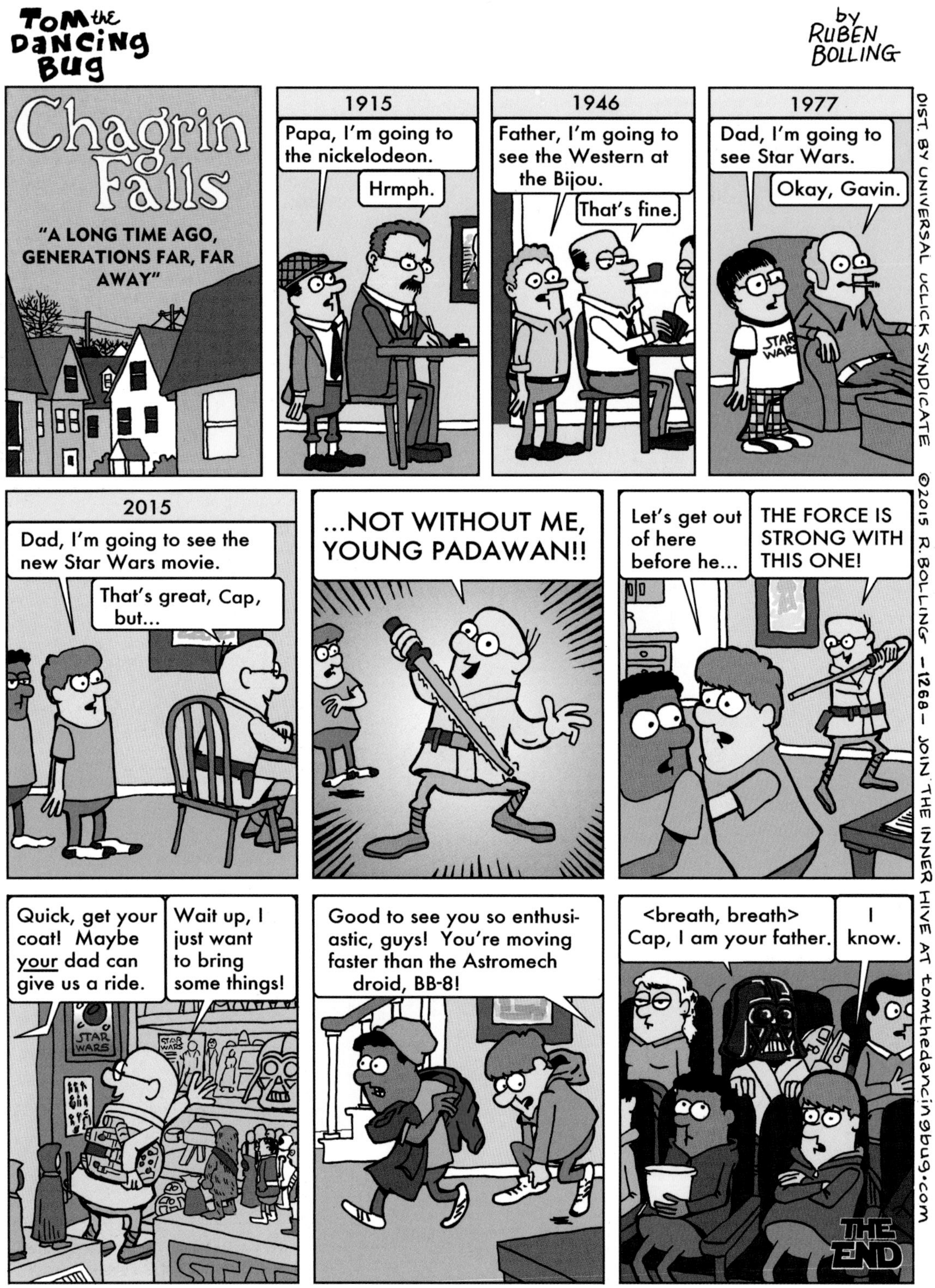

TOM the DANCING BUG
by RUBEN BOLLING
Chagrin Falls
"A LONG TIME AGO, GENERATIONS FAR, FAR AWAY"
1915
Papa, I'm going to the nickelodeon.
Hrmph.
1946
Father, I'm going to see the Western at the Bijou.
That's fine.
1977
Dad, I'm going to see Star Wars.
Okay, Gavin.
STAR WARS
2015
Dad, I'm going to see the new Star Wars movie.
That's great, Cap, but...
...NOT WITHOUT ME, YOUNG PADAWAN!!
Let's get out of here before he...
THE FORCE IS STRONG WITH THIS ONE!
Quick, get your coat! Maybe your dad can give us a ride.
Wait up, I just want to bring some things!
STAR WARS
Good to see you so enthusiastic, guys! You're moving faster than the Astromech droid, BB-8!
<breath, breath> Cap, I am your father.
I know.
THE END
DIST. BY UNIVERSAL UCLICK SYNDICATE ©2015 R. BOLLING —1268— JOIN THE INNER HIVE AT tomthedancingbug.com

12/14/15

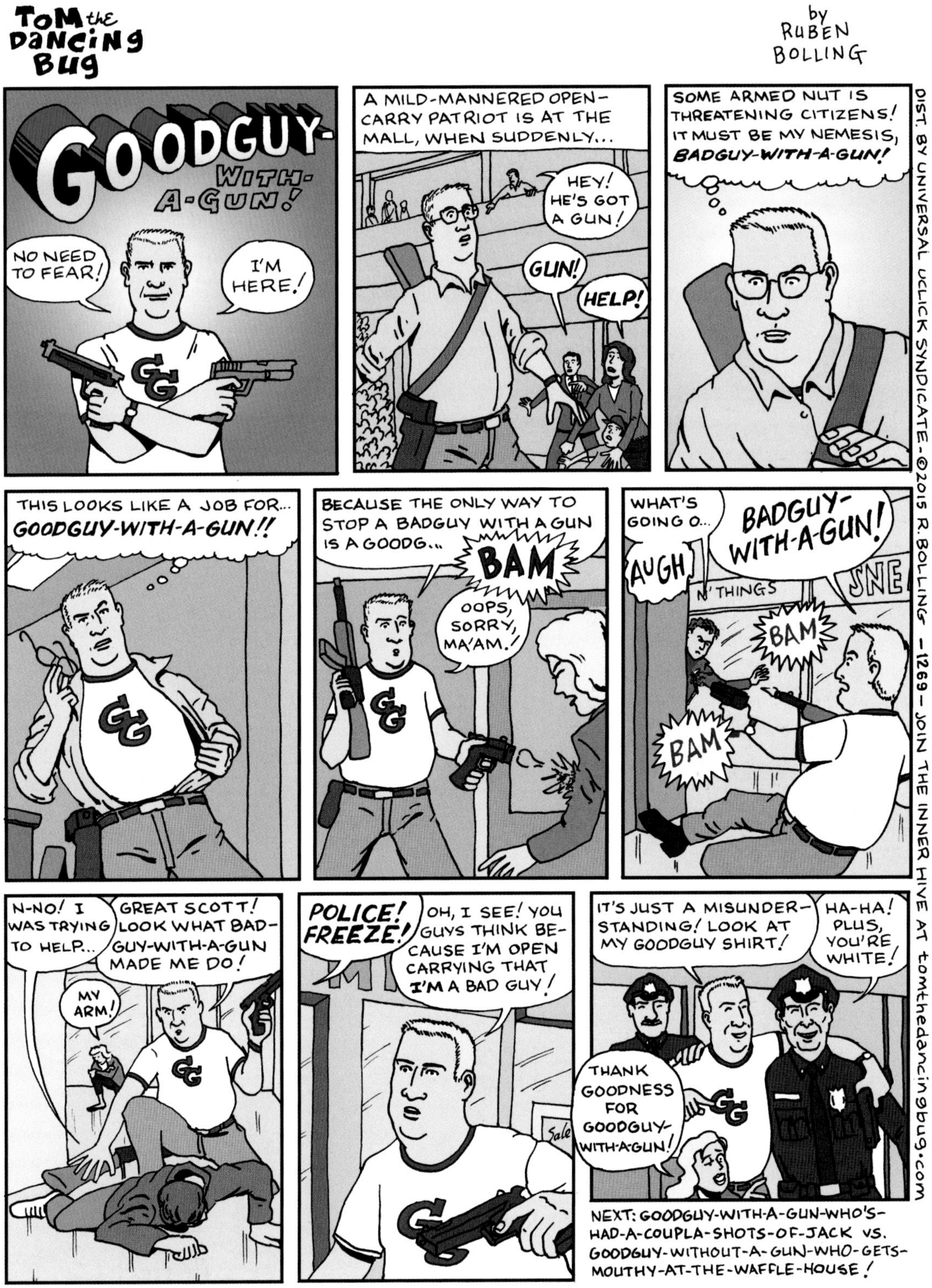

TOM the DANCING BUG
by RUBEN BOLLING
GOODGUY-WITH-A-GUN!
NO NEED TO FEAR!
I'M HERE!
A MILD-MANNERED OPEN-CARRY PATRIOT IS AT THE MALL, WHEN SUDDENLY...
HEY! HE'S GOT A GUN!
GUN!
HELP!
SOME ARMED NUT IS THREATENING CITIZENS! IT MUST BE MY NEMESIS, BADGUY-WITH-A-GUN!
THIS LOOKS LIKE A JOB FOR... GOODGUY-WITH-A-GUN!!
BECAUSE THE ONLY WAY TO STOP A BADGUY WITH A GUN IS A GOODG...
BAM
OOPS, SORRY, MA'AM.!
WHAT'S GOING O...
BADGUY-WITH-A-GUN!
AUGH
N' THINGS
SNE
BAM
BAM
N-NO! I WAS TRYING TO HELP..
GREAT SCOTT! LOOK WHAT BAD-GUY-WITH-A-GUN MADE ME DO!
MY ARM!
POLICE! FREEZE!
OH, I SEE! YOU GUYS THINK BE-CAUSE I'M OPEN CARRYING THAT I'M A BAD GUY!
Sale
IT'S JUST A MISUNDER-STANDING! LOOK AT MY GOODGUY SHIRT!
HA-HA! PLUS, YOU'RE WHITE!
THANK GOODNESS FOR GOODGUY-WITH-A-GUN!
NEXT: GOODGUY-WITH-A-GUN-WHO'S-HAD-A-COUPLA-SHOTS-OF-JACK VS. GOODGUY-WITHOUT-A-GUN-WHO-GETS-MOUTHY-AT-THE-WAFFLE-HOUSE!
DIST. BY UNIVERSAL UCLICK SYNDICATE -©2015 R. BOLLING -1269- JOIN THE INNER HIVE AT tomthedancingbug.com

12/21/15

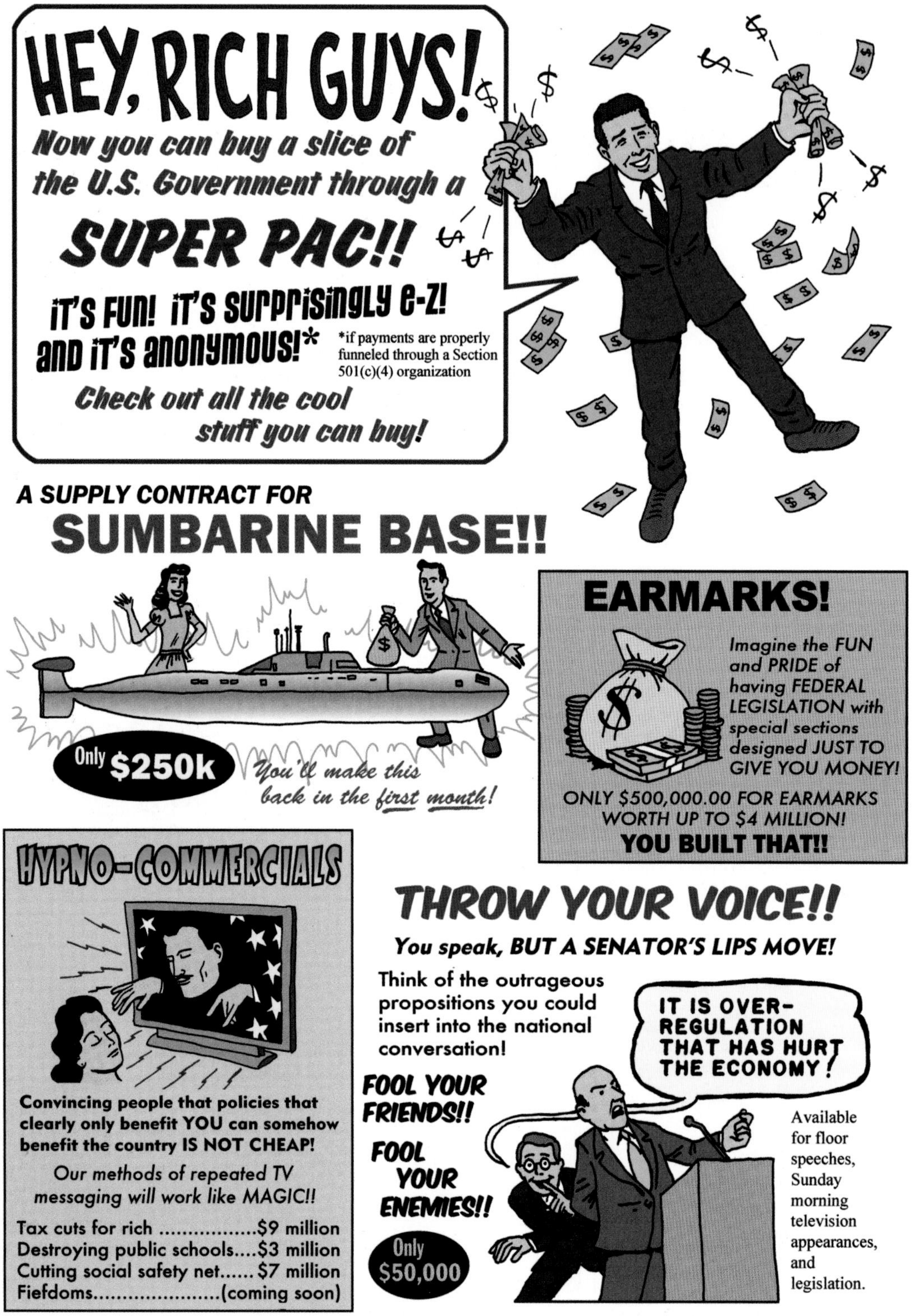
HEY, RICH GUYS!
Now you can buy a slice of the U.S. Government through a
SUPER PAC!!
IT'S FUN! IT'S SURPRISINGLY E-Z! AND IT'S ANONYMOUS!*
*if payments are properly funneled through a Section 501(c)(4) organization
Check out all the cool stuff you can buy!
A SUPPLY CONTRACT FOR
SUMBARINE BASE!!
Only $250k
You'll make this back in the first month!
EARMARKS!
Imagine the FUN and PRIDE of having FEDERAL LEGISLATION with special sections designed JUST TO GIVE YOU MONEY!
ONLY $500,000.00 FOR EARMARKS WORTH UP TO $4 MILLION!
YOU BUILT THAT!!
HYPNO-COMMERCIALS
Convincing people that policies that clearly only benefit YOU can somehow benefit the country IS NOT CHEAP!
Our methods of repeated TV messaging will work like MAGIC!!
Tax cuts for rich ....$9 million
Destroying public schools....$3 million
Cutting social safety net...... $7 million
Fiefdoms.......................(coming soon)
THROW YOUR VOICE!!
You speak, BUT A SENATOR'S LIPS MOVE!
Think of the outrageous propositions you could insert into the national conversation!
IT IS OVER-REGULATION THAT HAS HURT THE ECONOMY!
FOOL YOUR FRIENDS!!
FOOL YOUR ENEMIES!!
Only $50,000
Available for floor speeches, Sunday morning television appearances, and legislation.

This comic appeared in *The New Yorker*, 9/24/12 issue, across two full pages.

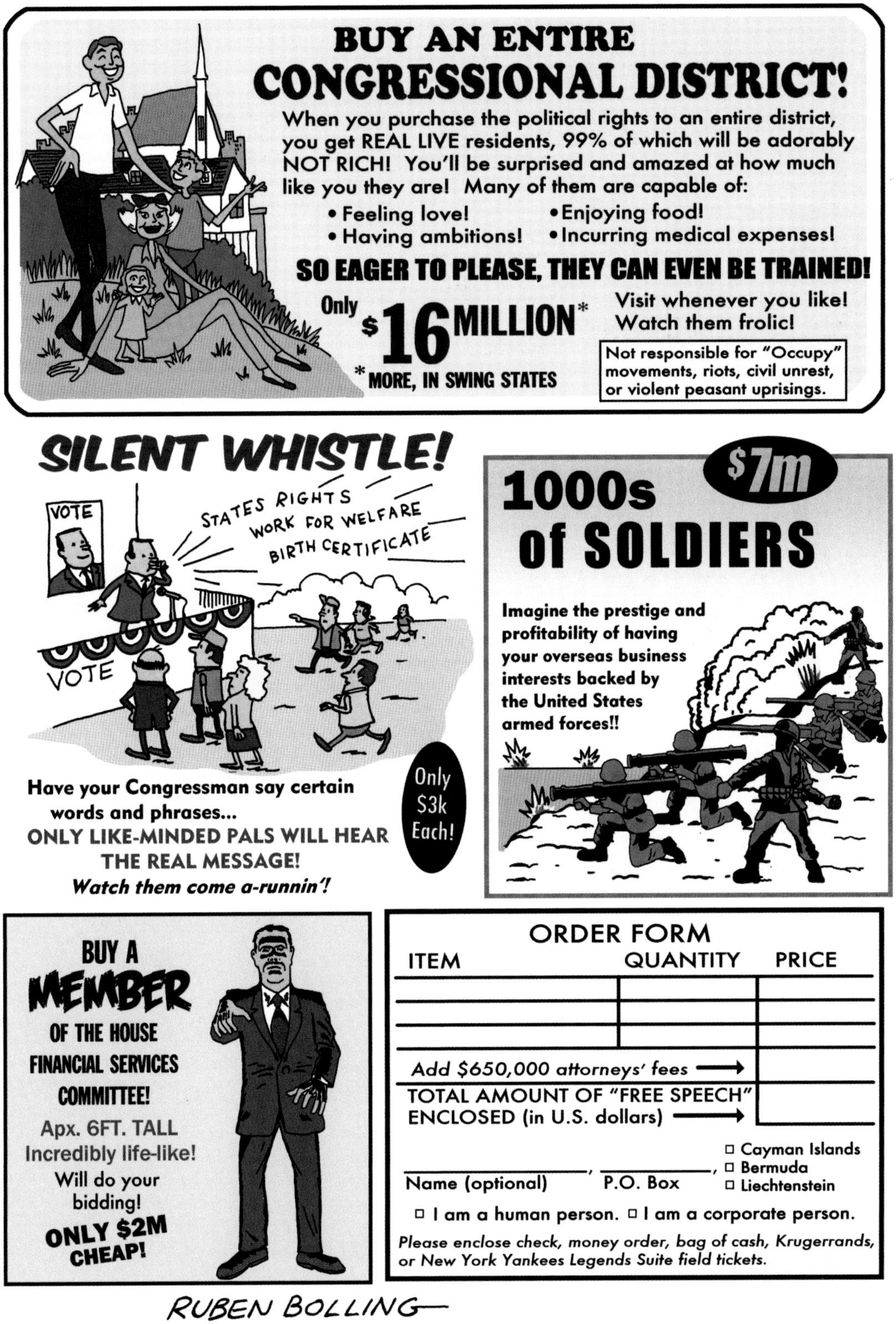
BUY AN ENTIRE
CONGRESSIONAL DISTRICT!
When you purchase the political rights to an entire district, you get REAL LIVE residents, 99% of which will be adorably NOT RICH! You'll be surprised and amazed at how much like you they are! Many of them are capable of:
• Feeling love!
• Having ambitions!
• Enjoying food!
• Incurring medical expenses!
SO EAGER TO PLEASE, THEY CAN EVEN BE TRAINED!
Only $16 MILLION*
* MORE, IN SWING STATES
Visit whenever you like! Watch them frolic!
Not responsible for "Occupy" movements, riots, civil unrest, or violent peasant uprisings.
SILENT WHISTLE!
VOTE
STATES RIGHTS
WORK FOR WELFARE
BIRTH CERTIFICATE
VOTE
Have your Congressman say certain words and phrases...
ONLY LIKE-MINDED PALS WILL HEAR THE REAL MESSAGE!
Watch them come a-runnin'!
Only $3k Each!
$7m
1000s of SOLDIERS
Imagine the prestige and profitability of having your overseas business interests backed by the United States armed forces!!
BUY A MEMBER OF THE HOUSE FINANCIAL SERVICES COMMITTEE!
Apx. 6FT. TALL
Incredibly life-like!
Will do your bidding!
ONLY $2M
CHEAP!
ORDER FORM
ITEM
QUANTITY
PRICE
Add $650,000 attorneys' fees →
TOTAL AMOUNT OF "FREE SPEECH" ENCLOSED (in U.S. dollars) →
Name (optional)
P.O. Box
□ Cayman Islands
□ Bermuda
□ Liechtenstein
□ I am a human person. □ I am a corporate person.
Please enclose check, money order, bag of cash, Krugerrands, or New York Yankees Legends Suite field tickets.
RUBEN BOLLING

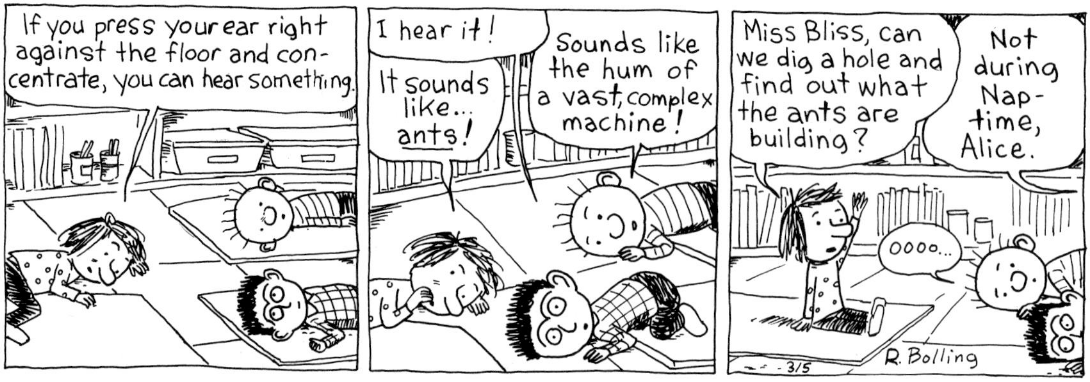
If you press your ear right against the floor and con-centrate, you can hear something.
I hear it!
It sounds like... ants!
Sounds like the hum of a vast, complex machine!
Miss Bliss, can we dig a hole and find out what the ants are building?
Not during Nap-time, Alice.
Oooo...
3/5
R. Bolling

3/5/12

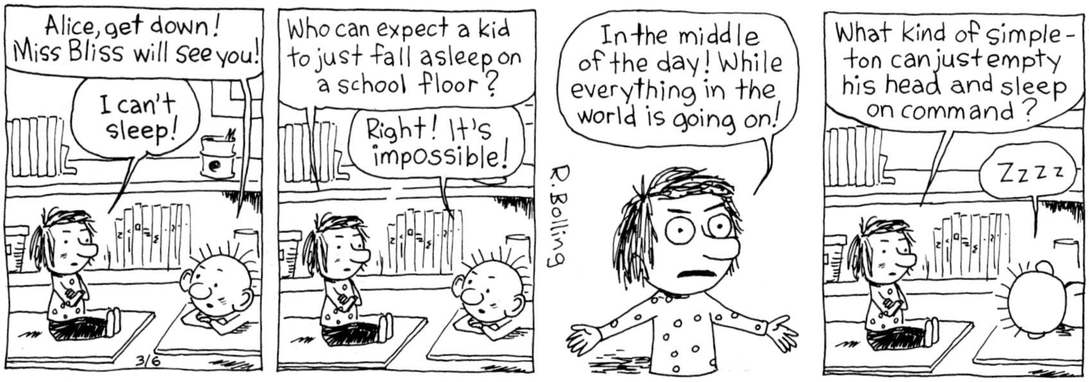
Alice, get down! Miss Bliss will see you!
I can't sleep!
3/6
Who can expect a kid to just fall asleep on a school floor?
Right! It's impossible!
R. Bolling
In the middle of the day! While everything in the world is going on!
What kind of simple-ton can just empty his head and sleep on command?
Zzzz

3/6/12

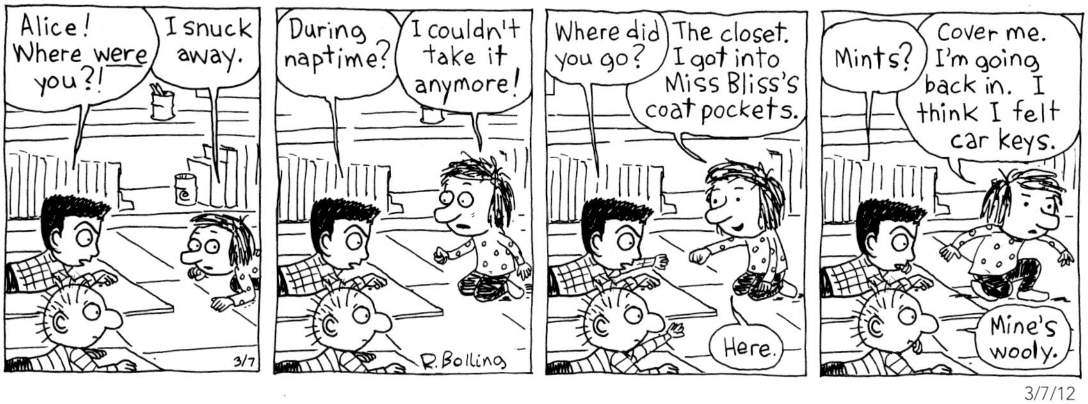
Alice! Where were you?!
I snuck away.
3/7
During naptime?
I couldn't take it anymore!
R. Bolling
Where did you go?
The closet. I got into Miss Bliss's coat pockets.
Here.
Mints?
Cover me. I'm going back in. I think I felt car keys.
Mine's wooly.

3/7/12

In March, 2012, the late, great, greatly missed cartoonist Richard Thompson needed some help with the deadlines for his daily comic strip *Cul de Sac,* as he underwent physical therapy. Ruben Bolling contributed with this week of comics.

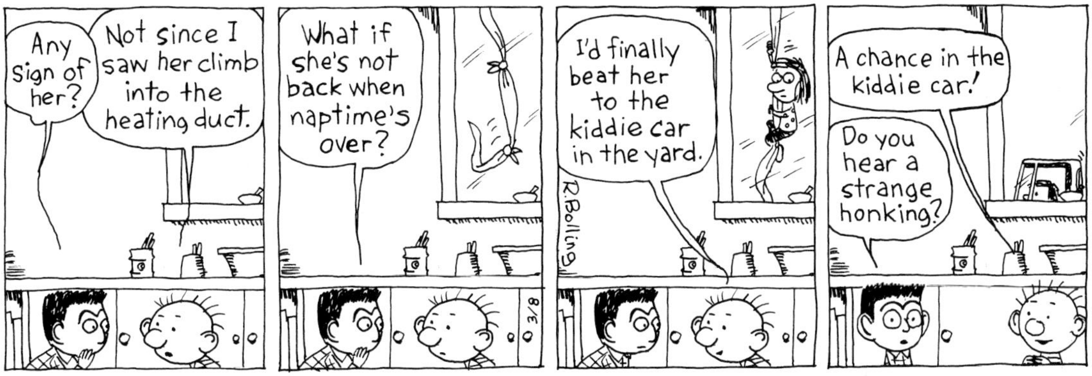
Any sign of her?
Not since I saw her climb into the heating duct.
What if she's not back when naptime's over?
I'd finally beat her to the kiddie car in the yard.
R.Bolling
3/8
A chance in the kiddie car!
Do you hear a strange honking?

3/8/12

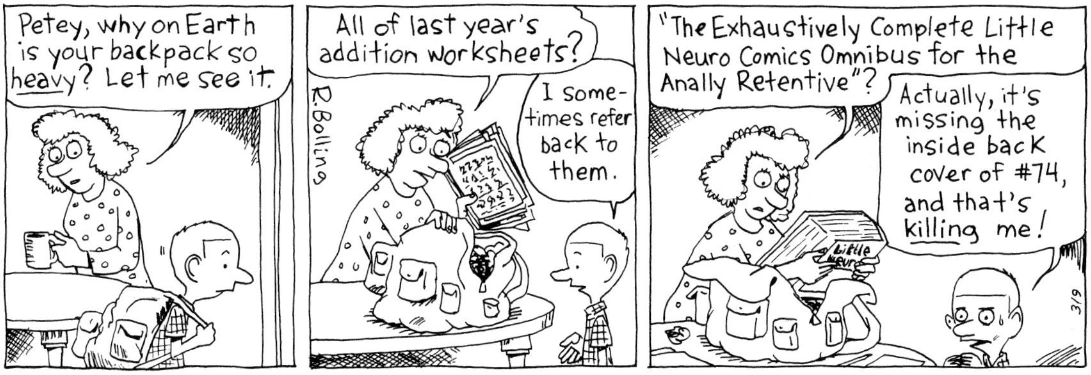
Petey, why on Earth is your backpack so heavy? Let me see it.
All of last year's addition worksheets?
R.Bolling
I sometimes refer back to them.
"The Exhaustively Complete Little Neuro Comics Omnibus for the Anally Retentive"?
Actually, it's missing the inside back cover of #74, and that's killing me!
3/9

3/9/12

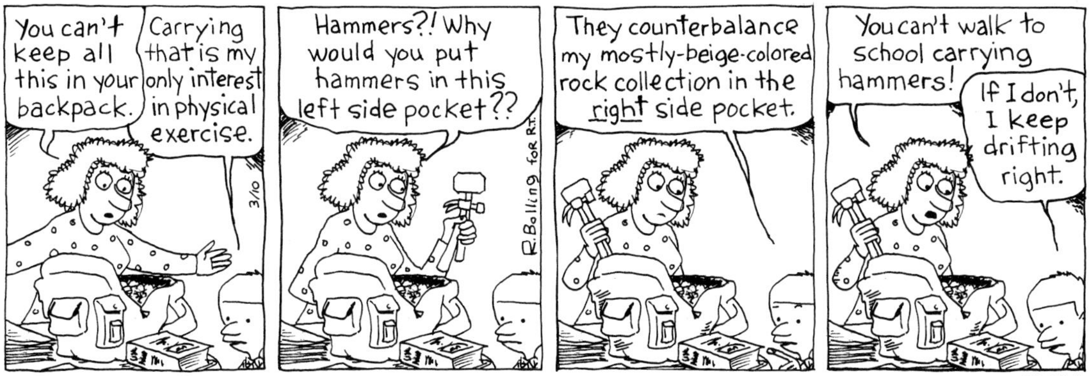
You can't keep all this in your backpack.
Carrying that is my only interest in physical exercise.
3/10
Hammers?! Why would you put hammers in this left side pocket??
R.Bolling for R.T.
They counterbalance my mostly-beige-colored rock collection in the right side pocket.
You can't walk to school carrying hammers!
If I don't, I keep drifting right.

3/10/12

TOM THE DANCING BUG FROM CLOVER PRESS:

The Complete Tom the Dancing Bug

TOM THE DANCING BUG
AWAKENS
THE COMPLETE TOM THE DANCING BUG, 2012-2015
Comics by Ruben Bolling

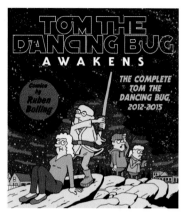

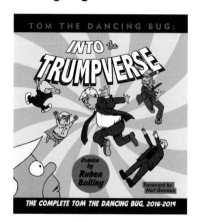

VOLUME 6
Tom the Dancing Bug Awakens
ISBN: 978-1-951038-35-9

TOM THE DANCING BUG:
INTO the TRUMPVERSE
Comics by Ruben Bolling
Foreword by Neil Gaiman
THE COMPLETE TOM THE DANCING BUG, 2016-2019

VOLUME 7
Tom the Dancing Bug: Into the Trumpverse
ISBN: 978-1-951038-08-3

COMING SOON: VOLUME 5!

$12.99
The SUPER-FUN-PAK COMIX Reader
Ruben Bolling
THE COMPLETE SUPER-FUN-PAK COMIX, 1997-2019
from the comic strip Tom the Dancing Bug

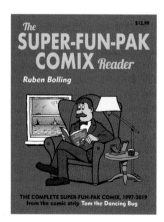

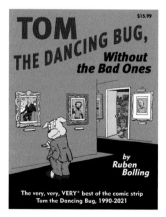

The Super-Fun-Pak Comix Reader

$15.99
TOM THE DANCING BUG,
Without the Bad Ones
by Ruben Bolling
The very, very, VERY* best of the comic strip
Tom the Dancing Bug, 1990-2021

Tom the Dancing Bug, Without the Bad Ones
ISBN: 978-1-951038-40-3